After Lives

After Lives

A Guide to Heaven, Hell, and Purgatory

JOHN CASEY

Fellow of Caius College, Cambridge

OXFORD
UNIVERSITY PRESS
2009

OXFORD
UNIVERSITY PRESS

Oxford University Press, Inc., publishes works that further
Oxford University's objective of excellence
in research, scholarship, and education.

Oxford   New York
Auckland   Cape Town   Dar es Salaam   Hong Kong   Karachi
Kuala Lumpur   Madrid   Melbourne   Mexico City   Nairobi
New Delhi   Shanghai   Taipei   Toronto

With offices in
Argentina   Austria   Brazil   Chile   Czech Republic   France   Greece
Guatemala   Hungary   Italy   Japan   Poland   Portugal   Singapore
South Korea   Switzerland   Thailand   Turkey   Ukraine   Vietnam

Published by Oxford University Press, Inc.
198 Madison Avenue, New York, NY 10016

www.oup.com

Oxford is a registered trademark of Oxford University Press

Library of Congress Cataloging-in-Publication Data
Casey, John, 1939–
After Lives : a guide to heaven, hell, and purgatory / John Casey.
p.   cm.
Includes bibliographical references. (p.).
ISBN 978–0–19–509295–0
1. Future life—History of doctrines.   I. Title.
BL535.C37 2009
220'.3—dc22   2009007204

9 8 7 6 5 4 3 2 1

Printed in the United States of America
on acid-free paper

In memory of my parents

Contents

PART III   Heaven

Acknowledgments

I am grateful to several friends who read earlier drafts of the book—
Paul Binski, Colin Burrow, and Ruth Scurr, who read it in full, and
Paul Foote and Cally Hammond, who read it in part. Jeremy Dimmick
gave very useful directions about reading at the very beginning of the
project. Ed Brambley took care of the illustrations.

Oxford University Press were heroically patient during the
lapse of time between their commissioning the book and my
finally getting down to work on it. I am grateful to my original
commissioning editor for that; to my present editor, Cynthia Read,
for extremely helpful comments; and to the reader to whom the
manuscript was sent for constructive, indeed invaluable,
suggestions. My very warm thanks go to my magnificent copy
editor, Mary Sutherland, whose intelligence and alert attention to
detail, combined with an unerring sense of the book as a whole,
made her a pleasure to work with. Thank-you as well to Joellyn
Ausanka, who ably shepherded the book through the production
process.

My greatest debt—obvious and here warmly acknowledged—
is to those many writers whose fundamental work opened paths
into areas hitherto unknown to me (which includes just about all
the writers cited on ancient Egypt) and intimated a structure for
the book, but especially Alan Bernstein, S. G. F. Brandon, Piero
Camporesi, and Colleen McDannell and Bernard Lang.

After Lives

Prologue: Stephen Dedalus's Hell

Beliefs held almost without question for centuries, and enforced by the authority of venerable institutions, can unpredictably evaporate. For almost nineteen centuries the great majority of Christians had accepted, even embraced fervently, certain doctrines about man's final end. These beliefs were at the center of the Christian imagination. Among Protestants in Northern Europe there had been some dilution of belief among intellectuals and the growth of liberal theology; but this did not begin to affect the masses until the early twentieth century. The Roman Catholic Church preserved the orthodox teaching on heaven and hell with energy and rigor until the Second Vatican Council (1962–65), after which the deliquescence of serious belief in damnation (heaven remained an attractive, if vague, possibility) was astonishingly rapid. Although the doctrines remained officially in place, they were played down and lost most of the resonance they used to have with the faithful. It could be that the new model army of enthusiastically orthodox priests, which emerged during the pontificate of Pope John Paul II (1978–2005), will eventually reconvert Roman Catholics to a lively terror of the possibility of damnation—but at the moment that seems unlikely. You will rarely meet a Catholic who believes (to use Browning's words) that God watches him "As he believes in fire that it will burn, / Or rain that it will drench him."[1]

Yet in the nineteenth century, and even in the twentieth, people converted to Roman Catholicism in the conviction that by this means, and this only, could they save their immortal souls. Gerard

Manley Hopkins was afraid that his favorite composer, Henry Purcell, was in hell because he was a heretic. Graham Green wrote novels in which damnation was the central theme. A vivid assent to the reality of another world was everywhere to be found. My own interest in the profound culture change in Catholicism is rooted in childhood memories. These include a dying nun, serene, impatient to "see Our Lady and the Holy Family"; being told by my mother, at the first Mass I can remember attending, to keep looking at the altar, because an angel might fly across it; on learning the catechism at my elementary school: "Of which must you take more care, your body or your soul?" "I must take more care of my soul, for Christ has said: 'What doth it profit a man to gain the whole world and suffer the loss of his own soul?'" The "Enemy" who might tempt one to prefer the world to one's own soul was always near at hand. After the end of every Mass the priest read prayers ("for the conversion of Russia"), which ended: "Blessed Michael the Archangel, Prince of the heavenly host, thrust down to hell, we beseech thee, Satan and with him all wicked spirits that wander through the world for the ruin of souls." It is hard for modern Christians—at least in the West—to conceive how seriously all this was taken not much more than a generation ago.

I was educated by the Irish Christian Brothers in an austere, puritanical, Augustinian version of Catholicism. We learned by heart the five proofs of St. Thomas Aquinas for the existence of God—from motion, causality, contingency, design, the universal consent of mankind. Among the devotional practices encouraged was the wearing of the Miraculous Medal. Not only might this preserve you from a fractured skull if you fell off your bicycle or had an accident on the rugby field, but you were certainly promised that you would not die in a state of Final Impenitence. On special occasions, such as the annual "retreat" in which the whole school took part, the local Jesuits were called in to give instruction on a higher level. Their sermons encouraged us to meditate on the Four Last Things (death, judgment, hell and heaven). It was only later that I realized that virtually all the images they used to body forth the reality of these tremendous subjects go back not only to the sixteenth century (when the Society of Jesus was founded) but even to the church fathers of the first Christian centuries.

There was, therefore, a live tradition that united the boys of a provincial English grammar school with Cardinal Newman, Ignatius Loyola, Calvin, Luther, Dominic, Francis, Augustine, John Chrysostom, Lactantius, and Tertullian. And in primary school we learned a catechism text that takes you back to the very beginning: "What will Christ say to the wicked?" "Christ will say to the wicked: 'Depart from me, ye cursed, into everlasting fire that was prepared for the Devil and his angels.'" "What will Christ say to the just?" "Christ will say to the just: 'Come ye blessed of my Father, possess ye the kingdom prepared for you from the foundation of the world.'"

Yet although this was a live tradition, the spiritual imagination it nourished seemed to many outside and some within its fold deliberately to cut itself of from the most vital developments in the contemporary world. The church, reacting to the intellectual mainstreams of the nineteenth and twentieth centuries, had turned itself into a fortress, vigilant against error, much as it did in reaction to the Protestant Reformation of the sixteenth century. From the Council of Trent (1545–63) until 1966, the Roman Catholic Church had published and regularly updated an *Index of Prohibited Books*, which included most of the best philosophers and many of the greatest creative writers (Erasmus, Machiavelli, Descartes, Spinoza, Kant, Hume, Pascal, Montesquieu, Milton, Flaubert, Swift, to name but a few). The integrity of the "deposit of faith" in the world of Darwin, Marx, Freud, Einstein, Stalin, and Hitler was preserved by an authoritarian, managerial discipline.[2] That is why the valiant attempt of Rome to hold on to the ancient convictions is more striking than what happened in Protestantism. It is also why the changes brought about by the Second Vatican Council were also of great significance. For although that council did not formally change any articles of faith, it produced a climate in which some central doctrines seemed to lose their purchase on the Catholic imagination, shaped as it had been by the Counter-Reformation. The cultural change is still working itself out, and its full implications may not be understood until many more years have passed. Before the council, many even among those who rejected the faith were profoundly colored by it. In the early twentieth century there were those brought up in the Roman Catholic tradition who both intimately and imaginatively understood the doctrines about the next life, but who found them so at variance with modern experience that they could only treat them with a profound—if not necessarily unsympathetic—irony. One of these was James Joyce.

The most famous evocation of hell in modern times is to be found not in a work of theology or of piety, but in a novel—Joyce's *A Portrait of the Artist as a Young Man*—which includes some sermons delivered by a Jesuit priest, Father Arnall, to a congregation of Catholic schoolboys. The setting is a religious retreat in the school of the hero of the book, Stephen Dedalus. The sermons are on the Four Last Things. At this time in the full flood of his adolescent sexuality, Stephen is paralyzed with shame at the sins of impurity he has committed, both in the form of what the Church calls "self-pollution" and with prostitutes. He had lain "for hours sinning in thought and deed; his monstrous dreams, peopled by apelike creatures and by harlots with gleaming jewel eyes...a cold sweat broke out on his forehead as the foul memories condensed within his brain."[3] For nearly a year he has avoided going to confession, and has therefore remained in a state of mortal sin, which "kills the soul" and merits eternal damnation.

In Jesuit style, Father Arnall invites his audience to "make . . . the composition of place." Spiritual exercises in the Jesuit tradition encourage the faithful to move from what Cardinal Newman called "notional" to "real" assent by imagining as fully as possible (for instance) Christ's sufferings for the sins of mankind, our own mortality, the reality of hell, and the sufferings that the damned will experience for all eternity.[4] Father Arnall maps these things in precise detail.

He describes the "straitness" of the infernal prison house "expressly designed by God to punish those who refuse to be bound by His laws. In earthly prisons the poor captive has at least some liberty of movement, were it only within the four walls of his cell or in the gloomy yard of his prison. Not so in hell. There, by reason of the great number of the damned, the prisoners are heaped together in their awful prison, the walls of which are said to be four thousand miles thick: and the damned are so utterly bound and helpless . . . that they are not even able to remove from the eye the worm that gnaws it."

Heaped promiscuously upon each other, the damned lie in darkness, for the fire of hell gives out no light. Of the plagues with which God afflicted the land of the Pharaohs "one plague alone, that of darkness, was called horrible." The horror of darkness and straitness is increased by the "awful stench." All the offal and filth of the world shall run there as into a vast, reeking sewer. The burning of the huge mound of bodies, which are never consumed, fills all hell with an intolerable stench.

The torment is increased by "the company of the damned themselves." The mouths of the lost souls are "full of blasphemies against God and of hatred for their fellow sufferers and of curses against those souls which were their accomplices in sin." The company of the damned inflicts a punishment far more horrible than that ordained in ancient times for the crime of parricide— being cast into the sea in a sack containing also a cock, a monkey, and a serpent; for nothing in the animal world can compare with the fury of execration with which the damned turn on their accomplices and curse them.

Then there are the devils: "The devils will afflict the damned in two ways, by their presence and by their reproaches. We can have no idea how horrible these devils are. Saint Catherine of Siena once saw a devil and she has written that, rather than look again for one single instant on such a frightful monster, she would prefer to walk until the end of her life along a track of red coals. These devils, who were once beautiful angels, have become as hideous and ugly as they were once beautiful."[5]

With brilliant economy, Joyce summarizes in these sermons the doctrine of hell as it developed in the Christian imagination (and Jesuit rhetoric). The punishments are partly physical or external—the fire, the stench, the crowding. But they are also internal. The malice of the damned and of the devils is at the limits of what we can comprehend—and the state of the damned and the ugliness of the devils essentially symbolize this malice. The imagination of hell in Christian tradition is also an imagination of sin, its true inner nature. Hell as a state of justly imposed suffering at or beyond the limits of what we can imagine is a way of producing "real assent" to this understanding of sin and its malice.

For Christianity, the malice of sin has a significance that transcends any other evil—so that Jesus can suggest that the innermost motions of the heart can merit damnation. The Gospel of Matthew has Jesus teaching that whoever looks upon a woman so as to lust after her has committed adultery with her already in his heart, and "if thy right eye offend thee, pluck it out, and cast it from thee: for it is profitable for thee that one of thy members should perish, an not that thy whole body should be cast into hell" (Matt. 5:29).

There are pictures of eternal punishment in both Homer and Virgil, but they have little of the horror of the Christian hell. In the *Odyssey*, Homer depicts the punishment of several notorious sinners. Tityos, who had offered violence to the wife of Zeus, lies stretched on the ground while two vultures tear eternally at his liver and bowels. The thirsty Tantalus stands in a pool of water that comes up to his chin but which vanishes every time he tries to drink it. Sysiphus has to roll a huge stone up a hill, and every time it reaches the top it rolls down again.

Tityos appears again, in Virgil's *Aeneid*, along with other rebels against the gods, punished in similar way. Virgil includes whole classes of sinners—adulterers, cheats, those who hated their brothers or struck their fathers, traitors, misers—and briefly mentions their punishment: "some roll a huge stone, or hang outstretched on spokes of wheels."[6] But there is little detail—"I could not sum up all the forms of crime, or rehearse all the tale of torments."[7]

The Christian story is a narrative of human sin and redemption. The sin of Adam entailed death on all his descendants—indeed, his descendants are children of perdition, hopelessly corrupt in their very nature, meriting eternal damnation. They can be saved only through the atonement achieved by Christ and by grace freely offered to them. Sin and human corruption are therefore at the center of the Christian imagination. Depictions of hell are at the same time depictions of human malice. Correspondingly, punishment for sin is immensely more horrible than anything that could be imagined in either the *Odyssey* or the *Aeneid*. The Christian hell is equipped to inflict on sufferers both "extension" and "intensity." Each torment adds extra force to every other, and every pain is experienced with an intensity that cannot be dulled by habit but is experienced as though for the first time.

Father Arnall's second sermon is on the purely spiritual torments of hell. Of these the greatest is the pain of loss. Since God is infinitely good, the loss of God through an obstinate turning away from him must be a loss infinitely painful. In life we have only a fitful idea of what this loss might be, but at the moment of judgment we realize what we have deprived ourselves of through our sins: "At the very instant of death the bonds of flesh are broken asunder and the soul at once flies toward God as toward the center of her existence." Knowing full well that this loss is the result of her own choice, the soul experiences this *poena damni* as the greatest torment.

Going with this is the pain of conscience. The damned remember their own past pleasures that have deprived them of God—"the proud king will remember the pomps of his court, the wise but wicked man his libraries and instruments of research, the lover of artistic pleasures his marbles and pictures . . . he who delighted in the pleasures of the table his gorgeous feasts, his dishes prepared with such delicacy, his choice wines." Murderers will recall their deeds of blood and violence, and the impure and adulterous "the unspeakable and filthy pleasures in which they delighted."

Last comes the torment of eternity. The pains of hell are destined to last for ever. At this point Joyce uses an image that often recurs in literature on hell—a mountain of sand a million miles high. Imagine that at the end of every million years, a little bird comes to the mountain and carries away in its beak a tiny grain of the sand. By the time the bird has carried away the whole mountain "not even one instant of eternity could be said to have ended."

Joyce fills these sermons with themes that have recurred in Christian thinking over the centuries. Not a single image is new. Many of the images can be found in English Protestant writings of the seventeenth and eighteenth centuries (including the mountain of sand—an especially popular trope), in the psychologically vivid sermons of baroque, Counter-Reformation Catholicism, in the church fathers of the early Christian centuries. The images of the unbearable stench of hell and of flames that burn but give no light go back even earlier—to the apocryphal New Testament scriptures.[8]

In Father Arnall's rhetoric, the sublimities and paradoxes of the Christian sense of the contrast between the goodness of God and the malice of sin have become commonplaces. There are moments of crass materialism—"the prisoners are heaped together in their awful prison, the walls of which are said to be four thousand miles thick." And a Christian paradox that many would find outrageous is uttered as though it were a truism: "even venial sin is of such a foul and hideous nature that even if the omnipotent Creator could end all the evil and misery in the world, the wars, the diseases, the robberies, the crimes, the deaths, the murders, on condition that he allowed a single venial sin to pass unpunished, a single venial sin, a lie, an angry look, a moment of willful sloth, He, the great omnipotent God could not do so because sin, be it in thought or deed, is a transgression of his Law and God would not be God if He did not punish the transgressor."

It is very likely that Joyce has in mind here a notorious passage from John Henry Newman, whose prose style Joyce greatly admired: "The Catholic Church holds it better for the sun and moon to drop from heaven, for the earth to fail, and for all the millions on it to die from starvation in extremest agony . . . than that one soul, I will not say, should be lost, but should commit one single venial sin, should tell one willful untruth, or should steal one poor farthing without excuse."[9]

This may seem to us to have less rationality than it had for Newman. Certainly one will be tempted to see Newman's almost casual (although he certainly means to provoke a response) mention of Catholic orthodoxy about the smallest sin being worse than the greatest possible physical evil that could afflict the world as mad—or bad. Father Arnall expresses the thought with ridiculous confidence. Instead of seeing the idealization of the spiritual, according to which sin is infinitely more significant than suffering or physical destruction, as leading to colossal, troubling paradox—paradox that should force one to reconsider the line of thought that has brought us to this point—Arnall is simply repeating words, failing to see that this might be a *reductio ad absurdum*. If it is better for the moon to drop from the sky, for twenty million to perish on the Eastern Front in the Second World War, for a million souls to be bludgeoned to death in Cambodia than for a man to be irritated when his wife overcooks the chicken—then we seem to be in a mad world. Could even Newman give "real assent" to such a conclusion?

Father Arnall's attempt to make hell morally and physically real almost backfires. His conscientious detailing of the torments (part of what one writer has described as the Jesuit strategy of "computerized terror"[10]), the insistence that the guilt of even the smallest sin is worse than the torments of all those who suffer the pains of hell, the confident pushing of the theology of eternal punishment up to and well beyond the boundaries of comprehension mean that the picture can seem simply impossible when brought up against the common light of day.

Stephen does for a time "really" believe in the fact of eternal punishment. After Father Arnall's sermons he goes to confession and resolves to amend his life. But even after the first sermon Joyce insinuates two worlds—the world of the church's teaching, and the world of common experience—when he points a contrast between Stephen's terror and the matter-of-factness of the other boys and one of the Jesuit teachers:

> Hell! Hell! Hell! Hell! Hell!
> Voices spoke near him:
>> On Hell.
> I suppose he rubbed it into you well.
>> You bet he did. He put us all into a blue funk.
>> That's what you fellows want: and plenty of it to make you work.

Yet the contrast between the daylight world of material reality and the infernal other world is exactly what many Roman Catholic preachers, especially of the seventeenth and eighteenth centuries wanted to concentrate on. Or rather, they wanted to give people an imaginative sense how the other world was as real as this one, and how the sinner might find himself precipitated with terrifying unexpectedness into it. The sensualist might find a hideously sudden change in his sensations:

> That evening, in a blithe and cheerful mood, he lay down on his bed, and after a turbid and long sleep, he suddenly awaked and, turning over on to one side and then the other, he stretched out his arms, and oh God, he could not find the soft feathers any more, he could not find the bolsters, or the linen; but with one hand he grasped a fistful of worms and with the other he found a toad's hole. He felt other equally repulsive insects crawling over his body and realized he was covered with disgusting rotten matter.... He tried to stand up, and feeling his way with trembling steps, here he bumped into a corpse, there he came up against a crumbling and dripping wall; here he trod on a pile of picked bones, there his foot sank into a sewer of rotten guts. From the stench, from the loneliness, from the darkness, from the horror, he finally realized that he was enclosed in a deep tomb: he was buried.[11]

Catholic baroque sermons, on which those of Joyce's *Portrait* are especially modeled, aim to make the infernal world so real that it is this material one that seems to be the dream. Stephen's sense of tension between the voices of the boys and the master and the terrors that have so filled his mind actually enacts what these preachers are trying to achieve.

The line of thought underlying Father Arnall's sermons is clear. Man's soul is made for God and finds in God its supreme good and happiness. The essence of sin is the willful turning away from God, especially when moved by pride. St. Augustine writes that there are three sources of sin: *superbia*, *curiositas*, and *lascivia*—"the pride of life," the "lust of the eye," and the "lust of the flesh." These were the three temptations that Christ overcame when tempted by Satan in the wilderness. They are above all sins of pride, choice of the lesser good—oneself—over the greater good, which is God. Pride, says Augustine, is the *radix omnium malorum*, the source of every evil, the sin of Satan himself. And the only answer to pride is humility before the goodness and perfection of God.[12]

In some deep way human beings know this, even though the vices of a lifetime may veil it from them. They may hide it from themselves, until in the encounter with God after death they see with absolute clarity both what their true good is, and that they have lost it by their own choice. Therefore, in their outcast state they will both recognize God's justice toward them and at the same time hate God for his justice, because their will is now fixed in rebellion against God. This is in itself an infernal state of being.

So the Christian tradition that Arnall's sermons epitomize internalizes hell. The punishments that afflict the damned have something in common with the simple torments for wickedness and rebellion that you find in texts such as the *Odyssey* and the *Aeneid*, but they also move a long way toward seeing these torments as giving insight into the sins that they punish. It is orthodox to hold that the greatest torment is spiritual—the pain of loss and the self-loathing of the sinner. From very early times theologians were inclined to see the pains of hell as symbolic as well as literal. The eternal flames and the worm that never dies express the unavailing remorse and chagrin of the damned.

The church developed an elaborate psychology of sin, and the pains of hell kept pace with this. Although the doctrines of eternal punishment and eternal bliss did have a use in persuading the faithful to lead virtuous lives, fearing punishment or looking for justice in the next world, that was not all they did. In the case of hell the immense effort that went into imagining what it must be like was also an effort of persuading people to see their sins in all their loathsomeness—as they are seen by the eyes of God.

The logical conclusion was indeed to hold that the worst evil that can befall man is the state of sin. Since sin is the effect of a wrong choice of the will, an evil will is intrinsically an infinitely greater evil that any natural catastrophe—hence the idea that even a venial sin is worse than "all the evil and misery in the world."[13]

Although the church greatly elaborated the doctrine over the centuries, it can still be seen as deriving from the ethics of intention of Jesus in the New Testament. We should fear not those who can kill the body, but those that kill the soul.[14] We should take more care of our soul than of our body, for "What doth it profit a man that he that he gain the whole world and suffer the loss of his own soul?"

In *Portrait of the Artist* Joyce has in effect given us a secular version of this central Christian spiritual tradition. Stephen Dedalus is faced with a series of choices—from the childish dilemma whether he should tell the other boys at school that he kisses his mother goodnight, to his decision to complain to the rector of his college about an unjust beating inflicted upon him by Father Dolan, to his final decision that his destiny is to be not an Irish patriot nor a Jesuit priest but an artist who will "forge in the smithy of my soul the uncreated conscience of my race." Joyce sees Stephen's adolescent sense of sin and his consequent fear of hell as epiphanic moments in this journey of self-discovery, and not a final destination. Nevertheless, the journey itself owes everything to the spiritual tradition in which Stephen's Jesuit teachers breathe and move and have their being. A sense of the infinite significance of choice that life imposes upon one has been transferred into creative literature from a religious tradition that continues to feed Joyce's imagination. This may suggest to us that the vitality of the tradition, in some form or other, is not exhausted.

PART I

Dark Futures

I

After Lives

The hell depicted in *A Portrait of the Artist as a Young Man* obviously carries with it an elaborate and sophisticated set of beliefs about immortality, the human soul, sin and retribution. It is rooted in the conviction that the infinite significance of the soul's choices is best understood as the *eternal* significance of these choices. The immortal soul is what is essential to human beings[1] and therefore what harms the soul—sin—is the worst evil that can befall it. In late Judaism (that of the Pharisees and of Jesus) in Christianity and in Islam, belief in immortality has always been a belief in individual survival, in rewards and punishments meted out by divine justice, and in a fullness of life and consciousness in the world to come. This differs strikingly from beliefs about postmortem existence in many other cultures.

Belief in an afterlife may go back as far as we have knowledge of human beings. There is certainly abundant archaeological evidence from remote prehistory that people have been careful to protect and provide for their dead, often apparently giving them all that was necessary for a life beyond the grave. It is even possible that belief in postmortem survival goes back to Neanderthal man; and burial rites that could point to such a belief are of immemorial antiquity and well-nigh universal.

Not a few philosophers have argued that a hope for survival is intrinsic to human nature, and that this explains its apparent universality. Plato, famously, held the soul to be an immortal substance imprisoned within the body, from which the soul escapes at death. St. Thomas Aquinas argued that man does not just shun death instinctively, as animals do— he conceives of and desires eternal existence:

> It is impossible that a natural desire should be in vain. But man naturally desires to remain in perpetuity. This is clear from the fact that it is existence which is desired by all things. Moreover, man apprehends existence intellectually, not simply existence here and now, as the animals may be said to apprehend it, but existence as such. Man therefore attains perpetual existence in his soul, by which he apprehends existence as such and without temporal limit.[2]

Spinoza says that every being endeavors to persist in itself, and that this endeavor is its actual essence and implies indefinite time, and that the soul, sometimes with a clear and distinct idea, sometimes confusedly, tends to persist in its being with indefinite duration and is aware of its persistency.[3]

Yet have human beings agreed on what postmortem survival might be? The answer is certainly no. In animism—possibly the earliest form of religion—the dead may be thought of as spirits who may depart for a paradisal land, perhaps encountering terrors on the way, but who can equally be imagined as ghosts hovering around their graves and making nuisances of themselves to the living. The ancient Sumerians of what is now Iraq, and the Homeric Greeks, if they thought of survival after death, imagined a half-life, a barely conscious existence in a place of darkness—very like the place that the book of Job refers to as *sheol* or the pit—"a land of darkness itself; and of the shadow of death, without any order, and where light is as darkness" (Job 10:21–22). This half-life was infinitely inferior to life in the world we have left behind, indeed it was something to be dreaded—the inevitable cheerless destiny of all men. This has nothing in common with the beliefs of the ancient Egyptians, the Jews of the time of Jesus, Christians, and Muslims that there will be a restoration to fullness of life in the next world, including a continuing existence or resurrection of the body, and a future of joy or punishments, depending on the life one has lived.

Despite heroic attempts by Plato and Aquinas and many others who have theorized about immortality, it is impossible to find, by philosophical reflection, a common thread in all the ideas that human beings have entertained about the afterlife. These spring from customs, religious and ethical convictions, pictures of the world so heterogeneous that no one formula could capture them all. Two ideas, though, have seized the attention of many thinkers—fear, and the desire of justice. Pictures of an afterlife, it has been suggested, derive from fear of extinction; or alternatively from a hope that a future world might compensate for the evils of this one.

George Bernard Shaw is credited with the remark that when a man says that his faith in immortality has conquered his fear of death, we know that on the contrary his fear of death has conquered *him*. Thinkers in antiquity took seriously the idea that fear of death is simply fear of extinction, and they argued that such a fear is irrational. In Plato's *Apology*, Socrates, after sentence has been passed upon him, says that if death is indeed unconsciousness—mere extinction—then the prospect of it is something to treasure:

> If it is unconsciousness like a sleep in which the sleeper does not even dream, death would be a wonderful gain. For I think that if one were to pick out that night in which he slept a dreamless sleep and, comparing it with the other nights and days of his life, were to say, after due consideration, how many days and nights of his life he had passed more pleasantly than that night,—I believe that . . . even the Great King [of Persia] would find that they were few in comparison.[4]

Lucretius argued that it is as irrational to feel horror at the eons ahead in which one will have ceased to exist as it would be to feel horror at the blank eons before one was born. And if we dread the pain of separation from the loved ones we shall leave behind, this simply shows that we falsely imagine that we shall have a conscious existence that will enable us to feel this pain of loss. But in fact we shall be unconscious, as unable to suffer pain as we were unable to suffer anxiety about the Carthaginian invasion of Italy in the ages before we were born.[5] Lucretius presumably approved of the words of Hector in the *Iliad* when, having predicted to his wife, Andromache, the destruction of Troy by the Greeks and her own miserable enslavement, he rejoices that his own certain death means that those things will not be able to grieve him.[6]

Socrates and Lucretius are both arguing that what is irrational is the fear of extinction. Lucretius also argues that equally irrational is terror at the thought of postmortem punishments. Therefore, there are no grounds whatsoever to fear dying. A second great theme in reflection upon death has been justice. Hamlet's famous meditation on "something after death, / That undiscovered country" in which there may be dreams, contrary to Socrates' musings, reminds us how often fear of death has been fear not only of extinction or of a miserable half-existence but of just punishments for misdeeds in this life. Those religions that have most vividly portrayed the joys of heaven (Christianity and Islam) have also most powerfully enforced the fear of hell. Who can say whether the fear of one or the hope of the other has had the strongest hold on the imaginations of believers throughout the centuries?

At least as powerful has been the hope that justice will compensate for a world in which the good are oppressed and the ungodly powerful prosper.

"One dieth in his full strength, being wholly at ease and quiet. His breasts are full of milk, and his bones are moistened with marrow. And another dieth in the bitterness of his soul, and never eateth with pleasure. They shall lie down alike in the dust, and the worms shall cover them" (Job 21:23–26). Ancient Israel looked to God to right the wrongs of his people at some future time in the world. Later, Christians looked to a future life where God would have rewarded the meek and humble, and put down the mighty from their seats.

Nietzsche argued that from such a sense of impotence was generated a whole response to life in the world, which he called the "slave morality."[7] This morality reflected the values of the excluded, the downtrodden, the disappointed, the *chandalas*, and it resented and hated all the values that were cherished by the fortunate, the strong, the possessors: self-affirmation, pride, ruthlessness, exuberance, cruelty, and contempt toward the outcast. The values cherished by the slave morality—meekness, obedience, charity, humility, self-renunciation—are opposed to "the world," which accordingly becomes a term of infamy to the "slaves." Slave morality, therefore, ultimately sets its values in a world apart, a realm opposed to the actual world—for instance, a paradise within, or a heaven where the humble and meek shall indeed be exalted.

Slave morality does not, therefore, express attachment to the world; its attitude to death will not be that of those who hate death because they love life.[8] The bliss that is promised to the humble, or to those who thirst after justice and righteousness in a transcendent realm because they do not find it in this world, becomes, for Nietzsche, a sickly asceticism, a negation of healthy human instinct.

In a curious way, Nietzsche, in looking for the genealogy of modern ideas, is trying to push us back to a more primitive understanding of death. An afterlife in which the powerful of this world will have to answer for their unjust domination over the impotent and their excessive enjoyment of the good things of the world represents not a development of moral thought, but a defeat of our natural and healthy love of this life and its possibilities. In effect he argues that a primitive fear of death can express a love of life that is fundamentally more healthy and intelligible than the Christian hope of immortality.

Yet this suggests one more reflection on ideas about postmortem survival. The most ancient versions of it seem to escape even Nietzsche's attempt to capture origins. It is possible that the earliest beliefs entertained about immortality that we know of in what Claude Levi-Strauss termed "the savage mind" (*la pensée sauvage*) have nothing to do with a desire for justice, fear of a future punishment, depreciation of this world in comparison with one that transcends it, *nor with fear of one's own death*. That at any rate has been the speculation of some early twentieth-century anthropologists and archaeologists, who suggested that early beliefs about immortality were rooted not in hope for a survival of the living, so much as in fear of the dead. Immortality meant ghosts and the fear of ghosts, spirits and the appeasing of spirits. Ghosts are expected to be malevolent if not appeased and, even when appeased, not truly friendly. They also have immense power—especially if they are ghosts of powerful men such as chiefs. Sometimes the dead are buried bound, in a fetal position, and hemmed in by heavy stones—so that they cannot come back to plague and terrorize the living: "The dead are honored, but at the same time kept under restraint, by the contrivance of burial."[9] The realm of the dead needs to be barred in order to keep the departed spirits from pouring into the world of the living. The dead have to be persuaded to accept that their new abode is the grave.

This is a theme that continues to the present day among many tribal peoples. Here is a contemporary example from a hill tribe of Burma:

"There he comes," said Grandma.

Our own dogs barked from the house. Their barks became friendly, as though with recognition, and then quietened down. I was intensely curious to know whether Grandfather would behave as he did when he was alive, always entering the bedroom from the corridor through a window. The stairs door opened with a long creak . . . the steps sounded steady and deliberate. The sound of footsteps continued toward the direction of the veranda of his bedroom window. "That's him," I thought. We were waiting apprehensively inside the room as the footsteps approached the window. We heard the window being opened, but its flaps did not open as I expected. An expectant silence ensued.

Grandma spoke: "Is it you, La Pen? I did everything you ordered for your funeral. I hope I have been a dutiful and faithful wife to you. But this house belongs to the living, not the dead. You know that. Please go back to the grave, to your new home. I will meet you again when I am dead."

There was no answer. We heard footsteps going back through the window, into the hallway, and down the stairs. The barking of dogs accompanied him as he went away.[10]

Fear of the dead in their ghostly form, or at least the desire to separate them from the living, is extremely widespread among many of the earliest religions we know of: "Whether a man has one soul or several, his personality, far from being extinguished by death, emerges from the sepulcher in a new, powerful and terrible form."[11] Rites of mourning have often involved head-shaving and self-mutilation,[12] which looked like a frenzy of grief but was actually intended (at least according to some early twentieth-century anthropologists) to convince the spirit of the departed that it was getting its due and was not being overlooked:

A great lamentation and wailing is made by all the relations and friends of the deceased. They cut off their hair close to the head and besmudge themselves with oil and pounded charcoal. The women besmear themselves with the most disgusting filth. All beat and cut themselves and make a violent show of sorrow; and all the time that the corpse, rubbed over with grease and red ochre, is being dried over a slow fire in the hut, the women take it by turns to weep and wail before it, so that the lamentation never ceases for days. Yet . . . for one minute a woman will appear in the deepest agony of grief and tears; a few minutes after . . . will laugh and talk with the merriest. The principal motive, in fact, for all this display of sorrow would seem to be a fear lest the jealous ghost should think himself slighted and should avenge the slight on the cold-hearted relatives who do not mourn sufficiently for the irreparable loss they have sustained by his death.[13]

Some anthropologists have traced religion to the cult of the dead, with powerful ancestors being transmuted into gods, these often starting as chthonic gods, later ascending and becoming sky gods. The appeasing of ghosts (on this account) mutates into worship of the gods.

This reinforces the sense of difficulty we should have in trying to find general formulae about beliefs in an afterlife. For here we find the possibility that immortality can begin as something for *others*, and that it can be based not in hope but in fear, and fear not of one's own death but of the dead; not in a desire for justice, or dread of it, but in dread of the terrifyingly capricious things the dead are deemed capable of inflicting upon the living. It can begin simply as the appeasing by ritual of the terrifying dead. If these accounts of some of the earliest cults of the dead are accurate, then one of the most profound developments in human thought will have been the metamorphosis of this into an individual's hopes and fears for *himself*. How generally true this is, it is hard to say—but it certainly seems to have been true about some "primitive" beliefs about an afterlife, and points to a source of those beliefs that is, not hope for oneself but fear of others. So different is this from convictions about an afterlife in all the world-religions that it should convince us that there is unlikely to be one root, or one set of motives for such beliefs.

To trace religious beliefs and practices back to a primitive root does not, however, necessarily explain them in their developed form. Japanese Shinto is rooted in the shamanism that is found all over east and central Asia, from Japan through Korea to Tibet and Mongolia. But the refined aesthetic of Shinto has turned it into something far removed from the vestigial, ritually crude shamanism that survives (for instance) in post-Soviet Siberia and central

Asia.[14] Even were we to know (as seems possible) that ancient Egyptian beliefs about immortality began in some sort of animistic ghost culture, that would not explain the stately structure of dynastic Egyptian religious beliefs or religious psychology.

But if the cult of the dead did indeed begin in a need that was felt to appease them, this does at least remind us how difficult it is to find a formula that captures all, or even most human beliefs about postmortem survival. For the Mesopotamians, Greeks, and Romans, the next world is a joyless realm—Hades—inhabited by beings that have only a lamentable half-existence, which is quickened only if they are given warm blood to drink. For the Egyptians, later Jews, Christians, and Muslims there can be an immortal future that includes physical survival, rewards, and punishments. The Greeks and Romans, again, entertained the idea that true immortality consisted in fame and honor after death—a belief that may or may not fit with their folk belief about a joyless Hades.

This may mean that in thinking about after lives one is free to choose one's narrative. And I shall be keeping my distance from religious anthropology. I shall be concerned only with those beliefs in postmortem existence that can be thought to have something to say to each other, that can enter into a debate, be seen as part of a tradition, however loose and interrupted this may be. I shall be looking at ideas of afterlife in cultures that have produced works of art, literature, and religious speculation, works that resonate both one with another and with later literary or philosophical traditions. These cultures give rise to what we can recognize as conscious reflection upon ethics; bodily and psychic identity; tragedy, the nature of evil, repentance, and forgiveness; skepticism versus belief; the ethics of honor. In this category I include the Egyptian pyramid and Coffin texts and the *Book of the Dead*, the epic of *Gilgamesh*, the book of Job and other texts of the Hebrew Bible, Greek and Latin texts, including those of Plato and the mystery (Orphic) religions, the Christian scriptures, the apocryphal New Testament, the writings of the fathers, such as Tertullian, Lactantius, Origen, Augustine, Irenaeus; Dante, as well as some of the classic Christian writers on the afterlife in the Catholic and Protestant traditions; doubters, heretics, spiritualists, moderns.

If the list is heterogeneous, anything tighter could be accused of excluding even more arbitrarily than I may be guilty of doing. It may seem odd, for instance, to include *Gilgamesh* in a discussion of the afterlife when *Gilgamesh* is essentially a poem that enjoins the reader to give up any belief in personal immortality, and is about neither heaven nor hell. But *Gilgamesh* embodies a tragic sense of life that has strong affinities (as do other Mesopotamian texts) with the book of Job, and, denying as it does that immortality can be rationally desired, is at least in the same realm of discourse as religions that teach the opposite.

From the Egyptians through Mesopotamians, Greeks, and Romans, early Christianity, medieval Catholicism, Reformation and Counter-Reformation to Swedenborg, the Spiritualists and the optimistic American landscape memorial parks of the early twentieth century, it seems likely that beliefs about the afterlife have been a function of how we understand and value this present one. The sayings of Jesus about everlasting punishment seem to go with his urgent conviction that the spiritual has primacy over all else, and that hardness of heart and all uncharity, the corruption of the innocent, attachment to riches and power, make a life worthless: "And if thine eye offend thee, pluck it out: it is better for thee to enter into the kingdom of God with one eye, than having two eyes to be cast into hell fire" (Mark 9:47). In developed Christian thought, the doctrine of hell (to a greater extent than that of heaven) becomes a means of evolving a richly detailed moral psychology, which culminates in the *Inferno* of Dante. Even the doctrines of original sin and predestination, although they claim to derive from scripture, are rooted, as we find them in Augustine, Luther, and Calvin, in a picture of the human soul that has an interest even apart from its theological origins.

The spiritual is thus idealized only in advanced civilizations, and it goes with a particular evaluation of the individual soul, of personal responsibility, and the intrinsic worth of each person. It is only against the idealization of the spiritual that both the terrible punishments of an everlasting hell, and the joys beyond utterance of heaven and the beatific vision can even be formulated. It took a long time for theologians to work out a topography for the pains of hell and rewards of heaven that would rationalize those words of Jesus. But the whole elaborate (and sometimes apparently mad) structure of their speculations may be a sincere attempt to do just that.

I do not aim at an inclusive theory to capture the genesis of beliefs about postmortem existence, because such a theory, if it aimed to find a pattern that underlies all such beliefs, or an element they all have in common, would inevitably fail. All we can hope for are family resemblances, and these will be not so much in content as in form. All the beliefs and practices are found only in sophisticated cultures, and those who formulated them were aware how their beliefs interlocked with other values, ethical, political, aesthetic, so that they could be entertained in subtly different ways. They have been treated allegorically, transmuted into works of art and literature (where that was not their original form), mythologized and demythologized. Even to treat them with naive literalness (as did some Jesuit preachers of the Counter-Reformation) may be to make an artful decision.

If there cannot be an inclusive theory, there may at least be a narrative. There is a pattern in the development of thought about an afterlife, even in its contradictions. For ancient Egypt (at least in the earliest times), Greece, and Rome, only kings, demigods, or the most powerful can inherit a pleasing afterlife. In the earliest Greek and Roman traditions, fame through great achievement—patriotic courage, for instance—is the only immortality worth having, from which it follows that immortality will be possible only for the tiniest of minorities. Yet the Egyptians, in the cult of Osiris, and the Greeks and Romans with the mystery religions, came to allow the possibility that there might be personal immortality for many, even all. But the stronger the belief in personal immortality—among the Egyptians, for instance, the Christians, and Muslims—the stronger also became the terror of judgment after death. The Mesopotamian, Greek, and Roman conviction that after death we become shades in a dark underworld may have been pessimistic—but at least it never led to the fear of eternal damnation that weighed so heavily on Jews of the time of Jesus, and on the other two Abrahamic religions. Even where ancient peoples entertain the idea of postmortem judgment, they do not (with the exception of the Egyptians) seem to be preoccupied with it. If the Homeric Greeks saw even the greatest of heroes, Achilles, as destined to a melancholy existence as a shade casting "a longing, lingering look behind" at the world he has lost, they did not in general fear an eternity squashed into a stinking sewer of rotten guts, burning in a huge mound of bodies, overcome by an intolerable stench, and tormented by devils so hideous to behold that St. Catherine of Siena, rather than look upon one again, would prefer to walk until the end of her life along a track of red-hot coals.

Yet the astonishingly elaborate structure of thought about the next life reared by the church, the cultivation of ideas that hover on the very edge of intelligibility does indeed find its origin in the simpler ideas of earlier faiths and philosophies. It does not represent simply the free play of imagination. In this book we explore some of the various paths that led to this remarkable destination.

2

Egypt

ma'at: Righteousness and the Afterlife

The first culture, of which we have evidence, that systematically connected an afterlife with good and evil conduct in this world, and with a judgment after death was that of ancient Egypt. The Egyptians were also the first people who developed fully worked-out beliefs about personal immortality. Indeed, since so many of the surviving monuments are tombs and funerary temples, the strongest impression that most of us will form of the Egyptians is bound to be that of a race preoccupied with death. "The houses of the living, even the palaces of the kings, were constructed chiefly of perishable materials such as mud-brick, reeds and wood. The tombs of the dead, for the most part, were made of stone."[1] This impression may, of course, be misleading, and Egyptologists remind us that the Egyptians were an exuberant, peaceful people, who loved life and hated the thought of death.[2] A typical greeting to visitors on a tomb was "O you who love life and hate death!"[3] The Egyptians have been depicted as a happy, light-hearted people: "Their folk-tales, their music, their comic-pictures and caricatures, their dancing and singing, their games, play, and buffoonery, their love and use of flowers, their bright colors and gaudy garments, and even the names they give to their children, "Eyes-of-love," "Cool Breezes," "Beautiful Morning," all go to indicate their buoyant, happy and gay disposition."[4] It has been suggested that the Egyptians were constantly aware of death, for the

Nile Valley "is a long thin strip of cultivable territory surrounded by lifeless desert; no one in central or Upper Egypt could ever forget the sharp dividing line between fertile land and desert...[pointing] the lesson taught by our ancient liturgical text: 'In the middle of life we are encompassed by death.'"[5] One may think of Nietzsche's suggestion that the Greek invention of tragedy, in its steady contemplation of suffering and death, springs from an attachment to life. That the elaborate death-culture of the Egyptians expresses just such a love of life is an attractive idea—and there is plenty of evidence to support it.

In the Valley of the Nobles, near ancient Thebes (Luxor) are the tombs of Menna and Nakht. Nakht was an astronomer of the god Amun; Menna was an inspector of the royal estates, and a scribe to the Pharaoh, Tuthmoses IV. Whereas the tombs of the pharaohs and their consorts in the Valley of the Kings and the Valley of the Queens are hieratic and otherworldly in character, these two tombs are much more free in their decoration. These rightly famous wall paintings suggest an intense attachment to the vitality of the world the dead have left behind. Nakht's tomb shows enormous bunches of grapes, many loaves of bread, and also the harvesting of grapes, sowing, plowing, treading the harvested grain. The lives of animals are also vividly suggested. Some scenes depict them being killed for food; but others seem simply to celebrate animals for their own sake. A cow is shown being slaughtered for a feast. But we also see a cat getting stealthily at some cooked fish under the table—almost under the noses—of Nakht and his wife. A trussed duck, destined for the pot, pecks hopefully at some grapes. Maidens dance to a harp; nubile women are massaged.

Menna's tomb is even more sharply the scene of the joys—or perhaps the sheer fact—of living. A scribe measures a field of high corn for tax purposes; and a man is shown being beaten for not paying his taxes. Wheat is cut with a sickle; men and women tread the vintage. In this tomb, abundant fields of ripe wheat are prominent in the wall paintings. As the wheat is trodden, two young girls are seen, carrying baskets and picking the grain out of each other's hair. A cat climbs a tree hunting for birds' eggs—while unbeknownst to it a mouse follows a foot or two behind. Men spear fish. Menna sits cupping his wife's breast in his hand. Pilgrims seek the tomb of Osiris at Abydos. Horus is shown judging the heart of a dead man.

Yet to see all this purely as nostalgia for the world the dead have left behind may be a mistake. This world of fertility and abundance is perhaps a representation of the next life, a life of bright, comfortable existence where, even though the dead have to work the lands for the gods, they will actually get the tasks done by magical substitutes (*shabtis*) while they attend to the serious business of enjoying themselves. The next world is the Kingdom of Osiris, a place where the dead will joyfully inhabit "the Land of Reeds"—modeled on actual Egypt, but better: "He shall come into the Fields of Reeds, and bread, wine and cakes shall be given to him at the altar of the Great God, and fields and an estate [sown] with wheat and barley, which the Followers of Horus shall reap for him."[6] The pictures in the tomb, because of the particular way in which Egyptians identified images with what they represent, actually make this ideal next life magically available to the dead.[7]

If it be true that the Egyptians were the first to decide that one's lot in the next life depended on one's conduct in this one, we need to ask what their ideals of behavior were. We already have the sense that they were not ascetic, that they did not despise the world nor think that human life was a mere worthless shadow of something more real and glorious. Were they simply hedonists—as some of the tomb paintings might suggest?

Vital to the Egyptians was their concept of *ma'at*. This immensely rich idea takes in truth, order, justice, being in touch with the fundamental law of the universe, hence with the sun god, Re, whose incarnate son ruled Egypt in the person of the pharaoh.[8] Hence it also suggested civic obedience. There was also a goddess, Ma'at, who personified truth, justice, physical and moral law, and order. She was the daughter of the sun god.[9]

For the Egyptians, living in accord with *ma'at* meant being in harmony with life—and therefore wishing to live forever.[10] It is an optimistic view of life, a belief that the good person is the one who achieves this harmony, and who is therefore happy. It is an ethic that connects wisdom with moral goodness. Its precepts link living morally with enjoying a good outcome, in the manner of much ancient Wisdom literature, including the book of Proverbs. When the wicked man is foundering in storm and flood, you should rescue him—both because this is the right thing to do, and because you will gain advantage over him:

> Lift him up, give him your hand,
> Leave him in the hands of the god.
> Fill his belly with bread of your own.
> That he be sated and weep. (*Moral Values*, 46)

In its connecting of righteousness with utility this resembles another text: "If thine enemy be hungry, give him bread to eat; and if he be thirsty, give him water to drink: For thou shalt heap coals of fire upon his head, and the LORD shall reward thee" (Prov. 25:21–22).

The person with *ma'at* was characterized by kindness, calm temper, justice, generosity, and respect for traditional rights. In showing these virtues, he also showed humility toward the gods (*Moral Values*, 48–49). Tomb inscriptions abound where the dead person claims the virtues that flow from *ma'at*. But these are not simply boastful, for they reflect a genuine belief in the judgment of the dead, a weighing up of the deeds of the deceased by an impartial, stern judge whose edicts reflect what the souls' own conscience tells.[11] There is a tomb inscription from the Tombs of the Nobles at Aswan, dating from about 2300 BC (Sixth Dynasty) that in its direct connection of one's state after death with good or evil deeds in this life has been called "one of the most significant documents both in the history of ethics and the evolution of the idea of post-mortem judgment."[12] The tomb belonged to one Herkhuf, and he writes of himself both egotistically but also according to the universal code of moral behavior that is *ma'at*:

> I dug a lake, and I planted trees. The King praised me. My father made a will for me, for I was excellent—a man beloved of his father, praised of his mother, whom all his brothers loved. I gave bread to the hungry, clothing to the naked, I ferried him who had no boat . . . never did I say aught evil to a powerful one against my people, for I desired that it might be well with me in the Great God's presence. Never did I judge two brothers in such a way that a son was deprived of his paternal possession.[13]

Herkhuf does not claim good treatment in the next life purely because of his excellent moral character. He has also performed the necessary magical rites that are a central part of the ancient Egyptians' preparations for passage into the next world: "I am an excellently equipped spirit, a ritual priest whose mouth knows."[14] Part of his declaration seems to be a spell or curse to deter anyone from interfering with or seizing his tomb—"As for any man who shall enter this tomb [i.e., take possession of it], I will seize him like a wild fowl; he shall be judged for it by the Great God."[15]

There is no question but that Herkhuf believes that his having lived well and done good deeds, in accordance with *ma'at*, is an essential part of his claim that he be well received in the afterworld—as well as the spells and incantations he has arranged.

Ma'at was very much an active virtue of public life as we see from the following tomb inscription:

> I am a worthy noble, a leader in the nomes,
> a thoughtful one who knows the good;
> successful, resourceful, weighty,
> knowledgeable, who finds the missing word,
> a solver of problems, discreet, dignified.
> Who speaks the good, repeats the good,
> does what his god praises,
> does what people love:
> A man of right, beloved of all the gods.[16]

There is worldly prudence in this, but it also commends a goodness of heart, not far removed from the Christian works of corporal mercy (comfort the afflicted, feed the hungry, clothe the naked, bury the dead):

> I saved the weak from one stronger than he as best I could
> ... I gave bread to the hungry, clothes to the naked,
> I landed one who was stranded,
> I buried him who lacked a son. (Ibid., 14)

It can also be a quality of debonair courtesy appropriate in one in high office in his behavior toward his inferiors:

> Generous, good-natured,
> open-hearted, free of glumness,
> whom this land holds in affection. (Ibid., 30)

Judgment

More striking is a story found in a tomb inscription some two thousand years later, around 300 BC, that recalls a parable, central to the Christian imagination of judgment after death, from the Gospel of St. Luke; the story of Dives and Lazarus:

> There was a certain rich man, which was clothed in purple and fine linen, and fared sumptuously every day:
> And there was a certain beggar named Lazarus, which was laid at his gate, full of sores,
> And desiring to be fed with the crumbs which fell from the rich man's table: moreover the dogs came and licked his sores.
> And it came to pass, that the beggar died, and was carried by the angels into Abraham's bosom: the rich man also died, and was buried;
> And in hell he lift up his eyes, being in torments, and seeth Abraham afar off, and Lazarus in his bosom.
> And he cried and said, Father Abraham, have mercy on me, and send Lazarus, that he may dip the tip of his finger in water and cool my tongue, for I am tormented in this flame.
> But Abraham said, Son, remember that thou in thy lifetime receivedst thy good things, and likewise Lazarus evil things: but now he is comforted and thou art tormented.
> And besides all this, between us and you there is a great gulf fixed: so that they which would pass from hence to you cannot; neither can they pass to us, that would come from thence. (Luke 16:19–26)

In very late Egyptian religion a similar contrast between the values of this world and those of the divine world seems to have been envisaged. The Egyptian story is inscribed in the tomb of Petosiris, a priest.[17] It tells of Satmi, a prince in Memphis, who one day observes the funeral procession of a rich man with all the pomp and ritual lamentation that you would expect. Immediately afterward he sees the pathetic funeral of a poor man, carried out of the city in a mat, with none to mourn him. Satmi is shocked by the contrast and utters the wish that his own end might be like that of the rich man.

Now, Satmi has a son, Senosiris—who is actually an ancient sage, miraculously reincarnated—and the son, to his surprise, contradicts him. Senosiris says: "May there be done to thee in the land of the dead ['Amentit'—the Beautiful West, which is the realm of the dead ruled by Osiris] that which is done for that poor man in the land of the dead, and may that not be done to thee in the land of the dead what is done to that rich man there."

To the amazement of Satmi, his son then takes him on a trip to the underworld, where they see Osiris enthroned. On their way to see Osiris in his Great Hall, they notice that the pivot of the door turns in the right eye of one of the damned. Senosiris says to his father:

"Satmi, seest thou that exalted personage, clothed in garments of fine linen, who is close by where Osiris sits? That poor man, whom you saw carried out from Memphis, with none to follow him, and rolled in a mat, the same is he! He was brought to the underworld, his misdeeds were weighed against his merits, and his merits were found to outweigh his misdeeds . . . it was decreed that he should be assigned a place among the venerable souls . . . close to the seat of Osiris. That rich man whom you saw, he was brought to the underworld, his misdeeds were weighed against his merits, and the former outweighed the latter . . . and it was he, whom thou saw, with the pivot of the door . . . planted in his right eye whenever the door is closed or opened, whilst his mouth utters great cries."

But although this particular rich man is tormented after death, there is no sense that being rich and happy in this life might in itself imperil a person's happiness in the next—no sense that it is easier for a camel to pass through the eye of a needle than for a rich man to enter heaven.[18] On the contrary, the proper use of riches is one of the things that marks the character of a good man. One autobiographical tomb inscription has:

> White-robed feast watcher with his brothers,
> Lucky with crops, good with the spear
> Generous, free of meanness,
> Shining at dinner, happy at breakfast
> Lord of food, free of stinginess.[19]

Visions of happiness that we find in these inscriptions include the idea that the good person is happy, but that this happiness implies certain material conditions. There is a picture of contentment in a villa:

> Its barns are full of grain and bulge with abundance.
> Fowl yard and aviary with geese; byres filled with cattle.
> A breeding pool with geese; horses in the stable.
> Barges, ferry-boats, cattle boats are moored at its quay.
> Young and old and poor have come to live nearby.
> ...Joy dwells within. (Ibid., 58)

As Miriam Lichtheim puts it: "What rings true in this fantasy is the joyous feeling for a bountiful, cultivated land teeming with life." In putting the value they usually do upon the civilized enjoyment of prosperity (notwithstanding the story of Satmi) the Egyptians stress, not a great gulf between this life and the next, but continuity. Yet this continuity needs to be striven for. They certainly do connect the rewards and punishments of the next life with a good and bad conscience. The evidence for that is the terrifying ordeal that the departed soul had to face—the judgment by the dog-faced divinity, Anubis, in the presence of Osiris. In *The Book of the Dead*[20] the soul is presented with a list of forty-two possible crimes that it might have committed, and claims to be innocent of all of them. The denials include:

> I have not laid violent hands upon an orphan; I have not done what
> God abominates; I have not slandered a servant to his superior ... I
> have not made anyone weep; I have not killed ... I have not had sexual
> relations with boys ... I have not debased the measures; I have not
> taken milk from a child's mouth; I have not driven small cattle from
> their herbage.[21]

After the dead man's soul has uttered these denials, Anubis—in a scene that one sees in an enormous number of tomb paintings—weighs the dead person's heart against a feather, the symbol of *ma'at*. At this point the dead person utters a prayer that his conscience—his heart[22]—will not rise up and accuse him:

> My heart of my mother, my heart of my mother, my breast, the heart of
> my being! Rise not up as a witness against me, turn not against me
> before the tribunal. Act not as my enemy before the keeper of the
> balance ... Cause not my name to smell evil in the nose of the
> tribunal. Speak no lie against me before the good gods.[23]

It is true that much of *The Book of the Dead* gives instruction for spells that the soul can use to influence the divine powers, and this is not purely a matter of

Anubis weighs the heart of the dead against a feather, the symbol of righteousness (ma'at). The hearts of the righteous are no heavier than the feather—they are not burdened with sin. From *The Ancient Egyptian Book of the Dead*, translated by R. O. Faulkner, spell 125, page 14.

conscience and divine judgment. Indeed it often looks like a crib for a frighteningly thorough general knowledge quiz in which the dead have to acquit themselves outstandingly well if they are to have any chance of successfully completing the journey through the land of the dead to the Halls of Osiris. As well as declaring its innocence, the soul has to show that it knows the names of all the forty-two assessor gods, for to know the names of the gods and demons who beset one on the journey to the next world is essential—the Egyptians believing that to know someone's name is to have power over them.[24] The soul even has to know the names of all the different gates and halls it will traverse:

> "We will not allow you to enter past us," say the jambs of this door, "unless you say our name." Accurate Plumb-bob is your name. "I will not allow you to enter past me," says the right lintel of this door, "unless you say my name." Pan for Weighing Truth is your name.[25]

The information—the spells—that will allow the soul to answer these questions is written on the tomb walls, or inside the coffin, or even on a roll of papyrus buried with the mummy. Because *The Book of the Dead* seems to offer the departed a cast-iron guarantee that if its instructions are followed to the letter he will pass the examination, it has been suggested that "there never really was any doubt concerning the success of the soul in making the journey, because the papyri always record that the individual for whom they were written overcame all difficulties and eventually reached the realm of Osiris."[26]

So traveling to the next world is like taking an examination when one already knows the questions.

Yet surely the very fact that an authoritative, powerfully magical religion offers to assist the soul on its journey and to guarantee success if all the rules are followed, suggests real terrors and dangers that are overcome. Even if the soul "ritually always claims innocence, and never offers to repent its past sins,"[27] the very claim of innocence shows that, as well as the arcane knowledge expected to be displayed by the departed, there is an irreducible element in which the person's conscience is weighed against truth (*ma'at*). The eloquence with which the soul calls on its heart not to betray it conveys a powerful terror of judgment, and of a "second death." You might compare this with the Catholic assurance that confession and the last rites before death do assure the forgiveness of sins. Yet the (old) funeral service includes such prayers as "*A porta inferi . . . Erue, Domine, animam ejus*" ("From the gate of hell . . . Deliver his soul, O Lord"). A ritual is something between a spell and a personal prayer; it is assumed to have power, but at the same time it expresses both hope and fear.

The dangers threatening the departed as they made their way to the halls of Osiris are depicted in such vivid detail that it is very hard to think that they were thought of complacently: the dead might be burned in a pond of fire, cooked or roasted and then devoured by demons, decapitated by baboons, mutilated, have their hearts torn out, lassoed and dragged to the slaughtering block, or seized by demonic pigs, snakes, crocodiles, dogs. It seems unlikely that the devout Egyptians, contemplating death, were confident that such a fate could be overcome *simply* by uttering certain words.

An Afterlife for Whom?

In the development of Egyptian beliefs about the afterlife there was a sort of gradual democratization.[28] In the earliest period—the Old Kingdom—it was believed that pharaoh and his family alone could ascend to a life of bliss in the heavens, while ordinary people went to the underworld. Later the privilege of joining the god Re in the heavens was extended to members of pharaoh's court and his highest officials. Finally, by the time of the Middle Kingdom, the "solar" realm of the dead became open to all.[29]

In the earliest dynastic times the ruler could expect to be translated to the heavens purely on account of his status. Even so, many were the spells that were meant to assure this. The earliest texts—the *Pyramid Texts* (so called because they adorned pyramids at Saqqara[30])—are entirely devoted to the afterlife of pharaoh. They proclaim and ensure that pharaoh has ascended to the sky as a star,[31] that he is joining the sun god, Re-Atum (ibid., utterance 217), primordial god of the earth and sky, lord of the cosmic order and father of *ma'at*, that he becomes the universal governor (ibid., utterance 224). There are, at the same time, spells against noxious creatures, such as snakes and scorpions, which could presumably harm him—but the overwhelming impression is of pharaoh joining his fellow divinities in the skies (ibid., utterances 226, 230, 233, 324). Nevertheless, there are a few moments when even pharaoh seems to regard himself as a possible object of judgment, a feeling that he has to justify himself not simply by his status but by his deeds as well: "I desire to be vindicated by what I have done" (ibid., utterance 260); "I have set right [*ma'at*] in the place of wrong" (ibid., utterance 249);[32] "O you female apes who cut off heads, I will escape safely from you.... Those whom I have caused to eat, they eat their food, those whom I have caused to drink, they drink of their water-flood" (ibid., utterance 254 (286).

The death of the pharaoh was a matter of the greatest consequence for the whole nation. In Egypt all religion was, in a sense, the cult of the king, since "Pharaoh alone was in direct communion with the gods as the one who offered to them and received blessings from them on a cosmic, eternal level."[33] It was pharaoh who thus took responsibility for ensuring that the gods sent the yearly inundation at its proper level, and who therefore agonized over the omens that foretold famine or plenty—as the story of Joseph interpreting pharaoh's dreams suggests in Genesis (Gen. 41). It was imperative that he should find his proper way to the heavens from which, as one of the gods, he would continue to watch over and guide the destinies of Egypt. Some have even seen the shape of the pyramids as providing a sort of symbolic launching platform for the king's ascent among the stars. So it is not surprising that nearly all these early funerary texts are to do with the royal rites of passage. The king was going to meet and be reunited with his *ka*—his divine element that unites him with the divine element of the god that created the world, and indeed of all the gods. In the earliest times, only pharaoh was deemed to possess a *ka*, but this gradually became the prerogative of all persons.

It is very easy to conclude that the world view of the ancient Egyptians was profoundly material. The immense importance they set on actually preserving the body for all eternity, as well as their picture of an afterworld of eating and drinking, adds to our sense of that. But this would be to overlook their particular ideas of how the human person is constituted. To the Egyptians, human beings are not a compound of body and soul as we have come to understand these terms. We are made up of three elements. First there is the *het*—the physical body, which is corruptible. (The body of a god—a *det*—is incorruptible.)[34] When the body was mummified, it was given a different name, which seems usually to have meant "image."[35] Mummification was a sacred, highly ritualized procedure that turned the material body into some-thing fitted for its special role in the afterlife.[36] One has a sense of what this means from the mummy coffins themselves, which represent an idealized version of the dead human form. Mummification aimed both physically to preserve the body as it was in life and at the same time give a sense of the person as he would be in the afterlife—radiant, transfigured.[37]

Mummification is also founded on the elements that constitute the human person: the body with its heart—the seat of its life; a shadow, the fleeting shade of a human being; the *ka* and the *ba*. The *ba*—which is sometimes represented as a bird with a human head—is sometimes translated as "soul"; it was "sometimes thought to be a kind of dream-soul, then a being which survived death, again a being which came into existence only after the death of the body to which it was related."[38] In earliest times it seems to have meant the power of king and gods to make their presence manifest in the world and which therefore was not possessed by ordinary people.[39] The *ba* could be thought of as living in the tomb, flying out of it in its bird-form, and returning. It might partake of the food offerings left for the dead.[40]

Perhaps the most difficult concept to understand, but one that tells us most about ancient Egyptian beliefs about the afterlife and the actual mortuary and embalming practices, is the *ka*. The *ka* could be thought of as a twin or double. It was connected with reproduction and male potency, and was a continuous link with earlier generations.[41] In the earliest hieroglyphic texts it meant both "bull" and "food."[42] It was a sort of life force, and therefore even had connotations of food and crops.[43] It is interpreted as a life principle, as character, as ancestral spirit, as personality, as essence, as protective spirit, and as temperament.[44] The *ka* is what makes someone divine. A god is a *ka* and so is a pharaoh. When a pharaoh died he went to his *ka* and so, eventually, did all men. The *ka* gives human beings life, good fortune, health, and joy as well as magical power, strength, glory, wealth, nobility, and intelligence.[45]

The *ka* has corporeal aspects (it, too, could partake of the funeral offerings of food, although this could also be done by a statue of the deceased *representing* his *ka*), but it is imperishable and in heaven. When a human being died, his soul (*ba*) went to join his *ka*, while the body remained lying in the grave. The essential thing is that the *ka* needed a physical form to inhabit after death. It is at this point that the belief peculiar to Egyptian religion comes into play and which explains a central part of their mortuary tradition. In order to achieve resurrection after death, it was necessary to preserve the relation between *ka* and *ba* in the afterlife, and therefore essential for the body to be kept as whole and perfect as possible.[46] The corpse must not corrupt in the tomb. From this arises the celebrated Egyptian invention of mummification—first described outside Egypt by Herodotus.[47] Originally, only the deceased pharaoh could comprise a *ka*, a *ba*, and a body spiritualized like that of a god's.[48] The elaborate mummification rituals found in the *Pyramid Texts* are partly devoted to producing this spiritualized body. Later, mummification offered this possibility to all.

What may be hardest for us to understand is how extremely detailed the prayers and spells are in their attempts to preserve and resurrect the body of the deceased. They describe in fairly shocking detail what has to be prevented, and the incantations to that end: the deliquescence of the corpse ("Chase away the fluid of your corpse");[49] the body's becoming maggoty ("You do not become maggoty, you do not smell, you do not suppurate") (ibid., 59); *rigor mortis*; loss of warm breath; darkness, loneliness, stillness, silence. There is an extraordinary sense of what is vital, and what contradicts the joyous vitality we enjoy here and now: "I am the master of the light, I detest dying. . . . Celebrate a gay day, follow your heart" (ibid., 2).

(Moderns, you could argue, medicalize death in a way that superficially resembles but is actually remote from the attitude of the Egyptians. The mouth of the corpse is sewn up, and cosmetics are applied, and embalming [in America at least—much less so in Europe] is also usual. But this is a way of sanitizing the physical. The Egyptians are not afraid to contemplate the realities of decomposition even while being determined to halt it.)

The future life offered to all was clearly a true resurrection. The dead may have spiritualized bodies, but this meant that they had the fullness of life of the gods, who possessed imperishable bodies. Yet if a future life was offered to all, so was the possibility of future punishment, for the Egyptians were also the first people to work out an idea of future punishments and hell. This is the price of "democratization"—one's future state no longer depends purely on social status.

Just as the happy life depicted in the tombs of Menna and Nakht, insofar as it is an envisaging of the next life and not purely a nostalgic recall of the delights of the present one, is a perfection of life in this world, so the punishment of the wicked will be a reversal of the natural order. They will walk upside down, will drink urine, and eat feces. They walk upside down because, having formerly walked on the earth, they now walk with their feet against the bottom of the flat disk of the earth (ibid., 9). Since they walk with their feet against the ceiling, the digestion goes into reverse, and the excrements arrive in the mouth (ibid., 73). The reward of the just is described with typical explicitness: "I do not walk bent for you. I walk upright. My phallus is united with me. My *anus* is united with me. I eat with my mouth. I have a motion with my *anus*" (ibid., 77).

Even in the *Pyramid Texts*, so devoted to the glories of the king in the heavenly realm, pharaoh is represented as capable of anxiety about that. Having expressed an interest in barley, emmer, bread, and beer, and having called, in several utterances, for roast leg of calf, he says: "What I detest is feces, I reject urine . . . I will never eat the detestableness of these two."[50]

In the later *Coffin Texts*—in which resurrection has become available for just about everyone—these fears are very frequently reiterated. Many are the spells "for not eating feces in the realm of the dead": "What I detest is feces, and I will not eat; filth, I will not eat; the vulture, the servitor of the dead, shall not bring to me, he shall not wipe his lips on me, he shall not coil his neck on me, because I sit between the two great gods, I live on bread of white emmer. . . . What I detest is efflux, and I will not eat . . . I will live on sweet stuffs [offerings of cakes and other sweet things left for the dead] which have issued from the shrine . . . I ward off feces, I reject urine."[51] "I will live on the white bread of emmer washed down with zizyphus [a rootlike herb] beer . . . warm will be the food . . . the foreleg, the hind leg, the haunch . . . I will not eat feces for you, I will not drink urine for you, I will not go upside down for you."[52] The *Book of the Dead* has a large number of spells against having to eat feces.[53] The belief that underlies this is that the hope for resurrection derives from the ever-renewed processes of nature, the yearly return of the inundation, the bursting to life of the seed planted in the damp mud. For the wicked, the natural order is reversed, the world turned upside down, natural processes perverted.

One of the chief fears about the afterlife was that for the wicked there would be a second death. This was not the nothingness that moderns may fear—but the dread that they would be hacked and torn to pieces and thrown into a fiery lake. So there are spells "for being saved from slaughter"[54] and for passing safely by the fiery lake of the knife-wielders.[55] Another text describes the task of certain gods (or demons) in the next life as to "hew and hack souls in pieces, and set restraints upon shadows, and to destroy such doomed beings as have their being in the place of destruction which blazes with fire."[56] Gods are represented who "stand at the blocks of torture" and who "annihilate the dead, who hack in pieces shades of men and women, who destroy and cut in pieces the dead, who avenge Osiris" (ibid., 110, 115). To be cut in pieces, eaten by an avenging beast, menaced with fire are among the penalties visited on the soul that has failed the test as its heart was weighed by Anubis in the balance. But the wicked dead are not to be punished eternally, nor even for a long time, for the task of the spirits who assault them, spirits "whose faces are of flames" is to "hack asunder the dead, and to cause the spirits to be destroyed" (ibid., 138).

The text shows a number of pits in which the wicked are consumed with fire. In one, a goddess with the head of a lioness holds a large knife in her hands and pours fire into it from her mouth (ibid., 249–50). Another shows a very large pit with vaulted roof, in which are immersed, head-downward, four male figures. The name of this pit is Ant-Sekhetu, "the valley of those who are turned upside down" (ibid., 251). The text reads: "Hack in pieces and cut asunder the bodies of the enemies and the members of the dead who have been turned upside down, O my father Osiris ... My father having once been helpless has smitten you, he has cut up your bodies, he has hacked in pieces your spirits; you shall never more exist ... you shall be cast down headlong into the pits of fire; and you shall not escape therefrom, and you shall not be able to flee the flames that are in the serpent" (ibid., 254–55).

Apostates and blasphemers against the god, Re, are to be bound in fetters before being cut up so that their souls "shall have no existence."[57] Enemies of Osiris will be assaulted by a great serpent, which is urged on by the faithful son of Osiris, Horus, to open its jaws and "belch forth your fires against the enemies of my father, burn up their bodies, consume their souls."[58]

The blessed, by contrast, are summoned to felicity in terms very slightly reminiscent of "Come ye blessed of my father, inherit the kingdom prepared for you from the foundation of the world" (Matt. 25:34): but here we read "wash with shouts of joy, perform that which is your right to do, and let your souls be in the following of created things."[59] There are even words that might remind us both of Ezekiel in the valley of the dry bones (but are no doubt to do with the revival of the mummified dead) and the Christian idea of resurrection: "Hail to you! Your souls live ... your flesh is to you, you have gathered together your bones, you have knit together your members, and you have collected your flesh."[60]

There is also a place where Osiris, addressing Atum, promises spiritual consolation to the departed souls: "O Atum, what means it that I proceed to the necropolis, the silent land, which has no water, no air and is very deep and very dark and all is lacking, wherein one lives in quietness of heart and without any sexual pleasures available? "I have given blessedness instead of water, air and sexual pleasures; quietness of heart instead of beer," says Atum."[61]

There is also no doubt that the rewards of the blessed are very often reassuringly material. They will especially enjoy pastry;[62] they will eat bread made from red grain cakes (or "bread-cake"), and drink good beer, ale, and even wine. They will even be seven cubits broad in their buttocks.[63] An invocation for the benefit of the pharaoh in one of the Pyramid Texts is in the same spirit: "be seated before a thousand loaves, a thousand mugs of beer; the roast, thy double-rib piece comes from the slaughtering bench."[64] Yet sometimes the food and drink seems also to have a spiritual connotation: "I have decreed for you that ye shall have your being [in Amentet] ... with *ma'at* [truth, order], and without defects. ... Their bread shall be *ma'at* cakes, their drink shall be of wine."[65]

Skeptics?

Herodotus records a *memento mori* of the Egyptians. He relates that at feasts they were accustomed to pass around a deceased person in a container (apparently a statuette version of a mummy) so as to remind themselves of death, and hence to reaffirm their joy in life.[66] This is typical of the Egyptian tendency to hold opposite ideas and emotions together in the mind. In the midst of an undoubted profound faith in an afterlife with a restored body and soul, there is to be found a precisely opposite attitude: "Thou who wast rich in people, thou art in the land that likes solitude. He who loved to spread his legs in walking is bound, enwrapped and obstructed. He who liked to dress himself in rich fabrics sleeps in yesterday's cast-off garments."[67] It was usual at a funeral for the widow to clasp the mummy's feet as if she wants to keep her husband with her and is full of doubt about the efficacy of funeral ritual and magic.[68]

Nebneteru, a priest of Amon, having celebrated the joys of life, laments: "The end of life is sorrow, it means the inadequacy of that which was formerly with thee, it means sitting in the hall of unconsciousness at the dawn of a morning which does not come ... it means not knowing, it means sleeping when the sun is in the east, it means being thirsty at the side of beer."[69] The last touch is poignant, for beer was among the gifts of food and drink offered at tombs, in the belief that the dead would thereby be refreshed. But here the suggestion is that the dead are incapable of ingesting beer or anything else.

Siegfried Morenz quotes the words of a contemporary of Nebneteru: "The fleeting moment when one receives the rays of sun stands for more than eternity, since one is ruler of the nether world." This seems to refer to Osiris, ruler over the dead, and Morenz reminds us of the famous words of Achilles to Odysseus, when he refuses to be consoled by the thought of being "king of all the dead that are no more."[70] Still more intense are the words of a woman, Taimhotep: "Death, 'Come' is his name, he summons everyone to himself. They come immediately to him, although their hearts shudder with fear of him."[71]

You could take these utterances as expressing doubts "about a spiritual existence and about rites intended to revive the dead."[72] Yet one could also see such a tone of pessimism and skepticism as a necessary part of a sophisticated culture, of a reflective, philosophizing system of belief. To entertain doubt, to state the opposite of what one's rituals entail is to show, surely, that one's beliefs are held in a conscious way—what I earlier described as beliefs connected with conscious reflection upon ethics, human nature, tragedy.[73] Beliefs of primitive societies in the afterlife seem different. They may be enacted in rituals, which have no explanation beyond the fact that this ritual is performed, and fits into a pattern of ritual practices. Egyptian beliefs are sophisticated; they embody a philosophy as well as a mythology, an ability to stand back and ponder as well as to believe and enact. These utterances need not express "doubt" but only an intelligent attitude to experience corresponding to T. S. Eliot's definition of metaphysical wit—"a recognition, implicit in the expression of every experience, of other kinds of experience which are possible."[74]

Osiris

Any sense we may have that a material afterlife is somehow in conflict with a spiritual one is dissipated when we reflect on a cult the importance of which to Egyptian religion cannot be overstated—the cult of their best-loved god, Osiris. The balance between the material and spiritual looks different in the light of that great popular devotion.

Osiris (who may have been an actual king or chieftain in pre-dynastic Egypt) was a peace-loving vegetation and fertility god, who taught his originally pastoral and nomadic people the arts of agriculture, who became the god of the dead, Lord and judge of the underworld.[75] He weaned his subjects from their miserable and barbarous manners, and taught them to till the soil, sow, and reap crops. He discovered the use of the vineyard, was the first to drink wine, and taught these arts to men. He built canals and floodgates to control the yearly inundation of the Nile.[76] His role as Lord of the dead is taken for granted in the *Pyramid Texts*, which means that he must have had this character from the very earliest times.[77] He was a corn god, and his influence extended over barley, corn, spelt, wheat, and grain.[78] He had a sister-wife, Isis, and a brother, Set. In a battle between Set and Osiris, Set defeated Osiris and slew him at Abydos, cutting up his body into sixteen parts. But with the assistance of Isis, who collected nearly all the parts, Osiris rose from the dead, became eternally the judge and ruler over all the dead, and eventually, a sign of resurrection for all. In one version of the story, there was one part—the phallus—that Isis could not recover. So she created, by magic, an artificial phallus, squatted over Osiris and conceived a son, Horus (who went on to avenge Osiris, defeating and mutilating Set). A wall painting in the temple of Abydos depicting this in conscientious detail somehow managed to escape mutilation by Copts and Muslims.

The underworld realm of Osiris somehow became merged over time with the solar realm of the sun god, Re-Atum, who was also the great god of creation. The result is that the Osirian underworld, in one of those unresolved contradictions in which Egyptian religion abounds, also seems to be thought of as being in the sky. So Osiris became the god of suffering and resurrection, defeat and triumph, kindly yet a judge, Lord of the dead, of creation, and of fertility. He is always associated with water and the Nile, and, as corn god, is sometimes shown lying prone with grain sprouting from his recumbent body, or with a tree growing out of his coffin. Because he was the first man to have raised himself from the dead, and now sat upon a throne in heaven, he offered hope of resurrection to every human being.[79] The dead were said to drink the emissions of Osiris and eat what comes forth from him—i.e., to live off the water and grain that the god brings forth.

Myth and Metaphysic

Egypt was, in the famous phrase of Herodotus *doron tou potamou*—"the gift of the river (Nile)."[80] The whole of the Egyptian delta was created from the Nile silt. Even the Egyptian account of creation draws on the picture of the Nile waters receding after the inundation. In the same way, the creator-god made land rise out of the aboriginal waters and the world came into being. Clearly all food is the gift of the divine river, and Osiris comes to preside over sowing and the harvest. Therefore all forms of food that grow from the Nile inundation, and by extension the cattle and sheep that graze upon it are divine gifts. This gives a sacral quality to the land of Egypt and all the good things it produces, all that supports human life and civilization. In the light of that, the pleasures of food and drink—of beer, wine, sweet cakes, the white bread of emmer, haunch, foreleg and rib—are not, in our sense, "material" as opposed to "spiritual" things. The same would apply to sex and human fertility, and indeed to the pleasure of being alive. Osiris brings all these good things to man, and to enjoy them is to partake in a sacrament.

To be admitted into the kingdom of Osiris required a good and upright life—a life lived according to *ma'at*. But *ma'at* itself implied living in respectful accord with the rhythms, the customs, the laws of Egypt, being thankful for the gifts of the gods, obeying lawful authority that had existed from time immemorial and was of divine sanction. Ancient Egypt was regarded by its inhabitants as a "land of the gods"—rather as Japan was regarded by ancient Shinto.

Many in the European Enlightenment found in Egyptian myths a philosophic wisdom.[81] This belief was not misplaced. We can reasonably elicit from the stories of the Egyptian gods and, in particular, the creation myths, metaphysical and ethical ideas. Atum (the primordial creator-god) spat out, sneezed, or masturbated two offspring from himself. These were his "son," *Shu*, which means "dry air," and his "daughter," *Tefnut*—"corrosive moist air."[82] Tefnut becomes the consort of Shu. According to Quirke, these are two life-giving principles. Shu embodies dry air as the force of preservation—that force that kept the earliest Egyptian burials in the sands of the desert from decay and perhaps suggested the idea of mummification. He thus suggests life itself and also time as an endless cycle of eternally repeated events. Tefnut, as moist, corrosive air is the opposite and expresses time as "the relentless rule of change," and, conversely, time as a series of unique events in a single line.[83] The first is the cycle of the seasons and of the movement of sun, moon, and stars. The second is the passage of generations and of life and death.

These ideas were not in the modern sense abstract, for they found the most vivid possible representation in the greatest event in the Egyptian year, the profoundest recurrent phenomenon in Egyptian experience, the repeat before their eyes of the original creation of Egypt, in the annual inundation (which came to an end with the building of the Aswan High Dam.)

> Every summer the low-lying fields and marshes in the Nile Valley were
> returned to the condition of primordial waters as the river swelled
> from the summer rains at its Ethiopian and Sudanese highland
> sources; every autumn, as the floodwaters drained to the
> Mediterranean Sea, the fields would emerge not as they had been
> before the flood but coated in a layer of new silt brought down by the
> river from higher up the valley to the south. In Egyptian terms each
> new occurrence repeated the "first time," when the waters receded to
> reveal the first shallows out of which a lotus-flower could bloom to
> support the sun god, and then the first dry land upon which the sun
> god could find solid ground to rest. The fragrant lotus ... played the
> role of revivifying the sun god, just as the scent of lotus revivified the
> Egyptians in their leisure.[84]

The Egyptians seem to have been preoccupied with the strife between order and chaos. The world comes back into existence each year after having seemed to have been swallowed up in the waters from which it had first emerged. The sun dies each night and is reborn each morning. This was another threat of chaos; and the sun was supported in its orderly progress across the sky by religious cult. The practices that assisted the sun were religious cult and justice.[85] Egyptian religion and ethics both spring from the actual conditions of the land, express themselves in myths that describe that condition, issue in rites that are meant to help in preventing the ever-possible collapse into chaos, and root themselves in this understanding and these hopes and fears. *Ma'at* is therefore related to the daily effort of imposing order upon chaos, as it is with the daily rebirth of the sun.[86] The inundation itself is a reenactment of creation and a reminder of one of the basic requirements of *ma'at*—justice between man and man. This is beautifully expressed in the *Hymn to the Flood*:

> there is no-one whose hand weaves with gold,
> there is nobody who becomes drunk with silver,
> true lapis-lazuli cannot be eaten;
> barley is the fundament of all being;
> when you rise for the hungering town-dwellers,
> they sate themselves on the produce of the country . . .
> goodness is strewn in the streets,
> and the whole land frolics afoot.[87]

The rising of the Nile brings sustenance to all, rich and poor, reminds us of what is truly precious in life, and is an emblem of human solidarity.

Perhaps this is why we may feel that the Egyptian preoccupation with immortality does not proceed from a morbid fear of death but from a healthy hatred of it—"O you who love life and hate death." There are texts of a poetic beauty that can still move us depicting the pleasures of the senses and the desire that these continue eternally:

> Delight your heart.
> exult in joy,
> unite with happiness,
> summer-lotus at your nose,
> myrrh-oil on your brow! . . .
> . . . . receive the lotus that comes from your garden . . .
> May you do as you wish in it for all eternity![88]

Grieving does not prolong life:

> Follow thy desire, as long as thou shalt live.
> Put myrrh upon thy head and clothing of fine linen upon thee . . .
> Set an increase to thy good things . . .
> Until there come after thee that day of mourning . . .
> . . . wailing saves not the heart of a man from the underworld.[89]

Egyptian beliefs about the afterlife are fully integrated into their total picture of the universe, of a world where order is constantly menaced by chaos, but in which what opposes order also brings vitality. There is the opposition between a cyclical eternal movement of stars, planets, crops, and seasons, set against the uniqueness of an individual life. Osiris lives, is murdered, is reborn. The inundation covers the land of Egypt; its waters recede, crops spring up, the land is magically restored more fresh than it was before. Man may have a fresh existence after death just as the crops spring up after the flood. As Osiris finally defeated Set, so pharaoh will master the forces of dissolution.[90]

This all suggests a theology, a metaphysic and, indeed, an aesthetic that mirrors, explains, and sacralizes the experience of Egyptians over the millennia. Egyptian ethics correspond to what Hegel called *sittlichkeit*—a social ethic that emerges out of inherited human customs and tradition. It is an ethic that affirms life, as powerfully as any we know of. Yet it goes beyond *sittlichkeit* precisely in that it has these complex roots and relations, this intellectual superstructure reared over, but also re-creating, the experience of the nation and of the land.

The Egyptian sense of sin has the balance one might expect from such a wonderfully poised philosophy. All the spells for the safe passage of the dead to Osiris are devoted to claiming that each soul is without sin. The sins themselves imply an eminently sane attitude to life. The "negative confessions" deny pretty obvious and central transgressions, and they never suggest the doctrine of total human depravity that we find in some central Christian traditions. The punishments of the Egyptian hell are terrifying enough but, assuming that the incantations and spells do their job, it turns out to be a hell mostly (to use the words of T. S. Eliot on the *Hell* cantos of Ezra Pound) "for other people, not for ourselves and our friends."[91] On the whole one can expect to be received into the loving arms of Osiris. The wicked are not punished eternally. Rather, they cease to exist.

Egyptian religion, because of its roots and ramifications, seems not to be vulnerable to some simple attribution of motives. If we ask why the Egyptians longed for eternal life, it would be no use answering that it was because they feared death. For they *consciously* feared death, feared it in a way that makes that fear the expression of a way of living, a set of ethical values and an imaginative response to nature itself. Their sense of the vitalizing processes of nature is the obverse of their bizarre (as it might seem to a modern sensibility) preoccupation with all the hideous processes of bodily decay—the maggots, the suppurating flesh, the decomposition of the body into liquid, the rigidity of the corpse. Yet all this testifies to realism. Whatever else the Egyptian hope for the resurrection was, it was in no sense a deluded or sentimental thing. It is as if the effort of a whole culture, an entire understanding of the cosmos, along with a noble ethical sense went into their view of the afterlife. Their avoidance of a pessimistic expectation that the dead would end up in Hades, or in the dark and dismal pit of the Sumerians, or the *sheol* (pit) of the ancient Israelites—was not easily won. It is hard to see a way of subverting or deconstructing this immensely subtle and rich view of the world. There is no way of having an overview of the Egyptians that enables us to sum them up and feel we have gone, philosophically speaking, decisively beyond them. Indeed, it is later belief systems that could, by comparison, seem primitive, or, at least, simplifying. It is very hard not to admire the sanity, balance and humaneness of the view of things we can take from ancient Egypt.

3

Mesopotamia and Israel

"He Who Saw the Deep"

Until around the second century BC there was no general belief in immortality, in the sense of personal bodily resurrection, in ancient Judaism. But the sense that God's power could restore Israel (as in the vision in Ezekiel of the reclothing in flesh and restoration to life of the valley of dry bones) was a vision that could gradually turn—as it did after many more centuries had passed—into a more personal hope. And there was the possibility of debate about man's relation with God, and how that relation radically affected his fulfillment in life, in the absence of such a hope and such a belief. From Mesopotamia and Israel we have a number of texts, and two in particular, that stand as sophisticated works of conscious skepticism, of abstinence from easily satisfying hopes and explanations. One is the book of Job. The other is a text that remained lost to the world until fairly recent times.

In the mid-nineteenth century an English archaeologist and his Assyrian assistant found a collection of clay cuneiform tablets, mostly broken into pieces, in the ruins of the palace of King Sennacherib of Assyria—the king whom Byron depicts coming down "like a wolf on the fold" when he invaded Israel. A few years later many more tablets were found in the palace of Sennacherib's grandson, Ashurbanipal. It was from the piecing together and deciphering of these ancient tablets—which had lain undisturbed for 2,500 years—that the ancient Mesopotamian poem, *The Epic of*

Gilgamesh, was recovered for the modern world. The language of the poem was Akkadian, a Semitic language spoken by peoples who conquered most of Mesopotamia, approximately in the middle of the third millennium BC. The conquered people were the Sumerians, a non-Semitic, non–Indo-European people, who had entered Mesopotamia in the fourth millennium BC, and who invented the cuneiform script. The earliest versions of *Gilgamesh* were actually written in Sumerian, a language that was not decoded until the late nineteenth century. They may date back five thousand years. The tablets on which the surviving portions of text were inscribed have been dated at around 1750 BC. *Gilgamesh* and the other Sumerian works of literature so far deciphered have been described as "the oldest literature of any appreciable and significant amount ever uncovered."[1]

Gilgamesh is a poem about the acquiring of wisdom, about the fear of death, and about the impossibility of hoping for immortality. Its hero, Gilgamesh, appears first as a man who exults thoughtlessly in his strength and vitality—a little like that thoughtless hero of Wagner's *Ring* cycle, Siegfried—and is led by that conscious strength to attempt astonishing deeds, finally even crossing the Waters of Death to seize the secret of eternal life. It is a story that ends in defeat, a defeat that is the condition of wisdom. And the wisdom that Gilgamesh acquires is that the best thing for man is to enjoy life: "Make merry each day, / dance and play day and night" and enjoy the love of his children and the embraces of his wife. Just as beliefs about immortality and how to obtain it issue logically in the Egyptian rituals for the safe passage from this world to the next, and in the whole elaborate cult of the dead, so the skepticism about eternal life that we find in *The Epic of Gilgamesh* issues in an impressively mature sense of human limitations, and in a stern realism.

Gilgamesh is the king of Uruk, a city in ancient Sumer, midway between what are now the cities of Baghdad and Basra in Iraq, and not far from Ur of the Chaldees, the traditional birthplace of Abraham. By the end of his life Gilgamesh has become a man of surpassing wisdom. He built the walls protecting Uruk; he built the temple of the chief goddess of Uruk, Ishtar; and above all he had "seen the Deep," brought back a tale of the times before the Flood, restored the temples that the Flood had destroyed, and eventually found peace in resigning himself to the common fate of all men—death.[2]

The ancient Mesopotamians—the Sumerians, the Akkadians, and the Babylonians—had a view of death infinitely more somber than that of the Egyptians. There was no happy afterlife in which the whole human being could be restored to full vitality, but only a dark, gloomy, silent netherworld of the dead, who have become mere shades, the "land of no-return." The entrance to this netherworld is only a few feet below the surface of the earth.[3] To go to this land of no-return was the fate of all. Those who go there—all the dead—immediately become terrifying and malevolent ghosts, unless they are appeased by constant offerings at their tombs.[4] Great kings, priests—and heroes—must all face this destiny. Kings and priests lose all their rank and wait at table, and heroes become as weak as birds held by their wings:

> In the house of dust into which I entered,
> I looked at the kings, and behold! Their crowns had been deposited.[5]

Nothing can avert this fate or hold out to humans any hope of salvation or resurrection. That is the burden of *Gilgamesh*. And because its hero is a great and mighty man who hopelessly pits himself against this common fate, the epic is a tragic drama—the first in all literature.

We first meet Gilgamesh in Uruk, where he walks about showing himself superior like a wild bull.[6] His hair grows as thick as barley, and he is of consummate beauty. He tyrannizes over the young men of Uruk, allowing none of them to "go free to his father."[7] He allows no girl to go free to her bridegroom, for he exercises over all brides the *ius primae noctis*. Not only that—he makes the young men take part in incessant contests. He mounts piggy back on a band of widows' sons who groan with his weight, crying "O my neck! O my hips!"[8]

Having introduced us to a king whose greatness runs also to tyranny and a good measure of joyous egoism, the poem switches to a very different sort of man. This is Enkidu, the warrior, "offspring of silence."[9] The gods decide that Gilgamesh needs this man, of strength equal to himself, to be his dearest comrade. Enkidu is a wild man of the hills. His body is covered in shaggy hair, so that he seems scarcely human. He roves over the hills all day, and he is a strong as a meteorite ("a rock from the sky")[10], grazes on grass with the beasts of the field, runs with the gazelles, and drinks at watering places with cattle. A hunter sees this terrifying apparition, and tells of him to Gilgamesh. Gilgamesh bids him take "Shamhat the harlot"[11] and get her to seduce and tame Enkidu. The strategy is successful:

> Shamhat unfastened the cloth of her loins,
>   she bared her sex and he took in her charms.
> She did not recoil, she took in his scent:
>   she spread her clothing and he lay upon her.
> She did for the man the work of a woman,
>   his passion caressed and embraced her.
> For six days and seven nights
>   Enkidu was erect, as he coupled with Shamhat.[12]

The result of the seduction is that Enkidu agrees to become civilized. A barber grooms his hairy body and anoints it with oil. He turns into a human

Gilgamesh and Enkidu slaying Humbaba. From *The Epic of Gilgamesh*, edited and translated by A. R. George, figure 6, page 45.

being, dresses properly, and learns to eat bread and drink ale. After drinking seven goblets of ale "His mood became free, he started to sing, / his heart grew so merry, his face lit up."[13] In becoming civilized, and especially in embracing Shamhat, he loses part of his strength. The beasts of the field shrink away from him, and the gazelles effortlessly outrun him. He is no longer part of innocent nature.[14]

Shamhat leads Enkidu into Uruk to meet Gilgamesh, who has already been advised in a dream that there will be brought to him by the gods a friend whom he will love, caress, and embrace like a wife.[15] Enkidu comes upon Gilgamesh just as he is about to exercise his privilege over a newly married girl, and challenges him to a fight. They strive mightily, but then vow to become bosom friends. As friends, both mighty in strength and courage, they must obviously do great deeds. So they decide to go and slay a terrifying monster, Humbaba, whose voice is the deluge, whose speech is fire, who lives among the cedars of Mount Lebanon.

Gilgamesh and Enkidu travel to the Forest of Cedars and duly slay Humbaba. Back in Uruk, the beauty and courage of Gilgamesh provoke the desire of the goddess, Ishtar—"Grant me your fruits, O grant me!"[16] However, Gilgamesh knows full well that Ishtar had murdered all her other loves, not only the human ones but a bird, a lion, and a horse! So he brutally rejects her. Mad with rage, Ishtar runs to her father, Anu, chief of the gods, and demands that he give her the Bull of Heaven (the constellation Taurus) so that she can use it to take

Gilgamesh and Enkidu slaying the Bull of Heaven. From *The Epic of Gilgamesh*, edited and translated by A. R. George, figure 7, page 53.

vengeance upon Gilgamesh. The Bull of Heaven comes down to earth, dries up marshes and rivers, and causes numerous citizens of Uruk to fall into huge pits. But then, Enkidu and Gilgamesh between them get hold of the bull's tail and horns, and slaughter it. (Enkidu holds the tail while Gilgamesh deftly plants his dagger in the nape of the neck, like a Spanish matador.) In a notable gesture of contempt, Enkidu hurls a haunch of the slaughtered bull all the way up to heaven and Ishtar.

So far, Gilgamesh and his dear comrade, Enkidu, have had it all their own way. Their courage and strength are godlike, and their boldness in the face of the gods themselves has something semi-divine about it.[17] But it is at this moment—immediately after Enkidu has done the amazing deed of throwing the haunch of the Bull of Heaven at Ishtar, presiding goddess of Uruk—that the limitations of human power show themselves. As punishment for this boldness—or *hubris*—Enkidu sickens and dies. As he sees death approach, he curses Shamhat the harlot who had taken him away from his wild way of life...may she eke out the rest of her life without house, in penury, and without the erotic attentions of men. But the god to whom he prays rebukes him, pointing out that it was through Shamhat's influence over him that he was magnificently clothed and acquired as companion the handsome Gilgamesh. The people of Uruk will lament and mourn for him, and the hair of Gilgamesh will be matted in mourning for his friend.[18] The heart of Enkidu grows calm, and he withdraws his curse of Shamhat:

My mouth that cursed you shall bless you as well!
  Governors shall love you and noblemen too!
At one league off men shall slap their thighs,
  at two leagues off they shall shake out their hair!
No soldier shall be slow to drop his belt for you,
  obsidian he shall give you, lapis lazuli and gold!
Earrings and jewelry shall be what he gives you![19]

I have used the world *hubris* in describing what Enkidu does. The ancient Greeks understood by *hubris* an overweening confidence in men that provokes the jealousy of the gods and brings down upon them *nemesis*. In slaying the Bull of Heaven, and Humbaba, Enkidu has been guilty of something like *hubris*. But the main feeling we have is that his arrogance and over-boldness result not so much in punishment imposed from the outside, but in a recognition of the common destiny of man. The strength and boldness of Gilgamesh and Enkidu can overcome everything, except death itself. Furthermore, Enkidu is made to realize that his cursing of Shamhat is intrinsically unjust—for she it was who brought to him what he actually values: civilization and the friendship of a great and wise king. He felt that in coupling with a woman he has become tainted and hence weak. But now he ceases to resent that. There is genuine self-knowledge in his withdrawing of his curse, and in its place something like humility. That the magnificently strong and bold Enkidu can at this moment acknowledge the claims of what is so different from the qualities he values in himself is a moment, for him, of profound inner change. We could also see it as a case of civilization and its discontents. In becoming civilized, Enkidu lost his oneness with nature, his sense of untrammeled freedom and power. Now he accepts that loss as a necessary fate—as necessary, perhaps, as death.

Enkidu has a vision of death and of his entering the netherworld—the "world of no return." The ancient Sumerians and Babylonians seem to have thought of the netherworld as above all a dingy place, and of the dead as clothed in dusty feathers like birds. Enkidu has a dream in which all his strength is "but as yesterday." A being with lion's paws and eagle's talons seized him by the hair, crushed him as a mighty wild bull could, drenching his body in poisonous slaver.[20] The mighty Enkidu is "turned into a dove." The specter binds his arms "like the wings of a bird." (Anyone who has been at a fowl market in the Near East, with housewives casually carrying by one wing live chickens or geese destined for the pot, thereby completely disabling them, will appreciate the power of this everyday image.) The specter leads Enkidu into the house of darkness, where lie priests and kings who had offered sacrifices regularly to the gods—yet here they are, lying in this dusty gloom:

to the house whose residents are deprived of light,
>   where soil is their sustenance and clay their food,
> where they are clad like birds in coats of feathers,
>   and see no light, but dwell in darkness.
> "On door and bolt the dust lay thick,
>   on the house of dust was poured a deathly quiet.[21]

Enkidu dies, and Gilgamesh is plunged into the bitterest grief. He keeps the body near him for a time and cannot accept that Enkidu is finally dead and decaying until a maggot drops from his nostril.[22] His grief is mixed with fear of his own death, that he, like Enkidu will "also lie down/never to rise again, through all eternity."

It is extraordinary that the poem manages to convey the impression that the idea of death is new and shocking to Gilgamesh, and that it does so through the sharply specific image of the maggot dropping from Enkidu's nose—a commonplace but irrefutable proof of Enkidu's mortality and an indication of the nature of that mortality.

Death simply is a horror, not because it involves judgment on a life (which was an idea alien to the ancient Mesopotamians), but because it is the direct negation of anything we can value—strength, energy, pride, ambition, glory—all that makes us infinitely better than shades. Gilgamesh is right to hate this, and the epic will not go on to declare that he is wrong, or that there can be any more consoling vision—only that he *cannot* fight the inevitable.

Gilgamesh resolves to travel beyond the limits of the known world to find Uta-napishtim, the Mesopotamian Noah, the one human being whom the gods allowed to survive the Deluge and who was thus granted immortality. He gets on the boat of the Mesopotamian Charon, Ur-shanabi, whose boat across the waters of death is rowed by mysterious "Stone Ones." For reasons that are obscure, but in character, Gilgamesh smashes all the Stone Ones and therefore has to punt the boat over the bitter waters, using a punt pole made out of a huge number of forest pines attached end to end to reach the immense depth to the bottom.

Having crossed the waters of death, the first person Gilgamesh meets is a female tavern-keeper.[23] It is the tavern-keeper who denies the possibility of immortality and gives Gilgamesh advice to cherish the essential consolations of human life:

> O Gilgamesh, where are you wandering?
> The life that you seek you never will find:
>   when the gods created mankind,

> death they dispensed to mankind,
>> life they kept for themselves.
> But you, Gilgamesh, let your belly be full,
>> enjoy yourself always by day and by night!
> Make merry each day,
>> Dance and play day and night!
> Let your clothes be clean,
>> let your head be washed, may you bathe in water!
> Gaze on the child who holds your hand,
>> let your wife enjoy your repeated embrace!

This has something in common with Hebrew Wisdom literature:

> He hath made every thing beautiful in his time: also he hath set
>> the world in their heart, so that no man can find out the work
>> that God maketh from the beginning to the end.
> I know that there is no good in them, but for a man to rejoice, and to
>> do good in his life.
> And also that every man should eat and drink, and enjoy the good of
>> all his labour, it is the gift of God. (Eccl. 3:11–13)

Finally Gilgamesh encounters Uta-napishtim, who devises a very simple way to convince him how entirely beyond the power of even the strongest man is the gaining of eternal life. He suggests that Gilgamesh try the much simpler feat of going for six days and seven nights without slumber.[24] The weary Gilgamesh squats down on his haunches and instantly "sleep like a fog already breathes over him." Uta-napishtim's wife bakes a loaf of bread for every day that Gilgamesh sleeps. By the time he wakes up, the first loaf is all dried up, the second one is leathery, the third soggy, the fourth has turned white, the fifth has a gray mold, the sixth is fresh baked, and the seventh still on the coals. Gilgamesh, waking up, assumes that he has slept for only a few minutes—until he sees the evidence of the bread. On seeing the evidence he bursts out afresh in lamentation of his mortality.

The response of Uta-napishtim is in the same spirit as that of the tavern-keeper. Gilgamesh has wandered to the ends of the world, exhausted, with matted hair, filthy body. and wearing the pelts of animals. This is not a human life. In searching for immortality, Gilgamesh has forgotten how to live, forgotten that he is a civilized man and a king. The man who lives and dresses like that is a fool; and whereas a king gets the best food and the attention of all others, the fool lives on leavings and is ignored. So Uta-napishtim orders Ur-shanabi to take Gilgamesh to the washtub, take away the pelts, wash him, soaking his body until he is handsome again, and give him royal robes, fresh and new, that befit his dignity.

But then he does offer Gilgamesh the secret of immortality. He tells him of a plant that lives deep down in the water, which, if it be eaten, will renew Gilgamesh's youth. Immediately, Gilgamesh ties heavy stones to his feet and plunges down into the depths of the ocean that Mesopotamians (like the author of the book of Genesis) envisaged as lying below the earth.[25] He finds the plant, brings it to the surface, and journeys back toward his homeland over the waters of death.

But just before reaching Uruk, Gilgamesh sees a pool of cool water and descends into it to bathe. A snake, drawn by the fragrance of the plant, comes up silently and glides off with it, sloughing its skin as it leaves—evidence of the restorative powers of the plant. Immortality is finally impossible. At this point the epic breaks off.

It is an epic of disillusion. It has been suggested by many commentators that *Gilgamesh* reveals the spirit of profound pessimism in which life was viewed by those who meditated upon it, and that this pessimism goes with the "appalling grimness" of the Mesopotamians' picture of the afterlife.[26] But if we read the epic as a *drama*, which it surely is, then we might be less ready to take it simply as a piece of didactic writing. The great thing about *Gilgamesh* is that it takes for granted a philosophy of life and energetically dramatizes a man's experience in the light of it. The very dramatization is a triumph, a sort of freedom, a way of presenting to oneself, and therefore freely possessing, that philosophy. I suggest that one no more comes away from a reading of *Gilgamesh* possessed by a spirit of pessimism than one does after watching *Oedipus Rex* or *King Lear*.

The tone is not one of abandoned pessimism. At every point when hope is betrayed, there are subtle reminders of the true hope to be found in living the civilized life. Even the snake that sloughs its skin may not really be a proof of the plant's restorative power—for it is of the nature of snakes, anyway, to slough their skin. It is not in the nature of man to slough this life and find a new one. The very simplicity of the proof that eternal life is an impossible quest—that we cannot even go without sleep—is a gentle reminder of what our nature is.[27] The days of Gilgamesh's sleep are counted out by the daily loaves— a reminder that life is a matter of receiving our daily bread, and all that goes with it.

Gilgamesh has something of the child about him, but his quest ends in something consoling. He accepts reality, maturity, the common human lot. Set against what our experience teaches us to value about life, the desire for eternal life loses its hold, or ceases to seem like a real desire. *Gilgamesh* has been called "a document of ancient humanism."[28] There is a tone of unillusion not very remote from Voltaire's *Candide*, or of Samuel Johnson's *The Vanity of Human Wishes*.

What is astonishing about *Gilgamesh* is not just the wisdom and courage it embodies but that it presents this wisdom and courage as topics for debate and philosophic reflection. It clearly rebukes the belief in immortality that can be seen as springing merely from fear or wish-fulfillment. Can we use it to rebuke Egyptian beliefs in the afterlife? Perhaps not, for these are rooted in a serious philosophy about the meaning of this life, the fragility of cosmic order, and the fearfulness of a final judgment. *Gilgamesh* does, though, suggest that the intelligent, or truly courageous, or truly noble consciousness sees things clearly and sees them whole. Any metaphysic that tries to establish the meaning of life outside of the ambitions, pleasures, pride, attachments and fear of normal human existence does indeed stand rebuked as blind, immature—even base. From the author of Gilgamesh to Nietzsche there is a line of thought, often submerged, which holds that a belief in immortality contradicts the values that make an admirable human life possible, and should thus be regarded with contempt. It is a philosophy that radically opposes much that springs from late Judaism, Christianity, and Islam.

There are other, earlier stories of Gilgamesh, written in Sumerian. In one of them he brings up his beloved Enkidu from the netherworld in the form of a phantom, and hears what he saw there. Enkidu tells him that in going down to the netherworld he will be like "an old garment...infested with lice, / like a crack in the floor...filled with dust."[29] Enkidu describes a realm in which the dead are simulacra of what they achieved, or failed to achieve, in their lives. He sees a man with one son, who bitterly laments. A man with two sons "seated on two bricks...eats a bread loaf." A man with four sons "like a man with a team of four donkeys his heart rejoices." He sees a palace eunuch. How does he fare? "Like a useless *alala*-stick he is propped in a corner." A leper abides apart from the rest, eating uprooted grass. He sees stillborn babies. How do they fare? "They play amid syrup and ghee at tables of silver and gold."

This does not quite read like an account of how the lives we lead on earth determine our status in the next world—although it has some coloring of that.[30] It seems more like an evaluation of what it is to lead the different sorts of life here, to suffer the several destinies of man. The chief emphasis seems to be on the desirability of exactly the wisdom that Uta-napishtim and the tavern-keeper seek to convey to Gilgamesh—that a fulfilled and fortunate human life is what is to be cherished. As for the mysterious and touching picture of the stillborn babies playing amid syrup and ghee—perhaps it simply conveys a sense of regret and innocence.

Job's Wisdom

Gilgamesh reads, then, essentially as a poem about wisdom. It would no doubt be anachronistic to describe it as a secular wisdom, since the interventions of the gods are inextricably mixed up in the action. It is also extremely important that the eternal life that Gilgamesh desires belongs exclusively to the gods (apart from Uta-napishtim and his wife.) There is another, indirect way in which the epic *feels* secular, and that is the context of the story of the Flood. It is generally agreed that the Babylonian story of the Flood—originally in Sumerian—is the source for the biblical account.[31] But the Mesopotamian and biblical accounts differ. In *Genesis*, God sends the Flood as a response to human wickedness: "And God saw the wickedness of man was great in the earth, and that every imagination of the thought of his heart was only evil continually. And it repented the LORD that he had made man on the earth" (Gen. 6:5–6). In the magnificently vivid account of the Flood in the "standard version" of *Gilgamesh*, no reason at all is given for the intention of the gods to destroy mankind. Insofar as any reason can be discovered, it is that human beings had greatly multiplied and had therefore become very noisy. So the gods decided to cull or exterminate them. The only moral one could draw from this is that the gods are extremely powerful and capricious, and that human beings should understand their own impotence.

Babylonian literature has some sophisticated expressions of ironic pessimism, which seem to suggest that we cannot set our hearts on any one particular view of things. There is a dialogue between a master and his servant, in which the Servant gives all the proverbially wise reasons for the Master to do what he says he is going to do, and then equally proverbial reasons against, when the Master changes his mind:

> "Slave, listen to me." "Here I am sir, here I am."
> "Quickly, fetch me water for my hands, and give it to me
>   so that I can dine."
> "Dine, sir, dine. Repeated dining relaxes the mind."
> "No, slave, I certainly will not dine."
> "Do not dine, sir, do not dine.
> Hunger and eating, thirst and drinking, come upon a man."
> . . . .
> "Slave, listen to me." "Here I am, sir, here I am."
> "I am going to love a woman." "So, love, sir, love.
> The man who loves a woman forgets sorrow and fear."
> "No, slave, I will by no means love a woman."

"Do not love, sir, do not love.
Woman is a pitfall, a hole, a ditch,
Woman is a sharp iron dagger that cuts a man's throat."[32]

There are also skeptical reflections on what man can expect from the gods:

In my childhood I investigated the mind of the god,
In humility and piety I have searched for the goddess:
And yet a corvee without profit I bear like a yoke;
The god brought me scarcity instead of wealth . . .
The mind of the god, like the center of the heavens, is remote;
His knowledge is difficult, men cannot understand it.[33]

The theme of the powerlessness of man, and of a wisdom that comes from the awareness of this, is found elsewhere in the "wisdom" literature of the Babylonians. There is an astonishingly eloquent work, the "Poem of the Righteous Sufferer" in which a just man laments the undeserved misfortunes the gods—and in particular, Marduk, the chief god of Babylon—inflicted upon him; or have allowed to be inflicted without intervening on his behalf, even though he is a man devoted in service to the gods. He is a nobleman who has been forsaken by all the gods and by men. His lament resembles biblical psalms:

Their hearts rage against me, and they are ablaze like fire.
They combine against me in slander and lies.
My lordly mouth they have held as with reins . . .
My lofty head is bowed down to the ground . . .
They have excluded the harvest cry from my fields . . .
By day there is sighing, by night lamentation,
Monthly—wailing, each year—gloom.
I moan like a dove all my days.[34]

All these afflictions are sent by Marduk ("His hand was heavy upon me, I could not bear it"). The question is why the god should do this to a just man who has committed no transgressions. It has one very obvious parallel—the book of Job. The whole theme of the book of Job is the problem of how a righteous God can punish the innocent. Marduk was also seen as a good and merciful god: "Merciful one among the gods. / Compassionate one, who loves to heal the dying. / Marduk, sovereign of heaven and earth."[35] Only in this case there are no false comforters, and Marduk does not reply to the Righteous Sufferer, unlike God who replies at length to Job. However, Marduk does show mercy. He sends a wind that takes away the diseases with which the sufferer has been afflicted:

My clouded eyes, which were cloaked in a deathly shroud—
He drove it a thousand leagues away and lightened my vision.
My ears which were clogged with sand blocked like a deaf man's—
He removed their wax and opened my hearing . . .
He wiped away the gangrene and purged its filth.[36]

Finally, Marduk completely restores the Sufferer—"The Lord gave me life, / He rescued me from the pit." The Sufferer ends being anointed with sweet cedar perfume, slaughters fat oxen and butchers sheep, and drinks honey-sweet beer and pure wine.[37]

Of course this can hardly be called a secular poem, since it is all about a man's faithfulness to a god even when afflicted by him. But it is at the same time entirely worldly. Marduk's power is simply a fact, and there is no way of knowing why the righteous sufferer has been afflicted. It is presumably better to remain loyal to Marduk, lest worst evils befall. Perhaps Marduk's eventual mercy is a response to this loyalty—in which case this makes the loyalty even more obviously prudential.

There are other Babylonian "psalms," with a strong biblical feel about them, that convey a similar submission to a powerful god, and a plea that he come to the aid of the sufferer:

In the billows of the flood he is thrown, the deluge has mounted
    over him.
The shore is far from him, out of his reach is the dry land.
He is perished in a deep place, upon a reef is he caught.
He stands in a river of pitch, he is held in the morass.
Take thou his hand; thy servant it shall not attain.
Cause his retribution to depart, bring him up from the river
    of pitch.[38]

Absent from all these prayers is any hope for a recompense in some future life for the evils and injustices of this one.

There are striking similarities of both theme and treatment in the much later and incomparably grander book of Job.[39] Job is the story of a good, upright, prosperous, and God-fearing man who dwelt in the land of Uz, had seven sons and three daughters, as well as seven thousand sheep, three thousand camels, five hundred yoke of oxen, five hundred she-asses, and a very great household. Job's sons feasted in their houses every day and called their three sisters to come and feast with them. After their seasons of feasts, Job would send his blessings to them and would get up early in the morning to offer burnt offerings to God for all his children, "for Job said, It may be that my sons have sinned, and cursed God in their hearts. Thus did Job continually" (Job 1:5).

Satan comes to God, who asks him "Hast thou considered my servant Job, that there is none like him in the earth, a perfect and an upright man, one that feareth God and escheweth evil?" (Job 1:8). Satan satirically points out that Job has very good reasons for fearing God—God hedges him about on every side, keeping him from harm and continually increasing his prosperity: "But put forth thine hand now, and touch all that he hath, and he will curse thee to thy face" (Job 1:11). God gives Satan *carte blanche* to attack everything Job has and, later, physically to afflict Job himself.

Job's oxen, sheep, and camels are seized by marauding tribesmen; his sons are all killed by a tornado while they are entertaining their three sisters to a feast (and it seems the sisters are also killed). Many of Job's servants are killed; Satan smites Job with boils from head to toe; Job sits amid ashes scraping himself with a potsherd. Job's wife enters on the scene: "Then said his wife unto him, Dost thou still retain thine integrity? Curse God and die" (Job 2:9).[40]

One cannot but be struck by the fact that it is God who sets Satan up to test and afflict Job, by bringing up the case of Job out of the blue. In giving his cynical answer, Satan is simply doing the devil's work. Is God doing God's work? If so, what is it? God's work is to reward the godly and punish wrong-doers. So how does God treat Job? Part of the time he simply seems to hide himself from Job: "Oh that I knew where I might find him! That I might come even to his seat! . . . Behold, I go forward, but he is not there; and backward, but I cannot perceive him" (Job 23:3, 8). But Job also finds God oppressively present, as a beast of prey: "Thou huntest me as a fierce lion: and again thou shewest thyself marvellous with me" (Job 10:16).[41]

Job sees himself as being in God's hands in the most absolute way, for he has a vivid sense of how God as a craftsman, or even housewife, made him:

> Remember, I beseech thee, that thou hast made me as the clay; and
>   wilt thou bring me into dust again?
> Hast thou not poured me out as milk, and curdled me like cheese?
> Thou hast clothed me with skin and flesh, and hast fenced me with
>   bones and sinews. (Job 10:9–11)

Job's sense of his having been fashioned by God means that he sees himself as belonging to God, and hence that he can claim some sort of protection from God in response to his "integrity." And this is exactly what the orthodox cult of YHWH promised—it was the bargain between God and his people. The sufferings of individuals, and of the nation of Israel, were supposed to be the result of impiousness, or of whoring after Baal and other seductive deities in the high places. Job's comforters, traditional believers all, try to preserve this faith by claiming that Job must be sinful. But he knows that he is not: "Thou knowest that I am not wicked; and that there is none that can deliver out of thine hand" (Job 10:7). [42]

Job both complains at God, and seeks to justify himself. Ultimately, he does claim that the bond between man and God necessitates that God play his part in protecting his loyal servants. Yet although no such bond is being honored, Job does not cease to be loyal.

Job's lamentations over his physical sufferings certainly resemble those of the Righteous Sufferer—"My flesh is clothed with worms and clods of dust; my skin is broken and become loathsome" (Job 7:5). Job's vision of the underworld—*Sheol*, the pit—is also reminiscent of Mesopotamian thinking:

> The eye of him that hath seen me shall see me no more: thine eyes
>   are upon me, and I am not.
> As the cloud is consumed and vanisheth away: so he that goeth down
>   to the grave shall come up no more. (Job 7:8–9)
> . . . .
>
> Are not my days few? Cease then, and let me alone, that I may take
>   comfort a little,
> Before I go whence I shall not return, even to the land of darkness
>   and the shadow of death;
> A land of darkness, as darkness itself; and of the shadow of death,
>   without any order, and where the light is as darkness. (Job
>   10:20–22)

The Mesopotamian emphasis on the *dust* of the house of death is also to be found in Job: "They shall; go down to the bars of the pit (*sheol*), when our rest together is in the dust" (Job 17:16). [43]

Job's hope in God is not a hope that a future life will recompense him for his sufferings in this one, or make up for the fact that wicked men prosper in this life. Indeed there is no belief in a future resurrection:

> As the waters fail from the sea, and the flood decayeth and drieth up:
> So man lieth down and riseth not: till the heavens be no more, they
>   shall not awake, nor be raised out of their sleep. (Job 14:11–12)

Ancient Judaism did not entertain thoughts of personal resurrection, nor a judgment after death. Job makes this quite plain:

> One dieth in his full strength, being wholly at ease and quiet.
> His breasts are full of milk, and his bones are moistened with
>   marrow.

And another dieth in the bitterness of his soul, and never eateth with
  pleasure.
They shall lie down alike in the dust, and the worms shall cover them.
  (Job 21:23–26)

One could easily imagine that the book of Job might not have been accepted
into the Bible at all. It does not fit there easily. It does not display God's justice, let
alone his compassion—only his sublimity. Job's refusal to curse God and die,
and his dogged refusal to attribute blame to himself, has its own sublimity.

The context of the book of Job is the orthodox ancient Israelite belief that
the worship of YHWH is the whole and exclusive religious duty of the
Israelite people and constitutes its national religion; that it abolishes all other
forms of piety, including the cult of the dead; that the individual Israelite has
significance only as part of the worshipping people; and that there is
no resurrection of the dead to an afterlife.[44] The worship of YHWH excludes
a cult of the dead in a way that must have offended the instinctive piety of
many—just as the prohibition of ancestor worship profoundly distressed the
Japanese when they heard it from Christian missionaries. The dead in the Near
East, and in the land of Canaan, had always been buried with precious objects
that testified to a belief that they needed somehow to be sustained in a future
existence. In Canaan it seems that there were even funnels from the surface
down into the grave through which wine and beer could be poured to console
the departed.

As national god, YHWH was to reward faithful service, and, in particular,
the faithful service of Israel. (Some writers have suggested that the exclusive
worship of YHWH went with the need to bring together the various Israelitish
tribes under one warrior god for the conquest of Canaan.[45]) He would reward
loyalty with military victory, and punish defection with defeat, enslavement,
and captivity. The whole emphasis was on rewards and punishments here and
now, in this life. The great heroes of Israel were those glorified by YHWH for
their signal service—Abraham, Jacob, Moses, David. These were not heroes in
the manner of Gilgamesh or Hercules or Achilles or Odysseus—men with
outstanding personal qualities—but men chosen and inspired by God and
elevated purely because of their service to him.

The worship of YHWH rigorously excluded the dead. They went to *Sheol*—
translated by the Greeks as *Hades* and, often, in the Authorized (or King James)
Version of the Bible as the "pit." *Sheol* was not hell (of which the Hebrew
equivalent is *gehinnom*, i.e., gehenna, which signifies a place of burning)[46] but
a gloomy underworld just like that described to Gilgamesh by Enkidu. Sometimes the Old Testament suggests that *Sheol* is completely outside God's realm,

or at least his care.[47] Sometimes it is suggested that God may even be present in *Sheol*.[48] But the ancient Jews were supposed to abstain from the practices of all the people who lived around them—such as slashing their bodies in mourning for the dead,[49] worshipping the dead, or getting in touch with the dead by necromancy.

Job's description of *Sheol* is, of course, irredeemably bleak. It is at best an immense pit located deep beneath the ground, indeed, even beneath the waters of the great abyss upon which the whole world rests.[50] It is even possible that Job, in referring to the abode of darkness and the shadow of death may even really be referring, in metaphorical terms, simply to the grave itself.[51] But what is plain is that Job is afflicted by the God of Israel whose whole claim upon the allegiance of his people is that he will reward and punish loyalty and disaffection here in this life. The wicked will infallibly come to destruction and disgrace, while the good will flourish and be blessed with worldly joy and prosperity. Given that this is how God is supposed to be, we can predict the answers that will be given when he seems to be different. So one of Job's "comforters," Eliphaz the Temanite, tries to suggest that no innocent man has been destroyed by God, that Job will come to the grave in the fullness of age, and that "thy seed shall be great, and thine offspring as the grass of the earth. Thou shalt come to thy grave in a full age, like as a shock of corn cometh in his season" (Job 5:25–26).

Job, however, refuses to accept this specious comfort, in which he does not believe. Nor will he accept, what is suggested by his "comforters," that he is guilty of secret sins, for he knows he is innocent. What, therefore, is the solution? One possible solution is that which occurs in what has been called "the best loved passage . . . which has been sung into the hearts of millions":[52] "I know that my redeemer liveth, and that he shall stand at the latter day upon the earth: And though after my skin worms destroy this body, yet in my flesh shall I see God" (Job 19:25–26). These magnificent words have been "sung into the hearts of millions" because they have been interpreted through two Christian millennia to mean that Job hopes for a resurrection of the body and life eternal in the presence of God. Some biblical scholars support that interpretation; many others do not.[53] Many simply find the passage obscure.[54] It is very hard for the reader, approaching the passage without preconceptions, if that be possible, not to find the idea of a glorious resurrection here out of kilter with the whole tone of the book of Job.

Job does not seek an intellectual solution to a theological riddle. Rather it takes the orthodox view of YHWH as a rewarding and punishing God, and imaginatively enacts a situation where that idea is brought radically into question. The book of Job has been called both skeptical literature, and literature in the tradition of the absurd.[55] Both descriptions seem right: skeptical in that it does not commit itself to any solution to the conundrum of why the virtuous suffer; absurdist in that there is the sense that no solution can even be seriously entertained. The role of the false comforters is further to bring out the paradoxes, and hence to draw out the courage, honesty, and tragedy of Job's response. Wisdom here means Job's seeing through false comfort because of his character—the comfort and, indeed, the orthodox doctrine are tested against a massively authentic man who has been tormented beyond endurance but who never gives up his faith and loyalty. Job's refusal to "curse God and die" flows not from some answer he has to the dilemma he confronts but from his character and will. His will is as strongly turned toward God as was Abraham's when he submitted to the command to sacrifice his first born son, Isaac.[56]

Job ends with the notoriously interpolated ending in which God rewards his servant and makes him even richer and more blessed than he was before his troubles began.[57] (He is even given more children, on the apparent assumption that these will satisfactorily replace those whom God allowed to be killed.) But the real burden of the book comes a few chapters earlier with God's answer to Job "out of the whirlwind." God's "answer" is an assertion of his own supreme power, and of a nature beyond anything that Job could comprehend:

> Where wast thou when I laid the foundations of the earth? Declare if thou hast understanding.
> ... When the morning stars sang together, and all the sons of God shouted for joy?
> Or who shut up the sea with doors, when it brake forth, as if it had issued out of the womb?
> When I made the cloud the garment thereof, and thick darkness a swaddling band for it ...
> Canst thou bind the sweet influences of Pleiades, or loose the bands of Orion? ...
> Canst thou draw out leviathan with an hook? Or his tongue with a cord which thou lettest down ...
> He maketh the deep to boil like a pot: he maketh the sea like a pot of ointment.
> He beholdeth all high things: he is a king over all the children of pride. (Job 38:4, 7–9, 31; 41:1, 31, 34)

To this assertion of the sublimity of God's power and knowledge, Job can only wisely and with humility abase himself: "I have heard thee by the hearing of the ear: but now mine eye seeth thee. Wherefore I abhor myself, and repent in dust and ashes" (Job 42: 5–6).

In the book of Job we have the most complete confrontation with YHWH-ism that it is possible to imagine. This official doctrine of Israel offered salvation to the nation when it obeyed God, which might be thought, and often was thought, to entail aid to the individual who did the same. This help and salvation was to be in this world, not in some future one. God's testing of Job is to see whether he will refuse to curse God when not only does he offer no succor but takes away, for no humanly graspable reason, all that Job has. Job's refusal to "curse God and die" is rooted in his recognition that God's unsearchable power is indeed such that man can make no claim upon him, and that this greatness makes God a proper object of worship. There is not a bond between man and God such that each has to keep his side of a bargain. But God's assertion of his own unsearchable power and hidden wisdom is more than just an example of horrible cosmic bullying. God is actually pointing out to Job that any belief that runs counter to the facts of nature is ridiculous. If Job really believes in the greatness of God, then he ought to know that God must be infinitely beyond human comprehension, as nature itself—in all the wonders of it that are so marvelously conveyed in these words of God—is beyond comprehension. And these wonders are not simply to do with the vastness of things, for they also show themselves in smaller matters that man thinks exist for his own convenience. For instance, men think that the warhorse is their servant. God suggests, on the contrary, that the horse lives in its own wonderful world and fights because it sublimely loves to:

> He paweth in the valley, and rejoiceth in his strength: he goeth on to
>   meet the armed men . . .
> He swalloweth the ground with fierceness and rage . . . He saith
>   among the trumpets, Ha, Ha; and he smelleth the battle afar off,
>   the thunder of the captains and the shouting. (Job 39:21, 24, 25)

Therefore Job's patience is as much a matter of wisdom and facing reality as is the acceptance by Gilgamesh that all men are subject to death. Job's lack of belief in compensation in a future life for the ills of this one could scarcely be more explicit:

> For there is hope in a tree, if it be cut down, that it will sprout again,
>   and that the tender branch thereof will not cease . . .
> But man dieth and wasteth away: yea, man giveth up the ghost, and
>   where is he?
> As the waters fail from the sea, and the flood decayeth and drieth up:

> So man lieth down, and riseth not: till the heavens be no more, they
> shall not awake, nor be raised out of their sleep. (Job 14:7, 10–12)

These two masterpieces, the book of Job and the *Epic of Gilgamesh*, have in common that they dramatize the possibility of entertaining certain beliefs. They are works of dramatic literature, not mythology. In both cases they imaginatively present experience that has a depth of reality that in effect excludes a hoped for immortality as a solution.

It has long been accepted that in ancient Judaism there is no clear belief in resurrection and judgment until the very late book of Daniel, with the Second Temple and then with Rabbinical Judaism.[58] The famous passage in Ezekiel about the valley of the dry bones, in which the bones are clad again with skin through the power of God and come back again to life, is an image of the restoration of the nation of Israel, not the resurrection of individuals. In any case, in context, the vision is about Israel regaining hope, after the Babylonian captivity, that its national life can be renewed: "these bones are the whole house of Israel: behold, they say, Our bones are dried, and our hope is lost: we are cut off for our parts." So when God is represented as saying that he will open the graves of his people and bring them to the land of Israel, this seems like a promise to rescue them from despair and restore them to their land: "[I] shall put my spirit in you and ye shall live, and I shall place you in your own land" (Ezek. 37:11, 14). The vision is a metaphor about spiritual and political hope, and to interpret it literally—as has often been done—is to import ideas that do not fit into Ezekiel as a whole.

It is only in the (rather childish, as Matthew Arnold thought) book of Daniel that something like a belief in resurrection and judgment is to be found with apparent clarity—and then only in two verses:

> And many of them that sleep in the dust of the earth shall awake,
> some to everlasting life, and some to shame and everlasting
> contempt.
> And they that be wise shall shine as the brightness of the firmament;
> and they that turn many to righteousness as the stars for ever and
> ever. (Dan. 12:2–3)

By the time of Christ, however, personal immortality had become established orthodoxy among the Pharisees. Josephus writes of three sects in Judaism. Of the Pharisees he writes: "They . . . believe that souls have an immortal vigor in them, and that under the earth there will be rewards or punishments, according as they have lived virtuously or viciously in this life; and the latter are to be detained in an everlasting prison, but that the former shall have power to revive and live again: on account of which doctrines they are able greatly to persuade the body of the people."

Of the Sadducees he says: "the doctrine of the Sadducees is . . . that souls die with the bodies." And of the Essenes: "They teach the immortality of souls, and esteem that the rewards of righteousness are to be earnestly striven for."[59] The Sadducees are closest to the pure doctrines of YHWH-ism.

Although it seems clear that there was no established belief in personal bodily resurrection in ancient Judaism, let alone disembodied survival, it has recently been suggested that this does not entail that the Jews assumed that the destiny of all was a miserable half-existence in the darkness of *Sheol*. Jon D. Levenson has argued persuasively that for the Jews *Sheol* as a human destination had a more complex and ambiguous significance than the land of no return had for their Mesopotamian and Canaanite neighbors. For the latter it simply is the fearful end for all of us. But in parts of the Hebrew Bible there seems to be a distinction between the fate of those who die in the fullness of years, fulfilled, blessed by God and rejoicing in their children and grandchildren—like Abraham and Moses—and those who die violently, unjustly, unnaturally. The first will be "gathered to their forefathers" and are not usually described as descending into *Sheol*.[60]

Indeed, the deaths of the righteous, such as the Patriarchs, do not seem to have the finality with which death is seen by the Mesopotamians and Canaanites. Abraham, Isaac, and Jacob continue to exist after they have died, not as spirits that survive the body in a personal immortality, but in the hearts and minds of the Jewish people whose fathers they will always be.[61]

It is clear that this argument is not intended to show that the ancient Jews had any belief in a personal survival after death in the way that Platonists believed in the survival of a disembodied soul, or that Jews of the Second Temple period, and then Christians and Muslims believed in personal resurrection. Rather Levenson's argument is about the concept of a person in ancient Judaism. A person for the ancient Jews is not simply a center of consciousness—as in, for instance, Cartesian philosophy—but a member of a people, an ancestor, a descendant: "to be a Jew means to be a member of a natural family, the people of Israel, the descendant of Abraham, Isaac and Jacob. It is, in other words, a bodily state and not exclusively a spiritual or intellectual one. . . . To live as a disembodied spirit . . . is to live in disconnection from peoplehood."[62]

The Patriarchs are not those "which have no memorial; Who are perished as though they had never been, And are become as though they had never been born, And their children after them" (Ecclus./Sirac 44:9). The Wisdom literature of the Hebrew Bible is close to the pessimism—or clear-eyed realism—of the Mesopotamians and Canaanites; but there is a tension between that and a growing affirmation of the power of God even over the terrifying netherworld of *Sheol*. The conviction that the Patriarchs and other just and great persons live on in their people's memories—and that therefore they do not go down into *Sheol* in the way that Jacob, thinking that his beloved son, Joseph, has been devoured by wild beasts says that he *will* go down into *Sheol*—gradually prepares for the belief of the Pharisees, Jesus and the Jews of the Second Temple period, and into modern times in a personal resurrection.[63] It is a development of belief made possible by the peculiarly Jewish emphasis on the overwhelming power of God to overcome the greatest evils, such as disease and misfortunes—eventually becoming, in late Judaism, a power to overcome death itself.

Gilgamesh might more properly than Job be called a work of ancient humanism. Job dramatizes resignation. It is an obedience that is never made fully intelligible, and which confronts the paradoxes that the cult of YHWH makes inevitable. If *Gilgamesh* consoles, it does so (in the way that parts of Ecclesiastes do) with the injunction that a certain way of enjoying life and seeing it whole represents a certain sort of wisdom. But each gives full range to the human desire to see things as they are not or, rather, to find premature explanations. In controlling such prematurities, each gives an excellent sense of the complexities of the world we are tempted to abridge and simplify. Both are dramas, rather than simply works of didacticism, enacting the movement of the mind of the protagonist as he is drawn to fuller understanding. Each dramatizes an idea of a possible recompense for the ills the flesh is heir to. And each abstains from assenting to any such belief. But in the *Epic of Gilgamesh* we find a hero who is astonishingly autonomous, astonishingly not compelled either to be in thrall to nor to rebel against an external divine will. Since the wisdom of Gilgamesh himself comes from self-discovery, and since the self-discovery arises from an heroic assertion of the human spirit, the *Epic of Gilgamesh* can indeed be called a document of ancient humanism.

4

Greece and Rome

In ancient Greece a new idea of immortality emerges. What we might hope for is not personal survival, as in ancient Egypt, but fame and eternal memory. True, the idea is not *entirely* new, for it is also to be found in the Wisdom literature of the Hebrew Bible. In Ecclesiasticus, rich, godly and wise men, living peaceably in their habitations, and men who created music and poetry will leave behind a name which "liveth for ever more"; whereas others—the majority, it would seem—leave no memorial and vanish as though they had not been born "and their children after them" (Ecclus./Sirac 44). In *Gilgamesh*, the hero will strive to conquer the terrible Humbaba so that he will "establish a name eternal."[1] In the Greece of Pericles, however, and of Aristotle, a civic ethic emerges, which seems officially to endorse honor and fame as the only sort of immortality that we should care about. A name that will live for ever is earned by martial heroes (Homer), by founders of cities and states, and by those whose heroic courage leads them to die for their city in war. In Rome this civic immortality goes with a virtual deification of the state and empire as consecrated by fate, so that *pietas*—a respectful pride in the City and Empire going with a readiness to die for them—becomes the grandest virtue.

Those who "discovered musical tunes and set down psalms in writing" are not forgotten. Horace is confident that his verses will make his name live for ever more, as long as eternal Rome shall last.[2] This official doctrine of Greek and Roman civic paganism becomes an unofficial, but not disapproved of, doctrine in later Christian Europe, pithily expressed in one of the greatest of English poems:

> Fame is the spur that the clear spirit doth raise
> (That last infirmity of noble mind)
> To scorn delights and live laborious days . . . [3]

But Christians were able to conjoin this classical paganism with the Christian hope in personal resurrection—something entirely denied by the "official" civic doctrine of fifth- and fourth-century Athens and pre-Christian Rome. Civic, impersonal immortality is an extraordinarily austere doctrine—sternly elitist and unillusioned. Since the vast majority will vanish as though they had not been, and their children after them, you could argue that the culture that enforces such a doctrine must have had a grandeur that does not hold out false hopes and a nobility that does not indulge them.

But did people—did the masses, did even the nobility who mostly were not going to leave an immortal name behind them—really believe in it? We soon discover that there were plenty of beliefs in the ancient world that warred against the official civic view: there was skepticism about the political world (the Cynics); there were philosophical sects that stressed the possibility that the individual could transcend the state (Stoics); there were philosophers who taught an immortality of the soul (Plato); and there were mystery religions that offered their devotees a blissful future life (e.g., Orphics).

The problem is not just that (in the words of Blake) to generalize is to be an idiot, but something deeper. What was certainly the ancient, real folk belief of both Greeks and Romans—that we become sad, impotent shadows after death—seems psychologically so opposed to the high civic ethic that it is hard to feel how the two can be reconciled. And there is a fair amount of evidence that some people felt exactly that.

Greece

The Shades

There are two celebrated passages in European literature concerning the spirits of the dead that imitate a Greek original. In Canto 3 of the *Inferno*, Dante depicts the souls of the damned as they are summoned by Charon into the boat over "the dismal stream of Acheron." He describes the vast throng ("I had not thought death had undone so many" [*Inferno* 3, 56–57; Eliot, "The Waste Land," 62–63]) who cast themselves from the shore into the boat at his command, each like a bird obeying the call of its leader, or like autumn leaves:

Come d'autunno si levan le foglie
    l'una appresso de l' altra, fin che 'l ramo
    vede la terra tutte le sua spoglie. (*Inferno* 3, 112–14)

[As the leaves fall away in autumn one after another, till the bough sees all its spoils upon the ground . . .]

The scene imitates a passage in Virgil's *Aeneid*, which also describes souls of the dead transported in Charon's vessel:

huc omnis turba ad ripas effusa ruebat,
matres atque viri, defunctaque corpora vita
magnanimum heroum, pueri innuptaeque puellae
impositique rogis iuvenes ante ora parentum:
quam multa in silvis autumni frigore primo
lapsa cadunt folia, aut ad terram gurgite ab alto
quam multae glomerantur aves, ubi frigidus annus
trans pontum fugat et terris immittit apricis.
stabant orantes primi transmittere cursum
tendebantque manus ripae ulterioris amore. (*Aeneid* 6, 305–13)

[Hither rushed all the throng, streaming to the banks; mothers and men and bodies of high-souled heroes, their life now done, boys and unwedded girls, placed young on funeral pyres before the eyes of their parents; thick as the leaves of the forest that at autumn's first frost drop and fall, and thick as the birds that from the seething deep fly shoreward, when the chill of the year drives them overseas and sends them into sunny lands. They stood, pleading to be the first ferried across, and stretched out hands in yearning for the farther shore.]

Although the scene in Dante has the same structure as the Virgil, the effect is profoundly different. The shades in Dante do not rush to be the first into Charon's boat, nor do they stretch out their arms longingly toward the farther shore. Dante tells us that their consciousness of their sins propels them toward their destiny. Yet those who linger are beaten into the boat by Charon—for their destiny is not a Virgilian underworld populated by mournful shades, nor the Elysian Fields reserved for the noblest souls, nor Lethe—the river of forgetfulness, passing through which people regain their innocence and a new life—but the eternal torments of the Christian hell.

Nor are Dante's shades the melancholy phantoms of the Greeks, who can speak and be conscious only when they have drunk of sacrificial blood, nor the equally impotent *animae* of the Romans. On the contrary, they are filled with rage and savage despair:

Bestemmiavano Dio e lor parenti,
l' umana spezie e 'l loco e 'l tempo e 'l seme
di lor semenza e di lor nascimenti.
Poi si ritrasser tutte quante insieme,
forte piangendo, a la riva malvagia
ch' attende ciascun uom che Dio non teme. (*Inferno* 3, 103–8)

[They cursed God, their parents, the human race, the place, the time, the seed of their begetting and of their birth. Then, weeping loudly, all drew to the evil shore that awaits every man who fears not God.]

Dante's damned souls have the full consciousness of living people. Their grief and rage are very different from the melancholy sadness with which the shades of the pagan underworld recognize their fate. It is not simply that Dante's souls are damned and fear their eternal torments. (Virgil's Hades also contains a fair measure of punishment for the wicked.) The essential difference is that the sadness of Virgil's shades is directed at the universal human lot. The image of the birds flying south to escape the chill of winter has a conscious, artful sympathy, characteristic of Virgil. The chill of death sends the shades not to warmer and brighter climes, but to the darkness of the underworld.

The Greek passage that both Dante and Virgil are imitating is the *nekuia* in Homer's *Odyssey*, which describes the visit of Odysseus to the gates of the underworld. The spirits of the dead flock to drink the blood of a sheep that Odysseus has sacrificed:

αἱ δ' ἀγέροντο
ψυχαὶ ὑπὲξ Ἐρέβευς νεκύων κατατεθνηώτων.
νύμφαι τ' ἠίθεοί τε πολύτλητοί τε γέροντες
παρθενικαί τ' ἀταλαὶ νεοπενθέα θυμὸν ἔχουσαι,
πολλοὶ δ' οὐτάμενοι χαλκήρεσιν ἐγχείῃσιν,
ἄνδρες ἀρηίφατοι βεβροτωμένα τεύχε' ἔχοντες.

[Then there gathered out of Erebus the spirits of those that are dead, brides and unwedded youths, and toil-worn old men, and tender maidens with hearts yet new to sorrow. And many, too, that had been wounded with bronze-tipped spears, men slain in fight, wearing their blood-stained armour. (*Odyssey* 11, 36–41)]

In Homer you do not find the conscious plangency with which Virgil creates an aesthetic distance that comforts even as it pities. Instead there is a naked simplicity of grief that comes simply from these spirits being deprived of "honey-sweet life" (*thumos meliedes*), the loss of which Anticleia, the dead mother of Odysseus, speaks (*Odyssey* 11, 203) as she talks to her son, using the same word Teiresias employs to prophesy Odysseus's own return ("thy honey-sweet return") to his homeland (*Odyssey* 11, 100). The chief sorrow of death is expressed as the loss of light—reminiscent of the blankness of the netherworld of the Sumerians and Babylonians, and the pit (*Sheol*) of Job—also in the words of Teiresias: "Why has thou left the light of the sun and come hither to behold the dead and a region where is no joy?" The flitting, gibbering, or faintly shrieking wraiths that Odysseus encounters in Hades enforce the sense that this shadowy survival after death is not an existence worth having. Although a few privileged souls might go to Elysium, the overwhelming majority will simply be *eidola* (phantasms).

Much has been written on how the Greeks understood the word *psyche* (ψῡχή), and it has become a large and debated subject. It does not mean what we have come to understand by the word "soul." The *psyche* is not the person—unlike Dante's shades; it is not the self, the bearer of consciousness. In the living person it is something like the breath of life (indeed the word *psyche* in its origins is to do with breathing).[4] When a person dies, the *psyche* is the breath that has left the body. From the moment someone dies, the *psyche* becomes an *eidolon*, a phantom image "like the image reflected in a mirror which can be seen, but cannot be grasped."[5] The *psyche* in its apparition as *eidolon* had special relation to dreams—the dead, through these images, come to the living in dreams. The most famous example of this in all Greek literature is in the *Iliad*, when the spirit (*psyche*) of the beloved, slaughtered Patroclus comes to Achilles in sleep, standing above his head. The Trojan hero, Hector, had slain Patroclus and in his turn had been slain by Achilles. In his grief, Achilles has delayed cremating Patroclus because he cannot bear finally to give up the corpse of his friend:

> You sleep, and have forgotten me, Achilles. You were not unmindful
> of me in my life, but you are now, in my death. Bury me with all speed,
> that I may pass within the gates of Hades. The spirits (*psuchai*) keep
> me afar off, the phantoms (*eidola*) of men that have done with toils,
> neither will they allow me to join myself with them beyond the
> River. . . . Give my your hand, I pitifully entreat you, for never more
> again shall I come out of Hades, when once you have given me my due
> of fire. Never more in life shall we sit apart from our dear comrades
> and take counsel together . . . And you yourself, god-like Achilles, are
> doomed to be brought low. . . . Lay not my bones apart from yours, but
> let them lie together.

Achilles promises to do what Patroclus asks but begs for a last embrace: "I pray you, draw nearer. Even if it is for but a little space, let us clasp our arms one about the other, and take our fill of doomed lamenting." He reaches out his hands "yet clasped him not; but the spirit, like a vapor, was gone beneath the earth, gibbering faintly" (*Iliad* 23, 68–100). These virile, deep-throated males in their feeble squeaking have in effect been feminized.

Nothing could be harder and sterner than this instant transformation of Patroclus from mighty warrior into a something that makes feeble noises like a bat. (In the *Odyssey*, the suitors, slain by Odysseus and his son, become "like

Achilles Searching for the Shade of Patroclus. Johann Heinrich Füssli (Henry Fuseli), 1803. © 2009 Kunsthaus, Zurich.

bats that squeak and in the depths of some mysterious cave when one of them has fallen from the rocky roof" [*Odyssey* 24, 6–9]). Throughout the *Iliad* we have warriors who are reduced to nothing as their soul flees to Hades. It is as though human greatness must include a sense of the nothingness that awaits us, and that the hero have a clear sense of this nothingness.

For the educated Greek, the appearance to Achilles of Patroclus, and the *nekuia* of Odysseus were the most powerful passages in all literature.[6] The dead are hardly more than dream images. The mother of Odysseus, Anticleia, whom he had left still alive in Ithaca, comes up from below and addresses her son. She tells him that she died, not of disease but from longing for him. Three times Odysseus tries to clasp her, and three times she slips from his embrace "like a shadow or a dream." Odysseus in his anguish asks whether she is simply a false image, an *eidolon* sent up by Persephone, queen of the dead, to make him grieve the more. Anticleia replies with the orthodox teaching: "... this is the appointed way with mortals when one dies. For the sinews no longer hold the flesh and the bones together, but the strong might of blazing fire destroys these, as soon as the life leaves the white bones, and the spirit, like a dream, hovers to and fro" (*Odyssey* 11, 197–222). The fire sunders the *psyche* from this world and allows it to enter into the gates of Hades. And it *is* only an *eidolon*—although not a false image sent up by Persephone. The most notable quality of the meeting between Odysseus and the *psyche* of his dead mother is that no consolation is offered, but only a stern recitation of the realities of life and death that exclude consolation or hope. There is in this an unblinking realism, the note of which has scarcely been sounded again in post-ancient literature.

And has the real Patroclus come to Achilles, or is it simply a dream? There is not a simple answer. It is a real message—but it is also a dream-image. You could say that since what Patroclus tells Achilles is true and timely, it is a *real* apparition, because apparitions of the dead were real to the Greeks when they had something important to communicate. But the passage makes it plain in how many ways this Patroclus is not real—Achilles tries to embrace him, just as Odysseus tries to embrace his mother, who escapes him "like a shadow or dream" (*skie eikelon e kai oneiro*); the *psyche* slips through their arms like a shadow or like smoke. The spirits in Hades have only a slight relation to the people they were when they lived physically on earth. They are not genuinely conscious (and only fleetingly regain a conscious life when they drink of the blood)—and then all they can do is remember. The representation of Anticleia herself is like a *memory* in the mind of Odysseus.[7]

But we do not need to know all about the various Greek understandings of *psyche* and *eidolon* to understand how Homer represents the afterlife—and therefore what many generations of Greeks believed about it. For their beliefs about the next world do not spring from a set of opinions or theories about the soul or the person. Rather, their ideas about the soul reflect and spring from their picture of the afterlife; and their picture of the afterlife reflects their valuing of this life.

Scholars tell us that the ancient Greeks could not have feared the dead in the way they are feared in many cultures, for the shades are without force and without consciousness: "There are no ghostly terrors, no imaginings of decomposition, and no clatterings of dead bones; but equally there is no comfort and no hope."[8] But the Greeks imagined the shades to be without force and without consciousness just because they had such a bleak view of the next world and of our existence in it. The next world simply is a loathsome place: "When the earth shakes during the battle of the gods, Hades leaps from his throne and roars with terror lest the earth break open and his realm be exposed to the light, ghastly, moldering and an abomination to the gods—as when a stone is overturned revealing putrefaction and teeming larvae."[9] The gods loathe Hades simply because it is the abode of death; they hate death—just as do the ancient Greeks (and the Egyptians and Mesopotamians). The shades are impotent because death takes everything away from us except sadness and (fleeting) memory.

In the face of this fear and loathing of death, of the sense that (nearly) all of us are doomed to a half-existence of melancholy darkness, what we have called the official Greek view of the ethics of honor strikes an exceptionally severe tone. In the archaic Greek world, as represented in the Homeric epics, the severity can hardly be missed. In Homer, action and the ability to act is everything. But the shades can do nothing at all. This ability to act the Greeks called *arete*—sometimes translated as "virtue." It denotes every human excellence (and even, in the case of women, beauty). The *arete* of a nobleman consists in the sorts of things his birth, wealth, and character make possible for him. If he is enslaved, he loses half his *arete* and becomes not much better than the common people and slaves who have no *arete* at all.[10] The greatest reward of *arete* is praise, honor. The greatest *arete*—that of the hero—is shown in warfare, in manly courage, and the readiness to die. The greatest praise, therefore, is accorded to the hero who dies in battle.

It is this that explains one of the great tragic scenes in Homer. In the *Iliad*, Hector's parents, Priam, king of Troy, and Hecuba, his queen, make one last attempt to dissuade Hector from fighting with Achilles. Hector will assuredly be slain, and Troy, bereft of its greatest protector, will fall. Hector acknowledges this but decides nevertheless to fight, simply for honor. Lest he be "ashamed before the Trojan men and the women with trailing robes," he will fight and fall in single combat, bringing down the city with him.[11] The defining quality of the nobleman is his sense of the honor (*time*) due to his rank, which will constrain him to give up his life for an honorable end. His *arete* is his very self. In later writers it will be claimed that it survives in glory after death.[12] But that is not what Hector says.

There are just a few who will have a happier fate, not through their merits, but because of their semi-divine birth. (Achilles is not of their number, despite his own divine origins.) In the *Odyssey*, Menelaus (the theft of whose wife, Helen, by the Trojan prince, Paris, was the sole cause of the Trojan War) is promised a fate far better than that of most men: "But for thee, Menelaus, son of Zeus, it is not ordained to die and meet thy fate in Argos ... but the Immortals will convey thee to the Elysian Plain at the ends of the earth. ... There life is easiest for men; there is neither snow, nor heavy storms nor rain, but Ocean ever sends zephyrs with soft-breathing breezes to refresh men. ... For thou hast Helen to wife, and in the eyes of the Immortals thou art son in law to Zeus" (*Odyssey* 4, 561–69).

So Menelaus is not going to be a pathetic shade, but properly immortal. But notice that what this means is not that Menelaus will be resurrected, but that he will not die at all—his *psyche* will not be sundered from his body. Why will he not die? Well—he is a hero. But that is not enough—he is related by marriage to Zeus, king of the gods. It is because Menelaus is already divine that he will be translated to the Elysian Fields. The only idea in Homer of personal immortality is that it belongs to the gods and to a few people favored by them or related to them. Some of the greatest heroes undergo apotheosis—they become truly divine. They are not sad shades—on the contrary, they appear of superhuman stature, are surrounded by a radiant nimbus, and their resplendent beauty strikes with admiration all who perceive them.[13] Other heroes may be transported to the Isles of the Blest, where the weather is equally favorable, where the earth bears fruit three times a year.[14] Such a fate is offered to only a tiny minority, to heroes whose virtues spring from their semi-divine origin. The vast majority of human beings, however well they have lived their lives, can hope for no such thing.

Civic Virtue

Alisdair MacIntyre has written that death in Homer is an unmixed evil. This informs how courage is understood in heroic (e.g., Homeric) societies. This sharp sense both of the sorrow of death and its inevitability colors all aspects of life: "one central theme of heroic societies is also that death waits for both alike. Life is fragile, men are vulnerable and it is of the essence of the human situation that they are such. ... The man therefore who does what he ought moves steadily towards his fate and his death. It is defeat and not victory that lies at the end. To understand this is itself a virtue; indeed it is a necessary part of courage to understand this."[15]

The brave man follows a destiny that has been laid down for him. Both Hector and Achilles accept that death is their destiny. The hero is born into a society with family, friends, comrades, fellow citizens . . . and this determines what he ought to do. But what he ought to do leads him to the "unmixed evil" of death. This is the germ of what later becomes civic virtue. The Homeric picture of *thumos*—the passion, spirit, courage of the fighting man, a spirit that prompts to spectacular deeds in war, to love of friends, family, and comrades, and of a city, such as Troy, which is in effect an extension of such particular loyalties—becomes something more impersonal. The city makes colder demands on one's allegiance, and the courageous citizen becomes more like a cog in a machine. This is, at any rate, how Pericles, in his funeral oration over the first of those who died for Athens in the Peloponnesian War, exalts the city over the individual in a way that, although it can be traced back to Homer, is chillingly un-Homeric:

> And these men were of such character as to benefit the city. It is necessary for the rest of you to pray, to be sure, for a safer conclusion, but with a purpose no less fixed to meet the enemy; you must analyze the benefit of such an attitude not merely by the words of a speaker, for a speaker could spend no little time in enumerating the benefits of defeating the enemy to you who know it clearly yourselves. Rather you must day by day contemplate the power of this city and become her lovers, and when you have thoroughly digested her greatness, become mindful that men who were bold and knew what was necessary and in the execution of deeds were moved by a sense of honor—these were the men who acquired this city. If they failed in an attempt, they thought it right that the city should claim their bravery, and sacrificed to her their fairest offering. They gave their bodies to the state and for themselves won a praise which is endless and the most distinguished of tombs, not the one in which they are in fact buried, but the one in which their glory survives for ever. . . . For the whole world is the grave of famous men . . . there is an unwritten memorial of them planted in the mind rather than written on a tombstone. . . . It is not the wretched who have the best justification for tossing away their lives, for they have no hope of improvement; but rather those in the opposite condition.[16]

Aristotle systematizes, and therefore changes the feel of the old ideas, when he says that most like true courage will be the fortitude of the citizen soldier who faces death in battle because of the penalties imposed by the laws, and motivated by a love of honor and fear of disgrace.[17] Aristotle's reasons for saying this include the conviction that the *polis* (city state) is the highest object of our loyalty, and the fullest expression of man as *zoon politikon* (political, or city-dwelling animal). So courage in war carries with it all the social virtues. Courage deals with what is most terrible—imminent death—and aims at what is most excellent—the safety, or greatness of the *polis*.

Civic courage of the sort invoked by Pericles and Aristotle sets an extremely high value—in theory, at least—on life in this world while at the same time demanding the virtue that leads men to sacrifice it. The *polis* makes absolute claims upon its citizens: there is nothing higher or better than being alive in a city-state—except the honor of dying for it. The next world, being the abode of impotent shades, has nothing at all to be said for it. Actual death is indeed an unmixed evil. So to sacrifice one's life for the city, for what is best and greatest in the world, manifests a supremely conscious attachment to the world that is being sacrificed. This merits honor and the highest gratitude of our fellow-citizens. Honor after death, therefore, is an immortality worth having, and the only immortality to which we can rationally attach a value. Courage, as Aristotle defines it, does require that one understand that.

It is hard to fault Aristotle's brilliant rational reconstruction of Homeric ethics. Aristotle is writing as a philosopher, and Pericles is making a claim to political loyalty early in a disastrous war. So one cannot really complain that what they say is immensely remote from the Homeric spirit. Or rather, it is remote from Homeric physicality and the passions that feel almost physical themselves. The longing of the dead for the light, for a life that is honey-sweet; the loss of bodily existence expressed by the swarming of the shades to drink blood and regain a momentary human consciousness ("Unsheathed the narrow sword, / I sat to keep off the impetuous impotent dead"[18]); the urge to embrace the dead so that you can take your fill of lamenting, as in life you took your fill of meat and wine—all these moments enforce a sense of the gulf between life and death in the face of which the official ethic, the willed belief that an immortal name will somehow compensate for what is gone, seems very like faking it. It may be a virtue that the courageous man understand what necessarily awaits him, but that does not stop many brave warriors in the *Iliad* clasping the knees of their victorious antagonist and begging for their lives. In Homer "no hero, not even the greatest, is spared the shameful experience of fear." The great Hector flees headlong from the bloodthirsty Achilles; Ajax flees trembling; even Achilles can be alarmed by the spear of an opponent.[19] The Homeric physicality pervades the descriptions of death in battle that, though stylized, are far more bloody—and sometimes visceral—than almost anything we find in Virgil. Guts pour from wounds, eyes are knocked out, brains are extruded, people grasp the dust while their body convulses.[20]

But the Greeks must have understood this, for the most celebrated of all rejections of the idea that posthumous fame is a sort of life comes in the *Odyssey*, when Odysseus tries to sooth the spirit of Achilles, greatest of heroes, by assuring him that he is eternally honored by the Argives and now rules mightily among the dead: "Therefore grieve not at all that thou art dead, Achilles." The reply of Achilles is the definitive rejection of what was to become the civic promise of immortality: "Do not try to persuade me to make light of death, Odysseus. I should choose, if I could live on earth, to serve as the bondsman of another, of a man with no property, rather than be lord of all the dead who are no more" (*Odyssey* 11, 488–91). That a great lord, a semi-divine hero should prefer a hideous existence as slave of a landless peasant, just so that he might be alive again, to any posthumous glory, must have had an immense impact on those who heard the poem, as well as carrying the ring of truth. In their deepest being, the Greeks saw the sweetness of life as the only thing worth having. Yet civic virtue aimed to cancel these instincts, offering honor as the compensation for the loyalty unto death that it demanded. This has provoked skepticism over many centuries: "Can honour set a leg? No. Or an arm? No. Honour hath no skill in surgery then? No. What is honour? A word. What is in that word honour? What is that honour? Air."[21]

Jasper Griffin has persuasively argued that what finally patterns the heroic readiness to face death is the sense—not that of the heroes but of the poem and its audience—that all this is devised by the gods "so that out of the destruction of men there should be a theme for song in later generations" and "from suffering comes song, and song gives pleasure."[22] This explains how the pleasure the gods take in what they have ordained is like the pleasure of an audience at a tragedy. So Zeus can take a tragic pleasure in the deaths of heroes whom he loves and the destruction of a city that he loves. "Like a tragic figure carrying out the decrees under which the fates had placed him at birth. Many people have, at some period, serious trouble in their lives—so serious as to lead to thoughts of suicide. This is likely to appear to one as something nasty, as a situation which is too foul to be a subject of tragedy. And it may then be an immense relief if it can be shown that one's life has the pattern rather of tragedy—the tragic working out of a pattern which was determined by the primal scene."[23]

Yet whatever doubts there may have been about the official doctrine, any rebellion against it does not seem to have taken the form of a widespread demand for personal immortality for all. Greek sepulchral inscriptions, until the middle of the fifth century BC, make no mention of any future existence:

"The dead person speaks only of his life, his city, his family, clan or children, and often of his own achievements with pride or love . . . they were more closely attached to the civic and social existence [than later Greeks], less insistent on the individualistic soul-theory and therefore more likely to look back than to look forward."[24]

A common wisdom? Frequent skepticism? Some Greek and Roman epitaphs

> "Charidas, what goes on down there?" "Deep darkness." "But
> what about all those journeys upwards?" "All lies." "And Pluto?"
> "A fable." "Then we really are f****d!"
> —Callimachus, Epig. 15, 3[25]

Greek epitaphs are a particularly valuable record of attitudes to death, ranging as they do "from simple faith to aggressive skepticism."[26] Some reiterate the civic virtue orthodoxy: perhaps they were civically commissioned:

> If dying well is the greatest part of virtue
> Fate has apportioned it to us of all men.
> For we, hastening to bestow freedom on Hellas,
> Lie here enjoying a good repute that will never grow old.[27]

This fame after death can be almost a resurrection:

> These men bestowed unquenchable glory upon their dear country
> And took upon themselves the dark mist of death.
> They have died, but are not dead, since their virtue
> Glorifies them and leads them up out of Hades' home.[28]

Most famous, and most austere of all the epitaphs of patriotic immortality is that on the grave of those Spartans who fell at Thermopylae resisting the Persian invasion:

> Stranger, announce to the Lacedaemonians that here
> We lie, obedient to their commands. (Herodotus 7, 228)[29]

There is, though, quite a difference between those and many other epitaphs that seem clearly to express what individuals and families actually felt. Perhaps a common wisdom emerges, but this is something different from a common faith—the faith that made sure that epitaphs on Christian graves characteristically have carried "in sure and certain hope of the Resurrection." The variety of attitudes we find in Greek epitaphs almost suggests a debate—which is not what you find in a churchyard. They often have a particularity, which is like a minimal narrative. Many commentators on Homer have noted how he gives a thumbnail sketch of a warrior, never before mentioned, just as he is about to die. It may be that these mininarratives are in this tradition:[30]

> Under the walls of this tomb the earth conceals Kydimachos,
> Who was rich and well along in years before he sailed into the harbour.
> He saw his grandchildren, and his old age was free of care.
> Now, dead, he shares our common fate.[31]

The very finality of death is sometimes a consolation:

> There is nothing left—for nothing awakens the dead—except to afflict the souls of those who pass by. Nothing else remains.[32]

Others, though, express a fierce skepticism about received beliefs:

> Do not pass by my epitaph, wayfarer,
> But stand, listen, and when you have heard, go on your way.
> There is no boat in Hades, no ferryman Charon,
> No Aiakos, keeper of the keys, no dog Cerberus.
> All of us who have died and gone below
> Are bones and ashes, nothing else.
> I have spoken to you truthfully. Go away, traveler,
> Lest I appear to you, though dead, to be an idle talker.[33]

There are plenty of Roman epitaphs that express just such skepticism. The following was especially popular with gladiators:

> Non fui, fui, non sum, non curo.
> [I was not; I was; I am not; I don't care.][34]

Or:

> Nil sumus et fuimus, mortales, respice, lector,
> In nihil ab nihilo quam cito recidimus.

[We are nothing and we were nothing. Reader, consider how mortals so quickly return into nothingness from nothingness.][35]

Life is light, and death deprivation of light: "At four years I left the sweet sunlight" [dum claram cernere lucem contingerit].[36] Marriage is one of the sweets of life that death takes away—it is an absolute loss, frequently mourned (for the unmarried can have no offspring to tend their memories): "My parents did not enjoy my young beauty, nor my fine brother, nor my husband, but gloomy

Hades." "I never cut my beard, nor was I garlanded in the bridal chamber."[37] There is sometimes a poignant exactness: "We . . . have acquired this funerary edifice for our sweet son Titus Aelius Saturninus, who lived 6 years, 8 months, 16 days and 6 hours . . ."[38] There can be lengthy and frank character sketches: "In this respectable tomb Glyconis lies, serenely sweet in name [i.e., Gk. *glukus* "sweet,"] but even sweeter in her soul. She never cared for splendid honors but rather preferred to be wild and pleasant, to be inebriated by Bacchus and to perform songs. . . . Worthy to enjoy blessings and eternal light she hurried herself to where the good fates call us."[39] "For the sweet Geminia Agathe Mater. My name was Mater, but I was never destined to become a mother. I do not deny having lived only 5 years, 7 months and 22 days. During the time that I lived, I enjoyed myself . . . I had the face of a little boy, not of a girl . . . with red hair, short on top and long behind. Now all of you offer me nice drinks, and pray that the earth lie light upon me . . . [whom] premature death stole and brought at a tender age to Tartarus. This is all, more cannot happen, this is decreed for us."[40]

Some Romans seem to have enjoyed affirming a cheeky Epicureanism on their tombs: "When I was young, I drank willingly; drink ye who live."[41] Some silver goblets were found in the ruins of Pompeii. On one of them, Epicurus himself is shown, his hand stretching toward a cake on a table. Between his legs is a little pig lifting his feet and snout to take his share of the cake. Above the cake are the Greek words: *to telos hedone*—"The supreme end is pleasure."[42] A still cheekier Roman epitaph runs:

> amici quit legitis, moneo, miscete Lyaeum
> et potate procul redimiti tempora flore
> et venereos coitus formosis ne denegate puellis:
> cetera post obitum terra consumit et ignis

[Friends who read this, I urge you to prepare wine, and drink it with your temples wreathed all around with garlands, and do not disdain having sex with beautiful girls: when we die the earth and the fire will consume everything else.]

One finds in Greek texts a note of pessimism about the very fact of being alive that is quite different from the humane realism of *Gilgamesh*, and that is not found at all among the Egyptians, nor in Latin texts:

> Best of all things is it, never to be born upon this earth, never to see
>   the rays of the burning sun.
> And, when a man is born, it is best that he should journey with all
>   speed to the gates of Death, and, wrapping himself in a close
>   covering of earth, should lie at rest.[43]

Then there are these famous, and similar, lines from Sophocles:

Not to be born is best of all; next best by far, to look on the light and
return with speed to the place whence one came.[44]

This fatalism goes right back to the beginning. One of the most eloquent
expressions of it is to be found in the elegiac poet, Mimnermus of Colophon,
who lived in the seventh century BC:

We are like the leaves that the hour of spring, rich in flowers, shoots forth,
which suddenly bloom in the rays of the sun. Like them we take our
pleasure in our span of youth, not knowing whether evil or good shall
come from God. For dark Fates stand beside us, the one contains the end
of painful old age, the other the end of death. For the bloom of youth is
short lived, so long as the sun spreads over the earth. And when this hour
passes by, then death is better than life. Many woes are born for the soul.
At one time a household is worn out, and the painful works of poverty
appear. Another man longs for children, and though he longs for them
he goes beneath the earth to Hades. Another has pain which destroys the
soul. There is no man for whom Zeus does not have many woes.[45]

This reminds us of a passage in the *Iliad*, which very likely influenced it:

Like leaves on trees the race of man is found,
Now green in youth, now with'ring on the ground,
Another race the following spring supplies,
They fall successive, and successive rise;
So generations in their course decay,
So flourish these, when those are past away.
(*Iliad* 6, 181–86, trans. Pope)

That is from Pope's translation of the *Iliad*. In his notes of the passage,
Pope notices the resemblance to the words of Mimnermus of Colophon—and
also to a passage in Ecclesiasticus 14:18–19: *As of the green leaves on a thick tree,
some fall, and some grow; so is the generation of flesh and blood, one cometh to an
end, and another is born.* (Ecclus./Sirac 14, 18–19). And this returns us to Virgil
and Dante, with human souls compared with the leaves of the forest that fall at
autumn's first frost drop.

Yet one also finds an equally vehement insistence on the value of being alive,
which rejects both the pessimism of Mimnermus and the glory of civic virtue—
for instance, in Euripides: "Daylight is the loveliest thing for men to look upon.
What is below is nothingness. It is madness to pray for death. Better a life of
wretchedness than a glorious death" (Euripides, *Iphigeneia at Aulis*, 1250–52).

In truth, it would be a mistake to look for an orthodoxy in ancient Greek (or Roman) religion. While most might pay lip service—and some would pay more than lip service—to the idea that true immortality is found in a glory after death that is won by heroic loyalty to the state (a tiny minority even of that minority of those who could afford epitaphs), a more skeptical opinion is extremely widespread. Skepticism may question the value of life itself. It may equally insist that since life is the supreme value, an immortality of honor is meaningless. There is no faith in a personal immortality, except in the mystery religions. Correspondingly, the punishments of evildoers after death depicted by Homer—and more fully by Virgil—do not seem to have had any great hold on people's minds. They seem to be midway between religious beliefs and poetic fictions. Although Virgil depicts Aeneas meeting various shades of individual people in the underworld in book 6 of the *Aeneid*—including his abandoned lover, Dido, and his father, Anchises—what he wants his readers to take most seriously is Anchises' predictions of "the long Glories of Majestick Rome" (*Aeneid* 1, 10, Dryden trans.).

Neither Homer nor Virgil is very interested in the punishment of ordinary sinners in the next life. Homer (as we have seen) represents the state of the dead as impotent and barely conscious, but he does—inconsequentially, we might feel—depict unending punishments in Hades for the wicked. They are condemned by Minos, son of Zeus, sitting in his judgment seat, scepter in hand. But only three notable sinners are mentioned—Tityos, Tantalus, and Sysiphus. These are all safely mythical figures who had rebelled against the gods. Their punishments reflect the nature of their sins, something that will become a typical feature of all later descriptions of postmortem judgments. Two vultures tear perpetually at the liver of Tityos; Tantalus, in terrible thirst, stands with water coming up to his chin, but is prevented from drinking it. Sysiphus, bathed in sweat, has to keep trying to raise with his hands a monstrous stone that for ever rolls back down upon him. But none of these punishments suggests a fate that awaits ordinary sinners.

Virgil's account is more elaborate, but he, too, is concerned with mythical figures who rebelled against the gods. He includes Tityos, Salmoneus ("who paid a cruel penalty while aping Jove's fires"—i.e., he claimed divine honors), the Lapiths, Ixion, Pirithous and Tantalus (*Aeneid* 6, 585–603). But Virgil does go on to mention the punishment of generic sins: "Here were they who in lifetime hated their brethren, or smote a sire, and entangled a client in wrong; or who brooded in solitude over wealth they had won, nor set aside a portion for their kin—the largest number this; who were slain for adultery; or who followed the standard of treason" (*Aeneid* 6, 608–13). But he is vague about the punishments: "Seek not to learn that doom.... Some roll a huge stone, or hang outstretched on spokes of wheels." The only individual sinners mentioned by name are Theseus and Phlegyas, but their punishments are not described. The truth seems to be, as one writer has suggested,[46] that the ancients did not regale themselves with thoughts of others' damnation.

There may have been exceptions to this. Pausanias, in his guidebook to Greece, describes a building that contains an astonishing picture by the famous artist, Polygnotus.[47] It seems to have been an enormous wall painting, on the scale of Michelangelo's frescoes in the Sistine Chapel. Part of the painting depicts the sack of Troy by the Greeks. Another part illustrates the underworld, starting with Odysseus's descent thither in the Odyssey, book II. The painting featured among other things the river Acheron and Charon's boat. On the banks of Acheron one saw a man who had been undutiful to his father, with the said father throttling him[48] ("For the men of old held their parents in the greatest respect"). Another man who had also been undutiful to his father was shown being forced to drink "a cup of woe" administered to him by a woman "skilled in poisonous and other drugs." There is also a demon, by name of Eurynomus, "who eats off all the flesh of the corpses, leaving only their bones...he is of a color between blue and black, like that of meat flies, and under him is spread a vulture's skin." (One could imagine the picture as a Doom on the wall of a medieval English church.) There is Ocnus (sloth) who plaits a cord, and by him stands a she-ass, eating up the cord as quickly as it is plaited. ("They say that this Ocnus was a diligent man with an extravagant wife"—which seems rather hard on Ocnus.) But in fact very little of this enormous painting seems to have been concerned with punishments. Its Hades simply contains all the great heroes of antiquity, records their tragic deaths, their adventures, their lives—Hector "sitting with both hands clasped about his left knee, in an attitude of grief...Paris, as yet beardless..." and so on.[49]

Did such a painting have the same function as depictions of the Last Judgment in Christian art? It is hard to say. There is some evidence that educated people did not take this sort of thing seriously. In Plato's *Republic*, Cephalus talks to Socrates of "the tales that are told of the world below and how the men who have done wrong here must pay the penalty there." The man who may have laughed at such tales, as death approaches "is filled with doubt, surmises, and alarms and begins to reckon up and consider whether he has ever wronged anyone."[50] The suggestion is that most people do not take these stories seriously during the greater part of their life. There is little sense that the threat of future rewards and punishments is something that people felt as part of their day-to-day lives, as Christians have during the greater part of two thousand years. They seem to have been vague popular beliefs, which had never died out entirely.[51]

Rome

Against the Fear of Death: Lucretius

If for both Greeks and Romans a postmortem existence is a state of half-being, a world of shades who at best remember with sad longing the world they have left behind, or at worst are tormented by the deities of the underworld, then death must have been looked on with fear and horror. Only a radical departure from the traditional picture could remove that fear. One departure would be that of some mystery religions that promised individual immortality. Another would be a denial that the nature of the soul and its relation to the body is such that the traditional picture is even intelligible. This was the doctrine of the Roman poet Lucretius (?95–?55 BC). In his great philosophical poem, *De Rerum Natura*, Lucretius gives purely moral or psychological arguments against the fear of death—e.g., why be horrified at the infinity of time ahead of us when we will not exist, when we have no horror at the eons before we came into existence?—but he buttresses such arguments with his specific, monist beliefs about the body-soul relationship.

Lucretius has sometimes been regarded as simply a religious skeptic, even as an atheist who could not quite bring himself to avow his disbelief. This seems not to have been so. Although he frequently attacks *religio*, what he really opposes is mistaken ideas about the gods and the human readiness to attribute to them powers that they do not possess, and an interest in human affairs that is quite alien to them. The gods are beautiful, strong, and live a life of everlasting tranquility and blessedness, in a place that sounds very like Homer's Elysian Fields:[52]

> ...sedesque quietae
> quas neque concutiunt venti nec nubila nimbis
> aspergunt neque nix acri concreta pruina
> cana cadens violat semperque innubilus aether
> integit, et large diffuso lumine ridet. (ibid., 3, 18–22)

[...their peaceful abodes, which neither the winds shake nor clouds soak with showers, nor does the snow congealed with biting frost besmirch them with its white fall, but an ever cloudless sky vaults them over, and smiles with light bounteously spread abroad.] The gods in tranquil peace pass placid years.

Living in such felicity, why should the gods bother with the petty affairs of mortal men? Humans think that the gods interfere, because they notice the order of nature—the circulation of the planets, the seasons. Then they see and fear thunderstorms, and dread them as a special revelation of divine power and anger against the misdeeds of men. But if the gods hurl thunderbolts, why do the guiltless suffer as frequently as the wicked, and why do they so often hurl them at their own temples, or into the midst of the desert, where there can be no question of someone's being punished (ibid., 2, 1095–104)? The movement of the spheres, the progression of light and darkness have nothing to do with the gods but are caused by the nature of things—ultimately by the various movements of atomic particles.

So there is no need for *religio*—superstitious fear of the gods, and a blasphemous attempt to tear them from their lives of ease and involve them in human affairs, including punishing men after death.

There are deeper arguments with which to free man from his fear of mortality. The soul is inextricably involved with the body, and neither can exist without the other. The soul, in effect, is the principle of unity within the living organism, and without the body, the soul itself must die. Lucretius argues with persuasive eloquence that we simply cannot think of the soul as something subsisting on its own. If we feel terror in our mind, then throughout the body the limbs sweat and pallor breaks out, the eyes grow misty, the ears ring, the limbs give way beneath us. The soul is clearly linked in union with the flesh (ibid., 3, 151–60).

Lucretius accepts the atomic theory of Epicurus and uses it to explain all phenomena. The human body is made up of biggish particles, but the mind, being very nimble, is composed of exceedingly round and exceedingly tiny seeds, which can be set moving by the slightest thing (ibid., 3, 185–88). These atoms are hot or cold, moist or dry, and this explains the passions of animals. Lions are full of hot elements, hence are angry and fierce, and "as often as they groan break their hearts with roaring, and cannot contain in their breast the billows of their wrath" (ibid., 3, 296–98). Deer are damp and cold, hence fearful and always ready to run away from danger.

This may sound quaint as medical science, but it is making an important point. The soul of any creature is inextricably involved with the nature of its body. If souls could leave or enter bodies, then why could not the soul of a dove enter into a lion, rendering it fearful, or the spirit of a lion create a ferocious deer? By nature the soul is protected by the whole body, is the guardian of the body:

> Nam communibus inter se radicibus haerent
> Nec sine pernicie divelli posse videntur. (Ibid., 3, 325–26)

[For the two cling together by common roots, and it is seen that they cannot be torn asunder without destruction.]

We see understanding growing in a child as its body grows, for as children totter with feeble and tender body, so weak judgment of mind goes with it. When the body is sunk beneath the burden of old age "the reason is maimed, the tongue raves, the mind stumbles, all things give way and fail at once." As smoke dissolves into air, so the soul which Lucretius sometimes likens to smoke, wearies and fades with the aging body (ibid., 3, 445–57).

These are perennial arguments (leaving aside the theory that everything can be explained by the movements of particles) for a monist understanding of man—that body and soul/mind form a unity. Another great monist, Spinoza, wrote in remarkably similar terms nearly seventeen hundred years later:

> they say . . . that if the mind were not fit for thinking the body would be inert. They say, again, it is in their experience that the mind alone has power both to speak and be silent, and to do many other things which they therefore think to be dependent on a decree of the mind. But with regard to the first assertion, I ask them if experience does not also teach that if the body be sluggish the mind at the same time is not fit for thinking? When the body is asleep, the mind slumbers with it. . . . all have discovered that the mind is not equally fitted for thinking about the same subject, but in proportion to the fitness of the body.[53]

So the soul cannot survive the body, and even if it could, it would experience nothing unless it had the bodily five senses. So there are no sad shades, no Hades, no punishments—and no Isles of the Blest. Death is a sleep, no more to be feared than the sleep we experience every night. Death is nothing to us. Just as we felt no fear or horror when the Carthaginians brought Rome almost to destruction before we were born, so, when our body and soul are parted, by whose union we are made one, we shall feel nothing, and therefore now need fear nothing:

Non si terra mare miscebitur et mare caelo. (*De Rerum Natura* 3, 842)

[Not even if earth shall be mingled with sea, and sea with sky.]

It is only because we do not understand this that we have this illusory fear of death, of the loss of our loved ones, and theirs of us. In Thomas Gray's words:

> For them no more the blazing hearth shall burn,
> Or busy housewife ply her evening care:
> No children run to lisp their sire's return,
> Or climb his knees the envied kiss to share. (Gray, "Elegy in a
>   Country Churchyard.")

Virtually those words occur in Lucretius (whom Gray had certainly read), but Lucretius goes on to rejoin;

> illud in his rebus non addunt "nec tibi earum
> iam desiderium rerum super insidet una." (*De Rerum Natura* 3,
>   894–901)

[Yet to this they add not: "Nor does there abide with thee any longer any yearning for these things."]

The fear of death is in every way an illusion. If we have lived full lives, it is contemptible not to accept that we have had our pleasures and should now bid them farewell. Age is indeed nature's kind signal to retreat,[54] and one should calmly leave what one has to future generations. Above all, there are no postmortem terrors, no Tityos eternally eviscerated by birds as he lies in Acheron, no Tantalus for ever trying to drink water that vanishes. It is here on earth we have these torments—we are eaten up with unrequited love as Tityos is by birds, we are condemned to frustration, like Sysiphus rolling his stone. We are buffeted to and fro by restless, mad passions; but if he saw all this clearly, every man would leave all else, and study, first, to learn the nature of things (*rerum naturam*) understanding what will be his for all eternity:

> proinde licet quot vis vivendo condere saecla;
> mors eterna tamen nilo minus illa manebit,
> nec minus ille diu iam non erit, ex hodierno
> lumine qui finem vitai fecit, et ille,
> mensibus atque annis qui multis occidit ante.
>   (*De Rerum Natura* 3, 1090–94)

[Therefore you may live on to close as many generations as you will: yet no whit the less that everlasting death will await you, nor will he for a less long time be no more, who has made an end of life with today's light, than he who perished many months or years ago.]

This great exorcism of fear is also an exhortation to rational pleasure—the doctrine of the master of Lucretius, Epicurus. But this Epicureanism recommends a pleasure that is constantly aware of its ephemeral nature, rather than a mindless jollity or sensuality.

Horace

In Latin poetry the theme of inevitable extinction is often linked (as it is in *Gilgamesh*) with the injunction to seize the present moment—*carpe diem*—notably in the lines of Catullus that have influenced such famous English *carpe diem* poems as Marvell's *To His Coy Mistress* and Herrick's *Corinna's Going a-Maying:*

> vivamus, mea Lesbia, atque amemus,
> rumoresque senum severiorum
> omnes unius aestimemus assis.
> soles occidere et redire possunt:
> nobis cum semel occidit brevis lux,
> nox est perpetua una dormienda.[55]

[Let us live, my Lesbia, and love, and value at one farthing all the talk of crabbed old men.

Suns may set and rise again. For us, when the short light has once set, remains to be slept the sleep of one unbroken night.]

But those lines are part of a seduction poem. It is to Horace, more than Catullus, that we turn for a meditation on inevitable extinction that seems to epitomize a philosophy, and that at the same time leads to another topic. A. E. Housman, himself a pessimist of a rather showier sort than Horace, regarded the ode, *Diffugere nives* (*Odes* 4, 7) as "the most beautiful poem in ancient literature,"[56] and which he—uniquely—translated, and—again uniquely— read out to his lecture audience with an actual show of feeling. The ode begins with spring and the return of grass and foliage:

> Diffugere nives, redeunt iam gramina campis
>   arboribusque comae;
> mutat terra vices et decrescentia ripas
>   flumina praeterunt;
> Gratia cum Nymphis geminisque sororibus audet
>   ducere nuda choros.
> immortalia ne speres, monet annus et almum
>   quae rapit hora diem. (*Odes* 4, 7, 1–8)

[The snows are fled away, leaves on the shaws
    And grasses in the mead renew their birth,
The river to the river-bed withdraws,
    And altered is the fashion of the earth.
The Nymphs and Graces three put off their fear
    And unapparelled in the woodland play.
The swift hour and the brief prime of the year
    Say to the soul, *Thou wast not born for aye.*][57]

Nature returns through death to a rebirth, but it is this very circle of the seasons that points, by contrast, to human mortality.

> frigora mitescunt zephyris, ver proterit aestas
>> interitura, simul
> pomifer autumnus fruges effuderit . . .

> [Thaw follows frost; hard on the heel of spring
>> Treads summer sure to die, for hard on hers
> Comes autumn, with his apples scattering . . .]

These regular renewals in earth and heavens are precisely what man cannot expect to participate in:

> damna tamen celeres reparant caelestia lunae;
>> nos ubi decidimus,
> quo pius Aeneas, quo Tullus dives et Ancus,
>> pulvis et umbra sumus.

> [But oh, what e'er the sky-built seasons mar,
>> Moon upon moon rebuilds it with her beams:
> Come *we* where Tullus and where Ancus are,
>> And good Aeneas, we are dust and dreams.]

In setting human fate against the cycle of the seasons familiar to all of us, Horace aims at a grave wisdom that we will recognize as a common inheritance. Mortality, in its secular inevitability, almost becomes part of the beauty of things. Such consolation, if that is what it is, that the poem offers is our capacity to hold on to the treasures of our hearts, for they are not goods that will be seized on by a greedy heir:

> quis scit an adiciant hodiernae crastina summae
>> tempora di superi?
> cuncta manus avidas fugient heredis, amico
>> quae dederis animo.

> [Torquatus, if the gods in heaven shall add
>> The morrow to the day, what tongue has told?
> Feast then thy heart, for what thy heart has had
>> The fingers of no heir shall ever hold.]

It may seem that Horace is uttering commonplaces, or—should we say?—presenting a distilled wisdom in this ode—a mature and sane vision of things, understated and calm, compared with the almost theatrical intensity of the Catullus. There is, though, another implied contrast, with a view of life and its seasons that was extremely influential in Horace's time, and which one could almost think of this poem as systematically opposing. This is a tradition, which in ceremonies of all sorts lays stress on the renewal of life, in its initiation ceremonies for infants, in marriage, in its celebration of the fertility of animals and plants, that sees all these things as giving "the assurance of a new and better life beyond the grave."[58] We are talking of the mystery religions that include the Eleusinian Mysteries and Orphism. The latter, far from holding that the cycle of the seasons cannot hold any promise of human immortality, envisages a sort of savior, a divine being who "dies in the decline of every year to be reborn in Spring [so that] its immortality must consist, not in exemption from death, but in recurrent resurrection. Similarly for human life immortality means a perpetual rebirth into this earthly life, not an escape from the wheel of becoming into a deathless future."[59]

Orphism and the Future Life

If we are to look for people in Greek and Roman antiquity who believed firmly that this life is a vale of tears and death a welcome deliverance from it, we will find them among the Orphics.[60] Orphism was a collection of beliefs and rituals that held out the promise of a future life far removed from the shadowy existence of Homer's *eidola*, one that is open not only to heroes or demigods, but to all. It therefore offers a hope to ordinary people that is entirely absent from the civic, Olympian religion, for the Olympian gods (like Homer himself) had no interest in ordinary people.[61]

Orphism reproduces in the Greek and Roman worlds some Egyptian beliefs about a future existence. In particular it takes seriously the idea that a person's future state will depend upon how righteously or wickedly he has spent his earthly existence. And as with the Egyptians, the idea that moral conduct determines one's fate in the next world was bound up with equally strong convictions that rituals can also influence those powers who judge human souls. It was, indeed, widely believed among the Greeks that Orphic religion was so called because it had originally been brought to Greece from Egypt by Orpheus himself.

Plutarch mentions the belief that the Oceanus of Homer (i.e., the water that surrounds the earth) is really Osiris, since Osiris is the lord of water "the source and origin of all things." He even suggests that the Zeus of Homer is partly derived from the "careful planning and thoughtfulness of Osiris."[62] Diodorus of Sicily in the course of a long account of Egypt, its religion, and customs writes:

> Orpheus brought from Egypt most of his mystic ceremonies, the orgiastic rites that accompanied his wanderings, and his fabulous accounts of his experiences in Hades. For the rite of Osiris is the same as that of Dionysus, and that of Isis is very similar to that of Demeter, the names alone having been interchanged: and the punishments in Hades of the unrighteous, the Fields of the Righteous, and the fantastic conceptions, current among the many, which are figments of the imagination—all these were introduced by Orpheus in imitation of Egyptian funeral customs. Hermes, for instance, the Conductor of Souls, according to the ancient Egyptian custom, brings up [a certain body] . . . and then gives it over to one who wears the mask of Cerberus [i.e., the monstrous dog, one of the guardians of the underworld in Greek and Roman mythology].

The point is that Cerberus is akin to Anubis.[63]

But who was Orpheus? There is a mass of legend about him, but some recurrent elements are these: Orpheus was the son of the muse Calliope. He was a superb musician, playing the lyre; he accompanied the Argonauts on their quest for the Golden Fleece. His playing and singing could enchant all creatures, even rocks and trees. He charmed the Clashing Rocks so that the ship of the Argonauts, *Argo*, could pass safely between them. He calmed a stormy sea and called down sleep on the eyes of the dragon that guarded the Golden Fleece.

Orpheus had a wife, Eurydice, who died after being bitten by a serpent. So overcome was Orpheus by grief for her death that he himself descended to the underworld to persuade the rulers of the dead to permit her to return to the light. He took his lyre with him. Having arrived in Hades he began to play. "The shades crowded round him as birds to a leafy tree at evening or in time of storm. The Eumenides and Cerberus himself were softened, and Ixion's wheel stood still."[64] Eventually he obtained his prayer that he be allowed to lead Eurydice back to the light and upper air. However (according to some versions of the legend), he broke a command of the rulers of the underworld by looking back at Eurydice before they had attained the realms of light. The result was that she was sent back into Hades.

Because of losing his beloved Eurydice, Orpheus thereafter shunned the company of women. Instead, he enchanted with his music the men of Thrace. Resentful at this enchantment of their husbands, the women of Thrace plotted to kill him. Orpheus was a follower of Apollo, hence gentle and civilized. These

Orpheus fascinated the men of Thrace with his music, which led to his being murdered by the women, jealous of his power. Attic vase, 5th century, plate 6 in W. K. Guthrie, *Orpheus and Greek Religion.*

women were Maenads, devotees of Dionysus, driven to Bacchic frenzy. They tore Orpheus to pieces. His head, along with his lyre, was thrown into the river Hebros, whence both floated to the isle of Lesbos, the head singing as it went:

> What could the Muse her self that *Orpheus* bore,
> The Muse her self, for her enchanting son
> Whom Universal Nature did lament,
> When by the rout that made the hideous roar,
> His goary visage down the stream was sent,
> Down the swift *Hebrus* to the *Lesbian* shore.[65]

There are several different versions of the story, but in most Orpheus becomes a power in the underworld. He has a role in determining the punishments there. Those who have lived lives according to those ideals Orpheus is thought to embody will be purified souls, and will be rewarded by him with bliss in the world to come.

And what were these ideals? Orpheus stands for civilization and gentleness, as against violence and barbarism. According to the legends he introduced the arts of husbandry and agriculture into Greece, corn, and viticulture. These are the arts of peace, as are the arts of music and song. His music calmed the savage breast, even in beasts, as it were. "His music was of the lyre; it did not excite to orgiastic excess, but tamed the beasts themselves to mildness."[66] In these respects, and in his suffering and dismemberment, he very strikingly resembles Osiris—also lord of the dead. And it is through his suffering, ritually remembered by his devotees, that Orpheus can initiate his followers into an afterlife.

The devotees of Orpheus aimed to lead ascetic lives of piety and purity. This meant abstaining from things that are polluted. The Orphics seem to have been vegetarians. In the *Laws* Plato writes: "We see in fact that the practice of human sacrifice persists to this day among many races; whereas elsewhere we hear of the opposite state of things, when we could not bring ourselves to taste even of the ox, when the sacrifices made to the gods were not of animals, but of cakes, and the fruits of the earth soaked in honey, and other similarly pure and bloodless offerings. Men abstained from flesh on the ground that it was impious to eat it or to stain the altars of the gods with blood. It was a kind of Orphic life . . . that was led by those of our kind who were alive at that time, taking freely of all things that had no life, but abstaining from all that had life."[67]

This ritual purity featured largely in the Orphic ethic, so much so that some writers have concluded that the Orphics were mere ritualists, formalists who abstained from certain forbidden acts merely as taboos—like Jews and Muslims abstaining from pork. Their object was simply to save their own souls, and the chief path to that was to achieve a state of ritual purity. But Judaism, Christianity, and Islam are not merely systems of ritual observances, but also lay an obligation on their followers to *perform* certain moral actions—for instance, to love one's neighbor as oneself.[68] So the Orphic religion was "the height of individualism."[69] Compared (later) with Christianity, with its insistence on the practical expression of human brotherhood and love for all men, Orphism is more like one of the philosophical schools than a faith that compelled human hearts. When Julian ["the Apostate" who tried to restore paganism] wished to show the world that the gods of paganism were as well worth worshipping as the God of the Christians, one of the things he had to do was to found hospitals and asylums for the poor in the name of Apollo.[70]

The Orphics taught that life should be a "practice for death."[71] They thought also that the human race was involved an aboriginal sin, as the result of which the soul was imprisoned in the body.[72] The way to expiate this inherited guilt was to lead a life of ascetic purity, which would make the soul fit to fly, after death, to its proper place in the *æther*—the element that contained the starry heavens, but was also the material of the soul itself. The body is evil, and the soul suffers from being imprisoned within it. Our souls are literally etherial, in that they are made of the divine element in which the gods live above the moon—hence the common statement that the souls of the righteous actually become stars. Man has a double nature, spiritual and earthly, and therefore there is a perpetual war in our members. We should condemn the sense world in which we are imprisoned and regard life as a sort of purgatory.[73] Life on earth is a constant struggle against the lower passions that arise from the body. Our natural passions and appetites have to be subdued if we are to arise to the heights to which the soul should aspire. The purified soul, having lived the ascetic life, can claim that it has come "from the pure," is one of the saints, and is hence ready to enter on the final stage of bliss.[74] We shall see that Plato works over these ideas philosophically, and is able to give an ethical content to this idea of purification.

This Orphic faith in the future life is expressed in some inscriptions on gold plates, which were discovered in graves in Italy and Crete.[75] The words of the inscriptions are often beautiful and give us a very good sense of the attractiveness to its devotees of the Orphic faith. They are in the form of instructions for the soul as it enters the next life:

> You will find within the walls of Hades a spring on the left
> And close to it a white cypress standing.
> Do not go near this spring.
> You will find another, cool water pouring
> From the Lake of Memory. Guards stand in front of it.
> Say, "I am the child of earth and starry heaven,
> But my race is of heaven alone. This you know yourselves.
> I am parched with thirst and perishing. Quick, give me
> Cold water pouring from the Lake of Memory."
> Then they will freely allow you to drink from the sacred spring,
> And thereafter you will reign with the other demi-gods.[76]

And another:

> But as soon as the spirit has left the light of the sun,
> Go to the right as far as one should go, being careful in all things.
> Be glad you have suffered what you never suffered before.
> From a man you have become a god.
> A kid you are fallen into milk.[77]

The Orphic religion offers its followers a future radically different from the shadowy half-existence to which Homer and the Olympian religion condemn the departed. Indeed, it proclaims the opposite—that it is only in the next world that our souls are truly themselves, truly alive. Our souls aspire to the stars—although we are children of earth, our true race is of the starry heavens. Indeed, in Orphic literature and ritual the soul is often represented as a spark that flies upward to join its native element, the ether. So the next world is a fulfillment, rather than a state of melancholy impotence:

I have flown out of the sorrowful, weary circle.
I have passed with swift feet to the desired crown.
I have sunk beneath the bosom of the Mistress,
    Queen of the Underworld.
And now I am become a suppliant to holy Persephone,
That of her grace she will send me to the abodes of the blessed.
Happy and blessed one, you will be a god instead of a mortal.
A kid I have fallen into milk.[78]

This idea of a vibrant and happy new existence after our earthly life was unknown in Greek religion, until around the middle of the fifth century. The Greek idea of the *psyche* alone made it virtually unthinkable. (And that was an idea that sprang from, as much as it produced, the pessimistic picture of the shades in the underworld.) Yet there was a way in which the Orphics did not make a clean break with the past. The condition of *psuchai* in Hades, except where they were very notably wicked, was not determined by how they had behaved in this life. Hades simply was the sad abode for all. The Orphics did not make morally good behavior the supremely important thing in deciding whether the soul would join the ranks of the blessed. Their emphasis was, instead, on rituals and ritual purity. True, the pure man would not be (for instance) a mass murderer—but the rituals loomed still larger in the Orphic imagination than morally good and bad actions. In this, Orphism did not anticipate Christianity. The real emphasis was on the ascent of the soul, its escape from the entrapment of the body, and from cycles of reincarnation. The implicit idea was of a person who achieves wisdom. And the delights promised to the blessed are very much those that would appeal to philosophers—they soared above the realm of clouds, snow, burnings, and lightning until they reached the starry sphere. This would be part of a journey where they would be blown about by violent winds and plunged into watery gulfs. Purified by these tribulations, they would rise to heaven, to the seats of the Blessed, to be bathed in celestial light, contemplate the eternal truths, and hear with unspeakable joy the sweet harmony produced by the rotation of the spheres.[79] Man alone among the animals stands in order to gaze upon the skies, so it is his fulfillment to be among the stars; and to look at them for ever is to commune with the gods eternally.[80]

Philosophical Religion: Plato

The Orphic beliefs about the afterlife took the form of myths and legends. The Orphics insisted upon them in a way that few if any had insisted on the veracity of Homer's description of the Isles of the Blessed or the Olympian gods. But to insist upon tales of a future world in which the soul is immortal and is either rewarded or punished is not equivalent to propounding a philosophy about the immortality of the soul. Pindar reflects the beliefs of the mystery religions in one of his Olympian odes:

> ...immediately after death, on earth, it is the lawless spirits that suffer punishment, and the sins committed ... are judged by One who passeth sentence stern and inevitable; while the good, having the sun shining for evermore, for equal nights and equal days, receive the boon of a life of enlightened toil, not vexing the soil with the strength of their hands ... a life that knoweth no tears, while the others endure labour that none can look upon—But [for the courageously pure] ocean-breezes blow around the Isles of the Blest, and flowers of gold are blazing...[81]

Orphism needed a philosopher, and it found one in a man who argued more powerfully than any other single human being for the existence of a spiritual realm beyond the world of the senses, and correspondingly for the doctrine that the human soul is independent of the body, superior to it, and immortal.

To say that the Orphics found in Plato their philosopher is very different from saying that the Roman Catholic Church found in St. Thomas Aquinas the thinker who could systematically expound its beliefs. Rather, Plato's doctrines about the soul do strikingly support Orphic beliefs from the outside as it were; while there is at the same time reason to think that Plato was himself influenced by Orphism. The idea so central to Greek imagining of the state of human beings after death—that only something shadowy and half-real survives—is frontally attacked in Plato's insistence that the soul is the true human reality. Plato not only transforms Greek notions about postmortem survival but recasts our ideas of how one could even imagine survival. Rather than a realm of sorrowful memories carried by shades that are only half-conscious, in which recollection of the world they have left behind, in its light and color and sensory splendor is the fundamental source of suffering, Plato depicts the world of the senses itself as at best a dim approximation to a fuller splendor. So immortality can be looked forward to joyfully, for we will enter a realm of supreme clarity, wisdom, and beauty both moral and spiritual, of which our experience in this life offers only intimations, "hints followed by guesses."[82]

Plato's conviction that the soul is independent of the body, and perhaps to be thought of as imprisoned within the body, finds expression in numerous dialogues, not only in the philosophical arguments he produces for immortality or in his mythic pictures of the souls after death, but in his picture of Socrates himself, the man whose life is transformed by philosophy.

In the *Phaedo*, which describes the last moments of Socrates and his discussion of arguments for the immortality of the soul, the soul is the means by which we see absolute beauty and absolute goodness—things hidden from the bodily senses.[83] The body, by contrast, contaminates the soul and hinders its spiritual vision (ibid., 66B). The body "fills us with passions and desires and fears . . . and truly makes it impossible for us to think at all" (ibid., 66C). The body prevents our seeing the truth through philosophical reflection; and purification comes only through separating the soul from the body so that the soul collects itself together and so comes to itself (ibid., 66C, 67C). Virtue comes from release from the passions and appetites, and temperance, justice, courage, and wisdom are together a sort of purification (ibid., 69C).

Socrates goes on to say that "those men who established the mysteries [the word Plato uses here is *teletas*. The *teletai* are, precisely, the Orphic rites of purification.] were not unenlightened, but in reality had a hidden meaning when they said long ago that whoever goes uninitiated and unsanctified to the other world will lie in the mire, but he who arrives there initiated and purified will dwell with the gods" (ibid., 69C) The soul of the wise, therefore good and temperate person, departs after death into that which is like itself—invisible, divine, immortal and wise, and when it arrives there it is freed from "error and folly and fear and fierce loves and all other human ills" (ibid., 81A) But a soul may be defiled and impure when a person is enchained in sensuality, and after death it may haunt the places it cannot bear leaving—"it flits about the monuments and the tombs, where shadowy shapes of souls have been seen, figures of those souls which were not set free in purity but retain something of the visible; and that is why they are seen" (ibid., 81D).

For Plato it is virtues such as temperance, justice, courage, and truthfulness that reveal the soul's true nature (ibid., 114E–115A). The soul of an unjust or self-indulgent person is sick, and this sickness can be healed only by the application of justice to that soul. For instance, the soul should be punished. In the *Gorgias*, Socrates argues with Callicles, an avowed amoralist who proclaims the doctrine that all human pleasures—of the senses, of power—are good, and that human fulfillment consists in experiencing just as many pleasures as possible. Socrates confutes Callicles by mentioning some pleasures that even Callicles has to admit he finds disgusting. He also ridicules Callicles' very picture of the pursuit of pleasure by comparing it with ceaselessly trying to carry water with a sieve to pour it into a leaky jar—and he mentions a fable of Pythagoras in which this activity, far from being a human felicity, is a punishment for the wicked in Tartarus.[84]

In the *Gorgias* Socrates has represented men who are at variance with themselves because they lack philosophic wisdom. His two chief opponents in that dialogue, Polus—who argues that the traditional virtues of temperance and justice are simply fraudulent checks upon the normal human desire to seek power at all costs—and Callicles are corrupt as well as confused. They are corrupt because they are teaching doctrines, which in effect would prevent people from sharing in a common human life, for only those with an harmonious soul—i.e., a soul that is not at variance with itself—can share in this common life.[85] Unless Callicles alters his thinking he will be at variance with himself for the rest of his life. This, then, is Socrates' picture of the soul: it benefits from just punishment, it is healthy only when under the control of the virtues, especially temperance, which in turn supports justice and practical wisdom. The happy human being will be he who lives most as a soul, independent of the ills of the flesh and the accidents of human life. He might be the man who is fearless as a soldier, who can walk barefoot over the ice, drink everyone under the table, and then go about his business unaffected, who can resist the sexual blandishments of the charismatic Alcibiades, and can discuss philosophy right up to the moment of his execution entirely without fear[86]—in other words, the Socrates whom Plato presents, whom one would very much like to have existed in just the form in which Plato presents him.[87]

Plato's Socrates can do all this because he is a philosopher. Most human beings inhabit that world of half-knowledge that Plato calls "opinion" (*doxa* as against *episteme*). The hilarious/touching passage in the *Symposium* where Alcibiades—the most handsome man of his time—recalls his attempt to seduce Socrates perfectly dramatizes the idea. Socrates was notoriously ugly. One way of seeing the failed seduction is that Alcibiades, without understanding that this is so, is attracted by the beauty of soul of the man he admires. Socrates, says Alcibiades, is like one of those Silenus figures, outwardly ugly "but if you opened his inside, you cannot imagine how full he is. . . . Whether anyone else has opened him, and seen the images inside, I know not; but I saw them one day, and thought them so divine and golden, so perfectly fair and wondrous, that I simply had to do as Socrates bade me. . . . Now I have been bitten by a more painful creature, in the most painful way that one can ever be bitten: in my heart, or my soul . . . I am stricken and stung by his philosophical discourses, which adhere more fiercely than any adder."[88]

The Alcibiades who has been stung by philosophy in the shape of Socrates is not simply a man prouder of his own physical beauty than of his soul. The historical Alcibiades was touched with the spirit of oligarchy (e.g., in the mutilation of the *hermae*), but in the *Symposium* he has the inauthentic or wavering soul of the democrat or demagogue, who therefore in Plato's eyes spends his time flattering the masses rather than obeying reason. This "love of the popular" (*pandemon*) is itself opposed to that nobler love that craves the soul over the body. This becomes explicit in Alcibiades' encomium of Socrates: "he brings home to me that I cannot disown the duty of doing what he bids me, but . . . as soon as I turn from his company I fall victim to the favors of the crowd."[89]

One of the best things about the *Symposium* is that it is not simply propaganda for the Platonic view of the relation between body and soul. Alcibiades does feel the pull of philosophy, and hence the spiritual and rational, and knows that it challenges his own addiction to the world and the flesh. But to the end he remains Alcibiades, drunk, charming, with vine-leaves and violets in his hair.

So Plato in a piece of dramatic writing suggests that our sensory experience drives us—should drive us—toward an intimation of the real that lies beyond the sensuous curtain. This leads to his further suggestion that a belief in the superiority of the soul and, eventually, of its immortality, is necessary if we are to make sense of our experience.

Nothing could be farther from the traditional, Homeric picture of the human state after death—the melancholy shades—than Plato's doctrine of the soul. The soul is the human reality, its health is the human health, and death releases the soul of the virtuous person into a fullness of life that is rarely possible on earth except to a very few wise men—philosophers. In the *Gorgias*, Callicles had ridiculed Socrates' "childish" pursuit of philosophy: "You neglect, Socrates, what you ought to mind . . . if someone should seize hold of you . . . and drag you off to prison, asserting that you were guilty of a wrong you had never done, you know you would be at a loss what to do with yourself, and would be all dizzy and agape without a word to say. . . . Such a person . . . can be given a box on the ear with impunity."[90] Callicles is proleptically describing (more or less) what actually did happen to Socrates—he was tried on trumped-up charges and executed. It is partly in response to Callicles that Socrates produces his magnificent myth about the judgment of the soul after death (ibid., 523–27). Here, the soul will be stripped bare of the body and revealed as it really is—its crimes and vices will show themselves in all their deformity, analogous to the deformities of an unhealthy or misused body; the soul that is guilty of perjuries and injustice will be a mass of wounds; luxury, insolence, and incontinence will show as disproportion and ugliness. Judgment will be given in a meadow, whence are two ways, one leading to the Isles of the Blest, and the other to Tartarus (ibid., 523A–524A).

In the *Phaedo* Socrates envisages great sinners plunged into the lake formed by the river Acheron, while the virtuous are freed from the underworld and "mount upward into their pure abode and dwell upon the earth. And of these, all who have duly purified themselves by philosophy live henceforth altogether without bodies, and pass to still more beautiful abodes" (*Phaedo* 114B–C). In the last book of the *Republic*, in the myth of Er, Plato describes the souls about to enter into their second lives on earth. The wicked are seen coming up from the earth "full of squalor and dust" (*Republic* 614D), while from heaven come the just, clean and pure. The wickedest men—tyrants in particular—are hideously punished, bound hand and foot, flung down and flayed, carded on thorns, and hurled into Tartarus (ibid., 625D–E). Savage men enter the bodies of beasts, wise men (such as Odysseus) choose the life of the quiet, private citizen; Orpheus chooses to become a swan—symbol of immortality, the creature that sings before it dies. Here again, the bodily form is taken to be an emblem of the inner, spiritual state.

Orphism had many attractions. It was a sect that promised its members salvation on not very arduous terms; its rituals were aesthetically appealing; it replaced the ancient grimness of death with the sense of a right to eternal felicity. But it was a system of myth. It did draw on philosophy—for instance, on the ideas of Pythagoras, who taught the transmigration of souls—but it was not systematically rational. Indeed, popular Orphism seems to have developed into a system of superstitious observances that was mocked by the satirically minded.

In several places Plato refers with reverence to Orphic teaching, to the Orphic initiations, and to Orphic images of the next world. His own myths of immortality, in the *Gorgias*, the *Phaedo*, and the *Republic* leap beyond what he thinks he has demonstrated by purely philosophical argument. They are what he regards as probabilities—ways of expressing intuitively convictions that philosophy cannot prove, but toward which it might point.[91] The combination of Plato's philosophy of spirit with the myths of Orphism certainly produced the most powerful idea of immortality that the ancient world knew (outside of Egypt).

But Plato's picture of the soul, while it has mythical elements, certainly forms part of a system of philosophy. The world itself is a pale imitation of the spiritual reality that underlies the appearance of things—what Plato at one point called the ideas. It is through our own rational principle, which is indeed the soul, that we human beings are equipped to see reality as it actually is beneath the shifting play of appearances. Therefore the soul, when it leaves the body, "comes home" in that it is united with that which shares its very nature— the spiritual reality that constitutes the universe. From time to time Plato strives to give a sense of how the soul will instinctively love the spiritual reality when once it is exposed to it. In a celebrated passage in the *Symposium* Diotima describes to Socrates how the soul approaches a vision of the Form of the Good:

When a man has been thus far tutored in the lore of love, passing from view to view of beautiful things, in the right and regular ascent, suddenly he will have revealed to him, as he draws to the close of his dealings in love, a wondrous vision, beautiful in its nature . . . it is ever-existent and neither comes to be nor perishes, neither waxes nor wanes; next, it is not beautiful in part and in part ugly, nor is it such at such a time and other at another. . . . Beginning from obvious beauties [man] must for the sake of that highest beauty be ever climbing aloft, as on the rungs of a ladder, from one to two, and from two to all beautiful bodies; from personal beauty he proceeds to beautiful observances, from observance to beautiful learning, and from learning at last to that particular study which is concerned with the beautiful itself and that alone; so that in the end he comes to know the very essence of beauty.[92]

The soul will have arisen from its desire for food and drink and such like sensual delights, from its enthusiasm for beautiful boys, to understand and love what lies behind all of these, and is the soul's real fulfillment—beauty in and of itself, which is also the good in and of itself. Diotima draws a picture of the soul's being ravished by this vision. It clearly influences Father Arnall's picture in *Portrait of the Artist* of the soul after death urgently desiring to fly toward God—but held back by a sense of its own unworthiness.

Plato's picture can persuade because he has shifted the human reality inward. The real world is not the phenomenal world of light and color, the loss of which the sad shades of Homer and Virgil deplore, but the world of ideas, which the soul only is equipped to grasp. This will make it possible for the successors of Plato, and those influenced by him—and, in particular, Christians—to find intellectual justification for a faith that this world is a faint shadow of a world to come, and that the goodness or wickedness of our souls has a reality beyond anything we can ascribe to the body or to our present physical existence.

Aristotle: The Soul as the "Form" of the Body

There is another great philosopher whose thought profoundly influenced ideas of the soul in a direction very different from Plato's—Aristotle. Aristotle does not uphold the idea of an active soul that is imprisoned in and can be thought of as existing independently of the body. A human being is not something—a soul, say—that *has* a body—it *is* a living body of a particular kind. For Aristotle, the soul is that which unifies all the powers—the potential—of any particular living organism. Plants have a vegetative soul, which is the process of their growth and sustenance. In addition to a vegetative soul, animals have also a sensitive soul—feeling, hearing, seeing, fearing, having an instinct for self-preservation. Human beings have the power of reason—mind, the power of consciousness and reflection. But in man these three souls are a single, composite form—the rational soul, which embraces the whole of human nature. In man, as a rational being, the fear of particular occasions of danger of death, which he shares with animals, becomes a fear of death in itself. (Later Aristotelians, St. Thomas Aquinas in particular, built on this the idea that man naturally desires immortality.)[93]

The soul in man enables the powers of his organism to come to fruition, for his potential to be actualized. Soul, you might say, is simply the unifying and organizing power of the complex human animal. When we die, the soul departs—in the sense that the power of organization ceases, the body decays, ceases to be a human body, becoming instead a heterogeneous mass of organisms. The soul is the "form" of the body. It is man, the specific human organism, that grows, feels, reasons—not some ghost within the human machine. The single composite form that makes up the whole, rational human organism could not survive the body—for in a sense it *is* the body, the body of a rational animal.

To describe the soul you cannot do better than describe what human beings characteristically do—speak, walk upright, live in cities, make music, philosophize—rather than some entity that stands behind what they do. This obviously makes it almost impossible to envisage a disembodied spirit—whether this be the *eidolon* of Homer, the souls escaping from the body of Plato, or the blissful spirits of the Orphics. A crucial question is whether Aristotle makes impossible a bodily resurrection from the dead.

It was not until around the thirteenth century that Christians (and then not all of them) thought it safe to use Aristotle to understand the soul. St. Thomas Aquinas seizes on an idea which he thinks can be drawn from Aristotle, that there might possibly be a part of the mind—a purely ratiocinative faculty—that can in principle survive the body. At best this would be purely a sort of repository of memories, incapable of receiving any new experience, since it would lack all bodily senses. Aquinas, however, thinks that the ratiocinative soul would be capable of having a vision of God (who is himself pure spirit) and through God could have knowledge.[94] This is very far from Plato's picture of the soul realizing man's true selfhood as it flies up from the body to the starry sphere. On the contrary, the separated soul is in an imperfect state without its body, and has a sort of longing to regain its body.[95]

It is very hard, though, to see how this might be possible in terms of the philosophy of Aristotle. For him, it is not the soul that thinks and wills but the person, the human being, who is a mind-body identity. To be a human being is to be capable of doing the things human rational animals by nature do. In other words, to be a person, to be human involves a certain mode of living, which is possible only for those with a human organism. A disembodied soul that thought and willed seems to be a contradiction in terms. Even could we envisage some sort of disembodied consciousness that contemplated God and hence had knowledge—perhaps even universal knowledge—it seems that we would be imagining, not that a person is contemplating, but that "contemplating is going on," or thought is going on.[96] Aquinas sometimes writes as though the soul causes a human being to be what he is, and his body to be a human body, just as heat causes water to boil. But more often he thinks that it is the cause of our being what we are, in the same way that it is the shape of the Great Pyramid that causes it to be a pyramid. It is in this sense that the soul is the form of the body—not something that (from the outside, as it were) affects the body.[97]

Aristotle, therefore, seems to make it impossible for a soul to survive without the body into a future life. Aquinas, compelled by faith to believe in a period between death and the general resurrection at the Last Day, tries to envisage souls that have something like a full human consciousness (unlike the *eidola* of Homer). His disciple, Dante, assuages his Aristotelian conscience by having souls long for reunion with their bodies, which will one day occur. But what neither Dante nor Aquinas can do is show that the being who experiences this longing is the same person who once composed a particular mind-body identity, whose memories are therefore those of the particular person who was once alive on the earth. Luckily, faith also compels Aquinas to believe in the resurrection of the body. So we might think that the gap that he has to bridge, in an un-Aristotelian way, between death and resurrection at the Last Day is a comparatively short one, even though it goes on getting longer as the millennia pass.

5

The Christian Beginnings

It is with Christianity that the doctrines of heaven and hell reach their full development. The Nicene Creed says that Jesus "propter nos homines et propter nostram salutem descendit de coelis . . . et crucifixus est sub Pontio Pilato . . ."—"for the sake of us men and for our salvation came down from heaven . . . and was crucified under Pontius Pilate." The earliest part of the message of Jesus is also the message of John the Baptist—"Repent ye, for the kingdom of heaven is at hand" (Matt. 3:2, 4:17; Mark 1:4, 15; Luke 3:3). Repentance is the first and urgent message. The time for repentance is short, because the last days, the judgment, the kingdom would come very soon—perhaps in Jesus's own generation or shortly thereafter. Whether the kingdom was to be the restoration of Israel in its power and its justification against its enemies; or that *plus* a Last Judgment in which all the nations of the earth should be held accountable for their actions, and especially for their oppression of Israel; or a judgment of all individual sinners—it was the nearness of this end that gave extreme urgency to the preaching of John the Baptist and formed the character of Jesus's own teaching. The apparent impracticability of many of his injunctions—to give up family and all possessions and follow him, to take no care of the morrow, for God will provide, to turn the other cheek, love your enemies and do good to them that hate you—has to be seen against his astonishingly heightened sense of the providence and fatherhood of God, and of the imminence of God's kingdom. The unworldliness, or otherworldliness of Jesus, his failure or refusal to legislate in the manner of Moses or Mohammed, or to include in his teaching a concern with politics or the welfare of the nation of Israel,[1] testify to his certainty that the present order of things is as nothing compared with what is to come at any moment, so that there is no need to "take thought" for one's raiment, or one's life for the morrow—"for the morrow shall take thought for the things of itself" (Matt. 6:25, 28, 34; "Sermon on the Mount").

Yet we could equally say that Jesus's certainty that the present order of things was soon to pass *derived from* his heightened sense of the spiritual. We should "seek first the kingdom of God, and his righteousness" as the one thing needful. For this singleness of purpose, Jesus uses the image of the eye: "The light of the body is the eye: if therefore thine eye be single [the Greek is *haplous*, which implies an opposition to what is double], thy whole body shall be full of light. But if thine eye be evil, thy whole body shall be full of darkness. If therefore the light that is in thee be darkness, how great is that darkness!" (Matt. 6:22, 23). If a man is not endued with the spirit of God, he is utterly cast out—as the body without proper transparency of the eye is in total darkness.[2] The Sermon on the Mount is full of the sense that an attachment to the things of this world—to spiritual pride, to money, even to the anxieties of living—is a very darkness compared with the light that is the realm of spirit. Jesus exalts the love of God over every other value with an astonishing absoluteness. This will go with the refusal of Jesus to be seen as the Jewish Messiah in at least one of the forms traditionally expected—earthly king.[3] He will not restore independence and greatness to Israel. Rather he will save the individual by getting each of us to repent and accept the fatherhood of God, for "My kingdom is not of this world" (John 18:36).

John the Baptist likens those who cut themselves off from the kingdom of God to useless trees that do not bring forth good fruit and that are hewn down and cast into the fire. Another image is of harvest and winnowing: "Whose fan is in his hand, and he will thoroughly purge his floor, and gather his wheat into the garner; but he will burn up the chaff with unquenchable fire" (Matt. 3:12).

There is an absolutism in all the teachings of Jesus. Either you have an absolute trust in God, or you have no faith in him at all; either you give up family and worldly goods to follow Jesus, or you fail entirely to follow him. Jesus is asked by a rich young man what he should do to have eternal life. Assured that the young man has all his life kept the commandments of religion, Jesus tells him: "If thou wilt be perfect, go and sell all thou hast, and give to the poor, and thou shalt have treasure in heaven: and come and follow me." But the young man goes away sorrowful "for he had great possessions" (Matt. 19:16–22; Mark 10:17–23; Luke 18:18–23). This scene is recorded in three gospels, and in each of them, immediately afterward, Jesus utters one of his most celebrated remarks of an absolutist character—that it is easier for a camel to pass through the eye of a needle than for a rich man to enter heaven (Matt. 19:24; Mark 10:25; Luke 18:25).

Matthew Arnold set "Hebraism" as a foil to "Hellenism." A little blandly, perhaps, he said that while the uppermost idea in Hellenism is "to see things as they really are," the guiding spirit in Hebraism is "the unequalled grandeur of earnestness and intensity" with which it enforces what Arnold called "strictness of conscience." Arnold goes on to sat that "the space which *sin* fills in Hebraism, as compared with Hellenism, is indeed prodigious."[4] Jesus enforces the need to live in obedience to and love of God, and the sense that failure to do so forfeits everything, with a power that is indeed prodigious. The conviction that sin is an absolute evil goes with a belief in eternal damnation for the unrepentant sinner.

It is in late Judaism, Christianity, and, later, Islam that future union with or eternal separation from God, salvation and damnation, came to occupy the central place in the religious imagination.[5] The drama of salvation is immeasurably heightened in Christianity with the doctrine of original sin—that all mankind shares in the guilt of the sin of Adam by which we are all cut off from God and destined to damnation, unless we can be saved through the sacrifice of Jesus Christ. To be saved rather than damned becomes the business of life. If one takes seriously the various Christian doctrines about predestination, then to discover whether one is saved or damned will be of the highest possible importance.

Yet from the beginning there have been tensions within Christianity about this central doctrine. There is a tension between Christ as Redeemer, and the Christ who will come at the end of time to judge the quick and the dead.[6] There is also an apparent tension between the teachings of St. Paul who may not have thought, and certainly did not clearly preach that the torments for those not saved will be eternal, and passages from the Synoptic Gospels, which represent Jesus as believing exactly that.[7]

Here are three crucial passages in which Jesus is represented as teaching an eternity of punishment for the wicked. The first is Mark, now generally regarded as the earliest gospel:

> And if thy hand offend thee, cut it off: it is better for thee to enter into life maimed, than having two hands to go into hell, into the fire that shall never be quenched:
>> Where their worm dieth not, and the fire is not quenched.
> And if thy foot offend thee, cut it off: it is better for thee to enter halt into life, than having two feet to be cast into hell, into the fire that never shall be quenched.
>> Where their worm dieth not, and the fire is not quenched.

And if thine eye offend thee, pluck it out: it is better for thee to enter into the kingdom of God with one eye, than having two eyes to be cast into hell fire.

Where their worm dieth not, and the fire is not quenched. (Mark 9:43–48)[8]

Hell and an eternal fire are plainly present in the Synoptic Gospels. Near the beginning of Matthew, John, baptizing in the wilderness, predicts someone mightier than he who will come after, who will baptize with fire "and gather his wheat into the garner; but he will burn up the chaff with unquenchable fire" (Matt. 3:12). Matthew also has Jesus speak of the servant who will be cast into outer darkness where there shall be "weeping and gnashing of teeth" (Matt. 25:30). And those who refused charity "shall go away into everlasting punishment: but the righteous into life eternal" (Matt. 25:46).

Luke has the story of Dives and Lazarus (Luke 16:19–31). In Matthew there is the description of the Son of man coming in his glory at the Last Judgment, separating the sheep from the goats—i.e., the saved from the damned. He will say to the sheep on his right hand: "Come ye blessed of my father, inherit the kingdom prepared for you from the foundation of the world: For I was an hungred, and ye gave me meat: I was thirsty, and ye gave me drink: I was stranger, and ye took me in: Naked and ye clothed me: I was sick and ye visited me: I was in prison, and ye came unto me" (Matt. 25:34–36).

The blessed then inquire when it was that they gave Jesus food and drink, clothed him and visited him; to which the reply is "Inasmuch as ye have done it unto one of the least of these my brethren, ye have done it unto me" (Matt. 25:40).

The wicked, accused of not having fed, clothed, or visited him, ask in their turn when it was that they neglected these offices of charity. The reply is: "Inasmuch as ye did it not unto one of the least of these, ye did it not unto me" (Matt. 25:45). He will say to the goats on his left hand: "Depart from me ye cursed, into everlasting fire, prepared for the devil and his angels." The conclusion is: "And these shall go away into everlasting punishment: but the righteous into life eternal" (Matt. 25:46).

That passage from Matthew—like Luke's story of Dives and Lazarus—is remarkable in that it shows the wicked sinning ignorantly. Alan Bernstein argues persuasively that Jesus identifies himself with those helpless and innocent ones who are treated by the powerful as of no account, who are neglected, despised, or corrupted by them.[9] Jesus says: "And whosoever shall offend one of these little ones that believe in me, it is better for him that a millstone were hanged about his neck, and he were cast into the sea" (Mark

9:42). Bernstein comments that the offense against the child, like the offense against any innocent believer, is thereby interpreted as an offense against Christ himself and his Father, for "Whosoever shall receive one of such children in my name, receiveth me: and whosoever shall receive me, receiveth not me, but him that sent me" (Mark 9:37). Jesus identifies himself with children in their innocence, and with the poor in their need, the helpless in their impotency.[10]

The refusal of charity proceeds from ignorance, but not from an ignorance that excuses. There is a terrible sternness in this. The rich, the powerful, the corrupt would no doubt not have refused charity had they realized that the one whom they were refusing was not a helpless child or beggar, but the Lord of the world—they would have been only too happy to oblige. But that is the point—the poor and helpless are beloved by the Lord just for their innocent helplessness, and so their appearance is a sort of trap into which the charitable would not fall. Or, you could say, not to be able to see Jesus in the poor, the innocent, the helpless is just what it is to fail in charity, to fail in any sense of solidarity—and that is why an offense against charity is such a great and fearful sin.

The "goats" did not, therefore, realize that their indifference to the poor and unfortunate would turn out to be indifference toward him who shall come to judge the quick and the dead. The rich man in the parable did not understand the nature of his indifference toward Lazarus until he found himself in hell and saw Lazarus in Abraham's bosom. The nature of Dives's uncharity is shown in his own urgent need for charity when their positions are reversed, when his need for a drop of water to moisten his tongue amid the flames of hell gives him an insight into Lazarus's need, when in life, for the crumbs that fell from his table. Jesus is preaching human solidarity—a solidarity that is now for ever impossible between Dives and Lazarus because, between the saved and the damned (as between the living and the dead), "there is a great gulf fixed." Perhaps only the dogs, in licking Lazarus's sores, represent a faint image of charity. Or perhaps his being surrounded by these (to the Jews) unclean creatures adds to the sense of his helplessness. In either case we see a radical failure of human solidarity that denies our human nature.[11]

The same is true of the passage from Matthew. Ignorance does not excuse, for the hardness of heart that goes with a failure to see the need of the hungry, the thirsty, strangers, naked, sick, and imprisoned is a failure to respond to and see others as persons like oneself. Likewise, one of the Jewish exhortations to charity toward strangers involved recalling that the Jews were once themselves bondsmen in the land of Egypt (Deut. 15.15). For Jesus, in effect, such failures amount to a denial of one's own humanity.

In the Gospels, it is those who fail in charity who are most in danger of damnation. To tarnish the innocence of children (which may mean to undermine their childlike faith in Jesus), to be hard of heart toward the poor in their need, the helpless in their impotency is to sin against charity and thereby to incur divine wrath. Bernstein argues that the punishment that these sins against charity bring down is "reflexive." It is more than retribution. The sinner refuses to help someone in need. Christ, who will one day be the sinner's judge, identifies himself with the needy. Therefore harming one of the needy offends the one who will judge the offender. Thus in harming another, one harms oneself.[12] Hence the Christian law of charity does not simply appeal to the sense of human solidarity—it also involves the idea that human solidarity is demanded by our relationship to the Creator of all men. To refuse to see that is to deny humanity in oneself as well as in others.

This helps explain why sins against charity are to be punished by hellfire—something that would be strange if charity were simply a human virtue, such as Hume's virtue of benevolence.[13] To refuse charity is to deny the image of God in all human beings, which comes close to blasphemy. (It has always been a catholic orthodoxy that in loving one's neighbor, one is loving Christ in that neighbor. This is the basis of Flaubert's story about St. Julian the Hospitaller, about a knight who gives shelter to a beggar freezing to death, and warms him with his own body, only to discover that the beggar is Christ himself.)

This is taken further with the famous extension by Jesus of the idea of obeying the Law to a person's inner state. Intention becomes all. Adultery is forbidden, but Jesus goes further—"whosoever looketh on a woman to lust after her hath committed adultery with her already in his heart" (Matt. 5:27–28). And the prohibition of murder becomes a prohibition even against anger. Hence not only "whosoever shall kill shall be in danger of the judgment" but "whosoever is angry with his brother without a cause shall be in danger of the judgment ... whosoever shall say, Thou fool, shall be in danger of hell fire" (Matt. 5:21–22). Those who obey the imperative of charity will be those who reject pride and love of the world. They are, precisely, those singled out by Jesus in the Beatitudes: "Blessed are the poor in spirit: for theirs is the kingdom of heaven ... Blessed are the meek, for they shall inherit the earth. ... Blessed are the pure in heart, for they shall see God" (Matt. 5:3, 5, 8).

One day, in the Temple, Jesus watches as many people cast money into the treasury, and many that were rich cast in much: "And there came a certain poor widow, and she threw in two mites, which make a farthing." Jesus tells his disciples that this poor widow has cast in more than the rich had done: "For they did cast in of their abundance; but she of her want did cast in all that she had even all her living" (Mark 12:42–44).

Paul: Is There Eternal Punishment?

The Epistles of St. Paul are now generally regarded as the earliest of all Christian texts, probably antedating even the Gospel of Mark. If so, it is very possible that the first Christian texts did not contain a threat of eternal punishment for the wicked.[14] At any rate, St. Paul neither preached eternal damnation, nor had any clear notion of hell.[15] You could even call Paul's expectations of human destiny optimistic, for he seems torn between envisaging salvation, in the end, for all, and an eternal reward for the just, where the wicked will simply cease to exist. This seems on the face of it at variance with later Christian teaching and with several sayings of Jesus in the Synoptic Gospels.

Famously Paul talks of death as being swallowed up in victory: "O death, where is thy sting? O grave, where is thy victory?" (1 Cor. 15:55).[16] The impression Paul overwhelmingly gives is of a hope and confidence that when the kingdom of God is finally and fully established through Christ, both death and hell will fade away. At times Paul seems to hope that even the wicked will eventually be absorbed within Christ's kingdom, when God will be the sole reality—will be "all in all": "For he must reign til he hath put all enemies under his feet. The last enemy that shall be destroyed is death . . . And when all things shall be subdued unto him, then shall the Son also himself be subject unto him that put all things under him, that God may be all in all" (1 Cor. 15:25, 26, 28).

Slightly earlier, Paul seems to suggest that Christ's redeeming power is such that no one will fail to be saved: "For as in Adam *all* die, even in Christ shall *all* be made alive" (1 Co. 15: 22 [my italics]). He also writes of those who lack faith that God would indeed have mercy upon all.[17] This idea that human failure or sin is the occasion of divine mercy appears elsewhere in Paul, in relation to Jews and Gentiles. He explains that the failure of the Jews to accept Jesus Christ—what he calls their "disobedience"—was a cause of divine grace to the Gentiles, because they can learn from that failure not to be unreceptive themselves. So the Gentiles, having previously been disobedient, are saved through the current disobedience of the Jews and hence have "received mercy." In this way, the disobedience of the Jews gives God the opportunity to display his mercy to the Gentiles. But Paul at the same time hopes that the current disobedience of the Jews will, analogously, give God the opportunity to show his mercy to the Jews as well! "For as ye in times past have not believed God, yet have now obtained mercy through their [i.e., the Jews'] unbelief: Even so have these also now not believed, that through your mercy they also may obtain mercy. For God hath concluded them all in unbelief, that he might have mercy upon all" (Rom. 11:30–32). Paul's thought and expression are convoluted, but he seems to mean that the Jews, having seen God do the unthinkable and make the Gentiles into a new chosen group, will realize that God's merciful goodness is so overwhelming that they, too, want to share in it after all.

So there is a strong impulse in Paul to hope for universal salvation—a hope that finds very little echo in later Christian tradition, at least until modern times.[18] As we shall see, the Christian thinker who tries to turn such a hope into doctrine—Origen—comes to be condemned as a heretic. Yet at the same time—contradictorily—when Paul is concentrating upon human sinfulness, his thoughts are much sterner. The hope that God might be "all in all" hardly covers the fate of those destined, either through their wicked lives or their lack of faith, not to enter the kingdom: "Know ye not that the unrighteous shall not inherit the kingdom of God? Be not deceived: neither fornicators, nor idolaters, nor adulterers, nor effeminate, nor abusers of themselves with mankind, Nor thieves, nor covetous, nor revilers, nor extortioners, shall inherit the kingdom of God" (1 Cor. 6:9–10).

Those who are to be saved are they who manifest the fruits of the spirit as against the fruits of the flesh. The fruits of the flesh include "hatred, variance, emulations, wrath, strife . . . envyings, murders . . ." The fruits of the spirit include "love, joy, peace, longsuffering, gentleness, goodness, faith, meekness, temperance . . ." (Gal. 5:20–23).

Those who manifest the fruits of the spirit belong to Christ and have crucified their own fleshly desires; they and they alone shall inherit the kingdom of God. Paul shows little interest in the ultimate fate of those who shall not inherit the kingdom. The predominant suggestion is that they will simply cease to exist; or perhaps that they will suffer tribulations when judgment comes "like a thief in the night" (1 Thess. 5:2) and then be annihilated—as the enemies of Christ will be annihilated. So God will truly and literally be all in all because those who through their wicked lives cannot belong to him will have ceased to exist.

It is clear that Paul both sees man's destiny as decided by his own sinful or godly will, yet also suggests that salvation is a sort of natural force, a necessity. The two ideas seem contradictory. The redemption of man from Adam's fall by Christ is a kind of natural process—as described in the famous image of sowing:

> So also is the resurrection of the dead. It is sown in corruption; it is raised in incorruption; It is sown in dishonour; it is raised in glory; it is sown in weakness; it is raised in power;

It is sown a natural body; it is raised a spiritual body. There is a natural body, and there is a spiritual body. And so it is written, The first man Adam was made a living soul; the last Adam was made a quickening spirit.

Howbeit that was not first which is spiritual, but that which is natural; and afterward that which is spiritual. (1 Cor. 15:42–44)

Bernstein comments on how complex an analogy Paul is developing: "The spiritual body will succeed the physical one just as the plant succeeds the seed, just as Christ succeeded Adam, as power succeeds weakness, and the imperishable the perishable."[19] But it is hard to see how this fits with Paul's insistence that we become worthy of immortality because we have put off the old Adam, died, and been reborn only through the sufferings of Christ and through faith. These seem to be supernatural, not natural, processes.

The passage continues with a contrast between the man who will return to the dust from which he was created and the man of heaven:

The first man is of the earth, earthy: the second man is the Lord from heaven. As is the earthy, such are they also that are earthy: and as is the heavenly, such are they also that are heavenly. And as we have borne the image of the earthy, we shall also bear the image of the heavenly.

Now this I say, brethren, that flesh and blood cannot inherit the kingdom of God; neither doth corruption inherit incorruption.

Behold I shew you a mystery; We shall not all sleep, but we shall all be changed, In a moment, in the twinkling of an eye, at the last trump: for the trumpet shall sound, and the dead shall be raised incorruptible, and we shall be changed.

For this corruptible must put on incorruption, and this mortal must put on immortality. (1 Cor. 15:47–53)

So there is a duality running through Paul's thought about salvation. On the one hand, Christ's reversal of the consequences of the sin of Adam is seen as a natural fulfillment, even a necessity. On the other, there is the sharpest possible distinction between sinners and saved, the works of the flesh and the works of the spirit. The righteous will receive "glory and honour and immortality, eternal life" while the children of perdition will receive "indignation and wrath, tribulation and anguish" (Rom. 2:7–9). But Paul, although he promises an eternity of rewards to the good, never threatens the wicked with an eternity of punishment. His thought about the fate of the reprobate hovers between a hope that even they will somehow eventually be reconciled with God, and the sterner expectation of their ceasing to exist.

There is one other criterion that Paul cites for deciding who shall and who shall not be saved, and it is not to do with moral character and actions: faith. Only those with faith will accept the message of Christ and hence be suitable for salvation—those enveloped in "the righteousness of God which is by faith of Jesus Christ unto all and upon all them that believe" (Rom. 3:22). Faith in Christ cancels out the punishment due to the sin of Adam:

> For if by one man's offence death reigned by one; much more they which receive abundance of grace and of the gift of righteousness shall reign in life by one, Jesus Christ.
>
> Therefore as by the offence of one judgment came upon all men to condemnation; even so by the righteousness of one the free gift came upon all men unto justification of life. For as by one man's disobedience many were made sinners, so by the obedience of one shall many be made righteous. (Rom. 5:17–19)

But who are those who will receive the free gift of grace? It is clear that Paul thinks these are only those whom God has chosen. Here the distinction between the saved and the reprobate derives not from how we lead our lives, but from God's election from all eternity of those whom we wishes to save and those from whom he withholds his grace. His granting and withholding of mercy is entirely a matter of God's will—he even seems to have created certain people in order to display his mercy, and others in order to show his wrath:

> For he saith unto Moses, I will have mercy on whom I will have mercy, and I will have compassion on whom I will have compassion. So then it is not of him that willeth, nor of him that runneth, but of God that sheweth mercy.
>
> For the scripture saith unto Pharaoh, even for this same purpose have I raised thee up, that I might show my power in thee, and that my name might be declared throughout all the earth. Therefore hath he mercy on whom he will have mercy, and whom he will he hardeneth. (Rom. 9:15–18)

This passage in Paul's letter to the Romans provides a basis for the doctrine of predestination that will loom so large in Christian history and become one of the precipitating causes of the Protestant Reformation. In those words Paul first formulates the idea that human beings cannot be saved by their own efforts, but only through the arbitrary "election" (i.e., choice) of God, an election made from all eternity in the unsearchable counsel of his own will. Paul is clearly aware of the difficulties—indeed, the crisis of faith and ethics— to which this doctrine can give rise, for he himself seeks to answer the obvious objection that such an arbitrary decision by God cannot be just. Paul's words seem drawn from those of God in the book of Job, when he answers Job "out of the whirlwind," and asserts his own transcendent power: "Where wast thou when I laid the foundations of the earth? Declare, if thou hast understanding . . . When the morning stars sang together, and all the sons of God shouted for joy . . . When I made the cloud the garment thereof, and thick darkness a swaddlingband for it . . . Canst thou bind the sweet influences of Pleiades, or loose the bands of Orion? . . . Canst thou draw out leviathan with an hook?" (Job 38:4, 7, 9, 31; 41:1).

Paul answers the objections to predestination with an identical assertion of sheer power on the part of God—if in language less sublime than that of Job:

Nay but, O man, who art thou that repliest against God? Shall the
thing formed say to him that formed it, Why hast thou made me thus?
    Hath not the potter power over the clay, of the same lump to make
one vessel unto honour, and another unto dishonour?
    What if God, willing to shew his wrath, and to make his power
known, endured with much long-suffering the vessels of wrath fitted
to destruction: And that he might make known the riches of his glory
on the vessels of mercy, which he had afore prepared unto glory."
(Rom. 9:20–23)

This is, in its own terms, unanswerable. But we might think that its terms are objectionable—for a man is not like a lump of clay but a sentient and moral being. It also takes away any reason for love or even piety toward God. For if the only thing we can say of God's actions is that he does them and that his power cannot be called to account—that if he hardens pharaoh's heart in order to "shew his wrath" then that is his business and not ours (all we can do is be impressed)—then there is no reason for calling God just or good. But if terms such as "just" and "good" do not apply to God's acts nor to his nature, then there is no difference between a powerful God who condemns men to perdition to "shew his wrath" and a powerful devil who might do the same. (The same applies to God's answer to Job.) It is difficult indeed to reconcile such a God with the Christian deity who "so loved the world that he sent his only begotten Son." This will be a perennial stumbling block to what develops as the orthodox Christian teaching about predestination. It is true that Paul, unlike Augustine and Calvin, does not have God condemn men from all eternity to eternal punishment, since as we have seen he does not envisage an everlasting hell, nor indeed any sort of hell. But it makes no logical nor moral difference whether people will cease to exist purely through a decision of God and regardless of their own merits, or whether they will burn in hell for all eternity.

There are some words of Jesus that seem to make the terrible prospect of eternal damnation a matter not of our own willed actions but of some destiny: "For many are called, but few are chosen" (Matt. 22:14). There is also the parable about the man who has sown weeds in another man's wheatfield. (For Jesus, the Galilean countryman, to sow weeds in the midst of another's crop is one of the most malicious of sins.) It seems that human individuals are from birth either good seeds or bad seeds. Jesus explains the parable in these words:

> He that soweth the good seed is the Son of man; The field is the world; the good seed are the children of the kingdom; but the tares [i.e., weeds] are the children of the wicked one; The enemy that sowed them is the devil; the harvest is the end of the world; and the reapers are the angels. As therefore the tares are gathered and burned in the fire; so shall it be in the end of this world.
>
> The Son of man shall send forth his angels, and they shall gather out of his kingdom all things that offend, and them which do iniquity; And shall cast them into a furnace of fire: there shall be wailing and gnashing of teeth.
>
> Then shall the righteous shine forth as the sun in the kingdom of their Father. (Matt. 13:37–43)

But this is not exact language. The "children of the wicked one" may simply be a way of referring to people sunk in vicious ways, unwilling to hear the Good News. A doctrine about human beings predestined to hellfire is not to be based on such fluid and poetic language. And most of Christ's sayings in the Synoptic Gospels that envisage eternal damnation plainly make it the outcome of the voluntary actions and character of individuals. That is clearly implied in the injunction "If thy right eye offend thee, pluck it out and cast it from thee: for it is profitable for thee that one of thy members should perish, and not that thy whole body should be cast into hell" (Matt. 5:29). The damnation of Dives because of his lack of charity (unless it be simply because of his wealth—which is quite possible) also points to an individual's sin. The suggestion there is of a salvation that flows from good actions and not only from the faith given by the grace of God.

Paul's Transformation of the Message

The original message of Jesus—as we find it in the Gospels of Mark and Matthew—mixes a call for repentance with the belief that Jesus is the prophesied Jewish Messiah: "Jesus came into Galilee, preaching the gospel of the kingdom of God, And saying, The time is fulfilled, and the kingdom of God is at hand" (Mark 1:14–15).

For Jews, the imminent end of the present world order will usher in the reign of the Messiah—and his essential role will be to "restore the kingdom" to Israel.[20] Christians envisage a Last Judgment—the judgment when Christ will accuse those who lacked charity. In Judaism this Last Judgment is an occasion on which God will judge not individuals, but the nations. He will vindicate Israel against its enemies, and will cast down those nations that have persecuted Israel. The saved will be those Jews who kept the Covenant, obeyed the Law—and are thereby part of God's people. The Last Judgment is the occasion on which the Gentile nations will be forced to see how they have mistreated the people of God.

The Christian vision of the *parousia*—Christ's Second Coming, when he will judge the living and the dead—obviously draws on this Jewish idea, but introduces a crucial difference. Instead of nations, it is individuals who will be judged: "When the Son of man shall come in his glory, and all the holy angels with him, then shall he sit upon the throne of his glory: And before him shall be gathered all nations: and he shall separate them one from another, as a shepherd divideth his sheep from his goats: And he shall set the sheep on his right hand, but the goats on the left" (Matt. 25:31–33).

But whereas the Jewish idea is that this scene of judgment will be the occasion when the nation of Israel is justified against her enemies and persecutors, here Christ's words will be addressed to individuals. The sheep are those who clothed the naked, the goats those who refused these acts of charity. The former will be received into the kingdom prepared for them from the foundation of the world; the latter will be cast into everlasting fire.

This already represents a new vision of the Messiah. He will not be the national hero who will restore the kingdom, but the judge of individual sinners. So although the imagery of the Jewish Messiah is used to depict a Last Judgment, there is no necessary relation to the Jewish nation at all. (As we shall see, Christian apologists sometimes see the Last Judgment as the occasion on which Christ will vindicate his followers against those who persecute them, and against those who did not believe in him, both Jews and Gentiles.[21] In this way they develop a Christian application for the idea of a Last Judgment.)

But do the Gospels contain the doctrine that the death of Jesus was necessary to the salvation of men? That they do is at the centre of Christian orthodoxy. That they do not is the contention of some biblical critics.[22] These latter argue that the overwhelming impression is of a Jesus who confidently looks to the imminent coming of God's kingdom, as do his followers. So when the tragedy happens of the arrest, trial, and execution of Jesus, the disciples are astounded and terrified. This is simply a catastrophe, the destruction of their hopes, the end of the dream. Jesus never doubted that he was chosen by God to lead Israel into God's kingdom, and they looked forward to participating in its inauguration. Therefore his anguished cry, *"Eloi, Eloi, lama sabachthani"* ("My God, my God, why hast thou forsaken me?" Mark 15:34]) is not, as Christian commentators have always argued, a deliberate reference to a prophetic Psalm 22 ("For dogs have compassed me: the assembly of the wicked have inclosed me: they pierced my hands and my feet.... They part my garments among them, and cast lots upon my vesture" [Ps. 22:16–18]) but a true cry of amazement and desolation.[23]

The resurrection turns catastrophe into triumph. Paul's decisive contribution to Christian thought is to show how this triumph was inevitable, and to explain its meaning. He turns history into myth, in the sense that he finds an explanation of the life of Jesus and its tragic end that goes back to the beginning of time, even before human history begins, and that will find its final consummation at the end of time. Paul sees his mission as being to convert the Gentiles. Since Judaism is about the Jews as the chosen people of God, and about the Messiah as the savior and restorer of the Jewish nation, there would not seem to be much that could attract the Gentiles. So, instead of presenting Jesus to the Gentiles essentially as the Jewish Messiah (an idea which would have meant nothing to them, and would, indeed, seem to exclude them) Paul develops a quite different theory about Jesus: the savior-god.[24] This does not mean that there is anything insincere or ad hoc about Paul's teaching. It is very believable that it is the outcome of his own struggle to decipher the significance of the extraordinary life and tragic death of Jesus of Nazareth.

Paul does believe that Christ as Messiah will come again to establish his kingdom—even within the lifetime of some of those then alive. But he does not see the story of Jesus as simply the tragic narrative of one who "came unto his own, and his own received him not" (John 1:11)—the Jewish Messiah rejected by his own nation. Nor is it simply the story of this tragic rejection of Christ overcome by his resurrection and forthcoming return. Rather, Paul wants to see the life of Jesus as an image of salvation planned from all eternity. That is why he evolves the idea of the savior god.

The world before the coming of Christ had labored under the rule of evil powers, perhaps because of some original sin, some aboriginal calamity. Indeed, demonic powers ruled the world in the form, as later Christian writers would say, of the pagan gods. God sent the savior—himself a divine being who had existed from all eternity—in the unexpected form of Jesus, so deceiving the powers of darkness: "Which none of the princes of this world [i.e., infernal powers] knew: for had they known it, they would not have crucified the Lord of glory" (1 Cor. 2:8). They "not recognizing the true nature of their victim . . . crucified him, and thereby forfeited their control over men."[25] So Paul concentrates not on the details of the teaching of Jesus, but on his death and resurrection, things intended by God from all eternity.[26]

In spirit, this is entirely out of keeping with Jewish tradition. It is much closer to pagan ideas of the death and resurrection of a savior god—for instance, Osiris. Whereas Jewish history in the Hebrew Bible is a depiction of events, governed by divine providence to be sure and full of miraculous elements, but nevertheless sequential history, the story of Jesus that Paul evolves has the timelessness of myth. The Jewish Messiah might have rescued the Jews from Babylon[27] or driven the Romans out of Palestine. Or he might have come—as the Gospels suggest—in the entirely unexpected form of a humble man calling to repentance and preaching that the kingdom is within us. What he would not have been was a divine being who would overcome an ancient curse by suffering death. Paul preached that. He also preached that salvation would come through something more complicated and esoteric than men listening to the message of Jesus and repenting. Rather, they would identify themselves with his suffering, death, and resurrection, and by that means participate in his kingdom and glory. They would crucify their old selves, and be born again as new people without sin:

> Know ye not, that so many of us as were baptized into Jesus Christ were baptized into his death?
>
> Therefore we are buried with him by baptism into death: that like as Christ was raised up from the dead by the glory of the Father, even so we also should walk in newness of life. . . .
>
> Knowing this, that our old man is crucified with him, that the body of sin might be destroyed, that henceforth we might not serve sin. (Rom. 6:3–4, 6)

The influence of Paul's vision on what became Christian orthodoxy cannot be exaggerated. (Indeed, some have argued that Paul was the true creator of Christianity, the religion that claimed to have superseded Judaism and abrogated the Law of Moses, the religion that turned Jesus the Jew into Jesus the Christian.) The world is under the sway of evil powers and some sort of original sin. Only Christ's sacrificial death can save us. So Paul evolves those ideas that became central to Christian orthodoxy—that through the saving merits of Christ, his followers are new beings, saved from the original sin, destined to eternal glory. The essentially new idea is that of atonement. It is what Christ did that saves us if we have faith in him—not our own good deeds. For Paul it is the atonement of the son of God that justifies us, rather than our repentance. Paul's welding of the savior-god on to the ancient idea of the Messiah is what makes Christianity so radically different in spirit from Judaism—and, for that matter, Islam.

What relation do Paul's ideas have to the Gospels and Christ's actual sayings? His doctrine of the atonement seems starkly at odds with those many sayings of Jesus that plainly suggest that our own repentance, acceptance of the word of God, trust in God, and charity toward our neighbors are what save us from eternal damnation. They do, however, fit squarely many other texts: predictions attributed to Jesus that the Son of man will have to be betrayed, insulted, and suffer death, and then be raised from the dead (Mark 8:31; Matt. 16:21; Luke 9:22); his assertion that all this was prophesied in the Law of Moses, which had to be fulfilled in him (Luke 24:26–27); and his saying to the apostles that his blood is shed for the remission of sin (Matt. 26:27–28; Mark 14:24; Luke 22:20). But here the great argument is about whether these sayings are part of the original or authentic Gospel of Jesus, or whether they were developed post hoc by Paul and the church as a means of explaining his life and mission as part of a cosmic drama of the fall and salvation of man. The ancient traditions of Christian orthodoxy maintained that there is no difference between the Christ of the church and the Jesus of the Gospels, no differing strands of the Gospels, which could allow one to separate the lowly Galilean preacher and healer from he who would return in his *parousia* in great power and majesty, surrounded with his angels to judge the quick and the dead. If these ancient traditions, rather than the conclusions suggested by much modern biblical scholarship[28] are true, then it would be false to say that Paul is indeed the true inventor of Christianity. It is, of course, possible that Paul's influence is there from the beginning, influencing the very formation of scripture in the early church.

Early Visions of Hell

Christian accounts of the torments of hell and the joys of heaven, starting from the extremely brief hints to be found in the Gospels, were not long in coming. Two of the earliest and most influential are *The Apocalypse of Peter* and *The Apocalypse of Paul*. In them we see the beginnings of a mapping of the afterlife that will reach its summation in Dante. These two apocalypses form part of the apocryphal New Testament—those accounts of Jesus and certain of the apostles that were not received by the church into the scriptural canon.

The newcomer to the mass of apocryphal writing is liable to be startled at the extreme crudity and silliness of much of it by comparison with the canonical scriptures. There is, for instance the Gospel of Nicodemus, once famous and influential. This gospel is an anti-Judaic, pro–Pontius Pilate tract written with the obvious intention of ingratiating the Christians with the Romans. Then there is the "Infancy" Gospel of Thomas, which depicts the infant Jesus as a little monster with magic powers, who causes another child who had brushed against his shoulder to drop down dead. When the afflicted parents of the dead child complain to Joseph, the irritated Jesus causes them to be struck blind. The apocryphal scriptures, where they do not replicate the writings in the canon, make up a farrago of absurdity. But *The Apocalypse of Peter* and the *Apocalypse of Paul* contain nothing so outlandish, are not full of absurd miracles, and are in spirit orthodox.

The Apocalypse of Peter is the earliest extant Christian document that describes heaven and hell.[29] It may date from the first half of the second century AD, in which case it was written not long after the Gospel of John.[30] The *Apocalypse of Peter* takes its starting point from a scene in Matthew's Gospel (which follows an equivalent one in Mark), where Christ, sitting upon the Mount of Olives, is asked by his disciples what will be the signs of the Second Coming and the end of the world. Jesus replies by predicting wars and rumors of wars, the rising of nation against nation, and the abomination of desolation—"Then let them which be in Judaea flee into the mountains. . . . pray that your flight be not in the winter, neither on the sabbath day: For then shall be great tribulation, such as was not since the beginning of the world" (Matt. 24:16, 20–21; Mark 13:14, 18).

In the *Apocalypse of Peter*, Christ, in response to the questions of his disciples, of whom Peter is the spokesman, opens the palm of his hand, and in it the disciples see hell and its torments and, much more briefly, the state of the blessed in heaven. In hell the sufferings of the damned usually reflect the nature of their sins—as they will do, with incomparably more subtlety and imagination in Dante's *Inferno*. Near the beginning, there is a vision of the Last Day, which obviously draws on the words of Jesus ("let them that be in Judaea flee to the mountains") but here is exaggerated so that it becomes more like a game of Changing Places: "As soon as the whole creation dissolves, the men who are in the east shall flee to the west, and those who are in the west to the east, and those who are in the south shall flee to the north, and those who are in the north to the south."[31] The unrighteous are shown plunged into a fire, there to be punished everlastingly.

Then comes a vision of specific sins and their punishments:

> And I saw another place, very squalid; and it was a place of
> punishment, and those who were punished and the angels that
> punished them had dark raiment in accordance with the air of the
> place. And some were hanging by their tongues; and these were the
> ones who blasphemed the way of righteousness, and under them was
> laid fire flaming and tormenting them.... And again behold two
> women: they hang them up by their neck and by their hair; they shall
> cast them into the pit. These are those who plaited their hair, not to
> make themselves beautiful but to turn them to fornication, that they
> might ensnare the souls of men to perdition. And the men who were
> joined with them in the defilement of adultery were hung by their
> loins, and had their faces hidden in the [boiling] mire and said, "We
> did not believe we would come to this place."[32]

The sinners are being punished in that part by which they offended. The
women suffer through that by which they set out sexually to attract their
paramours, and the adulterous men suffer through their loins. (The fact that
the heads of the men are hidden in the boiling mire suggests reason overcome
by passion.) Elsewhere, blasphemers suffer in the tongue that uttered the
blasphemy; idolaters suffer in the fire with which (perhaps) they burnt their
offerings to the false gods.[33] We find murderers in a gorge that is full of
noxious, creeping things, venomous beasts that torment them without rest—
"and their worms shall be as many in number as a dark cloud."[34] This
symbolizes their own beastly character as murderers—just as does the
Roman punishment for parricides, who (as Joyce's Father Arnall recalls)
were put into a sack along with a cock, a snake, and a monkey, and tossed
into the Tiber. Meanwhile, the souls of their victims "stood and looked upon
the torment ... and said, "O god, righteous is your judgment." (This anticipates
the opinion of Thomas Aquinas and other theologians that the blessed in
heaven shall look upon and rejoice in the sufferings of the damned in hell.[35])

Adulterous women are confined within a pit "very great and deep" into
which flows "all manner of torment, foulness and excrement."[36] Men and
women who trusted to riches are shown clothed in filthy rags. Usurers (in a
passage reminiscent of the Hell cantos of Ezra Pound)[37] stand up to their knees
"in a great lake full of foul puss and blood and boiling mire." Although *Peter* does
not say so explicitly, this suggests that part of the punishment for both usurers
and adulterers will be a horrible stench. Stench is as old an image of hell-
punishments as is flame. *The Acts of Thomas* mentions sinners in hell cast into
"a very dark cavern, exhaling a very bad stench."[38] The image is a long-lasting

one; Father Arnall also mentions how the burning of the bodies which are never consumed "fills all hell with an intolerable stench."[39]

One of the more powerful passages depicts murdered and aborted infants, who stand opposite their guilty parents in "a place of delight" and cry to God: "These are those who . . . delivered us to death: they have cursed the angel that formed us and begrudged us the light which you have given to all creatures." The milk of their mothers, who should have nursed them, flowing from their breasts, congeals, and noxious creatures come out of it to devour their flesh. From the eyes of the murdered children "went forth rays of fire, and smote the women in the eyes; and these were those who conceived out of wedlock and caused abortion."[40]

Children who refused to obey their parents and did not honor their neighbors are afflicted with flesh-devouring birds. (This symbolizes the perversity of such disobedience—giving and receiving the breast is an image of love: birds gnawing at flesh are an alien intrusion. This becomes a rich image in later iconography: Christ is the pelican who wounds his own flesh to feed his young with his blood. Shakespeare's Lear talks of his own "pelican daughters."[41]) Disobedient servants gnaw their tongues for ever.

The apocalypse concludes with a brief vision of the state of the blessed, including Moses, Elijah, Abraham, Isaac, and Jacob. The manifestation of Moses and Elijah obviously recalls the transfiguration of Christ when "his face did shine as the sun" (Matt. 17:2–3), his garments became white as snow, and the two patriarchs were seen conversing with him. *Peter* has "And behold there were two men there, and we could not look upon their faces, for a light came from them, shining more than the sun, and their raiment also was shining."[42] Elijah has the color of "flower of roses" and the hair of both patriarchs is like "the rainbow in the water."

Finally, "Peter" is vouchsafed a vision of "a very great region outside this world, exceedingly bright with light, and the air of that place illuminated with the rays of the sun, and the earth itself flowering with blossoms that do not fade, and full of spices and plants, fair-flowering and incorruptible, and bearing blessed fruit." A delicious odor wafts from that region. Angels "ran about" there, and all the inhabitants "praised the Lord God, rejoicing in the place."

What is perhaps most interesting about this vision is not the infernal punishments—which are improved on in precision, vivacity, and horror in the later church—but the reaction to these torments of both the disciples of Christ and of Christ himself: "We beheld how the sinners wept in great affliction and sorrow, until all who saw it with their eyes wept, whether righteous or angels, and he himself also."[43] Again, "Peter" (quoting Christ on the betrayal by Judas [Matt. 26:24][44]) says to Christ of the sinners that "it were better for them that they had not been created,"[45] for which he is rebuked by Christ: "You resist God. You would not have more compassion than he for his image: for he has created them and brought them forth out of not-being." The catalogue of sins and their punishments is meant to show that God, in punishing these sinners, however hideously, is just.

From the earliest times, then, in Christian depictions of hell, we find the human temptation to weep for the damned that regularly shows itself in Dante, in tension with the need to acknowledge the justice of God. This temptation of compassion rises, for a moment, to an imaginative height in the later *Apocalypse of Paul*.

In the Epistle to the Corinthians, Paul, apparently speaking of himself, describes a man who was "caught up into paradise, and heard unspeakable words which it is not lawful for a man to utter" (2 Cor. 12:1–4). The *Apocalypse of Paul* takes this hint as the starting point for its description of "Paul's" vision of heaven and hell. This became the best known and most widely translated Christian text describing the afterlife before Dante.[46] This apocalypse is more sophisticated and more dramatic than the earlier one of "Peter." It includes such startling images as angels (taking the souls of the damned) "without mercy, having no pity, whose countenance was full of madness, and their teeth sticking out beyond their mouth; their eyes shone like the morning star of the east, and from the hairs of their head or from their mouth sparks of fire went out."[47]

The scenes in *Paul* have individually a dramatic quality that has sometimes been compared with Dante—although they never come up to Dante's level of intensity or reality. Early in the vision the soul of an impious man is seen going out of his body, just at the moment he is saying "I know nothing else in this world, but eating and drinking and enjoying what is in the world; for who is there that has descended into hell, and, ascending, has declared to us that there is judgment there?"[48]

It is, of course, Jesus who has done exactly that. As soon as this man's soul departs the world, he changes his tune: "It were better for me if I had not been born." He is led both by his own guardian angel and evil angels toward heaven and the judgment that awaits him there at the throne of God, as voices from above are heard saying: "Present that wretched soul to God, so that it may know that it is God whom it despised" [i.e., in the person of Christ who "descended into hell"]. Its own angel, and the divine spirit that dwelt within the soul both urge that it should be expelled from the sight of God because "the stink of it crosses to us angels." God decrees that the soul be "handed over to the angel Tartaruchus" [i.e., the angel of the Tartareous pit].[49]

This straightforward example of obvious sin and its immediate punishment is succeeded by something slightly more subtle. Another soul is brought before God, and pleads for mercy. God rebukes it by pointing out that it never showed mercy in life, and adjures it to confess its sins. The soul replies "Lord, I did not sin." God summons the soul's guardian angel who produces a document containing a record of all the sins of this soul from its tenth year of age. The angel, aware, it would seem, of God's compassion, suggests that only the sins from its fifteenth year ought to be relayed. God answers: "By myself I swear, and by my holy angels, and by my virtue, that if it had repented five years before it died, on account of a conversion one year old, oblivion would now be thrown over all the evils which it sinned before, and it would have indulgence and remission of sins; now indeed it shall perish."[50]

We then learn how bad its sins were, for its victims appear and compel the soul to confess: "Lord, it is not a full year since I slew this one and poured his blood upon the ground, and with another I committed fornication; not only this, but I also greatly harmed her in taking away her goods." Tartarus and everlasting punishments follow.

After an interlude during which we enter through the gates of paradise, where we meet the Old Testament "scribe of righteousness," Enoch, whose countenance shines as the sun, and view the Acherousian lake with waters white as milk, and four rivers of honey, milk, wine, and oil,[51] we are shown a fuller vision of hell. We see men and women up to the knees, the navel, the lips, their hair in "a river boiling with fire." These souls turn out to be "they who were neither hot nor cold, because they were found neither in the number of the just nor in the number of the godless." These people sometimes prayed—and sometimes fornicated.[52] Those immersed in the fire only up to their knees were accustomed to go out of church and "occupy themselves in idle disputes." Those up to their navel took the body and blood of Christ in Holy Communion, but went on to fornicate, not ceasing in their sins until they died. Those up to their lips in the fire are slanderers, while those immersed to their eyebrows are "those who nod to each other and plot spite against their neighbor."[53]

The punishments enact the nature of the sins, as they do in Dante, but in a fairly obvious way. Those who took the body of Christ did not receive him so as to eschew the lusts of their lower natures. Slander is a misuse of speech—a slanderer is the opposite of the prophet on whose tongue a coal of fire is placed—and so their lips are burned for ever.[54] The burning of the eyebrows of those who gossip spitefully together is a symbolically obvious punishment.

Those who were "neither hot nor cold"—the lukewarm—correspond to those souls whom Dante places in the vestibule of hell.[55] The allusion is to the words of St. John about the church of Laodicea: "I know thy works, that thou are neither hot nor cold: I would that thou wert cold or hot. So then because thou art lukewarm, and neither cold nor hot, I will spue thee out of my mouth."[56]

These passages in *Paul* try to make the punishments fit the sins of the damned, and do so with some success. But here where we can make a direct comparison, we see how much more suggestive and dramatic Dante's treatment will be. In Dante these "lukewarm" have never really lived—because they never attached themselves to life through a true allegiance—and so they have no hope of death. They follow after a whirling banner that keeps abruptly changing direction—another symbol of their lukewarm natures, their lack of conviction: "These wretches, who were never alive, were naked and were much stung by gadflies and wasps."[57] This "ignominious and comparatively trivial punishment of the lukewarm reflects the nature of these souls and thus is right and just for them."[58] The *Apocalypse of Paul* cannot rival this imaginative exactness: the punishments that illuminate the sins only fitfully have symbolic power, and sometimes degenerate into mere catch-all penalties of flames and filth.

So we are shown an old man whose bowels are pierced by "Tartaruchean angels" (i.e., devils) who use an iron instrument with three hooks. He turns out to have been a presbyter who not only broke the fast but fornicated before saying Mass. There is another old man tormented by evil angels who "pushed him into the fire up to his knees, and struck him with stones and wounded his face like a storm, and did not allow him to say "Have pity on me!"[59] This was a bishop who enjoyed his episcopal status, but "did not give just judgment and did not pity widows and orphans."

Possibly the bishop's being wounded in the face by a storm of stones is meant to suggest helplessness—the helplessness of widow and orphan in the face of the buffetings of the world. His being unable to ask for pity may reflect his not having shown pity himself. But the ideas do not get beyond the obvious and are swallowed up in the repetitive beatings and burning. When we find, a little later, men and women, their hands cut off and their feet naked in a region of snow and ice, devoured by worms, and learn that these, too, are souls who "harmed orphans and widows and the poor, and did not hope in the Lord"—we begin to note a certain paucity of invention, let alone moral imagination. This is not simply an aesthetic defect—Dante's brilliance in making the punishment enact the character of the sinner actually helps us to see the punishment not simply a something imposed arbitrarily from the outside by a powerful God, but as in the nature of the evil acts themselves.

Much the same applies to the rest of the punishments. People who broke their Communion fast are stretched over a pit, tantalized by fruits they cannot grasp to slake their thirst; whoremongering husbands are hung up by their eyebrows; sodomites are in a sulfurous pit. There are certain correspondences—the snow and ice that engulf those who harmed the helpless suggest hardness of heart. But why the sin of sodomites should be punished by their being "covered with dust . . . their countenance like blood" is hard to say. These penalties lack the backing of any exact philosophy.

The final vision is of unbelievers and heretics. We are shown heathens who gave alms, but knew not God. Their lack of faith takes away all merit from their charity—they are dressed in bright clothes, but are blind, and are engulfed in a pit. Then we are shown those who deny that Christ came in the flesh, the son of the Virgin Mary; and "those who say that the bread and cup of the Eucharist of blessings are not the body and blood of Christ." They are in a covered well. When the well is about to be uncovered, the angel who is leading "Paul" (rather as Virgil will lead Dante in the *Divine Comedy*) warns him: "stand far off that you may be able to bear the stench of this place." When the well is opened, immediately there arises from it "a disagreeable and evil stench, which surpasses all punishments."[60]

The most memorable moment in *Paul* comes from compassion for the damned. "Paul," having seen the souls of those who denied that Christ rose from the dead and who also denied the resurrection of the body set in a place of cold and snow, gnawed by two-headed worms each a cubit's length, weeps bitterly, and utters that common refrain (derived from Christ's stern words about those who scandalize any of "these little ones") "it were better for us if we had not been born, all of us who are sinners."[61]

At this a general wailing breaks out, involving all the damned souls, who see the archangel Michael descending in judgment with all the heavenly host. They beg the archangel for mercy: "we now see the judgment and acknowledge the Son of God! It was impossible for us before these things to pray for this, before we entered into this place; for we heard that there was a judgment before we went out of the world, but impediments and the life of the world did not allow us to repent."[62] Michael assures them that he prays for the human race, prays that God will send dews and refreshments to the world, and that now he weeps for these lost souls, that he will pray "if by chance the merciful God will have pity and give you refreshment." At this, all the souls, and "Paul," cry out to God for pity and mercy.

The Son of God reveals himself, descending from heaven crowned with a diadem. At first Christ reminds them sternly how his blood had been poured out for their sakes, that instead of the diadem he had worn a crown of thorns and been buffeted, thirsting on the cross had been given instead of water vinegar mixed with gall; had been wounded with a spear. Yet he goes on to grant them what Michael had asked for—refreshment. Because of the prayers of Michael and Paul and all the faithful upon earth "who offer oblations" he will give to all damned souls a night and day of refreshment for ever—every Sabbath.[63]

> Around the wicked
> In hell's abysses
> The great flame flickered
> And eased their pain.[64]

The Fathers

Damnable Spectacles: Tertullian

Descriptions of hell and its torments were soon to be found outside the apocryphal literature of alleged revelations. Since hell was to become one of the central *topoi* of Christian preaching throughout the ages, it is no surprise to find it taken into the tradition of Roman forensic eloquence as early as the second century. One of the most memorable, if also one of the briefest, examples of damnation as a theme for declamation is the *De Spectaculis* of Tertullian.[65] Tertullian's depiction of hell does not pose as revelation or scripture, but is avowedly a work of Latin declamation.

Tertullian (ca. 160–ca. 225) was born in Carthage. His upbringing was pagan. He was learned in the Latin classics, and in history and philosophy. In his *Apology* (where he denounces philosophy [*Apologeticus* 46]) he says that he was once among those who laughed at God—"Christians are made, not born" (*Apologeticus* 18). Later in life he deserted the orthodox Church for the heresy of Montanism (a severely ascetic movement in the early church, which seemed to exclude from salvation all but the exceptionally pure). He is widely regarded, nevertheless, as the writer who both created a Christian Latinity, and laid the foundation of Latin Christianity.[66]

Tertullian's brief treatment of hell is famous and notorious because Gibbon took it as evidence of the inhumanity of Tertullian and, by extension, of Christianity itself.[67] It is interesting that what caught Gibbon's attention—the very end of *De Spectaculis*—jumps out at the reader after sections of vivid denunciation of the inhumanity of Roman spectacles, and particularly the gladiatorial combats and other bloodthirsty shows in "the Amphitheater."[68] Tertullian's exultation at the prospect of the enemies of the church burning in hell flames is an obvious subject for Gibbon's scorn and contempt. But the central aim of Tertullian's book—an astonishingly sustained exercise in denunciation, almost worthy of Juvenal—is to contrast the life of the Christian, blessed with the gifts of the Holy Spirit, with the soul-threatening passions of the public spectacles—games, theatres, wrestling matches, indeed, virtually all the mass entertainments offered by the city of Rome. It might be possible to read the passage with a little more sympathy than Gbbon was prepared to show.

Tertullian is a writer without charm. Much of *De Spectaculis* reads like the rantings of a Scotch Covenanter who has fallen surprisingly in love with the riches of Roman forensic oratory. The resulting mix is potent, if startling. Tertullian's fundamental assumption is that Rome is ruled by demons. All her gods are really demons; her public entertainments are demonic; the duty of a Christian is to avoid demon-haunted places; Christianity's ultimate destiny is to exorcise the demonic world and replace the rule of the devils by the kingdom of Christ.

Tertullian strives mightily to show that all games, chariot races, indeed, all public shows are rooted in rituals honoring the pagan gods of Rome, and in this he is certainly right. This "assemblage of heathen people" (*conventum ethnici populi*)[69] is impious, a gathering of the enemies of Christ (Tertullian, *De Spectaculis* 3). The whole equipment of public shows is "idolatry pure and simple" (ibid., 4) Rome is the city where the demons sit in conclave (ibid., 7). All the architectural symbolism of the Circus Maximus, where chariot and other races were held, is pagan, therefore demonic. The temple of the sun is in the middle of it; seven egg-shaped balls (which were displayed in the Circus, one of which was removed on completion of each of the circuits of the chariots) "are assigned to the honor of Castor and Pollux by those who do not blush to believe them sprung from the eggs of the swan, Jove."[70] The Circus's ornamental dolphins spout in honor of Neptune. Equestrian skill is not wicked in itself, but Tertullian finds a peril in the fact that horse-racing is mixed up with Neptune—who in Greek is called *hippios* (Tertullian 9).

Turning his disapproving gaze on athletics, Tertullian decides that running and jumping cannot be approved—they are injurious and useless displays of strength (ibid., 18). Wrestling is "the devil's own trade." Was it not the devil himself, in the guise of a serpent, who in paradise first crushed men? "[Wrestling's] very grips are the snake's, the grip that holds, the twist that binds, the suppleness that eludes." As for the theater, it is, properly speaking, the shrine of Venus or, rather, of Venus and Bacchus together, the place of "demons of drunkenness and lust" (ibid., 10). The supreme charm of the theatre is filth—filth in the gesture of the actor, filth in the behavior of the man taking the part of a woman.[71] Tragedies and comedies are bloody, lustful, and prodigal; hence they encourage such vices in the audience (ibid., 17).

So far, so caricaturable—the Scotch Covenanter side of Tertullian is in the ascendant. Gradually, though, an argument emerges that is to some extent independent of his theology, and which conveys a serious moral purpose. The gifts of the Holy Spirit, which should above all characterize the Christian, include "tranquility, gentleness, quiet and peace." These are to be contrasted with "madness, bile, anger and pain"—those demonic states of soul that are

manifested at public games and other spectacles, and especially in the sangui-
nary displays of the Colosseum. Every public spectacle in Rome is filled with
frenzy: "Look at the populace coming to the show—mad already! Disorderly,
blind, excited already about its bets! The praetor is too slow for them; all the
time their eyes are upon his urn, in it, as if rolling with the lots he shakes up in
it. The signal is to be given. They are all in suspense, anxious suspense. One
frenzy, one voice. Recognize their frenzy from their empty-mindedness (*de
vanitate*)" (ibid., 16).

Tertullian could easily be describing many sporting spectacles of our own
day. It gradually becomes clear that he is building up a picture of the "popular"
soul,[72] the soul riven by disordered passions, torn hither and thither by rage,
lust, frenzy, bile. This picture is ultimately rooted in Plato, with his picture of
the *logos* (reason) that should rule the soul constantly in danger of being
mastered by the lower, irrational passions and appetites. This is also that
"popular" soul that for Plato goes with those twin political perversions, democracy and tyranny.

It is in the Flavian Amphitheater—"the temple of all demons" (ibid., 19)—
that we see these passions at their most damnable. The shows of the Colosseum were often defended on the grounds that they exhibited, either as gladiators or as victims of wild beasts, criminals who had already been condemned to
death. But the innocent, Tertullian insists, cannot take pleasure in the punishment of another "when it better befits the innocent to lament that a man like
himself has become so guilty that a punishment so cruel must be awarded
him" (ibid.). A Christian does not even have to be told that he should hate such
a spectacle. (So—can the saved rejoice in the sufferings of the damned?
Tertullian will soon suggest that they do.)

Tertullian rises to heights of eloquence as he goes on further to describe the
passions let loose by the spectacles in the Colosseum: "he who shudders at the
body of a man who died by nature's law the common death of all, will, in the
Amphitheater, gaze down with most tolerant eyes on the bodies of men mangled, torn to pieces, defiled with their own blood; yes, and that he who comes to
the spectacle to signify his approval of murder being punished, will have a
reluctant gladiator hounded on with lash and rod to do murder" (ibid., 21).

With great skill, Tertullian is evolving an image of a soul so disordered that
it is infernal, that it anticipates the state of being damned. But this soul is
precisely that of the pagan world, of imperial Rome in all its works and pomps.
This is the plight of all souls which lack the gifts of the Spirit. Hence the
present world is itself infernal—so we can prove from experience the validity of
Tertullian's fundamental claim that the world before Christ is a realm ruled by
demons, and that Rome is *civitas diaboli*—the opposite of *civitas dei*.

It is this conviction—fired, no doubt, with an orator's forensic sense that a "turn" of the argument, its unexpected move in a new direction is required—that now leads Tertullian into his exultant vision, with which *De Spectaculis* ends, of the triumph of Christ in his Second Coming, the spectacle to end all spectacles, that earned Gibbon's contempt. The passage deserves to be quoted at length:

> Would you have fightings and wrestlings? Here they are—things of no small account and plenty of them. See impurity overthrown by chastity, perfidy slain by faith, cruelty crushed to pity . . . have you a mind for blood? You have the blood of Christ.
>
> But what a spectacle is already at hand—the return of the Lord, now no object of doubt, now exalted, now triumphant! What exultation will there be of the angels, what glory that of the saints as they rise again! . . . Yes, and there are still to come other spectacles—that last, eternal Day of Judgment, that Day which the Gentiles never believed would come, that Day they laughed at, when this old world and all its generations shall be consumed in one fire. How vast the spectacle that day, and how wide! What sight shall wake my wonder, what my laughter, my joy and exultation? As I see all those kings, those great kings welcomed (we are told) in heaven along with Jove, along with those who told of their ascent, groaning in the depths of darkness! And the magistrates who persecuted the name of Jesus, liquefying in fiercer flames than they kindled in their rage against the Christians! Those sages, too, the philosophers blushing before their disciples as they blaze together, the disciples whom they taught that God was concerned with nothing, that men have no souls at all, or that what souls they have shall never return to their former bodies! And, then, the poets trembling before the judgment-seat, not of Radamanthus, not of Minos, but of Christ whom they never looked to see! And then there will be the tragic actors to be heard, more vocal in their own tragedy; and the players to be seen, lither of limb by far in the fire; and then the charioteer to watch, red all over in the wheel of flame; and, next, the athletes to be gazed upon, not in their gymnasiums but hurled in the fire—unless it be that not even then would I wish to see them, in my desire rather to turn my insatiable gaze on them [i.e., the Jews] who vented their fury on the Lord. "This is he," I shall say, "the son of the carpenter or the harlot, the Sabbath-breaker, the Samaritan, who had a devil. This is he whom you bought from Judas; this is he, who was struck with reed and fist, defiled with

spittle, given gall and vinegar to drink. This is he whom the disciples secretly stole away, that it might be said that he had risen—unless it was the gardener who removed him, lest his lettuces be trampled on by the throng of visitors!" Such sights, such exultation—what praetor, consul, quaestor, priest will ever give you of his bounty? And yet all these, in some sort, are ours, pictured through faith in the imagination of the spirit. But what are those things which eye hath not seen nor ear heard, nor even entered into the heart of man? I believe, things of greater joy than circus, theater or amphitheater, or any stadium.

As we have noticed, the *De Spectaculis* is now the most famous work of Tertullian for the simple reason that Gibbon denounced his inhumanity in chapter 15 of his *Decline and fall of the Roman Empire*. Gibbon says that he will draw the "'veil over the rest of this infernal description'" out of regard for "the humanity of the reader." He notes with disapproval that Tertullian was regarded as an immense authority: "In order to ascertain the degree of authority which the zealous African had acquired, it may be sufficient to allege the testimony of Cyprian, the doctor and guide of all the Western churches. As often as he applied himself to his daily study of the writings of Tertullian, he was accustomed to say, 'Da mihi magistrum, Give me my master.'"[73] Tertullian certainly is a master of rhetoric and psychology. Whether his forensic brilliance adds anything solid to the stock of human wisdom is another matter. What he does is to use all the resources of Latin eloquence to damn the very culture that produced it. You could call that *trahison des clercs*.

Lactantius

Lactantius (ca. 250–ca. 324)—otherwise known as Lucius Caecilius Firmianus—lived through one of the great turning points in the history of Europe.[74] Having been converted to Christianity from paganism ca. 300, he suffered dismissal from his academic posts during the persecution of the Christians by Maximian Galerius; saw the edict of toleration issued by Galerius in 311; Constantine's Edict of Milan in 313, which made Christianity the semi-official religion of the Empire; and survived to become tutor to Constantine's son, Crispus. Lactantius was a Christian apologist, swaying educated Romans by his mastery of Ciceronian eloquence, and attempting to persuade them of the truth of Christianity on the basis not so much of scripture as of pagan philosophy and literature.

Lactantius is probably best known for his lively little work of savage polemic, *De Mortibus Persecutorum*[75]—an account of the agonizing ends of

THE CHRISTIAN BEGINNINGS 131

several persecutors of the Christians, and in particular, of Maximian Galerius, the colleague of Diocletian, who unleashed the tenth persecution of the church—the last, and most severe of the General Persecutions. One of Lactantius's chief aims as a Christian apologist was to show how God's providence ruled the world, and that it was part of this providence that the good and evil acts of men would be rewarded and punished, if not in this life, then in the next. The punishment of Galerius was inflicted on him—according to the celebrated account of Lactantius—in this life. Galerius, having inflicted hideous tortures upon Christians, burning them by slow fires so that their whole skin and all their inward parts were destroyed very gradually—ought in justice to suffer similar torments himself. His death, from an agonizing and horrible disease, is not unlike accounts of sufferings of the damned in Christian literature, and could well have influenced these. Anti-Christian tyrants being devoured by worms is a quite popular theme:

> It was during the eighteenth year of his reign that God struck
> Maximian with an incurable malady. A malign ulcer appeared on the
> lower part of his genitals and spread more widely. Doctors cut and
> then treated it, but the wound split open . . . the more it was cut away,
> the more virulently it spread . . . the malady became much
> worse . . . his entrails putrefied from the outside, and his whole seat
> dissolved in decay . . . worms were born inside him. The smell
> pervaded not just the palace but the whole city. . . . Cooked meats still
> warm were placed near his dissolving buttocks so that the heat could
> draw out the worms; when these were broken up, countless numbers
> of these creatures swarmed around. (Lactantius, *De Mortibus
> Persecutorum* 33, 1–2, 4, 7–8)

This is certainly a description of an infernal punishment in this life and fits well that Christian imagination of exquisite, ever renewed and unending tortures that becomes central to the imagination of hell.

The chief work of apologetics by which Lactantius sets out to commend Christianity to those steeped in Latin culture is his *Divine Institutes*.[76] This seems to have been the first treatise in Latin setting out the Christian attitude to life.[77] The book includes a vision of the end of the world and of judgment in which Lactantius freely mingles biblical passages with the prophecies of the Sibyls. It is interesting—and tells us something of Lactantius's project to reconcile the Christian world view with Latin pagan culture—that when he comes to describing the end of the world, not only are the so-called Sibylline prophecies treated as having the same authority as holy writ—they vastly outnumber passages from the Bible.

There is nothing in Lactantius about original sin or of Christ's atoning sacrifice for man. Christ came to teach wisdom and the way to God. Lactantius gives a classical account of the virtues and vices—one that would have been instantly recognizable to Plato, Aristotle, or Cicero. But the point of keeping to the virtues is to be rewarded by God. God deliberately made the way to heaven difficult and steep, so that it is climbed by man only with the greatest labor. The virtues of justice, temperance, faith, patience, chastity, abstinence, wisdom are given to help in this ascent. But God also puts in our way poverty, disgrace, labor, pain, and all bitterness—so that the virtues will have a field of operation, and so that we will know good from evil (Lactantius, *Divine Institutes*, 6, 4). The virtues lead to heaven. And the vices lead inevitably to hell (ibid., 6, 3).

This is how Lactantius manages to turn his picture of virtue and vice in a Christian direction. Among the animals, only man is born capable of "beholding" (rather than simply seeing) the heavens (ibid., 2, 1). But man has been surrounded by temptations and passions that turn him toward the earth. There is an inherent weakness in man, for his mind is "wrapped in a fragile case and enclosed in a shade-like domicile" (ibid., 7, 2). Man does not perceive truth clearly—something only God can do. Man's damaged vision does not allow him to see, except fitfully, that "the goods of the soul are evil to the body, namely, flight from wealth, ban on pleasure, contempt of pain and death" (ibid., 7 5). "Hence, to live well eternally is to live badly in time, and to live well in time as worldly persons understand this is to incur eternal punishment" (ibid.).

But this theoretical structure is entirely subservient to Lactantius's eloquent—sometimes magnificent—depiction, using all the resources of Latin oratory, mixing words of Jesus with Sibylline prophecies, of the last days, and of heaven and hell.

In the last days, civil discords will break out. Ten kings will rise to divide the world equally between them. But these rulers, having increased their armies to an immense size by forced recruitment—thereby leaving the earth destitute of tillers—will suddenly be confronted by a powerful enemy from the North, who will pillage and contaminate the earth, confound the human with the divine, plunder, despoil, and kill. Cities will be torn from their foundations, and men will perish from fire, sword, constant earthquakes, frequent epidemics and prevailing famine (ibid., 7, 16).

After that, things can only get worse. There will be a mixture of pollution and global warming: "The air will be vitiated and will become corrupt and pestilential; now from unseasonable rains, again from unusual dryness. At one time it will be too hot, at another too cold" (ibid.). No plant, tree or vine will bear anything. Springs will dry up and other water supplies will be changed to blood or bitterness. Therefore animals, birds and fish will start to die out. There will

THE CHRISTIAN BEGINNINGS   133

be comets and eclipses and stars will fall from the sky. The moon will slip into extraordinary meanderings, and will be covered with blood. Eventually the whole sky will turn black, and "lest anything be lacking to the evils of men, the trumpet from heaven will be heard, which the Sibyl announces in this manner: "The heavenly trumpet will blow its sound of many notes" (ibid.).

As I have mentioned, many of the prophecies are taken from the Sibylline oracles. These are Jewish and Christian adaptations or imitations of collections of sayings ascribed in Greek and Roman paganism to female seers who presided over shrines in various parts of the Greco-Roman world. The Christian versions date from the second century on. (Lactantius mentions seven Sibyls—the Persae, the Libyssan, the Delphic, the Cimmerian, the Erythraean, the Samian, and the Cumaean—the last of whom leads Aeneas through the underworld.[78]) This goes with early Christian efforts to demonstrate that there were anticipations of and affinities to Christian revelation among the pagans. Virgil's *Fourth Eclogue*, with its picture of the return of the Golden Age as a son is born, was given virtually a Sibylline status as the "Messianic Eclogue." The tradition continues until at least the twelfth century, for in the *Dies Irae*, which dates from that time, and the use of which was until very recent times normal in masses for the dead, we find the verses:

> Dies irae, dies illa,
> Solvet saeclum in favilla,
> Teste David cum Sibylla.
> Tuba mirens spargens sonum
> Per sepulchra regionum,
> Coget omnes ante thronum.[79]

[That day of wrath, that dreadful day, which will turn the world into ashes, David witnesses, along with the Sibyl. The trumpet scattering sound through the sepulchral regions compels everyone to come before the Throne.]

Lactantius's vision of the End of Days is, then, a mixture of scripture, the apocryphal scriptures, the Sibylline oracles, and other sources. He explains that a great prophet will appear to convert men back to God. If people refuse to hear him, he will close heaven, hold back the rains, change water to blood, create famine, and send forth flames from out of his mouth. Not surprisingly, these prodigies will convert not a few (Lactantius 7, 17). However, an Evil one—Antichrist, undoubtedly—will appear who will show even greater signs and wonders—such as causing the sun to stand still, and a statue to speak. He will try to overturn the temple of God (i.e., the church) and will persecute Christians. He will make the earth desolate for forty-two months, and turn everything upside down: "No law nor order nor military discipline will be observed; no one will reverence grey hairs; men will not recognize the duty of piety; nor will they show mercy to sex or infancy; all things will be confounded . . . in one common game of freebooting, as it were, the whole world will be destroyed" (ibid.).

However, according to the *Sibylline Oracles*,[80] a king will be sent from the East who will "rescue the world from evil war." The Sibyls and the *Apocalypse of John* agree that the middle of the heavens will be opened and there will be "a brilliant fire in the midst of darksome night"[81]—i.e., God descending in judgment. A sword will fall from the heavens; Antichrist will be defeated, and "Chaos shall then show Tartarus; then the earth will gape open (Lactantius 7, 20; *Sibylline Oracles* 8.241, 242), and all will come before the tribunal of their God and King."

God will then proceed to the Last Judgment. (Lactantius denies that there is a judgment immediately after death for each soul—all the souls are detained "in one common custody" [Lactantius 7, 19], until the Great Assize.) The souls will again be clothed with their bodies, so that the wicked who have sinned with their bodies can be punished, and the just rewarded. A special sort of flame will burn the wicked. It will not be the type of flame with which we are familiar in this world, which has a tendency "to fly upwards toward the sky in a jumpy movement" (ibid., 21), but one that lives for ever of itself without need of being fed, which both cremates and at the same time re-creates the bodies of the impious so that they can be tortured for ever. The same flames (which anticipate the late mediaeval Roman Catholic doctrine of purgatory) will scorch with fire and burn also the bodies of those who are just and therefore saved, but stained with sin. However, "when the fullness of their justice and maturity of virtue has been boiled free of dross, they will not feel the fire, for they have something of God in them which may, then, repel and ward off the power of the flame" (ibid.).

Lactantius finds it important to confront the common pagan belief (to be found in Plato and Virgil) that the souls of the dead, having been steeped in the waters of Lethe, will, after a thousand years return with new bodies to the realms of light, forgetting the past. He insists that the impious will be consigned "to the shadows and the fire," having no second chance, and that only the just will return to earth, clothed with new bodies, God giving them "spirit and honor and life" (ibid. 7, 22).

A brief, tantalizing vision of heaven follows. The sun will become seven times brighter than it is now (which not all would regard as paradisaic);[82] the earth will produce crops of its own accord; honey and wines will flow through mountain streams, and rivers will overflow with milk.[83] Beasts will become vegetarian, and so, apparently, will hawks and eagles, since they will cease to be birds of prey. Children will play with snakes. Honey will ooze from oaks, rams will voluntarily color their fleeces the way we like them,[84] and lambs will be born with scarlet coats. Lions will eat bran from the feed box and (more mysteriously) dragons will go to sleep with asps (Lactantius 7, 24; *Sibylline Oracles* 3, 787–91). Men will be transformed into the likeness of angels, white and shining as snow, while the impious "will be burned in perpetual fire for ever in the sight of the angels and the just" (Lactantius 7, 26).

Both Tertullian and Lactantius are masters of Latin eloquence, of passionate declamation. But what is entirely lacking in both is any intellectual structure, any philosophic spirit. The first Christian Father to buttress his doctrine with a seriously worked out philosophy—a philosophy that led his thought in a direction ultimately condemned as heretical—was Origen.

Hell Not Eternal? The Humane Heresy of Origen

Origen was born around AD 185, probably at Alexandria, of Christian parents. At the age of seventeen he narrowly escaped martyrdom in a persecution by the emperor Septimus Severus. Origen's father, Leonides, actually was martyred, and Origen wrote a letter to him encouraging him to persevere in the faith. Indeed, it is said that he was dissuaded only with difficulty from embracing the same fate for himself.

He pursued a career as theologian and teacher, fell out with his superior, the patriarch of Alexandria, and spent the rest of his life in Caesarea. His devoted his greatest efforts to scriptural exegesis. Tradition has it that he wrote a thousand books, including a fifty-volume commentary on the Greek text of the Old Testament (the *Septuagint*), hardly any of which survives because the scribes were too bored to copy it out. Tradition also has it that he castrated himself in order that he could remain pure while instructing his female pupils.[85] Certainly he lived a life of immense labor, asceticism, and courage. He was imprisoned during another persecution and severely tortured, but "bore his suffering with the same undaunted spirit that he had displayed since boyhood."[86] Released from prison, but broken in health, he died at Tyre in 253 in his seventieth year.

Origen was the first great Christian philosopher and theologian, and the first to attempt a synthesis of faith and reason on the most general possible level. Unlike Lactantius and Tertullian, he is not essentially a master of Latin eloquence, but of Greek philosophy, a truly systematic thinker, and a man of extraordinary speculative audacity. It was this audacity—his attempt to reconcile scriptural passages about eternal punishment with reason and justice— that eventually, after his death, got him condemned for theological error.

Origen was anathematized by the Second Council of Constantinople (AD 533) for a number of theological opinions that were thereafter deemed to be heretical. The condemnations are detailed, but the burden of Origen's heretical teachings is summed up pretty well in some pithily hostile remarks of St. Jerome: "one who is now a man may in another world become a daemon, while a daemon, if he lives negligently, may be bound to a grosser body, that is, may become a man. Thus he mixes up everything, so that one may be changed from an archangel into a devil, and on the other hand a devil may turn into an angel."[87] The fundamental scandal that Origen caused for Christians—or to what later became orthodox Christian teaching—lay in his teaching that hell will not be eternal; in the connected claim that the free will of all rational beings entails that they can always make their condition better or worse by their own free choice; and that there were worlds—possibly numerous—before the one that saw the Fall of man and Christ's redemption, and which will be the scene of the Second Coming of Christ; and that in the end man and God share the same substance.[88]

Origen puts forward many doctrines that are strange to the modern ear—such as that the sun and stars are living beings (an idea found in Plato and many other ancient writers), beings that may have become what they are through their own choice—but the source of all he writes can be found in some lucid philosophico-theological ideas. One guiding idea is that God first created, not material things but rational beings—minds with the power of free choice and movement. These minds (many of them, at least) became slothful and wearied of the effort required ceaselessly to love the good, and so began a process of withdrawing from the good and moving toward evil. In these movements were the seeds of that variety and diversity that characterize the world as we know it, with higher and lower regions, where dwell pure minds, angels, human beings, and demons. The idea seems to be that the original universe would have been perfect and unchanging (and pretty boring by the sound of it) and that change is the result of this fall from grace. The descent from goodness toward evil is also a descent into material bodies of beings that were originally pure minds (Origen, *First Principles*, 130–31).

This idea is the germ and structural principle of all of Origen's thought about damnation and salvation. Eventually there will be a "restoration" (*apocatastasis*) of the universe to its original state, when (and here Origen quotes Paul's words) "God will be all in all."[89] In this restoration all rational beings and, eventually, even the devil himself will have a share.

It is another fundamental principle that it is, above all, as minds that we exist, and that all rational beings are endowed with free will. Their exercise of their free will extends to their choosing in what sort of being their minds will express themselves. Those who through weariness of God and the good sank in the scale of existence took to themselves bodies—moving from an existence as ethereal beings to ever grosser bodies, tying themselves to human flesh, and finally "to the gross body of one of the irrational animals" (*First Principles*, 40–41 and 125–26). Those who descended only a little way from God became archangels, cherubim, thrones, dominations and angels. Those who fell a very long way became daemons (ibid.).[90]

We can to some extent separate this from its theological context by seeing it as essentially a doctrine about free will and the development of habit or character which, as Aristotle says, becomes a sort of second nature.[91] Our choices determine our character through becoming ingrained. Through the course of habitually making cowardly choices one becomes a coward. The self-indulgent person acquires his character in the same way. In learning habitually to act courageously, we become brave. Hence the character we end up with is profoundly the result of our own choice, even though through habit we may find it virtually impossible to break out of the patterns of behavior our own previous choices have imposed upon us.

For Origen, minds take on a character in a similar way—but his account of moral development (and degeneration) is hugely more speculative than Aristotle's. The first bad choice that a mind can make, the first sin it can commit, is to fall away from loving God: "some sinned deeply and became daemons, others less and became angels; others still less and became archangels; and thus each in turn received the reward for his individual sin" (*First Principles*, 67). Souls of the better sort enter into stars and planets, which Origen envisages as being governed by intelligences (which is why they move in a fixed order [ibid., 61]) while the more fallen exist on earth as human beings, and the worst as devils in the underworld. God made the present world and bound the soul to the body as a punishment (ibid., 67).

We might notice another conclusion drawn by Origen that would certainly offend the orthodox: if we human beings are what we are because of some choice made long ago before we were born, it follows that human souls had a prior existence. Indeed, Origen teaches that the sins that made us what we are were committed before the creation of the present world. He therefore leaves open the possibility of transmigration of souls, of our having several, or many lives in which to work out our salvation or damnation.

The downward descent can become unstoppable. A mind, which has become a human soul, can descend through sensuality and grossness to taking on animal or even plant life. It can then do nothing to help itself. But, short of turning into an irrational being, a soul can always in principle help itself begin the painful ascent back toward mind: "For the cessation of evil-doing means the beginning of an impulse toward virtue; and among irrational beings virtue does not exist" (ibid., 73).

Origen sets the scene for his "heretical" account of hell by seizing on the sayings of Christ in the Gospel of John: "Verily, verily I say unto you, Except a corn of wheat fall into the ground and die, it abideth alone: but if it die, it bringeth forth much fruit" (John 12:24). Origen argues that the risen body is no more a mere reproduction of our present body than the wheat is a reproduction of the seed: "Therefore, we do not say that after the body has been corrupted it will return to its original nature, just as the grain of corn that has been corrupted will not return to be a grain of corn. For we hold that, as from the grain of corn an ear rises up, so in the body there lies a certain [life] principle which is not corrupted from which the body is raised in incorruption."[92]

The risen body is, for Origen, a spiritual body—as it is for Paul—"It is sown a natural body; it is raised a spiritual body" (1 Cor. 15:44). Future bodies will be immaterial in a future world in which material nature will have been destroyed.[93] Origen begins to build his heterodox theory of postmortem punishment on these texts. For if the risen body may be profoundly unlike the present material body, then the punishments of hell may be interpreted in a far from literal sense. This is what Origen suggests. Interestingly, there is some analogy here with Tertullian's account of the hellish nature of the disordered souls who enjoy the Roman spectacles—their "frenzy, bile, anger and pain"[94]— as a preview of hell itself. For Origen, the risen body is one which God refashions out of the natural, earthly one, and it is a spiritual body that is fitted to dwell in the heavens.[95] Analogously, the risen body of the damned is one suitable for a life of spiritual torments. For the torments are indeed spiritual— not grossly material. In discussing the meaning of scriptural "eternal fire" Origen acutely points out that in the Isaiah, where it is first used,[96] the fire by which each man is punished is described as belonging to himself. For it says, "Walk in the light of your fire, and in the sparks that ye have kindled."[97] Origen's conclusion is that "every sinner kindles for himself the flame of his own fire, and is not plunged into a fire which has been previously kindled by someone else or which existed before him."[98]

It is not easy to see how this could possibly fit with "Depart from me ye cursed, into everlasting fire, prepared for the devil and his angels."[99] It is exactly on this point that Jerome moves in to attack Origen and convict him of heresy: "As for the fire of Gehenna and the torments, with which holy scripture threatens sinners, Origen does not make them to consist in punishments but in the conscience of sinners, when by the goodness and power of God the whole memory of our offences is placed before our eyes. The entire crop of our sins springs up as it were from seeds which have remained hidden in the soul, and every shameful and impious act that we have done is represented in an image before our eyes, so that the mind, beholding its former acts of self-indulgence is punished by a burning conscience and stung by the pricks of remorse."[100]

This an accurate resumé of some passages in Origen, but it brings out what is actually attractive in Origen's teaching. Origen writes: "the whole mass of evil boils up into punishment and is kindled into penalties; at which time also the mind or conscience, bringing to memory through divine power all things the signs and forms of which it had impressed upon itself at the moment of sinning, will see before its eyes a kind of history of its evil deeds, or every foul and disgraceful act and all unholy conduct. Then the conscience is harassed and pricked by its own stings, and becomes an accuser and witness against itself" (First Principles, 142).

Origen makes the fire of hell symbolic—exactly as Jerome accuses him of doing. It is symbolic of "those faults of passion which often occur in men, as when the soul is burnt up with the flames of love, or tormented with the fires of jealousy or envy, or tossed about with furious anger, or consumed with intense sadness" (ibid.). The "outer darkness" of hell is allegorized. It is not a place of murky atmosphere, lacking all light, but rather "a description of those who through their immersion in the darkness of deep ignorance have become separated from every gleam of reason and intelligence" (First Principles, 145). Origen even speculates that just as the saints will receive back the very bodies in which they have lived in holiness and purity during their sojourn in this life, bodies made bright and glorious as a result of the resurrection, so, too, "the wicked who in this life have loved the darkness of error and the night of ignorance, will after the resurrection be clothed with murky and black bodies, in order that this very gloom of ignorance, which in the present world has taken possession of the inner parts of their mind and being, may in the world to come be revealed through the garment of their outward body" (ibid.).

Origen and Tertullian are united in seeing in the disordered soul an image of damnation, of a hellish state. From this it is easy to understand the sufferings of the damned—as Origen wishes to understand them—in a nonliteral way by internalizing them. A powerful tradition develops in later Christian thinkers in which the psychology of evil is explored in such a way that the wicked soul is seen as subject to self-imposed suffering, which has analogies with the sufferings of hell. The most eloquent passage among the Fathers in this tradition is to be found in St. Augustine—certainly no denier of the objective reality of hell—when he writes of "libido" or lust (i.e., unbridled desires):

Lust dominates the mind, despoils it of the wealth of its virtue, and drags it, poor and needy, now this way and now that; now approving and even defending what is false as though it were true, now disapproving what it previously defended, and rushing on to other falsities; now refusing assent and fearing clear reasoning; now despairing of fully discovering the truth and clinging to the deep obscurities of stupidity; now struggling into the light of understanding and falling back again from weariness. Meanwhile the reign of lust rages tyrannically and distracts the life and whole spirit of man with many conflicting storms of terror, desire, anxiety, empty and false happiness, torture because of the loss of something that he used to love, eagerness to possess what he does not have, grievances for injuries received and fires of vengeance. Wherever he turns, greed amasses, extravagance wastes, ambition entices, pride bloats, envy twists, sloth buries, obstinacy goads, submissiveness harasses, and all other innumerable things that throng and busy themselves in the kingdom of lust. Can we think that this is not punishment which, as you see, all must endure who do not cling to wisdom? (Augustine, *On the Free Choice of the Will [De Libero Arbitrio]*, 11)

Origen develops his symbolic account of the flames of hell in a manner that leads irresistibly to his notorious denial of the eternity of punishment for the damned. Instead of seeing the fire simply as the tormenting of sinners—as retributive justice—he understands it as a means of purging and healing. He argues that when the soul has become separated from "that order and connection and harmony in which it was created by God for good action and useful experience and not at concord with itself," it must suffer something analogous to the excruciating pain felt in limbs if they are dislocated and torn away from their proper connections and functions: "When the soul, thus torn and rent asunder, has been tried by the application of fire, it is undoubtedly wrought into a condition of stronger inward connection and renewal" (Origen, *First Principles*, 143).

God becomes the physician of the sick soul. We occasionally find it necessary to take unpleasant and bitter medicine as a cure for the ills that result from self-indulgence. Sometimes it is even worse: "We need the severe treatment of the knife and a painful operation...should the disease have extended beyond the reach even of these remedies, in the last resort the ill is burnt out by fire" (ibid.). God, our physician, wanting to wash away the ills we have brought upon our own souls "makes use of penal remedies of a similar sort, even to the infliction of a punishment of fire on those who have lost their soul's health" (ibid.).

Since God-as-physician uses this fiery punishment to purge and heal rather than simply torment, to recall each sinner to the memory of God, it must be assumed that the treatment will be efficacious. Origen certainly assumes that: "There is a resurrection of the dead, and there is punishment, but not everlasting. For when the body is punished the soul is gradually purified, and so is restored to its ancient rank.... For all wicked men, and for daemons too, punishment has an end, and both wicked men and daemons shall be restored to their former rank" (Origen, *First Principles*, 146).[101]

Origen's ideas obviously look heretical—because other ideas triumphed and therefore formed the orthodoxy. Even Origen himself sometimes seemed to disclaim the most radical of his doctrines, or to suggest that they were advanced simply for discussion. There is no doubt that some of his erstwhile supporters— including Jerome—retreated in timid outrage when they discovered that the Master entertained the idea of ultimate universal salvation, even for the devil and his angels. Jerome denounced the idea of an ultimate restitution of all things, when it will be "the same for Gabriel as for the devil, for Paul as for Caiaphas, for virgins as for prostitutes." These were poisonous heresies.[102]

But the argument in favor of these poisonous heresies is strong, both philosophically and morally. Origen's strongest point is his unshakeable belief in free will. He thinks that the holiness that existed in minds as they were first created by God was an "accidental" quality of them, rather than an essential one—and "what is accidental may also be lost" (*First Principles*, 50). Created beings chose to lose this holiness by their own free will—by their consenting to the impulses of sloth that led them to fall away from God. True, in consenting to vicious impulses—sloth, anger, lust, greed—we develop (as Aristotle sug-gests) a character that makes it extremely difficult for us to turn back toward the good. Nevertheless, this is a character that we have chosen, and it is in principle possible that we could repent or be converted.[103]

It is this emphasis on free will that leads directly to Origen's belief in the ultimate salvation of all. For even if we assume that a soul sunk in vice is extremely unlikely to overcome the habits of a lifetime, we still have to consider the effects on such a soul of punishment after death. Since Origen interprets the fire as the flames of conscience, the torments as the stings of remorse, and the worm that never dies as the gnawing of guilty conscience, then the state of the wicked soul after death must be offering it unparalleled chances of repen-tance. Indeed, these torments may themselves represent the workings of a yeasty conscience.

This is strengthened by Origen's insistence that in punishing the wicked God is also purging and healing them. God punishes people for their good (*First Principles*, 104). Even the God of the Old Testament, so often represented as a vengeful tyrant, does this. Tertullian quotes Ezekiel: "Sodom . . . shall be restored to her former estate"—the very Sodom upon which God rained down fire and brimstone [ibid.; Gen. 19:24; Ezek. 16:55]. . . . Hence, the God of the Law [i.e., the Old Testament or Hebrew Bible] and the gospels is one and the same . . . "he does good with justice and punishes in kindness, since neither goodness without justice nor justice without goodness can describe the dignity of the divine nature" (*First Principles*, 104–5).

Would the infliction of hideous torments for all eternity be an example of justice without goodness? It is clear that Origen thinks it would. God takes away from those whom he would save their "stony heart" and replaces it with a "heart of flesh" (ibid., 186, quoting Ezek. 11:19). But the purging and cauterizing that is hellfire must itself take away the stony heart from all but the most resolutely obdurate. And why must God intend the punishments as a means of healing and purging, rather than simply tormenting? Origen takes it as a fundamental principle that we should never understand scripture as showing God doing something wicked, unjust, or disgusting.[104] Eternal torment that produces no good would be indeed wicked and disgusting.

But can Paul be the same as Caiaphas—can Mother Theresa be the same as Hitler, Stalin, and Pol Pot—when all things are restored? Origen envisages the periods of suffering of the most wicked as stretching over eons. (We might think of them as light-years.) No doubt it is fanciful metaphysics and theology—but is it rational as moral thinking? It is at this point that our moral concepts seem to lose any purchase on a slippery surface, so removed are these speculations from the world as we know it. We know what it is to regret, to repent, to suffer remorse and stings of conscience. These can flow from small faults, petty selfishness, small failures to be kind or charitable—to much greater offenses against human solidarity. For Jesus the coldness of heart shown by Dives toward Lazarus; the failure to give meat to the hungry, drink to the thirsty, clothing to the naked; causing scandal or offense to innocent children—all these sins merit damnation. Yet even here, it is not difficult to see how those who have sinned can genuinely repent. People can regain a sense of human solidarity, and accuse themselves of uncharity, in a specific way, really rather than notionally.[105] Suffering himself, in hell, Dives can see what it is to need charity and mercy from another, not having shown these to Lazarus in life. Peter, having realized the depth of his betrayal of Jesus and the thoughtless insincerity of his earlier declaration that "Though I should die with thee, yet will I not deny thee" (Matt. 26:35), goes out and weeps bitterly.

Catholic teaching on confession demands from a penitent admission of sins, contrition and satisfaction.[106] In the case of serious sin "attrition" may also called for—weeping, for instance. If there is to be a final restoration—*apocatastasis*—for great criminals, bitter weeping would only be the beginning of remorse—perhaps to be followed by a lifetime's attempt at restitution. Given that a refusal of charity to even one person can be a sin meriting damnation—so that a refusal to love his parents might be a source of guilt in someone for the rest of his life—the remorse for crime that would be demanded of the greatest sinners defeats imagination. He who has caused the death of one innocent must grieve over it for the rest of his life. How much more so the despot who condemned millions! Remorse would indeed take eons. Yet unless we think that repentance has no moral significance, it would have to be in principle possible, and effective. Repentance and remorse purge the sinner of the malice that underlay his evil acts. If there is to be a temporal punishment for the sin ("satisfaction"), then punishment even for the greatest sins cannot be unlimited.

The Christian understanding of hell has not, on the whole, held that certain sins are of their nature unforgivable (except what Jesus referred to as the "sin against the Holy Ghost") but rather that after death the possibility of repentance is removed, and the will is fixed in the malice that led to the sin. Clearly Origen did not take that view, so his belief in a final *apocatastasis* is entirely logical. His was, though, a logic that would have fatally compromised what has been central not only to Christian faith but to Christian psychology— the conviction that how we live this short life on earth, and the moral choices we make, is of infinite significance. As usual, the church understood the long term implications of Origenism. Instead of a "Doctor of the Church," Origen became one of the greatest heresiarchs.

To Islam: Some Muslim Traditions of Hell

Sura 17 of the Qur'an has the title "The Night Journey." It begins:

> Glory be to Him who carried His servant by night
> from the Holy Mosque to the Further Mosque
> the precincts of which We have blessed,
> that We might show him some of Our signs.[107]

From this brief suggestion of a visionary journey, or a vision in a dream, has arisen a vast body of exegesis and commentary. In popular Islam, this vision of a journey (*mi 'rāj*) is taken to be an actual journey, in which Mohammed was taken up by the angel Gabriel from Mecca, and led, mounted on a miraculous flying horse (called Buraq) to the Temple Mount in Jerusalem. There he ascended through the layers of fire of the seven levels of hell, where he saw the damned roasting in fire, and up through the seven heavens, where he was vouchsafed a vision of the blessed in paradise, and in the last and highest of which he was allowed to see and converse with God. Visions of hell and paradise become at least as important in Islamic as in Christian tradition.

The Muslim doctrine of hell is not at variance with that of Christianity— although it is pictured with what one might call the sensuous sublime style of the Arabic imagination. Although there are numerous references to hell and Gehenna in the Qur'an, they are pretty formulaic and hardly at all descriptive. Those in hell will moan and sigh, and endure there as long as the heavens abide (ibid., sura 11). The damned will burn in fire and be forced to drink pus, and boiling water that scalds their faces like molten copper, which they will lap down like thirsty camels (ibid., sura 18, 44, 56). It is in later tradition, and especially in the *hadith* attributed to Mohammed, that we find a development of descriptions of hell imbued with the extraordinary Arabian capacity to find arresting visual images for scarcely graspable ideas. One *hadith* has Mohammed saying that a stone thrown from the top of hell takes seventy years to reach hell's base, and that the heat of the fires of hell is sixty-nine times greater than the heat required to burn a body on earth.[108] In hell there will be snakes like the necks of Bactrian camels, the poisonous bite of which will hurt for forty years, and scorpions the size of mules.[109] The wicked dead will be resurrected afflicted with physical horrors appropriate to their sins. People who refused to give *zakat* (charity) will be gathered from their graves having stomachs like mountains filled with snakes and scorpions; the envious will arise clad in trousers of tar.[110] The arrogant shall be brought forth in the form of small ants trodden by both the good and the depraved.[111]

One of the special features of the Muslim imagination of the next life is the overwhelming sense of terror of the moment of dying, and a vivid conceiving of the suffering of a damned human being in the very grave itself. This is emotional, but again has that quality of intensely imagined physicality that seems typical of the Arab Muslim tradition. A dead man feels anguish at seeing his body washed and prepared for burial, and may feel pain if the water used is too hot or too cold, or the winding sheet too tight.[112] He hears with grief the footsteps of the mourners as they leave the graveside. The torment of the grave is mostly the consequence of three things: slander, calumny, and not guarding oneself against being soiled with urine. One *hadith* says: "Much of the grave's torment is from urine."[113] Angels will test the soul in its grave, and it will sweat with terror.[114] And at the Last Judgment, as the resurrected dead stand before God, their fear is so intense that they stand in their sweat up to their ankles, hips, even necks.[115] There are two angels who have the task of interrogating the deceased in the grave—Munkar and Nakir. It seems that they play tricks on the dead, sometimes giving a soul the impression that it is damned, only to reassure it a few moments later that it is destined for paradise. The questioning includes interrogation about the good and evil deeds of the deceased—but above all about his Muslim faith: Who is your Lord? What is your faith? Who is your Prophet? Any pious Muslim will know the answers to those questions; God, Islam, Mohammed. If the deceased gives the correct answers, an angel will open a window at the top of the grave, through which he can gaze at the gardens of paradise and feel sweet breezes wafting in.[116]

What I called the sensuous sublimity of the Muslim tradition—the insistence on turning an idea into an impossible but compelling image—shows itself in the Angel of Death (*Izrā'īl*): "He has a thousand wings, stretching from the heavens to the earth, from the farthest point of the east to the farthest point of the west, holding within his hands the entire earth with its mountains, plains and jungles. So huge is he that if all the waters of the oceans and rivers were poured on his head, not a drop would reach the earth.[117] For the faithful his wings spread wide in reception; for the disobedient they become like pincers."[118] So terrifying was *Izrā'īl* when God created him, that all God's angels fell into a swoon for a thousand years. But the Angel of Death also has compassion for the damned. Seeing them, he weeps. Had not Allah prevented his tears, his weeping would have filled the earth, and it would have become like the flood of *Nuh* (Noah) (ibid.).[119]

The same imagination locates the scene of the particular judgment of each dead person in the grave itself. Part of the terror of death is finding oneself sitting up in one's grave facing the interrogation of Munkar and Nakir. Indeed, the torments of the damned seem to be suffered—at the beginning, at least—in the tomb itself. Several stories are told of the Prophet himself passing by the tombs of the damned and becoming aware of their torments. His camel was afraid of going through a cemetery because—as animals can—it heard the shrieks of the damned, which no human being could hear, as it passed their graves. Another story has Mohammed, walking with his friends through a graveyard, and becoming aware that two people buried there were being tormented. So they cut off shoots from a tree and placed one on each grave to cool them off (ibid.).

The sense of guilt over sin also finds a sensuous image. Having faced the two angels, another horror awaits the wicked man: "a man with an ugly face and rotten smell comes to him. He says: 'May Allah recompense you wrong for what you did. By Allah, you were slow to obedience and quick to disobey Allah.' The dead man says: 'Who are you? I have never seen anyone uglier than you in the world!' So he says: 'I am your wicked actions'" (ibid.).

But the image that most vividly captures the Muslim sense of the strait way between salvation and damnation is the bridge (*Sirat*) over which all the dead have to pass. The Qur'an often talks of the "path" or "way" to salvation, and this was turned into an actual bridge over the abyss of hell-flames, a bridge wide and easy for believers to pass over (and they will have the undoubted advantage of being led by the Prophet himself), but sharper than a sword and thinner than a hair for evildoers and infidels. For the wicked the bridge "will shake like a ship on the sea in a tempestuous gale" (ibid., 101). But those who have been obedient and sincere toward God "will pass over it like a flash of lightning or a wind, and will go on" (ibid.).

The Muslim doctrine of hell, then, differs in imaginative construction from that of Christianity, but not in any essential doctrine. True, the Muslim hell (at least in some well-established traditions and in keeping with certain Qur'anic verses) will have Christians and Jews howling in torment (separated from each other in two circles) but that is simply the Muslim version of the Christian dogma: *extra ecclesiam nulla salus*—outside the church there is no salvation. And among Muslims, as among Christians, there have been differing hopes about the proportion of those who will be saved. Although the overwhelming Muslim orthodoxy, supported by several passages of the Qur'an, is that that damned will roast in hell's fires and be scalded by pus and boiling water eternally, there have been some who hoped that the torments of hell would be a purgation, so that all Muslim believers, and perhaps all others as well, as Origen taught, might eventually be saved. According to some *hadith*, Muslims in hell but now repentant will be released from the fire after a thousand years, whence they will be taken to the River of Life, will "bathe in it and come out of it young, beardless, and hairless with kohl on their eyes. Their faces will be like the moon" (ibid., 119–21). However there is no doubt but that Islam as received by the vast majority of believers upholds a doctrine of the eternity of hell's torments that corresponds with that of the severest versions of Christianity.

Muslim tradition has developed one idea that finds no echo in Christianity—the temporary extinction of the entire universe on the Last Day. After the third sounding of the angelic trumpet announcing the end of days, God will seize the seven heavens and the whole of creation, accusing them of having misled man, through their beauty, into forgetting who is truly supreme and beautiful—God alone. At that moment, the universe will go out like a light being turned off, and nothing will be left except God. After this demonstration of the oneness and omnipotence of God, God will bring the universe, with the angels and human souls, back into existence, and time will come to an end with the blessed being ushered into the gardens of paradise, and the damned consigned to hell. The central Muslim insistence that there is none like to God, and that his will is supreme and unsearchable, could hardly find more dramatic expression.

6

Dante: *Inferno*

Aristotle thought that every art, inquiry, and action aimed at some good. Furthermore, all actions, as well as aiming at specific goods— health, wealth, power—aimed at a general human good, which could be seen as the final end of human endeavor. This most general of goods, indeed the supreme good, was happiness, and man achieved that through his possession of the virtues, which can be seen as our rationality being expressed in action. Intelligence—or what Aristotle called *phronesis*, practical wisdom—was necessary for man to achieve the good, along with such virtues as courage, temperance, and justice. Aristotle's chief emphasis was on the life of intelligent action, in which the highest sphere was the political realm, the life of *time*, honor. Yet beyond that—surprisingly, perhaps—he thought that there was a still higher activity—contemplation, which characterized, above all, philosophers, and was godlike. Of all, activities, contemplation was most completely an end in and for itself.

St. Thomas Aquinas adopted Aristotle's account of the human good, in general structure, and in most of its details. He, too, placed emphasis on the active virtues, and he, too, taught that contemplation was the highest expression of the rational soul. But Aquinas believed that the greatest object of man's contemplation was not philosophy or mathematics or science (as Aristotle in effect assumed) but God. Contemplation is not simply godlike, but aims at God. Therefore man's pursuit of the good should naturally rise from the happiness we can achieve in the exercise of the normal human virtues, to a participation in what Christians have called the gifts of the Spirit—the characteristic Christian virtues of humility, meekness, readiness to court suffering, a consuming love of righteousness, compassion for the poor, weak, and suffering, mercy, and purity of heart. These are, indeed, the Beatitudes of the Sermon on the Mount: Blessed are the poor in spirit . . . the meek . . . they that mourn . . . they that hunger and thirst after righteousness . . . the pitiful . . . the pure in heart . . . the peacemakers.

All these gifts of the Spirit imply a rejection of egoism and the lusts that go with egoism—pride, vengeance, an obsession with earthly wealth, honor and power, self-indulgence, hardness of heart.[1] Thomas Aquinas's adapting of Aristotle to Christian tradition provides an intellectual and moral scaffolding to the account of hell, purgatory, and heaven that we find in Dante, who was a master of the thought both of Aristotle and of Aquinas. A guiding principle in Dante's thought, taken from Aquinas, is that sin is the choice of the lesser good over the greater. In surrendering to the lusts of the flesh or disordered passions, in plunging into cruelties, fraud, and injustice, man essentially chooses self over the true good, which is God. The *Inferno* is so structured that as the gravity of the sins increases, so the damned souls are farther and farther from God, who is light and love, and are finally immersed in ice and darkness.

Symbolic Punishments

Dante's vision of the condition of souls in hell, purgatory, and heaven is without doubt the supreme imagining of the afterlife in all literature. Its greatness lies in his ability to find images for what starts from but transcends human experience, and to do so with such emotional and sensuous precision that the *Divine Comedy* is perhaps the greatest example of what Aristotle called a "probable impossibility."[2] The eighteenth-century English writer Jonathan Swift, in his *Gulliver's Travels*, famously created an impossible but probable world. Swift had a visual imagination that strongly resembles Dante's and gives us a sense of the mighty effort with which Dante evokes his heaven, hell, and paradise as regions through which a soul in pilgrimage might imaginably travel. When Gulliver first sees the flying island of Laputa, it is a very hot day, and Laputa comes between him and the sun which "on a sudden . . . became obscured." Gulliver notes that this obscuring of the sun was "in a manner very different from what happens by the interposition of a cloud." He turns around and perceives "a vast opaque body between me and the sun, moving forwards" and notices that the air is not much colder nor the sky more darkened "than if I had stood under the shade of a mountain."[3]

Dante produces just such precise details. The spirits in hell notice that the poet, unlike them, casts a shadow (*Purgatorio*, Canto 3, 88–91, and Canto 5, 4–6). Dante has to board the boat of Phlegyas, preceded by Virgil, who is a shade without solidity, and it is only when he gets in that the boat sinks into the water under his weight (*Inferno*, Canto 8, 27). One of the tormentors in hell, Chiron, is suspicious when he notices that as the pair go past, Dante alone moves things that he touches (ibid., 12, 81). When the poet meets some spirits in the gloom of a low circle of the *Inferno* they knit their brows at him *come'l vecchio sartor fan e la cruna*—"as the old tailor does at the eye of his needle" (ibid., Canto 15, 21).[4] And as Swift uses the physical as a correlate of the spiritual and moral, especially in the voyage to the Houyhnhnms (where depraved humanity is represented by malicious and dirty apelike creatures), so Dante finds precise visual and physical images in the *Inferno* to depict punishments that express the inner nature of the sins for which particular souls are damned.

Far beyond what we find in the *Apocalypse of Peter* or the *Vision of Paul*,[5] and exceeding anything in Lactantius, Tertullian, Origen—or even Augustine—we have in Dante a philosophical structure that is fully worked out and exactly imagined to its smallest details. In the words of T. S. Eliot: "It happened that at Dante's time thought was orderly and strong and beautiful, and that it was concentrated in one man of the greatest genius . . . the thought behind [the *Divine Comedy*] is the thought of a man as great and lovely as Dante himself: St. Thomas."[6] Dante's debt to Thomas Aquinas is evident throughout the *Divine Comedy*.

Unlike (again) the *Apocalypse* or the *Vision*, the *Divine Comedy* depicts someone who is no mere spectator, but also a character in the drama. The poem begins with the poet "midway in the journey of our life"—i.e., the age of thirty-five, which is half the biblical life span—lost in a dark wood, a place of terror such that even now the very thought of it *rinova la paura*—"renews the fear." The commentators tell us that the darkness of the wood comes from "the darkness of ignorance and sin, which blinds us and makes things dark. Ignorance and sin seek darkness, for those who do evil and hate light."[7] Fear "always besets the sinful life and enslaves the sinner."[8] The poet is in fact in danger of damnation through sins that have led him astray from God and the path to salvation. Dante's poem merits just such a density of interpretation, for it exists on several levels. For instance, early in Canto 1 Dante is terrified by three animals that menace him and block his way, a leopard, a lion, and a she-wolf (*Inferno*, Canto 1, 31–54). The three animals stand for worldly sins—the leopard for worldly pleasure, the lion for ambition, and the she-wolf for avarice, cupidity, or concupiscence. They also stand for Florence, the royal house of France, and the Papacy.[9] Such multilayered symbolism pervades the *Commedia*. Fear pervades the *Inferno*, sometimes as a fearful pity for the damned, or a response to the fearful announcement of eternal damnation over hell-gate, and finally horror at the monstrous figure of the gigantic Satan, immersed to his waist in ice, weeping frozen tears at the bottom of the universe.

The Roman poet Virgil appears to Dante and tells him that he will be his guide for the greater part of the way. With Virgil's aid, Dante is to see "the ancient tormented spirits who all bewail the second death" (*Inferno*, Canto 1, 117 [Singleton]). The "second death" refers to two passages from the *Revelation of St. John*: "And death and hell were cast into the lake of fire (*Apocalypse* 20, 14). This is the second death"; and to the fate of murderers, whoremongers, sorcerers, idolaters, and all liars who shall have "their part in the lake that burneth with fire and brimstone: which is the second death" (*Apocalypse* 21, 8). Virgil will also show Dante "those who are content in the fire [i.e., the souls in Purgatory, confident of eventual salvation] because they hope to come among the blessed, whensoever that may be." Dante's last guide, though, in heaven, will not be the pagan Virgil, who sighs in Limbo, but one of the Christian blessed—Beatrice.

One of the recurrent motifs of the *Inferno* is the pity Dante feels (and knows that he will feel) for some, at least, of the damned souls. This is a pity very much sharper than what we saw in the *Vision of Paul*.[10] It is also something for which Dante is rebuked by Virgil.[11] Because of this pity, he sees his journey through the circles of hell as a *Guerra*—a war:

> Lo giorno se n'andava, e l'aere bruno
> toglieva li animai che sono in terra
> da le fatiche loro; e io sol uno
> m'apparecchiava a sostener le guerra
> sì del cammino e sì de la pietate,
> che ritrarrà la mente che non erra.

[Day was departing, and the dark air was taking the creatures on earth from their labors; and I alone was making ready to sustain the strife, both of the journey and of the pity, which unerring memory shall retrace.] (*Inferno* 2 1–6)

By contrast, Beatrice, among the blessed, experiences no pity:

> I' son fatta da Dio, sua mercé, tale,
> che la vostra miseria non mi tange,
> né fiamma d'esto 'ncendio non m'assale.

[I am made such by God, of his grace, that your suffering does not touch me, and no flame of this burning assails me.] (*Inferno* 2, 91–93)

This derives from a passage in Aquinas—*Et ideo beati qui erunt in Gloria nullam compassionem ad damnos habebunt.* [Therefore the blessed who will be in glory will have no pity on the damned.]

With the first spirits that we meet in the *Inferno* we become aware of the principle that Dante calls *contrapasso*[12]—an appropriate retribution for a crime, defined by Aquinas as "equal passion repaid for a previous action; and the expression applied most properly to injurious passions and actions, whereby a man harms the person of his neighbor; for instance, if a man strike, that he be struck back."[13] So among the first of the damned whom the poet encounters are "the sorry souls of those who lived without infamy and without praise." They are mingled with those angels who at the time of Satan's rebellion "were neither rebellious nor faithful to God, but stood apart" [*che non furon ribelli fur fedeli a Dio, ma per sé fuoro*] (*Inferno* 3, 34–36, 38–39). These spirits were rejected by both heaven and hell—they are the lukewarm of whom the *Revelation* says "so then because thou art lukewarm, and neither cold nor hot, I will spue thee out of my mouth" (Rev. 3:16). With utterances of woe, accents of anger, voices shrill and faint they swirl in the air unceasingly *come le rena quando turbo spira*—"like sand when a whirlwind blows." Having no hope of death, these lukewarm envy every other condition.

In Canto 5 the poet encounters two famous, doomed lovers, Paolo and Francesca. The historical Francesca had been unhappily married to an ugly and deformed man, Giancotto, and had fallen in love with her husband's beautiful brother, Paolo. (One version of the story relates that she had actually believed she was marrying Paolo.) This region of hell contains the carnal sinners, and the titanic power of lust is aptly expressed by these sinners being swept about on an infernal hurricane (*bufera infernal*) that "never resting, sweeps along the spirits with its rapine; whirling and smiting, it torments them" (*Inferno* 5, 31–33). Yet Dante subtly modifies the image when he begins to compare the wind-blown spirits with birds: "And as their wings bear the starlings along in the cold season…and as the cranes go chanting their lays, making a long line of themselves in the air, so I saw the shades come, uttering wails" (ibid., 5, 40–48). As the birds both act by instinct yet aim at an end, so lust is natural and at the same time something consented to. The change of feeling continues in the beautiful image of the approach of Paolo and Francesca in response to the summons of the poet: "As doves called by desire, with wings raised and steady, come through the air, borne by their will to their sweet nest, so did these issue from the troop where Dido is, coming to us through the malignant air, such force had my compassionate cry" (ibid., 5, 82–87).

The lustful pair are now amorous turtle doves. Their desire is attractively natural because it is connected with the fidelity even unto death of doves. The lustful are in the second circle, which is the beginning of hell proper. Lust is a yielding to natural desire, and one of the least of the mortal sins. In Dante's scheme by far the gravest sins are those against charity.

Francesca describes their downfall, how they were one day together, without ill intent, reading a romantic novel about the illicit passion of Lancelot for Guinevere. Several times during the reading their eyes met, and their faces became pale, until they came to a place in the story that described how the two lovers had kissed. At that moment, Paolo kissed Francesca on the mouth *tutto tremante*—"all trembling," after which "that day we read no further." Murdered by the jealous husband, their guilty souls fled to hell. On hearing the tragic tale, Dante for pity swoons as if in death and falls as a dead body falls.

The canto dramatically and physically enacts the moral theme. The sinners are shown swept along on the gusts of their carnal passion, and the voice of Francesca gives the reader a sense of the sweetness of carnality. (Francesca's words even now suggest that she had and has no sense that she might have resisted her lust.) The poet is himself caught up in the storm of sensibility as he swoons away at the pitiful spectacle of the weeping lovers. So we both feel the temptation and attractiveness of the sin from the inside, and yet accept an objective judgment, a setting of lust within the greater scheme of things. The inner sweetness of carnality is implicitly judged by its being set in the howling gale that drives the lustful hither and thither. The evil of lust is affirmed as certainly as its attractiveness. This is typical of the *Inferno* as a whole. Sinners ceaselessly and obsessively re-enact their sin, as though being damned is an imprisonment in one's favorite vice, and as though mortal sin itself is an imprisonment.

In the next canto the poet encounters the gluttons. They are constantly flayed by the dog Cerberus. The rage of gluttony is expressed in Cerberus's having three heads, his always craving to devour, and his being satisfied with fistfuls of earth thrown into his three "ravenous gullets"—*bramose canne* (ibid., 6, 27).[14] The gluttons lie, appropriately, in a constant downpour, in mud and filth. An inordinate obsession with eating turns them into simply machines for producing ordure. One of the gluttons, Ciacco, having spoken to the poet, "twisted his straight eyes asquint, looked at me for a moment, then bent his head and fell down with the other blind ones" (*Inferno* 6, 91–93).

The cross-eyed look of Ciacco denotes *hebetudo*—the "dullness of sense in the understanding, on account of the fumes of food disturbing the brain.... Secondly, as regards the appetite, which is disordered in many ways by immoderation in eating and drinking, as though reason were fast asleep at the helm."[15] For Aquinas this dullness of sense is one of the five "daughters of gluttony," the others being "unseemly joy, scurrilousness, dirtiness and loquaciousness."[16]

Aquinas teaches that all mortal sins are sins against charity.[17] Gluttony entails an inordinate desire for the pleasure of food, and hence a falling away from our rational nature. This immersion in the pleasures of food can therefore amount to a turning away from God, who is our ultimate end and the proper, rational object of our love. Pleasure is part of the essence of happiness,[18] but happiness lies in man's fulfillment as a *rational* animal—and not just as an animal. Abandonment to gluttony is against man's rational, hence true, nature, and hence a turning away from man's true end.

The picture of the filthy wallowing of the gluttons dramatizes the following passage in Aquinas: "Dirtiness is chiefly a matter of vomiting, according to Isaiah, *All tables were full of vomit and filth* . . . Ecclesiasticus, *Art thou forced to eat too much? Then sick it up and you will be refreshed.*" Aquinas quotes scripture on "any kind of incontinence resulting in any way from lust." And he invokes St. Gregory: "so long as the vice of gluttony has a hold, all valiant deeds are in forfeit, so long as the belly is not confined, all the virtues are swallowed up."[19] After all, Esau forfeited his birthright for a mess of pottage.[20]

It is noticeable that in describing one of the lesser mortal (or "capital") sins, Dante paints a strikingly repulsive picture. Yet the poet shows compassion even for the gluttons—a compassion that will vanish in the lowest reaches of hell.

In Canto 7 we meet the avaricious, the prodigal, the wrathful, and the sullen. The wrathful are "a muddy people"—*genti fangose*—plunged in a bog "all naked and with looks of rage. They were smiting each other not with hand only, but with head and chest and feet, and tearing each other piecemeal with their teeth" (*Inferno* 7, 110–14). One of them, an "irascible Florentine spirit," called Filippo Argenti, actually bites himself. The wrathful are called dogs ("Away there with the other dogs") because the dog is a wrathful animal.[21] These are people whose souls were overcome by anger.

Aquinas writes of "the sharp-tempered, the sullen-tempered, and the harsh-tempered." The sullen-tempered are implacable and remain angry for a long time.[22] These are important distinctions for Aquinas. For him anger can be righteous—he writes that anger and justice have the same object.[23] This is because "anger . . . seeks evil only by way of just revenge. When the evil inflicted exceeds the measure of justice, according to his estimation, the angry man will relent. Hence . . . the angry man is appeased if many evils befall, whereas the hater is never appeased."[24] The argument is that righteous anger is directed against the other as a person, at some unjust or contemptuous thing he has done. So if the person with whom one is angry apologizes and makes restitution, one's anger is necessarily appeased, one forgives. But someone whose anger is unappeasable is withdrawing human recognition. He becomes fixed in his obsessive wrath, which reveals itself as a deadly hatred. That is why Dante depicts such people as continuing to vent their rage, smiting each other with hand, head, chest, and feet, tearing at each other with their teeth—to all eternity. As always in the *Inferno*, the eternity of punishment is not something simply imposed from the outside: it reflects the nature of the sin itself.

The same applies to the punishment of the sullen—*tristi*. Down under the water "are people who sigh and make it bubble at the surface.... Fixed in the slime they say, 'We were sullen in the sweet air that is gladdened by the sun, bearing within us the sluggish fumes; now we are sullen in the black mire.' This hymn they gurgle in their throats, for they cannot speak it in full words" (*Inferno* 7, 121–26).

The plight of the *tristi* expresses the understanding, richly developed in medieval times, of the deadly sin of sloth—in Latin, *acedia*. It seems that Aquinas and his predecessors had thought a lot about *acedia*—for they write about it like experts. *Acedia*, according to Cassian, "greatly troubles monks at noon. It strikes like a recurring fever; it lays the soul low with sultry fires at regular and fixed intervals."[25] St. John Damascene (quoted by Aquinas) says that *acedia* "is a kind of oppressive sorrow (*tristitia aggravans*) which so depresses a man that he wants to do nothing."[26] *Acedia* is a kind of sorrow over the spiritual good; it shrinks from that good as laborious or irksome to the body.[27] Later, Aquinas quotes Isidore to the effect that despondency (*tristitia*) engenders "spite, pusillanimity, bitterness and despair," while spiritual apathy (*acedia*) engenders "idleness, drowsiness, verbosity, idle curiosity."[28]

For Aquinas, *acedia* is intrinsically joyless, a morbid state of soul. It is a sin against charity, and hence a mortal sin, because it is sorrow over the spiritual good precisely as the divine good. The physical lassitude—torpor—that he associates with sloth, the torpor of those damned souls submerged in the waters of the marsh, is not simply a physical state but brings with it a despairing, joyless, loveless attitude of mind and soul. *Acedia* carrying these meanings survives into much later thought. As *accidie* it becomes a property of the French *symbolistes*, in particular Baudelaire. *Ennui*—one of the sins mentioned in the introduction to *Les Fleurs du Mal* is essentially *accidie* or *acedia*. And in *Fuses* Baudelaire actually writes (quoting both Seneca and St. John Chrysostom) of *l'acedi*, the *maladie des moines*, and of *tedium vitae*—among the sufferers from which he includes Nero.[29]

So *acedia*, far from remaining a purely scholastic idea of not much more than antiquarian interest, has passed via seventeenth- and eighteenth-century ideas of melancholy through Romanticism to *Symbolisme*, to become a cherished late nineteenth- and early twentieth-century allegory of the human condition. Its has developed far beyond what Aquinas and other scholastics envisaged. If they thought of it as a capital sin that merited damnation, the moderns have developed a Romantic and post-Romantic version of it that depicts *poetes maudits*. Baudelaire, as T. S. Eliot discerned, is one of the most notable of them. Eliot described Baudelaire as "man enough for damnation."[30] Much of Eliot's own work, including "The Waste Land," "Mr. Eliot's Sunday

Morning Service," and, especially, "Gerontion" can be seen as explorations of *acedia* and hence of damnation. ("The Love Song of J. Alfred Prufrock," another exploration of *acedia*, is actually prefaced by the words of a damned soul in the *Inferno*.) Sloth as a deadly sin and a constitutive despair becomes in modern times characteristic not simply of individuals but of a civilization; and not only of a civilization but of a culture that values and creates inwardness, self-awareness, self-consciousness—and even the idea of a profound distinction between being saved and being damned.

Over the Styx

Dante and his "master," Virgil, are ferried over the river Styx to lower hell and the City of Dis. Here we are in the sixth circle of the *Inferno* where the sins are much graver, more perverse, and the punishments consequently more terrible. The lustful, the gluttons, the wrathful, and the gloomy-sluggish are not within the City of Dis, the city of Satan himself which occupies the sixth to the ninth circle. Virgil explains to Dante that what God hates is the malice of sin, for malice aims at injustice; and the injustice attained by either violence or fraud is "an evil peculiar to man" (*Inferno* 11, 22–27). Canto 11 is crucial in that it provides a key to the whole scheme of punishments in the *Inferno*—in only forty lines (ibid., 22–66 and 75–111) Virgil explains the whole scheme to Dante.

The sins of the incontinent—the lustful, gluttonous, wrathful, and sullen—are punished in the upper circles of hell because they are not sins that proceed from a full human intention and, for that reason, are not malicious. Sins of malice are punished in the lower circles precisely because they *are* malicious. The malice, for Dante, characteristically takes the form of violence or fraud. Virgil tells the poet that among those in these three circles are the violent. Violence can be offered to God, to one's self, and to one's neighbor. So the first of these three circles torments "all homicides and everyone who smites wrongfully, despoilers and plunderers." A man may "lay violent hands upon himself and upon his own property; and therefore in [the second of the three circles] must everyone repent in vain who deprives himself of your world, gambles away and dissipates his substance, and weeps there where he should be joyous" (ibid., 11, 40–45).

Virgil goes on to explain that violence can also be committed against God "by denying and blaspheming Him in the heart, and despising Nature and her goodness" (ibid., 11, 37–48). Therefore this circle contains sodomites and usurers, as well as heretics and schismatics. He goes on to explain that still deeper within the City of Dis, and approaching the very bottom of hell, are those who practiced fraud. Unlike incontinence, fraud proceeds from an evil will. Fraud destroys the very fabric of human community, and severs the "bond of love which nature makes." Hence hypocrites, flatterers, sorcerers, thieves, and cheats ("barrators")—all examples of fraud—are hideously punished. And the worst example of fraud is treachery, either to the human order, or to God himself.

We can see the coherence and moral plausibility in this, even when it is presented thus abstractly. It comes into its own fully when Dante embodies it in actual examples of sinners and depictions of their punishment.

The poet encounters those who were violent against their neighbors. Their sin is *cieca cupidigia e ira folle*—"blind cupidity and mad rage, which in the brief life so goad us on, and then, in the eternal steep us so bitterly!" (ibid., 12, 49–51). This cupidity and rage is figured strangely like the raging wind that blows the lustful hither and thither, only in this case, instead of a wind, those lost souls who in life were dominated by passions darker than lust are plunged into "a river of blood . . . in which boils everyone who by violence injures others." We encounter Alexander the Great, a tyrant who "took to blood and plunder" (ibid., 12, 105–7) and who produced "a hurricane that swept the whole East in its fury . . . insatiable for human blood . . . always thirsty for fresh slaughter."[31] Alexander is plunged in the "crimson boiling" along with other bloodthirsty tyrants, who are submerged to their eyebrows, "uttering piercing shrieks." On one side, the boiling stream gradually diminishes, until we find ordinary murderers who, their crimes less heinous than those of the tyrants, are plunged in up to their necks only. Virgil, however, tells Dante that in the other direction there is a still deeper reach of the stream where a sinner is plunged in so deep that he cannot be seen. He is Attila the Hun "who was a scourge on earth" (*Inferno* 12, 134).

The violent against others are succeeded by the violent against themselves—those who took their own lives. Dante and Virgil enter a mysterious wood, where there are no green leaves, but only dusky ones, and "no smooth boughs, but gnarled and warped; no fruits were there, but thorns and poison" (ibid., 13, 4–6).[32] This is the sad wood of suicides. Four harpies, which have broad wings, human necks and faces, feet with claws, and great feathered bellies, make their nests "and make lament on the strange trees" of this wood. The poet hears on every side a wailing that seems to come from among the trunks of the trees—as though people are hidden among them. Instructed by Virgil, he breaks a twig off from a great thornbush, at which the stub cries out "Why do you tear me?"—and it becomes dark with blood. A brilliant image follows:

Come d'un stizzo verde ch'arso sia
    da l'un de' capi, che da l'altro geme
    e cigola per vento che va via,
sì de la scheggia rota usciva insieme
    parole e sangue... (*Inferno* 13, 40–44)[33]

[As from a green brand that is burning at one end, and drips from the other, hissing with escaping air, so from that broken twig came out words and blood together.]

This is the spirit of Pier della Vigna, a minister of the Emperor Frederick II, who after falling from power had committed suicide in prison by dashing his brains out against a wall. He tells the poet that his proud mind "in scornful temper, thinking by dying to escape from scorn, made me unjust against my just self" (ibid., 70–72).

These "fierce souls" who had thus uprooted themselves from their bodies are dropped by Minos, judge of the dead, into the seventh circle, falling wherever fortune flings them, where they sprout "like a grain of spelt." They

Dante and Virgil in the Wood of Suicides. Dante Alighieri, *The Divine Comedy*, illustrated by Gustave Doré (London 1874, 1875), *Inferno*, Canto 13, 34.

shoot up wildly, and the harpies come to feed off their leaves, which causes them exquisite pain.

The punishment—the *contrapasso*—for these sinners vividly and precisely expresses the inner evil, the malice of their sin. The imagery perfectly captures the idea of violence against our own bodies, of alienation from them. The self-destroyer treats his body as no more than a thing—and so that is what it becomes, something vegetative, but with human sensations. Not respecting his body, the suicide does not deserve human form. The insensate way in which the harpies feed on these bodies-turned-to-shrubs reflects the attitude these spirits had to their own flesh when they wrought violence upon it. We have to remember that Dante's master, Aquinas, following Aristotle, regarded the human person as a body-soul identity. Hence contempt for the body is contempt for the soul as well. It is contempt for the human person created by God. Because the self-destroyers had shown contempt for their physical selves, their spirits will never share the privilege of being reunited with their bodies at the general resurrection. Instead, "hither we shall drag them, and through the mournful wood our bodies will be hung, each on the thornbush of its nocuous shade" (ibid., 106–8).

The Violent against Nature and Art: Blasphemers, Usurers, Sodomites

The principles set out in Canto 11 explain the damned of the next four cantos—blasphemers, usurers, and sodomites. Force and fraud are the sins most obnoxious to God. Force can involve violence against others, against self, and against God by blaspheming him in the heart, and by denying nature. For Dante, as for Aquinas, homosexuality is a sin against nature; and the *contrapasso* reflects this.[34] Some of these sinners are lying supine and naked on the ground; some sit crouched, while others move about incessantly. They are in a parched, sandy plain in which nothing grows. As they have offended nature, so the plain rejects all natural growth, while "huge flakes of fire" are falling slowly on them "like snow in the mountains without a wind." There is no possibility of repose as these unfortunates use their hands in vain attempts to "beat off fresh burning" (*Inferno* 14, 6–9, 19–24, 28–30, 40–42).

The rain of huge fiery flakes brings to mind the fire and brimstone that annihilated Sodom and Gomorrah. But it also points to the inner nature of the sin of the sodomites. The lust of the incontinent sinners was symbolized in the raging wind that bears them to and fro—a wind, however, that also suggests the sweetness of their sexual desire. Here the flames bring a picture of dry, unappeasable, barren lust. In the next Canto (15) the poet meets "a troop of souls" each of whom "looked at us as men look at one another under a new moon at dusk; and they knit their brows at us as an old tailor does at the eye of his needle" (ibid., 15, 16–21). As we have seen, the image of an old tailor screwing up his eyes to thread his needle caught the attention of T. S. Eliot (for whom Canto 15 was one of the most important moments in the poem) as an example of the extreme sensory precision of the Dantean style. It might even conjure the picture of people on the sexual prowl, ever ready to respond to an answering glance. Indeed, the images of the sodomites are all images of restlessness—they are not allowed to stay still, but must constantly be kept running. They have to keep circling back if they want to keep Dante and Virgil in their view. (They are described in the next canto as "each wheeling [directing] his face on me, so that his neck kept turning in a direction contrary to his feet" (ibid., 16, 24–6)—a way of glancing that Proust took as a signifier of the homosexual.[35]) The carnal sinners, Paolo and Francesca, in Canto 5 had been likened to "doves born by their will to their sweet nest." That is, despite the circumstances and the torment, an image of natural fulfillment and rest. The eternal running about of the sodomites conveys the opposite.

The blasphemers of the previous canto—who are fewer in number than the sodomites—do not move about. They lie supine and are the more tormented. Lying as they do, their faces are turned upward to receive the flakes of fire—the fire of the God they had blasphemed, when by nature they should have worshipped him, and from whom in life they had turned their faces.

Sitting "all crouched up" are the usurers—who have done violence to both nature and art. They sit, defending themselves against the burning flakes as dogs in summer do "now with muzzle, now with paw, when they are bitten by fleas, flies or gadflies" (*Inferno* 17, 47–51). Each of them has a pouch or purse hanging from his neck, on which he seems to "feast his eyes" (ibid., 46–57). In a tradition that goes back to Aristotle,[36] usury is a sin against nature, for the charging of interest—unlike the profits achieved through trade—is money breeding upon itself, hence unnatural. Aristotle's discussion of this curiously resembles the scene in which Dante's usurers are punished. Aristotle had been discussing the acquisition (*chrematistic*) that comes from the fruits of the earth, animals, the retail trade, and household management. This is the context of normal human society and work. Currency came into existence as a means of exchange, whereas usury tries to make money increase as though that were an end in itself. It is like a son unnaturally begotten by a father alone.[37] That is why we have what to the modern mind[38] is a curious yoking together of apparently heterogeneous ideas: blasphemers, sodomites, and usurers. They are all sinners against the natural order, violent against nature and art.

Yet it is here that we see how Dante's allegiance to an objective scheme of moral judgment, one that he and Aquinas see as based on natural law, allows him both to accept wholly God's judgment on sin, and at the same time to show respect for the virtues of the sinner. In Canto 15 (which T. S. Eliot imitates in "Little Gidding") Dante meets a poet whom he terms his "master"—Brunetto Latini, who is among the sodomites. Brunetto, like the others, has to run incessantly. He tells Dante that if any of them was to stop, even for an instant, he would have to lie a hundred years without brushing off the fiery flakes.

Dante and Brunetto engage in conversation, in which Brunetto prophesies glory for Dante. In reply Dante speaks of the "dear, kind, paternal image" of Brunetto that is fixed in his memory and now saddens his heart, an image of one who "when in the world, hour by hour" had taught him "how man makes himself eternal" (*Inferno* 15, 82–85). At the end of this memorable encounter, the incessant running of the sodomites is, in Bruno's case, converted into something heroic, an unending assertion of will—for he becomes like a man running a race: "Then turned he back, and seemed like one of those who run for the green cloth at Verona, and of them he seemed he who wins, not he who loses" (ibid., 121–24).

The Frozen World: Cocytus

Finally, Dante and Virgil arrive in the ninth circle, the realm of the frozen river, Cocytus, a place of eternal cold. It is often assumed that the Ptolemaic picture of the universe, in which sun and planets circle the earth, exalts man and his world by placing them at the center of things. Yet you can also see Dante's earth as being at the bottom of the universe, at the furthest remove from God. And the center of the earth, where the lowest hell is, is at the uttermost remove from divine light and the source of warmth. It is a place of punishment for traitors and is divided into four rings. First, there are those who (like Cain, from whom one of the rings, *Caina*, is named) slew their own kindred. Next is the ring for those who were traitors to their country; then, traitors to their friends or guests; finally, traitors to their lords and benefactors. As the crimes increase in heinousness, so the criminals are plunged ever deeper in the ice, until eventually the poet treads above those sunk and fixed completely, like straw in glass (ibid., 34, 12). The symbolism of this immersion in ice—an image of the final egoism and hardness of heart—needs no gloss. The malice of these traitors reveals the final extinction of charity, which participates in the warmth of the divine love. This ultimate human depravity is a sheer coldness. Franklin Delano Roosevelt, in a speech delivered in 1936, used the idea excellently: "Men may err, governments may make mistakes, but the immortal Dante assures us[39] that the eternal justice weighs the sins of the hot-blooded and the cold-hearted

Dante and Virgil with the sinners in lowest Hell. *The Divine Comedy*, illustrated by Gustave Doré (London 1874, 1875), *Inferno*, Canto 32, 20–22.

in different scales." Roosevelt went on to accuse his opponents of being "frozen in the ice of their own indifference."

At the very center of this "dolorous realm" stands the great traitor, Satan himself, gigantic, up to his chest in ice, with three heads, six eyes weeping frozen tears, impotently flapping his six huge batlike wings and producing thereby a wind *quindi Cocito tutto s'aggelava*—("whereby all Cocytus was congealed" [*Inferno* 34, 52]). Each of the mouths of Satan champs a sinner, skinning him constantly with his teeth. The sinner whose head is inside the central mouth, while his legs dangle outside, is Judas Iscariot. The other two, whose heads hang down outside—and whose torture is therefore slightly less severe—are Brutus and Cassius. The three represent treason against lords and benefactors—against Jesus Christ (and therefore God) and against Julius Caesar (who had forgiven Brutus and Cassius their previous enmity and received them into friendship) and hence against the Roman Empire, which for Dante had a divine sanction.

Dante has used the picture in Aristotle and Aquinas of the rational good for man to depict degrees of wickedness. To move away from God is to deny our rational nature, and to prefer ends that take us away from ourselves and any source of joy. At no point do we feel that the punishments of the damned are simply inflicted by God as a punishment. Rather they seem a doom eternally embraced by the sinners. A Dante scholar writes of a "quite simple student" of his who exclaimed with a certain bewilderment of the souls in hell, "But they don't seem to *want* to get out." That is quite true. They are the same in death as in life, and the ultimate aim of the preferences that had hardened in them in life is now hideously apparent.

Eternity

Origen had argued that God's punishment by fire of sinners in hell is a way of purging and healing. Fire cauterizes the sick soul. Therefore punishment, having such an end in view, cannot be everlasting. Origen sees infernal punishment as something aimed at sinners as free agents, which brings home to them the reality of their sin and gives them an opportunity and motive to repent, and choose freely the good over the evil.

This is plainly not the vision we find in Dante. Dante's lost souls certainly are punished eternally. Yet such a bald statement does not quite catch the retributive scheme of the *Inferno*. It is certainly true that God is the author of their sufferings, since he created hell and maintains it in existence. Here, though, we remember the astonishing paradox contained in the inscription over hell gate:

GIUSTIZIA MOSSE IL MIO ALTO FATTORE;

FECEMI LA DIVINE PODESTATE,

LA SOMMA SAPÏENZA E 'L PRIMO AMORE. (Canto 3, 4–6)

[Justice moved my high maker, the divine power made me, the highest wisdom and *the primal love*.]

Dante's hell is to express all these divine attributes—even love. To understand that, we have at least to find a way in which the eternity of punishment is not something merely cruel or unintelligible—as Origen thinks it must be. Given that it is easy to see how the specific punishments symbolize the inner nature of each particular sin, can we connect that with the fact that the punishments are everlasting? Is there, perhaps, something characteristically —even necessarily—obsessional, repetitive, or psychologically imprisoning about capital sins and the states of character to which they give rise?

Take the sullen (*tristi*) bubbling eternally immersed in the water of their marsh. Sloth (*acedia*) is a "mortal" or capital sin because it kills the soul by cutting it off from divine grace. Its deadly quality lies in its shrinking from the spiritual good in general and giving rise to (for instance) "idleness, drowsiness, verbosity, idle curiosity." These vices pretty much incapacitate any human being from engaging in serious enterprises, undertaking anything strenuous—or, as the Ancients would put it, anything noble.[40] Idle curiosity betokens a failure actively to impose a pattern on what one knows or experiences; it is the opposite of intellectual boldness. Verbosity dissipates rather than concentrates. Drowsiness can be thought of as a shrinking from the world. If it is true (as Isidore, quoted by Aquinas puts it[41]) that despondency (*tristitia*) engenders "spite, pusillanimity, bitterness and despair," then these two lists give us a picture of human beings comprehensively incapacitated for life.

We might understand people in this predicament as suffering from psychological illness. Medieval people thought rather in categories of moral character. The two ways of thinking are not so sharply distinct, and it is not obvious that to prefer to think in medical terms is any more than that—a preference.

There are surely states of character—what Aristotle and Aquinas would regard as vicious states—to sink into which is to become dominated by patterns of thought and feeling from which it is practically impossible to escape. It may not even be possible to want to escape, to have any idea of escape because the mind and will have become darkened. Dante, following his philosophical masters, depicts sloth or *acedia* as torpor, despair, bitterness. This is precisely a state of mind that would lead us to envy the good of others, pity ourselves, shrink from any effort to save ourselves, indeed from all serious effort. We can think of such a state of mind as feeding upon itself, reinforcing itself, finding always more excuses not to confront the truth of its own condition. This is a mental state that of its nature goes on indefinitely, engulfs one more and more. Despair is its natural end. This is why, for Dante, the sins that constitute these mental states are so terrible and damnable. They are a way of going on digging deeper the hole in which one finds oneself.

In enforcing so sharply the difference between vice and virtue, the moral psychology of Aristotle and Aquinas is describing something dynamic. The virtues and vices promote different patterns of behavior. The virtues are active in a special way: they tend to integration of character. They open a person to the world. Aristotle had held that "most like the truest courage" was the courage of the citizen soldier, voluntarily fighting for his city, facing death on the battlefield, acting under orders and out of a desire for honor and fear of reproach.[42] This may seem strange to us, but it has a rationale. It enmeshes the citizen soldier in a rich context of values. The citizen soldier—who is a volunteer—is loyal to his city and intends to put his loyalty into action. ("Greater love hath no man than this, that a man lay down his life for his friends" [John 15:13].) He fears reproach because he truly accepts the obligation of being brave, which arises from the obligation of being patriotic. To be honored is to get respect because one is a true member of a political community. One's life does not exist on a purely individualistic, selfish level, but reaches out to the good of one's fellow citizens. To be attached by love and honor to one's city and one's fellow citizens is honorable— indeed it is the most honorable thing a man can aspire to.

The vices are characteristically a lapsing from rationally active awareness into fantasy, willfulness, unfocused restlessness, inactivity. Courage in its truest expression has to overcome obstacles in aiming at the good—obstacles of fear, self-regard, smallness of mind. The courageous man sees things differently from the way in which the coward sees them. He does not blindly panic but sees what can be done, what must be done, what honorably ought to be done. Aristotle expressed this by saying that his courage involves *phronesis*, or practical wisdom, and also justice. To be able to see in the way the brave man sees is to have a character that is open to experience, organizes experience, is active both intellectually and emotionally. We can think of people as hopelessly sunk in sloth, or lust, or self-pity, or passively negligent of the common good. We cannot think analogously of the *temptation* to lapse into courage, or into practical wisdom or justice. These are by their nature active and integrative dispositions. The virtues, as Aristotle and Aquinas see them, come together to produce people who are free rather than enslaved, who choose what we all can choose if we have minds undarkened by sloth, egoism, and other vices—a growing picture of the human good. So a virtuous character involves a constant effort of liberation from those obsessive yet passive states that Dante depicts as the character, and hence the punishments of the damned.

This gives us insight into the sins of the violent and treacherous. The image of a river of boiling blood into which savage murderers are plunged is an image of an appalling temptation to which any human being might succumb. It indeed requires religious belief and a theological opinion. We tend to see murderers as special sorts of people, people with an abnormal psychology. They are psychopaths, for example. But for Dante, to yield to the impulse to murder is to succumb to a temptation that does not set us apart from but shows us as typical of the common run of human beings. The first murder is recorded in Genesis 4 and springs from wounded *amour propre*. The tyrant who—like Dante's Alexander the Great—murders and pillages, is not a freak or mentally ill. He is simply someone in a position to do what any of us, if not restrained by moral education and virtuous dispositions, would do, given the opportunity. As it is, most of us commit smaller evils, our "crimes confined, / Forbade to wade through slaughter to a throne, / And shut the gates of mercy on mankind" (Gray, "Elegy Written in a Country Churchyard"). The temptation is a terrible one precisely because in yielding to it, we become enslaved by it.

The scheme of the *Inferno* does provide something of an answer to Origen's claim that eternal punishment makes no sense and cannot possibly be just. The punishments make real the sins they penalize. The sinners obsessively re-enact their past, and they do so not just because God has doomed them to do just this, but also because this obsessiveness and inability to turn back is seen as in the nature of evil. They suffer, therefore, a genuine punishment rather than simply a torment. It is true that Dante subscribes to the theological opinion that after death the will of the sinner—or the saint—is fixed for ever. To hold to that with the security he does indeed requires theological belief. Yet the picture of virtue and vice that he draws from Aristotle and Aquinas at least gives the scheme of punishments an essential plausibility. The same picture will give Dante an equally sure compass as he navigates purgatory and heaven.

7

Predestination: Augustine to Calvin and Beyond

Augustine against the Pelagians

We have seen that in the earliest Christian texts there can be found the suggestion that souls may be saved and damned purely by the will of God alone: "Therefore hath he mercy on whom he will have mercy, and whom he will he hardeneth" (Rom. 9:18). Jesus, also, in the parable of the man who has sown weeds in another man's wheatfield, implies that from birth we are either good or bad seeds. The good seed "are the children of the kingdom; but the tares [i.e., weeds] are the children of the wicked one" (Matt. 13:38), Yet this must be set against the many sayings of Jesus that call on men voluntarily to repent for "the kingdom of heaven is at hand." Indeed, in the very same chapter where Jesus explains the parable of the sower, there is a version of the parable that clearly implies that to accept or reject faith in the word is indeed voluntary. A sower went forth to sow, and some seeds fell by the wayside, and were eaten by birds; others fell on stony places, sprang up quickly but were soon scorched by the sun and died; others fell among thorns, which choked them; but others fell on good ground, and brought forth fruit "some an hundredfold, some sixtyfold, some thirtyfold" (Matt. 13:3–8).

The explanation Jesus gives of this parable is that the seed which fell in stony places is the word of God heard joyfully, but not fully rooted in the affections of the person that hears it, so that when any persecution or tribulation arises, he does not persevere. The seed fallen among thorns is the word received by someone who allows the cares of the world and the deceitfulness of riches to choke his faith. The good ground receiving the seed "is he that heareth the word, and understandeth it" (Matt. 13:8, 23).

Whether one's acceptance of Jesus and his message is voluntary or not is obviously of momentous significance, for the weeds will be gathered together in bundles to be burned, while the wheat will be gathered together in his barn. And "so shall it be in the end of the world."

> The Son of man shall send forth his angels, and they shall gather out
> of his kingdom all things that offend and them which do
> iniquity;
> And shall cast them into a furnace of fire: there shall be wailing and
> gnashing of teeth.
> Then shall the righteous shine forth as the sun in the kingdom of
> their father. (Matt. 13: 30, 40–43)

From the earliest times, therefore, there has been an apparent contradiction in the Christian promise, between salvation offered to all who will repent and hear the word of God, and a salvation and damnation that has been decreed for every individual by God's will alone, regardless of what he actually does in life. Are we free to accept or reject God's word and his grace, or is our eternal future eternally predetermined? To resolve this question has been the preoccupation of some of the greatest thinkers in the history of the church; and a determination to end uncertainty about it once and for all was the spirit that above all brought about the Protestant Reformation.

The Christian thinker who first made a systematic attempt to impose upon the church a doctrine of predestination was Augustine of Hippo (354–430). His ultimate disciple, equaling if not exceeding Augustine in logical rigor was John Calvin. Augustine's doctrines of original sin and the consequent depravity of human nature, of the absolute necessity of God's grace in procuring man's salvation, and above all his unrelenting insistence upon a doctrine of predestination have indelibly marked all subsequent theology. Augustine was the greatest single influence on Calvin, whose own account of predestination molded and terrified millions through the Protestant centuries. The Augustinian understanding of human depravity has continued to inform our understanding of human psychology even in a post-Christian era.

Augustine's whole career was a mixture of searching and polemics. When he achieved certainty within the fold of the church, he turned with ferocious indignation on the beliefs he had earlier embraced. In his youth, despite having Catholic parents, he had attached himself to the Manichean heresy for nine years, before converting to the Catholic faith. The Manicheans believed that the whole universe reflected a primeval struggle between light and darkness, the good and evil principles. Salvation could come only by a release from this world and by a state of perfection achieved through a life of extreme asceticism.

A chief text for the Manicheans was the saying of Jesus: "A good tree cannot bear bad fruit, nor can a bad tree bear good fruit" (Matt. 7:18). This was interpreted to mean that from a good will no evil can come forth, nor any good from an evil will. Therefore evils come from evil natures, and goods from good natures. Everything God makes is good, including the human will before the Fall, and therefore evil must come from something not made by God, but at war with God—an evil principle, such as a Satan-figure who would be co-eternal with God.[1]

The answer to this by orthodox Catholic thinkers, including Augustine, was (in brief) that evil could indeed arise from what was originally good—original human nature—when the human will turned or fell from God, turning toward itself, thus depriving itself of possession of the highest good, which is God. Evil, therefore, is a privation of good, rather than something that has a positive existence in itself.[2] (This doctrine will allow for the thinnest of partitions dividing Augustine from his even more radical disciple, Calvin.)

Even after Augustine was converted to orthodox Catholicism (an orthodoxy in the shaping of which his own ideas had a powerful influence) the psychology of Manicheanism still colored his thought. That, at any rate, was what some of his enemies alleged against him.

Augustine faced and tried to give a consistent answer to the fundamental question of Christianity: Why did Christ live, suffer, and die at all? Was it to save us all from eternal damnation, and open the gates of heaven to all mankind? If Christ's death was necessary for the salvation of sinners, was this simply because he presented a model of holiness and perfection, which might inspire us to follow his example, to imitate his virtues—as people might aspire to follow the example of Buddha, or of Socrates? If that were so, then Christ's life and death was not in itself either necessary or sufficient for salvation—for it could be seen simply as encouraging the rest of us to live better, more perfect lives, with the implication that to do so is within our own power. Much in the gospel writings would allow us to see Jesus as essentially an inspiring exemplar, a shiningly good man whose life we should strive to imitate, and whose death would have been simply a tragedy but for the resurrection. It was Paul who made Christ's death an essential part of the scheme of salvation and saw the merits of this death as being applied to sinners simply through the decision of God. This is the doctrine of the *atonement*—implied in words ascribed to Christ himself in several Gospel texts[3]—that the merits of Christ's sacrificial death are applied to sinful human beings so as to lift from them, through no merit of their own, the burden of depravity and the sentence of eternal damnation.

The doctrine that it is within our own power to follow Christ, and therefore to move voluntarily toward salvation, was one that Augustine spent much of his life combating. It is called Pelagianism and is the only great British contribution to Christian heresy.

Pelagius was a British monk who taught at Rome in the late fourth and early fifth centuries. He seems to have been a cultivated, charming, and pious man. He opposed the grim view of the world entailed by Manicheanism, and stressed man's power to be virtuous, and even to achieve salvation through the free exercise of his will. Pelagius rejected any doctrine of original sin. Indeed, he argued that to insist on the depravity of human nature, on man's inability through his own efforts to avoid sin, was to make God responsible for the sins of mankind. God had created human nature, and if after the Fall men are born so radically defective, they cannot be blamed for their iniquities.

The vast majority of Christians—at least, in the West—are now Pelagians without knowing it. The changes of liturgical forms and words in many of the churches reflect a systematic downplaying of any idea of essential, inherited human depravity, and of the powerlessness of human beings to achieve anything good of their own efforts—"there is no health in us."[4] In effect they attenuate the fear of hell that has been central to Christian practice throughout the centuries. Augustine thought that Pelagianism was perhaps the most deadly of all heresies precisely in that it reduced Christ to a role model, and denied that his death had of itself atoned for the sin of Adam; that faith in Christ was sufficient for salvation and that such faith was a free and unmerited gift of God; and that human beings could not, through their own unaided efforts do anything to overcome the power of sin. Augustine was convinced that it was only those very doctrines, which the Pelagians denied, that could explain how Christianity was unique, and why *extra ecclesiam nulla salus* [outside the church there is no salvation].

In all this Augustine was consciously following Paul. The Pelagians were held to deny the Christian teaching that the world since Adam's death had been involved in a calamity, which included physical death itself: "In the sweat of thy face shalt thou eat bread, till thou return unto the ground; for out of it wast thou taken: for dust thou art, and unto dust shalt thou return" (Gen. 3:19). Paul taught that it was because of the sin of Adam that we all die (Rom. 8:10, 11; 1 Cor. 15:22). To the Pelagians, death was simply part of nature—not at all a punishment for sin. Adam would have died in the course of nature, even had he not sinned. Adam's sin harms man simply because it gave a bad example, which we are tempted to imitate, another conclusion rejected by Paul (Rom. 5:12–21).

The Pelagians were, in effect, humanists and sprang from a great pagan tradition. Aristotle, for instance, had seen moral education as the perfecting of what is inherent in man's nature. Virtues such as courage, temperance and practical wisdom could be taught, and they usually involved our preserving the role of reason as ruler over the passions and appetites. The virtuous person was someone in whom the natural human capacities had been educated into a harmony one with another. To be truly brave goes with being also just and practically wise—otherwise courage might be no more than a reckless bullying. The temperate person pursued the higher and more rational human pleasures over simple animal satisfactions. But virtuous people did not overcome or suppress human nature. Rather they found the best way of subordinating the passions and appetites to reason, hence bringing them into the happy life of a rational animal. For Aristotle, then, human beings need moral education to perfect themselves and are subject to the temptation to fall away from rational living. But human nature as such is certainly not depraved.

The Pelagians held some ideas in common with Aristotle. He did not think of the passions and appetites as evil—simply that they needed to be ordered by reason. Within a harmonious human personality the passions and appetites are actually good. The anger of those who are brave and just is something noble. A chief claim of the Pelagians, similarly, was that human passions and appetites, are not *in themselves* evil—it depends what one does with them. In themselves they are neutral. They become evil only if evilly used. The sexual instinct is natural and to that extent good. Within the context of marriage, sexual desire is good. It becomes evil only if wrongly used.[5]

Augustine assaults Pelagianism root and branch. Our passions and appetites cannot be looked on as neutral, for they are in revolt against the good. They express the whole of man's nature as it seeks self rather than the external, objective good which is God. Man's passions from their very birth—at least since the Fall—are filled with his perverse will. They are therefore evil in themselves in that they are infected by the evil of the human will. Hence what is evil in man is not just the appetites and passions when they rebel against reason, but the human heart itself in its perversity: "The heart is deceitful above all things and desperately wicked: who can know it?" (Jer. 17:9).[6] Man is thoroughly depraved; he cannot even genuinely desire the good. Fallen human nature cannot of itself perform any good act. God's grace is required. Without the free gift of grace we are all headed to perdition.

How does Augustine *know* that we are depraved, utterly incapable of doing anything on our own to achieve the good? How does he know that we all inherit the sin of Adam, that we are born tainted with original sin, so that we are incapable of doing the right without the assistance of God, and hence damned to all eternity?

In the first place he knows it from revelation. Paul writes that human beings can never be justified by works, but only by faith (Rom. 3:27–28). It was Paul who introduced the idea of our inheritance of some original sin to atone for which Christ's suffering and death were necessary. It follows from Paul's teaching that we can achieve nothing good except by having righteousness imputed to us through Christ's sacrifice—and that, therefore, we are depraved. The Pelagians denied, in effect, that we can find convincing evidence of this depravity in human experience. Can Augustine?

In his *Confessions* Augustine does find evidence of an inherent perversity from his own infancy. It is rooted in willfulness—a willfulness that is to be found even in the baby at its mother's breast: "what then were my sins at that age? That I wailed too fiercely for the breast? For if today I were to make as gluttonously and as clamorously, not of course for my mother's breasts, but for the food I now eat, I should be ridiculed and quite properly condemned. This means that what I did then was reprehensible, although since I could not understand words of blame, neither custom nor common sense allowed me to be blamed. . . . [Yet] surely it was not good, even for that time of life, to scream for things that would have been thoroughly bad for me; to fly into a hot rage because older persons—and free, not slaves—were not obedient to me; to strike out as hard as I could with sheer will to hurt, at my parents . . . for not yielding to my demands" (Augustine, *Confessions*, bk. 1, chap. 7). Every infant is born "wrapped . . . in the hereditary rags of his vitiated origin" (*Against Julian* 2, 6 (15), 76). All children are born into death unless they are reborn through Christian baptism.

Augustine takes as another proof of original sin that infants are often born physically diseased or maimed—"sometimes born blind; sometimes deaf . . . sometimes . . . feeble-minded." This shows that they are conceived and brought forth under the power of the devil (ibid., 2, 4–5, 114–17).

For Augustine, the innocence of children is not a quality of their minds, but lies simply in the helplessness of their bodies. The true horror of infantile willfulness would come out if a grown man—perhaps a man with worldly power—had the unchastened will of an infant. He would be a terrifying monster—a Caligula, a Hitler, or an Idi Amin. Even before the use of reason, infants can show what is monstrous in human nature: "I have myself seen a small baby jealous; it was too young to speak, but it was livid with anger as it watched another infant at the breast" (*Confessions*, bk. 1, chap. 7). (Interestingly, Augustine does not say that the jealousy arises from the infant's feeling excluded from the breast of its own mother. It is possible that he is describing sheer motiveless malignity—envy toward another infant at the breast of *its* own mother.)

What Augustine is describing is the titanic willfulness of the infant, a willfulness that gets its satisfaction in opposing the will of another, or bending the will of another to its own, or simply wishing to obstruct another's satisfaction. Or it may express itself by lusting after what is forbidden simply because it is forbidden. Augustine famously tells the story of his theft, in adolescence, of some pears: "I stole things which I already had in plenty and of better quality. Nor had I any desire to enjoy the things I stole, but only the stealing of them and the sin. There was a pear tree near our vineyard, heavy with fruit, but fruit that was not particularly tempting either to look at or to taste. A group of young blackguards, and I among them, went out to knock down the pears and carry them off late one night. . . . We carried off an immense load of pears, not to eat—for we barely tasted them before throwing them to the hogs. Our only pleasure in doing it was that it was forbidden. . . . The malice of the act was base and I loved it . . . I loved . . . simply the evil" (*Confessions*, bk. 2, chap. 4).

But the place where Augustine most urgently—one might say, obsessively—finds evidence of inborn depravity is human sexuality. Augustine wrote extensively on Christian marriage and was profoundly influenced by the constant early Christian tradition that voluntary celibacy is a higher state than wedlock. His fundamental assumption is that sexual desire—concupiscence—within marriage, let alone outside it, is a pardonable fault at best, and at worst the equivalent of adultery within the marriage bed itself. By concupiscence in marriage, a husband is "the adulterer of his own wife."[7] One proof he gives of this is our sense of shame, which came with the Fall. When Adam and Eve had eaten of the apple "the eyes of them both were opened, and they knew that they were naked" (Gen. 3:7). For Augustine, we have to understand the new knowledge that came to them as their "perceiving and recognizing the new state which had befallen their body" (*On Marriage and Concupiscence*, bk. 1, chap. 6, 266). This new state was sexual desire. Man's disobedience to God in eating the apple is punished by the new phenomenon of the disobedience of his own flesh to himself. This was the opening of Adam and Eve's eyes. After the Fall, the genitals refuse to obey the human will:

> Well, then, how significant is the fact that the eyes, and lips, and
> tongue, the hands, and feet, and the bending of the back, and neck,
> and sides, are all placed within our power—to be applied to such
> operations as are suitable to them, when we have a body free from
> impediments and in a sound state of health; but when it must come to
> man's great function of the procreation of children, the members
> which were expressly created for this purpose will not obey the
> direction of the will, but lust has to be waited for to set these members

in motion, as if it had legal right over them, and sometimes refuses to act when the mind wills, while often it acts against its will. Must not this bring a blush of shame over the freedom of the human will, that by its contempt of God, its own Commander, it has lost all proper command for itself over its own members? (Ibid.)

It is not only this "shameless novelty"[8] of the unwilled stirring of the sexual parts that reveals the shamefulness of lust or concupiscence, but also the fact that parents seek to hide their sexual activities from their children, that privacy is typically sought for in sex, and that human beings cover their private parts. Even wet dreams reveal the taint that comes from original sin (*Against Julian*, bk. 4, chap. 2, 10, [174]; *Confessions*, bk. 10, chap. 30, 190–91). In Paradise human beings would have copulated in a purely willed way, without lust (*Against Julian*, bk. 4, chap. 11, 57, [215]). The best that can be said for marriage is that it is better than fornication, although inferior to consecrated celibacy (*On Marriage and Concupiscence*, 1, 15, 271); but it would be better still if the sole justifying purpose of marriage and the sexual act—procreation—could be performed without any sexual desire at all. Jesus is born sinless just because he was conceived without carnal intercourse between two human beings and born of a virgin (*Against Julian*, bk. 2, chap. 2, 58).

The inheritance of original sin is, for Augustine, bound up with sexuality, as it is in Genesis, when Adam and Eve, having eaten of the forbidden fruit, realize for the first time that they are naked. The offspring of human copulation are the children of perdition, the sons and daughters of wrath. Augustine quotes a psalm: "He sent upon them the wrath of his indignation; indignation and wrath through evil angels" (Ps. 78:49). He quotes with approval a remark of Cicero's that many infants are possessed by devils (*Against Julian*, bk. 6, chap. 21, 67, [379]). It is through sexual desire that original sin is transmitted (*On Marriage and Concupiscence*, bk. 1, 24). Sexual desire without the immediate intention of procreation can just be tolerated in marriage as a venial sin when it is not too powerful, but only lest the devil tempt couples to be incontinent outside the marriage bed (ibid., bk. 1, chap. 16).

In *Paradise Lost* Milton represents Adam and Eve after they have eaten the apple as passing from an innocent, if enthusiastic desire for each other to blamable sensual connoisseurship:

> But come, so well refresht, now let us play,
> As meet is, after such delicious Fare;
> For never did thy Beautie since the day
> I saw thee first and wedded thee, adornd
> With all perfections, so enflame my sense

> With ardor to enjoy thee, fairer now
> Then ever, bountie of this vertuous Tree.[9]

Lust came into marriage only after the Fall. When it did, it brought with it the embarrassment of periods and the pains of childbirth. There would otherwise have been no female orgasms in response to virile male activity—that is to say, virgins would not have been excited to conceive "by the force of turbid heat" but would rather have been "submissive to the power of the gentlest love " (*On Marriage and Concupiscence*, bk. 2, chap 41). (We also would have had no fear of animals—which were, presumably, noncarnivorous. In proof of that, Augustine quotes St. John Chrysostom's contention that if man had been afraid of beasts in the garden of Eden, Eve would have run away from the serpent rather than stopping and talking to it.[10] The results would have been better, of course.) In our fallen state, it is only conjugal modesty that makes sexual activity morally bearable at all (*Against Julian*, bk. 4, chap. 6, 36, [200]). Perhaps in Paradise we were able to come together purely to beget offspring, like birds, or to procreate without any copulation at all—like honeybees (*Good of Marriage.* bk. 1, chap. 2, 2, and *On Marriage and Concupiscence*, bk. 1, chap. 5).

Augustine writes as though he finds sexual desire to be the area of human life where original sin most vividly manifests itself. This is strange and does not seem warranted by his general argument. For the real evil of concupiscence is that it is an example of the flesh warring against the spirit. He writes that the activity of the male member before the Fall did not cause shame "because it was moved only by the command of the will" (*Against Julian*, bk. 4, chap. 13, 62, [219–20]). But this war between flesh and spirit shows itself in many areas of human life. Augustine thinks it a sin if we take too much pleasure in eating. Indeed, he comes close to suggesting that any sensual delight in food at all is sinful: "What sober man would not prefer to take food . . . without any stinging carnal pleasure, if he could, as the air he draws in and lets out . . . This food, consumed continually through mouth and nose, neither tastes nor smells, yet we cannot live without it even the shortest time, whereas we can live a very long time without meat and drink" (ibid., bk. 4, chap. 14, 68, [225]). He even quotes, with semi-approval, "some writers on scripture" who think that in Paradise human beings did not need food at all, and that "only such nourishment as delights and sustains the hearts of the wise" would have existed there. (Given that it was a widespread opinion among the Fathers of the church that Adam and Eve were actually in Paradise for only a few hours before they sinned, this does not seem an hypothesis that could easily be tested.)

The point is that human nature is depraved throughout. Natural man is sinful through and through, and it is only when human nature is suffused with

God's grace that there is any good in it at all. The coming of Christ and his grace has made all the difference. Since Christ it is definitely better to remain celibate than to marry—even than to have a continent (i.e., nonlustful) marriage (*On Marriage and Concupiscence*, bk. 1, chap. 14). Those who do not believe in Christ are incapable of doing anything truly good, however hard they try and however noble their motives may seem to be. Augustine attacks Julian of Eclanum, a follower Pelagius, for lack of rigor on just this point: "You say: 'If a Gentile clothe a naked man, is it a sin because it is not done by faith?' Insofar as it is not done by faith it is truly a sin—not that the thing done, clothing the naked, is a sin in itself; but only an ungodly man denies that it is sin not to give glory to the Lord in such a work" (*Against Julian*. bk. 4, chap. 3, 30, [194]).

Not only can no purely human motives make an act good—they bring in sin. Even mercy dictated simply by a merciful will can be evil—a mercy that simply is motivated by sympathy or pity (ibid., 31, [195–96]). If unbelievers do manage to do good works, these are not really their works but those of God who decides to use them. Their sins, on the other hand, are theirs alone (ibid.). Good works, without faith, are not truly good.

We might say that although for Augustine human depravity is a universal fact, it shows itself dramatically in certain phenomena—such as sex and the malice of babies. But in the case of a high-minded pagan who clothes the naked, visits the imprisoned, and performs other corporal works of mercy, Augustine does not seem to think it necessary to look for *evidence* at all. Indeed, he seems even to rejoice in the fact that on the surface the behavior of honorable unbelievers looks as though it is inspired by the highest motives. It is only by revelation that we know it to be worthless. It is through revelation that we know that the high-minded pagan—all high-minded pagans throughout the ages, indeed all non-Christians—are damned. So why should we place so much weight on the evidence of depravity as it is found in human sexuality? It is as though he thinks that we know when the flesh wars against the spirit when we see it palpably doing so—but if all human actions are without merit when carried out without faith, how can some be more palpably worthless than others?

The doctrine of original sin is meant to explain how the whole world is involved in catastrophe and suffering. It is a world ruled by Satan, a world disordered and chaotic. This reflects Augustine's inheritance from both Plato and the Manicheans—the sense of the actual world as a damaged or inferior version of something better and more real.

These beliefs in man's depravity and need of grace, added to the picture of nature itself as damaged beyond repair, are the background to the doctrine of predestination. Augustine meditates on the scriptural texts that suggest that

God has from all eternity chosen some for perdition and some for salvation, with unprecedented intellectual rigor and passion. This intellectual rigor brings to the surface as plainly as possible the central difficulty of predestination. If man is profoundly depraved, capable of doing nothing good for himself but dependent entirely on the grace of God so that only those freely chosen by God can be saved, the obvious question arises: Why should God extend his grace to some and not to others? For Augustine, as for Paul, faith is essential to salvation. But faith is itself a free gift of God. Augustine is absolutely certain that the choice of believing does not lie in the human will "because in the Elect the will is prepared by the Lord" (*On the Predestination of Saints*, chap. 10). This choice by God—this "election"—has nothing to do with human merits (ibid., chap. 11). and there can be no explanation in human terms why some are given faith, and hence rescued from eternal damnation, while others are lost, except simply that it *is* God's will: "For it is better in this case for us to hear or to say, "'O man, who art thou that repliest against God?' than to dare to speak as if we could know what he has chosen to keep secret" (ibid., chap. 16, quoting Rom. 9:20).

Augustine's ultimate argument for denying that God's arbitrary choice of one human being for salvation and another for damnation is wickedly unjust is indeed based on his doctrine of original sin. Since all of us, from our inheritance of the sin of Adam, are guilty, none of us *deserves* or *merits* salvation, whatever we do. What God is doing is according mercy to some guilty people and withholding mercy from others. But he has no obligation in justice to spare any at all—his doing so even in only a few cases would be an overflowing of his compassion. In saving one and not another, he no more does injustice than I do if I give alms to one beggar rather than to another.

This is logical so far as it goes—but it runs up against an obvious problem. I did not create the two beggars, whereas God *did* create all human beings. All babies since Adam are born in a state of original sin, and therefore all of them are destined to hell for all eternity unless the guilt of Adam's sin be removed by baptism. (Augustine certainly believed in the damnation of unbaptized babies, although he seems to have thought they would go to the least painful parts of hell.) God foresaw from all eternity which babies would be baptized and saved, and even, among these, which would persevere in their faith, and which would fall from grace and be damned (*On the Gift of Perseverance*, chap. 32). Hence God foresaw which human beings he would save, and which he would condemn to hell. (Augustine seems to have thought that the proportion of the saved would be very small.) God's grace is "gratuitous, and thus genuine grace; by not giving it to all, he has shown what all deserve" (ibid., chap. 28). If God does give grace, he is merciful; if he does not, he is righteous.

Augustine thinks this pretty much answers the case. God foresees Adam's sin, that in his Fall he will involve all men and the world in the catastrophe. But although he foresees it, he does not cause it. Adam could have willed not to sin: "I made him just and right, / Sufficient to have stood, though free to fall."[11] After that, God can freely choose whom among the guilty freely to pardon—for none of them *deserves* a pardon.

This answer has satisfied millions of Christians over the centuries. But it can hardly quell our doubts. For the further question is: It may be true that God cannot be accused of injustice in predestining some to hell and some to heaven for no fault of their own, purely from the unsearchable counsel of his own will, but given that he foresaw how the world would be through the free choice of Adam and Eve, why did he create it at all? Now, this is a problem only if God is to be thought of as good. If he is malicious or evil there is no problem. But all scripture and tradition maintains that God is good, and that he intended a good world: "And God saw everything that he had made, and, behold, it was very good" (Gen. 1:31). But the doctrine of original sin sees the world as not very good—indeed, as extremely evil. That God created the world knowing it would turn out as Augustine sees it to be—and it is a dark and tragic world indeed— seems unintelligible on the assumption that God is supremely good. It may be that terms such as "good" apply to God only in an analogical way—that they are very remote from the sense they have when we apply them in ordinary human life—but in that case it is hard to see where it gets us, or any Christian theologian, to insist upon them. We might agree to *call* God good, but that might be just like agreeing upon the use of a certain *word*. The argument that may convince us that we cannot convict the Creator of evil seems also to show that we cannot meaningfully call him good.

And this was the starting point of the Manicheans. The existence of evil in the world, a world that an omnipotent Creator could have ensured was purely good, shows that there are *two* divine principles struggling for mastery—the principles of good and evil. Augustine's whole doctrine of original sin can be seen as a mighty attempt to answer the fundamental claim of the sect that had possessed his loyalty for nine years of his life.

Augustine's doctrines of original sin, and of the predestination of souls to heaven and hell purely through God's unsearchable counsels and through no merit or fault of their own, became Christian orthodoxy. It was certainly an orthodoxy that made sense of passages of scripture. Above all, it marked the intellectual triumph of the beliefs of St. Paul. The triumph seems retrospectively to have been inevitable. But it was not. The Pelagians were not defeated by argument. Rather they were destroyed by papal condemnation and the power of the Roman emperor of the time.

> Whatever we inherit from the fortunate
> We have taken from the defeated
> What they had to leave us—a symbol.[12]

It is worth remembering that the defeated party produced at least one man of outstanding ability, whose loathing of what became orthodoxy expresses some of the central convictions of pagan humanism. Against his Roman stolidity, the sinuous eloquence of Augustine takes on some of the character of fanaticism. At the time of his death, Augustine was engaged in a polemical work (his second) against Julian of Eclanum, an Italian bishop who had been deprived of his see (along with seventeen other Italian Pelagian bishops) by the pope. This is the gravamen of his charge against Augustine:

> You ask me why I would not consent to the idea that there is a sin that
> is part of human nature. I answer: it is improbable, it is untrue; it is
> unjust and impious; it makes it seem as if the Devil were the maker of
> men. It violates and destroys the freedom of the will . . . by saying
> that men are so incapable of virtue, that in the very wombs of their
> mothers they are filled with bygone sins. You imagine so great a power
> in such a sin, that not only can it blot out the new-born innocence of
> nature but, for ever afterwards, will force a man throughout his life into
> every form of viciousness . . . [And] what is as disgusting as it is
> blasphemous, this view of yours fastens, as its most conclusive proof,
> on the common decency by which we cover our genitals.[13]

Pelagius and his followers were indeed defeated, yet their spirit so permeated men's minds that the battle had to be fought many times over. Yet who can say that the spirit of Augustine is more alive in the modern Christian church than that of Pelagius?

Luther versus Erasmus

A ferocious exchange (ferocious, on Luther's part, at least) between Luther (1483–1546) and Desiderius Erasmus (1466–1536) reveals a percipience on the part of the reformer that some Catholics wanted to tone down the doctrine of predestination, and to allow that the human will can to some extent cooperate with divine grace. Luther was an uncompromising Augustinian and a wholehearted follower of St. Paul in his insistence that the whole of man "body, soul and spirit" is "fleshly,"[14] that the universal sinfulness of man nullifies free will (ibid., 222), that there is therefore no such thing as free will (ibid., 293–95), and that God does directly cause enslaved man to sin, as when he hardens the hearts of the reprobate—as he hardened the heart of Pharaoh (ibid., 164); and that, in short, God's foreknowledge of man's sin imposes on man the necessity of sinning (ibid., 164).

Erasmus had, in fact, argued only for a modest contribution of the will to human goodness, and had allowed an extremely limited scope for the will's freedom. He asserted that if the will is simply enslaved, as Luther suggests, and if all human sins are predetermined, there would be no point in passages of scripture that seem directly to call people to repentance. For instance "Repent, for the kingdom of heaven is at hand" (Matt. 4:17; Mark 1:15) and Paul's adjuration: "Let us cast off the works of darkness" (Rom 13:12) along with Paul's demand for a "sloughing off of the old man and his acts." How, Erasmus asks, can we be ordered to throw off and strip off our old bad selves if we really cannot do anything for ourselves at all?[15] Erasmus proposes a "middle way" in which the human will is not completely passive, but cooperates with God's grace.[16] Just as reason had been dulled but not extinguished in those who lack grace, so "it is probable that the power of the will has not been absolutely extinguished in them either, but only rendered incapable of doing good."[17]

Luther's rage at the middle way of Erasmus (which would later be confirmed as Catholic orthodoxy by the Council of Trent)[18] may testify to his almost psychotic sense of sin and of personal impotence in the face of the perfection of God. It also shows, though, that he had a very good instinct for the way things were going. The Catholic Church, while keeping predestination in theory, would be in practice ready to soften it and adapt it to more humane instincts—indeed, to something like humanism.

The Sorcerer's Apprentice? Calvin

John Calvin (1509–64) was born in Picardy, studied the arts in Paris and law at Orleans. He was destined for the Roman Catholic church but became convinced by the principles of the Reformation. He therefore fled Paris in 1533 and eventually settled in Geneva, where, after many vicissitudes, he set up what was in effect a theocratic state ruled according to his own religious, moral, and political principles. He had no direct political power—only the immense influence of his own prestige and moral authority. His greatest work, the *Institutes of Christian Religion*, had an enormous influence upon French Protestants (Huguenots), and, indeed, even though it was first published in Latin, upon the development of the French language itself.[19]

In Calvin, Augustine finds his greatest disciple. Here we find Augustine's Latin rhetoric stripped away, the sense of an immediately recognizable individual personality, whose faith is passionately rooted in personal experience, removed. Instead you have the doctrine of predestination expressed in impersonal, armor-plated logic—the "army of unalterable law."[20] There is, nevertheless, a sort of intellectual passion, somewhat akin to the intellectual passion of the not less impersonal Spinoza. It is possible that *total* human depravity is even more certainly a doctrine of Calvin's than it is of Augustine. This is because Calvin does not seem to share Augustine's vision of evil as the privation of good. In the *Confessions* Augustine writes that all things are good even if they are corrupted. Man's being consists in his enjoyment of God's goodness; so if his corruption is so total as to deprive him of that utterly, he would cease to exist. So if evil possessed man totally (as Calvin in fact contends) then in consuming all that was good in man, it would consume itself.[21] In his *Enchiridion* Augustine similarly argues that since every being is good insomuch as it exists, as created by God, man cannot be totally evil without ceasing to be man, and hence ceasing to exist.[22] So Augustine's philosophical theory about the good does—just—mean his picture of human depravity is not quite as thoroughgoing as Calvin's. But it is a close-run thing.

Calvin does add something to Augustine's account of original sin and human depravity. For him man is *totally* depraved. Yet for Calvin the sense of impotence and even of despair that the conviction of sin engenders, the misery of the human predicament and the sense of a fallen world, are not purely negative, because he sees them as the starting point of our knowledge of God: "For, as a veritable world of miseries is to be found in mankind, and we are thereby despoiled of living raiment, our shameful nakedness exposes a teeming hoard of infamies. Each of us must, then, be so stung by the consciousness of his own unhappiness as to attain at least some knowledge of God."[23] It is precisely because of our own awareness of our ignorance, vanity, poverty, and infirmity that we are impelled to recognize that all true wisdom and righteousness repose in God alone. Calvin argues, symmetrically, that it is only when we have "first looked upon God's face" and then descended to scrutinize ourselves that we see fully our own unrighteousness, foulness, and folly (ibid., 37). So without knowledge of God we lack knowledge even of ourselves. And we know God through our own sense of sin and inadequacy.

There is no desire more deeply rooted in human nature than the desire to be flattered (ibid., vol. 2, chap. 1 sec. 2, 242). This blind self-love was the root of Adam's rebellion. Adam's sin was unfaithfulness, which gave rise to ambition, pride, and ungratefulness (ibid., sec. 4, 245). Original sin produces "the depravation of a nature previously good and pure." Adam, as far as he was able, "extinguished the whole glory of God" (ibid., 246). Contagion crept into human nature, which was left despoiled and destitute, with rotten branches springing forth from a rotten root, so that Adam's corruption "was conveyed in a perpetual stream from the ancestors into their descendants" (ibid., chap. 1, sec. 7, 250). This corruption makes us all liable to God's wrath, and brings forth in us the works of the flesh (ibid., chap. 8, 251).

In the same Augustinian spirit, Calvin concludes that the whole of human nature is overwhelmed by original sin "as by a deluge," so that all which proceeds from man "is to be imputed to sin" (ibid., sec. 9, 253). It is not just the brute appetites that need to be obliterated, but the whole of man's corrupted heart and mind—indeed, his whole rebellious spirit. Calvin criticizes Plato and Aristotle for believing that reason, though clogged and sometimes conquered by the senses, nevertheless "like a queen governs the will." He rejects utterly their conviction that to be virtuous is, in the end, a matter of free human choice (ibid., vol. 2, chap. 2, sec, 2, 257).

Thomas Aquinas had upheld a doctrine of predestination that looks very like that of Augustine. He taught that "some people God rejects" and that this rejection can properly be called "reprobation." There is hardly any softening—for instance, Aquinas says that reprobation does not indicate God's foreknowledge only; for as predestination includes the will to confer grace and glory, so reprobation "includes the will to permit someone to fall into fault and to inflict the penalty of damnation in consequence."[24] Nevertheless, the reprobate abandon grace out of a free decision of their own. Within the general scheme of God's providence Aquinas allows a free choice of the individual will.

It is a tiny concession, but one not to be found in Calvin who (as we shall see) will teach the stern doctrine of "double predestination"—i.e., that God not only determines some souls, before their creation, to eternal bliss but also consigns others, in the unsearchable counsel of his own will, to everlasting torment. (Calvin's Catholic critics accused him of teaching that God actually wills the sins of the damned.) Calvin reserved some of his harshest strictures for those Catholic theologians who even hint that man can, of his own free will, cooperate with God's grace, or that he does, sometimes, even if ineffectively, "somehow seek after the good."[25] He quotes with approval St. Augustine's insistence, in his reply to Julian of Eclanum, that without the Spirit the will is not free.[26] Not even one single good work is possible without grace.[27]

There is just one virtue that Calvin seems to allow to man without its being a direct gift of God—humility, man's sense of his own "calamity, poverty, nakedness and disgrace." That at least gives man some self-knowledge (*Institutes*, vol. 2, chap. 2, sec. 10, 267). (It could, of course, give rise to despair, which is traditionally regarded as a sin against the Holy Ghost. Calvin does not discuss that possibility.) All that remains uncontaminated in human nature is our sense of "civic fair dealings and order," our feeling for law and politics, and our grasp of the arts and sciences (ibid., sec. 13, 272).[28]

Since man's will is so corrupted, he actually sins willingly. So, although the will is not free, and man is subject to the necessity of sinning, his very wickedness ensures that he sins with gusto and determination—hence, guiltily. So he sins of necessity, but without compulsion (*Institutes*, vol. 2, chap. 2, sec. 5, 294–95).

It obviously follows that good works avail us nothing—and Calvin, while grimly praising Augustine because "he admirably deprives man of all credit for righteousness, and transfers it to God's grace," complains nevertheless that Augustine does not go far enough, since he "subsumes grace under sanctification, by which we are reborn in newness of life through the Spirit" (ibid., vol. 3, chap. 11, sec. 15, 746).

Calvin moves without apparent hesitation to the conclusion that defines "Calvinism"—since man is totally depraved, and since only God's grace, freely granted, can save him, a grace that includes the gift of faith in Christ, which is both necessary and sufficient for salvation; and since God has known from all eternity whom he would chose to favor with his grace and whom he would pass over, it follows that all human beings are, from all eternity, predestined by God to everlasting bliss or everlasting torment—the notorious doctrine of double predestination comes in. As we saw, the Roman Church would put the darkest construction on Calvin's doctrine—that God does not simply permit the sins of those who will (as he foresaw) be damned—he actually *wills* them. Not only did he permit Adam to sin, he *willed* it. He furthermore wills every actual sin.[29]

There is no doubt but that the doctrine of original sin, grace, and predestination as developed by Augustine and Calvin has a magnificent logic. If man's nature is indeed as depraved as the doctrine of original sin entails, so that moral evil proceeds not from the appetites and passions overcoming reason—as Plato and Aristotle thought—but in a taint that runs through all of human nature, then it is entirely plausible to conclude that from human nature alone nothing good can proceed. Hence, any good in man comes from the free granting of God's grace, which none of us merits. Therefore we are, through the unsearchable counsel of God's will from all eternity, either of the elect or of the reprobate, and if of the latter, we are condemned to an eternity of torment through a decision God took before time began.

Depraved?

Christian churches have reared an immense structure of doctrine and practice on the premise of man's depravity (in the case of Calvin and Luther, almost matched by Augustine, man's *total* depravity.) The idea of original sin gives

Christianity its ultimate validation. It is only if there is an urgent need for salvation through the merits and grace of Christ that the church can claim a unique role—that of being the conduit of that grace through baptism, or, as the Roman Church claims, through that and the other sacraments. Even in these unconsciously Pelagian times, it is very hard to see how the church could dispense with these doctrines without renouncing its historic mission. (And contemporary Pelagianism sits uneasily with another feeling to which the horrors of the twentieth century gave rise—that man is indeed vitiated by some perversity that we might even choose to call "original sin.")

Yet we have to stand back and ask ourselves what the evidence is for this tremendous teaching (apart from Revelation). If man is as depraved as Augustine thinks, and totally depraved as Calvin (not to mention Luther) holds, one might assume that the evidence for this massive deformation of humanity would be everywhere evident. Is it?

Augustine was happy to provide, in his *Confessions*, anecdotal evidence of the restless perversity and rebelliousness of the will. There was his infant wailing "too fiercely" for the breast, his flying into hot rages because "persons—free, not slaves—were not obedient to me." There was his observation of infantile malice and envy, of the baby livid with anger as it watched another infant at the breast.[30] Then there was his recollection of his theft of pears that he took only because they were forbidden.

We know that such anecdotes point to something characteristic of human nature and specific to it. There is no equivalent perversity in animals, even when it looks as though there may be. A fox may get into a henhouse, kill all the hens but carry off only one to eat. People sometimes think that this shows that foxes are possessed by sadism or some perverse lust for destruction. But then we may be offered an explanation: foxes typically kill all they can in an opportunist way, but then they normally set about burying their prey in diverse spots, which they dig up one by one afterward to get their meal. A henhouse will not usually be near the fox's usual place for storage, and thus the fox will not get the chance to complete its work. Whether or not that explanation is right, it is the *sort* of explanation we look for in the behavior of animals. It does not seem intelligible to attribute to them sheer perversity.

Many pre-Christian thinkers, including Plato, Aristotle and the Stoics, and some post-Christian ones, such as Hume, found no place for sheer perversity in their accounts of human nature either. The nearest Aristotle gets to confronting the question is in his treatment of *akrasia*—weakness of will. We often act against our own better judgment, doing things we know to be wrong or against our own interests. We may drink too much, knowing that this will ruin our lives and even hating ourselves as we do it. How is this to be explained?

Aristotle's answer is both plausible and curiously unpersuasive. I am offered that extra glass of wine. I know that too much wine makes me ill and spoils the next day. And I know that on the next day I will regret drinking to excess. But I take it—I take it because of *akrasia* or weakness of will. Aristotle thinks that weakness of will is a sort of ignorance—at the moment I make the bad choice, I forget something that I know, some general proposition—such as "too much wine is bad for you." I don't forget this in a theoretical way—I could, even as I accept the drink, say that too much wine is bad. But according to Aristotle I do not know this in a practical way—it does not enter into my *boulesis*, my deliberation.[31] I do not bring my general knowledge to bear on the particular case. So practically speaking, I do not know. Aquinas refines this. What I do as I yield to the temptation to drink against my better judgment is to bring my action under a true, but at this moment irrelevant "desirability characterization."[32] So, wishing to drink, I bring what I am about to do under the characterization "cheerful sociability is good" rather than "excessive drinking is bad"—and this, as it were, allows me to do what I am tempted to do. It drives out the better, relevant principle.[33]

Here Aristotle is answering, and modifying, Socrates' paradoxical doctrine that no one does wrong knowingly.[34] If I choose the worse course of action, I do not really know it for what it is. Socrates, Aristotle, and Aquinas agree that to choose what I normally know to be wrong, or what goes against my own better judgment, is to suffer some sort of failure of knowledge. None of them entertains the idea that I may be driven by some sort of perversity.

The Aristotelian account does allow for a course of self-deception that can amount eventually to perversity and even depravity. For the man who wants to embark on a life of deceit or crime may very well adopt just those principles of conduct that put his actions in a favorable light. The confirmed liar typically does not know that he is lying. Lying has become instinctive so that he almost believes that his motives or intentions are what he claims them to be. The burglar will convince himself that "property is theft" or that to burgle is bold and manly, or shows his superiority to softer people. People can adopt whole philosophies that justify monstrous conduct—Bolshevism, Nazism. There is a virtue in receiving evidence, and the more partial we are toward our own wishes, the more we will lack that virtue. So in the end we may have a responsibility for our beliefs. There can be a corruption of mind that goes with false opinions.

Nevertheless, when we enter the world of Augustine and Calvin, we are presented with a picture of human nature that is darker than Aristotle's. Aristotle does not really pay attention to the human capacity for *evil*, for malice or sheer malignity, wanton destructiveness, mad vanity and egoism, sadistic cruelty, vindictiveness, hatred of another's good simply because it *is* his good and deprives us of nothing that we could hope to have. Augustine's descriptions of sins of infancy—sins that the infant has to be educated out of, even forced out of—suggest that such perversity is powerful, innate, inescapable—*original*. It seems beyond possibility that the child can turn from it through its own will. It is not at all implausible to extend this picture to man's life as a whole, to see the whole of human nature as containing the perversity of the infant, but with a much greater capacity to put this perversity into effect—sometimes on a gigantic scale.

Post-Enlightenment pictures of human nature have tended to move toward an Augustinian pessimism. At any rate, our being in the grip of forces that we can neither acknowledge nor control is an idea to be found, in one way or another, in Nietzsche, Marx, and Freud. Augustine's account of concupiscence also finds echoes in modern philosophy. Sartre finds sexual love to be a locus of conflict, a source of impossibly self-contradictory desires. In desiring another, I want to reduce him to his flesh, to abrogate his freedom, convert his subjectivity into an object of my own will. My means of achieving this is to evoke in the Other sexual desire for myself. If the Other gave himself freely, and not through dissolving into erotic desire, I would feel cheated of the response I need. Yet at the same time, contradictorily, if the Other did not give himself freely, then also I would not feel genuinely loved.[35] For Sartre the problem is that our relations with others as persons are compromised in sexual love by the very fact that the erotic involves physical (and emotional) responses that escape rational control and seem to have a will of their own. This has analogies with what Augustine says of concupiscence, and why he finds in the involuntary movement of the sexual parts in erotic love a deformity, a product of original sin.

But can evidence of perversity, irrationality, the power over us of unconscious forces support a doctrine of human nature since the Fall as fundamentally depraved? In consequence of the horrors of the twentieth century it became quite common for people to say that they had rediscovered a belief in original sin. But did they really mean that they see human nature as depraved? That we cannot possibly bring about any good through our own efforts?

For we can bring contrary evidence—of a mother acting with heroic self-sacrifice to save her child; of people sacrificing their lives for the good of their country; of those whose sense of justice overcomes self-interest; those with a generous love of fine qualities in other people; others who struggle with increasing success to overcome childish jealousies and resentments.

In pointing to such things, we need not be falling into some optimistic trap, a Panglossian view of human nature. The question is whether we could even grasp the concept of depravity unless we could set this against actions, desires, and motives that are not depraved. Were our understanding as depraved as Augustine and Calvin suggest, it is very hard to see how we could know our own depravity. They argue, of course, that we see our own blackness when we contrast ourselves with God. But this does not help their argument. Whatever our conviction of the supreme goodness of God, it does not follow that we have a clear idea of the profound depravity of man. Even though God be infinitely superior to us in goodness, that does not help us to understand how, say, a moment of irritation with someone is no different in its gravity from mass murder (as Newman appeared to suggest).[36] Nor would the fact that God is entirely just show that we cannot see some human acts as more just than others.

The very idea of depravity, of perversity, depends on our being able to think of some actions and motives as being better than others. We could not understand human actions at all unless we were capable of seeing some people as acting courageously and honorably, others as moved by spite or envy, of distinguishing between kindness and sadism, generosity and mean spiritedness. We know that some people are more dominated by irrational fears than others, that some are more mature and others more childish. Some can subordinate their own urgent desires to the common good, can defer gratifications, can see a situation as it really is. At any rate, some of us—probably, most of us—can exercise some of these virtues some of the time and fail in them at other times.

If we acknowledge that for practical purposes—for the purpose of seeing intelligible patterns in human action—this is true but nevertheless add "But it is not strictly true, for we are helplessly depraved," then that remark and others like it would become simply a sort of incantation or a cog unattached to a wheel. It would be like saying "I have no real belief in the solidity of physical objects" while unconcernedly sitting on a chair or mounting a staircase.

If we accept that we can in practice understand the moral distinctions that we make all the time, but insist that these have no ultimate validity in theory, it is unclear what we are doing. It seems that we are denying that any evidence can come to bear. But this again would seem to be paying lip service to an idea that has no actual purchase on our experience. Augustine based his belief in human depravity not primarily on experience but on revelation. The support for the idea that he found in experience—especially in sexual desire—was a sort of optional extra. But even revelation cannot make the idea of total depravity ultimately intelligible if does not answer to our experience, and, indeed, if it conflicts with it.

Augustine's picture of fallen nature has power and persuasiveness, but it can never escape its inherent paradoxicality. To refuse to distinguish between different degrees of goodness, or virtue, or benevolence in human motivation makes it impossible, in the end, to describe and understand human actions at all.

The Council of Trent and Afterward

The Council of Trent (which lasted, with intervals, from 1545 to 1563) was concerned to reaffirm Catholic orthodoxy against the Protestants. Calvin's *Institutes* appeared in Latin in 1535, and thus his doctrines about justification and predestination came within the ambit of the council's deliberations.

Trent upheld the essentials of Augustine's teaching, in the usual robust fashion of Christian ecumenical councils: "If anyone says that a person can be justified before God by his own works, done either by the resources of human nature or by the teaching of the law, apart from divine grace through Jesus Christ: *let him be anathema!*"[37] But there is a rebuke for the Calvinist position when the council denounces the idea that "a person's free will when moved and roused by God, gives no co-operation by responding to God's summons and invitation to dispose and prepare itself to obtain the grace of justification; and that it cannot, if it so wishes, dissent but, like something inanimate, can do nothing at all and remains merely passive."[38] A soul can cooperate to receive justifying grace, but only when it has already been invited and summoned by God to do so—i.e., from the free grace of God. Yet Trent has allowed a tiny space for the soul's freedom to choose which may have been the pigmy lance intended to pierce Calvin's armor-plated logic. More obviously directed against Calvin is Trent's condemnation of the doctrine that "after the sin of Adam, human free will was lost and blotted out, or that its existence is purely nominal, a name without a substance, indeed a fiction introduced into the Church by Satan" (ibid., Canon 5). The council also condemned what it understood as Calvin's doctrine of double predestination—"that God is the agent for evil acts just as for good, not only by permitting them but also in a full sense and by personal act, so that the betrayal of Judas no less than the call of Paul is an act fully his" (ibid., Canon 6). It condemned the teaching that all human actions, before justification, are sins—again a rebuke to Calvin and the radical Protestants. It decreed that not only faith but also a preparation by "a movement of our own will" is necessary for man to be justified (ibid., Canon 9). The Council defended good works as both preserving and increasing justice, as this has been received as a gift of God (ibid., Canon 24, 680). Trent anathematized those who deny that the just who perform good works should "expect and hope for an eternal reward from God through his mercy and the merit of Jesus Christ" (ibid., Canon 26). and also anyone who says that the good deeds of any justified person are only the gifts of God and not also "the good merits of the one justified" (ibid., Canon 32, 681).

It is true that the Council of Trent officially upheld the doctrine of predestination and seemed to allow only a small—indeed, apparently tiny—space for the human will to cooperate with God's grace. Whether this concession—which we might consider humane—was logically possible within the somber doctrine of election is debatable. What is certain is that Trent, whether intentionally or not, and despite its official loyalty to the Augustinian doctrine of predestination, opened the way to a radical change in emphasis, which amounted de facto to a shift in doctrine in the direction, ultimately, of Pelagianism. The tiny space opened for free will was soon to be vastly expanded by theologians eager to humanize the church's teaching. It is hard not to suspect that the church—as so often before and since—overtly supported the hard teaching of Augustine, while knowing full well that the (apparently) tiny concession was the leak that would finally sink the Augustinian ship.

Jansenists contra Jesuits

What happened is revealed most clearly in the bitter dispute within French Catholicism in the seventeenth and eighteenth centuries between the Jansenists and the Jesuits. The Jansenists were followers of Cornelius Jansen (or Jansenius), bishop of Ypres, who died in 1638. Jansen was a strict Augustinian who wrote a book in which Augustine's doctrine of predestination and human depravity was upheld in a form so austere and rigorous as to sound suspiciously like Calvinism. Pope Innocent X condemned Jansen's book, first in 1643 and again in 1653, and the Jesuits began a vigorous campaign against his followers. In 1709 the convent of Port Royal—the center of Jansenism—was destroyed on the orders of Louis XIV; and in 1713 Clement XIII issued the papal bull *Unigenitus*, which condemned the central claims of Jansenist theology as heretical.[39]

Jansenism came to stand for an essentially Christian view of human nature that was profoundly out of sympathy with the spirit of the French Enlightenment. Teachings central to traditional Christianity—not just the Augustinian doctrine about human depravity but the stern morality that went with that[40]—were being challenged by an increasing belief in the power of the human will to do good unaided, in natural virtue, and even in the essential innocence and nobility of the human heart.

Enlightened opinion in France had in effect begun to dispense with the supernatural. Man could be virtuous if his actions and sentiments were in accord with Nature. Nor was it only the essentially non-Christian *philosophes* who promoted such ideas. They found what on the surface looks like an improbable set of allies—the Jesuits.

The Jesuits had a strategy, which they pursued with a certain resolution and what some—e.g., the Jansenist-influenced Blaise Pascal—considered to be Jesuitical cunning. They wanted to free Christianity from the shackles of Augustine and therefore from any serious belief in original sin. They wanted to accommodate Catholicism to the modern world, to reassure sophisticated moderns that Christianity was not an especially difficult faith to live by, not innately opposed to natural human inclination.

The Jansenists denied that virtue and morality could be derived from nature, for nature itself was corrupted by the Fall. Unlike the Jesuits, who thought in effect that original sin had merely taken supernatural life from man and left him as he would have been by nature had he not sinned—mortal, and in many ways weak but capable of all the moral virtues—the Jansenists denied that man is essentially a natural being at all.[41] Man's true nature is revealed only as he lives a life that united him with the divine life. Separated from God by sin, he is thereby alienated from his own real self and thus incapable of living a truly human life. The Jesuits comforted the average man—*l'homme moyen sensuel*—by suggesting that sins committed without full knowledge and deliberation might not be sins at all. A state of character that blinds men to the moral law, or a state of "invincible ignorance" that hides the divine from individuals, would excuse from sin. The Jansenists, by contrast, asserted that even those unconscious, unacknowledged impulses that lead people to sin are part of our selves, part of depraved human nature. Every man is either the child of sin, or the child of grace.[42]

In other words, the Jesuit doctrine was really a return to Pelagianism, the assumption that human nature is of itself morally neutral, or even innocent. Their practical teaching looked forward to the Sentimentalism of Rousseau, to the idea that the untutored, natural human heart, rather than being deceitful above all things and desperately wicked, was the source and locus of innate human goodness. Against this, the Jansenists clove to Paul, Augustine, and (almost) to Calvin. There is an irony in the fact that the Pelagianism of the Jesuits triumphed over the essential orthodoxy of the Jansenists using the same methods of persuasion by which Augustine had triumphed over the Pelagians— censorship, royal and papal disapproval, and physical destruction.

The user-friendly language of the Roman Catholic Church after the Second Vatican Council shows Rome's ability to soften a doctrine without formally repudiating it. The *Catechism of the Catholic Church*, published in the light of that council, mentions predestination only to disavow it: "God predestines no one to hell; for this a willful turning away from God (a mortal sin) is necessary, and persistence in it until the end."[43] Yet the doctrine of grace in the catechism is essentially the same as that of Trent—that it is a free gift of God, unmerited by man, by which man is sanctified and shares in the supernatural life of God. Merit comes, first, from God as a free gift, and secondly from human collaboration with this gift.[44] Yet the Council of Trent, like Augustine, clearly thought that this doctrine of grace entailed some sort of predestination. Calvin would certainly have thought that the Catholic formulations opened the way to Pelagianism. Indeed, the strongest Protestant objection to Catholicism was that it substituted good works for divine grace. The tone of the new catechism is humanist and consoling. Even though there is no formal repudiation of the terrifying doctrine of predestination, the Roman Catholic Church now in practice allows the faithful to be as cheerfully and unconsciously Pelagian as everyone else.

8

The Decline of Hell

Jesuit Hells

Dante's hell had been ordered, even infernally hierarchical. There was a gradation of punishments in accord with the severity of the sin, and each class of sinners occupied its particular domain. There is even, at times, a sense of spaciousness in Dante's infernal world. This changes with the Protestant Reformation and the Catholic Counter-Reformation. Protestantism—at least in its more radical forms, such as Calvinism—denied that there was any gradation in sin at all. Either you were destined to salvation or you were not. The state of reprobation was an absolute separation from God, and there was no point, or theological validity, in imagining some sinners punished more severely, or differently, from others. Therefore any ideas of an ordered hell, to which an imagination such as Dante's provided a sort of map, was meaningless. There is no point in distinguishing the varieties of damnation.

The Counter-Reformation, starting from different premises, came in practice to the same conclusion. Catholics certainly did regard some sins as graver than others. It was mortal sins, as distinct from venial ones, that killed the soul and merited eternal damnation. Dante's conception of punishments of varying horror, fitting the different degrees of wickedness of each mortal sin, so that the greatest sinners would turn out to be those who betrayed God and the political realm (Brutus, Cassius, and Judas Iscariot) was never rejected by the church. What changed was the style of teaching. Roman Catholicism of the Counter-Reformation developed a rhetoric and psychology that aimed at bringing hell home to the faithful in the most dramatic manner possible, at making hell a reality in the imaginations of those listening to the sermons that became so important in its reinvigorated propaganda. This preaching, above all by the Society of Jesus—the Jesuits—created to produce the counterattack on Protestantism, was actually quite close to Protestantism in its psychology, for in effect it did not distinguish among the capital sins but simply tried to inspire an absolute horror at the infernal torments, even though the various sorts of torment (e.g., physical and spiritual) are distinguished. The Jesuits sought to bring hell alive by their "composition of place"—a vivid realization of what hell must actually be like. The damned are all in the same boat, and, even worse, they are hideously squashed together. Different sins do not have their own space.[1]

On the whole, Catholic attempts to imagine hell remain exercises in psychological rhetoric, mixed with theological argument. They aim to have the same dramatic immediacy that characterizes baroque art of the period. Counter-Reformation Catholicism developed an immensely effective dramatic psychology of the Last Things, death, judgment, hell, and heaven. In Protestant, empirical England there was an early growth of quasi-scientific speculations about the physical nature of hell, its actual location in the universe, the exact chemical constitution of its fires. Going with this is a gradual strengthening of humane sentiment that eventually undermines belief in hell.

A Fierce Jesuit

A famous exponent of Jesuit eloquence was Jeremias Drexel (or Dresselius), a Bavarian Jesuit who lived from 1581 to 1638. His specialty was eternity. He sought to dramatize for his listeners and readers the idea of everlasting punishment, using every possible rhetorical technique. He talks of a "stone in Arcadia, called Asbestos," which being set on fire burns continually; and of a certain kind of flax "which is so far from being consum'd by the Fire, that it is wash'd and cleans'd by it.... Thus shall the Damn'd Burn, but the Fire shall never be Extinguish'd; they shall always Burn, but never be consum'd; they shall seek for Death in the Flames, but shall never find him."[2]

The pain of loss of the beatific vision will never have an end, because in hell there is no possibility of satisfaction—i.e., paying for sin: "Their Torments shall continue many Millions of Years without one sweet or refreshing Moment.... They shall gnash their Teeth with cold, and the Fire shall force them to lament and weep.... If the Gout or Stone is in one short Night ... severely painful and grievous to us, consider we with ourselves how shall we endure to lie in the Flames Night and Day for Thousands of Years" (ibid., 23–24).

even a momentary (mortal) sin brings damnation, for every sin is against the infinite majesty of God, so even a momentary lapse can incur eternity. Drexel's eternity is expressed in virtually the same words as his (fictional) Joycean fellow-Jesuit, Father Arnall used: "shou'd God say to the Damn'd, let the Earth be cover'd with the finest Sand, and let the World be fill'd therewith; let Heap be pil'd upon Heap, till it reaches up to the highest Heavens, and let an Angel, every Thousand Years, take a grain from it [and, after all has been cleared, the dead would be released from hell]. . . . how would the Damn'd rejoice? . . . But alas! After millions and millions of years, there remain more Millions, and still more Millions for Ever and Ever" (ibid., 71). And if you were to take from eternity as many years as there are stars in the firmament, drops in the ocean, spires of grass in the field, motes in the sun, or atoms of sand upon the sea-shore, not one moment of eternity would have passed. If one of the damned were to shed a tear every hundred years, and all the tears shed were to be kept together, until they made a sea as large as the ocean that surrounds the earth "how many Millions of Years may we reasonably suppose to pass away, before this tedious Effusion of Tears wou'd make a little River, and what is a River, to the vast great Ocean? And yet if this could possibly be done, we might then truly say, now begins Eternity" (ibid., 180–81).

Drexel is also an expert on the imagery of exclusion—in capturing the dread sense of how few shall be saved. He speaks of the vision of a woman miraculously brought back from the dead, who stood before God's tribunal together with sixty thousand souls who were summoned from all parts of the universe to stand before their judge "and they were all Sentenc'd to Eternal Death, Three only excepted" (ibid., 187).[3]

But why should we be surprised? Only eight human beings were saved in Noah's ark, the rest of mankind being drowned.[4] When Moses led out of Egypt six hundred thousand men on foot, besides women and children, a promiscuous multitude also following the camp, only two of so great a number came into the fruitful land of Canaan, while "to the rest the Wilderness was a capacious Grave" (ibid.). The statement in the Apocalypse that 144,000 shall be saved means that of all the Jews from Abraham to the end of the world, less than one in a thousand will escape hell (ibid., 289).

Drexel lists the torments of hell as darkness (inner and outer), weeping, hunger, intolerable stench, fire.

> *Tenebrae*: Of all the plagues of Egypt described in Exodus, the outer
> darkness is alone called "horrible." The inner darkness is even worse,

for the deprivation of the sight of God is the greatest punishment of the damned. We will know that when we die. The falcon, when its head is covered with the leather cap, its eyes blindfolded, has no desire to go after magpies or doves or herons. But once the *pileolus* is removed, nature rushes him on—it is impossible to hold him back, except with extreme force—he breaks chains and thong, and no one can do anything with him, even with the hunter holding his feet in his arms. Held back, he would be injured, so violent is the force of nature as soon as he sees what he desires at a distance. Man is the same. As soon as we see God we want to rush to him. While we exist in this life, *our* eyes are hooded; *we* are in darkness. But as soon as we see God the veil is removed—the cover is removed by death, and we are freed from it for all eternity. So if we are excluded from God for ever and ever, this is to us an unspeakable punishment. Of the pains of *Gehenna*, by far the most unendurable is to be shut out from the glorious sight of Christ and God.[5]

Fletus: Weeping is another grievous torment. *Tempus vivendi, tempus flendi*—the time of living is the time for tears. After death they are useless. Angels find tears of repentance in the living fragrant, for they reveal holy grief, divine love—"Blessed are they who weep, for they shall be comforted." But in hell the tears stem from rage, pain, despair, envy, and obstinate malignity. Hell will be filled with the hideous howling of the damned—a horror in itself—as they gnash their teeth from rage (*stridor dentium*), filled with the despair of the fire that can never be quenched and the worm that never dies. In the cruel gardens of Nero, where Christians were burned to make nocturnal torches, what sad outcries, what lamentations there must have been! Imagine thousands and millions and thousands of millions impaled over the flames, what hideous screams! Add to that the howlings of the demons who will be yelling at them from close to! (ibid., 37–40). Among the damned there will be no sleep, no quiet, not even for a single moment. Whereas in heaven there would have been the choir of angels, the songs of martyrs and apostles, here you will be among ulcerated, diseased cadaverous human beings yelling as in a super-heated hot room at the baths, their skin a venomous mass of slavering putrefaction, weeping and screeching as they experience pain and stench, hearing the howls of others in the same state. These are the *mores* in the Hall of Satan, everyone burns with ardent hatred of everyone else, and every one would, if he could, tear everyone else with his teeth.

Fames: Hunger will be a punishment designed especially for
  gluttons—people who, like Heliogabulus, *vomunt ut bibant, bibunt ut
  vomant*—who vomited in order to drink, and drank in order to vomit.
  Gluttons will eructate in the most frightful way, their stomachs will
  rumble thunderously, and they will always be shouting out with
  hunger.

Foetor: Drexel was particularly interested in the intolerable stench of
  hell. The damned will be in a very strait prison house into which the
  filth of the whole world pours. It is a cloaca most filthy (actually
  "shitty"—*faeculentissima*), a cavern most noisome (*graveolentissimam*).
  All the concentrated sulfurous rotten-egg smells of this world put
  together are as nothing in comparison with the *foetor* of hell. And the
  very bodies of the damned themselves, crammed into this tiny space,
  hugely increase the foul stench, for every one of the damned is an
  immensely smelly, wormy, putrid corpse. There will be flatulence,
  corrupt air from the huge multitude, and all the smells from the
  World Sewer (ibid., 70–75).

  At this point Drexel engages in a memorable—perhaps
  unique—calculation, as he works out how tightly the damned will be
  squashed together in hell: There will be a hundred thousand million
  of them, and they will have to fit into one square German mile. They
  will be penned like dogs or pigs, or like grapes in a winepress, like
  pickled tuna in a barrel, like bricks in the furnace of a lime-kiln, like a
  ewe-lamb on the spit, like plums being flambed, like sheep having
  their throats cut in the market (ibid., 129). No wonder they will stink
  to high heaven![6]

Ignis: Who among us dares touch fire, let alone put his whole finger in
  the flame of a candle, let alone his whole arm—his whole body?
  Nothing is more excruciating than fire. But the difference between
  fire on earth and in hell is that here it produces light and splendor.
  But the fire of hell burns without light, except with such light as
  enables the damned to see the foul society in which they live (other
  damned souls and demons). Our fire consumes what it burns—hellfire does not. Our fire burns only while it has material on which to
  feed; but there it is nourished for ever by divine justice, which never
  sleeps and is inextinguishable.

So there the damned will lie for millions upon millions of years, millions of
centuries, millions of millennia, in a place that is *profundissimus, tenebricosissi-
mus, foetidissimus, et quod lugubre cogitatu, remotissimus a caelo, mille clathris ac*

feris, repagulis ac claustris mille obseratus—"most deep, most dark, most fetid, and, what is lamentable to think on, most remote from heaven, with a thousand bars and grates, bolts and doors, shut up a thousand times over" (ibid., 150).

A Smoother Jesuit

The Frenchman Louis Bourdaloue (1632–1704), also of the Society of Jesus, was a famous preacher in his time, although his memory has largely been overshadowed by his contemporary, Bossuet. (He was also famously long-winded. Fashionable ladies at his sermons used to keep chamber pots, which they called "bourdaloues" under their long dresses in case of necessity.)[7] In a sermon preached before Louis XIV, Bourdaloue offered a vision of hell, which, while not in the least departing from orthodoxy, gave a very different color to the horrors from that of the rougher Bavarian.

There is no need of demons nor of specters to make hell a place of torment. The crimes committed by each of the damned—these will be the demons by which he is surrounded: "Those abominable impurities, those enormous injustices, those profanations of holy things, those signs of contempt toward God, those inveterate hatreds against one's neighbor, those perfidies and treasons . . . those scandals of atheism . . . those black impostures of calumny . . . these are the monsters that infest the reprobate, who encompass him around, who seize him with the most lively terrors."[8]

In stressing the spiritual pains of hell much more strongly than the pains of sense, and in identifying these pains as essentially those of remorse of conscience, Bourdaloue comes close to Origen, whose overwhelming emphasis on remorse got him branded a heretic. Bourdaloue thinks that we can discover hell through our own conscience—which implies that scripture is not the only source for our knowledge of what it is like. It is not even necessary to be a Christian to be convinced by what he says "since the very pagans have recognized and made it the matter of their fables. But what we call fables are at bottom nothing less than the most sublime principles of their theology, the best established principles of their morality . . . these fictions reinforce the same truth that our faith insists upon, and . . . give us a witness . . . that one of the greatest penalties of hell will be to have sinned, and to be soiled by the crimes committed during one's life" (ibid.).

The sinner can never forget the shame of his sin—it torments him eternally. In hell, instead of a holy sadness there is a remorse that lacerates, sadnesses that crush, repentance that deranges, drives to madness and rage. The penalty God reserves in hell is that the soul will constantly see the sights that it sinfully loved in life—"secret assents, criminal desires . . . scandalous connections, lascivious invitations, liberties, glances, dissolutenesses, soft-nesses." God will rub the soul's face (as it were) in all these: "'Gaze,' he will tell it, 'for each moment of eternity, behold the fruits of your incontinence, behold what your heart brought forth!'" (ibid., 555).

Bourdaloue will not try to set before Louis and his court the pains of sense in hell, for other preachers have a thousand times made the useless attempt to get them to comprehend the horror. All he will say is that all the cruelties tyrants have invented, all the patience of which martyrs have been capable, are but a shadow of that fire (ibid., 561). Bourdaloue passes over the fire rather quickly, wondering that we who are so delicate, so tender to ourselves, so sensible of pain are so little affected by the thought of torments to come. The best thing is for us to let the fire of hell serve to ignite in us another fire—the fire of charity (ibid., 563).

But in hell not a drop of that ocean of mercy and of goodness that is in God will be poured on these unfortunate creatures, not a single drop of the blood of redemption to relieve them—"'What serves their weeping and their mournful accents? They strike my ear but do not reach my heart—there is no remedy, no turning back'" (ibid., 566). God's holiness is eternal, and eternally the enemy of sin, and, it necessarily follows, always hates sin, always pursues sin, always punishes sin. So the sin itself endures for ever (ibid., 567).

So Bourdaloue is not the "soft Dean" who "never mentions Hell to Ears polite."[9] In addressing these immensely polite ears, he formally keeps the fires, the physical torments of hell—but de-emphasizes them with the subtlety one would hope for from a French Jesuit at the court of the Sun King. Indeed, there even seems to be the bat-squeak of possibility that the pains of hell may end up on the same level as the "fables" of the more polite pagans.

England: The Common Vision

By the early seventeenth century in England some common themes had become established in the writing and preaching of hell. Some of them date from the earliest centuries of the church. They last into the twentieth century (and in Ireland they make a grand final appearance in Father Arnall's sermons in *Portrait of the Artist*). The great majority of English preachers and writers, empirical in their instincts, think of the torments of hell in overwhelmingly literal terms. This sometimes turns into attempts to work out where hell is, the nature of its flames, the exact physiology of the suffering inflicted on the damned. This literalism eventually comes to be used to discredit and even ridicule hell, and to provoke a reversal of feeling—what came to be called

"Sentimentalism"—that rebelled, not so much intellectually as emotionally, against the very idea of eternal torment.

Protestant England is not interested in an exact mapping of hell, of the gradation of sins and their punishments such as we find in Dante. This reflects the influence of Calvinism, with its insistence (as we saw) that we are all either justified or damned, that no sin is more serious than any other, meriting more severe punishment. Every sin is a deadly one: "Let the children of God hold that all sin is mortal. For it is rebellion against the will of God, which of necessity provokes God's wrath."[10] Although the English divines do find connections between particular offenses and particular punishments, this is not part of a worked-out moral and theological scheme. The horrors of hell are presented vividly, and are certainly believed in, but they do not systematically illuminate the nature of the offense for which souls are damned.

There is something crude in the English Protestant literalism—even compared with the ferocities of Drexel. The psychological acuteness of Counter-Reformation Catholicism passes them by. This might possibly be because they have no tradition of private confession to a priest, and so no building up of expertise in diagnosing, probing, healing the human soul. In Catholic hellfire preaching (at least among sophisticated preachers like the Jesuits) the physical horrors are in balance with a brilliantly composed picture of spiritual loss and despair. The English Protestants seems much less at home in this.

A representative example toward the end of the seventeenth century is Sir William Dawes, who sometimes preached on hell before King William III, and whose sermons were issued in two books in 1696, *The Greatness of Hell Torments* and *The Eternity of Hell Torments*. They bring together tropes that recur through most of the century, are anticipated in the sixteenth century and survive into the eighteenth.

Dawes attempts to bring together the inner conviction of sin with the material reality of hellfire. The conscience of sinners makes them suffer, even in this world, some intimation of the torments of hell—although this is feeble in comparison with the terrible reality to come.[11] The five greatest torments of hell are: (1) banishment from the enjoyment of God, (2) the lashes of our own guilty minds, (3) the "loathsomeness of the place of hell" and the "troublesome conversation of devils," (4) the pain of the fire of hell, and (5) "eternal durance."

The mental torment of the damned will be increased by the memory of God, whom they will have seen for an instant before being damned, and the continual sight of heaven—as Dives from his place of torment sees Lazarus in Abraham's bosom. Furthermore, the angels, even (presumably) guardian angels, protectors of the sinner in life, will now mock him—a version of the more terrible doctrine that God himself will mock and laugh at the damned (ibid., 8, 9). The lashings of our own mind and conscience, which even in life gave a dim foretaste of what was to come, will be inconceivably great, and all the fears of the wicked will be heightened into despair (ibid., 10, 11). The loathsomeness of the place will include utter darkness, devils, and wicked men "jangling, snarling, biting" (ibid., 12). The flames of hell will be real and material, but mixed with them will be guilty conscience, the "worm that dieth not." Yet although the fire of hell will be hideously intense, the damned will also simultaneously suffer extreme cold. They will be certain that there will be no intermission for their pains (ibid., 14).

Dawes is producing a somewhat pallid version of a literal hell that we find in more red-blooded terms more than forty years earlier in the work of a Puritan divine, Christopher Love. His *Hell's Terror* was the companion piece to a (sadly) much slimmer volume, *Heaven's Glory*.[12] Love throws together speculations of the church fathers about the intensity of infernal torments, the pain of the loss of God, the necessity that hell be eternal because an infinitely good God has been offended, with the Calvinist-influenced assumption[13] that the number of the saved will be lamentably small in comparison with the legions of the damned.

Love's mind is incurious, literal, and pharisaical. He exults in the shock that people will feel when their commonplace vices meet with such an unexpected punishment: "did they but know that they can swallow bowls of wine, and drink to excess, they shall one day drink draughts of burning brimstone in hell."[14] His few attempts to think of hell as *spiritual* deprivation soon lapse into a more congenial materialism. There is a moment when he suggests that there is an argument from conscience in favor of the existence of hell—"those horrors and terrors of conscience that are in wicked men when they are dying" (ibid., 226). And he briefly adverts to the ancient view that the chief pain of hell is the loss of God: "if there were a thousand worlds (saith Chrysostom) the loss of the favor of one God, is more than a thousand worlds." Apart from that, Love's vision of hell is essentially physical. The loss of God is soon shorn of the mystical character it has in Chrysostom: "when thou art scorching in the flames, when thou art howling in thy torments, then God shall laugh at thy destruction, and then the saints of heaven shall sing and rejoice, that thou art a vessel for his justice, and so his power and wrath be made known in thee" (ibid., 257). Chrysostom's ease with a spiritual interpretation is not something the English empiricist shares.

This picture of a Laughing God, who will mock the damned in hell, seems to have been developed by followers of Aquinas. Aquinas thought that one of the pleasures of the blessed in heaven would be their sight of the sufferings of the damned. He meant not that the suffering of the lost would give pleasure for its own sake, but that the blessed, having a clear vision unmixed with sheer sentiment, will rejoice in the clear operation of God's justice—*Giustizia mosse il mio alto fattore*. Aquinas himself quotes Psalm 57: "The just shall rejoice when they shall see the revenge: he shall wash his hands in the blood of the sinner."[15] Some interpreted these special pleasures of the saved on the model of Lucretius's *suave mare magno* ("It is good to stand on the shore in a great storm and observe a ship in distress—not for the pains of those in danger, but because of a sense that you have escaped these dangers"[16]). Others envisaged a more wholehearted pleasure in the pains of others: "as the damned souls shall, from hell, see the saints' happiness, to increase their own torments, so shall the blessed, from heaven, behold the wicked's misery to the increase of their own joy."[17] The American Calvinist Jonathan Edwards suggested that the saved exult in the sufferings of the damned even when among then they see "those who were near and dear to them in this world."[18]

We remember that Tertullian in *De Spectaculis* had invited the Christians to laugh at the punishments to be inflicted on the deluded and persecuting pagans, for which he was rebuked by Gibbon (and, as we shall see, by the liberalizing divine, Dr. Thomas Burnet).[19] The image of the Laughing God had also become current in Counter-Reformation Catholic theology.[20] That God will laugh at those he has consigned to an eternity of exquisite torment is a peculiarly horrible thought. It has, though, its logic. If the blessed rejoice in the sufferings of the damned, then they might also be thought to exult, for to exult is to manifest a sense of one's own felicity. If Hobbes is right in describing laughter as "sudden glory," then this exulting would be close to laughter.[21]

Age cannot wither nor custom stale the infinite variety of hell torments: "There is not one way, but a hundred, a thousand, ten thousand ways to torment you. Indeed, were you sick here, it may be you should have but one kind of disease upon you at once; it may be stone, it may be plague . . . but you have not variety: had you plague, and stone, and gout, and fever concurring in one to afflict your body, how miserable would you be with all? But in hell there is not one kind, but variety to torment you: unquenchable fire to burn you, a lake of brimstone to choke you, eternal chains to tie you, utter darkness to affright you, and a worm of conscience to gnaw you."[22]

None of this has the systematic matching of punishment to offense that we find in Dante. On the contrary, the aim is to show that every soul in hell suffers all imaginable torments at once and without remission. The eye shall be "tormented with the sight of devils, the ear shall be tormented with the yelling and hideous outcries of the damned in flames. The nostrils shall be smothered with brimstone to choak you . . . the tongue with a flame . . . the whole body (in a word) tormented in flames of fire." Not only that, the imagination "will be tormented with thoughts of present pain; the memory with thoughts of what a heaven and happiness you have lost" (ibid., 259).

Then there is the horror of the society of the devils, devilish and damned persons like yourself. To be in their company "is worse than living in Bridewell among thieves, or bedlam among mad men"—for these have better compassion than have the damned (ibid., 262).

As I have suggested, most of the English divines draw on the ancient stock of ideas about hell which go back to the church fathers—the same stock of images that pervade Drexel's terrifying calculations and the hell sermons in *Portrait of the Artist*. The damned in *Portrait* are described as howling and screaming at one another; all laws are overturned, all sense of humanity forgotten. These ideas come up repeatedly in seventeenth- and eighteenth-century England. Christopher Love brings in another idea, which is to reappear in Joyce. Love quotes St. Anselm as saying, "I had rather endure all the torments that art or nature can devise, than see the devil with my bodily eyes" (ibid., 264). ("We can have no idea of how horrible these devils are. Saint Catherine of Siena once saw a devil and she has written that, rather than look again for one single instant on such a frightful monster, she would prefer to walk to the end of her life along a track of red-hot coals."[23])

Love insists that the torments of hell must be eternal "because the justice of God, which they have wronged by their sins, can never be satisfied"[24]—an argument that recurs in all the orthodox defenders of hell, but which comes under attack in the late seventeenth century and in the eighteenth, amid growing skepticism about eternal punishment. But Love does not even need this argument, which he seems to include simply because it is to hand, for he goes on immediately to claim that the wicked—conveniently—will *want* to sin to all eternity: "Their cursings are their hymns, howling their tunes, and blasphemies their duties. There the wicked blaspheme God that made them to condemn them to hell eternally . . . they blaspheme his justice, because he judged them, his wrath because they feel it" (ibid., 271).

As writers try to depict this unimaginable blending together of all torments in hell, so they attempt to hint at the equally unimaginable idea of their eternity. Drexel's and Arnall's depiction of eternity—the mountain of sand a million miles high, visited once every million years by a bird which carries away in its beak one grain of the sand, occurs in Love, where it is attributed to a Mr. Bolton:

> Mr. Bolton, upon this subject, hath this expression: Suppose all the mountains of the earth were mountains of sand, and many more

mountains were added thereto, till they reached up to heaven, and a little bird should come once in every thousand years and take one sand of this mountain, there would be an innumerable company of years pass over us before that mass of sand should be consumed and taken away, and yet this time would have an end and it would be happy for men if hell were no longer than this time; but this is man's misery in hell, he shall be in no more hope of coming out after he hath been there millions of years, than he was when he was first cast in there; for his torments shall be to eternity without end, because the God that damns him is eternal. (Ibid., 273)

Love disposes briskly of the worry that a high proportion of mankind may be doomed to this eternity of torment, using the arguments of Augustine and Calvin: "it stands with God's decree that most of men should perish . . . for God to damn most of men, it is so far from impeaching his mercy, that it doth set a greater lustre on the mercy of God to the elect" (ibid., 302). Far from shrinking from the consequences of the Augustinian and Calvinist arguments, Love is eager to entertain them: "God would show more mercy if he should save but one man in the world, than he should show extreme justice in damning the whole world" (ibid., 303).

John Bunyan

John Bunyan (1628–88) stands out from the mass of English preachers and writers on hell, not because he differs from them in belief but because of his palpable spirituality. He is untroubled by the eternity of damnation and its torments as a *doctrine*, but he breathes an unmistakable pity for the lost souls, even as he depicts the ugliness of sin. There is nothing merely rhetorical in the horror he expresses at the prospect of damnation. Instead there is a fearful pity.

In *The Resurrection of the Dead*, Bunyan describes, symmetrically, the rising from death, first, of the just, and then of the unjust. The just will rise from their graves "glorified in their bodies," as the risen Christ was glorified in his. Bunyan imagines the body of someone who had suffered for Christ's sake—"the body that feels the stocks, the whip, hunger and cold, the fire and rack, and a thousand calamities . . . the body in which we have the dying marks of the Lord Jesus."[25] The bodies of the saints "dishonorably tortured, killed and sown in the grave" will be raised by God in incorruption, glory and honor (ibid., 210). The just will rise "in a far more glorious state" than when they were sown in the grave; but though their bodies will have a transcendent splendor, they will be the same bodies that were buried and which rotted in the grave (ibid., 216).

Bunyan uses Paul's similitude of the seed of corn sown in the earth—"that which thou sowest, is not quickened, except it die" (1 Cor. 15:36). As the corn after being buried in the soil quickens and revives "so shall it be with our body. . . . It is sown a dead corn, but raised a living one. It is sown dry, without comeliness, it riseth green and beautiful." The body is buried like "a poor, dry, wrinkled curnel . . . and there it lyeth, and swelleth, breatheth, and, one would think, perisheth . . . yet it is the same that riseth that was sown . . . after a far more glorious manner, not with the same husk, but without it."[26]

The wicked will have an opposite fate. They will arise in deformity, in death "and shall be under it, under the gnawings and terrors of it. . . . As it were a living death shall feed upon them, they shall never be spiritually alive, nor yet absolutely dead." They will come out of their graves "having yet the chains of eternal death hanging on them, and the talons of that dreadful ghost fastened in their souls. So that life will be far from them, even as far as heaven is from hell" (ibid., 248–49). Bunyan paraphrases those verses from Daniel (Dan, 12:2.), which are the most explicit among the very few verses in the Old Testament that possibly suggest future torment: "The good shall rise to everlasting life; but the wicked to shame and everlasting contempt." He comments: "Never was toad or serpent more loathsome to any, than these will be in the eyes of God on their rising forth from their graves. . . . The ungodly at their death are like thistle-seed; but at their rising, they will be like the thistle grown; more noysom, offensive, and provoking to rejection in abundance."[27]

It is interesting that Bunyan, unlike many of the English writers, has too much literary tact and too keen a moral imagination to attempt any physical description of the loathsomeness of the risen damned, only a sense of their spiritual ugliness "meer and naked lumps of sinful nature," bodies with "the hot scalding stink of hell" upon them. Above all, the wicked will be in despair: "They shall not be able to lift up the head for ever, pangs shall take hold of them, and their hands shall faint, and every man's heart shall melt" (ibid., 250). Conscience will be a witness against the soul in the day of God (ibid., 269).

Bunyan cannot conceive of hell as other than a material reality, a place of actual physical torments, and in this respect he is as literal minded as most writers of his age, but he does manage to blend the imagining of these things with a sense of spiritual loss. He meditates on "the terrible word, 'depart'" and does so with a fearful compassion for those to whom the direful word will be addressed:

"Depart from me ye cursed." Thus will these poor ungodly creatures be stript of all hope and comfort, and therefore must needs fall into a great sadness and wailing, before the judge; yea, crying out, as being loath to let go all for lost, and even as the man that is fallen into the river, will catch hold of anything, when he is struggling for life...so...these poor creatures, as they lie struggling and twining under the ireful countenance of the judge; they will bring out yet one more faint and weak groan, and there goes life and all; their last sigh is this, Lord, when saw we thee an hungered, and gave thee no meat? Or when saw we thee thirsty, and gave thee no drink? (Ibid., 285–86)

Now the damned begin to see "the worth of Christ, and what it is to be smiled upon by him; from all which they must depart...they shall have the view of this, so they will most famously behold the pit, the bottomless pit, and the flaming beds that justice hath prepared for them of old" (ibid.).

Despair and the sense of loss have become as palpable as any physical description of hell torments, which seem, indeed, almost ancillary to the spiritual and moral drama.

In another of Bunyan's mediations on damnation, *A Few Sighs From Hell*, spiritual and physical torments are more evenly matched. Indeed, this book is an exposition of the parable of Dives and Lazarus:

Verse 23: *And in hell he lift up his eyes being in torment, and seeth Abraham afar off, and Lazarus in his bosome.*

That some are so fast asleep, and secure in their sins, that they scarce know well where they are, till they come into hell, and that I gather from these words, *In hell he lift up his eyes*. He was asleep before, but hell makes him lift up his eyes.[28]

Dives is in the actual, eternal hell, where the torments are not simply those of conscience: "one part of the torments will be this, thou shalt have a full sight of all thy ill-spent life from first to last...the guilt [of all your sins] shall lie on thy soul as if thy belly were full of pitch, and set on a light fire...all the sins that ever thou didst commit since thou camest into the world, all together clapt on thy conscience as at one time, as one should clap a red hot iron to thy breast, and there to continue to all eternity, this is miserable" (ibid., 273). This is at least as well imagined as the remorse of conscience described by Bourdaloue.

The physical torments are hideously precise: "set case you should take a man, and tie him to a stake, and with red hot pincers, pinch off his flesh by little pieces for two or three years together.... Nay, but besides all this...we will serve you thus these 20 years together, and after that we will fill your mangled body full of scalding lead, and run you through with a red hot spit...here thou mayest lie and fry, scorch and broil, and burn for ever" (ibid., 300–301).

The damned soul will behold people he has never seen before, and these complete strangers "shall sit down with thy friends, and thy neighbors, thy wife and thy children in the kingdom of heaven, and thou for thy sins and disobedience shall be shut, nay, thrust out. O wonderful torment!" (ibid., 274). Instead of the friends and neighbors he has now lost, his companions will be devils "howling and roaring and screeching and yelling in such a hideous manner, that thou wilt even be at thy wits end, and be ready to run stark madde again for anguish and torment" (ibid., 274–75). And Bunyan uses familiar images to evoke the eternity of this torment: "here must thou be for ever: when thou lookest about thee, and seest what an innumerable company of howling devils thou art amongst, thou shalt think this again, this is my portion for ever. When thou has been in hell for many thousand years as there are stars in the firmament, or drops in the sea, or sands on the sea shore, yet hast thou to lie there for ever" (ibid., 279).

Bunyan always relates the fear of hell to the familiar vices that bring something as unfamiliar as eternal damnation. They are always vices of worldliness—in effect, levity and lack of any sense of eternity. They are lusts of the flesh, lies, and some quite innocuous pleasures: "they were light, stout, surly, drinking themselves drunk, slighting God's people, mocking at goodness . . . following the world, seeking after riches, faring deliciously . . . painting their faces, feeding their lusts, following their whores, robbing their neighbors, telling of lies, following of playes, and sports to pass away the time; but now they are in hell and they do cry" (ibid., 279).

Even as Bunyan describes the damned cast off from all human community into the company solely of devils, he gives a powerful sense of what human society is, even in its familiar vices. It is not far from the Shakespearean society of Mistress Quickly, Falstaff, and Bardolph in Cheapside. Bunyan is describing ordinary people damned for, on the whole, ordinary vices. In that there is an implicit sympathy with the damned. There is an intimacy in his imagining of the vices of l'homme moyen sensuel and of the hideous danger these vices expose him to. Bunyan undoubtedly takes for granted the doctrine that any sin committed is the worst sort of evil there can be, and that it is better for many millions to die in extremest agony than that any one venial sin be committed.[29] A human life is the time of testing, something of infinite meaning, eternal significance. So every human project, every moral effort and failure has the coloring of eternity. This is what we mean by the Puritan conscience, and it demands that we see every person as a candidate either for salvation or for damnation.

Fire and Brimstone from Heaven

In the later seventeenth century a stout literalism about hell and its pains was beginning to merge with a curiosity about how hell might be explained in natural terms, what is the exact composition of its fire, and where on the globe it might actually be. The beginnings of scientific speculation had begun, in a somewhat haphazard way, to look with interest at the infernal regions. Not unnaturally—and with ancient precedent—some writers began to take an interest in volcanoes. Fifteen years before Bunyan's *A Few Sighs From Hell*, Thomas Vincent published *Fire and Brimstone from heaven, from earth, in hell ... Concerning the burning of the wicked eternally ...*[30] This is an attempt to fit the fires of hell into an empirical picture of the world and is distinguished by its hyperliteralism. Vincent begins with a lively account—apparently firsthand—of a recent eruption of Mount Etna. He describes the horror and fear of those whose homes are on the slopes of the mountain. With unconcealed relish he recalls how, being papists, they had run hither and thither carrying their most sacred images, and attending a votive mass to divert the flow of the lava—all without success. Vincent aims to demonstrate both that the Etna eruption shows that the earth contains within itself fiery forces of a power sufficient to produce the fire and brimstone that destroyed Sodom and Gomorrah (Gen. 19:24), and hellflames of all the intensity and unquenchableness ascribed to them in the Bible: "God, who hath power to kindle a fire in the earth, hath power to kindle the fire of hell, and he that hath power to keep alive the fire of this mountain for some thousands of years, hath power to keep alive the fire of hell, unto eternity."[31]

Vincent is not actually arguing that Etna may be a gate of hell, only that hell exists somewhere under the earth, and that the activity of volcanoes is evidence that the earth really can produce violent and unending fires. This was not uncontroversial in his time, for many believed that what lay under the earth's surface was not fire, but water. In recounting the Flood, Genesis says that "all the fountains of the great deep [were] broken up, and the windows of heaven were opened" (Gen. 7:11). The idea—also to be found in ancient Mesopotamia—is that there are great waters both over the heavens and under the surface of the earth. Vincent is citing volcanic eruptions to paint a picture different from the biblical one.

Vincent sees the flames as real and material. Yet he also wants to understand them symbolically—as signs of the wrath of God directed at sinners, at the obviously benighted papist inhabitants of Italy, at the sinners of Sodom and Gomorrah, and eventually at all the wicked of the world on the Last Day. The flames of Sodom (and presumably of Etna) "are but shadows of future flames" and are like mere painted fire in comparison with the stream of fire and brimstone, which shall consume the wicked eternally in hell (ibid., 87). The eruption of Etna is a foretaste of that final burning of the world itself in the eventual consummation—in comparison with which it is a little thing:

> O what a dreadful fire this will be! It will be dreadful to behold it, how dreadful will it be then to feel it! As the wicked shall be in their passage to the eternal flames of hell; when they shall see the heavens on fire, and the earth on fire, and fields on fire, head, back, breast, belly, hands, arms, legs, feet every part on fire, and that such fire, though it doth torment them, yet shall not be able to consume them; when they shall see the heavens, which have endured so long to melt, stones to be broken, and the hardest metals to be dissolved by the fervent heat of this fire, and yet their bodies made so strong, that their flesh shall not be consumed hereby; O how fearful will this be! Tongue cannot utter, thought cannot conceive, the anguish of the wicked on this day, and in this place of fire. Mr. Doolittle in his book of *Rebukes* [ibid., 85], doth pathetically set forth the woe of the ungodly through this fire, from page 297 to page 305.

Even without the extra pathos provided by Mr. Doolittle the picture is clear.

The fire of hell, then, is real. Yet it is also (as we have seen) a sign of "the fierce anger and wrath of the sin-revenging God, who is himself called a consuming fire" (ibid., 98). Even as he piles up material images, Vincent seems to be trying to convey the spiritual. The fire of God's wrath will be more dreadful than if the most furious creatures in the world were mustered up together, and let loose upon the damned to tear them in pieces and devour them. Any physical torments of this world are "no more than the biting of a flea, or the prick of a pin in comparison with the immediate strokes of God's vengeance, and the burning under the fire of his indignation" (ibid., 99).

If Vincent's apparent vacillation between the symbolic and literal seems curious, so that the wrath of God is sometime symbolized by, but is sometimes the direct cause of actual physical torments, the explanation may be that, like many of his contemporaries, he still sees the world in fundamentally symbolic terms. Events in the physical world are real in themselves, but may also be read as though the world were a text conveying the mind of God. The flames of Etna are truly fire and brimstone. This shows that there really *is* fire and brimstone, and that hell may be made of the same materials as those that that erupt from the volcano. At the same time, these phenomena reveal the nature of God. Volcanoes are among those signs by which God reveals himself to us. Whether or no the flames of hell might be actually volcanic, they certainly reveal God's wrath to sinners.

So when Vincent turns to describe hellfire, his language does not change—he might just as well be describing Etna or other immense phenomena of nature: "of all the objects of this sense [i.e., feeling, or touch] fire is the most afflictive and painful . . . other senses will be afflicted too, the ear with hideous noises, shrieks, and yellings of fellow damned sinners; the eye with fearful ghastly and horrible spectacles, the smell with suffocating, odious and nasty stench, worse than carrion, or that which cometh out of an open sepulcher; but the feeling will be most afflicted by the devouring and eternally burning fire, which the wicked will be thrown into" (ibid., 100).

The fire of hell will be a great fire; it will be a dark fire; it will be an irresistible fire; a fierce fire; a continual fire; an unquenchable fire; an everlasting fire. It is surely unnecessary for Vincent to point out, as he does, that it will be rather more serious than the Great Fire of London of 1666.

Finally Vincent comes to the notorious "darkness visible"[32] of the flames of hell, and here again his language hovers between the symbolic and the material, cleverly so, for he manages to suggest that the darkness of the infernal fire is both a spiritual symbol and material fact:

> There will be no light of God's countenance, not the least smoothing of his brow. . . . There will not be the least light of comfort, nothing but weeping and wailing and gnashing of teeth; there will not be the light of the sun, or the moon, or the candle, and the fire itself will give no light, all will be dark and black, black devils, black bodies, black souls . . . or if there is to be a duskish light there, to represent one another's ruful countenances, and other frightful spectacles, be sure there will be no refreshing light, there the damned will be in a place and state of darkness for ever.[33]

Vincent has none of Bunyan's sense of human solidarity, none of his imagination of the ordinariness of the sins that lead to this prison. His final assessment, in Calvinist terms, of the probable numbers of the damned compared with that of the saved, therefore, may strike the reader as infernal priggery: "The whole world may be divided into two parts, they are either such as are in a state of nature, or such as are in a state of grace, the former are many thousand times the greater . . . the children of wrath, which are also called the children of the devil, are heirs of hell."[34]

But where is it?

> ('tis an old mistake
> To place hell at the bottom of the earth)
> —Robert Browning, "Bishop Blougram's Apology"

If we think of hell as an actual place with real fires, we might reasonably ask not only whether the fires are fed from the same source that fuels volcanoes, but whether hell might be located in the very place that is the source of volcanic fire—the center of the earth. That hell, Tartarus, Hades (or rather, *Gehenna*), lies beneath the earth's surface is an ancient belief. The shades of Homer and Virgil, no less than the damned souls of Dante's *Inferno*, are deprived of the sweet light of the sun, which is one of their most grievous losses. According to Lucian the Greeks commonly thought of the abode of the shades as "a certain large and dark place under the earth."[35] By the Greeks and Romans the underworld was variously located under Lake Avernus in Campania, or under Laconia in the Peloponnese. Christians were also encouraged to think of hell as subterraneous through the words in the Apostles' Creed: "He descended into hell."

The spirit of English empiricism comes out in Tobias Swinden, who tried to work out how the various scriptural statements and theological traditions about hell could be accommodated in what we know of the actual composition and geographical features of the earth.[36] Swinden is an undoubting believer in the literal fires of hell that consume without destroying. He quotes Isaac Barrow: "In the state of everlasting death, our bodies shall be afflicted continually, by a sulfurous flame, not only scorching the skin, but piercing the inmost sinews; and our souls shall be incessantly gnawed by a worm (the worm of bitter remorse, for our wretched perverseness and folly, the worm of horrid despair)" (ibid., 44). He quotes Tertullian on an eternal fire in which "the mountains burn and endure, and why not also the guilty and enemies of God?" This is not "a mere metaphorical fire" but a literal one, and one that needs to be explained scientifically. Were the fire and brimstone that rained upon Sodom and Gomorrah the same fire and brimstone as those with which the wicked will be eternally tormented? Does the same material erupt from volcanoes? Or will God perhaps produce a special recipe that mixes brimstone with the fires of hell to make them burn "not only the darker and sharper, but also the

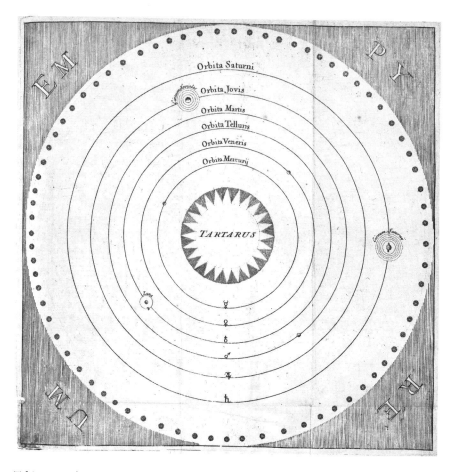

Tobias Swinden argued that the most plausible location for Hell was in the sun. Tobias Swinden, *An Enquiry into the Nature and Place of Hell* (London, 1714), 116–17.

loathesomer, and so grieve the sight, smell and taste of the wicked, which have here surfeited with so many vain pleasures" (ibid., 48).

But can hell indeed be at the center of the earth? Swinden suggests that perhaps it cannot. In the first place, there is not nearly fuel enough at earth's center to sustain the gigantic and ever-burning flames of hell (ibid., 66–67). Still more telling, the center of the earth is too small a space to contain all the lapsed angels and the uncountable numbers of the human damned. This is no small difficulty, because the fallen angels were as a third part of the stars of heaven, which, even with the astronomical knowledge available to Swinden, let alone in the age of the Hubble telescope, would suggest an impossible crowding. Of course, hideous overcrowding is itself one of the more unpleasant aspects of hell, as Swinden acknowledges when he quotes Dresselius on the numbers of the reprobate

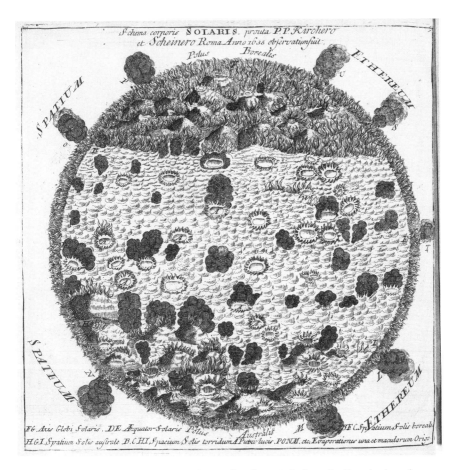

Sunspots indicate the abodes of the damned. Tobias Swinden, *An Enquiry into the Nature and Place of Hell* (London, 1714), 210–11.

amounting to not less than a hundred thousand million, all to be squeezed into one German square mile. (Swinden thinks such crowding unlikely.)

But the killing argument for Swinden is that the center of the earth simply is not hot enough. Indeed, it is not hot at all, for the simple reason that it is largely water, or, rather, water and earth. Insofar as fire and air are imprisoned beneath earth's surface, they are there by sheer accident (ibid., 67). The deeper you go into the earth, the more water will you find, a fact that confirms Psalm 24.2: God founded the earth "upon the seas, and established it upon the floods." Water is much more likely to be at the center of the earth than fire.

What about volcanic activity? This may suggest heat—but that is misleading. Volcanoes such as Vesuvius, Etna, Hecla, and those of Guatemala are really "only fires of nature's kindling in some extreme parts of the earth, and not the results of a general *Tophet* [i.e., hell, Gehenna] about the center of it" (ibid., 78–79). It is obvious that Swinden is still under the influence of the ancient theory of the four elements, according to which those of water and earth sink downward, while those of air and fire have a natural tendency to ascend.

So, if hell is not at earth's center, where is it? Swinden hits upon a theory that is as simple as it is ingenious: hell must be in the sun. Consider: the sun has easily enough fuel to go on burning for ever and at the right intensity needed to fry and roast the damned. The body of the sun is a real, corporeal fire: "If anyone be so stupid as to doubt, or hardy to deny this, let him only betake himself to those parts of the world that lie directly under the Line, and there expose his naked body to its scorching beams, when in its full meridian strength; Or, if that be too long a voyage for him, let him even in these cooler climes, on a clear summer's noon, lay himself open to its piercing rays, when collected into the focus of a reflecting concave, or other burning glass" (ibid., 108).

The sun is more than a million times bigger than the earth, so there is plenty of room for "the punishment of an innumerable company of devils and wicked men" (even if the number of the latter, as Drexel taught, should turn out to be not less than a hundred thousand million). So the body of the sun is the "Tartarus or local hell." The sun is at the center of the solar system, at the extreme edge of which is the orbit of Saturn. Beyond Saturn is the empyrean, the region of angels and happy souls. So the sun is at the extreme opposite in the solar system from the abode of the righteous and God's ministers. Hence it is the *lowest* part of creation, and therefore what could be more rational than to suppose it to be the seat of devils and miserable sprits? And is it not equally rational to assume that there is the greatest distance from the one to the other (i.e., from the devils and damned to the blessed, as from the sun to the empyrean)? The inhabitants of the two spheres are opposite in character and functions: "the former are angels of light, the latter of darkness: the former are ready and cheerful executioners of the wills and command of God; the latter are forced drudges and tired slaves of Satan" (ibid., 122).

The sun is that fire that shall last for all eternity, and certainly to the Last Day, the true *pur aionion* of which scripture speaks. Swinden deals with the difficulty that hell is often spoken of as a place of darkness as well as of fire. Do not maps of the sun show many dark spots? *That* is where the damned souls, lapped in darkness visible, are imprisoned.

After this scientific deduction of the probable location of hell, and the corresponding certainty of a literal fire that will burn for ever, Swinden returns briefly to the problem of the justice of this eternal punishment. Here his ingenuity falls away, for he disposes of the problem quite briskly. Not all punishment aims at amendment. Anyway, the damned have offended obstinately and willfully: after death they have no freedom of will that could allow them to repent: "For though God may indeed be considered under the notion of a physician, yet he may be supposed to meet with them whose case are lost, who are corrupt, putrefied, and gangreen'd members, and are therefore without mercy to be cut off, and like the unprofitable tree, fit for nothing but to be hewn down and thrown into the fire" (ibid., 240).

With that clinching medical metaphor, Swinden consigns his (and Drexel's) hundred thousand million damned souls to roast in the sun for ever—or until it becomes a dwarf star.

The Merciful Doctors

Samuel Richardson

Few, if any, writers on hell have interpreted the worm that gnaws for ever as other than a metaphor for remorse and the unappeasable stings of conscience. But they all (with rare exceptions, such as Origen) insist upon an irreducibly literal element in the flames of hell, even though these fires do not obey the laws of nature as we at present understand them. Accounts of hell agree that its eternal fires are dark as well as light, cold as well as hot, all consuming while yet they do not consume. There are attractions in thinking that the flames are at least partly metaphorical, for they can then symbolize feelings of guilt and just punishment rather than simply the torments of a wrathful God. But this suggests that hell torments understood as metaphors—of guilt and justice— are more intelligible than when they are understood merely literally. Arguments about the literal flames seem to mask deeper anxieties about the intelligibility and morality of an eternal hell. It was in England, home of empiricism, that the most persistent attempts were made to understand hell fires literally and scientifically. In England, as well, the spirit of skeptical inquiry was not easy to suppress, and it led gradually to almost open skepticism. The center of attack was the *eternity* of hell torment, and the arguments eventually called into question any belief in hell.

Sir William Dawes had tried to answer the arguments of that growing number of skeptics about the eternal punishments of the damned. Dawes's arguments are in the mainstream of Christian orthodoxy. In offending an infinitely good God, the soul is guilty of such monstrous folly and ingratitude that this alone would be sufficient grounds for God to punish it eternally "if he shall think fit."[37] Also, since it is just for human judges to inflict for outrageous crimes such punishment on offenders as shall last the whole duration of their lives, it is not unjust in God to punish sinners for the duration of their beings (i.e., eternally) since he has the power to do so (ibid., 8). Anyway, sinners would sin eternally if they *could* (ibid., 9). Hellfire does not (contrary to the opinion of Origen) *purge*; it simply punishes—for evil lies in the will, not the body, of spirits. And men in terrible torments cannot freely and voluntarily repent. Through bad habits they have quenched the holy spirit within them (ibid., 10).

Dawes's final suggestion is the traditional one that the everlasting torments of the damned may eternally minister to the saints and angels in heaven in their enjoyment of their own happiness, since the sight of everlasting torment gives them a motive to be "still more sensible" of their own felicity (ibid., 11).

In 1660 a Baptist divine, Samuel Richardson, launched a spirited attack upon hell. His arguments include a curious mixture of the scriptural and the empirical. Like others after him, Richardson tried to reinterpret scriptural passages that had been used to support the doctrine of eternal damnation. He cites places in the Bible where you might expect hell to be mentioned, but where it is not.[38] He points to inconsistencies in the idea of a corporeal hell fire.[39] He also seems to think that the distance a soul would have to fall to get to hell is an argument against it: "Others say, hell is above, near the third heaven . . . if so, it is very far to hell. Astronomers say that there are three heavens above the firmament, where the fixed stars are . . . a hundred and sixteen million miles above the earth, which is so high that if a stone or weight should fall from thence, and continue falling an hundred and fifty miles an hour, it would be eighty-eight years, two weeks, four days, five hours, and twenty minutes a falling down to earth" (ibid., 16).

But his essential argument is that hell as traditionally taught is both unjust and inhumane. A note enters discussions of hell—outrage at the cruelty that is seen as essential to the orthodox doctrine, but impossible to attribute to a merciful God—that grows stronger until it will eventually drive hell from center stage in the Christian consciousness to the wings, or even into oblivion. Richardson's arguments certainly proceed from the heart more than from the head: Christ said "Let not your hearts be troubled," but the fear of hell causes many evil and hard thoughts of God—"fear troubleth the hearts of many of the Lord's people and makes them sad with their lives" (ibid., 47). Hence the doctrine of hell causes sin, hinders faith, and disables the soul from every good work.

Richardson regards the very notion of condign punishment after death— whether or not it be eternal—as fundamentally opposed to the spirit of Jesus: "Fear is a weight that oppresses the soul and makes it weak, it straiteneth the heart; but hope comforteth and enlargeth it." Clearly Richardson is thinking of the Calvinist doctrine of predestination, for it is that, and scruples about whether one is of the number of the elect, which radically depresses the soul and causes "an exceeding and unreasonable trouble of mind and melancholy." The doctrine of hell has caused "many to murder themselves, casting themselves out of windows, and from high places to break their necks, and by other deaths, that they might not live to increase their sin, and increase their torments in hell." But "freedom from fear causeth love" (ibid., 48).

Richardson does not engage seriously with the theological and philosophical arguments of the orthodox. Yet that is what is so striking about him—he expresses a sentiment about hell torment in the light of which these arguments seem irrelevant. His confidence in sentiment is as strong as would be that of his famous namesake writing about a hundred years later—the novelist, Samuel Richardson. Yet our Richardson was writing just at the end of the Commonwealth. He goes on to argue a priori that the Christian God could not have created hell, because it is impossible that the God of nature should in this way go against nature. Man has a universal love for his fellow man, and especially for his offspring. We are the offspring of God. We cannot endure seeing other men suffer pain, least of all our own offspring—so how could God condemn *his* offspring to eternal torments? (ibid., 49).

The fundamental objection to the eternity of hell torments is that it is an unintelligible doctrine. If it be not the purpose of hell fire to purge and purify, nor simply to torment, then it must be solely intended to punish. But what does that mean? Why should punishment go on for ever? The answers traditionally given have come down to two: first, the damned go on sinning—their wills are frozen into rebellion. That is the answer of Dante. Second, a sin against an infinitely good God demands an infinite punishment.

But this assumes that we can make sense of a punishment that entails eternal torment—i.e., that the unending suffering is a work of justice (*Giustizia mosse il mio alto fattore*). Richardson is certain that we cannot. He embraces the logic of Origen's teaching about the purging effect of any punishment after death—that in the fullness of years, or of centuries, or of eons, even the most wicked, even devils, even Satan himself will be saved, that there will be a final *apocatastasis*—restoration (ibid., 50). It is against God's glory that only *some* shall be saved—let alone that a hundred thousand million should be damned. He denies that God's justice would be vindicated if he saved one man alone and damned the rest of the human race. As for hell's being necessary to fulfill the justice of God, his reply is that, on the contrary, it contradicts justice, for justice requires proportionate punishment, a death for a death, rather than infinite suffering: "a great and terrible punishment belongs to cruelty, not justice" (ibid., 55, 58).

Many defenders of hell—and even some worldly skeptics—had argued that a fear of damnation was necessary to maintain civil order among the masses. Richardson's riposte is that it is the punishments inflicted by magistrates, more than a fear of hell, that keeps men from abusing others.

Richardson's is not a subtle mind, and he cannot be said to engage closely with the theological arguments that over the centuries had been used to develop the doctrine of hell. He has, though, a massive confidence that he understands the mind of Jesus and the spirit of his teaching. It is a confidence close to the spirit of liberal churchmen of modern times, and strikingly far removed from the legalism and literalism of the mid-seventeenth century. His scriptural interpretations can hit the nail on the head, as when he reminds the reader of the occasion on which Christ's disciples asked him to call down fire from heaven to consume his enemies. Jesus rebuked them. Since he would not suffer his enemies to suffer a short death by fire, how much less so "a more terrible fire never to end?" But in the end, Richardson simply sets his own moral sense and spiritual intuition against religious orthodoxy: God is love; love is infinite, without bounds; delights in mercy and in love, not in the punishing of sin. Sin cannot overcome God's love, for "where sin hath abounded, grace did much more abound" (Rom. 5:20). Remarkably for his time, Richardson is prepared to read scripture on principles that are fundamentally humanist and that appeal to our moral sentiments. In reading scripture, we must not understand any text in a sense "that is not plain in scriptures, or contrary to scriptures, or contrary to the law of nature, or against the general goodness of mankind, or to lessen the goodness of God, or contrary to the gracious spirit and mercifulness of a saint, or contrary to the mind of Christ . . . or contrary to the fruits of the blessed spirit, the nature of the love, goodness and mercy of God" (ibid., 55). It is a comprehensive list of exclusions. If Richardson is right, the God of Augustine and Calvin, Bunyan, Tertullian, Aquinas, and Dante is not the God of scripture, or nature or mercy, and the Christian church had misunderstood him for nearly seventeen hundred years.

A Free Thinker: Thomas Burnet

The attack on orthodoxy is pressed further by Thomas Burnet, in *Hell's torments not eternal*.[40] Burnet (1637–1715) was widely suspected in his own time of being a freethinker. He cautiously introduces his critique of orthodoxy by quoting St. Augustine on certain "merciful doctors" who did not believe in the eternity of torment. Burnet's point is that although Augustine himself believed in what became the orthodoxy, he treated these merciful doctors with respect as upholders of an alternative opinion—rather than as heretics at whom anathemas should be hurled. So perhaps even now it is possible to re-open the question.

Like Richardson, Burnet relies to a great extent on our moral intuitions in condemning the doctrine. He adds a certain touch of irony savoring of the Enlightenment, suggesting that the idea of a "material fire" at the center of the earth as the abode for the wicked is just a bit ridiculous: "so remote from us, and so far below, the wicked will have an almost inaccessible place for their torments, and vast solid tracts of earth to perforate in their voyage; and how long, how tedious a journey will it be? The semi-diameter of our earth is alone 34,000 of miles, an impenetrable distance" (ibid., 3). The devils, curiously, will have allotted to them "the large prisons of the air" rather than this narrow place to dwell in (ibid., 15–16). This is a new note—not warm indignation, but cool irony, deftly implying that a material hell with a precise location is absurd. That the torments of hell might be literal he rejects with similarly dismissive irony: "flames, darkness, and extreme cold do not combine well together; how can worms live in flames or be immortal in their generations? Whereas in other places they are said to die" (ibid., 7–8).

When Jesus talked of an eternal fire prepared for the devil and his angels, he was simply using the ordinary notions of the Jews of that time. On grounds of natural reason he cannot be taken literally: "Reason, the nature of God, and the nature of things are on the milder side; they plead for temperate sentence . . . that Christianity may not receive an irrecoverable wound" (ibid.). Burnet is ready simply to oppose his own dogma to that of the church: "it is certainly repugnant to the divine wisdom, justice and mercy, to condemn his creatures to eternal misery" (ibid., 9).

Burnet is one of the few theologians to confront head-on the common argument for the justice of eternal punishment—that the damned cannot repent, that their will is fixed in everlasting malice. Why should they not repent? It injures the dignity of God if it be thought that he formed human nature "in such a manner as to degenerate into a state of incurable pravity" (ibid.). If human beings remain rational creatures, with understanding and will, they may repent; but if they have neither the one nor the other, they cannot sin (ibid., 11).

Burnet is making a serious point. We can imagine people so steeped in habits of vice that repentance is, for all practical purposes, impossible. They mentally exclude the possibility; they justify themselves to themselves; they suppress consciousness of their own wrongdoing. One way of putting this has been that they "resist the known truth"—which is one of the sins against the Holy Ghost. The traditional teaching has been that the human will becomes fixed at the moment of death. Dante makes psychological sense of this when he depicts the damned obsessively re-enacting the vices that damned them. If we have an intelligible idea of a disembodied soul surviving death, we can perhaps understand this. The power of desiring and willing seems connected with the possession of a body, and with the possibility of new experiences. We could, possibly, think of a disembodied soul as fixed in the memories it might retain from life, but with no possibility of new experience. So in some way we could imagine its will as eternally fixed. But Christian doctrine is that the soul will eventually be re-united with the body. If that is so—and if the risen body has characteristics in common with the earthly body (and if it has none, it becomes unclear what bodily resurrection would mean, what the continuity between former and risen body might be)—then it would seem that the risen soul-body identity would be capable of new desires, thoughts and intentions. If the new experiences are sufficiently shocking—for instance, the exquisite tortures of the fires of hell—then the damned would have a very good reason to repent. Burnet imagines exactly such a moment when the wicked see Christ coming in his glory at the Last Day:

> there will be no room for their infidelity . . . concupiscence will be no
> more . . . ambition, avarice and evil affections will be taken away;
> why, therefore, and with what motives can they adhere for ever to their
> sins, unless they are hardened by heaven? But if they are driven
> away by any external force without any freedom of liberty, or of reason,
> they cannot in that case be called men. (ibid., 10)

As to the contention that sin is infinite in its guilt because it is committed against an infinite God, Burnet points out that that makes all sins equal (which is what Calvin asserted), so that it would follow that (as Calvin also asserted) "the lightest and most trivial sin may be punished with eternal misery" (ibid., 11).

Burnet clearly sees no need to argue with the orthodox in their own terms. He insinuates, instead, a confident rationality and an equally confident moral sense, which takes itself to be superior to theirs. He knows in advance of any argument that the doctrine of eternal torment is cruel, absurd, and contrary to reason. If scripture supports this doctrine, then scripture must be cavalierly reinterpreted to exclude such a pernicious belief, for the God of scripture must not be seen as creating man frail, and then punishing him eternally for falling (ibid., 10).

Like Richardson, Burnet anticipates the Sentimentalist doctrine of the later eighteenth century that will mold its God in the light of its moral certainties. This culminates (in a more abstract form) in Kant, who argued that we are not obliged to obey a commandment simply in that it is ordained by God, but only if we can see that it is right in itself—and *therefore* that it is ordained by God. Burnet and other skeptics are sweeping away the theological justifications of eternal punishment on the grounds, essentially, that a God of unending torment would not be a God fit to love and obey—precisely the argument against the God of Calvin's logical deductions. Given that scripture frequently describes God as merciful, we have a right and duty so to read scripture that it is this picture of God that emerges from it. Reason, nature, and this canon of scriptural interpretation make virtually unthinkable the hell of Augustine, Aquinas, and Calvin.

Burnet is not arguing that there are no savage punishments in hell—only that they do not last for ever, and that the damned may eventually be allowed to sink into nonbeing. So he does not actually consider seriously the question of how far the hideousness of the torments—except, perhaps, for the greatest criminals (murderers of millions, for instance)—is in itself abhorrent to the moral sense. Nevertheless, he is on strong ground when he suggests that the development of the orthodox doctrine from the early church fathers is a sort of moral *reductio ad absurdum*, which those theologically captured by it were too benighted to realize. To that end he quotes from an "unmerciful doctor"—Tertullian: "such is eternity . . . that if a damned person, in a thousand years, were to squeeze one tear from his eye, it would afford enough water, in time, to drown the whole earth."

Burnet writes: "The time will come, when that opinion will be as absurd and ridiculous as Transubstantiation" (ibid., 17).

Dives Saved?

Just about the most audacious reinterpretation of scripture at this time so as to deny the eternity of hell was that of William Whiston (1667–1752) in a book entitled *The Eternity of Hell Torments Considered*. Whiston's book is a determined exegesis of scripture that will explain away any hint of eternal punishment. Like others before him, including Thomas Burnet, he explains that the Greek words *aion* and *aionion* do not mean "eternal" but denote simply an indefinitely long period of time. He also argues that *Hades* is a place of detention underground, known to the pagans, and not the Jewish place of fiery torment, *Gehenna*. With this in mind he takes it upon himself boldly to reinterpret that parable of Christ that (as we have seen) has always been taken to express Jesus's own belief in the eternity of hellfire: Dives and Lazarus.

Whiston notes that the parable has raised horror in the minds of "imperfectly good Christians"—as well as in the minds of the more perfect. But this is based on misunderstandings. The rich man is not in Gehenna but in Hades.[41] He is, therefore, punished "in close confinement" rather than prison, so that remission may be hoped for. The purpose of this punishment is to amend him.[42]

Abraham does not treat Dives as "a damned wretch that deserves no compassion, or answer." Rather he calls him "son" and "puts him coolly in mind" of his changed circumstances and those of Lazarus (ibid., 120). On Abraham's words about there being "a great gulf fixed" between Lazarus and the rich man, Whiston "coolly" interprets this as meaning that "Providence had put an invincible obstacle to Lazarus's coming to his assistance, as he desired, and as Lazarus would otherwise readily have done" (ibid.). Dives now repents his former indifference to Lazarus and is filled with compassion toward his own five brothers, whom he wishes to prevent from coming to this place of torment. All this shows that Dives, far from showing infernal obstinacy or savage cruelty—which is how orthodox Christians saw the damned—reveals something more like "a preliminary to true Christian charity, and to a real repentance toward Lazarus before" (ibid., 121). So Dives is brought by this punishment to true repentance, and this shows that forgiveness is sometimes denied in this world but granted in Hades.

With the saving of Dives—the parable about whom has always been taken as the strongest evidence that Jesus did believe in an eternity of suffering for the lost—the English tradition of free religious enquiry reaches the point of no return.

PART II

Purgatory

9

Rome's Happiest Inspiration?

A Cause of Scandal

Of all the doctrines of the Roman Catholic Church, purgatory is the one that historically has attracted the greatest hostility from Protestants. The alleged Catholic exalting of works over faith may be the nub of the differences that led to the Reformation rupture between the two traditions. But the immediate occasion for Luther's revolt was the selling of indulgences by Tetzel. The theory of indulgences derived from the ancient practice of canonical penance. The sinner, in the earliest years of the church, had to repent publicly in atonement for a sin that he had openly confessed (before private confession had become the norm) and for which he had received absolution. The penance counted as the temporal punishment, or satisfaction, for this sin, of which the guilt had already been removed. (In some cases—stolen goods, for instance—he would also have to make restitution.) Since the church imposed these temporal penalties, it also began to claim the right to remit them—as a state may declare an amnesty and release prisoners.[1] Certain pious acts might attract these indulgences, which had the effect of remitting the temporal punishment due to already pardoned sins.

Although the doctrine of purgatory did not necessitate the practice of indulgences, that practice had long enhanced the authority of the church and promoted the doctrine of purgatory. Purgatory left an indelible stamp on late medieval Christianity. It can even be said to have transformed it. What started as shadowy intimations of a possible middle state of souls between salvation and final condemnation, evolved into a doctrine that so shaped the actual religious practice of the Christian West as to constitute a profound psychological break with the first ten Christian centuries. It was the liveliness of the belief in purgatory that led to many of the greatest works of ecclesiastical architecture. People of means made sure, in dying, that they left funds sufficient for numerous, even perpetual masses, by means of which the suffrages of the faithful would assist the souls of those who died in the faith but in a state of venial sin, to pass more easily through the purgatorial sufferings to paradise. One Oxford College, All Souls, was founded with the specific purpose of praying for the souls of those English warriors who fell on the field of Agincourt.[2]

What is purgatory? The first dogmatic statement about the prayers of the living assisting the souls of the dead came at the Council of Lyons in 1274. According to the Council of Trent (1545–63), "there is a Purgatory," and the souls there detained "are assisted by the suffrages (i.e. prayers and oblations) of the faithful, and most especially by the acceptable sacrifice of the altar."[3] It is a place, or, as Trent also says, a state, where souls are purified between death and resurrection. The souls in purgatory have left this world in a state of grace but are subject to that temporal punishment due to mortal sins, of which the eternal punishment has been remitted, but which have been imperfectly expiated, and also to unconfessed venial sins still on the soul. According to some theologians, the severity of the punishments in purgatory, like those of hell, exceed the most bitter pains that mortals can conceive. But souls in purgatory are immensely consoled as they endure their punishments, which they do willingly, in the assured hope of final salvation.

If the Protestants wanted an example of Romish innovations they needed look no further than purgatory. If they wanted a clear example of a doctrine that exalted the power of the church and the priesthood, and also filled ecclesiastical coffers, then there, too, purgatory was a perfect instance. As Jacques Le Goff in his magisterial book, *The Birth of Purgatory* puts it: "For the Church, what a marvelous instrument of power! The souls in Purgatory were considered to be members of the Church militant. Hence, the Church argued, it ought to have (partial) jurisdiction over them, even though God was nominally the sovereign judge in the other world. Purgatory brought to the Church not only new spiritual power but also, to put it bluntly, considerable profit.... Much of this profit went to the mendicant orders, ardent propagandists of the new doctrine. And finally, the "infernal" system of indulgences found powerful support in the idea of Purgatory."[4]

A common Protestant ground for scandal was the belief that Rome's promotion of purgatory had financial motives: "you may buy as many masses as will free your soul from Purgatory for 29,000 years, at the church of St. John Lateran, on the feast of that saint; at Santa Bibiana, on All Souls' day, for 7,000 years; at a church near the basilica of St. Paul and at another on the Quirinal Hill, for 10,000 and 3,000 years, and at a very reasonable rate."[5] A papal document published in France in 1691 was alleged to contain a tariff for indulgences and dispensations covering certain offenses: for absolution of the crime of apostasy, £4; absolution and dispensation for bigamy, £1051; heresy, £80; murder, £95; being an accessory to murder, £85; permission to read forbidden books, £25; dispensation from vows of chastity, £15.

Ancient Christian traditions—this was the Protestant view, and it was largely consonant with the facts—set a "boiling gulf"[6] between salvation and damnation, between the broad gate that leads to hell and the strait one that admits to heaven, and saw life's drama as the choice of (or predestination to) one or the other. And now, here was the church claiming to erect a bridge over the abyss, to elide the opposition between a sinful and hence damned state, and a state of justification, hence salvation: "[The papists] have paved a large causeway over this wide gulf, and have opened a very easy passage from a life of torments to one of eternal happiness. For by virtue of some prayers, oblations and indulgences, they have made the way broad to heaven and narrow to hell. A man that hath money in his pocket cannot be damned, and a camel may as soon pass through the eye of a needle as a poor man be saved."[7]

Then the very fact that the church had defined as of faith a doctrine that had such slight warrant in scripture, and not much in tradition, pointed, for Protestants, to a perversion of the very idea of the church. Nothing could better illustrate the hubris of medieval Catholicism than that from the late twelfth- to the sixteenth-century popes and councils should have elaborated and imposed (as an article of faith) belief in the existence of a place that was hardly imagined in the early church, and was (and is still) denied in Eastern Orthodoxy. Over the years, Protestants built up a huge case history of papist abuses centering on the practices associated with purgatory:

"A certain rich proprietor at Alicante having died, left sufficient money to the Church for the purchase of twelve thousand masses for his soul; but after a few of them had been said, the masses were discontinued. A lawsuit was in consequence instituted by the heir, for the recovery of the sum left for the masses. The defence, however, was, that upon application being made to the Pope to be relieved from saying so great a number, he had granted a dispensation, at the same time declaring that twelve were as efficacious and beneficial to the soul of the deceased as twelve thousand."[8]

Another favorite topic for Protestant polemic was St. Patrick's Purgatory, a famous pilgrimage center at Lough Derg in County Donegal. The original legend was that St. Patrick, having crossed the river Derg on the back of a salmon, which he mistook for a stepping stone, and having fasted there for the whole of Lent, was granted the privilege of bringing souls out of hell—"seven persons on every Saturday until Doom."[9] This became the basis for a pilgrimage to a cave on the island of Lough Derg, which was popularly believed to be the entrance to purgatory. From the twelfth century on, pilgrims entered the cave, or were shut in at night, and later told how they had experienced the terrors of postmortem punishment, including visions of demons. English governments under Elizabeth I, and later, tried to close down the pilgrimage site, but it always revived, until an imposing basilica was erected over the cave. (Hamlet, on seeing his father's ghost, who is detained in purgatory, swears an oath "by St. Patrick.")[10] Popular piety was convinced that whoever underwent penance at St. Patrick's Purgatory was assured of salvation, for they had seen what awaits the impenitent in hell: "[It] contains numbers of men which no arithmetic can reckon up, all lying on the ground, pierced through the body. They uttered hoarse cries of agony, their tongues cleaving to their jaws. They were buffeted by violent tempests, and shattered by repeated blows of devils. The devils drove them into another plain, horrible with exquisite tortures. Some, with iron chains about their necks and limbs, were suspended over the fires; others were burned with red hot cinders. Not a few were transfixed with spits and roasted, melting metals being poured into them. Alas, for those who do no penance in this world."[11]

In attacking purgatory, Protestantism was assaulting what was most dear to late mediaeval piety. It was a doctrine that put into practice in the most literal way the doctrine of the Communion of Saints. The dead were still among us, because prayers for their souls, which would have direct and continuing effect on their progress in the next world, went on indefinitely.[12] A huge effort of piety went into prayer for the dead. Perpetual chantries were established in cathedrals and parish churches. Indulgences could be earned by the living and applied to the dead. When at the Reformation all the chantries were destroyed and prayers for the dead forbidden and declared vain, this must have seemed to many like the destruction of the soul of their religion—a sense sharpened by the fact that the mass itself, which had been seen as a perpetual sacrifice for both the living and the dead, was also outlawed.

Yet purgatory—hardly existent in scripture, shakily supported by tradition, productive of numerous abuses, responsible for a vast extension of clerical power—could claim to be Rome's happiest inspiration. Its distinction, between the unrepented mortal sin that merited damnation, and the venial faults that could be purged after death, as well as the allowance that forgiven sins still required satisfaction, may well have been a softening of the sublime and terrible gulf between saving and losing one's soul, but it was shaped both by something humane and by the sense of justice. It is true that in traditional religion purgatory is very much like hell, where "the sexually promiscuous were tormented in the loins, the gluttonous forced to drink scalding venom or nauseous filth,"[13] but the accompanying doctrine that those in purgatory, in the midst of their torments, were sure of salvation made possible a picture of repentant suffering infused with charity. Dante developed this possibility so as to transform the traditional picture of purgatory.

Scripture

Catholic apologists for purgatory ransacked the scriptures for evidence that it was anciently believed in. A few texts were quoted again and again. Judas Maccabeus sent money to Jerusalem to procure sacrifices in the Temple for his soldiers who had been slain in battle.[14] Paul, apparently referring to a primitive Christian practice in which Christians lay under the coffins of their unbaptized (pagan) relatives and were baptized on their behalf: "What shall they do which are baptized for the dead, if the dead rise not at all?"[15] Then there was: "And whosoever speaketh a word against the Son of man, it shall be forgiven him: but whosoever speaketh against the Holy Ghost, it shall not be forgiven him, neither in this world, neither in the *world* to come" (Matt. 12:32). Again: "If any man's work shall be burned, he shall suffer loss: but he shall himself be saved; yet so as by fire" (1 Cor. 3: 11–15). Christ's descent into hell between his death and resurrection was interpreted as Christ's releasing from hell (or Limbo) the virtuous Patriarchs who were deemed to have looked to salvation from him *avant la lettre*, and perhaps even one or two virtuous pagans. Hence there was a place in which those destined for heaven might be kept for a while after their deaths before entering into their glory.

A number of ancient liturgies offered prayers for the dead. From the Liturgy of St. Basil: "Be mindful also of all who have slept in the hope of a resurrection to life everlasting." St. John Chrysostom: "For the memory and remission of their sins who were the founders of this habitation." St. Mark of Alexandria: "Give rest O Lord Our God to the souls of our Fathers and Brethren, who have slept in the faith of Christ."[16]

These were hardly convincing arguments to the Protestant opponents of purgatory. The texts cited are either hard to interpret, as in the case of the two Pauline texts and the text from Matthew, or uncanonical—the Protestants did not accept as canonical the books of Maccabees. The ancient liturgies certainly show that the early church prayed, in general terms, for the dead—but this was far from the medieval practice by which named individuals hoped to be assisted in the next world by perpetual masses. Nevertheless, someone sympathetic to the idea of purgatory could possibly find creative interpretations for the scriptural passages that might just, barely, press them into service for a "development of doctrine" (a Catholic more than a Protestant notion, to be sure). But the truth would remain that, compared with the plain and obvious sense of some New Testament sayings of Jesus about heaven and hell, the bits of scripture cited to support purgatory are fragmentary, dark, and almost nugatory.

Purgatory, nevertheless, answered profound needs. If it reduces the terror of judgment that had been centrally important to Christian tradition, this can count as an argument in its favor. For it tempers terror with justice and, indeed, mercy. It had always been a hard doctrine to swallow that a man who died with any unrepented sin should suffer for all eternity. Equally, the idea that a last-minute repentance could cancel all the punishment due to the sins of a misspent life and admit instantly to paradise, troubled others—especially those who had always had a certain *tendresse* for the elder brother in the parable of the prodigal son.

It is interesting that both supporters and opponents of purgatory could appeal to intuitions about the fundamental character of Christianity. The Protestant John Hartcliffe, writing in 1685, argued that Jesus fundamentally teaches that heaven and hell are fixed for the two eternal states of good and bad men, and that if after this life they had any hopes of gaining the first, or escaping the second by the prayers or gifts of their surviving friends, this expectation "would in great measure frustrate the intent of Christ's coming into the world, which was to teach men how in *this present life* they must work out their salvation, how through patient continuance in well-doing they must here be brought to goodness and real virtue."[17] The Church of Rome seems to assume that human beings are incapable of the goodness to which they are called, whereas a true "Godly great fear" awakens all our powers, quickens our motions, gives our feet wings "and enables men to do things with ease, which without so strong a motive, they would never be persuaded to attempt."[18] Or, as Kant writes, a man may say that he is incapable of withstanding the temptation to commit adultery; but if he knows that a gallows is constructed outside his house ready to punish the act, he will certainly find the strength to remain chaste.[19]

Believers in purgatory could call on their own intuitions: "the infinite goodness of God can admit nothing into heaven, which is not clean, and pure from all sin both great and small. . . . There must of necessity be some place or state, where souls, departed this life, pardoned as to the eternal guilt or pain, yet obnoxious to some temporal penalty, or with the guilt of some venial faults, are purged and purified, before their admittance into heaven."[20]

Much of the a priori argument in favor of purgatory bears an interesting resemblance to Origen's "heretical" arguments against the eternity of hell, especially his doctrine that all just punishment must be remedial. God is the physician of the sick soul when he punishes sin. In extreme cases he "makes use of penal remedies . . . even to the infliction of a punishment of fire on those who have lost their soul's health."[21] Origen (as we saw) makes the fires of hell symbolic of "those faults of passion which often occur in men, as when the soul is burnt up with the flames of love, or tormented with the fires of jealousy or envy, or tossed about with furious anger, or consumed with intense sadness."[22] God the physician, therefore, *heals* the souls he punishes. Flames of punishment and other tortures that were not remedial would be simply the inflictions of cruelty, not of justice, let alone of love. That is why there will in the end be an *apocatastasis* (restoration) in which all rational beings, even the devil himself, will have a share.

Upholders of purgatory never went so far as to envisage Origen's *apocatastasis*—but sometimes his language crept into their arguments. Thomas White insists that the punishments of purgatory will not be externally inflicted torments, but will be "such punishments as naturally spring from the sins themselves, as the delay of Beatitude till the Day of Judgment and the dissensions any intestine Warre of Appetites [produces]."[23] The pains are not corporeal—the fire, darkness, gnashing of teeth are not to be taken literally: "that Darkness is a faint Expression of the Privation of the Beatifical Vision . . . [That] Fire and Burning describe Love and Grief . . . the Worm of Conscience and Gnashing of Teeth implies Repentance."[24]

Given that the whole idea of purgatory was of a place or state where the soul is afforded the grace to repent, Origen's insistence that the torments are symbolical of inner states, and that as punishments they are remedial, becomes very plausible. And the sting in the tail—that Origen denied the apparently clear scriptural teaching about the eternity of hell torments—is removed.

Unspeakably Pleasant Torments: St. Catherine of Genoa

The developed orthodoxy of purgatory is to be found in simple and limpid form in a *Treatise on Purgatory*, by the fifteenth-century saint, Catherine of Genoa (1447–1510). It is an orthodoxy that seeks to explain how, although the purgatorial sufferings are unimaginably severe—perhaps as severe, extensively speaking, as those of hell—the souls in purgatory are nevertheless joyful. One reason for this, according to Catherine, is that they are exempt from self-love. Since they do not think of themselves, they see in the pains only the working of the divine goodness: "They cannot see that they are in pain because of their sins; that sight they cannot hold in their minds because in it there would be an active imperfection, which cannot be where no actual sin can be."[25] It is only just at the moment in which they pass from this life that they see the cause of the purgatory they endure. They never see it again, for in another sight of it "there would be self."[26]

This is the purgatorial version of the happiness of the saints in heaven, which is not diminished, but actually increased, by the sight of the sufferings of the damned. For (as Aquinas suggested) the saved see in the infernal sufferings only the operation of God's justice.[27] Catherine says that no happiness can be compared with that of the souls in purgatory, save only that of the saints in paradise.[28] Another writer, having suggested that "all these pains are purely pleasures" gives the reason why: "They look upon these pains as a man of invincible courage, highly inflamed and passionately enamored of some achievement, would look upon his adventurous actions or sufferings in the pursuit; wherein reason and experience tell us he would feel unspeakable *pleasure*."[29] (The idea of a purgatorial painful pleasure probably stands behind lines from Crashaw's poem on St. Theresa of Avila: "O! how oft wilt thou complain / Of a sweet and subtle pain, / Of intolerable joys."[30] It is given sculptural expression in Bernini's *St. Theresa in Ecstasy* where a cherub, turning a spear in Theresa's viscera, causes her burning anguish as well as ecstasy.)

This may look complacent, even fantastical. Yet the idea, which many writers on purgatory entertain, at least as a possibility, that talk of flames and other torments in purgatory is symbolic of spiritual pains—guilt, regret, sense of one's uncleanness before God—makes it plausible. For our mental states are defined by their intentional objects. If my burning sorrow—so burning as to be experienced almost as a physical pain—is made up of the thought that I, an ungrateful sinner, have offended a God who loves me and whom I love, and with whom I know I will eventually be united, then this must be a significantly different sorrow from one that is directed at an offended God who casts me off for ever. When lovers quarrel and are reconciled, their pain at the rupture, mixed as it is with relief at restored affection, takes on in the memory a different character from an unrestored breach, which can turn into hatred. This will not take us all the way to the conclusion that the sufferers in purgatory are actually happy, let alone that that they feel "unspeakable pleasure"—but it does at least point in that direction.

Indeed, we could see the doctrine of purgatory as contributing to the psychology of repentance. The fundamental idea is of the difference between a pain of mind with, and one without, hope. Aristotle had suggested that the anger of a man directed at someone much more highly placed or much more powerful than himself would come out not as anger but as a sort of melancholy.[31] Anger is a painful perturbation of the mind but yet, as directed toward an outcome that is hoped for (the correction or punishment of the person who has provoked the anger) contains, in this very hope, an element that pleases. If the hope of achieving that fails, then all that is left is the pain of mind—which you could reasonably call melancholy. The character of the feeling is determined by such contexts and possible outcomes, by its intentional objects.

When one is talking about physical pain, it would be unwise to push this reasoning too far. Jesus says: "A woman when she is in travail hath sorrow, because her hour is come; but, as soon as she is delivered of the child, she remembereth no more the anguish, for joy that a man is born into the world" (John 16:21). Her pain may be different from the pain a terminally ill person suffers, just in that she knows it is a prelude to a great joy. But Jesus does not say that her knowledge that she will rejoice means that she does not suffer the pain, let alone that the pain is an unspeakable pleasure. Yet even to suggest that would not quite be nonsense—people do intelligibly say that suffering accepted for a loved one was not suffering, and they must at least partly mean it. Given that the theorists of purgatory are so often ready to treat its sufferings as anyway symbolic or mental, the idea that the pain turns into something like pleasure is not absurd.

Catherine of Genoa likes to express the difference between souls in purgatory suffering with hope and love, and those in hell who are merely tormented, in imagery of rust and gold. The rust—sin—is burned away by the purgatorial fire, with the result that the true character of the soul is uncovered, and it can be reached by the light and loving warmth of God. The soul that has not separated itself from God through mortal sin will turn out to be like gold. The more it is refined by fire the more golden it becomes. The fire melts it until it has destroyed in it every imperfection. Attachment to self rather than to God is annihilated. Insofar as the soul is in God, it cannot be destroyed: "When gold has been purified up to twenty-four carats, it can no longer be consumed by any fire; not gold itself, but only dross can be burnt away. Thus the divine fire works in the soul."[32]

The starting point for St. Catherine is that the soul, having been restored by baptism, finds itself back on the road to its first state—oneness with God. However, the lasting effects of original sin in this life's pilgrimage mean that most people die stained by some sins, and they then realize that their souls need to be transformed, cleansed of sinfulness so that they can approach their true end. This kindles in the soul "a fire so great that this is its purgatory." The soul's instinct to God, aflame and thwarted, makes purgatory.[33]

The image is certainly that of lovers. Separation between lovers can mean that their love is aflame and thwarted. But if they know for certain that they will be reunited, the suffering must needs take on a different character. Instead of melancholy or despair there will be hope and assured expectation. Since an emotion is identified by its intentional objects, the pain of the hopeful lovers will be so unlike that of people who love without hope that it might not be absurd to say that it is a different feeling. The understanding of their experience, the sense of the shape of their lives of those who love with assured hope, is different from that of those who despair.

Thoughts along these lines underlie the common descriptions and justifications of purgatorial sufferings. They go with the steady effort to discriminate between the sufferings of purgatory and the torments of hell. Although some writers thought that demons conducted souls to purgatory, just as they did to hell, this was a minority view. ("Albertus [Magnus] and Dr. Fisher assert that the ministers and executioners of purgatorial punishment are the holy angels: Sir Thomas More contends they are the devils.")[34] A tradition grew up that the soul's guardian angel conducted it to purgatory, whence it would lead it on to heaven after its period of probation was accomplished—a tradition that we find in Newman's *The Dream of Gerontius*. No one thought that demons tormented the souls as they were purged.

Dante: *Purgatorio*

Jacques Le Goff writes: "A little more than a hundred years after its inception, purgatory benefited from an extraordinary stroke of luck: the poetic genius of Dante Alighieri, born in Florence in 1265, carved out for it an enduring place in human memory."[35] Le Goff calls *Il Purgatorio* "the noblest representation of Purgatory ever conceived by the mind of man" and points out that Dante, while affirming the essence of the dogma, selects from among the many, often competing, images that the tradition of purgatory had introduced into the imaginations of Christians.

The nobility of Dante's vision in the *Purgatorio* is bound up with the superb evocations of repentance he achieves throughout the poem. He depicts the suffering souls eagerly seeking out their torments inspired by assurance of final salvation; and he does so with the concreteness of poetry again and again so that this state of mind is realized dramatically and psychologically. Dante develops a picture of the recovery of innocence, assisted by grace and such virtues as humility, pity, and gentleness.

Le Goff argues that purgatory was one of the main reasons for the dramatization of the moment of death, because repentance *in articulo mortis* could avoid the horror of final damnation through the lesser horror of a period of postmortem purging: "Final contrition increasingly became the last resort for those who wished to take advantage of purgatory. Life's final moments accordingly took on a new intensity: even though it was long since too late for most sinners to hope for direct admission to Heaven, there was still time to be saved by way of Purgatory."[36]

In the *Purgatorio*, Dante depicts a number of last-minute repentances. In Canto 5 he meets Buonconte da Montefeltro, who had been slain in battle and whose body had never been found on the battlefield. Encumbered in heavy armor, and wounded in the throat, Buonconte had fled to where a mountain torrent flowed into the Arno, and lying there, just before he died, he uttered the name of Mary:

> Io dirò vero, e tu 'l ridì tra ' vivi:
>> l'angel di Dio mi prese, e quel d'inferno
>> gridava: "O tu del ciel, perché mi privi?
> Tu te ne porti di costui l'etterno
>> per un lagrimetta che 'l mi toglie;
>> ma io farò de l'altro governo!"

[I will tell you the truth, and do you repeat it among the living. The Angel of God took me, and he from Hell cried, "O you from heaven, why do you rob me? You carry off with you the eternal part of him for one little tear which takes him from me; but of the rest I will make other disposal!"][37]

The devil refers contemptuously to "one little tear"–as though the physical fact of a teardrop is all there is. The church, however, had always made contrition, which might well include weeping, an integral part of repentance. Hence there is an immense metaphysical significance to the *lagrimetta*— although Satan, in his rage, affects not to understand this.[38] With magnificent literalness, the devil goes on to show exactly what he thinks of this drop of water that can snatch a soul from his grasp. He stirs up the mists and the winds of that part of the Apennines, and causes a raging torrent to sweep Buonconte's frozen corpse into the Arno. In dying, Buonconte had disposed his arms over his breast in the form of a cross: the devil has at least the satisfaction of having the waters loosen his arms.

In contrasting the torrent of waters, rolling along the corpse and burying it in the depths of the Arno, with the teardrop, Dante is dramatizing Catholic belief about the infinite significance of repentance—indeed, of that briefest of moments when repentance *in articulo mortis* saves the soul from Hell. The doctrine of purgatory fits this dramatization very well. The briefest moment is

The last-minute repentance of Buonconte da Montefeltro. *The Divine Comedy,* illustrated by Gustave Doré (London 1874, 1875), *Purgatorio,* Canto 5, 124–27.

sufficient for salvation—but this leaves us with a very strong sense of the temporal punishment due to sin. Catholic teaching is also enforced in Dante's pointing out elsewhere that a soul, which repents at the last moment of grave sin, needs the suffrage of someone on earth to get it into purgatory.[39]

Dante's purgatory, though entirely orthodox, is not traditional. Most writers about the "middle state of souls" had placed purgatory near hell, probably somewhere in the depths of the earth. Dante's, by contrast, is an immensely high mountain, in the Southern Hemisphere, directly opposite Jerusalem, on the other side of the globe. The progress of souls is one of climbing Mount Purgatory, a task that is initially extremely arduous, but which becomes progressively easier as each soul is freed of sin and becomes lighter and lighter until the advance toward the top is like a skiff sailing rapidly with the current (Canto 4, 91–94). The soul's progress in purgatory is also a gradual cleansing from pride, the root of all sin. Pride is shown weighing down repentant sinners as by great stones about their necks (Canto 11, 52–54), forcing them to look down rather than toward their goal. Dante himself becomes physically lighter as he is purged of the pride which he acknowledges as his greatest fault (Canto 11, 117–20; Canto 12).

Purgatorio shows deadly sins being purged by their opposite virtues. So pride is purged by humility, gluttony by fasting (indeed, famine), envy by pity, and wrath by *mansuetudo*, or gentleness. Hence repentance is not simply negative—a casting off of a vice—but also the acquiring of a positive good. In acquiring the good we learn to love it, and since God is the ultimate source of all good, we come to love God more and more. Therefore the essential plan of the poem is to show the growth of love.

Purgatory itself consists of seven circles, each ranged above the other, through which the poet passes as he ascends the mountain. Each of these circles purges sinners of deadly sins—the sins (in order) of pride, envy, wrath, sloth, avarice, gluttony and lust. The purging is produced by punishment and, secondly, by the soul's being brought to meditate on the sin and its corresponding virtue.[40] In Cantos 14 and 15 charity and pity are opposed to envy, and gentleness to wrath. One example, taken from Ovid, is of Aglauros, daughter of Cecrops, king of Athens. Her envy caused the god Mercury to turn her into a stone—an appropriate emblem of the hardening of the heart that goes with envy. Aquinas considers as a sign of the truest envy that it be a discontent about another's good, in so far as it surpasses ours. "That is true envy, and is always wrong."[41] Envy is directly and essentially a sin against charity. Envy feels pain at the good of our neighbor, whereas charity rejoices at it.[42] Pity is disconsolate over our neighbor's bad fortune, whereas envy is disconsolate over their good fortune: "The envious, then . . . are not men of mercy, nor are merciful characters men of envy."[43] Pride begets vainglory, which in turn leads to envy, because the vainglorious person is always discontented at the good of others, which might undermine his sense of himself. Disinterested envy is one of the worst sorts—grief at the prosperity of another simply because that enhances his good name.

Aquinas's account of envy, which Dante closely mirrors, makes it a sin that stains and corrodes the soul. It is what Aquinas would call a capital sin. Such a sin (to use Sartrean terminology) constitutes the whole of a person's being-toward-the-world. It is, therefore, not a vice that can easily be thought of as being cancelled out by an act of repentance. Or rather, divine mercy can be thought of as accepting an act of repentance and ipso facto cancelling the guilt of the sin; but the stain, or what Catherine of Genoa calls the "rust" of the vice can be purged only by a drawn-out process. This could be thought of as a punishment externally inflicted. More plausibly it can be envisaged as the opposite virtue invading the territory occupied by the vice. In Dante's scheme, charity and pity do the invading. In Canto 14, two of the repentant spirits express a charitable pity for the misfortunes of certain great Tuscan houses, and find that weeping for pity comes more naturally to them than speech.

In Canto 15 wrath is countered by what Aquinas calls *mansuetudo* (mansuetude—gentleness.) Dante is suddenly caught up in an ecstatic vision in which he sees "persons in a temple, and a woman about to enter, with the tender attitude of a mother, saying: 'My son, why have you done so to us? Behold your father and I sought you, sorrowing'" (Canto 15, 85–92). The reference is to the finding of the child, Jesus, in the Temple:

> But they, supposing him to have been in the company, went a day's journey; and they sought him among their kinsfolk and acquaintance.
> And when they found him not, they turned back again to Jerusalem, seeking him.
> And it came to pass, that after three days they found him in the temple, sitting in the midst of the doctors, both hearing them, and asking them questions.
> And all that heard him were astonished at his understanding and answers.
> And when they saw him they were amazed: and his mother said unto him, Son, why hast thou thus dealt with us? Behold thy father and I have sought thee sorrowing. (Luke 2:44–48)

Mary's response to the child indeed reveals not just the virtue of *mansuetudo* but also the scope of that virtue.[44] For in this gentlest of rebukes she is also seeking understanding—whereas a response of wrath would, for practical purposes, have excluded understanding. Understanding is not what she gets immediately, when the child answers: "How is it that ye sought me? wist ye not that I must be about my Father's business." But the chapter ends with that memorably understated recompense for Mary's *mansuetudo*: "And he went down with them, and came to Nazareth, and was subject unto them: but his mother kept all these sayings in her heart" (Luke 2:44–49, 51).

Again the virtue that casts out the vice is (as Aristotle thought) a quality that characterizes a whole life, a virtue that creates character, a second nature, not something that can be assumed in the twinkling of an eye through an act of will or of repentance. It is also a virtue that seeks, and finds, understanding. Wrath (*iracundia*) by contrast heats the blood. Aquinas quotes St. Gregory the Great as saying that "the heart that is inflamed with the stings of its own anger beats quickly, the body trembles, the tongue stammers . . . familiar acquaintances are not recognized." And Aquinas says that the fervor of anger is bitter and destructive.[45] Dante's example comes in another visionary moment (where he recalls the martyrdom of St. Stephen, the first Christian martyr): "Then I saw people, kindled with the fire of anger, stoning a youth to death, and ever crying out loudly to each other, 'Kill, kill!' and him I saw sink to the ground, for already death was heavy upon him, but of his eye he ever made gates unto heaven, praying to the high Lord in such torture, with that look which unlocks pity, that He would forgive his persecutors" (Canto 15, 106–14).

Canto 16 has a brief passage, put into the mouth of one Marco, a Lombard, describing the earliest loves of the infant soul and the need for these loves to be tempered by the divine law:

> From his hands who fondly loves it before it exists, comes forth after the fashion of a child that sports, now weeping, now laughing, the simple little soul (*l'anima sempleccita*), which knows nothing, save that, proceeding from a glad Maker, it turns eagerly to what delights it. First it tastes the savor of a trifling good: there it is beguiled and runs after it, if guide or curb bend not its love. Wherefore it was needful to impose a law as a bridle, it was needful to have a ruler who could discern at least the tower of the true city. (Canto 16, 85–96)

The description is of the immediately compelling goods that both point to and yet mask the underlying final good for the soul, which is God. This is only the beginning of a possible narrative of a life's journey in which the "simple little soul" will embark upon a lifetime of choices that will mark and stain it, and of which it will need eventually to be purged "as of by fire." T. S. Eliot's exquisite poem "Animula," recalling both Dante and the emperor Hadrian's farewell to his soul (*animula blandula vagula, / hospes comesque corporis*), excellently captures and expands Dante's lines:

> Issues from the hand of God the simple soul
> To a flat world of changing lights and noise,

To light, dark, dry or damp, chilly or warm;
Moving between the legs of tables and of chairs,
Rising or falling, grasping at kisses and toys . . .
                                    . . . taking pleasure
In the fragrant brilliance of the Christmas tree,
Pleasure in the wind, the sunlight and the sea . . .
Issues from the hand of time the simple soul
Irresolute and selfish, misshapen, lame,
Unable to fare forward or retreat,
Fearing the warm reality, the offered good,
Denying the importunity of the blood,
Shadow of its own shadows, spectre in its own gloom;
Leaving disordered papers in a dusty room;
Living first in the silence after the viaticum.[46]

Eliot has evoked the soul's seeking its first loves, then covering itself with the rust of habit, so that it fears the "offered good" and, rendered naked again after death, will have to face the reality of the good from which it had come to avert its eyes, after the *viaticum*—Extreme Unction, or last anointing, which also forgives sins.

Although the sins of the *Purgatorio* replicate, to some extent, those of the *Inferno*, the difference is that the sinners undergoing purgation are indeed open to the love and hence forgiveness of God. This openness, combined with the clarity of their consciousness of sin, is repentance and contrition. Purgation becomes a yielding to what is profoundly natural, a moving away from a sin that now seems against the natural. The release of gluttons from their obsession, at the end of Canto 24, is likened to the experience of awakening to the beauty of the natural order; "And as, heralding the dawn, the breeze of May stirs and smells sweet, all impregnate with grass and with flowers, such a wind I felt strike on my brow, and right well I felt the pinions move, which wafted ambrosial fragrance to my senses; and I heard say, 'Blessed are they who are so illumined by grace that the love of taste kindles not too great desire in their breasts, and who hunger always so far as is just.'"

The purgation of their sins (as St. Catherine of Genoa suggests) consists essentially in a contrition that is a direct consequence of their comprehending love. Therefore they can rejoice in the cleansing, even when this takes the form of a refining fire:

Ieu sui Arnaut, que plor e vau cantan;
consiros vei la passada folor,

> *e vei jausen lo joi qu'esper, denan.*
> *Ara vos prec, per aquella valor*
>   *que vos guida al som de l'escalina,*
>   *sovenha vos a temps de ma dolor!"*
> Poi s'ascose nel foco che li affina.

["I am Arnaut, who weep and sing as I go; contritely I see my past folly, and joyously I see before me the joy that I await. Now I pray you, by that power which guides you to the summit of the stair, in due time be heedful of my pain." Then he hid himself in the fire that purifies them. (Canto 26, 142–48)]

That this purificatory burning is essentially spiritual is shown by its leaving unscorched the hem of Dante's robe. That it is a suffering suffused with charity, and an urgent wish to reach salvation, is suggested by the poet's vision of the purgatorial spirits, in the midst of the flame "making haste and kissing one another, without stopping, content with brief greeting: thus within their dark band one ant touches muzzle with another, perhaps to spy out their way and their fortune" (Canto 26, 31–36).

The fullest expression of this is in Canto 31 where Dante's mounting remorse for sin makes him "burst under that heavy load, pouring forth tears and sighs, and my voice failed along its passage" (Canto 31, 19–21). This is purgatorial repentance—quite unlike the *fletus* of hell. Since repentance is now complete, a heavenly soul, Matilda, appears and plunges the poet into the waters of Lethe, by immersion in which the searing memory of sins already pardoned is erased.

That the pains of purgatory are *extensively* the same as the torments of hell has been a common teaching within the Roman Catholic Church, although it has never been part of official doctrine. *Intensively*, though, the sufferings are shot through with hope and charity—confident hope of eventual salvation, and love of God. As we have suggested, this intensive difference is enough to alter the sufferings in their essence—as Simon of Cyrene's carrying of Christ's cross was said to have become a privilege and a joy—which is why so many Catholic writers on purgatory went so far as to say that the sufferings are experienced as joyful. Hence also the growing conviction that the place of purging is not close to (let alone a part of) hell, as earlier theologians taught, but points toward and is spiritually and geographically close to heaven. Dante's Mount Purgatory has the Earthly Paradise at its summit, which provides the take-off point for the soul's journey through the successive heavenly spheres to the empyrean and God.

Protestant Reformers were right in pointing to the lack of any solid scriptural foundation for the doctrine of purgatory; to the abuses it occasioned (especially in the mechanical conception of remission of sin so often associated with indulgences); to the power and money it brought the church; to the astonishing difference between speculative ideas of a middle state of souls, and Christ's clarity on the subject of heaven and hell. Nevertheless, as Dante's *Purgatorio* suggests, it also develops powerfully the psychology of repentance; enforces that sense of solidarity between living and dead pointed to by the doctrine of the communion of saints; and softens, in a way that only the most austere will be unmoved by, the boundaries between eternal perdition and salvation. Why, then, should we not consider it to be one of the happiest inspirations of the Church of Rome?

PART III

Heaven

IO

Heaven: Egypt, Mesopotamia, Israel

Old-fashioned Marxism might tempt us to see the history of heaven as reflecting the history of human social relations. There are the gods—an aristocracy presided over by a king of the gods—who dwell on the heights and live for ever; and there are human beings, things of clay, created purely to serve the gods and destined to a short span only of life on earth. The gods live a life of exultant joy in heaven, whereas human beings are condemned to toil from dawn until dusk, before descending to an early grave—exactly how both the aristocracy and peasantry of the ancient Near East would see themselves and their relations to each other, if we leave aside the small fact that the aristocracy are not actually immortal.

It is certainly true that an ancient sense of an impassable gulf between the human realm and that of the gods mirrors earthly hierarchies; and the conviction that man can never join the gods to share in their life of joy reflects common ideas that aristocracies—or, at least, kings—are made of different stuff from commoners. For ancient Mesopotamia the gulf between the human and divine realms is impassable. No human being can hope to escape his fate, which is, at best, to exist after death in a shadowy, dusty, mournful underworld.

In Egypt, where full-blooded belief in immortality is first formulated, heaven is open, first, only to the king; then to the ministers of the king; and finally to all—or to any to whom Osiris shows favor. Perhaps this reflects changes within Egyptian society?

The trouble is that developments of ideas about heaven do not seem to be correlated with social change. Rather, they seem to develop autonomously. The "democratization" of heaven in Egypt does not seem to have reflected any dilution of social hierarchy. *The Epic of Gilgamesh* sees any hope of a happy afterlife as a delusion—but that does not necessarily tell us much about the society that produced the epic. To a great extent, therefore, the development of belief in a heaven to which many may go is a primary phenomenon.

Egypt

The idea of immortality was first systematically elaborated in ancient Egypt. But the possibility of human beings joining the gods in their heavenly dwelling-place was in the earliest times reserved for one man alone—the pharaoh, god-king of Egypt. We know this from the earliest surviving texts that contain prayers, rituals, and spells for the passage from this world to the next—the *Pyramid Texts*, so-called because they lined the chambers of the earliest pyramids.[1]

The Egyptians had several—to our minds, conflicting—images of the heavenly realms. First, they saw the heavens as a giant bird: "When many ancient Egyptians gazed skyward they imagined that they were looking at the underside of an enormous falcon flying above the earth."[2] As is usually the case with mythology, it would be pointless to ask whether the Egyptians *literally* believed that the heavens were a giant falcon, or whether this was metaphorical or poetic. These distinctions do not get a hold. They certainly talked of the sky as a giant falcon; a falcon—Horus—is the faithful son of Osiris, avenger of his father against Seth; as symbol and protector of the kings of Egypt, Horus is often portrayed with wings outstretched behind the head of the seated pharaoh.

Second, heaven is seen as a celestial cow. This cow may be the goddess Nut, but might also be the goddess Hathor. The sun god, Re, is often depicted as journeying across the sky in his boat through the stomach of the celestial cow.

Third, there is the celestial woman—the goddess, Nut. Many are the representations of her, with stars and sun proceeding through her belly as her body arches over the earth (*Geb*) while she is supported by the air god, Shu, who typically touches her nipples with one hand and her vulva with the other.[3] And last, the heavens are seen as a flat surface, a huge plane.[4] This great plane (sometimes a vault) rests upon mountain tops.

Whether or not these images fit together logically (and it seems that the Egyptians tended to add new ideas to the old stock, reluctant to jettison any), they give us the general sense of how ready the Egyptian imagination was to locate their religious convictions firmly in the material universe. There were pathways, gates, ladders connecting the earthly realm with the celestial world, a world to which, in the course of many centuries, the idea grew that all Egyptians could hope to be admitted.

The *Pyramid Texts* clearly concern the fate simply of this one man—the king for whom the pyramid would have been chiefly built. His destiny is to join the heavenly powers above; to join them among the circumpolar stars, indeed himself to become a star. Pharaoh will ascend to the sky: "you shall bathe in the starry firmament...the sun-folk shall call out to you, for the Imperishable Stars have raised you aloft."[5] The king becomes a star, rising above and sinking below the horizon: "You will regularly ascend with Orion from the eastern region of the sky, and you will regularly descend with Orion into the western region of the sky" (ibid., utterance 442). Pharaoh joins the sun god in the sky: "O Re-Atum, this King comes to you, an imperishable spirit...your son comes to you.... May you traverse the sky, being united in the darkness; may you arise in the horizon, in the place where it is well with you" (ibid., utterance 217). The king is identified with Osiris: "O Isis, this one here is your brother Osiris, whom you have caused to be restored, that he may live" (ibid., utterance 219). He will destroy the earth (*Geb*) if a place is not made for him in the heavens: "O Lord of the horizon, make ready a place for me, for if you fail to make ready a place for me, I will lay a curse on my father Geb, and the earth will speak no more, Geb will be unable to protect himself, and whoever I find in my way, I will devour him piecemeal...the earth [will be] entirely dammed up; the borders will be joined together, the river-banks will unite, the roads will be impassable for travellers" (ibid., utterance 254). Pharaoh virtually bullies the gods to admit him among their number.[6] The king becomes the supreme god—he even hunts and eats the gods:

> The King has appeared again in the sky,
> He is crowned as the Lord of the horizon;
> He has broken the back-bones
> And has taken the hearts of the gods...
> ...He has swallowed the intelligence of every god.
> (*Pyramid Texts*, utterances 273–74)

The pyramids themselves and all the funerary rituals, prayers, and spells were intended the assist the god-king of Egypt to ascend into the heavens from whence he will look down on and protect his realm.

The texts specifically *exclude* the common people—almost as though pharaoh needs to have his dignity protected from them: "Nut has commanded the King to Atum, he open-armed has commanded the king to Shu, that he may cause yonder doors of the sky to be opened for the King, barring (ordinary) folk who have no name. Grasp the King by his hand and take the King to the sky, that he may not die on earth among men " (ibid., utterance 361). "O King; receive your head, collect your bones, gather your limbs together, throw off the earth from your flesh . . . stand at the doors which keep out the plebs" (ibid., utterance 373).

It has been suggested that after the tumultuous times of the First Intermediate period in Egyptian history, during which pharaohs were overthrown, belief in their divinity was shaken, and that there was a gradual democratization of hopes for the future life.[7] What the *Pyramid Texts* had done for royalty, the *Coffin Texts* (coffins contained scrolls of spells and prayers) and then the *Book of the Dead* began to do for commoners. By the time of the *Coffin Texts*, the sun god is no longer supreme.[8] The Lord of the Dead has become Osiris, who welcomes all who have lived good lives to his bosom. Indeed, the deceased now becomes "the Osiris so-and-so." The spells of the *Coffin Texts* are sometimes for a safe passage for the deceased, but very often they invoke the hope of a delightful existence in the next world. The deceased is represented as praying to the gods, reminding them of the gifts he has brought, and begging for absolution: "I have brought you natron and incense . . . I have come that I may expel the evil which is in my heart and that I may remove the wrong that is in it."[9] Some spells are meant to bring it about not only that the deceased will rise into the skies as Horus, the falcon god, but that he will take vengeance on his enemies, as the son of Osiris takes vengeance upon the enemy of his father: "I am a human falcon who walks as a man. . . . It is granted that I have power over that foe of mine . . . I have grasped him with my talons . . . I fly up and alight upon his spine . . . I have crushed his family, I have thrown down his house . . . Osiris is joyful when he sees me mount aloft as a falcon" (ibid., spell 149). Many of the images are of the dead mounting to the sky, begging the gods to make a ladder: "O Lord of flame guarding the doors of the sky, open the doors of the sky, put the ladder together for me, make a way for me, for I am weary in chaos, in the Abyss, in darkness and in gloom" (ibid., spell 76).

The common people did not expect to be translated to the stars but hoped to go to the Field of Rushes, which would be an ideal version of agricultural life on earth in a sort of idealized Egypt. (Some spells aim at both at once—for the ancient Egyptians seem to have been happy to hold two conflicting ideas in their minds at the same time.) "I know that Field of Rushes . . . the height of its barley is four cubits, its ear is one cubit, its stalk is five cubits; its emmer is seven cubits, its ear is two cubits, its stalk is five cubits" (ibid., spell 159).

The inhabitants of the next world, whether this be the Field of Rushes or the sky, will be blessed with vigorous appetites: "O N [deceased] awake for this your warm bread which I have prepared for you, your thousand of bread, your thousand of beer, your thousand of oxen, your thousand of poultry, your thousand of figs, your thousand of grapes. . . . I have given to you your bread which does not grow moldy and your beer which does not grow sour" (ibid., spell 67). Immortality for the Egyptians was certainly quite unlike the immortality of fame and honor officially desired by the Greeks. To use Pope's words, "solid pudding" counted for more than "empty praise."[10]

The spells for not walking upside down, and therefore eating feces and drinking urine,[11] are the most numerous of all three collections.[12] As we saw earlier, they often include a joyful confidence that the deceased will have his normal bodily functions: "I will not eat feces for you, I will not walk upside down for you . . . my phallus is on me, it being attached; my anus is on me, it being attached. I eat with my mouth, I defecate with my anus."[13] In the Field of Rushes it is better not to have to work but to have *shabtis* doing this for one[14]: "O shabti, allotted to me, if I be summoned . . . to do any work which is to be done in the realm of the dead . . . you shall detail yourself for me . . . making arable the fields, of flooding the banks or of conveying sand from east to west: 'Here am I,' shall you say."[15]

The most glorious fate seems to be avian transfiguration: "I have flown as a swallow, I have cackled as a goose . . . I shall appear as a god, I shall eat and gorge in the Field of [Rushes] . . . O men and gods, I am bound for seven meals in the sky . . . I will set up a ladder among the gods, for I am one of them. BECOMING A GOOSE."[16] (In fact, the goose here stands for the creator-god—the Great Cackler—who sometimes takes the form of a goose.)

As we read in chapter 2, some of the tomb paintings, with their depiction of the world that has been left behind—the world of harvest, grapes, waterbirds trussed for the pot—give us a vivid sense of this belief in a virtual-earthly existence after death. The blessed will have offerings of water, of beer, of wine, of bread, and of cakes. He may receive a "seat in Heliopolis" (i.e., a throne),[17] or be transformed into a god, giving light and darkness.[18] And in the kingdom of Osiris the arisen man will meet his slaves and domestic servants, who will help cultivate the land that will be allotted to him. He will also meet "his ancestors, his father, his mother, his grown-up sons and daughters . . . and the concubine whom he loved and knew."[19]

Mesopotamia

As the *Epic of Gilgamesh* shows, the Sumerians of southern Mesopotamia had no faith that anyone—even kings—could attain to personal immortality. *Gilgamesh* conveys with astonishing power the sense that any hope of immortality is a tragic delusion. If anyone might be thought capable of overcoming death, it would surely be this legendary hero of superhuman strength and courage. Yet even he fails, and fails in a way that is almost absurd in its accidental quality, showing how vulnerable human efforts are to accident and fate. Having finally seized the plant that confers immortality, Gilgamesh, tired and dusty, takes the chance to bathe in a deliciously cool pool. While he is in the water, a snake glides by and eats the plant of immortality.

The Sumerian cosmology expresses the same ideas. There is a triple division (corresponding to that in Genesis) of sky, over which are waters, earth, with an Underworld, and the waters under the earth.

The Sumerians had an almost aristocratic disdain toward the longing for immortality. In this respect theirs was a culture of maturity and realism. "The Sumerians were dominated by the conviction that in death the emasculated spirit descends to a dark and dreary beyond where "life" at best was but a dismal, wretched reflection of life on earth. Humans toiled from birth to death and the grave was their end."[20] This underworld (see chap. 3) is a house

> where the entrants are bereft of light,
> Where dust is their fare and clay their food,
> Where they see no light, residing in darkness,
> Where they are clothed like birds, with wings for garments,
> And where over door and bolt is spread dust.[21]

Ishtar, the Babylonian queen of heaven (in Sumerian, *Innana*) went down to this Land of No Return, possibly to rescue her lover, Thammuz, the god who every year was slain, causing the river Orontes in Syria to run purple with his blood.[22] At every gate of this underworld, through the hatred of Ereshkigal, queen of the dead, Ishtar was stripped of her jewels, her scepter, and, finally, all her clothes. Stark naked, she has to kneel before Ereshkigal, who releases against her the gods of death. She dies and her corpse is hung from a stake. She is brought back to life, however, by means of the god Shamash (in the Sumerian version, *Enki*). But as she comes up from the Underworld, she is followed by bogies and demons. This reflects the Mesopotamian belief that the dead had to be kept firmly locked up in the next world lest they pour up from below to plague the living.[23]

Since the Sumerian cosmos consists of a heaven above, where the gods reside, earth and, below the earth, the Underworld, there is virtually no possibility that a human being can be translated from the earth or the Underworld to join the gods in their heaven. Yet there is an earthly paradise, rather like the Elysian Fields of Homer, which the Sumerians called *Dilmun*, or "the place where the sun rises," or "the land of the living."[24] It was a land of cedars, a pure, clean, and bright land:

The mountain of Dilmun is pure, the mountain of Dilmun is clean.
. . . In Dilmun the raven shrieked not,
The kite shrieked not kitelike

. . . .

The lion slew not.
The wolf plundered not the lambs,
The dog approached not the kids in repose.
The mother goat as it fed on grain he disturbed not[25]

Dilmun was a place where man lived healthily to an immense age:

Oh head ache thou art the "Head Ache" one said not.
As to the old man "Thou are an old man" one said not.

There is abundance of pure water to drink:

Dilmun may drink water in abundance.
Thy pools of bitter waters as a pool of sweet waters may flow.[26]

This paradise seems to have been identified with the island of Bahrain, or perhaps with "a strip of land from about 29th degree of latitude southward along the eastern coast of the Persian Gulf including the islands off the coast, perhaps as far as the Strait of Ormuz and the Arabian Sea."[27] Or it may have been in southwestern Persia, with its western boundary extending along the eastern part of the Persian Gulf from somewhere south of Elam in the direction of the Strait of Ormuz.[28] Yet it is always called "Mount Dilmun." In Dilmun, then, man had lived with perfect health, extreme longevity, and without toil.[29] But Dilmun was destroyed in the deluge sent by the creator god, Enki, who for some reason became dissatisfied with human beings. In the flood men dissolved "like fat, like tallow." In *Paradise Lost*, Milton most curiously anticipated (because the texts would not become known for another two centuries) the Sumerian account of the destruction of Mount Dilmun, in his account of the melancholy end of the Earthly Paradise:

. . . all the Cataracts
Of Heav'n set op'n on the Earth shall powre
Raine day and night, all fountains of the Deep
Broke up, shall heave the Ocean to usurp
Beyond all bounds, till inundation rise
Above the highest Hills: then shall this Mount
Of Paradise by might of Waves be moovd
Out of this place, pusht by the horned floud,
With all his verdure spoild, and Trees adrift

> Down the great River to the op'ning Gulf,
> And there take root an Island salt and bare,
> The haunt of Seales and Orcs, and Sea-mews clang . . .[30]

The similarity of this Sumerian myth to the book of Genesis, and therefore its probable influence on it, is obvious. But there are big differences. Before they sinned, Adam and Eve lived happily in paradise for only a very short time—often calculated as a few hours—and paradise continued to exist after their expulsion. Man's abode in the Sumerian paradise lasted quite a bit longer than that—for 432,000 years, to be precise. It was ruled by ten kings whose longevity puts that of the biblical patriarchs in the shade. King Alorus reigned for 36,000 years; King Amelon of Sippar for 46,200 years; King Amemnon, a Chaldean, for 43,200 years; King Megalarus, 64,800 years; King Daonus, 36,000 years; King Eurdorachus 64,800 years; Amempsimus, another Chaldean, 36,000 years; Opartes, 28,500 years; Xisdithrusd, son of Opartes, 64,800. The reign of King Alaparos was notably short—only 10,800 years.[31]

Only two Mesopotamians were thought to have ascended into heaven proper, i.e., the abode of the gods—and both lived before the flood. These were King Emmeduranki, who was assumed into heaven and taught the secrets of the gods, and Adapa, of the time of Hammurabi, king of Babylon, who was taken up to heaven where he, too, met the gods but was treacherously tricked out of immortal life and had to return to earth.[32]

Ancient Israel

Judaism originated from Canaanite religion.[33] The Canaanites had a pantheon in which the presiding god was El. They thought of El as the creator of heaven and earth. The ancient Israelites incorporated some of the character of El in their own tribal god, YHWH.[34] Some biblical texts admit that there are gods other than YHWH—"For all the nations walk each in the name of its god; but we walk in the name of YHWH our god for ever and ever."[35] There was even a suggestion that YHWH had a consort—the goddess Asherah. But gradually those in control of the Temple in Jerusalem were able to insist that YHWH was not only king of the gods, not only superior to the other gods of the Canaanites, but that he was the only real deity. The other deities, in becoming subordinate, lost their status as gods, and became the servants of YHWH—e.g., angels. (The ancient Israelites do not seem to have adopted the theory of the church fathers that the gods of the pagans were really fallen angels—i.e., devils.)

The eventual unchallenged supremacy of YHWH also affected beliefs about the dead. We have noticed that most of the peoples of the ancient Near East did not have any belief in heaven as a place to which kings, or heroes, or the righteous went after they died. Heaven was the realm of the gods alone, and the Underworld the place of dust and darkness where all human beings ended up.

The ancient Israelites were in this respect no different from their neighbors. The conviction that once a man had gone down into *Sheol*—the pit, Hades—he was reduced to a sad, shadowy existence, is expressed (as we saw in chapter 3) in Job's words, when he talks of *Sheol* as "a land of darkness as darkness itself and of the shadow of death, without any order, and where the light is as darkness" (Job 10:22). And Job talks of there being hope if a tree be cut down "that it will sprout again, and that the tender branch thereof will not cease" (Job 14:7), but "man lieth down, and riseth not: till the heavens be no more, they shall not awake, nor be raised out of their sleep" (Job 14:12).

So the dead continued to exist in this shadowy way. They lived for a while in the grave itself, and then, as the body decayed, they slipped away into *Sheol*. Although they were mostly thought of as impotent, they nevertheless could sometimes help or harm the living, and could themselves be helped or harmed by the living. The witch of En-dor calls up the apparent spirit of the prophet, Samuel, to prophesy to Saul that he would die on the morrow on the field of battle.[36]

The living could help the dead by keeping a *cultus* of them going, visiting their grave, leaving food offerings, and pouring libations. (There were even Canaanite tombs, some of them Israelite, where you could pour libations of wine down special funnels directly onto the corpse.) Those of the dead who were honored in this way were thought of as being in the higher, lighter parts of *Sheol*. The neglected dead slipped down into the dingier parts.[37]

McDannell and Lang suggest that Israelite beliefs about the afterlife went through four stages.[38] In the first they pictured the cosmos as other Semitic peoples understood it. There were three levels: earth, heaven, and the underworld. The gods live in heaven. Man, who was created from clay to serve the gods, is granted the surface of the earth. The dead reside in the lowest realm, a cavern underground, where they can be communicated with and placated by their living relatives.

The second stage of Israelite belief—sometimes called the "YHWH alone" tradition—rejected any idea of communication with the dead. Belief in any life after death was played down; there was to be no necromancy; ancestors were not to be venerated; only the God of Israel was to be worshipped. This policy was officially imposed in the seventh century BC by King Josiah, who also strictly forbad any conjuring of the dead. The realm of the dead was to be kept strictly separate from that of the living; ritual purity forbade any contact with a dead body, especially on the part of priests.[39]

The third stage carries this still further: it holds that the dead have no importance at all. What matters is the fate of the nation of Israel. The God of Israel (as depicted in Ezekiel's valley of dry bones) will one day resurrect those Israelites who have been faithful and give them an earthly kingdom in which to live for ever.

The fourth stage shifts its gaze from purely national concerns to those hopes that an individual may have in a hostile world. The hope is now in the ascent of the immortal soul to God it creator. This is the background to the varying beliefs of the contemporaries of Jesus—Pharisees, Sadducees, and Essenes—and gives a context to what became the Christian idea of heaven.

Before this fourth stage, the idea that the individual might hope after death to ascend to the realm of the gods was considered either unthinkable or blasphemous. The Tower of Babel had been erected for just that purpose, and God punished that act of hubris by confounding human speech. Three Old Testament figures overcame death: Noah was granted immortality, while Enoch and Elijah were miraculously taken up to heaven by God while still alive. It is only the (very late) book of Daniel that suggests unambiguously that whole categories of human beings—the righteous, for instance—will live in heaven after death, and that the wicked (or simply those who lack wisdom) will be punished: "And many of them that sleep in the dust of the earth shall awake, some to everlasting life, and some to shame and everlasting contempt. And they that be wise shall shine as the brightness of the firmament; and they that turn many to righteousness as the stars for ever and ever" (Dan. 12:2–3).

The passage in Ezekiel (celebrated in a well-known spiritual and by T. S. Eliot in "Ash Wednesday") describing the dry bones springing to life and being clothed with flesh—also frequently invoked as an image of the resurrection of the bodies of the just and unjust at the Last Day—seems to envisage, not the rising again of the individual but the renewal of the nation of Israel:

"Son of man, can these bones live? . . . So I prophesied as he commanded me, and the breath came into them and they lived, and stood up upon their feet, an exceeding great army. Then he said unto me, Son of man, these bones are the whole house of Israel: behold, they say, Our bones are dried, and our hope is lost. . . . Behold, O my people, I will open your graves, and bring you into the land of Israel" (Ezek. 37:3, 10–11, 12).

The triumph of strict monotheism in ancient Israel meant that all those domestic pieties involved in the cult of one's dead were redirected, absorbed into the insatiable demands of the "jealous God" the worship of whom was centered in the Temple at Jerusalem. But it did not actually make any difference to hopes and fears for a future life. Dusty Sheol was still all that could be looked forward to (except that, as we have seen, great and good men could hope to live in the memory of Israel).[40] The God of Israel does not promise immortality to those who serve him. Rather his promises and threats have to do with outcomes in this life, with the security and prosperity of the nation of Israel, of the disasters that will befall the Israelites if they turn from their LORD.

The trouble with this was that the greatest catastrophe that befell Israel (before the destruction of the Temple in AD 70)—the Babylonian captivity— followed the final triumph of monotheism, when YHWH singularly failed to protect his obedient people. There is a particular irony in this. Throughout the Hebrew Bible, God through his prophets constantly calls his people to come back to him when they have been whoring after such fun gods as Baal. It is only after he triumphs that they are led into captivity by a people who worship gods resembling Baal.

The idea of a world more real and more perfect than this one is something we inherit from both Platonism and Christianity. Otherworldliness is a possibility that we hold somewhere in our imaginations, whatever our beliefs. It is accordingly hard for us to put ourselves into the world of the ancient Mesopotamians and Israelites, for their imaginations seem to have lacked entirely the otherworldly possibility. The Land of No Return, *Sheol*, the place of dust and darkness are no doubt depressing prospects. But they suggest an unflinching realism—just in that they are the fate we could least hope for. The ancient Israelites set an absolute value on life in this world, and especially on the flourishing of the nation of Israel. This went with what had clearly become a genuine worship of the God of Israel and a genuine desire to obey his commandments. The welfare of the nation, as overseen by YHWH, was an actual religious imperative—as the Roman worship of their tutelary deities who would protect and bless the Roman state was a religious imperative. In *Job* and *Ecclesiastes* there is a vivid sense of what it is to flourish, how absolutely that is denied by misfortunes and misery, of how intensely life is to be valued and enjoyed as against the blank darkness of the underworld. We might very well conclude that the ancient Mesopotamians and Israelites had an apprehension of the joy of life that became clouded in a culture that stressed the future joys in heaven for the individual as the focal point of life in this world. To quote a passage from *Ecclesiastes* again: "I have seen the travail, which God hath given to the sons of men to be exercised in it. He hath made everything beautiful in his time: also he hath set the world in their heart.... I know that there is no good in them, but for a man to rejoice, and to do good in his life. And also that every man should eat and drink, and enjoy the good of all his labour, it is the gift of God" (Eccl. 3:10–13).

Jews, Persians, and Greeks

Zoroaster

In 586 BC a Babylonian army conquered Jerusalem and destroyed the Temple. Soon the kingship of Israel was abolished, and many prominent Jews were taken to live in Babylon. The reaction of many Jews, including the prophet Ezekiel (who wrote during the Babylonian exile in the early sixth century BC), was to hope that God would one day restore Israel to her rightful place in the world and bring back to bodily life the Israelite dead who had been steadily obedient to YHWH, and who would then inhabit the gloriously renewed kingdom. At any rate, whether this was an actual belief, it became an inspiring patriotic image. However, Babylon was also influenced by Persian ideas, and was eventually conquered by Cyrus the Great—who has the distinction of being honorably mentioned in Herodotus, the Hebrew Bible and the Qur'an—who allowed the Jews to return to Jerusalem and restore (in a rather inferior version) the Temple. The official religion of Persia was Zoroastrianism, and the ideas of this religion began to permeate Jewish religious thought.

Zoroaster (or Zarathustra [Persian], ca. 1400 BC) had preached the end of time and a bodily resurrection. There would be a coming together of the souls and bodies of the just in a renewed earth, where the just would live for ever serving Ahura Mazda, the benevolent creator. The Zoroastrians never buried their dead, because that would pollute the sacred earth.[41] Nor did they cremate them, because the element of fire is especially sacred in Zoroastrianism, the religion of Fire Temples. Instead, they left the bodies out in the open, often in "Towers of Silence" where they would be picked clean by the birds of the air. It has indeed been suggested that Ezekiel's vision of the valley of dry bones—"a vast plain covered with human bones bleached by the sun"—closely resembles a Zoroastrian burial ground.[42] There is, though, a huge difference. The Zoroastrians imagined this as a general resurrection of the just of all humanity in a renewed world at the end of time. Ezekiel's vision is narrowly nationalistic, of a glorious restoration of the kingdom to Israel. Nevertheless, this idea of a bodily resurrection of many thousands comes from Persia into Jewish thought for the first time.

Enoch Ascends to Heaven

Some psalms seem to imply that the faithful of Israel, after their deaths, might be received into heaven by God, rather than moldering in the underworld.

However, this is not at all clear. In Psalm 49 the rich man who trusts to his riches finds that wealth cannot bring it about that God will grant him that he should "still live forever and not see corruption." This is in keeping with the received tradition that death, decay and *Sheol* are what await all humans. The arrogant rich man is "like the beasts that perish.... Like sheep they are laid in the grave; death shall feed on them...their beauty shall consume in the grave." The psalm goes on: "But God will redeem my soul from the power of the grave: for he shall receive me." It is hard to see how this fits with the rest of the psalm, which suggests that the wise die and "carry nothing away," but there is at least the possibility of hope for something better than the underworld, and that this might be offered not just to the tiny number of patriarchs who were snatched up to heaven by God while still alive (Ps. 49:9, 12, 14–15, 17).

With the idea of resurrection as found among the Persians came the idea of imagining an ascent to the heaven of God. The apocryphal *Book of Enoch*, possibly written from the third to the second century BC, reflects just such an idea, and contains accounts of what the biblical patriarch saw after he had been taken up into heaven. The language is extravagant, but the vision is conceived in the most literal terms. "Enoch" enters the temple of God; its floor is fire, and above is lightning and the paths of the stars, and the roof is a burning fire; there are shooting stars or fireballs and hailstones all around the temple. There is a high throne that looks as if it is made of ice, surrounded with light as of the shining sun. He who sits on the throne has "a raiment brighter than the sun, and whiter than any snow." He is surrounded by fire and ten thousand times[43] ten thousand angels stand before him. (It is likely that "the opposing elements of fire and water can coexist only in heaven."[44])

Enoch is vouchsafed a view of how the cosmos works, being shown the winds that "turn heaven and cause the disk of the sun and all the stars to set."[45] In typical apocalyptic style (which is nothing if not extravagant) he sees seven mountains of precious stones: of pearl, of colored stone, of "healing stone," of red stone, of stibium, and of sapphire.[46] There are "seven stars like great burning mountains," and even stars that are rolled in an enormous fire as a punishment for their not having come out on time.[47] Interspersed with these visions are conversations with a large number of angels—not just with the usual ones—Michael, Uriel, and Raphael—but with Saraqael, Azazel, Arsyalalyur, Amezarak, Armaros, Baraqiel, Kokabel, Tamiel, and Astradel. Some of the conversations are about astronomy, some about the wickedness and punishment of a particular rank of angels—the Watchers—who defiled themselves by copulating with the daughters of men.

Any reader unsympathetic to what Gibbon called "the prophetic style"[48] will find nearly all of the *Book of Enoch* tedious and turgid, but there are several things of interest. There is a description of Enoch being welcomed by God into heaven and seated forever among the angels, having been anointed with the very best oil.[49] This does suggest that "the boundary between humanity and the divine is permeable."[50] The text also holds out the possibility to "all the righteous who escape God's judgment" that they will be "united with the great age, and the age will be united with the righteous, and they shall live eternally. And they shall have no more labour, nor suffering, nor sorrow, nor night, nor darkness, but ... about them a great light for ever ..."[51] Finally the images of God's dwelling-place may symbolize a heavenly version of a mixture of the first and second Temples, purged of all impurities, and existing in heaven[52]—a New Jerusalem. The difference between this and the vision of John is, of course, that in John's Revelation, Christ, instead of transporting the faithful to heaven, will bring the kingdom of heaven down to earth.[53]

The account of eternal bliss in *Enoch* sometimes makes it indeterminate whether this will be in God's heaven or in an earthly paradise: "When the whole creation that the Lord has made comes to an end, and every man goes to the Lord's great judgment, then the seasons will perish, and there will be no years any more, nor will the months nor the days and hours be reckoned any more, but there will be a single age.... And they shall have no more labour nor suffering nor sorrow nor fear of persecution, nor labour nor night ... but they shall have above them a great light for ever and an indestructible wall, and in the great Paradise shall they have the shelter of an eternal dwelling place."[54]

Nevertheless, the *Book of Enoch* directly contradicts the belief, common to the ancient Jews, the Sumerians, and the Near East in general, that man has no place in the realm of the gods, or of God. Enoch is to be transformed into one of God's angels, and the implied message is that if you live like Enoch, you too can be enrolled among the angels of light; and if you live wickedly, your destiny is to abide for all eternity with the fallen angels.

Judaism Hellenized: Philo of Alexandria

Confidence in a heavenward ascent for the soul did not enter Jewish thought until the Jews came into intimate contact with Greek philosophy. When Alexander the Great conquered the Persian Empire, the whole Jewish world came under the influence of Hellenistic ideas. Above all, Platonic doctrines about the immortality of the soul, its divine birth, and its innate desire to return to God, allowed Jews to have an intellectually much more sophisticated picture of an ascent to heaven than we find in the *Apocalypse of Enoch*.

The greatest of the hellenizing Jewish thinkers was Philo of Alexandria (20 BC–ca. AD 45). Philo was a brilliantly fluent Platonist who set himself the task—which he made seem utterly congenial—of finding a Platonic idea behind most of the Old Testament narrative, including the creation of the world, and behind the Law of Moses. He does this with brio and resource. Genesis says that God created the world in six days. But we must think of God as actually doing all things simultaneously, remembering that "all" includes, along with the commands he issues, the thoughts behind them. Six days are mentioned for the creation simply to indicate that order in the process is needed, and the number 6 is by nature the most suitable number to indicate creativity, for if we start with 1 it is the first perfect number, being equal to the product of its factors (i.e., $1 \times 2 \times 3$), as well as made up of the sum of them (i.e., $1+2+3$), its half being 3, its third part 2, its sixth part 1. The number 6 is both male and female. For among things that exist, the odd is male and the even female. It is right that the world, being the most perfect of things, should have come into existence in accord with a perfect number, and yet should spring from a mixed number, because that means that it contains within itself the male and female principles.[55] This number mysticism is a good example of Philo's symbolic reading of the Jewish scriptures and of the ease with which he transforms narrative into allegory (in which he is followed by St. Augustine and other Christian fathers).

When Moses (whom Philo regards, of course, as the author of the Pentateuch) says that God made man in his own image and likeness, the image must refer to Mind, the sovereign element of the soul; and man's mind is patterned after the Mind of the Universe as an archetype. In man this mind is godlike, for it rules man as God rules the universe. Invisible itself, it ranges over all visible things, soars to contemplate the upper air, the planets and the fixed stars, carries its gaze beyond what is perceivable by the senses, and reaches after the intelligible world, descrying in that world sights of surpassing loveliness—the patterns of all sensible objects—until "with Corybantic frenzy" it seems to be on its way to the Great King (*ho megas basileus*—usually just *ho basileus*) himself, longing to bath in his rays of concentrated light.[56]

In the light of this powerful form of intellectual levitation, the old means of ascent to heaven by Jewish patriarchs and prophets, such as via fiery chariots, are superseded. What had been rare, miraculous events become a possible destiny for all, for we are all souls come down from above. Some souls descend to take care of mortal man, but then are caught in the rushing torrent of the cares of human life and get swallowed up. Others can stem the current, rise to the surface, and then soar upwards back to the place from whence they came. These are the souls of those "who have given themselves to genuine philosophy, who from first to last study to die to the life of the body."[57]

When Jacob had his dream of a ladder (or stairway) reaching up to heaven, the stairway, when applied to the universe, symbolizes air, which extends from earth up to the moon (where heaven begins). Those going up the stairway symbolize the souls whose natural tendency is to rise, whereas those moving in the other direction mean souls of earthy tastes.[58] God is by definition the point toward which the rising souls move, so naturally Jacob says: "This is none other but the house of God, and this is the gate of heaven" (Gen. 28:17).[59]

So for Philo and many other hellenized Jews, Judaism became a philosophy, or purely a system of religious belief, and not the defining feature, the ideology, of a state.[60] Plato's otherworldliness, his preference for the contemplative over the active life—hence for individual piety rather than patriotic struggle—enters into Jewish consciousness. Life is a spiritual preparation for ascent to God, rather than any attempt to "restore the kingdom to Israel." Resurrection will be not of the nation, but of the individual. Philo gives a recipe for individualism that had hitherto been anathema in the eyes of the religion of Israel.

Yet Philo himself was not just an armchair philosopher. Rather, he was one of those souls who, as Plato recommended, conceive it to be their duty to come down and intervene in sublunar affairs. He took part, on behalf of the Alexandrian Jews, in an embassy to the crazed emperor, Gaius (Caligula). The occasion was the extremely grave crisis provoked by Gaius's wish to have statue of himself installed in the Temple at Jerusalem. The embassy had to convince him that the whole Jewish nation would die rather than allow this. Arriving at Caligula's collection of villas, they found him busy consulting his architects, and had to chase him from villa to villa, trying to present their case, while he fired scornful questions at them: "Why do you refuse to eat pork?" ("Majesty, some people choose not to eat lamb." "Quite right too. It is not nice.") The Jews assured Gaius that they were loyal, and sacrificed for him in the Temple: "That is all very well—but you do not sacrifice to me." The emperor now began dashing around his rooms, and the Jewish embassy were all compelled to run after him, trying to explain points of theology. It seems to have been successful after all, for, after numerous signs of hostility and expressions of menace, Caligula suddenly dismissed them with: "It is just their hard luck that they are such idiots as not to believe that I am a god."[61] Thus was a Jewish revolt and possible destruction of the Temple averted.

Jesus

This mixture of ideas prepares the way for the Christian idea of heaven. When we come to the Gospels we find a world in which competing ideas about a possible future life have been greatly reduced in number. There is no gloomy underworld where the dead will live a shadow existence, no Hades. (And in the parable of Dives and Lazarus, Dives is clearly damned and in *Gehenna*, despite the use of the word *Hades* in the Greek text.) Nor do we find Ezekiel's vision of the restoration of the dead into a new state of Israel. Instead, you have two opposed schools: the Pharisees, who certainly believed in individual immortality; and the Sadducees "which say that there is no resurrection" (Matt. 22:23). Then there is Jesus, whose doctrine of the kingdom of heaven is otherworldly, yet often sounds like a description of the holy life within this world.

The Sadducees appear as skeptics but, at the same time, literal-minded legalists. The Law of Moses had decreed that if a man die childless, his brother must marry the widow and beget children, as it were on behalf of the dead brother: "Now there were with us seven brethren: and the first, when he had married a wife, deceased and, having no issue, left his wife unto his brother: Likewise the second also, and the third, unto the seventh. And last of all the woman died also. Therefore in the resurrection whose wife shall she be of the seven? For they all had her" (Matt. 22:25–28).

The Sadducees obviously take it for granted that those who, like the Pharisees and Jesus, believe in an afterlife, assume that after the resurrection the faithful will be restored to a happy family life on earth in a renewed Jewish nation. The reply of Jesus famously pulls away the carpet: "Ye do err . . . For in the resurrection they neither marry, nor are given in marriage, but are as the angels of God in heaven" (Matt. 22:29–30).

Those words of Jesus explain why so many early Christian thinkers assumed that the best way to understand his doctrines philosophically was through Plato. True, Jesus teaches a resurrection of the body. But what he seems to describe are spiritual bodies, in which some of the natural functions are remitted—an idea that develops mightily in later Christian thought.[62]

The heaven in which the risen are as angels and do not marry is anticipated by self-sacrificing, obedient, and charitable lives on this earth. Even though Jesus does sometimes invoke a heaven and hell that will be places as real as any with a spatial location, the vast majority of his images of heaven make it seem like a state of mind here and now rather than a different world.

We remember that he offers his listeners a selection of images, which together might approximate to an idea of the kingdom of heaven, even though they differ one from another. What they all have in common is the suggestion that the kingdom of heaven is within you. To recapitulate: in the parable of the sower, seed falls by the wayside and is eaten by birds; or on stony places, where it springs up but soon perishes, having no roots; or among thorns that choke it. "But other fell into good ground, and brought forth fruit, some an hundredfold" (Matt. 13:8). The seed by the wayside is God's word, snatched away by the devil; the seed that falls on stony ground and is scorched by the sun is the word received by someone with no depth or sincerity, so that when troubles arise he abandons it; the seed among thorns is the word choked by the cares of the world. The seed that falls onto good ground is the divine teaching in the heart of someone who "heareth the word and understandeth it; which also beareth fruit" (Matt. 13:19–23).

It is in these inward motions of the heart and mind that the kingdom of heaven exists. It is something the heart cherishes. Hence, it is also like a treasure that a man finds buried in a field—so that he sells all he has in order to buy the field. Or it is a net filled with fish, of which the good are kept and the useless ones thrown away. Or it is one pearl of great price for which a man will sell all else he has (Matt. 13:44–46). Jesus also compares the kingdom with a man who owns a vineyard and hires laborers. To the ones who come at the beginning of the day he offers a wage. He offers the same wage to successive comers, so that at the end of the day those that have been working for only an hour get the same amount as those who have toiled all day. These latter, having born the heat of the day, complain. The owner tells them that he is entitled to do what he will with his own, "so the last shall be first, and the first last: for many are called but few are chosen" (Matt. 20:1–16). Most beautiful, perhaps, of the similitudes is the comparison of the kingdom to a grain of mustard seed, which a man took and sowed in his field: "Which indeed is the least of all seeds: but when it is grown, it is the greatest among herbs, and becometh a tree, so that the birds of the air come and lodge in the branches thereof" (Matt. 13:31–32).

It is very hard to sum up these similitudes. As usual in the teaching of Jesus, the emphasis not, in the first place, on what an individual *does*, but on the movements of the heart. The heart receives the word with joy and takes it deep within itself. So the heart becomes a rich soil in which a seed can grow and bring forth fruit an hundredfold. It can even bring forth a tree in which others can rejoice and find their shelter. But we can see it simply as that which the heart desires above all else—the pearl of great price. (An image that surely echoes in Othello's mind, having lost what his own heart most desired, when he compares himself with "the base Indian" who throws a pearl away "richer than all his tribe.")[63]

The parable of the laborers in the vineyard evokes a kingdom, entry into which no one can actually *merit*. It is more a miraculous gift, a calling by God on which we cannot presume. All the images suggest faith—an unmisgiving acceptance of the transcendent worth of the kingdom, a readiness to lose all to secure it. The images of fruitfulness, increase, all express confidence in a promise. We see here the origin of the belief that inheritance of the kingdom is a matter of faith rather than of works.

Yet these images of a kingdom that is within coexist with what appears to be Jesus's firm belief in a kingdom of heaven that is the next world—a world ruled directly by God, into which the righteous will enter, and from which the wicked will be cast into an everlasting fire that was prepared for Satan and his angels (Matt. 25:41). It coexists also with Jesus's visions of the end of the world when the Son of man will come in the clouds of glory, sending his angels who, with the great sound of a trumpet, "shall gather together his elect from the four winds, from one end of heaven to the other" (Matt. 24:30–31).

Yet even this Last Judgment seems to be a separation of those who have faithfully received Christ or his teaching in their hearts (from which good deeds spring as the mustard seed becomes a tree and supports the birds of the air, and those who recognized him in the poor, the naked, and the hungry) *from* those without charity and faith. The former will be taken individually to live with God, rather than be restored to an earthly kingdom.

There is a tension, which even seems like a contradiction, between the Jesus who preaches the heaven within, the fructifying heart, and the Jesus who will come as judge at the Last Day to receive the righteous into an actual kingdom somewhere, and cast out the wicked into the eternal fires. Yet Christians have felt obliged to reconcile the two and to believe that the future heaven will be an actual reward for those who manage to live the heavenly, selfless, charitable life on this earth.

The various images Jesus uses to suggest the kingdom that is within us also suggest a fulfillment here and now, a faith that is also hope. The hope is not for a redress of wrongs in a future life, but for a spiritual reward in this one. A sonnet by Gerard Manley Hopkins suggests how deeply these images have entered our imaginations:

> Thou art indeed just, Lord, if I contend
> With thee; but, sir, so what I plead is just.
> Why do sinners' ways prosper? and why must
> Disappointment all I endeavour end?

> Wert thou my enemy, O thou my friend,
> How wouldst thou worse, I wonder, than thou dost
> Defeat, thwart me? Oh, the sots and thralls of lust
> Do in spare hours more thrive than I that spend,
>
> Sir, life upon thy cause. See banks and brakes
> Now, leavèd how thick! Lacèd they are again
> With fretty chervil, look, and fresh wind shakes
>
> Them; birds build—but not I build; no, but strain,
> Time's eunuch, and not breed one work that wakes.
> Mine, O thou lord of life, send my roots rain. (Sonnet 50)

Hopkins has started from an invocation in the Hebrew Bible—a request that God will intervene to put right injustice of the world in which (as Job complains) the wicked flourish.[64] But the poem really asks that the just man should experience the consolation that Jesus promises in *this* world. The poet has accepted the word, but instead of putting forth fruit an hundredfold, he suffers from spiritual dryness. It is as if *his* roots are in stony ground and hence need rain. It is the "sots and thralls of lust" who seem favored with increase. Hopkins, a celibate priest, is indeed one of those who "have made themselves eunuchs for the kingdom of heaven's sake" (Matt. 19:12)—but, far from having a spiritual consolation for this, he has become also a spiritual eunuch who does not "breed one work that wakes." The chief images of the poem are drawn from those words of Jesus depicting the kingdom—images of hopeful growth. There may even be a reminiscence of the grain of mustard seed that will grow into a tree in the branches of which the birds of the air will rest ("birds build—but not I build"). The passionate desire for justice of the psalmist and Job has been internalized into a desire for spiritual refreshment.

St. Paul and St. John

Paul

Paul begins from the teaching of Jesus that in heaven there will be no marriage and giving in marriage, and therefore envisages the risen body as spiritual. Heaven will not be a renewal of life on earth—a restoration, for instance, of the kingdom of Israel in which the just children of the covenant will return to live on a gloriously refurbished earth. The insistence of Jesus that there will be no marriage or giving in marriage in heaven but that the just will be as the angels of God, clearly reflects his belief that the heavenly life will be different in kind from earthly life. The kingdom of heaven is within. It is hard to read all the words of Jesus as manifesting a belief in a physical resurrection. The Gospels themselves are full of ambiguity. The risen Jesus can eat fish and bread (Luke 24:42), and has wounds into which Thomas, doubtingly, can thrust his finger; but he can also pass through walls and locked doors (John 20:19, 26–28). On Easter morning, Mary Magdalene does not recognize him—mistaking him for the gardener (John 20:15). The disciples, out fishing, see him on the shore but do not immediately recognize him (John 21:4). Most movingly, perhaps, the two disciples on the journey to Emmaus walk with him and talk with him for (one supposes) several hours; but they do not recognize him until he breaks bread, blesses it, and gives it to them. Even then their recognition comes as much from the effect of his words upon them as from that gesture made significant to them at the Last Supper: "And they said to one another, Did not our heart burn within us, while he talked with us by the way, and while he opened to us the scriptures?" (Luke 24:13, 30–32).

Paul thinks of the risen body as spiritual. He writes of a man he knew in Christ—usually taken to be himself—who "(whether in the body I cannot tell; or whether out of the body I cannot tell: God knoweth;) such a one was caught up into the third heaven." And of a man (the same man?) who was "caught up into paradise, and heard unspeakable words, which it is not lawful for a man to utter" (2 Cor. 12:2–4). This man is physically still on earth, but yet at the same time in heaven—which suggests that heaven and earth are not simply two spatially distinct entities. For the risen body to be spiritual rather than fleshly means that the blessed will not be subject to the sins and temptations that beset us in our earthly lives. The flesh, in Paul, is that which wars against the spirit. The sins of the flesh include carnal lusts but also envy, covetousness, pride, and wrath. The risen body is spiritual just in that it has transcended these vices.

Paul had talked of the body in its resurrected form and raised in incorruption, a spiritual body (1 Cor. 15:42–44). Paul is obviously not simply speculating about the ontological status of the risen body, for notions of "corruption" and "incorruption" occur on the same level as "dishonor" and "glory." He makes this still plainer when he goes on to talk of the dead, at the last trump, in the twinkling of an eye, putting on incorruption and immortality: "O death where is thy sting? O grave where is thy victory? The sting of death is sin" (1 Cor. 15:52–55).

These words of Jesus and Paul allow both a literal and a metaphorical understanding of resurrection and therefore of the heavenly life. Paul undoubtedly believes in the actual rising from the dead of Christ—"if Christ be not raised, your faith is vain" (1 Cor. 15:17). The saved will be raised in the same way. Yet to be incorruptible is to be without sin. Hence "the wages of sin is death" (Rom. 6:23) does not mean simply that death is a punishment for sin, but that it is a necessary condition for incorruptibility that one be without sin. "And if Christ be not raised . . . ye are yet in your sins" (1 Cor.15:17).

This spiritual life implies *ascesis*—mortification of the flesh and the ego, the casting off of the Old Adam, a life not in society and family but through Christ alone: "I am crucified with Christ: nevertheless I live; yet not I, but Christ liveth in me" (Gal. 2:20). The life of the flesh is taken up into (or, to use a concept of Hegel) *sublated* into the life of the crucified Christ.

Christian thought about heaven is rooted in these texts. The mixture of the literal and metaphorical certainly produces ambiguity, and perhaps ideas that are not finally reconcilable. Later Christian theology will expend much ingenuity in trying to reconcile them. There is no doubt that scripture does insist upon actual resurrection. Equally, there is no doubt that this resurrection is to be understood in overwhelmingly spiritual terms and cannot be taken just literally or physically. There is plenty of warrant for Christians to understand heaven not (as a Platonist might have it) as a picture of the human soul released from imprisonment in the body, but of its release from the wretchedness of sin; and hell as the soul deprived of its own chief good—the possession of God.

The *ascesis*, both physical and spiritual, that this implies inaugurates the Christian tradition in which "the world"—wealth, power, egoism, and sexuality—is the enemy of the spirit. Hence arise the ideals of virginity and of monasticism with its vows of poverty, chastity, and obedience. From it also flows the (especially) Roman Catholic tradition according to which some exceptionally holy people are allowed in this world a glimpse of the bliss of the world to come.

There is a passage in Augustine's *Confessions* where such an intimation of beatitude comes to Augustine and his mother, Monica, just after he has been converted, and shortly before she dies. They are staying in a house at Ostia, on the Tiber, leaning in a window, looking into the garden of the house in which they are staying. They are discussing what the eternal life of the saints might be like, and, as they talk they find their minds and spirits are drawn from earthly to heavenly things:

> And our conversation had brought us to this point that any pleasure
> whatsoever of the bodily senses . . . seemed to us not worthy of
> comparison with the pleasure of that eternal light. . . . Rising as our
> love flamed upward toward that self-same, we passed in review the
> various levels of bodily things, up to the heavens themselves, whence
> sun and moon and stars shine upon this earth . . . and so we came to
> our own souls, and went beyond them to come at last to that region of

richness unending, where you feed Israel forever with the food of truth: and there life is that Wisdom by which all things are made, both the things that have been and the things that are to be.

Monica says that she now no longer hopes for anything from this world; and "within five days or not much longer she fell into a fever."[65]

The Revelation of John

Yet the ideas underlying this are to be found as early as the description of the apocalypse of John (Rev. 1). The colorful imagery of that book—the great red dragon with seven heads and ten horns, whose tail drew a third part of the stars of heaven; the great whore sitting upon seven hills—has been a chief reason for its fascination and an inexhaustible source of bogus prophesy. But at its core is a picture of a God-centered universe, in which heaven turns out to be a huge liturgical celebration of the glory of God. The New Jerusalem pictured is not the restoration of the kingdom of Israel on earth; rather, the New Jerusalem that descends from heaven is essentially a temple in which God is praised for ever.[66] Augustine and his mother feel that they are already near to entering that temple.

At the beginning of the apocalypse John's vision is of something between an imperial court and a grand liturgical ceremony. One who is "like unto the Son of man, clothed with a garment down to the foot and girt about the paps with a golden girdle" initiates a ceremony in which seven stars and seven golden candlesticks appear as the emblem of seven Christian churches (Ephesus, Smyrna, Pergamos, Thyatira, Sardis, Philadelphia, and Laodocia) which are admonished for their various lapses in faith or discipline (Rev. 1:13, 20; 2–3). Then John sees the throne of God in heaven. Unlike the heaven of Enoch, this one includes human beings—martyrs—as well as angels. God's throne is surrounded by four symbolic beasts, with eyes in both the front and back of their heads. One beast is like a lion, one like a calf, the third has the face of a man, and the fourth is a flying eagle. The beasts praise God continually, chanting Holy, holy, holy (Rev. 4:6–9).

There is another ceremony, part liturgical and part prophetic, when the beasts of the apocalypse are released to terrify the earth. The tribes of Israel to the number of 144,000 are then seen standing around the throne, and, after that a countless multitude from all nations, clothed with white robes, palms in their hands (a recollection of Christ's entry into Jerusalem on Palm Sunday). All wear robes made white in the blood of the Lamb which was slain (Rev. 7).

It is a liturgy accompanied with the greatest virtual reality show of all time as angels open seven seals which show in vivid detail the shape of things to come—including a third part of the sea becoming blood, the opening of a bottomless pit, which releases locusts wearing crowns, and breastplates of iron, and with human faces. There is the woman clothed with the sun, the Great Beast with seven heads and ten horns, the fall of Babylon, the Great Whore, mother of harlots and the abominations of the earth (Rev. 8, 9, 12–14, 17).

The notable feature of all this is that it is part of a ceremony, a liturgy, a show. It portrays God as a great Eastern potentate sitting on his throne, surrounded by a court of both angelic and human beings—as well as symbolic beasts—and it sees heaven as a place where the power of God is both worshipped and made manifest.

Finally, the new Jerusalem is seen descending from heaven (Rev. 21). This will be a city that is at the same time a glorified version of the destroyed Temple of Jerusalem. God will dwell there for ever, and his presence lights the whole city so brilliantly that no light of the sun is needed. The golden streets of this citytemple—the light of which must be blindingly intense, since it is entirely constructed of jasper, sapphire, chalcedony, emerald, sardonyx, sardius, chrysolite, beryl, topaz, chrysophrase, jacinth, amethyst, and pearl, as well as common or garden gold—are filled with uncountable numbers of pilgrims from all parts of the world. God's faithful will be with him, and he shall wipe away all tears from their eyes "and there shall be no more death, neither sorrow, nor crying, neither shall there be any more pain: for the former things are passed away" (Rev. 21:4).

The heaven of St. John can be seen as an ecstatic celebration of the death of an evil past, for it represents all the powers of the world and of wickedness overcome by the sacrifice of Christ. This celebration takes place always in the actual presence of God, enthroned at the center while the cosmic pageant unfolds. It is a strange, barbarous agglomeration, and has been taken to license the worst sort of prophetic superstition in the Christian centuries. But at its heart, redeeming its extravagances, and fundamentally setting it apart from the Apocrypha, is an intense vision of innocence set against corruption, and sorrow which will be assuaged in the final triumph of the kingdom.

II

Bodies Fleshly and Spiritual

An Earthly Paradise: St. Irenaeus

Ancient Jewish hopes for a resurrection of the dead were often really hopes (as in the vision of Ezekiel) for a restoration of Israel to her ancient might and glory. Christian belief in immortality and heaven was from early times powerfully influenced by the idea of compensation and restitution. The Christian community saw itself as existing in, but not of, a world of wickedness. Resurrection would mean the triumph of the meek, Christian godly over the carnal and worldly pagans. Still more to the point, in these early centuries of the church, it would mean the triumph of Christ's followers over their persecutors. Tertullian's vision of damnation was directed at those who scoffed at and persecuted the Christ and his Church.[1] Salvation and restitution became intimately connected.

The most distinguished early Christian thinker for whom heaven was closely linked with compensation was St. Irenaeus (ca. 130–ca. 200), bishop of Lugdunum (the modern Lyons.) There had been an outbreak of persecution of the Christians of Lyons between AD 75 and 77, in which the bishop Pothinus perished. Irenaeus, who may have been born in Smyrna, succeeded Pothinus as bishop, and hence his sense of what it meant to be a Christian, and perhaps his interpretation of the Christian hope in the next life, was colored by the circumstances in which he became bishop. Irenaeus had heard and been influenced by Polycarp, bishop of Smyrna (traditionally ca. 69–155), who also perished in a persecution. Polycarp was revered as a link between the Apostolic age and Irenaeus's own time, and it seems likely that Polycarp's martyrdom would have served to strengthen Irenaeus's own conviction that heaven was a compensation to Christians for sufferings on earth inflicted, especially, by the Roman secular power.

Irenaeus's wholehearted stress on compensation goes with a reading of scriptural texts and prophecies that could scarcely be more literal. The dinners that a just man might have given to the poor "will be a hundred times recompensed in the kingdom."[2] Irenaeus really seems to mean that for every dinner he charitably gave on earth, the just man will get a hundred dinners in heaven, and (apparently) that they will be a hundred times more delicious than the earthly ones.

Irenaeus thought that human history has three periods.[3] First was his own era—the time of persecution. Then would come the kingdom of the Messiah. The final age would be that of the kingdom of God the Father. The kingdom of the Messiah—which he describes in some detail—will last a thousand years. The kingdom of God the Father will last for ever—but Irenaeus shows little interest in working out what it will be like.

Irenaeus is not literal inadvertently, but by conviction. Literal interpretation of scripture is what he polemically insists upon against those who are drawn to allegorical readings. The possibility of bodily resurrection seems to him proved from actual historical events as these are recorded in the Bible. The book of Daniel has the three young men rescued from the fiery furnace of Nebuchadnezzar by the hand of God. This proves that God can re-create human bodies from whatever they have disintegrated into. God can give immortality to bodies—after all, the patriarchs of the Hebrew Bible lived for 700 or 800 or 900 years; and the patriarch Enoch was even "translated in the body."[4] These historical facts show that through God's agency there have actually been cases of physical resurrection and immortality. And think of Elias (Elijah) in the fiery chariot that carried him heavenward—"his flesh was not wasted in the flames" (ibid.). Furthermore, "Jonas, being cast into the deep, and swallowed up in the belly of the whale, was vomited up safe upon the earth" (ibid.).

To explain his emphasis on these solidly physical examples, Irenaeus sets forth his philosophy of the relation between the spiritual and physical in man. Perfected man is "a certain mingling and uniting of the soul, receiving the Spirit of the Father: which mixture is blended with that of the flesh, which is molded according to the image of God" (ibid., 5, 6). Flesh alone is not perfect man, nor is spirit alone. Man is truly a blending and union of the two. Man is tripartite—although the parts mingle and are united: flesh, soul, and spirit (ibid., 5, 9). Therefore we do and should believe that Christ rose "in the substance of his flesh" (ibid., 5, 7). Both Lazarus and the daughter of Jairus "rose again in the same bodies in which they died" (ibid., 5, 13).

One gets a sense of how controversial this could be for the early church by noticing how uncomplimentary some of the fathers are about *unrisen* flesh. Arnobius described the human body as "a disgusting vessel of urine" and a "bag of shit" (*saccus stercorum*). Ambrose saw it as only a wretched prison for the soul, which aches to escape from the pain.[5] There is an alleged patristic saying, *"inter faeces et urinas nascimur"* [Between feces and urine are we born].[6] It is not surprising that the opinion arose (attributed to Origen, and condemned by the Second Council of Constantinople in the middle of the sixth century) that we will escape all this nastiness by contriving to resurrect as spheres.

Irenaeus is close to the ancient Jews in envisaging resurrection as not merely an individual immortality, but a kingdom of the Messiah on earth. So it is necessary for him to work out how to predict not only the nature of this kingdom but also the date at which "Christ will destroy temporal kingdoms and bring in the eternal one."[7] The world will last for six thousand years; and the kingdom of the Messiah will last for one thousand years. The kingdom of the Messiah will have to arrive some time after the rule of Antichrist. Antichrist (whose name Irenaeus gives variously as "666," "Lateinos," "Titan," and "Eganthas") may have already manifested himself at the end of the reign of the emperor Domitian (AD 51–96). Antichrist was predicted to reign for three years and six months. (There is one difficulty about that, however. Antichrist was expected to take the Temple at Jerusalem as his seat, but since Titus destroyed the Temple in AD 70, it is hard to see how Antichrist would have found much to attract him to the site.)

Messiah's kingdom, then, will come into existence at a particular time and in a particular place. In the resurrection of the just, the church, taking the place of the Jews whom it has superseded, will receive the land God promised Abraham "from the river of Egypt unto the great river Euphrates." The meek shall inherit the earth, or at any rate, this substantial piece of the Near East (ibid., 5, 32). In this restored kingdom the fruit of the vine will be drunk, for "the resurrection shall be flesh." Compensation comes fully into its own in Irenaeus's invocation of the kingdom: "Vineyards shall grow, having each 10,000 main shoots: and in one main shoot 10,000 branches and in one branch again 10,000 sprigs, and upon every sprig 10,000 clusters, and in every cluster 10,000 grapes, and every grape when pressed shall yield twenty-five measures of wine. And when any of those saints shall lay hold of a cluster, another cluster shall exclaim, I am a better cluster, take me" (ibid., 5, 25). (It is worth reminding ourselves that in centuries to come, Christians would criticize Muslims for their belief in a "sensual paradise.")

Wheat, too, will be multiplied ten thousand by ten thousand times, and then by ten times when it comes to producing "clear and clean flour." Fruits, seeds, and grass will be equally abundant; and all the animals, being strictly vegetarian, will live at peace and in agreement with one another, presenting themselves to men with entire submission.

The poetically expressed hopes of Isaiah and Jeremiah are also quantified. Isaiah's verse "For the young man shall be an hundred years old" becomes an assurance that in the kingdom "Man is made young again, and hath become ripe for incorruption, so as never to be susceptible to decay from age" (ibid., 5, 36).

Jerusalem will be rebuilt after the pattern of heavenly Jerusalem, and God will dwell there with men, who will enjoy also communion with the angels. All the inhabitants of the kingdom will be members of the church. Irenaeus insists that all this is to be taken literally—"nothing can be allegorized, but it is all firm and true and substantial" (ibid., 5, 35).

The vision of Irenaeus is, then, a consciously literal rendering of Old Testament prophecies in Isaiah and Jeremiah. It is hard to see how it consorts with numerous sayings of Jesus about the kingdom of heaven within us. True, Irenaeus accepts the words of St. Paul that the risen body will be spiritual. He interprets that to mean that we will not be subject to fleshly lusts and temptations to sin. There is no doubt, though, that he is envisaging an earthly paradise with wine lakes and wheat mountains, a paradise swimming in the material good things of life. It has been suggested that Irenaeus's picture is what you might expect from a bishop of "a great clearing house for the commerce in corn, wine, oil and lumber . . . a manufacturing and distribution center for most of the articles consumed by Gaul, Germany and Britain."[8] It is hard to see why, in the midst of this materialistic picture of the good life in the kingdom to come—healthy, eternal, and festive—Irenaeus can find a way of agreeing that there will be no marriage or giving in marriage. He can hardly reject the plain words of Jesus on that subject—but it hardly fits the spirit, or (should one say?) the body of his argument: "For Christians who wanted to live in the world, carry on business and raise families, compensation in a glorified material world was God's great promise. Their loyalty to Christ had already been tested by torture and humiliation; now they were ready to experience a full life on earth."[9] The enormously rich land Irenaeus describes would certainly need merchants to deal with the reliably immense surpluses eternally guaranteed. In the midst of all this abundance and jollity, the absence of relations between the sexes and the raising of families might conceivably be overlooked.

A Spiritual Heaven: St. Augustine

We recall that Augustine was a Manichaean before he converted to Catholic Christianity (see chap. 7), and that in the *Confessions* he drew a picture of the struggle between flesh and spirit that is clearly informed by Manichaeanism, especially his account of the sinfulness of babyhood and boyhood. There was his own "hot rage" as an infant because "older persons . . . were not obedient to me."[10] There was the infant "livid with anger" as it watched another infant at the breast (ibid.). Infants are not really innocent, since such faults, found in a grown man, would be seen as monstrous: "These childish tempers are born with lightly, not because they are not faults, or only small faults; but because they will pass with the years . . . the same things would not be tolerated in an older person" (ibid.).

His idling at school (ibid., 1, ix), his refusal to learn Greek (ibid., 1, xiii) are part of his fleshly, willful rebellion against God. His sexual desires manifest the perversity of original sin: "I had no desire whatever for incorruptible food, not because I had it in abundance but the emptier I was, the more I hated the thought of it . . . my soul was sick and broke out into sores whose itch I agonized to scratch with the rub of carnal things . . . I polluted the stream of friendship with the filth of unclean desire and sullied its limpidity with the hell of lust" (ibid., 3, i). He sees his ambition as a young man to excel at rhetoric, his love of stage plays as expressions of carnal worldliness (ibid., 4, ii).

After his conversion, Augustine develops this memory of the struggle between fleshly desire, with its perverse will, and the spirit, into an ascetic philosophy. That, in turn, shapes his idea of heaven. His mystical experience with Monica at Ostia (ibid., 9, x, xi, 455) is an intimation of the life to come, where concupiscence and the rebellion of the will have been left behind. Nothing could be further from the kingdom of the Messiah invoked by Irenaeus. Such a grossly material heaven is unthinkable for Augustine.

In *The City of God* Augustine insists on an actual resurrection of the body. He argues against those Platonists who say that the body, being earthly, must exist at the level of the lower elements (earth and water) rather than the higher (air and fire) and that therefore by its nature it cannot be lifted to and remain in the heavens (Augustine, *City of God* 22, 12). Augustine's arguments make sense in terms of the theory of the elements, but what is more interesting is the fact that he thinks the argument worthwhile at all. The reason must be that he thinks the resurrection is in some sense literal, and that what rises is not pure spirit. He therefore addresses himself to the usual arguments of the pagans against the possibility of rising from the dead: What about abortions? Will they rise again? What about those who in part are turned to dust, in part evaporate into the air? Some people are consumed by wild beasts, others by fire, others by shipwreck. Their flesh decays and dissolves (ibid.). How can they be resurrected? What about someone eaten by cannibals? Into whose body will he return?

Augustine deals with these stumbling blocks. His answers give us the clue to how he regards the risen body. He is uncertain about abortions, but "As for little children, I can only say that they will not rise again with the tiny bodies they had when they died. By a marvellous and instantaneous act of God they will gain that maturity they would have attained by the slow lapse of time. For we may be sure that in the Lord's statement that 'not a hair of your head will perish' he promises that what was already there would not be lacking: but that does not deny that what was lacking will be supplied" (ibid., 22, 15).

His argument is that all human bodies develop according to an inborn form, one that all have in potentiality, even if in some cases this is not actualized. So God will intervene to realize the potential, and confer on each body the perfection that nature demands. All the resurrected will have bodies that correspond to what in nature is the human prime of life—which happens to be the age of Christ himself when he was crucified. Therefore all the blessed "will rise neither younger nor older than Christ. They will be of the same age, the same prime of life" that Christ had reached (ibid., 22, 16).

Next, Augustine deals with what to a modern mind is a surprising question: Will women retain their sex in the resurrected body (ibid., 22, 17)? It seems that some of Augustine's contemporaries had argued that women will be raised up as men. Their official reason for believing this was that God made men and women out of clay, and woman out of man—therefore the perfection of women is to become men. Underlying this is the notion found in Aristotle that the female sex is a sort of failure;[11] fetuses with less than sufficient vital heat fail to develop into males, who are the perfection of the human form.

Against this, Augustine argues that "a woman's sex is not a defect; it is natural."[12] But resurrected women "will be free of the necessity of intercourse and childbirth." Therefore female sex organs will not have their present function at all. So what will their function be? "they will be part of a new beauty, which will not excite the lust of the beholder—there will be no lust in that life—but will arouse only the praises of God for his wisdom and compassion, in that he not only created out of nothing but freed from corruption that which he had created" (ibid.). The human body can always been seen to have an aesthetic as well as a practical function (ibid., 22, 24)—the nipples on a man's chest and the beard on his face are there "for masculine adornment" rather than for function. Practical needs are transitory. In heaven we shall enjoy one another's beauty aesthetically, and without lust. Indeed, we shall see the human body with the same wonderment and delight with which we see the beauties of nature, the "abundance of light, and its miraculous loveliness, in sun and moon and stars; the dark shades of woods, the color and fragrance of flowers; the multitudinous varieties of birds, with their songs and their bright plumage . . . the mighty spectacle of the sea" (ibid.).

Our internal organs will be transformed. Livers and intestines will become transparent in paradise[13] (which makes it especially fortunate that we will not need to eat there, as Augustine says, for otherwise the *saccus stercorum* really would be unpleasant). All bodily change, all growth and decay, will cease. Tertullian invokes a legend about the children of Israel as they wandered in the desert to prove that such a suspension of change is perfectly possible for God: Their shoes and clothes did not wear out, nor did their hair and fingernails grow. If God can thus suspend natural laws in order to preserve shoe-leather and garments, how much more can he preserve flesh for resurrection?[14]

Augustine's tendency to absorb particular functions of the body into this detached aesthetic vision widens into his wish to understand the risen body as absorbed into the life of the church, which is the body of Christ. Are our risen bodies to resemble the perfect manhood of Christ? This is to be understood through the words of St. Paul: "he . . . gave gifts unto men . . . And he gave some, apostles; and some, prophets; and some, evangelists; and some, pastors and teachers; for the perfecting of the saints, for the work of the ministry, for the edifying of the body of Christ: Till we come in the unity of the faith, and of the knowledge of the Son of God, unto a perfect man, unto the measure of the stature of the fulness of Christ" (Eph. 4:8, 11–13).

So the perfection of manhood is the incorporation into the church, which is the body of Christ. Christ "is the head . . . through whom the whole Body is fitted and joined together, with strength supplied through every joint, while each separate part performs its orderly function."[15]

There is a curious mixture in Augustine of a vision of the risen body, which is virtually allegorical—or at least that sees the body's existence and reality as subsumed within the life of the society of believers—and a continued attempt to explain it in a semiliteral way. He comes back in the following chapter to such tricky points as whether all the hair and nails that we have cut off during the course of our lives will somehow have to be incorporated into our risen bodies, since "not a hair will perish," and whether thin people and fat people will change their shapes in the life to come. He answers these problems sensibly enough (the number of hairs on our heads will be those we had in our prime—our hair will not become immensely long); but his final stress is undoubtedly upon the spiritual body.

His understanding of this spiritual body is caught succinctly in what he says about Plato and the Neo-Platonic philosopher, Porphyry. Plato had said that souls could not exist indefinitely after death without bodies—they would eventually find new bodies to inhabit. Porphyry, by contrast, held that the soul, once it has been purified in going back to the Father, will never return to the evils of this world. Porphyry insists that the soul, if it is to be in bliss, must be free from all contact with a body. Therefore the soul cannot be blessed unless it escapes altogether from everything material (*City of God* 22, 26–27). Augustine reconciles the difference between Plato and Porphyry by saying that even the holy will return to their bodies, but they will not return to the evils that go with the body as it exists in this fallen world. For the bodies will be spiritual, and not under the influence of concupiscence (ibid. 22, 29).

What, above all, does he want to know about these spiritual bodies? He is chiefly occupied with the question how in our arisen bodies we shall see God. Shall we see him with our physical eyes? That does not seem right, for our physical eyes could have been focused—as were the eyes of the disciples on the journey to Emmaus, or when he appeared in the upper room—on the risen body of Christ without seeing his glory, i.e., the qualities of his divinity. (For they were overcome by spiritual blindness [ibid.].) Hence, in heaven we shall have to see in some other way.

Augustine's conclusion is that in heaven we shall "see" spiritually, without the need of bodily eyes. In seeing God, we shall not see a material substance—something visual—but God as present everywhere and governing the whole material scheme of things (ibid. 22, 30). We shall see this in our risen, spiritual bodies "wherever we turn our eyes." He uses an interesting analogy to illustrate the idea. When we see living creatures with which we come into contact, we do not *believe* them to be alive—we *observe the fact.* "We could not observe their life without their bodies; but we see it in them, without any possibility of doubt, through their bodies" (ibid. 22, 29). As Wittgenstein might say, our attitude to them is as to living beings, we see them as living (ibid. 22, 19).[16]

Analogously, we "see" God as present everywhere and governing the universe; but you might equally say that we "see" the universe as equally and everywhere governed by God—which is reminiscent of pantheism and Spinoza.

Seeing God in this way, we of necessity praise him and love him as the governor of the universe everywhere and in all its beauty. This is, for Augustine, the activity of the blessed in heaven. There will be nothing remotely like the heavenly kingdom of Irenaeus, with its suggestions of overflowing winepresses, and huge surpluses of corn and oil, of generous eating and drinking.

Augustine insists that the risen Christ, when he ate something in the presence of his disciples, did it because he had the power to do so, and not because his risen body would normally take or need nourishment (ibid. 22, 29). (That is why Augustine thinks that in heaven none of us will eat.) Because they will have this vision of God, the blessed will be incapable of sin (ibid. 22, 30). This will not be a restriction on their free will, for "the will is the freer in that it is released from a delight in sin and immovably fixed in a delight in not sinning." This will be a gift from God who, although omnipotent, himself cannot sin.

In the Heavenly City, therefore, there will be freedom of the will, an unfailing delight in eternal joys, and a forgetting of all past offenses and punishments. The blessed will have no sensible recollection of past evils. They will forget them not as a scholar does who neglects his studies, and hence lets them slip from his memory, but as the sufferer does in escaping from misery. Augustine is perhaps remembering the words of Jesus (if we may quote them again), where he is intimating his own death: "A woman when she is in travail hath sorrow, because her hour is come: but as soon as she is delivered of the child, she remembereth no more the anguish, for joy that a man is born into the world" (John 16:21).

Paradise of the Senses?: Islam

Christians have traditionally condemned the paradise promised by Mohammed to true Muslims on the grounds that it offers purely material and sensual delights and hardly any spiritual ones. In the Qur'an there are indeed one or two *suras* that promise satisfactions that we could call spiritual or moral, but the references are very brief: "There they shall hear no idle talk, but only 'Peace.'"[17] Some writers speak of the blessed seeing God (although whether God could ever be "seen" remains controversial among theologians). But far more representative are passages evoking delights that are certainly sensuous, if not sensual:

> surely for the godfearing awaits a place of security,
>   gardens and vineyards
> and maidens with swelling breasts, like of age. (Sura 78)

There will be rivers of water, of wine, of milk (that never goes sour) and of honey (sura 47). Dressed in silk brocade, and reclining on couches, the blessed will live among gardens and fountains, palm trees and pomegranates, calling for every fruit they desire, and espoused to wide-eyed *houris*, lovely as rubies, beautiful as coral: vessels of silver and goblets of crystal will be passed around, and they will drink cups of ginger wine served to them by immortal youths (suras 44, 55, 76).

Visions of paradise are further developed in the *hadith*. There is again that striking sublimity of visual exaggeration: "Abu Huraira reported Allah's messenger (may peace be upon him) as saying: In paradise, there is a tree under the shadow of which a rider can travel for a hundred years."[18] There is also the idea—not found in the Qur'an—that some in paradise will have, through their spiritual excellence, a higher place than others: "The inmates of paradise would see the inhabitants of the apartment over them just as you see the shining planets which remain in the eastern and the western horizon because of the superiority some have over others."[19] In general, though, you have an elaboration of the sensuous/sensual delights: For each believer there will be a tent of a single hollowed pearl, the breadth of which will be sixty miles.[20] "In paradise there is a street to which [the blessed] will come every Friday. The north wind will blow and will scatter fragrance on their faces and on their clothes and will add to their beauty and loveliness, and they will go back to their families after having an added lustre to their beauty and loveliness."[21] They will drink water on Saturday, liquid honey on Sunday, milk on Monday, wine on Tuesday. When they have drunk that, they will be intoxicated. When they get intoxicated, they will fly for one thousand years until they reach a great mountain of pure and pungent musk.[22] The first group to get into paradise will be like the full moon in the night. The next group will be like glittering stars. The first group will neither spit, nor suffer catarrh, nor void excrement, and will sweat musk. Their form will be the form of one single person according to the length of their father sixty cubits tall. Every one of them will have two spouses, so beautiful that the marrow of their shanks will be visible through the flesh, the same way red wine is seen through white glass. Not surprisingly (perhaps) there will be no dissension amongst them and no enmity. Their hearts will be like one heart, glorifying Allah morning and evening.[23]

One or two of the sayings are strikingly mystical: "Abu Huraira reported Allah's messenger (may peace be upon him) as saying: There would enter Paradise people whose hearts would be like those of birds."[24]

There have been Muslim thinkers in modern times, especially some hailing from the Indian subcontinent, who have sought to interpret the sensuous delights of paradise (and indeed the pains of hell) spiritually or symbolically.[25] Even some early *hadith* suggest that the sensual delights are quite unearthly: "The Prophet said: "Allah-ta-'ala created the faces of *houris* of four colors: white, green, yellow and red. He created their bodies of saffron, musk, amber and camphor."[26] The faithful are certainly promised some solidly sensual satisfactions: "the people of the Garden increase in beauty and handsomeness every day....One man is given the power of one hundred in eating, drinking and sexual enjoyment."[27] Islam has a strong mystical

Allegory of Earthly and Heavenly Drunkenness. From *Images of Paradise in Islamic Art*, ed. Sheila S. Blair and Jonathan M. Bloom (Hanover, NH: Hood Museum of Art, Dartmouth College, 1991), 60.

tradition, and no lack of philosophers who could provide a rationale for such reinterpretations. Some have argued that the resurrected body cannot possibly be identical with our earthly body, and even that it will not be a material object as we understand that, and cannot therefore enjoy the sensuous delights of paradise nor suffer the physical tortures of hellfire. However, popular and orthodox Islam holds powerfully to a literal interpretation of the Qur'an and the *hadith*, with the result that real assent to the actual existence of heaven and hell is immeasurably stronger and more unquestioned in Islamic countries than in those of the Christian (or post-Christian) world.

It is nevertheless true that not later than the twelfth century very many Muslim theologians, including the great Averroes, who was a major influence upon Thomas Aquinas, interpreted the delights of paradise as allegories of the beatific vision, and denied that they could be taken literally as pleasures of the senses. This was particularly true of the great Sufi tradition, in which all experience is finally to be understood (in a Platonic fashion) as pointing to the love of God.[28] And there are certainly early *hadith*, which attribute to the Prophet the opinion that the chief joy of the blessed will be that they will see God "without obstruction" as on a clear night we see the moon without obstruction.[29] The greatest, highest, most noble and perfect felicity is to see the Noble Face of God in the abode of honor and of bliss.[30]

We might be tempted to feel that there is something too easy in the traditional Christian horror at the sensuality of the Muslim paradise. In Christian tradition attempts to conceptualize, let alone describe the bliss of heaven, have often foundered on that very assumed need to understand it in purely spiritual terms. Only one great attempt has been both intellectually and emotionally successful—Dante's synthesis of his own poetic imagination with the philosophy of Aquinas. Christian thinkers have often hesitated between a purely spiritual heaven, which can come to seem boring or lifeless, and admitting sensuous elements, which have reduced the sense that in the next life God will be all in all.

It is worth remembering that the more spiritual versions of the Christian heaven have gone with the tradition of asceticism, one that elevates holy virginity above marriage, and which envisages a heaven (as Jesus did) as a state where there is no marrying and giving in marriage. Christian thinkers who have in one way or another abandoned that ascetic tradition—for example, Luther—become quite confused about how purely spiritual heaven could be. Muslims can argue that their paradise is at least consonant with the picture— accepted by Jews, Christians, and Muslims alike—of man as a body-soul identity. This does not, though, answer another objection we might bring— that paradise as described in the Qur'an and the *hadith* and accepted in popular tradition seems to leave no room for any lively activity of the intellect.

12

Dante: *Paradiso*

Beatitude

T. S. Eliot writes that "we have . . . a prejudice against beatitude as material for poetry." Such a prejudice might lead us to assume that the states and degrees of blessedness described by Dante in the *Paradiso* must be insipid or monotonous. Eliot suggests that whereas Shakespeare commands the greatest *width* of human passion, we find in Dante the greatest altitude and greatest depth.[1] The *Paradiso* is characterized by a sustained altitude—or sublimity—equaled by no other work of literature. It aims to evoke states of bliss. Yet this bliss is not intelligible simply as experience; it has to be understood through a philosophy in which contemplation is the highest human good. Aquinas had given an account of the philosophy of mind in which man's natural ascent to contemplation led to the acceptance of those Christian virtues that renounce the lusts of the world—for power, wealth, carnality—and stress instead the Beatitudes of the Sermon on the Mount.

In the *Inferno* Dante had depicted damned souls re-enacting throughout eternity the states of soul or character that merited unending punishment. In the *Paradiso* we do not have anything as pictorial and concrete. There is no equivalent, in the *Paradiso*, of spirits tormented by fiery flakes, or perpetually running, or buried in mud and ice, such as we find in the *Inferno*. Sinners are plunged into obsessive, grotesque activities that express their choice of self rather than the objective good. Virtue, or grace, by contrast, does not have this egoistic character. Indeed, throughout the *Paradiso* the blessed are seen expanding their love more and more, through an ever growing concentration on God, until love is also an *understanding* of God, and hence of reality as a whole. Or, as Dante puts it, the human will is merged with intellection. The ascent to God is an ascent of the understanding as well as of the will. One commentator writes: "the Almighty is disclosed to us, first through his works, then through Christian dogma, and lastly in his own essence."[2]

In the *Paradiso*, the poet encounters souls that, though blissful, are waiting to be perfected by being reunited with their bodies at the general resurrection. The bliss enjoyed by these souls is that of love—the love they experience from God and which they feel toward God and toward other souls. The enduring image of love that Dante uses is that of light. The first sighting of God is of a tiny but intensely bright point of light, surrounded by circles of light spinning with immense rapidity. These turn out to be the nine choirs of angels (angels, archangels, thrones, dominations, princedoms, virtues, powers, cherubim, seraphim).

As the *Inferno* depicted a descent into the lowest depths of depravity, and into a world of eternal cold that symbolizes the final rejection of charity, so the *Paradiso* is a poem of ascent. The poet quits the sphere of earth and moves successively through the spheres that constitute the Ptolemaic solar system— the moon, Mercury, Venus, the sun, Mars, Jupiter, Saturn, the fixed stars, the Primum Mobile—the outermost sphere of the solar system—until, finally, he reaches the empyrean where God dwells in his full glory. In each sphere he meets souls who represent different levels of bliss, each level corresponding to their capacity to love and understand God. There is little or no physical description of what it is like to exist on these spheres—there is no hint of space travel. Although one can read the *Inferno* without paying much attention to the symbolic scheme, this is not true of the *Paradiso*. The spheres are overwhelmingly symbolic, and the ascent through them is inescapably allegorical.

The lowest sphere of paradise contains the souls of people who succumbed to weakness and broke their religious vows but were nevertheless vouchsafed final salvation. This is the sphere of the moon—the "inconstant moon," as Shakespeare's Cleopatra calls it, the plane of fickle women, of people who could not hold with fortitude to one good course of life. In the moon the spirits are discerned as "faint translucent images of human shapes, like the reflections we sometimes catch in windowpanes or in shallow water."[3] Here Dante meets Piccarda Donati. She had been betrothed to a man whom she did not wish to marry. To avoid the marriage she had entered a convent. But her brother and some followers entered the convent, seized her, and compelled her to wed. Piccarda never wanted to abandon her nun's vows; or, as Dante writes: "From her heart's veil she was never loosed" (*Paradiso* 3, 117)—i.e., she remained a nun at heart. But she lacked the fortitude simply to refuse the marriage and take the consequences.

We get a good sense of Dante's symbolic scheme in this encounter. The souls in the sphere of the moon are not pure, burningly bright lights, as they become in the higher reaches of the *Paradiso*, but faint, elusive beings. They were not strong and constant enough to burn with the intense flame of divine love. Their comparative faintness accords with the blanched light cast by the moon. The symbolism goes further. In the Ptolemaic system the moon moves sluggishly. This is because it is near the earth, which is at the bottom of the universe and does not move at all.[4] As you rise through successive spheres, you find that each moves faster and faster, the outermost sphere— the Primum Mobile—moving fastest of all. Ever more rapid movement in the *Paradiso* regularly symbolizes ever more ecstatic love of God. This indicates the relatively low degree of love and beatitude in these saved, but fragile souls.

This ascent, although symbolic, does imply a picture of the universe as it was actually understood by the cosmography of Dante's time. The earth is literally as far as it is possible to be from the empyrean, which is the true heaven—and yet the ascent to the empyrean has to be understood spiritually. Yet again, the ancient theory of the elements enters. Fire naturally leaps upward. Souls, similarly, naturally seek to regain their rightful place among the stars.

Among the blessed there is a hierarchy of happiness, which depends upon the love each has for God. As souls approach closer to the empyrean, each soul's understanding of the divine nature deepens and increases, and so, accordingly, does the love and happiness of every soul. Since love is expressed as light, the happier a soul grows, the more brilliantly does it shine, and the more beautiful it becomes. Hence, Beatrice, as she approaches her proper place in heaven, and therefore nearer to God, shines ever brighter and more lovely. The brightness and happiness, along with the understanding, of the souls is often expressed in the rapidity of motion of the souls in their joyful circles:

> E come in fiamma favilla si vede,
>> e come in voce voce si discerne,
>>> quand'una è ferma e altra va e riede,
>> vid'io in essa luce altre lucerne
>>> muoversi in giro più e men correnti,
>>> al modo, credo, di lor viste interne. (*Paradiso* 8, 16–21)

[And as we see a spark within a flame, and as a voice within a voice is distinguished when one holds the note and another comes and goes, I saw within that light other lamps moving in a circle more and less swift according to the measure, I believe, of their internal sight.]

In the second division (or *cantica*) of the *Paradiso*, the poet visits in turn the planets Saturn, Jupiter, and Mars. Each of these heavenly planets symbolizes a particular form of life, or a virtue. Saturn, being cold and remote,[5] is aptly taken to be the abode of monks, for it can stand as the type of contemplation. Jupiter stands for Empire—the abode of those who upheld justice. Mars—symbolizing, of course, war—is the home of Crusaders who willingly gave their lives for the faith.

After passing these planets, Dante reaches the sun. This, the brightest of the heavenly bodies, appropriately houses the theologians. The first theologian to whom Dante speaks is also, possibly, the greatest: St. Thomas Aquinas. The souls of these theologians appear like blazing suns, and they circle three times around Dante and Beatrice "like stars neighboring the fixed poles." Dante uses an extraordinary image to suggest the bliss of these souls: they are like "ladies not released from the dance, but who stop silent, listening till they have caught new notes." (For Dante to imagine the souls of the greatest theologians on the model of dancing women waiting for the next movement of the dance to begin is a fine example of his using homely imagery to convey sublime ideas.)

The souls of these great theologians shine brighter than the sun. Dante is introduced by Aquinas to other brilliant lights, who include Solomon, Boethius, St. Dominic, and St. Francis. Dante represents all these spirits as not only shining with beatific light but as wheeling in dancing circles in their joy—"all the great festival of both song and flames, light with light, gladsome and benign" (*Paradiso* 12, 22–24). Throughout the *Paradiso*, the spirits whom Dante encounters tend to express their beatitude in such ecstatic whirling.

What is the nature of their joy? It is a mixture of love and knowledge. In the words of St. Bonaventure: "Tantum gaudebunt, quantum amabunt; tantum amabunt, quantum cognoscent" [They shall rejoice in proportion as they shall love; they shall love in proportion as they shall know.][6] Souls in heaven shine because of the fervency of their love of God. This fervency is less or more in proportion as they have a less or more clear vision of God, i.e., it flows from the depth of their understanding of the divine vision. Some souls are created to have a deeper understanding of God than others, and this is purely a result of God's grace, which is to say, of predestination.[7] The power to understand is given by God prior to the power to love. In the Dantean vision, then, understanding, rather than will, is primary and indispensable—although with the beatific vision understanding and will become united.

Aquinas: Soul and Body

Joyful though the souls are in their present state, they desire, nevertheless, to be reunited with their bodies. What difference will this make? "When the flesh, glorious and sanctified, shall be clothed on us again, our persons will be more acceptable for being all complete . . . so that our vision must needs increase, our ardor increase which by that is kindled, our radiance increase which comes from this" (*Paradiso* 14, 43–51).

The souls of the blessed, then, long to be reunited with their bodies. The thinker who makes the profoundest and most coherent sense of this idea is Aquinas. Aquinas derived from Aristotle a particular theory of the relation of soul to body on which Dante draws to understand bodily resurrection. For Aquinas, unlike for Plato, the human being is not a something that *has* a body: it *is* a body, a living body of a particular kind.[8] The body without the soul is not, strictly, the body at all. So a living body and a dead body are not bodies in the same sense. And although the soul does survive death, it is not strictly a human person when it is in a state of separation from the body. For a person is a "complete substance of rational nature."[9] Man is a soul-body unity, a single substantive form—the rational soul. A single, composite form unites man's whole being, his vegetative, sensitive, and intellectual "souls" (i.e., fleshly growth, sensation, and thought). It is therefore contrary to the nature of the soul to be without the body. The immortality of the soul therefore seems to demand the resurrection of bodies.[10] The idea that the soul is the "form" of the body, rather than imprisoned within the flesh as a Platonist might say, allows that a human being is more perfect when he forms a soul-body unity.

Theologians had argued over whether the risen body would be the same "flesh" that had moldered in the grave. If so, what of cannibals who had lived all their lives on the flesh of other people? Whose would be the body resurrecting in the next life? Some had laid great stress on St. Paul's language of the seed going into the earth and then germinating new life. Others had stressed the extreme *dis*continuity of the risen body from the old fleshly one, seeing it as above all spiritual. For Aquinas (and for his master, Aristotle), the soul is the form of the body, it is that principle of unity and organization by which the body lives, grows, feels as a human body. After death, the particles making up the body fall apart, for the body without soul is mere matter, mere potentiality. Bodily resurrection is the identical soul informing matter so as to organize the body of the very same person who has risen from the dead. The original body was a body only because of the soul that "informed" it. Whether and what original material elements remain in the resurrected body is irrelevant, so long as the matter is informed by the original soul.

So when the souls of the blessed are reunited with bodies, this is not the fulfillment of a longing as when lovers are reunited; rather the body completes the natural being of the soul.

Nevertheless, Dante expresses this as an increase in ardor, pictured as an increase of fiery brightness: "even as a coal which gives forth flame, and with its white glow outshines it, so that its visibility is maintained, so shall this effulgence which already surrounds us be surpassed in brightness by the flesh which the earth still covers" (*Paradiso* 14, 52–57). Being more perfect, this soul-body unity is more like God—for everything more resembles God the more perfect it is. Although bodiless souls in heaven are perfectly happy, they will, when reunited with their bodies, find an increase in joy, because they will know they are more perfect.[11] This increase in joy is expressed as an increase in light, in the image of the white-hot coal shining through the flames that surround it. The light symbolizes glory—which is the means by which God enables the blessed to see him.

The Approach to God

The poet's approach to God had been, first, through God's works; then through God's revelation in Christian doctrine; and eventually to see God face to face. As he comes to the last sphere of the Ptolemaic universe—the ninth heaven—he leaves the material world behind altogether and enters on a vision of the true spiritual world: the empyrean. Here he undergoes, appropriately, an examination in the three theological virtues of faith, hope, and charity. His examiners are Peter, James, and John. Having passed the examination with flying colors, the poet is at last ready to approach the vision of God himself—the beatific vision. All other light fades away, the light from the sun and stars, and from the nine choirs of angels fading before the ineffably greater light of God.

God's astonishing first appearance as that point of light of laser intensity for a time deprives the poet of sight. This point has revolving around it, with incredible rapidity, the nine choirs of angels. Then, in one of the most majestically beautiful images in the whole *Divine Comedy*, Dante is granted a vision of the grace of God, which appears to him as a vast, inexhaustible river of light:

> e vidi lume in forma di rivera
>   fulvido di fulgore, intra due rive

dipinte di mirabil primavera.
Di tal fiumana uscian faville vive,
   e d'ogne parte si mettien ne 'fiori
   quasi rubin che oro circunscrive;
poi, come inebrïate da li odori,
   riprofondavan sé nel miro gurge,
   e s'una intrava, un'altra n'uscia fori. (*Paradiso* 30, 61–69)

[And I saw a light in form of a river glowing tawny between two banks painted with marvelous spring. From out this river issued living sparks and dropped on every side into the blossoms, like rubies set in gold. Then, as if inebriated by the odors, they plunged again into the wondrous flood, and as one was entering another was issuing forth.]

Eventually he is granted a vision of the souls of the just seated in heaven, and the privilege of seeing them as they will be after the general resurrection, when they will have regained their bodies in the glorified form these bodies will then take—which includes their shining with a brilliant luminosity. The blessed form an enormous golden rose, divided between the saved of the Old Testament, redeemed by their faith in the future Messiah, who fill up one half of the flower, and those redeemed by their faith in Christ after he came into the world. There are still places left to be filled up—but not very many.

The moment has been prepared where the poet will look on God himself. As he does so, he sees the summation of all his, and of all human desires. Gathered up into the divine vision is the whole of reality united in God's love:

Nel suo profondo vidi che s'interna,
   legato con amore in un volume,
   ciò che per l'universo si squaderna . . . (*Paradiso* 33, 85–87)

[Within its depths I saw ingathered, bound by love into one volume, the scattered leaves of all the universe.]

Within the intense light he sees three circles, of three colors—God as Trinity. And within these the image of man is somehow imprinted—the second person of the Trinity as the human Christ. The poet, satisfied to the depths of his nature, finds that his own will becomes one with "the Love that moves the sun and the other stars"—[l'amor che move il sole e l'altre stelle] (*Paradiso* 33, 145).

T. S. Eliot describes the divine ascent in the *Paradiso* as following "the logic of sensibility."[12] This suggests that the vision is guided by a philosophy that at the same time expresses and answers to an emotional need. As the *Inferno* gave images of depravity that were also an exploration of its inner

The redeemed seen as petals of the divine rose. *The Divine Comedy*, illustrated by Gustave Doré (London 1874, 1875), *Paradiso*, Canto 31, 1–3.

nature, so the *Paradiso* philosophizes an emotional ascent toward the most serene, contemplative joy, a joy that we can understand in its own terms without necessarily giving our allegiance to Dante's own religious beliefs. Eliot expresses this finely: "If you can read poetry as poetry, you will 'believe' in Dante's theology exactly as you believe in the physical reality of his journey; that is, you suspend both belief and disbelief. . . . his private belief becomes a different thing in becoming poetry."[13] What we do have to do is take seriously—respond to imaginatively—the picture of the mind that structures these beliefs. Aristotle's *Metaphysics* had envisaged the highest human activity as a state of pure contemplation, where the mind, reflecting on itself, becomes more truly itself. This is a rare moment, where the austere objectivity of Aristotle's thought merges into aesthetic beauty and is even touched with emotion. He is describing contemplation as the highest activity, because it is an image of God's own activity and is hence the state in which man most closely approaches the divine:

> And thought thinks on itself because it shares the nature of the object of thought; for it becomes an object of thought in coming into contact with and thinking its objects, so that thought and object of thought are the same. For that which is *capable* of receiving the object of thought, i.e., the essence is thought. But it is *active* when it *possesses* this object. Therefore the possession rather than the receptivity is the divine element which thought seems to contain, and the act of contemplation is what is most pleasant and best. If, then, God is always in that good state in which we sometimes are, this compels our wonder; and if in a better state this compels it yet more. And God *is* in a better state. And life also belongs to God; for the actuality of thought is life, and God is that actuality; and God's self-dependent actuality is life most good and eternal. We say therefore that God is a living being, eternal, most good, so that life and duration continuous and eternal belong to God; for this *is* God.[14]

Aristotle's picture of the human mind and soul entails that the best states we can be in are the most active states. Paradoxically, the most active state is the activity of contemplation. This is the fulfillment of human nature and the truest happiness. Dante has taken Aristotle's metaphysics and philosophy of mind, and married it to the Christian belief in a God of love. So in the *Divine Comedy* contemplation is also an intense *amor*. You can certainly call this a logic of sensibility, because it unites the depiction of bliss as this can be captured in poetry with a philosophical doctrine about the degrees of reality of the universe itself and of our perception of it. Dante was uniting the depiction of states of bliss that communicate themselves emotionally to the reader with a doctrine about the degrees of reality of the universe.

Dante's heaven is a mirror image of his hell. The sufferings of the damned are unending re-enactments of the sins that led to their damnation. Hell is the state in which we exist as sinners, rather than simply a punishment imposed from the outside. His heaven is, analogously, a fulfillment of human nature, a depiction of the highest reach of human possibility. In all human acts there is a movement toward either integration—a union of self with the deepest reality which is God; or disintegration—a choice of self against this truest reality, a choice that becomes an enchainment in blindly obsessive states of degradation. In the *Paradiso*, Dante renders the former with an emotional and intellectual profundity that has no parallel in literature.

It is appropriate that the poet's eyes are finally directed toward the beatific vision of God himself by the saint who wrote so persuasively of the contemplative life—Bernard of Clairvaux. Bernard's understanding of divine punishment is essentially the same as Dante's: "What is God? No less the punishment of the perverse than the glory of the humble; for he is, so to speak, the spiritual principle of equity, unalterable and uncompromising, indeed, pervading everywhere; and every evil that comes in contact with this principle must necessarily be confounded."[15] Bernard understands the approach to God as the antithesis of perverse choice, for it is the soul exercising its highest faculties in contemplation. The great form of contemplation is that which scorns all sensible objects and soars to the sublime "not by gradual steps but by sudden ecstasies. I think the ecstasies of Paul are of this last type: ecstasies, not ascents, for he says that he was 'caught up' not that he ascended." That flight "is made with wings of purity and ardor."[16]

In the final canto of the *Paradiso*, Bernard commends Dante to the Blessed Virgin, whose supplication will lift to the sublime those whose desire for God would, without her favor, "seek to fly without wings" (*Paradiso* 33, 15). Nor would the poet's desire have been accomplished ("my own wings were not sufficient" [*Paradiso* 33, 139]) had his mind not been "smitten in a flash" (*Paradiso* 33, 140). This divine grace that lifts the poet so as to share for a moment in the divine life is also in essence—although far beyond our normal capacities—a philosophical contemplation, which satisfies our deepest desire just in that it satisfies our desire to know.

Clearly the whole structure of the *Paradiso* is intended to symbolize and to enact the ascent of the mind toward God. A mass of earlier Christian writing had understood the soul's progress to heaven as such an ascent, but in Dante the idea is enforced in a mixture of devotional imagery and philosophy of mind of unsurpassed cunning. What is enforced is a picture of man in which the contemplative life is incontestably superior to the active life. Dante sets out the theory with exemplary clarity in his *Convivio*, where he distinguishes between two sorts of angels, those who attend to the stars and planets and the affairs of the world, and those (the seraphim) whose "activity" consists purely in contemplating God: "And inasmuch as human nature, as it here exists, hath not only one blessedness but two, to wit that of civil life and that of the contemplative life, it were irrational did we perceive those others to have the blessedness of the active that is civil life, in guiding the world, and not that of the contemplative life, which is more excellent and more divine.... And because this life is the more divine...it is manifest that this life is more loved by God."[17]

The highest human blessedness must be in contemplating God as he really is—contemplating his essence so far as God allows human nature to do so. But since God's own life is a self-contemplation, and since God is the Unmoved Mover, out of love for whom the sun and the other stars revolve, it follows that the highest human bliss reaches toward an ultimate stillness. The life of contemplation is the life of peace, in part because it is the end of motion and of all restlessness. This is symbolized by the empyrean, which is the true realm of the blessed souls and of God's heaven, and which, beyond the other circling heavens, is itself perfectly still.

Therefore, the heaven of Dante and Aquinas is bound to be intensive rather than extensive. There is no room for a paradise of earthly delights, or for a human society, conversation, and recreation that stands outside the beatific vision. This is the heaven anticipated in the whole Catholic tradition of monasticism, celibacy, mortification of the flesh, and asceticism in general. Underlying those disciplines was always the belief that in quietening the demands of the flesh and the world, the mind and soul would become more open to the movements of the spirit. In Dante's heaven there is no logical space for animals, plants, the continuation into the next life of conjugal love, or the concerns of civil life. (It has to be admitted, though, that Dante does keep meeting blessed souls who retain the keenest interest in the affairs of Florence.) The Renaissance could not endure such an austere conception of heaven, and allowed aspects of the natural world to creep back in. The heaven of Protestantism, also, comes soon to diverge radically from Dante's, and more and more reproduces in the next life the most important or attractive features of this one. Post-Protestantism in the form of the visions of Swedenborg, and, later still, in the pallid reproductions of this world in the practices of Spiritualism, jettison the Dantean vision completely. It may well be that the synthesis of the Christian ascetic tradition with the Aristotelian philosophy of mind could only have lasted for a relatively short time. It is something of a miracle that it found the poet who could reproduce it with such profound dramatic realism.

13

Celestial Pleasures: Renaissance and Reformation Heavens

The Contemplative Heaven

In the heaven of Dante and of St. Thomas Aquinas, then, God is all in all. Souls in bliss are absorbed in contemplation of that one object—which is what is meant by the beatific vision—as the passage of Aristotle's *Metaphysics* indicates. In Dante, God's own self-knowledge involves love between the first and second persons of the Trinity, expressed in the Holy Ghost; and in the soul's contemplation of God there is a fusion of love and knowledge, as the soul sees in God's depths "ingathered the scattered leaves of all the universe bound into one volume."[1] No one who has this vision would ever want to turn his eyes from it.

Aquinas had thought that the souls in heaven would be motionless, because this final coming to rest is in itself supremely desirable. (Dante adds a new element when he has the spirits dance for joy and love when we meet them during the approach to the final revelation. But in heaven itself—where they miraculously still are at the same time that they seem to appear to the poet outside it— contained within the golden mystical rose, they are perfectly still as they contemplate the divine.) Dante's heaven contains only souls (eventually, at the Last Day, to be joined by their risen bodies) existing in ever more gloriously intense light. There is nothing else at all in this spiritual world of pure light—certainly no plants or animals.[2]

It is remarkable how strong a hold this picture of the afterlife— ecstatic, yet, in its distance from common human ideas of human pleasure, austere—had upon people's minds. No doubt this is partly due to its wholehearted adoption by Dante and Aquinas, the poet and theologian laureates, respectively, of Catholicism. Yet it also chimed in with practical religion, which, despite the powerful mediating presence of the church, and despite devotion to Virgin and saints, still kept the sense that God is the overwhelming reality, in comparison with whom man's hold on existence is tenuous indeed.

Early modern spirituality and theology did not soon depart from medieval orthodoxy. But Renaissance humanism, with its emphasis on action at the expense of contemplation, encouraged a conception of heaven that began to move away from Dante and Aquinas. In the fifteenth and sixteenth centuries less than purely spiritual human pleasures began to find an imaginative place in heaven.

There were gardens—earthly paradises, gardens of delight. This is hardly surprising. The Bible begins with mankind set in a garden—a paradise, planted in Eden. Virgil and other classical authors imagined that heroes and other distinguished spirits would disport themselves in the next life in the Elysian Fields. There was also the myth of the Golden Age, reflected in pastoral poetry and a popular subject for painters. It was natural that both Eden and Elysium would, in Renaissance thinking, come to mingle with the orthodox teaching about heaven.

The garden of Eden, the Elysian Fields, the Happy Isles, the Golden Age had power over the European imagination right up until late in the eighteenth century. Many of the ancients believed in the actual existence, in this world, of the Happy Isles. Diodorus Siculus (roughly contemporary with Augustus Caesar) describes a voyage in which one Iambulus traveled from Ethiopia to an island far south, near the equator. He found there inhabitants who were tall and well proportioned, and who had two tongues so that they could converse with two people at once. They experienced no illness and lived to the age of one hundred and fifty years. Their island produced large and useful, but harmless, animals, and plenty of both hot and cold springs. When they reached one hundred and fifty years, they would lie down on a special plant that lulled them asleep for all eternity.[3]

Christians continued firmly to believe that the garden of Eden still existed, even though they would be deterred from entering it by angels with fiery swords. It was certainly a most desirable place. St. Ephraim the Syrian (died 373) writes of "the silent fig-tree in the enclosure . . . the light-filled dwellings, the fragrant springs." He held that in paradise "shadowy February smiles like May, December is like August with its fruits, June like April." Flowers are abundant, the air is virginal and transparent, the soil yields an abundance of wine, milk, honey, and butter. The whole place is "a granary of perfumes" and "lambs feed, free of fear."[4]

There were many attempts to work out exactly where this wondrous place might be, somewhere in Mesopotamia being a favorite choice. (In the eighteenth century, though, a claim was made for Brazil, partly based on the extremely fortunate fact that the tree of good and evil still grew there.)[5] In general, the account of the garden of Eden in Genesis suggested that it would have to be somewhere near the Tigris and the Euphrates. There were many tales of people looking for paradise, but none of their ever having entered it. Christopher Columbus thought he had rediscovered it at the mouth of the Orinoco River: "Believing that fateful tract could not be entered without God's permission, he did not investigate further; but in an eloquent letter to his royal patrons, Ferdinand and Isabella, he marshaled the observations and precedents in favor of this conclusion. He was now of the opinion that the earth was pear-shaped rather than round, that the newly discovered hemisphere was shaped like a woman's breast, and that the Earthly Paradise was located at a high point corresponding to the nipple."[6] It was left to Milton to decide that Eden had perished "pusht by the horned flood" in lines that wonderfully capture the nostalgia with which paradise has existed in our imaginations.[7]

Dante's Celestial Paradise is revealed at the summit of Mount Purgatory. It is a place of transition to the heavenly paradise. All visions of an earthly paradise carry associations of Eden, of the garden, the *locus amoenus* of peace, rest, and sensuous—indeed, sensual—pleasures. Many ancient depictions of the earthly paradise suggested that the pleasures of erotic love are among its delights. None of this carries over into Dante's heaven, as we have seen. The Celestial Paradise is not a garden; it is not filled with people enjoying themselves in a garden of delights; and all love—which is, anyway, nonerotic— is subsumed into the love of God, *l'amor che move il sole e l'altre stelle.*

But the heaven of Dante, centered on the act of understanding, dominated the European imagination for a comparatively short time. Elements of the terrestrial paradise began to creep back. Subdivisions of the heavenly realm reappeared. There was the suggestion that the blessed might enjoy themselves in ways that did not utterly resolve into the beatific vision.

Humanist Heaven: Lorenzo Valla

"He does not understand that to contemplate is nothing other than to progress in learning. . . . To conceive of [the gods] as contemplating we consider exceedingly reprehensible; and to say that they do nothing is even worse. Don't the gods ever move, Aristotle? Don't they change place?"

The speaker is one Vegio, polemical Epicurean lauder of pleasure, in a dialogue by Lorenzo Valla (1405–57), *On Pleasure.*[8] His attack on Aristotle is also an attack on Dante's idea of heaven as pure contemplation, and it is a radical attack. Vegio has been arguing against the Stoic conviction that virtue—the highest human value—should be pursued for its own sake. On the contrary, he contends, everything at which we aim must offer us pleasure. Soldiers who try to be courageous hope for honor and praise. Even philosophers who claim to seek pure knowledge are motivated by a lust for fame. So even contemplation cannot be an end in itself—it must offer a pleasure; and the pleasure must be learning what one does not know. This could be the pleasure of curiosity, or ambition—but it is a pleasure in activity, the active attempt to discover, the delight in discovery. It is not a steady, passionless, motionless contemplation of an object, be that object mathematical truth or God. The arts (in which Valla includes what we now call the sciences) "have been brought to their highest development by the most vigorous human contemplation" (ibid.).

Vegio's point is that the only contemplation we can intelligibly value is indeed *human*—not something godlike, a state of stillness and superhuman calm. Philosophers may take as their typical objects of contemplation mathematical concepts, or the heavens, the earth, the seas. But according to Vegio contemplation is rooted in ordinary human behavior—as when we observe the qualities of human beings—"their characters, intentions, desires, feelings, bodies, habits, degrees of strength, actions." It can even include being interested in beautiful women and games (ibid.).

We can all understand these pleasures, which are rooted in normal, day-to-day human activities. What we could never grasp would be some sort of pleasure or happiness that lifts itself entirely into an empyrean of pure thought, abstracted from what we could ordinarily see as interesting, fascinating, attractive. Even the highest contemplation is rooted in curiosity—for instance, pleasure in complexity, contrivance, beauty—and never cuts its ties to such satisfactions.

It would follow from Vegio's argument that if we try to imagine intellectual activity that has outsoared all normal human activities and claims to be simply a pure concentration on the most abstract object—thought—we will be imagining, not the highest sort of human activity, a state akin to the life of God, but something like stark insensibility, brute isolation, loss of consciousness, or even death. Vegio's attack on Stoicism, therefore, is really an attack on a heaven in which the contemplation of God could be the sole and satisfying activity of the saved.

This points to a problem in Aristotle's *Ethics*. Through most of that book, Aristotle analyzes and commends the moral and intellectual virtues of the active life—courage, temperance, justice, practical wisdom. But then, unexpectedly, he begins to praise contemplation. This is because (as the passage from the *Metaphysics* shows [see chap. 12]) he believes that contemplation is most like God's essential activity of self-awareness. So Aristotle, the great philosopher of the active life—and, especially, the life of civic virtue—ends by making the contemplative life superior to the active one. Aquinas is able to relate this to the Beatitudes, which all suggest that a complete reliance on the fatherhood of God is superior to worldly appetites, striving, and power.

Vegio's criticism is that Aristotle has left behind anything of which we can make sense in our experience, extrapolating to an activity so rarified that it is unintelligible. This is a wholesale dismissal of Dante's heaven, because it insists that an eternity of pure contemplation of God cannot have value for human beings. Dante can reply that in contemplating God, the blessed are apprehending the whole of reality—the scattered leaves of all the universe bound by love into one volume. Yet that demands that we could apprehend in one act of contemplation the whole of reality without having to experience bits of that reality one after the other. Vegio is arguing that all our ideas of understanding, reflecting, concentrating derive from experience—the experience of finding individual objects, individual ideas fascinating, worthy of investigation, and beautiful. You cannot soar from this to an intellectual and spiritual activity that does all this in one blow while not doing any of it individually.

It also follows that the ideal which Dante and Aquinas envisage—stillness raised above the hurly and burly of ordinary human life—is not intelligible either. Nothing that dispenses with the fundamental conditions of human experience can have value—which casts doubt on self-abnegation as against active pride, virginity as against marriage, and an eternity spent contemplating God rather than in enjoying all sorts of humanly intelligible delights.

Valla, a humanist scholar (the man who brilliantly disproved as a forgery the alleged "Donation of Constantine" on which papal claims to temporal power in Italy were long based) was also an orthodox Catholic. His dialogue gives powerful arguments for the Epicurean preference for the life of pleasures over one of virtue for its own sake, but in the end it has to give an account of the delights of heaven that will accord with Catholic doctrine.

It does so. Yet Valla's heaven, although centered on God, allows in a large admixture of delightful experiences that are outside the beatific vision as Dante understands it. Freed of its bodily limbs, the soul becomes immediately aware of an atmosphere radiant with a preternatural light. The pleasure will be like that experienced by someone with lynx's eyes lifted into the heavenly region, gazing around at the sea with its ships, the sky with its many hues.[9] The soul's entry into heaven will be a grand and noisy affair. Twelve legions of angels will accompany it, rather like fighter planes escorting a bomber. There will be, naturally, a fight with demons, who will have scrambled to meet the soul, but the demons, mangled and weakened with wounds, will be put to flight with screams and horrible shouts. It seems that the twelve legions were there more for show than necessity, because we are told a bit later that "even one angel is enough against all the devils" (ibid., 291).

Our heightened awareness in the next life increases our apprehension both of beauty and ugliness. We men all think of ourselves as handsome, and imagine that we are falling in love with every woman, and that every woman should fall in love with us. But if we were to see the form of an angel next to our beloved, the beloved would seem so horrible and uncouth that we would turn away from her as from the countenance of a cadaver (*quasi a cadaverosa facie*) and direct all our attention to the beauty of the angel. If the angel were actually to speak to us, we should be ravished by the delicious sweetness of his voice. All this helps us to comprehend how inexpressibly hideous devils look and sound (ibid., 295).

But in heaven we shall not lose the pleasures of earthly life—rather they will be hugely improved. It will not be a life merely of contemplation, but of active and eternal success—"honors without toil, dignities without envy, rule without hatred and danger." Nor are the pleasures purely spiritual. Our bodies will be more brilliant than the morning sun—but not so as to hurt our eyes, which themselves will have been improved. We will hear the delightful music (presumably of the spheres), and will smell the preternaturally heightened scents of flowers and herbs (ibid., 299–301).

Will there be food and drink in heaven? Yes—but of a special kind. The body and blood of Jesus Christ will be perpetually administered, and will be of such sweetness that the sense of taste will conquer the other senses. We shall never be sated with this nourishment; it will not permit hunger and thirst to return but will leave a continuous sweetness in our mouths, and its power and suavity in all our parts, even to the marrow of our bones, so that our bodies will smell as deliciously as the most fragrant herbs and flowers (ibid.).

We will be able to fly, winged, and play with other winged souls in midair, over the mountaintops or the seas. Or we will be able to run about, like Virgil's Camilla, over the points of the young ears of grain without bruising them.[10] Or we will be able to live underwater like fish. However, we will have to give up hunting, because there are no dogs, hares, fish, or birds in heaven (Valla, *De Vero Falsoque Bono*, 303). But the greatest pleasures will be intellectual—literature, speeches, and thinking. We will speak and have mastered all languages, all learning, and every art and science (ibid., 305). We will never be sated with these mental pleasures.

A major part of the pleasures of heaven, it becomes clear, will be the visual grandeur. We will pass through vast pellucid spheres—the firmament, the Crystalline Heaven, and finally the empyrean, which will resound with an eternal song to greet every soul that arrives. Gigantic processions will accompany us as we ascend toward the father of all light, as Phaeton ascended toward Phoebus. We will be drawn on chariots, by comparison with which Phoebus's chariot of the sun will seem like a peasant's cart, into the New Jerusalem, the Solomonic temple of Christ. We will see David, wearing a golden tunic with a purple chlamys, and crown alight with great glittering jewels, holding a richly ornamented harp decorated in gold and ivory (ibid., 308–11).

We will be greeted by the bells of the city churches rung out to show their joy, and by the tens of thousands of citizens of heaven, and we shall recognize among them, as they throw their arms about our necks, parents, brothers, sisters, children, relatives, friends. We will find the defects of our earthly bodies remedied in paradise. If we were handsome, we will become even better looking (ibid., 308–15).

The Virgin Mary will arrive: "When she has come to meet you, she will clasp you to her virginal breast, on which she suckled God; and she will kiss you" (ibid., 315). Then Christ will arise from his throne with manly majesty, and take you to his breast, and welcome you, his voice breaking into tears (ibid., 317).[11]

Valla has preserved an orthodox picture of heaven. But it is nothing like as God-centered as the heaven of Dante. Jesus welcomes the soul and clasps it to his manly breast—but at that point the description of heaven comes to an end. There is no sense that the soul will spend eternity looking at God the Son, God the Father, and God the Holy Ghost. There is no reason why it would not prefer to spend much of its time skimming like Camilla, diving like a fish, and enjoying the pleasures of good conversation, and the consolation of reunion with those whom we have loved long since and lost awhile.

Pleasures for an Ascetic

The Dominican friar Girolamo Savonarola (1452–98) was a famous rigorist who for a while ruled his native Florence as a puritan dictator. He was excommunicated by the notably un-puritan Pope Alexander VI (father of the ruthless and brilliant politician Cesare Borgia, who came closer than any man to making the papacy hereditary), fell from power, and was burned at the stake. In 1497 he inspired the famous "bonfire of the vanities," when the noble ladies of Florence, conscience-stricken about their love of worldly luxuries, which the friar had eloquently denounced, committed their most precious jewels and richest apparels to the flames. Savonarola claimed immediate heavenly inspiration, and was guided in all his public acts by visions. In the early 1490s he was vouchsafed a vision of heaven. Savonarola's heaven turns out to have significant elements of a paradise of earthly delights—and even to include plants and animals. Earthly and celestial paradises have begun interestingly to mingle in the imagination of this austere figure:

> We lifted up our eyes and saw a very broad field, covered with delicious flowers of Paradise. Live crystal streams flowed everywhere with a quiet murmur. A vast multitude of mild animals, such as white sheep, ermines, rabbits, and harmless creatures of that sort, all whiter than snow, played pleasantly among the different flowers and green grass alongside the flowing waters. There were leafy trees of various kinds decorated with flowers and fruits, in whose branches a crowd of varicolored birds flying here and there in a wonderful way sang a sweet melody.[12]

Savonarola travels through the nine ranks of the angelic choirs and approaches the throne of the Blessed Virgin, who sits "most beautiful and gracious" holding in her lap "an infant brighter than the sun" (ibid., 247). Although Savonarola's heaven is a sort of pageant, in which the flowers and numerous precious stones have an allegorical significance—"tiny violets like gems . . . a heady fragrance of virtues like the sweet-smelling violet" (ibid.)—it nevertheless allows centers of devotion and delight that are partly outside the vision of God. Mary's throne is in a paradise garden, and people seem able to move from one paradisal location to another. It is not a sensualist's garden of delights, but it has moved radically away from the heaven of Dante where the contemplation of the divine vision alone will give satisfaction for all eternity.

McDannell and Lang note that when Madame Louise of Savoy—the mother of the French king Francis I—died in 1531, an elegy by Clement Marot (1469–1544) envisaged her arrival in the Elysian Fields:

> There, where she is, nothing has lost its bloom; never do the day and its pleasures die there; never dies the richly colored green. . . . For every ambrosial fragrance flourishes there, and they have neither two nor three seasons, but only spring, and never do they mourn for loss of friends. . . . In those fair fields and natural mansions Louise lives,

without fear, suffering or discomfort . . . there she eats fruit of inestimable price; there she drinks that which appeases every thirst; there she will know a thousand noble souls. Every pleasant animal is found there, and a thousand birds give immortal joy, and among them about the place flies her parrot, which departed before her.[13]

A still greater humanist than Valla—Erasmus of Rotterdam (1466–1536)—also imagined a heaven where sociability, especially in the form of conversation, would be central, and where the deceased would meet noble souls. In one of his *Familiar Colloquies*—"The Apotheosis of Caprio"—Erasmus relates a vision he has had of the ascent of his friend John Reuchlin from a paradise garden into heaven. Reuchlin, who had died a day or two before, is seen in "a wonderful pleasant Meadow; the emerald Verdure of the Grass and Leaves affording such a charming Prospect; the infinite Beauty, and variety of the Flowers, like little Stars, were so delightful, and every Thing so fragrant, that all the fields on this side of the River [i.e., in this life] by which that blessed Field was divided from the rest, seem'd neither to grow, nor to be green; but look'd dead, blasted and wither'd."

Reuchlin appears clad in a wonderful, shining white damask. He is followed by "a very pretty boy with Wings" who seems to be Reuchlin's "good Genius."[14] Reuchlin in life was a "famous triple-tongu'd Phoenix of Learning" (ibid., 218), and, appropriately, he is greeted and embraced by St. Jerome, great author of the Vulgate. Jerome conducts Reuchlin into a meadow and up a hill, where they embrace and kiss again. Then the heavens open, there appears an "unutterable Glory," a pillar of fire comes down and the two are assumed into heaven. Reuchlin, as a scholar, is going to enjoy the company of his peers, their intellectual and scholarly conversation. The only analogy in Dante is where the poet, in the company of Virgil, meets Homer, Horace, Ovid, and Lucan.[15] But that is in Limbo, not heaven. In heaven, Dante's meetings with the mighty dead are always connected with his spiritual growth—as when he is examined on his knowledge of the faith; they are not for the purpose of pleasant conversations.

This is significant, for where the blessed are envisaged as conversing among themselves, rather than wholly absorbed in the beatific vision, we have the germ of an idea of a sort of republic of the saved—or, at any rate, a state where distinguished persons enjoy the company of their peers, and where *that* is an important part of bliss. Standing behind this idea is the author who was the single greatest influence on Renaissance thought: Cicero. Cicero's dialogue, *The Republic*, was an exploration of republican virtue and of the high destiny of statesmanship. It is a defense of the practical wisdom that is

of the essence of politics, and of active virtue as against theoretical contemplation.[16] The knowledge of "those arts which can make us useful to the state" is
claimed by one of the speakers in the dialogue as "the noblest function of
wisdom, and the highest duty of virtue as well as the best proof of its possession." The *Republic* ends with the famous *Somnium Scipionis* (Scipio's Dream)
in which one of the speakers is granted a vision of the heavens, entry to which
will be the reward of the true statesman after death—"All those who have
preserved, aided, or enlarged their fatherland have a special place prepared
for them in the heavens, where they may enjoy an eternal life of happiness.[17]
Scipio is allowed by the African king Massinissa to see the whole system of
stars and planets, the latter being "round and globular bodies animated by
divine intelligences" (ibid., 15). Those who perform their duties to their parents
and kinsmen but, most of all, to their fatherland, will be translated to the skies
after death to dwell among these heavenly things and hear the music of the
spheres (ibid., 16). This, rather than mere transitory fame on earth, is the
reward for the active political life and practical wisdom. Scipio concludes,
replying to Massinissa,: "If indeed a path to heaven, as it were, is open to
those who have served their country well, henceforth I will redouble my efforts,
spurred on by so splendid a reward; though even from my boyhood I have
followed in the footsteps of my father and yourself and have not failed to
emulate your glory" (ibid., 24).

In his treatise *On Old Age*, Cicero depicts Cato the Elder talking to Scipio
Africanus and looking forward to conversation with the mighty dead to which
his military and political glory entitle him: "Really Scipio, I am carried away
with the desire to see your father, and yours too, Laelius, both of whom
I honored and loved; and, indeed, I am eager to meet not only those whom
I have known, but those also of whom I have heard and read and written."[18]

This is a heaven for republican virtue and those who incarnate it. Since
these virtues are above all active, we can presume that the heaven they will
enjoy will also allow their active dispositions to find expression. It diverges
radically from the contemplative, intellectual heaven of Aquinas and Dante. It
allows a development in ideas of heaven that will eventually lead to a much
more worldly view of the next life than had been earlier allowed in Catholic
orthodoxy.

Reformation

Nietzsche lamented the fact that when Luther irrupted onto the European
stage in all his literal-minded, fundamentalist zeal, he succeeded in reversing

that re-appropriation of pagan cultural values which had taken place under the patronage of popes such as Julius II and Leo X.[19] Luther's attack upon Roman "corruptions," his demand for a return to a Christianity undiluted with the culture of Greece and Rome, was also an attack upon the whole project of Renaissance humanism. (Even Augustine was not sufficiently austere for him. He said that he had once "devoured" Augustine, but that "when the door was opened for me in Paul, so that I understood what justification by faith is, it was all over with Augustine.")[20] Luther directed a significant amount of his apparently inexhaustible venom toward Erasmus, a man who wished to reform the church but to do so within both an orthodox and humanist framework. He described Erasmus variously as an "eel," an epicurean, and a wicked man who scoffs at religion, one who "makes no distinction between Christ and Solon."[21] Luther's hatred for Erasmus was inspired above all by the fact that (as Luther saw it) Erasmus did not put God at the center of human life, that he set a value on human life in itself, independently of our relation to God.

Luther goes as far as any Christian theologian—perhaps, farther than any—in making God "all in all." His God is certainly "the God of Abraham, Isaac, and Jacob" (and Paul) rather than the God "of philosophers and schoolmen."[22] God as judge, God as omnipotent and omnipresent yet essentially unknowable, can be found in the work of medieval nominalists who dissolved Aquinas's synthesis between religion and Aristotelian philosophy. Luther did not add anything philosophically significant to this picture, but his imaginative response to it was immensely powerful. Set against the majesty of God, fallen human nature is worthless. Human life itself, if considered apart from man's obligation to worship and obey God, is without value. To be in heaven just means to be in the presence of God. God will be all in all, and eternal life will be life without change, without eating and drinking, without anything to do.

Luther assumed the medieval picture of the universe (and rejected Copernicus out of hand)[23] in which everything becomes steadily more impure as we approach the bottom of the universe—i.e., earth.[24] After the Last Day, God will cleanse the sublunary world and make it as pure as the upper heavens. The earth will contain, it seems, plants and animals, restored to their prelapsarian innocence, and cleansed of the effects of original sin. (For instance, even noxious insects will become delightful and sweet smelling.)[25] But this restored world will exist for the blessed simply as an object of contemplation, not as a place to live. They will live simply in their vision of God and will enjoy contemplating the restored earth essentially as part of their vision of God's active goodness.

Calvin's vision was virtually the same. Calvin argued that without knowledge of God we have no knowledge of ourselves.[26] But in knowing God we know that we are as nothing before his majesty and power: "Hence that dread and wonder with which Scripture represents the saints as stricken and overcome whenever they felt the presence of God. Thus it comes about that we see men who in his absence normally remained firm and constant, but who, when he manifests his glory, are so shaken and struck dumb as to be laid low by the dread of death—are in fact overwhelmed by it and almost annihilated" (ibid., 1, 1, 3, 39). Our very being is nothing but subsistence in the one God (ibid., 1, 1, 1, 35).

Since human life depends so profoundly on God and the knowledge of God, heaven is bound to be nothing more nor less than being in God's presence: "If God contains the fullness of all good things in himself like an inexhaustible fountain, nothing beyond him is to be sought by those who strive after the highest good and all the elements of happiness" (ibid., 3, 25, 10, 1005).

Calvin refrains from speculating on different degrees of blessedness in heaven "how great the difference will be between prophets and apostles, and again, between apostles and martyrs; by how many degrees virgins will differ from married women"—questions he deems harmful and "contributing to the levity of others" (ibid. 3, 25, 11, 1006–7). Calvin does, though, confront the question of the restoration of the world in all its glorious plenty after the Last Day, because that is attested in scripture. The problem is that "the children of God will not be in any need of any of this great and incomparable plenty but will be like the angels, whose abstinence from food is the symbol of eternal blessedness" (ibid.). His conclusion is that the restored world will be simply an object of contemplation: "in the very sight of it there will be such pleasantness, such sweetness in the knowledge of it alone, without the use of it, that this happiness will far surpass all the amenities that we now enjoy. Let us imagine ourselves set in the richest region on earth, where we lack no pleasure. Who is not from time to time hindered or prevented from enjoying God's benefits by his own illness? Who does not often have the even tenor of his life broken by his own intemperance? From this it follows than a temperate rather than a sensual life, enjoyment, clear and pure from every vice, is the acme of happiness" (ibid.).

The Protestant Reformers in effect imagine a state of blessedness that is as God-centered as the vision of Aquinas. Cicero's charming picture of a future state in which civilized conversation will be a central part of the promised delights is dropped, as are various Renaissance hopes that families will be reunited in the next world. True, Melanchthon in his funeral oration for Luther imagined Luther holding conversation with "God, His Son, our Lord Jesus Christ, with the prophets and apostles."[27] But this will certainly not be conversation in the Ciceronian sense. And although members of the same family will, of course, end up in heaven, they will no longer be related to each other *as* family members. Luther memorably remarked that anyone who says that if his wife is in heaven he does not wish to go there is a fool.[28]

There is one important way in which the reformers depart from Aquinas. Thomas had taught that the greater the merits of each saved person, the greater will be his closeness to God, the greater his understanding of the beatific vision: "The various mansions of the saints are distinguished according to the various degrees of charity."[29] But for Luther and Calvin there will be no such distinctions. In heaven we will all be equal, even though "a particular [i.e., individual] crown is laid up for [each] in accordance with his labors."[30]

Luther's speculations on heaven and the risen body show his imaginative strengths at the same time as his philosophical weakness. His instinct is to reject the Thomist picture of heaven as stillness and contemplation—just as he rejects the Catholic monastic vision of the superiority of the contemplative over the active life, of the life of chastity over the married state. He obviously thinks that the risen body strongly resembles the earthly one but is purged of all sorts of embarrassing features.

In his commentary on 1 Corinthians 15 Luther meditates on the question St. Paul imagines put to him by those who do not believe in the resurrection:

> What kind of bodies will they have? . . . if we are all to be revived again, each with his present body restored to him, a teeming world and an innumerable multitude of people will surely forgather. Where will they all find enough to eat and drink? Where can enough grain, enough oxen, pigs and sheep be found to supply everyone with food? Just think how many people alone died in two or three centuries, to say nothing of thousands and more thousands of years! They would be enough to consume the whole store of the earth's meat and bread in one day.[31]

Luther is nothing if not practical.

And when we do arise, how will we live together? "Will I live with my wife and children, my master, my country's ruler and his father and grandfather? Where will all the emperors, Kings, lords and princes find room? Will they all . . . reign over one and the same country?" (ibid., 170–71).

Paul's solution was to distinguish between the animal body and the spiritual one: "Paul replies very briefly: "No, nothing whatsoever of this . . . But this is the way it will be: Everybody will remain what he was created, whether man or woman. For scripture says that God created male and female. . . . Therefore everyone's body will remain as it was created. But he will not eat, drink . . . nor . . . beget children, keep house, govern etc" (ibid.). Luther beautifully expands on Paul's words: "that which thou sowest is not quickened, except it die: And that which thou sowest, thou sowest not that body that shall be, but bare grain, it may chance of wheat, or of some other grain" (1 Cor. 15:36–37). Luther urges that we take the point of view of the husband-man who sows the grain: "He would picture [the kernel] as already standing and growing there nicely, with beautiful stalk and ears. And we too must let ourselves be pictured thus when we are cast into the ground.... And the cemetery or burial ground does not indicate a heap of the dead, but a field full of kernels, known as God's kernels, which will verdantly blossom forth again and grow more beautifully than can be imagined" (ibid., 178).

He expands on this in a way that would appeal to the German peasant:

> Go into a garden at this very hour [the date was December 22, 1534] to see how things are going, how all sorts of plants and trees are growing there now. You will find that everything is absolutely dead. But if you return in summer, you will find a far different picture. There all is verdant and is blossoming. There is sheer joy and life compared to this harsh dead winter. But if we had never witnessed this before, do you not suppose that we would regard it a great deed and miracle to transform one seed into a beautiful apple or cherry tree, which bears a thousand apples or cherries in place of this one kernel? Of course people do not see or heed that but pass it by and do nought but gorge and swill all that grows. They are like swine that run across a field or wallow in a garden and devour what they find. But if anyone wants to be a swine, let him. This illustration is not presented for swine but for those who are Christians, that they might be delighted at the sight of such beautiful blossoms and fruits and say: ... What a great God He must be who is able to fashion such a beautiful object from the dead winter? ... He is much more disposed to do the same with us when we similarly lie buried under the ground and the time comes for an eternal summer to dawn. Then we will come forth far more beautiful and glorious. (Ibid., 180)

This more glorious existence will be one in which we cease to eat and drink and digest (ibid., 182). For the human body in its animal state is an overwhelmingly shameful thing: as soon as we die corruption sets that is so disgusting that we hurry human bodies away for burial as soon as possible—which we do not feel we have to do with other animals. Yet we do not hate our bodies, despite the fact that "the nose is rendered so filthy by nasal mucus and other impurities, to say nothing of the belly and the whole body with its sweat and rash and all kinds of filth." Yet when the body rises from the dead "no matter how dishonorable or worthless it is at present, it will return in a form so honorable and precious that its future honor and glory will surpass the present shame and dishonor many thousand times. Every creature will be amazed over it, all the angels will sing praises and smile admiringly at it, and God Himself will take delight in it" (ibid., 187).

Luther insists that to call it a spiritual body does not mean that it no longer has physical life or flesh and blood. It means that it will have life yet not be a body that eats, sleeps, digests, but one that is nourished and preserved spiritually by God (ibid., 189). And the body that thus lives spiritually with God "will sally forth into heaven and earth, [and] play with sun and moon and other creatures." It will be as clear and light as the air, and will see and hear sharply to the ends of the world. Risen bodies will in fact be like the stars—which are so constituted that they need nothing for their existence and yet are physical creatures (ibid., 189–90). The entire body will be as pure and bright as the sun and as light as the air, and, finally, so healthy, so blissful and filled with such heavenly, eternal joy in God that it will never hunger, thirst, grow weary, or decline (ibid., 196). We will not have to drag "this heavy, indolent paunch" about with us. Rather it will "swish through all the heavens as swiftly and lightly as lightning and soar over the clouds amid the dear angels" (ibid). Merely viewing and looking at God will make the body so beautiful, vigorous, and healthy, indeed so light and agile that we will "soar along like a little spark, yes, just like the sun which runs its course in the heavens" (ibid., 143). Anyone who wants to possess acute sight and hearing that reaches farther than a hundred miles, or who wishes to be able to see through walls and stone will be granted those desires.

Amid all this, the world itself will be transformed. The sky will rain down Thalers and gold, and the Elbe with be filled with pearls and other gems (ibid., 146). If we wish, trees will bear nothing but silver leaves and golden apples, and the fields will bear grass and flowers which shine like emeralds (ibid.).

Although all the saved will enjoy equal bliss, because they will have the same essence, yet in heaven there will be different degrees of glory: "Peter's and Paul's will be the glory of the apostles; one person will partake of the glory of a martyr, another of that of a pious bishop or preacher; each one in accord with the works he has performed" (ibid., 185). Because God will be all in all, no one will need father, mother, servant, food, clothing, house, and the like.[32] God will clothe the saved more beautifully than any emperor was ever clothed, indeed, more beautifully than the sun and all jewels. All the garments and gold bedecking a king will be sheer dirt in comparison with us when we are illumined by the divine glance (ibid., 142). If someone wishes to be a lord, God will grant even more than he wishes (ibid., 144).

Luther doubted that in heaven we shall all be of the same stature, or that there will be marriage "otherwise everybody will want to be a woman or a man."[33] He admitted that he could not imagine what the joy of eternal life would be like, for he could not think how we would spend the time, since there will be no change, no work, no food and drink, and nothing to occupy us in heaven: "But I think we'll have enough to do with God."[34] He was scathing about the what he takes to be the Muslim vision of paradise: "The Turk says that the following will happen after the resurrection: A beautifully set table will stand there with tasteful salvers and excellent drinks. The food will be eels and tender liver. Around the table will stand attractive nude women, whom it will be a delight to look at." Dr. Pomeranus added: "Thus they'll go 'round and round' like a rooster among the hens.'"[35]

In all his writings, Luther comes across as both an intensely spiritual and intensely earthy man. It would have been temperamentally impossible for him to imagine an afterlife as static and sensuously attenuated as that set down in the *Paradiso.* The world of the senses was extraordinarily vivid in Luther's imagination. At the same time he is committed to a literal interpretation of scripture. Temperamentally, the allegorical accounts of scriptural meanings, so popular since the church fathers, are also alien to Luther. So he cannot help imagining a strongly sensuous heaven while denying that it is also *sensual.* There will be all sorts of ways in which the risen body will disport itself, and there will be an immense variety of visual and auditory delights. The body, though glorified, really will be the same as the one we had on earth. It will retain its nature, but the *use* of it will not be the same. So although we will retain stomach and all the organs of digestion, as well as genital organs, we will not actually eat, drink, digest, and excrete. There will be no sex and begetting of children, for "in the resurrection they neither marry nor are given in marriage, but are as the angels of God in heaven" (Matt. 22:30). And although we will have all the other human capacities and (presumably) emotions, of the sort that equip us for living in society, there will be no servants, maidservants, fathers, mothers, lords, princes, or kings.[36]

Luther gives no explanation of what will be the point of retaining all these human characteristics when they are not going to be exercised in any human way. What is the point of having digestive organs if we are never going to eat throughout eternity (with the possible exception of the Lord's Supper, which, if it is thought of as physical rather than purely spiritual food, would become infernally boring after the first few centuries.) Why acknowledge that our loved ones will be with us in heaven, while denying that any special relationship with them can survive? It is the very vividness with which Luther imagines risen bodies that so obviously replicate earthly ones that pushes these questions to the forefront of the mind. He says that we will not need food (nor malmsey!) because God will make us satisfied in both body and soul (ibid., 142), and that the sight of God will keep us always strong and vigorous, healthy and happy, as well as brighter and more beautiful than sun and moon. But this seems to make God something like a tonic. There is no overwhelming reason why we should rejoice everlastingly in seeing God when we can also have such fun swishing about in the air and filling the Elbe with pearls.

Luther's heaven certainly is God-centered, because he follows scripture. It is true, also, that he sees man as less than nothing without the assistance of divine grace. Therefore the prospect of heaven reinforces the conviction that the world is worthless and best quitted. Luther's last recorded thought, written on a bit of paper the day he died, was: "We are beggars. That is true."[37] Not many weeks before, he had set down his conviction that here is no abiding city or enduring stay in his own inimitable style: "I'm fed up with the world, and it is fed up with me. I'm quite content with that. The world thinks that if it is only rid of me everything will be fine, and it will accomplish this. After all, it's as I've often said: I'm like a ripe stool and the world's like a gigantic anus, and so we're about to let go of each other."[38]

Charmed into Heaven: St. Francis de Sales

Luther's ferocious attack on the "epicurean" Erasmus (see page 303) was part of his conviction that the Roman Church was prepared to tone down, if not abandon, the doctrine of predestination, and to allow the human will to cooperate with divine grace. As a follower of Augustine and, still more whole-heartedly, of Paul, Luther saw the sinfulness of man as nullifying free will.[39] The whole of man "body, soul and spirit" is fleshly (ibid., 222). There really is no such thing as free will (ibid., 293–95). God does directly cause men to sin, when he hardens the hearts of the reprobate—as he hardened the heart of pharaoh (ibid., 164). In short, God's foreknowledge of sin imposes on man the necessity to sin (ibid., 184). Luther hated Erasmus for what he saw as an attempt to transmute Christianity into something like humanism—a soften-ing that would change the whole tone and tenor of Christian teaching on sin and redemption.

Erasmus had pressed only for a modest contribution of the will to human goodness, arguing for an extremely limited conception of freedom. He sug-gested that if the will is simply enslaved, and if all sin is predetermined, there would be no point in the numerous scriptural passages that seem to call people to repentance, "sloughing off of the old man and his acts." Luther's rage at the middle way of Erasmus was (as we saw in chap. 7, page 180) prophetic. The Roman Catholic Church, while keeping predestination in theory, did adapt the doctrine to something like humanism. Nothing more illustrates the type of thought that Luther hated and feared (other than Erasmus himself) than Francis de Sales (1567–1622).

De Sales had to administer a diocese in a largely Calvinist area, at significant personal risk to himself, but through his "unfailing spirit of charity and his engagement in controversy in a conciliatory spirit"[40] he won many Calvinists to Catholicism. His "unfailing spirit of charity" pervades one of his two most famous works, *The Love of God.*[41] It is not as though de Sales departs in any way from Catholic teaching about grace and free will. But the spirit breathed in his writing insinuates into the mind of the reader a world wholly removed from the bleak determinism of Luther and Calvin. De Sales makes the whole process of the soul's advance toward God seem seductive, or, at least, charming.

Francis begins by suggesting that the will has some control over intellect, and over memory.[42] The will even has a powerful hold over the sense appetites. We cannot prevent concupiscence from becoming pregnant with sin; but we can certainly deter it from bringing sin to birth (ibid., 7). He even suggests that "in the long run [the sense passions] become subdued, weakened, quelled, all the life taken out of them; if not utterly dead, at least deadened, mortified" (ibid., 8).

Francis thinks that man has a natural capacity to love the good inborn in him, a capacity that is completed by the love of God—which, again, is partly natural, partly the effect of God's grace. Even our fallen nature instinctively loves God (ibid., 40–41). Human passions are good or bad, virtuous or vicious in exact proportion to the goodness or badness of the love from which they spring (ibid., 10).

There is no doubt that de Sales in practice allows great scope for human goodness, because he bases it in an innate capacity for love. We can, from the beginning, desire God's love. This means that we can take large strides toward the Christian virtues: "when we want God's love to reign in us, we deaden self-love. If we cannot repress self-love altogether, at least we weaken it; still alive it may be, but it has ceased to reign. Similarly we can do the opposite: we can forgo charity and cling to creature loves—the despicable adultery with which the heavenly bridegroom so frequently upbraids others" (ibid., 11–12).

Contrary to Luther's dark vision of man's nature as being corrupt in body, soul, and spirit, de Sales argues that sin has weakened the will far more than it has clouded the intellect (ibid., 80). The combination of intellect and will, even in its weakened form, leads us to cooperate with God's grace. Grace, *pace*

Luther, does not bring force to bear upon us: it goes with freedom (ibid., 80). It operates "not to compel the heart, but to allure it" (ibid., 43).

Luther would have been still more enraged by de Sales than he was by Erasmus could he have read the similitude by which Francis clearly suggests that the weakness caused by sin is not lethal: "Our nature, after all, is sickly with the distressing weakness of sin. It is like palm trees on this side of the world; they only sprout incompletely—trying, so to speak, to produce fruit, but not quite succeeding. The maturing of ripe dates is reserved to better climes" (ibid., 43).

The conscious charm with which Francis allures the reader is nowhere more evident than in the image he returns to several times of human souls, damaged by original sin, being like some birds he has read about in Aristotle. Aristotle had called a certain short-legged species of birds *apodes* ("footless"—a reference to the rudimentary feet of the sea swallow). "Once these birds had alighted in the ground, they were forced to stay there, unable to take off again as neither legs nor feet could propel them back into the air. There they would lie until they died, unless a sudden gust of wind happened to catch and lift them" (ibid., 72).

It is clear what the analogy is: We are the *apodes*, and the wind that lifts us is the grace of God. We human beings, if we happen to leave the atmosphere of divine love, and to settle on the ground and cling to creatures more than we do to God, are in mortal danger: "some faint emotions are left, like legs and feet, to make an attempt at love; but they are so weak, we cannot extricate our hearts from the slime of sin, cannot take off again on wings of charity, cannot resume the flight which—wretches that we are—we disloyally and deliberately abandoned" (ibid.).

Francis uses an image that would have shocked Luther even further. The grace of God that saves us from this mortal danger is "the favorable wind of his inspirations. Powerfully, but gently, they play upon hearts, striking them, moving them, raising our thoughts, impelling our emotions into the atmosphere of God's love" (ibid.). The conclusion is that "consent to grace depends more upon grace than upon the will, while resistance to grace depends solely upon the will" (ibid.).

The humanist tinge to de Sales is strikingly apparent where he argues that although theological arguments and miracles point to the credibility of Christianity, faith alone can be responsible for accepting it. And what leads us to faith? Is it simply the imposition upon us of grace? No—rather (in a curiously Keatsian formulation) de Sales suggests that "faith fills a man with love for the beauty of its truth, with faith in the truth of its beauty, through the charm it uses on the will, the certitude it gives to the intellect" (ibid., 80). God indeed "leads the soul by inexpressibly charming ways" (ibid., 135).

Heaven, for de Sales, is essentially a state of being intimately charmed by God for ever. Once the mind is lifted above the natural light of reason, it begins to see directly the truths promised by faith: "The human heart leaps with joy at the sound of the bridegroom's voice; *never was honey*, all human knowledge, *so sweet to its taste*" (ibid., 136–37). God's truths have great power to charm us even in "the dim light of faith." When we contemplate them in the noonday of his glory they will ravish us in the way the queen of Sheba was ravished at the wisdom and glory of Solomon—but to an infinitely greater degree (ibid., 136–37). The beatific vision is essentially to be understood as the most intimate union possible of mind and soul with God. De Sales happily mingles images of knowledge—we will see God face to face, we will see the eternal begetting of the Word in the Holy Trinity (ibid., 142–44)—with images of infantile bliss: "that is how it will be with us—privileged to share his nature, fostered on his very substance . . . like children suckled at the breast, strangers to a bottle-feed" (ibid., 139).

This absorption in the divine, where we find ourselves living in God, contemplating him as "the well-spring of bliss, of life eternal" obviously leaves no room for any activity other than contemplating and loving God. De Sales does not speculate on how our risen bodies will be able to move at infinite speed through space, or see through the thickest material objects. Indeed, there is no imaginative space *for* the body, even though de Sales must believe, of course, in a physical resurrection. There is no room for relations with other souls in bliss, let alone any remembrance of family ties, or any Ciceronian conversation with others of the mighty dead. De Sales's vision is intensely individualistic and at the same time seems to involve a sort of extinction of personality, since all our mental and emotional faculties will be swallowed up in the beatific vision. Indeed, de Sales's vision of heaven is closer to Plato's account in the *Symposium* of the vision of the Good than to anything else.[43] Anything resembling the pleasures of the earthly paradise has been winnowed out, as has any sense that a cleansed and restored world will have any significant place in the future life.

A Puritan's Everlasting Rest: Richard Baxter

England produced one divine in the seventeenth century who rivals St. Francis de Sales in what Matthew Arnold calls "sweetness and light." Surprisingly, he was a Puritan, but one who honeyed over the austerities of Puritanism with a manifestly sincere charity. Baxter was a moderate Calvinist, but in him—as in de Sales—the harshnesses of the doctrine of predestination are certainly not emphasized.

Baxter's chief work is *The Saints' Everlasting Rest*. This was a famous and much reprinted book both in his lifetime and afterward. It had a second lease on life when John Wesley rediscovered it and published an abridged edition. (More recent abridged editions of Baxter manage to emphasize his charity still more strongly by leaving out entirely what he has to say about the eternal sufferings of hell.)

Like Calvin and Luther, Baxter starts from a powerful picture of the miseries of human life. Our conception of the bliss of heaven is rooted in an overwhelming sense that life in this world is continuing trouble, pain, and sorrow.

> The Church on earth is a mere hospital; which way ever we go we hear complaining; and into what corner soever we cast our eyes we behold objects of pity and grief; some groaning under a dark understanding, some under a senseless heart, some languishing under unfruitful weakness, and some bleeding for miscarriages and willfulness, and some in such a lethargy that they are past complaining; some crying out of their pining poverty; some groaning under pains and infirmities; and some bewailing a whole catalogue of calamities, especially in days of common sufferings when nothing appears in our sight but ruin; families ruined; congregations ruined; sumptuous structures ruined; court ruined; kingdoms ruined. Who weeps not when all these bleed?[44]

Baxter suffered from severe ill health all his life and was often near death. Yet these are not the repinings of a querulous man. His sense of the evils of the world often rises into genuine eloquence, especially when it blends into what he knows, or has experienced of the troubles of his own times. He writes movingly of the destruction produced by the English Civil War and the Wars of Religion in Germany:

> What heart is not wounded to think of Germany's long desolations? Oh, the learned universities, the flourishing churches there, that now are left desolate! Look on England's four years of blood, a flourishing land almost ruined; hear but the common voice in most cities, towns, and countries through the land; and judge whether we have no cause of sorrow. . . . When a most wonderful Reformation by such wonderful means might have been well expected; and is this not cause of astonishing sorrows? (Ibid.)

Heaven, for Baxter, is rest. Echoing Aristotle and Aquinas, Baxter says that rest, the cessation from motion, is the end and perfection of motion (ibid., 7).

All motion "ends at the center"—which is God. This is not just a philosophical idea. For Baxter salvation comes only from the end of that which troubles, moves us, sets us astir. Salvation, therefore, is the state where "prophesying ceaseth, tongues fail, and knowledge shall be done away with" (ibid., 28).

Baxter indeed inspires a tradition of English quietism—in fact, melancholy—that has a literary life after him. You could say that Baxter's "rest" is essentially negative, a cessation of all that moves, lives, and grows in the world. He understands it as moving to a state of contemplation, and this contemplation is the love of God—quite reminiscent of the individualistic piety of de Sales: "As all good whatsoever is comprised in God, and all the creatures are but drops of this ocean; so all the glory of the blessed is comprised in their enjoyment of God" (ibid., 41).

The true, studious, contemplative man knows this to be true, for he "feels as sweet embraces [the connection] between his intellect and truth, and far more than ever the quickest sense did in possessing its desired object. But the true, studious, contemplative Christian knows it much more, who sometime hath felt more sweet embraces between his soul and Jesus Christ than all inferior truth can afford" (ibid., p 41).

All human relations as well as sorrows will be swallowed up in this sweetness—"No more parting of friends asunder . . . no more care of master for servants, of parents for children, of magistrates over subjects, of ministers over people . . . No more marrying or giving in marriage, but we shall be as the angels of God" (ibid., 173).

For Baxter the sorrows of religious division are as great as those of partings, poverty and death: "Could I have believed him that would have told me five years ago that when the scorners of godliness were subdued and the bitter persecutors of the Church overthrown that such should succeed them who suffered with us, who were our intimate friends, with whom we took sweet counsel, and went up together to the house of God? Did I think it had been in the hearts of men professing such zeal to religion and the ways of Christ to draw their swords against each other, and to seek each other's blood so fiercely?" (ibid., 161).

Although Baxter sees the active contemplation of God as constituting heavenly bliss, still, in practice, the emotional impetus is the profound desire for relief from the ills of the world, or a compensation for them. Will we know our old friends and relations in heaven? Baxter answers that we shall know them in a new and at present unimaginable way. But actually he imagines it as a grand reunion of the just. Not only shall we sit down with Abraham, Isaac, and Jacob, but we shall also live eternally with Peter, Paul, Augustine. . . . Wickliffe, Luther, Calvin, Zwingli, not to mention Cartwright, Brightman,

Bayne, Pemble, Twiss, Ames, Preston, and Sibbs (names that possibly now shine less brightly). We shall discover that Hampden and Pym are members of a triumphant Senate far grander than the House of Commons, which they graced in life.[45] The everlasting rest of the saints will be, then, positive as well as negative. But Baxter does put great emphasis on the negative. We shall rest from all our perplexing doubts, from the sense of God's displeasure that makes us wonder whether we are saved or damned; from the temptations of the world and the flesh, and of wicked men; from intra-Protestant divisions ("the names of Lollard, Huguenot, Puritan, Roundhead there are not used"), with bloody battles and massacres; from dolorous hours, sad thoughts and personal sufferings; from the sad affections that must arise in our earthly separation from God (Baxter, *Everlasting Rest*, 147–81).

Baxter hovers between envisaging the eternal heavenly contemplation as an extinction of knowledge and its completion: "In one hour shall I see all difficulties vanish; and all my doubts in physics, metaphysics, politics, medicine, etc., shall be resolved. . . . Yea, all the depths of divinity shall be uncovered to me. . . . For in knowing God, I shall know all things that are fit or good for the creature to know."[46]

An emphasis on knowledge as central to the happiness of heaven, where the blessed will know God to the greatest extent of which human nature is capable—resurfaces in William Beveridge.[47] Beveridge writes that the saints in heaven "shall see God . . . as he is in himself, which blessed sight must needs fill them with the highest joys their infinite nature is able to bear. To see Wisdom, and Power, and Greatness, and Justice, and Mercy, and Immensity, and Eternity . . . yea, to see him smiling, as it were, upon them. . . . Who is able to conceive how much their blessed souls are affected, delighted, transported with this blessed Sight?" (ibid., 9).

By the light of God, the blessed will have a perfect view of "all the animals and plants, and stones, and metals, and minerals, and whatever else God ever made either in heaven or earth" (ibid., 8). They will grasp the cause of the ebb and flow of the seas, and other great phenomena, and will understand "the secret and wonderful Powers that God hath put into all Animals and Vegetables . . . the several motions of the Sun and all the Planets, as well as the fixed Stars" (ibid., 11–12). This knowledge of nature will deepen into an understanding of the divine plan: "by this Light they look back upon their former lives, and see the steady hand of Providence ordering and over-ruling . . . even the least circumstances in them . . . how everything should be just as it is" (ibid.). Our corrupt nature on earth blinds us to this heavenly knowledge. Our minds "are so stuffed with vicious and gross Humours that they cannot see the light; and so wholly inclined and bent upon sensual Objects, that they can take no pleasure in the Joys of heaven." On the contrary, we have an antipathy to these pure delights because they are directly contrary to our corrupt nature (ibid., 13): "They cannot hear that heavenly Music; or if they did, it would sound harsh all Discords to them. . . . They cannot see the face of God; or if they did, they would not be pleased, but terrified and confounded by it" (ibid.).

Beveridge mixes a very English, empirical idea of heavenly knowledge—the knowledge, perhaps, of an intelligent amateur naturalist—with the slightly more Dantean notion that in seeing God we will have access to a higher order of knowledge altogether.

Baxter's marrying of contemplation with *contemptus mundi* and with his sense of *lacrimae rerum* would eventually flow into the eighteenth-century tradition of pastoral meditation, of which the masterpiece is Gray's *Elegy Written in a Country Churchyard*, where death merges into the pleasures of contemplation and melancholy.

In 1743 the Reverend Robert Blair published a poem titled *The Grave*. Despite its being a collection of entirely conventional thoughts about death-the-common-leveler—but without the lapidary quality of Gray's *Elegy* (to the sentiments of which, as Samuel Johnson put it "every breast returns an echo")—it achieved a huge success. Blair became known as the graveyard poet, and the book went through many editions. In 1808 *The Grave* achieved the distinction of being illustrated by William Blake. As a result it was transformed into something powerful. Whereas Blair's poem expressed a melancholy in the face of death that had become important to eighteenth-century sensibility (and which eventually went into the genre of *gothick* horror), Blake's illustrations transformed the atmosphere of Blair's poem. There is nothing of melancholy, nor of the gothick, but rather a tragic emphasis on separation, sin, the sundering of soul and body—and joyful resurrection and reunion.

In one plate, the virtuous soul (here portrayed by Blake as feminine), swooping down from above, is shown being reunited to the body of a virtually naked, muscular, curly-headed, and beautiful young man. She clasps her arms urgently around his neck and kisses him erotically on the mouth as they "rush together with inconceivable energy."[48] In the next plate we see a family reunited in heaven: "The sweet felicity, the endearing tenderness, the ineffable affection that are here depicted, are sufficiently obvious. The Husband clasps the Wife; the Children embrace; the Boy recognizes and eagerly springs to his Father." Indeed the husband does clasp the wife—his right arm is around her left shoulder, but his left hand is placed firmly on her buttock.[49]

The erotic element in Blake's heaven also appears in the depiction of the Last Judgment.[50] Again there is the insistence on the blessed being resurrected as family groups; and again there is the powerful eroticism as a couple

The soul reunited with the body. The soul (portrayed by William Blake as feminine) and the resurrected muscular young man "rush together with inconceivable energy." Illustration by William Blake from Hugh Blair, *The Grave* (London, 1783).

A family resurrected. Blake sees resurrection as a restoration of erotic love and family life. Illustration by William Blake from Hugh Blair, *The Grave* (London, 1783).

embrace, with the man touching the woman on her left thigh and right buttock. In the family groups, couples, clearly seen as lovers, are prominent. Another sign that Blake's heaven is not the purely spiritual place of Baxter, or of Blair's poem itself, is suggested by a bearded, thoroughly patriarchal-looking angel, very close to God's throne, who bears a tray on which rest two wine glasses and two loaves. Possibly—probably—these represent the Eucharist; but the impression is also one of the celebration of food and drink.

Dante's imagining of a heaven in which God is all in all went with a clear metaphysic and philosophy of mind, which made pure contemplation the highest human good. No later writer fully retained that austere metaphysic. In various ways they all—even St. Francis de Sales—let in some pleasures that can be thought of as being valued for their own sake and which are not all subordinate to the beatific vision. Luther insists upon a God-centered next life but has no philosophy to enforce the idea. The Puritan, Baxter, in making heaven so much the opposite of the evils of this world, also, despite his theological intentions, implies such extra pleasures—for instance in conversations with both great and obscure Reformers. Blake's illustrations for *The Grave* blatantly envisage a heaven in which our sexual desires and family love will be fully catered to. Once the austere joys of Dante have been compromised, it is hard to see what can stand in the way of a heaven which more and more reproduces the joys of this world. That is what McDannell and Lang call the modern heaven. Its greatest exponent was Emmanuel Swedenborg.

14

Heavenly Speculations

England during the later seventeenth century and the first half of the eighteenth was a fertile ground for lively speculations about the next life. The natural philosophers and theologians who engaged in the speculations were relatively uninhibited by Christian orthodoxy. Some will argue that all human beings will be saved; others that the pains of hell will not be everlasting. There was even a Member of Parliament who was also an amateur theologian, and who notoriously claimed that it is even now possible for any human being with faith not to die at all but to be "translated" into the heavenly life. That souls can exist independently of the body is strongly denied—and as stoutly affirmed. Most writers about bodily resurrection claim that the risen body will be in some sense physically identical with that of the person who died. But some insist that God will give each of us a brand-new body, which will so closely resemble the old one—if in a glorified form—that we will not be able to notice the difference. Mortalism—the opinion that the soul is naturally mortal, dies with the body, and will have to be re-created by God at the resurrection—has its supporters. Heaven is still, on the whole, centered on God; but plenty of other pleasures begin to gain admittance to the next life. Eventually, in the early eighteenth century, a work by a woman writer depicts various departed spirits recounting the joys of paradise; God, if he comes in at all, seems to be an afterthought.

This freedom of speculation is striking, and it goes with a characteristically English empiricism. Seventeenth-century science is brought up against the teachings of revelation. Scripture is never challenged, but it is robustly pressed to fit the available facts of contemporary science.

An extremely important topic for debate is the exact nature of the risen body. Will we resurrect with the bodies that we originally had? Is that even thinkable? Will there be a period—as most theologians had asserted—between a particular judgment of the individual soul and the Last Judgment? Will souls, separated from their bodies, enjoy the delights of heaven or suffer the tortures of hell? Various passages from scripture—in particular the parable of Dives and Lazarus, and the assurance of Christ to the Good Thief that "to day shalt thou be with me in paradise" (Luke 23:43)—seem to imply that souls will go straight to heaven or hell immediately after death, and before the general resurrection of bodies. But is that scientifically possible? Can souls without bodies know anything, or experience pleasure or pain?

What may strike us most forcefully is that two bodies of knowledge—scripture and science—exist side by side, and that the thinkers of this period are making heroic, honest, if rather literal-minded efforts to reconcile them. For instance, our knowledge of the body, combined with a materialist philosophy, might lead us to deny any possibility of disembodied souls. This could easily lead to a denial that there is any future life at all—an obviously abhorrent conclusion. We might instead prefer the idea that at death the soul falls asleep, and is only roused to life and awareness with the general resurrection of bodies at the Last Day. People who believed this, of whom Milton seems to have been one and Sir Thomas Browne another (in his *Religio Medici*), were called mortalists, or sometimes, "thanato-psychists."

One powerful upholder of mortalism was Richard Overton, who puts the case with a sprightly display of logic in 1675.[1] Overton denies outright the existence of anything we can call a soul. His essentially Aristotelian argument is that man is an organism, all of whose faculties express his organic being. Our ability to be rational depends upon our organism's being at a certain stage of development. Therefore there cannot be a rational soul that exists apart from an appropriate body. An infant, undeveloped physically, is not rational: "rationality in an infant, is no more in it than a chicken in the egg, only *in posse*; therefore a child cannot possibly ratiocinate, before it be actually rational; which cannot be before organical perfection; for reason cannot *be*, and cannot show itself; show itself and not *be*; for its being is its rationality, and its rationality is its being" (ibid., 15).

Orthodox Christian teaching about the future life is that man will see God—and it is only as rational beings that we can see God. But if our being rational depends upon our having mature bodies, then the very possibility of disembodied spirits seeing God, or knowing or seeing anything at all, is obviously ruled out. Overton argues, therefore, that man does not have an immortal soul: "Man is corruptible, and himself but a bundle of corruption, or curious mass of vicissitudes. If all of Man that goeth to his manhood be mortal, where, then, or what is this immortal thing the soul they talked of?" (ibid., 16).

Not only does Overton dismiss "this immortal thing the soul"—he does not even believe that the qualities we usually think of as proper to man as a rational being are peculiarly human. Rather, they exist in a sort of dissipated form throughout the animal kingdom but come together or are summed up in man. Reason characterizes man as a certain sort of animal organism; it is not a special spiritual quality. Hence we can find traces of its effects in other animals. Scattered forms of human qualities appear among the beasts: "the hare is eminent for memory, the dog for apprehension and fidelity, the serpent for wisdom, the fox for subtilty, the dove for chastity and innocency, the elephant for docility, modesty, and gratitude, the ape for imitation and understanding" (ibid., 18). So human nature, divided up as it were (*sensu diviso*), is to be found among the other animals; but in man they all come together (*sensu coniuncto*), and it is simply because man unites all these qualities in himself that he is, as a rational, physical creature, "capable of God" (ibid., 19). It follows that "if in man be an immortal spirit, then divers other creatures have the like, though not in the same degree" (ibid.).

Thus mortalism is a radical way of solving the conundrum that has always haunted Christian thought about the next life. If the soul flies to God, or to hell immediately after death, and is judged there and then, what is the point of the Last Judgment, since judgment has already been passed? Theologians have sometimes suggested that the point is that everyone's sins will thereby be made public—but that does seem to be a less than substantial reason for such an elaborate, worldwide ceremony. It also solves a question that we are aware of in both Aquinas and Dante: If spirits can see God and experience his glory, why, exactly, do they need to be joined by the body? Dante depicts the souls as expecting a fuller happiness when their bodies rejoin them. But this picture hovers between the full-blooded Platonic teaching that the soul is the true human being, simply imprisoned within the body and yearning to fly to the empyrean, and some sort of materialism. Even Dante quite often finds it natural to treat spirits—especially in the *Inferno*—as though they are embodied. We find, equally, that even those who believe that disembodied spirits exist, and enjoy and disport themselves in heaven, regularly imagine them as very like bodies, albeit glorified ones. And they find it much easier to envisage heaven when they envisage the resurrected body, and speculate about what it will be like.

A Heavenly Royal Society[2]

Isaac Watts (1674–1748) imagines a heaven in which the disembodied souls will be perpetually conscious, eternally awake. There will be no night in heaven. Watts explains the advantages of this: Where there is night we lose our way, fall into ditches, get lost among the briars. Night is also the time when we conceal our secret sins.[3] But the real reason why there shall be no night in heaven is that disembodied souls will have better things to do than sleep: "sleep was not made for the heavenly state. Can the spirits of the just ever sleep, under full blaze of divine glory, under the incessant communication of divine love?" (ibid., 265–66). We will never weary of this incessant communi-cation and blaze: "when the soul arrives in heaven, we shall be all warm and fervent in our divine and delightful work" (ibid., 274). There is something a little disconcerting in this heaven—for it seems a bit like a work camp always in the blazing sun, a sun that is "the bright emblem of divinity." But Watts goes on to meditate on the properties of the resurrected body; and it turns out to be so remarkably reconstituted that this life of unending response to the divine blaze might seem plausible. Indeed, the human senses as we know them, may, in the next life, be utterly transformed. We are not sure what senses the resurrected body may have—they may not involve separate organs of sight and sound: "what if the whole body shall be endued all over with senses of *seeing* and *hearing*? What if these sorts of sensation shall be diffused through all our present mortal flesh? What if God himself shall in a more illustrious manner irradiate all the powers of the body and spirit, and communicate the light of knowledge, holiness and joy, in a superior manner to what we can now conceive or imagine?" Darkness in every sense will be banished from the heavenly state.[4]

The reconstituted body will not feel pain (and anyway, there will be nothing in heaven to cause pain.) The reasons Watts mentions to prove that this will be a good thing, though sensible enough, are truistic: pain, fatigue, and anxiety unfit us for the enjoyments of life, as well as for life's labors and duties: "What joy can he find in magnificent buildings, in gay and shining furniture, or in all the glittering treasures of the Indies, when the gout torments his hands or feet, or the rheumatism afflicts his limbs with intense anguish?" (Watts, *World to Come*, 335).

In heaven, the soul has forsaken this flesh and blood, and risen as on the wings of angels to the heavenly world, leaving all pain behind. With no gout or rheumatism, there will be no violent passions or impatience, or any repining at the providence of God (ibid.).

It is in another work, imagining heaven in detail, that Watts allows his fancy free range.[5] He starts with the traditional idea that in heaven we will know things in a way different from that in which we know them on earth. We will know them "in a manner something akin to the way whereby God knows us . . . such a sort of knowledge as we have of a man when we see him face to face . . . a certain and unwavering knowledge . . . without error or mistake" (ibid., 72–73).

This metaphysical beginning soon turns into something more English and concrete. We are to imagine the lives of the spirits in heaven, and the nature of their heavenly pleasures. They will not be bored, for they will all have different tastes and pleasures. And why not?—after all, consider the varieties of nature: "think of the Leviathan, the eel, and the oyster, and tell me if God has not shown a rich variety of contrivance in them" (ibid., 94).

God's rich contrivance suggests the possibility that heaven will reflect the variety of the human world. At least, we may suppose so. May not all our various talents down here be put to good use in heaven: "may we not suppose [David and Moses] trained up in the arts of holy government on earth, to be the chiefs of some blessed army, some sacred tribe in heaven? They were directors of the forms of worship in the Church below under divine inspiration: and might not that fit them to become leaders of some celestial assembly, when a multitude of the sons of God above come at stated seasons to present themselves before the throne?" (ibid., 94–95). David is set to become Master of the King's Music: "Both of 'em knew how to celebrate the praise of their creator in sacred melody; but David was the chief of mortals in this harmonious work: And may we not imagine that he is or shall be Master of heavenly Music, before or after the resurrection, and teach some of the choirs above to tune their harps to the Lamb that was slain?" (ibid.).

The need for us to employ our talents in the next world allows Watts to construct a whole society which satisfyingly reproduces the social arrangements of his own time. Superiority of talent will be what wins the prize: those seventeenth-century founders of English science and Fellows of the Royal Society, such as Robert Boyle and John Ray, will be "fitted beyond their fellow Saints to contemplate the wisdom of God in the works of his hands" (ibid., 95–96), and plenty of theologians will see their theories confirmed by divine truth. Gilbert Burnet, bishop of Salisbury, the great John Tillotson, divine and archbishop of Canterbury, and Richard Baxter will set the intellectual tone. Watts also envisages (vaguely) a place for the lesser talents, so that artificers and traders may be "fitted by their character and conduct on earth for peculiar stations and employments in heaven" (ibid., 98)—although exactly how plumbers, carpenters, and shopkeepers will find the opportunity to exercise their skills in the celestial realms remains problematical.

Some saints and heroes of the Old Testament will clearly come higher in the heavenly hierarchy than others: "Can we think that Abraham and Moses, who were trained up in converse with God face to face, as a man converses with his friend . . . were not prepared for a greater intimacy with God, and nearer views of his glory in heaven, than Sampson and Jephthah, those rude heroes, who being appointed of God for that service, spent their days in bloody war, in hewing down the Philistines and the Ammonites?" (ibid., 110). Indeed, one has a sense that the intellectual Watts is not a wholehearted admirer of these rough and ready heroes: "we read little of their acquaintance with God, or converse with him, beside a petition now and then, or a vow for victory and for slaughter" (ibid.). (Watts is shocked that anyone might erroneously hold that the Good Thief, who lived by plundering and mischief, might be as glorious as St. Paul in heaven "just because he repented a moment before death" [ibid., 111].)

Much of what goes on in heaven will be worship, song, prayer, heavenly melody—and "humble addresses," expressions of zeal for the glory and kingdom of Christ. But for variety there will also be "entertainments," including sermons (which not all of Watts's readers might have classed among the delights to look forward to in the next life) and "lectures of divine wisdom and grace given to the younger spirits there by spirits of a more exalted station" (ibid., 120). And at solemn seasons in heaven there will be the equivalent of a *conversazione* of the Royal Society, when Jesus Christ himself may announce "new and surprising discoveries," which are "reserved to entertain the attention and exalt the pleasure of spirits advanced to glory" (ibid., 121).

Indeed, heaven soon begins to resemble a college or a research institute. The spirits, disencumbered of this load of flesh, may go off on sabbatical journeys of discovery "quick as sunbeams" to observe "the inhabitants of the various and distant globes" and then come back to exchange impressions and travelers' tales (ibid., 125). Adam will be among the guest speakers: he will "tell us the exact nature of the trees of knowledge and life. . . . Paul and Moses shall join together to give us an account of the Jewish law, and read wondrous and entertaining lectures" (ibid., 178–79).

As for the very top saints, they will join a celestial colonial civil service: They may "sometimes be appointed Visitors and Superintendants over whole provinces of intelligent beings in lower regions who are yet laboring in their state of probation" (ibid., 127).

Watts's book is written in memory of and includes a funeral sermon on Sir John Hartropp, Bart. that ends by bringing together Sir John's social gifts with his heavenly merits. Sir John had an obliging deportment and an affable temper that rendered him easy of access to all his inferiors. In heaven he "doubtless practices now all the same graces of conversation among the blessed spirits there, but in a far superior manner" (ibid., 206).

All Things New?

We have seen that in Dante's *Paradiso* the blessed spirits look forward to the time when they will be reunited with their bodies. Yet without their bodies they do not seem especially incommoded, and nor is their bliss palpably diminished. As suggested earlier, a simple and logical way of solving the problem about what happens to souls in the interim before their bodies resurrect is to deny that disembodied souls do or can exist at all. Until the general resurrection they sleep (a sleep that seems hardly different from death), to arise with their bodies either to eternal glory or to everlasting contempt.

A question that continued to exercise theologians was whether the risen body would be physically identical with that of the person who had died. Aquinas himself had dealt with the question about cannibals and the resurrection:[6] Suppose a cannibal who had lived exclusively on the flesh of other people: With what body will he resurrect? Has he a body of his own at all? A traditional answer had been that it really needed only an atom or two of his real body to survive, and God would reconstitute the whole. After all, God created us from blood and sperm, so would it be beyond his powers to re-create our bodies from the smallest bits remaining (from, for instance, a bit of DNA)? (The idea recurs several times in the Qu'ran.[7])

But why not deal radically with this question as well? Why not decide that the resurrected body is brand-new? An obvious objection would be that arising from personal identity: If the body is not in any literal way the same as the one that died, in what sense could it be said that the individual had been resurrected body and soul? One answer to this would be that the continuity of memories makes one the same person. It is not clear how this would work for bodily identity. Nevertheless, the idea of a newly created body does avoid many of the old difficulties, even if it creates new ones.

A confident expounder of the brand-new body option was Thomas Burnet (1635–1715), whom we have encountered in chapter 8 (pages 218–21) arguing against the eternity of hell's torments. We might see Burnet as marooned between two worlds, one dying and the other struggling to be born—the worlds of medieval philosophy and of modern science. Burnet is concerned to reconcile his theology with science. The result is a curious mixture of bold, almost heterodox speculation, literal-minded empiricism, and proto-science.

Burnet is intellectually extremely ambitious. He wants to describe, in the most general terms, the state of the dead:[8] He also constructs a "sacred theory of the earth," which is a mixture of theology and geology, complete with an account of what will happen to the earth after the general resurrection.[9]

Burnet begins with a fundamental argument against the possibility of disembodied souls. Soul without body cannot be conscious. It can have no perception of the external world.[10] It cannot suffer pleasure or pain (and therefore cannot be in heaven or hell). Neither scripture nor reason supports the notion of a particular judgment before the general one on the Last Day (ibid., 56–57). The dead can know nothing of the state of the living; they are "freed from the encumbrances of domestic cares, and rest from their labors" (ibid., 121). Burnet finds it impossible to imagine that an old woman who can neither write nor read,[11] much less understand statuary or painting, shall, as soon as she has been divested of her body "fancy an Image exactly agreeable to herself, with all the lineaments of her Face, and her outward Appearance, even the exactness of habit, with greater nicety than Apelles cou'd paint, or Phidias carve" (*State of the Dead*, 121).

Being unconscious, the souls cannot experience the beatific vision, which comes only with the resurrection of the body (ibid., 56–57). Burnet notes the rather tenuous reasoning by which Dante thinks that the bliss of souls will be increased when the body rejoins them, noting that papists say that the happiness of the blessed is not intensively, but only extensively increased by the resurrection of the whole body (ibid., 72–73).

Will we resurrect with the same body we had during life? Burnet pours scorn on the idea. Our old, battered bodies will be made good as new or, rather, will be replaced with completely new ones, with nothing in common with the old: "like the ship *Argus*, an hundred times repaired, it has only its name.... I had rather have a new habitation from heaven, than this old patch'd up one, mended, and botch'd in this manner" (ibid., 228).

Burnet is short with the notion that God will take the trouble to recollect the scattered atoms of our bodies: "It would be a very operose miracle to recollect the Particles of all the deceas'd humane Carcasses from the beginning of the World to the end thereof, to separate the Mass, and parcel it out into little Heaps" (ibid., 230). And anyway, the cannibal problem is worse than had previously been thought. We all eat each other—we eat our ancestors transmuted into herbs and animals: "Most carcasses are dissolved and dissipated, some return to their Mother Earth, the rest are exhaled into the Air, and fall down in Dews and Rain, are imbibed in the roots of Plants, Corn and Fruits; from whence they circulate back to our human bodies" (ibid., 231).

So our risen bodies cannot possibly be the same as those that have moldered in the grave. Far from it—they will be celestial and incorruptible, void of flesh and blood (ibid., 192); they will be like a flame or liquid ether, subtle matter, fluid and slender, like the bodies of angels (ibid., 208). In heaven we will be "light, vivid and volatile"; our bodies will obey the motions of the mind, easily shooting through space ("pervading, rarefying and condensing"). Like lightning they will penetrate and overthrow all in their way (ibid., 199–202).

All of this sounds far removed from anything like the natural human body—which is exactly Burnet's point. Our heavenly bodies are really nothing like our earthly ones and are certainly not identical with them. In particular, it is impossible that our earthly bodies could somehow be transformed into heavenly ones, for if we pursue that idea, it becomes absurd. Many theologians had argued, for instance, that the risen body will not need to eat nor to exercise other bodily functions. Burnet points out that if the body "shall want a Belly, it will likewise be without Bowels, and without Paunch, and all the inward Appurtenances of that Belly . . . and the Body will be maim'd and imperfect. . . . Moreover, the Parts below the Belly will be taken away likewise, or be entirely useless" (ibid., 189). We will not need legs, thighs, nor feet, which were designed for us to walk upon a firm and solid pavement. Since there will be no such thing in heaven, we will not move by walking but shooting around like the angels (ibid.). (A contemporary of Burnet, William Gearing, was of the opinion that the floor of heaven will be of precious metal and that "God will not suffer dirty feet of impure sinners to tread upon this pavement of pure gold."[12] In *Paradise Lost*, Milton depicts Mammon, while still an angel in heaven, perpetually looking down at heaven's golden pavement, which he prefers to the beatific vision.)[13]

Burnet pursues the self-contradiction of a body that does not need food. With no food there is no nourishment, hence no "tasting, chewing, swallowing, concocting, sanguinification, and distribution of the Chyle, together with many of the glands necessary for Nourishment and Secretion" (Burnet, *State of the Dead*). Who could possibly bear this mutilation of our organic bodies? The notion of the corruptible becoming incorruptible is simply absurd—for our bodies in their essential being are corruptible: Incorruptible blood is a contradiction, and flesh is "only a coagulation of Blood and Juices" (ibid., 191). Therefore our celestial and incorruptible bodies must be void of flesh and blood.

If the dead were to rise with the same bodies they had in life, it might follow that they would have the instincts of terrestrial human beings. For instance, they would need to live in societies, to live a political life. Burnet draws out this possibility in order to show its absurdity—in that skeptical tone that got him, in his lifetime, the reputation of unorthodoxy or even infidelity.

If they are to have political government, they will have to be divided, in heaven, into nations. The French, Italians, Germans, Spanish, and English will have to be separated from each other "in the air"—which will be difficult in an ethereal realm that lacks ditches, rivers, or clear demarcations (ibid., 114). Burnet warms to his theme: The Greeks will have their own native language in the other world, the Latins theirs. But if that is so, in this Babel of voices, how will different races, or different generations within the same race communicate? "the present Romans are entirely ignorant of the antient Latin tongue, so what communication will they have with Romulus or Numa? They who inhabit the Western and Northern parts of the Globe, understand not the Celtick and Scythian tongues" (ibid., 114–15). Even more disconcerting, we, the inhabitants of Britain, will not understand our own forebears—the ancient British, the Saxons, Normans.

And if people are to retain their race and nationhood, why not their religion? Will Jews be Jews, Muslims have their Prophet—and papists their pope?

We might think that Burnet's *reductio ad absurdum* so satirically dismisses all ideas of the identity of the earthly and risen bodies that any belief that human beings will in any sense survive into the next life is impossible. Our bodies will not be bodies in any sense we can now understand; they will have none of the properties of flesh and blood, and, by the sorts of arguments Burnet himself deploys, it is difficult to see how they can be sentient (or how angels can be, for that matter.) We will, presumably, have no instinct for society in the way in which we now understand that. And yet Burnet insists that the blessed will inhabit a real place in the next life as genuinely physical beings.

So the risen body will have to be more or less like the body of an angel. For angels also do have bodies—real ones. Burnet is indignant at any suggestion that angelic bodies might not be real. The guards and attendants of Christ at the Second Coming must be visible and have bodies of a superior quality. It would be intolerable to think that they simply put on bodies for the great day and then take them off again when the show is over. It is unthinkable that Christ should come in his full panoply of majesty with a guard of shadows and phantasms and thousands upon thousands of masquerade angels (ibid., 195).

Burnet is determined to give to the blessed a local habitation. He is (as we have said) an immensely ambitious thinker, and his notions about the state of the dead flow from his astonishing book about the history of the earth itself—the *Sacred Theory of the Earth*. As one editor says, this work, for all its eccentricity "has about it a certain epic grandeur both in conception and style, and Burnet might be described as a kind of prose Milton thirty years nearer to Addison."[14]

Burnet's starting point is that the earth must have once been subject to some aboriginal catastrophe. Far from being the beautiful product of God's handicraft that theologians had traditionally described, the earth is a sort of wreck or ruin of something that was *once* beautiful. What ruined the earth was the Deluge. The biblical flood was more catastrophic than we have hitherto understood. It was not produced simply by a great deal of rain falling upon the planet. Burnet proves, pretty conclusively, that there could never have been enough rain to bury the highest mountains. He calculates that eight oceans of water would be needed to bury the earth up to the tops of the greatest mountains. Forty days and nights of rain would simply have been insufficient for the job. There certainly could not be enough rain produced by the usual evaporation to do anything like what the Bible describes.

The only solution that fits the facts is this: The antediluvian earth was a beautiful smooth crust, formed out of oily substances, dust, and water. Under the crust was a vast world of water (*"He founded the Earth upon the Seas, and establish'd it upon the Floods"* and *"He stretched out the Earth over the Waters"*)[15]— the "fountains of the deep" that Moses mentions as being broken up and flooding the earth at the time of the Deluge. Neither the sea as it is at present, nor the subterraneous waters can correspond to that "Mosaical Abysse," which was sufficiently vast and capacious to contain waters to overwhelm the whole world (ibid., 74–75).

Because of human sin, God suffered this crust of the earth to dry, shrink, and eventually crack, so that parts of it collapsed and fell into the waters below. When the flood abated it left what we see now—the disordered, ravaged, ruined remains of what had originally been perfectly spherical and, hence, beautiful: "In this smooth earth were the first scenes of the world, and the first generation of mankind; it had the beauty of youth and blooming nature, fresh and fruitful, and not a wrinkle, scar or fracture in all its body; no rocks nor mountains, no hollow caves, nor gaping channels, but even and uniform all over . . . the air was calm and serene . . . 't was suited to a golden age, and to the first innocency of nature" (ibid., 64). (It is astonishing that such a boring landscape—which sounds like a idealized version of Cambridgeshire—should have so appealed to Burnet.)

Burnet holds that the resurrected dead will indeed be bodies, but new and perfect ones; and the heaven they dwell in will be a blissful place in which to live. The earth, being so ruinous, will not be blissful, and so the new kingdom of Christ could not exist on the surface of the present earth. Anyway, this world—so we are informed by scripture, and so was the opinion of the ancients, especially the Stoics—is due to end in a general conflagration. This final conflagration, like the Flood, will have a natural origin. The volcanoes (ibid., 272–76), emanating from the Central Fire (ibid., 268), will belch forth their flames (ibid.); there will be fiery meteors from above; and "the latent seeds of fire shall everywhere be let loose" (ibid., 274). In preparation for all this, there will be an extreme drought; the earth will become chapped and scorched, there will be an immoderate heat in the air, the woods and trees being ready fuel for the fire (ibid., 265). There is no terrestrial body that does not finally yield to the force of fire (ibid., 266). (There are all sorts of hidden and invisible materials within the earth, including minerals and mineral juices that are igniferous: sulfur, bitumen, inflammable salts, coal and other fossils that are "unctuous and inflammable.") The fire will, of course, start in Rome, the cause in nature being that Italy is a combustible country full of volcanoes (ibid., 273–74); and the providential cause being that Rome is the seat of Antichrist—i.e., the pope. Protestant England, though, over which Antichrist has no power, will not escape. On the contrary, it will be a particularly hot spot, because of its generous deposits of coal (ibid., 276).

After all this, by means which there is no need to go into but which Burnet elaborates with full ingenuity, something like the original earth will be restored, there will be a thousand years reign of Christ and the saints, a final, hugely destructive conflict involving Gog and Magog, and the final translation of the saints to heaven—the earth becoming a fixed star (ibid., 376). "There we leave it; having conducted it for the space of seven thousand years, through various changes from a dark chaos to a bright star" (ibid., 377).

There is undoubtedly something sublime in Burnet's vision. It is true that he is literal-minded, and that his attempt to reconcile scripture with the science of his time (including his calculation of seven thousand years as the total life span of the earth) might strike us—as it did not strike his contemporaries—as doomed. Yet he is making an heroic effort to produce a picture of the destiny of the world and of the human race that includes all available knowledge, and which tries to work out in empirical terms his fundamental thesis that heaven will be a real place containing actual, physical bodies. Burnet does indeed have something in common with the Milton of *Paradise Lost* (which he obviously knows well.) He can imagine a world in which biblical history is validated and the promises contained in the scriptures actually fulfilled, and he does so with real power. His heaven is not God-centered, but is much more powerfully a picture of a renewed and perfected human society.

A Sentimentalist's Heaven

It was to become a characteristic feature of modern thought about heaven to see the next life as closely replicating this one. Going with this was a decline in the sense that essential to heaven will be the vision of God, that God shall be all in all. A sense grew that the boundaries between the next life and this are porous, that there is no great abyss between the living and the dead, and that the dead depart by degrees, as it were. This becomes part of the vision of Emmanuel Swedenborg and issues finally into the beliefs and practices of Spiritualism.

There is an early intimation of this in the works—extremely widely read in their day—of Elizabeth Rowe (1674–1737). In her most popular book, *Friendship in Death: Letters from the Dead to the Living*, she has the recently dead communicate with friends and loved ones in this world, and describe their state in the hereafter. (A modern sensibility is suggested by the fact that none of them is writing from hell.) What is striking about these letters is that in the afterlife depicted, God is conspicuous by his semi-absence; and that the love that springs from the beatific vision is largely replaced by a sentimental eroticism.

In Letter 11 ("from a gentleman who died in Constantinople") this is patent. This man is awakened after death by a voice he perfectly remembers—"the charming Almeria's voice"—Almeria's own death "being the occasion of my travels." Heaven for this gentleman is reunion with the charming Almeria: "the first spirit that welcomed me to these new regions was the loving Almeria. But how dazzling! How divinely fair! Ecstasy was in her eyes, and inexpressible pleasure in every smile. . . . Her mien and aspect were more soft and propitious than ever was feigned by poets of their goddess of beauty and love."[16] Her softness and propitiousness clearly have an erotic meaning—so that her smiles have a rather different significance from the smiles of Dante's Beatrice. Almeria receives him into her ethereal chariot, which is sparkling sapphire, studded with gold, and which rolls with a spontaneous motion along the heavenly plains, until it stops at the Morning Star—not a public house, but the planet Venus, where the two lovers will have their eternal habitation.[17] (Almeria's chariot seems remotely inspired by Milton's description of the Messiah's chariot, with its sapphire throne, which puts the rebel angels to flight in *Paradise Lost*.[18] Here it is transformed from terrifying war machine to a charming conveyance for a pair of lovers on a date.)

This "enchanting land of love" consists of "delectable vales, flowery lawns, myrtle shades and rosy bowers, crystal rivulets and orient pearls" (a reminiscence of Milton's paradise of Adam and Eve).[19] Whatever can raise desire and give delight is found there; every wish is replenished with full draughts of vital pleasure.[20] It is like the Muslim paradise as that has always been understood by Christians, but more sensual. Indeed, the strong suggestion is of ever-renewed sexual activity; and now Almeria is extremely good at it—"as much superior to her former self as I thought her superior to the rest of her sex on earth."

There is no God, no saints and martyrs to welcome the young man—just his mistress with the implied promise of abundant good sex.

Another letter is from a soul who has been transported to "one of the millions of worlds God has created."[21] The inhabitants of this world, unlike Adam and Eve, never sinned. They live in sapphire and agate palaces with gates of carbuncle. There is an abundance of sylvan scenes, verdant avenues, flowery walks, streams, and groves, all pouring out music from every bush. A thousand feathered songsters warble to the measured fall of high cascades—there are tuneful reeds, warbling lutes, and sweet enchanting voices of the Lydian (i.e., sensual) strain.[22] It is Milton's paradise without God, and the heavenly Jerusalem without Christ. It also looks forward to Evelyn Waugh's depiction of Whispering Glades, a California cemetery full of recorded music emanating from speakers hidden in the extensive shrubbery.[23]

Another letter evokes another paradise. The (female) writer speaks of "your charming brother, gay as a cherubim."[24] This gay cherub sings meltingly, accompanying himself on his lute. The angels themselves get caught up in the erotic triumph, where "all desire is lost in full and complete fruition." The full face of love unveils its original glories and all is rapture and inexpressible ecstasy. Although the full face of love implies a reference to God, the main impression left is of the erotic.

Yet another writer from the Beyond is taken on a magical mystery tour through the liquid regions under the conduct of an ethereal messenger. Or rather, he makes the Grand Tour—in this case a tour of the universe, exploring the limits of creation with unspeakable agility. He moves from star to star, meets a thousand suns blazing in glory, without fear he follows the track of prodigious comets, and finally ascends with ease and swiftness to the "superior heaven, the imperial palace of the Most High," after which "description fails, and all beyond us is unutterable."[25] The Palace of the Most High does seem an afterthought. It is an astonishingly casual break from all traditional and orthodox pictures of heaven: a secular paradise dominated by a gently sentimental sensuality.

John Asgill Is Translated

Perhaps the most extraordinary attempt to break down the barriers between this world and the next, between life and death, is the argument by which John Asgill, Member of Parliament in the early eighteenth century, set out to prove that death itself can be escaped, and that we can be translated to the next world without passing through the portals of mortality.[26]

Asgill's essential argument is that dying is merely a custom, a habit that we ought to grow out of. He admits that it is a habit that has a very strong hold on our minds—but that is all the power it has: "the dominion of death is supported by our fear of it, by which it hath bullied the world to this day" (ibid., 8).

Asgill's argument is simply a blank denial of induction. Just because, up to now, everyone (with the exceptions of Elijah and Enoch who were translated, according to the Bible, straight to heaven) has died, it does not at all follow that any one of us has to do the same: "If my father was hanged, does this mean I will drown?" As the life and death of one man is no cause of the life and death of another, so "the multitudes of examples don't alter the case" (ibid.). After all, the Flood destroyed all but eight persons—"yet that was no argument that these eight should be destroyed as well." Therefore, the custom of the world to die is no argument one way or the other.

In case his rejection of inductive reasoning might not get him the whole way, Asgill invokes scripture. By the New Covenant of Christ, we are ransomed from the law under which we fell in Adam and are delivered into the eternal life that was promised us when Christ arose from the dead (ibid., 52). The fact that people have gone on dying is neither here nor there. Those that will be still alive at the Second Coming of Christ "shall be caught up together in the air with him" (ibid., 90). Asgill, meanwhile, is perfectly confident that he himself shall not taste death. He shall not be taken in the midst of his days "before I have done all my heart's desire" (ibid., 95). But when he has done his heart's desire "I know no business I have with the dead, and therefore do as much depend that I shall not go hence by returning to the dust . . . [but] I shall make my exit by Translation, which I claim as a dignity belonging to that degree in the science of eternal life, of which I profess myself a graduate . . . and if after this I die like other men, I declare myself to die of no religion" (ibid.).

Asgill's little book is "an engine in divinity, to convey men from earth to heaven" (ibid., 100). But he counsels his readers "man, woman or child" not to try it at home, or at any rate "not to venture themselves with him until they shall see his success" (ibid., 101). But he will go "by the way of an eagle in the air" (ibid., 103).

Sad to say, Asgill's contemporaries were not perfectly convinced. On December 18, 1707, he was expelled from the House of Commons of the first Imperial Parliament of Great Britain, for "many prophane and blasphemous expressions, highly reflecting upon the Christian religion."[27]

He seems to have created a stir, and some (including Daniel Defoe) thought it worth writing a rejoinder to him.[28] Others were content with satire. A pamphlet appeared, which purported to describe how Asgill would actually be translated.[29] The anonymous writer depicts Asgill as preparing himself to be removed out of this mortal state from the top of Hampstead Heath, having conveyed himself thither, along with a couple of friends, in a coach, in the early morning to avoid the multitude of people who will be bound to come to witness such an extraordinary spectacle.

Asgill will prepare himself with two bottles of champagne, because champagne is of an elevating nature, plus "a few pinches of plain Spanish [snuff]." He will reject any "very ingenious" machines, proposed to him by his friend Mr. Whiston (the same Whiston who rescued Dives from hell), such as a flying chair, a flying coach, or a flying boat. There will be scaffolding with raised seats for a million people, who will have paid for tickets ranging from one guinea to one shilling, and will each be provided with a paper of printed directions "how to direct their view to the true part of the hemisphere through which Mr. Asgill will pass."[30] Since there will be spectators not only around Hampstead Heath and Highgate Hill but tens of thousands on the roof of St. Paul's, the Monument[31], and all the church steeples, two bombs will be exploded fifteen minutes before Asgill mounts. His friends will have calculated the exact amount of luminous air needed to carry Mr. Asgill, and it has been worked out that a vortex of air five hundred yards in diameter will be sufficient to raise him up; and that "upon a mean computation he will be near the moon about two in the evening" and will thereafter continue his progress "north of Mars, and hold directly upon Jupiter, whose belt he will cross, and so leaving Saturn on his right, proceed on to the fixed stars, within three degrees of the great Polar North Star, where Mr. Asgill conceives he shall reside some thousands of years."[32]

Poor John Asgill, alas! was committed to prison for debt, his book having been burned by the public hangman, where he died, untranslated (but one hopes, unabashed) in 1738.

15

Heaven Heard and Seen: Swedenborg

The Seer

"[T]hat divinely chosen seer of our age, who was impregnated with the joys of heaven, to whom the spirits spoke through all senses and the entire body, in whose bosom the angels lived." The words are those of Goethe, comparing the "cold and bloodless" arguments of the author of a book, entitled *Prospects of Eternity*, that he is reviewing, with the visionary system of Emanuel Swedenborg.[1] The son of a Swedish bishop, Swedenborg had worked on the Royal Board of Mines in his native Sweden, until in April 1745 in London, he was vouchsafed a mystical vision of "the Lord God, the Creator of the world and the Redeemer," who permitted him to see "the worlds of spirits, heaven, and hell."[2] For the rest of his life, Swedenborg set out to describe in vivid detail, and virtually to map the worlds of spirits, the "heavens," the "hells," the character, habits, speech, and dwelling places of the inhabitants of these worlds, and of other planets in the solar system, and to explain their exact relation—the "correspondences" as he termed them—to the spiritual states of human beings. What makes Swedenborg unusual among eighteenth-century writers on heaven and hell is that he claimed, without the least embarrassment, that he had seen all these things for himself, that he had had visions of the Lord, talked regularly with angels, and visited the heavenly habitations.

It is interesting that not all, or even most, of Swedenborg's contemporaries considered him mad, or a charlatan, despite the detailed effrontery of his claims. One thing that made an impression on even the most skeptical was his reputation for extraordinary powers. Kant wrote a little book mocking Swedenborg and describing his "big work" *(Arcana Coelestia)* as "full of nonsense" and "void of the last drop of reason."[3] At the same time, he relates without obvious mockery several stories about the seer's occult powers. One of them concerns Swedenborg's apparent ability to be aware of things that were happening at a great distance: "toward the end of the year 1759 . . . one afternoon Mr. Swedenborg, coming from England, landed in Gothenburg. The same evening he was invited to meet some company at the house of a resident merchant. After being present a short while he proclaimed, with evident consternation, the news that, just at that moment, a terrible fire was raging in Stockholm, in the Sundermalm [where his own house was situated.] After the lapse of several hours, during which he had from time to time left the company, he reported to them that the fire was checked, and how far it had spread. This wonderful news was noised abroad the same evening, and the next morning was all over town. Not until two days after did the first report from Stockholm arrive in Gothenburg. It agreed entirely, it is said, with Swedenborg's visions."[4]

Swedenborg was seen as a frank, genial man, curiously matter-of-fact in his accounts of the wonders he has experienced. There is also in his writing a quality of authenticity, which, combined with the perspicuity of his style, goes some way to persuade us to read him as seer or visionary rather than charlatan. Some commentators compared his writings with Mohammed's account of his direct revelations from God in the Qur'an—no doubt intending that as a damning criticism. We might recall, however, some words of Carlyle, when he spoke of Mohammed's *"sincerity,* a deep, great, genuine sincerity."[5] The sense of the naked vision in Swedenborg must have been part of what impressed several Romantics, including Blake and Coleridge, as well as Goethe.[6]

Luther had been very willing to imagine earthly delights in heaven, as we saw in chapter 7.[7] Yet Luther, along with Calvin and the other Reformers, assumed that in heaven God would be all in all. Luther may have lacked good philosophical grounds for believing this, but theologically this God-centered next life was essential for him. Swedenborg evolves a picture of heaven that radically departs from Catholic, Protestant, and, in many ways, Christian doctrine. Swedenborg's heaven is really a continuation of our present life, but in a more realized form. It is not a place but a state: "We may . . . conclude that the state of our inner nature is what constitutes heaven and that heaven is within each one of us, not outside us."[8] Yet Swedenborg's visions of heaven are full of landscapes, parks, and houses. This is because even the way we occupy space, and the space that we occupy, is somehow the projection of our own inner states. God does not decide who enters heaven or hell. Human beings decide that in the lives they choose to lead and the affections they choose to nourish within themselves. It is with Swedenborg that (in the words of McDannell and Lang) the modern heaven emerges.[9]

Swedenborg's heaven and hell are, therefore, real, but their reality consists in the way they correspond to human spiritual or psychological states. If the wonders of heaven and the miseries of hell are to be seen as projections of the human soul, then human nature contains within itself heights and depths, powers and possibilities that accord with the high Romantic doctrine of man as potentially a microcosm of the universe. Swedenborg's vision of thin partitions only dividing man from the spiritual world flows smoothly into the picture of the Romantic artist being in touch with a higher reality, and with the truth of the universe being revealed above all to the creative imagination.

This was an idea seized on by William Blake (who had a love-hate relationship to Swedenborg). For Blake, to be a visionary (i.e., a seer) was to have a heightened sense of the allegorical, indeed, to read the world as allegory. Blake thought that the opposed way of understanding experience—what he called "corporeal understanding" and which he associated with such British empiricists as Locke and Newton—would never issue in true understanding. The opposite of corporeal understanding would be to see with the highest poetic power—metaphorically (as Aristotle says, metaphor is the highest gift for it enables one to see the similarity in dissimilars).[10] As Blake expresses it: "To see a World in a Grain of Sand, / And a Heaven in a Wild Flower, / Hold Infinity in the palm of your hand, / And Eternity in an hour."[11]

To see in the poetic way is to cleanse the doors of perception and so see things as they really are—i.e., to grasp their spiritual meaning.[12] Seen imaginatively, the human body itself fully reveals a meaning: "The head Sublime, the heart Pathos, the genitals Beauty, the hands and feet Proportion."[13] For Blake, these are not tokens of a reality that we can grasp independently of the poetic imagination: it is only in seeing the world in a grain of sand, of seeing the head as sublime that we can see a grain of sand, the human head as they really are. But what they really are exists only imaginatively. Blake, furthermore, creates images that can be grasped only through the emotional power they have over us—the Tyger burning bright, the Sick Rose. The Tyger and the Rose exist only as vehicles of expression. This was Blake's creative way of showing how to reject empiricism and materialism, which he thought closed the doors of perception.

Some of Swedenborg's ideas had been anticipated by earlier writers. Among them we can include Phillip Nicolai (1556–1608), a German poet and hymn-writer, and a Capuchin friar, Martin of Cochem (1634–1712).[14] Nicolai imagined a multicultural, globally unwarmed heaven on earth, where the oceans will have disappeared, the climate will be extremely pleasant and temperate, and everyone will live happily in their own ethnic and linguistic communities, traveling widely, and coming back to exchange reminiscences (and, presumably, to show their holiday snaps). Nicolai thought that the "many mansions" in our Father's house of which Christ speaks will be real buildings in real cities.[15] Martin of Cochem insisted that heaven is not spiritual, but corporeal—a place where the five senses will be delighted with "a real river, real trees, real fruit and real flowers that please our vision, taste, smell and touch in unsurpassable ways."[16] But although these writers anticipate details of Swedenborg, they entirely lack the philosophy and theology with which Swedenborg buttresses his visions.

Swedenborg sees the human world as surrounded by the world of spirits. Man is himself a spirit, attached during this life to a body, which he leaves at the moment of death, replacing it with a different sort of body. With these new bodies human beings become angels and inhabit worlds with houses, gardens, and cities spiritually appropriate to them. Immediately after death, human beings find themselves in the world of spirits. Some time passes before they either rise to heaven or sink down into the hells (*inferna*). No judge decides what evil people will suffer. Rather the character their actions produced in them in life determines their fate: "The evil within us is hell within us, for it makes no difference whether you say 'evil' or 'hell' . . . it is we, not the Lord, who lead ourselves into hell."[17] Heaven, similarly, is not outside anyone but within. You are not taken into heaven simply by an act of God—say, by being granted God's mercy—as the doctrine of predestination teaches (ibid., 54). On the contrary, "unless heaven is within an individual, nothing of the heaven that is outside flows in and is accepted" (ibid.). Those with the best spiritual qualities become the highest sort of angels, inhabiting the innermost heaven.

Heaven is within us. Not only can we not be admitted there if heaven does not correspond to the state of our souls—if by some accident or miracle we did manage to get in, we would feel so ill at ease there that we would quickly try to get out again. This even applies to anyone with the ambition of moving from one of the lower to one of the higher, or inner, of Swedenborg's several heavens. He tells a cautionary anecdote about celestial climbing—of some people from the outmost heaven who were pushy enough to gate-crash the heaven where the angels "with the deeper qualities" live: "They were allowed to visit them, but when they arrived, even though there were a great many angels there, they did not see anyone no matter where they looked. . . . before long they were seized by heart pain and eventually could not tell whether they were still alive or not. So they quickly made their way back to the heaven they had come from, and were delighted to be among their own people" (ibid., 35). They vowed after this never again to try for things that did not suit their own way of life.

Every human being is a heaven in miniature, and heaven is man writ large, and should be seen as a single human being (ibid., 30). Every heavenly inhabitant forms some part of that all-inclusive body: "each spirit finds himself in that place and in that apparent member which is in accordance with his peculiar office in such a spiritual body." Again, all societies of spirits together, and the world of all these invisible beings, finally presents itself in the appearance of the *Grand Man, Maximus Homo*."[18] The highest heaven is the head (of this *Maximus Homo*), the middle heaven constitutes the torso down to the genitals; and the lowest heaven is the feet.[19]

Swedenborg also had visions of the different worlds in space and the character of the inhabitants of each. The inhabitants of the different planets have characters corresponding to the nature of each planet and all together make up the one human form. Those who live on Mercury have no interest in earthly or bodily matters, but only in the constitutions, laws, and governments of peoples.[20] Some of the souls on Jupiter have sooty faces like chimney sweeps and are destined eventually to "make up a province of the seminal vesicles in the Grand Man or heaven."[21] In yet another world, beyond the planets, he comes across naked couples whose spiritual affinity for each other makes them look physically as those possessed of "conjugial" love, Swedenborgian for "married love."[22]

The Doctrine of Correspondences

Swedenborg has the very rare distinction—which he shares with Dante—of basing his account of heaven on a coherent philosophy, one that goes back, especially, to Plato and Plotinus. The philosophy is a species of Idealism, in that Swedenborg asserts that the phenomenal world has existence only as pointing to a spiritual (or "spirit") world.[23] Material things, for instance, the human body, exist only as *signs* of this spiritual world. To understand the body is to read the spiritual realm of which it is a part. No single human body corresponds to one single element in the spiritual world, but to that world as a whole.[24] So, just as we know the material universe by knowing how objects interact with each other, we know, by seeing material objects as signs, how the different elements of the spiritual realm interrelate. It is only if our windows of perception are cleansed that we can see through the shell of the material world to the kernel within; and only seers such as Swedenborg (and, perhaps, poets such as Blake) are thus spiritually enlightened.

Everything in this world is symbolic of an inner state, even space. So when Swedenborg in his visions sees gardens, whole countries, palaces, galleries, and arcades in which the spirits live after death, he must be understood as talking about his own spiritual state and that of the spirits. A spirit of a certain type will live in a palace, another in gardens, others in caves or mountains. And the fact that Swedenborg can see these things even while walking about the streets in broad daylight, so that he is actually among them, says something about *his* spiritual state.

This does not mean that the houses, gardens, galleries, and spirit-countries are unreal. They are just as real as this material world; but *its* reality comes from a correspondence to our inner spirit. That is why Swedenborg found that whenever he spoke to his recently deceased friends, they had difficulty in believing that they had died, for the world they found themselves in seemed just like the world they were leaving behind. This was because their spiritual state was still earthbound: it is only as their spirit develops in the other realm that the space they live in will change.

Since our experience of space is conditioned by our spiritual state, those spirits who are profoundly compatible one with another, such as loving friends, are really right next to each other, even though they may be materially separated by thousands of miles. People who to the corporeal eye are in the same room, may actually inhabit different worlds. The dead may be right next to us—in effect, in the next room—if we are in profound spiritual sympathy with them. So when someone dies, his soul does not move to another space, but only comes to grasp—usually for the first time—what the place was that it had always occupied in the spirit world.

Swedenborg clearly thought that this doctrine enables us fully to understand Christ's words that "the kingdom of heaven is within you" (Luke 17:21). Everything in heaven corresponds to the natural and human world, not just in general but in every particular.[25] We can see this in the human face. The face is the index of the mind, and unless a person has been taught to dissimulate, all the emotions naturally and pellucidly manifest themselves in the face with an unmistakable directness. In heaven, angels can always read facial expression correctly. Not that they really need to do so, for Swedenborg tells us that some hypocrites occasionally tried to steal into the heavenly communities but immediately revealed themselves when their faces turned blue (ibid., 48). Similarly our intelligence manifests itself in our manner of speaking and our will in our physical behavior (ibid., 91). The inner and outer man are thus intimately conjoined and yet are as separate one from another as heaven is from earth: "Everything that happens and comes forth in the outer or natural person does so from the inner or spiritual one" (ibid., 92).

This is not the only type of correspondence. The different communities that make up heaven are arranged like the members, organs, and viscera in a human being: "so there are communities that are located in the head, in the chest, in the arms, and in the particular parts of these members. . . . the ones in the head in heaven correspond to our head, the ones in the chest there correspond to our chest, the ones in the arms correspond to our arms . . . We continue in existence because of this correspondence, for heaven is the only basis of our continued existence" (ibid., 94). These three levels are three heavens. The communities located in the head correspond to the spiritual qualities of love, peace, innocence, and wisdom; those in the chest to thoughtfulness and faith. Reasonably enough, the qualities of "marriage love" are located in the groin. Natural spiritual goodness is to be found in the feet (ibid., 96). It is a sort of body politic.

Swedenborg had a sunny, optimistic personality, which is reflected in his philosophy. The overarching concept in his thought is love—love of God and love of our neighbor. Heaven is not a reward for love. Rather, it is our capacity for love that makes us suitable for heaven, or that allows us even to desire heaven. After death we are spirits—beings undetermined whether they will go to heaven or hell. But if we have led lives characterized by love of God and our neighbor, we will gradually discover that we are in heaven. We will have become angels. All angels are simply human beings who have risen to angelic status—as all evil spirits are human beings who, having lived loveless and malicious lives, have chosen to become part of the "diabolic crew."[26] All babies who die in infancy become angels (which means that babies and children are an extremely high proportion of the inhabitants of heaven).[27] The more that angels (which is what we will have become) are inwardly convinced that everything good comes from God, the more securely *are* they angels and in heaven (ibid., 7). Although Swedenborg's heaven is vast—encompassing not only all the planets in our solar system, which he believes are inhabited by angels, but all the unknown planets that (he is sure) circle thousands or millions of remote stars[28]—it is, from the corporeal point of view, not a spatial heaven at all. Angels in heaven move toward God the more they love him, and they face him just insofar as they love him.[29] The East—i.e., God—is always in front of the angels, no matter in which direction they turn their faces and bodies (ibid., 143). Love unites angels into a single individual. Love is our vital core—the essential reality of every individual life (ibid., 13–14). Since the summation of love is love of God, heaven itself sometimes takes on the appearance of a single individual—the Lord (ibid., 52).

Swedenborg's doctrine of angels is obviously heretical. In scripture (influenced ultimately by Zoroastrian beliefs) angels are God's messengers, and they also order the sublunary world at God's behest. Some of them fell and were damned for all eternity. Swedenborg's doctrine of angels may well be his most enduring legacy for popular religion—even if only a tiny number of people will actually know anything directly about his esoteric teaching on the subject. The idea that the dead, children especially, become angels, unknown to traditional Christianity but extremely popular since Victorian times, comes from Swedenborg.

As we have suggested, Swedenborg's doctrine of correspondences draws on facts with which we are all familiar. We read the expressions on people's faces as directly revealing what they feel: "We can see in the human face what correspondence is like. In a face that has not been taught to dissimulate, all the affections of the mind manifest themselves visibly in a natural form, as though in their very imprint, which is why we refer to the face as 'the index of the mind.' This is our spiritual world within our natural world" (ibid., 91). We might interpret him as holding that involuntary reactions are related to expression. You might say of a blush that it is both a physical and psychological fact. Blushing is distinguished from flushing in that the reddening of the cheek in a blush betokens self-consciousness; it is both a physical and a mental event.

Swedenborg draws on an ancient, prescientific way of thinking, which assumes that we can read the book of nature as though reading the divine mind or the divine plan. In particular, the bodily forms of animals and even of plants give us insight into the spiritual reality that they signify. So we can read the spiritual reality of man by reading his physical being. The fact that he stands upright, that his skin is not covered in a sheath of hair—everything about his body expresses his status as a rational animal.[30] Similarly, Milton thought that Eve's long tresses reveal her character as less rational than Adam's, whose manly locks hung no lower than his shoulders broad.[31]

It would certainly be a mistake to interpret Swedenborg allegorically or symbolically—if, that is to say, one is setting those terms against the *actual*. As we have seen, for him, as for Plato and Plotinus—and, indeed, the larger tradition of philosophical Idealism—the rational (or intelligible) is the real. The world of ordinary, corporeal experience is less real than the world as it is experienced by philosophers, poets, and spirit-seers. The world without imagination is (in the words of Coleridge) "a vast heap of littleness." So when Swedenborg says that "the activity of love and faith is what makes heaven";[32] that we become images of heaven in so far as we participate in love and faith (ibid., 57); or that heaven in its most perfect form is a person (ibid., 59)—this could be seen as a purely metaphorical way of speaking. But this is not how he himself understood what he was saying. Blake wrote one of his finest lyrics about a sick rose:

O Rose, thou art sick.
The invisible worm,
That flies in the night
In the howling storm:
Has found out thy bed
Of crimson joy:
And his dark secret love
Does thy life destroy.

We might see this poem as expressing a sexual guilt that eats away at erotic happiness; or as our being in death in the midst of life; or as Satan entering the garden of Eden to destroy the innocent love of Adam and Eve. Many readings are possible. In this poem Blake is creating a concept, one that can be grasped only through the emotional charge that comes with it; and the words of the poem are the objective correlative to the emotional charge.[33] The poem gives us a height-ened sense both of our experience and of the world. Blake's poem is not an allegory of something that can be stated in different words—as the papacy, in the *Inferno*, could be described in ways other than through the image of a she-wolf.

Analogously, the visions of Swedenborg are not a code for something that can be captured in other terms. Allegories, in the sense of conventional correspondences, are not *visions*. It was the palpably visionary quality of Swe-denborg's writing that appealed to those who looked for a heightened sense of the world, and who desired to see everything in it as alive with a life that could be captured by the imagination.

So there is no contradiction between saying that Swedenborg is thinking and writing symbolically, and holding that his heaven and hell, his visions of the departed spirits, and all his dealings with the spirit world are real and, by him, genuinely believed. It is this constant interplay between vision and corporeal knowledge that accounts for the weird immediacy of Swedenborg's visions—what Kant described as "the most extravagant and queerest of fancies in which all his dreams culminate."[34] The queer extravagance, with the quality of a waking dream proceeds from a fiercely sincere *belief*.

Hence his serene ability both to see heaven and hell as essentially inner states, and at the same time to describe goings-on there in strangely material terms. Someone who wishes to enter heaven but whose inner, spiritual state does not correspond with the part of heaven he wishes to enter finds heaven physically/psychologically impossible: "people who have lived evil lives and who arrive in heaven bring their souls with them and are tormented like fish out of water, in the air, or like animals in the vacuum in air pumps once the air has been pumped out."[35] We have already met hypocrites who are good at hiding their inner nature, but whose faces turn blue if they manage to steal into heavenly communities, because of "their opposition to the life that is flowing in and affecting them" (ibid., 48).

Swedenborg has the good fortune to meet and talk to angels and to be received by them in their beautiful homes (like some favored reporter from *Hello* magazine)—homes that contain chambers, suites, and bedrooms in abundance, and "courtyards with gardens, flower beds, and lawns around them" (ibid.). Some heavenly palaces have upper stories that shine as though they are made of pure gold, and lower ones as of precious gems. (As usual, the *Revelation of St. John* is mainly responsible for the otherwise inexplicable notion that a heaven consisting largely of gold and precious stones would not be an eyesore. There are equally garish parklands with leaves sparkling like silver and fruits like gold [ibid., 185]).

Swedenborg's heaven is obviously not God-centered, in the way in which the heavens of Augustine, of Aquinas and Dante, Luther and Calvin are. Swedenborgian angels lead very busy lives, often in the heavenly bureaucracy, in departments of ecclesiastical, civil, and domestic administration (ibid., 387). They clearly do not spend all their time in rapt contemplation of the beatific vision. There is divine worship in heaven; it does not consist in going to church or hearing sermons, but in "a life of love, thoughtfulness and faith" (ibid., 221–22). However, in order to understand what heavenly church services are like, Swedenborg has occasionally been allowed to go in and hear sermons. He gives a curiously minute description of the physical arrangements of what is very obviously a Protestant place of worship. The preacher is in a pulpit stationed in the east. Directly in front of him sit people who are in greater light of wisdom than others, while to his right and left are people who are in less light. The seating is circular, so there is nobody who escapes the preacher's gaze. No one is allowed to stand behind the pulpit; if anyone does, the preacher loses his train of thought (ibid.). The sermons (as one would have hoped) are very much better than those on earth.

Most angels wear clothes in heaven, and their garments correspond to their spiritual state. Some clothes gleam as though aflame, and others shine soft and white, and some are of many colors. Angels in the innermost heaven are nude, because they are in innocence, and innocence corresponds to nudity (ibid., 229).

Angels are powerful. They can level and overturn mountains, split cliffs from top to bottom, and scatter hundreds of thousands of evil spirits by a pure act of the will. That is why they are called Powers (ibid.). They cannot utter a single word of human language, but they have a language of their own, although there seem to be different dialects as between the different ranks of angels. With the heavenly angels *U* and *O* predominate; but among the spiritual angels, *E* and *I*. When angels "speak" to human beings they do so by letting their meanings flow, first into our thoughts and then into our hearts. Hebrew is the language closest to that spoken by the angels. However, talking with spirits is rarely allowed nowadays because it is dangerous (ibid., 237–49). (He is writing, of course, before the rise of Spiritualism.)

Cheerfulness Always Breaking Through

Swedenborg's heaven is not merely a pleasure palace. It is where human powers are exercised to the utmost. Surprisingly, perhaps, Swedenborg celebrates the potentialities of human nature as convincedly as would a representative man of the Renaissance. He rejects those Christian doctrines that degrade man's nature. He dismisses the idea that infants who die before baptism could be damned. On the contrary (as we have seen) they all become angels. Non-Christians can get to heaven (but possibly not Roman Catholics—Swedenborg was an anti-papist bigot). The seer has an enjoyable conversation with Cicero. Even heathen Chinese may get there. He notices a Chinese who, curiously, appears as, successively, a woolly goat, a cake of millet, an ebony spoon, and, finally, a floating city (ibid., 321, 322, 325). But at least he is there. Heaven, indeed, is easy to enter. All that is required is to live a civic and moral life—and if we do that properly we will ipso facto also be leading a spiritual life. A spiritual life is not something distinct from worldly living—it just is practicing honesty and fairness.

In other words, Swedenborg is an out-and-out Pelagian. Getting to heaven simply means having the motives and intentions that constitute us as spiritual rather than infernal beings. In spiritual beings, love for God, from which decent civic living flows, predominates. Hell is made up of those who are "wholly focused on the pleasures of the body and the flesh because of their love for themselves and love for the world" (ibid., 382a). The (Catholic) tradition of asceticism and contemplation as the highest goods is entirely rejected. Swedenborg has talked after their death to people who during their earthly lives had renounced the world and devoted themselves to the solitary, contemplative life. In reality they had envied those who were happier than they, and had coveted heaven excessively. When they got there, their anxieties upset the happiness of the angels. So they ended up betaking themselves to lonely places where they led the same miserable existences they had done on earth (ibid., 360).

Mortification is bad. There is marriage in heaven, because divine truth and divine good, the source of all intelligence, wisdom, and happiness, flow primarily into marriage love (the word Swedenborg normally uses is *conjugial*).

This means that marriage love is the essential matrix for the divine inflow because this inflow is itself a marriage of the true and the good (ibid., 370). Married love in heaven is extremely pleasurable—Swedenborg once saw it represented by an indescribably lovely young woman enveloped in a white cloud (ibid., 382a). Angelic lovers are united into one being and experience intense bliss. But in place of children, they procreate "what is good and true" (ibid., 382b).[36]

Swedenborg's cheerful ethic of intention, his insistence that the inner state is all that matters, leads him into some sunny complacencies. It has been granted him to know that rich people enter heaven just as easily as do poor people. Indeed, in heaven many of the rich are in greater splendor and happiness than the poor.[37] The Swedenborgian philosophy definitely allows you to take it with you, for the rich in general live in heaven more elegantly than others (ibid., 361). Indeed, the poor may find it harder to enter heaven than the rich, because, unaccountably, in life they are often not contented with their lot, and this draws their thoughts away from future joys (ibid., 364). There is no need to give to the poor "except as the spirit moves us" (ibid., 358).

He is not embarrassed by scriptural texts that seem to suggest the opposite. He interprets the parable of Dives and Lazarus thus: Dives, dressed in rich robes, is the Jewish nation who had God's revelation. The poor person lying in the rich man's gateway who longed to feast on the crumbs that fell from the rich man's table "means the non-Jews who did not have understandings of what is good and true but still longed for them" (ibid., 365). Needless to say, he sets at rest the minds of any who feel troubled by Christ's remark about the camel and the eye of a needle.

This can be seen as a Renaissance view of man, in which the active life is superior to the contemplative one, and enjoyment of the good things of the world to be preferred over a life of self-denial. It has also something of the complacency of an urban myth of the comfortable, if high-minded, bourgeois. A passage in his *Spiritual Diary* reinforces this impression. He is writing about beggars in the next life:

> They who have been long accustomed to begging, and at length have found pleasure therein, so as to contract an aversion to a life of useful labor that they may procure food and the necessities of life, appear, as it were, naked, or only covered with most filthy rags, so botched together as scarcely to conceal their nakedness. They beg alms of everybody whom they meet, employing one with a small vessel to receive it. I hear from them that it is true what is said of beggars, that they desire nothing but money, despising garments and food; that

they live impiously among themselves—in quarrels and similar things, abhorring labor, and sometimes living in all kinds of luxury, despising money, and eagerly enquiring what each has received.[38]

The good things of the world are not gross physical pleasures or the pleasures of egoism, but the more refined delights that can be sought for in a life informed with love and knowledge. Heaven is not a final coming to rest, a place of stasis. It sharply differs from the heaven of Aquinas who thought that motion of itself implied imperfection, so that the final state of beatific vision was also a state of eternal stillness. For Swedenborg, heaven is a state of eternal progress toward the good, not of having finally arrived. He expresses the idea in an eloquent, if relentlessly cheerful, passage—one that uncannily anticipates the modern American doctrine that life begins at some late age:

> People in heaven are continually progressing toward the springtime of life. The more thousands of years they live, the more pleasant and happy is their springtime. This continues for ever, increasing according to the growth and level of their love, thoughtfulness and faith.
>
> As the years pass, elderly women who have died of old age— women who have lived in faith in the Lord, thoughtfulness toward their neighbor, and in contented marriage love with their husbands— come more and more into the flower of growing youth and beauty that surpasses any notion of beauty accessible to our sight.[39]

They are enabled so to develop because the predominant love in our life, our ruling passion, is what makes us the persons we are and is thus able to manifest itself fully in the life to come. The predominant love of wicked people equally finds its fulfillment in the next world. Those who have taken delight in covert plotting live in dark cellars and whisper in each other's ears. "This is what becomes of the pleasures of their love." People who were "filthy misers" live in cubicles "and love the filth of pigs and the foul odors they breath out from half-digested food in their stomachs." Those who in life pandered to the gullet and the belly, loving this as the greatest pleasure in life, end up loving feces and latrines in the next world (ibid., 488). Swedenborg's hell with its evil spirits endlessly repeating actions that symbolize their sin is, at this point, not unlike Dante's. After death we become our love, and people purely of carnal love look "coarse, dim, dark and misshapen" (ibid., 479–81). Conversely, people who have loved divine truths live in sunny uplands, with a springtime climate, looking out over fields ripe for harvest and vineyards. They live in houses of precious stones and pure crystal. The truths from the Word they love "correspond to the harvest fields, vineyards, precious stones, windows and crystals." After death, love remains the same for ever, especially married loves (ibid., 489).

Swedenborg had said that in heaven, the Lord is always before the angels whichever way they look; or they are always facing the east, because their minds are always focused on the Lord, no matter in which direction they turn their faces and bodies (ibid., 143). Yet what is it to be focused on the Lord? Is it to praise him unendingly? In fact, when he writes of the traditional heaven where the blessed are engaged in perpetual worship of God, Swedenborg comes close to satire. In *Conjugial Love*[40] he describes one of his visions, in which an angel takes a party of visitors into a church with a packed congregation. There are guards at the doors to prevent anyone from leaving. This is the second day the worshippers have been there. When Swedenborg looks at them he discovers that most of them are asleep, and those who are awake cannot stop yawning. As a result of keeping their thoughts raised to God all this time, some are wild-eyed, and all are depressed at heart, and weary in the spirit from boredom. They turn their backs on the pulpit and shout out: "Our ears are stunned. Put an end to your sermons . . . the sound of it is beginning to become hateful." They rush the guards on the doors and get outside (ibid., 9). The priests try to get them back into the church, but to no avail.

Then an archbishop and three bishops (at least that is what they had been in their previous lives) turn up and rebuke the priests: "You do not know what glorifying God means; it means bringing forth the fruits of love, that is, faithfully, honestly and painstakingly doing the work demanded by one's occupation. For this is part of loving God and loving the neighbor; it is the bond which holds a community together, and it is the good it performs" (ibid.). The bishops even accuse the priests of insisting on formal divine worship because it brings them honor, glory, and reward.

It is hard to think of any more radical departure from virtually all Christian ideas about a heaven of eternal praise. Without the philosophical scaffolding of Dante and Aquinas, and lacking the varied delights of the Muslim paradise, a heaven of eternal praise has always run the risk of seeming a bore. John Wesley was intermittently interested in Swedenborg but rejected his ideas of heaven as "low, groveling, just suiting a Mahometan paradise."[41] He said of the Swedenborgian hell that "it leaves nothing terrible in it; for, first, he quenches the unquenchable fire . . . then he allows that the governor of it, the devil, sometimes orders the spirits that behave ill to be "laid on a bed of hot ashes." And, secondly, he informs you, that all the damned enjoy their favorite pleasures— "He that delights in filth is to have his filth, yea, and his harlot too!"[42] Wesley stuck stoutly to the belief in uninterrupted praise. Indeed, he was moved to a most uncharitable rejoinder to a "much applauded wit who has lately left the body" and who did not relish "sitting upon a cloud all day long, a singing praise to God." "We may believe him," Wesley darkly comments, "and there is no danger of his being put to that trouble."[43]

Conjugial Love

Swedenborg is certainly not of the cloud-sitting camp. He gives an account of some of the earthly delights of heaven—starting with delicious eating, progressing through sports, and culminating in a marriage ceremony. He depicts some celestial privy councilors and their guests sitting down on padded seats (and wearing breeches and stockings of iridescent silk) at a table on which, around a lofty pyramid of gold, are ranged a hundred dishes on their stands. There are sugared cakes and crystallized grape juice, together with delicacies made of bread and wine. Nectar gushes from the pyramid and automatically fills goblets made of translucent gems. As they help themselves from the various dishes, these automatically refill.[44]

The scene shifts to the outskirts of the celestial town, where boys play at sports such as racquets, and to theatrical performances. Then we find ourselves at a wedding. The bridegroom is dressed in a mantle of gleaming purple. On his head is a miter. The bride is in a red cloak over an embroidered gown, with a golden girdle below the bust, and a crown set with rubies. The groom makes certain pledges, and then tells the bride: "Now you are mine." A merry wedding party follows.

Marriage in heaven is probably at the emotional center of Swedenborg's vision, to which the reality of fields, streets, and parks, angels' houses and palaces, and the different levels of heaven are all subordinate. After death we remain as real, human persons, and hence we are fully male and female. Each of us keeps his (her) own love after death. For most people on earth, their strongest love is sexual. But those who reach heaven are they who have become spiritual on earth, and their chief love is "conjugial love."

What exactly does Swedenborg mean by *conjugial* love? He frequently contrasts it with sexual love and also suggests that it is love experienced only by a minority. And conjugial love is chaste. Does this mean it is platonic?

The question is put to some angels by a group of spirits—mostly young men, of course—who have just arrived in heaven and are having a look round. They want to know about sex in heaven (ibid., 44). Indeed, when they speak to the angels, their eyes glitter with the spark of sexual desire. The angels tell them that all the women in heaven are of unparalleled beauty and all the young men models of good character. The youthful arrivals ask whether in heaven sexual love is possible (remembering that Jesus had said that in heaven there will be no giving in marriage, but we shall all be as the angels of God). The reply is not entirely clear: "*Your* sort of sexual love is impossible, but there is angelic sexual love, which is chaste and free from all the allures of lust." That makes the young men groan: "How boring heavenly joy must be.... Is not such love barren and lifeless?"

The angel assures them that sexual love among the angels is full of the most intimate delights and invades parts of the mind and body that no other affection can reach. It is the very model of heavenly sweetness because it is pure. (One imagines that the angel might blush here, as does Raphael when he hints to Adam and Eve of the pleasures of angelic sexual intercourse.)[45]

Unsurprisingly, the young men are unconvinced: "What can chaste sexual love be but love stripped of its living essence?" The angels at this point become indignant and insist that true conjugial love is confined to one person of the opposite sex to the exclusion of all others, and is a love of the spirit leading to love of body, not the other way around. Crucially, it also includes the "ultimate delights" of married love. The only difference is that instead of children, it propagates via its ultimate delights spiritual offspring, which are love and wisdom. Furthermore, angels have an extraordinary potency with their wives, a potency that will grow throughout eternity.[46]

After death, then, we are ourselves, and we exist in our bodies—but bodies that are transmuted into a form suitable to spirits and then angels. These bodies are real. Indeed, the body as reworked in heaven is the real body, the body that fully expresses its intrinsic spiritual reality. Similarly with conjugial love: it is a love that has fulfilled its true—i.e., spiritual-nature. *Scortatory* love does not fulfill love's true character, because it is not essentially directed toward one person. True marriages transcend death. False, earthly marriages are broken off soon after death and eventually in heaven spirits find their true soul mates, whom they will love conjugially through all eternity.

We could interpret Swedenborg here as meditating on the difference of emotions in animals and in human beings. There are passions in animals and human beings, which seem strongly to resemble each other. Yet it could be said that the human version of the passion takes on a quite different character just because it is the passion of a rational being. So what might be the maternal instinct in a cow is, in human nature, a mother's love for her child. A mother who loves her child has, in one sense, the same passion as a cow that may bellow after her calf when it has been weaned. But a cow does not *love* her calf as a mother loves her child. Argo, the faithful hunting dog of Odysseus, pined away for its absent master and died as soon as he set eyes on him again. But the mother of Odysseus, Anticleia, died of grief for her son: "Nor did any disease come upon me, such as oftenest through grievous wasting takes the spirit from the limbs; nay, it was longing for thee, and for thy counsels, glorious Odysseus, and for thy tender-heartedness, that robbed me of honey-sweet life."[47]

We can express the difference between animal and human passion by saying that a human being has a particular sort of awareness of the object of his emotion. Love, in a human being, has a certain lucidity. It is not true to say that love is blind. Although explanations come to a stop as to why I love this particular person rather than that one, it is nevertheless true that my love is conscious of the character of its object. The lover finds, at least, things to say about what he loves in his beloved. If this were not so, we could not have the corpus of love literature that we do: "My beloved is like a roe or young hart . . . his legs [are] as of pillars of marble, that are set upon bases of gold. His form is as of Libanus, excellent as the cedars." Or: "A garden enclosed is my sister, my spouse; a spring shut up, a fountain sealed."[48] The lovers in using these words are presenting to themselves the objects of their love and giving their love a character. Love that did not or could not do this would have lost much of its character as *human* love. Awareness of beauty is part of human love. The lover finds something to say about the personal qualities of the beloved. Attraction to physical beauty may be the beginning of attraction to personal qualities—a love that remained fixed on the purely physical and went no further would hardly be human love. Sexual love reaches its full expression when it encompasses the qualities of character and mind of the beloved. It encompasses, in other words, the beloved as subject as well as object. A love that stopped short of doing this would lack essential qualities of the human, because human love is directed at a person. Insofar as what Swedenborg calls "scortatory" (i.e., purely sexual love) is not directed to a person, it stands for a love that shrinks back from its final end. Swedenborg expresses this beautifully: "In a human being conjugial love is in sexual love, like a gem in its native rock."[49]

This also derives from Swedenborg's doctrine of correspondences. The body is a signifier of a corresponding spiritual world. Behind lust, and semi-concealed by it, is the spiritual (or spirit) world of conjugial love. Conjugial love is not deprived of its erotic content. Rather, in its being purified from the taint of promiscuity that characterizes scortatory love, its true, powerful form emerges. The correspondence that gives it its character is a correspondence with the good and the true. For Swedenborg, man's love corresponds especially with the true; woman's love with the good. Man's love is truth flowing from the good, and woman's love is the good flowing from the true. That is the ultimate character of conjugial love between the sexes. Although sexual love is common to human beings and animals, conjugial love is found in human beings alone (ibid., 94–99). It corresponds to Christ's love of his church (ibid.

chap. 4, 62–63). It is worth remembering that a traditional Christian reading of the Song of Songs saw its eroticism as an allegory of Christ's love for his church, and this interpretation was dominant until historical criticism began to develop in the eighteenth century.

Conjugial love therefore gives us the truest picture of the heavenly state. Similarly, the truest picture of hell is a picture of those incapable of rising to conjugial love, unable to live as celestial lovers. They remain, instead, among the lower beings of the world, their forms of lust having as their correspondences crocodiles, dragons, and leopards (ibid., chap. 4, 79). It is in married love alone that the entire system of correspondences between the natural and spiritual worlds finds its focal point.

Sexual mysticism, in many of its varieties, from Blake to D. H. Lawrence, can be traced to Swedenborgianism. Swedenborg's peculiar version of philosophical Idealism had something in common with the Romantic movement and appealed to several Romantic writers. There is little doubt, though, that Swedenborg both generalized and eviscerated the historic Christian message. He may have found psychological equivalents for the love of God and of Christ, and have given some idea of sin, and consequently hell, as a withdrawal from unselfish love. But there is no real place for original sin, man's consequent innate depravity, nor the need for Christ's saving sacrifice. Swedenborgianism undermines anything like the orthodox view of heaven as an enjoyment of the presence of God, for, although conjugial love is explained ultimately by Christ's love for his church, what really emerges is an exaltation of *eros*, and an overwhelming emphasis on erotic love between two individuals who, in the next life, become as one. It is true that the whole heavenly community is swallowed up, in theory, in Christ, who sometimes embodies it in his own person. But God as an object of our attention, as something that transcends ourselves, has largely dropped out of sight.

Wesley grudgingly admitted that Swedenborg "had strong and beautiful thoughts and may be read with profit by a serious and cautious reader."[50] Such a reader might regard Swedenborgianism as a "probable impossibility."[51] Swedenborg's reasoning by correspondences has a venerable history in the interpretation of scripture and as part of a traditional religious consciousness. The firmament "declares the glory of God." There is a consistency that resembles the calm working out of consequences from certain premises—above all from the doctrine of correspondences. Even his regular and weirdly matter-of-fact visits to the spirit world and his conversations with angels have nothing of mystery-mongering about them. It could all be mad, but it is the madness of the dreamer of dreams and the seer of visions. They are related in the clear light of day.

Swedenborg brings out implications of the Renaissance and Protestant conviction that a life of activity is superior to one of contemplation. Perhaps this is the only sort of heaven that a Protestant ought logically to countenance—one in which the active virtues are paramount and which represents a purified version of a cheerful active society as it ought ideally to be in this life.

It would be possible, up to a point, rationally to reconstruct Swedenborgianism and thus play down its prophetic and visionary elements—even though these plainly make up by far the greater part of his writings. One could see him as mapping psychologically and metaphysically the human good, better, and worse states of consciousness. It would not be a gross distortion to see his doctrine as being, ultimately, about persons, and the nature of their deepest relations to each other. Stripped of its theological and metaphysical scaffolding, as well as its multitude of curious anecdotes, this doctrine becomes thin, relentlessly optimistic, and repetitively expressed. But in a creative writer such as Blake it clearly does have elements of what T. S. Eliot saw as the naked vision. Goethe was not wrong in seeing Swedenborg as one who was impregnated with the joys of heaven, to whom the spirits spoke through all the senses and the entire body; and in thinking that if ever angels did inhabit the human bosom, they might very well have chosen that of the Swedish spirit seer.

16

With Easy Intercourse Pass
To and Fro

The Birth of Spiritualism

Christian belief about the afterlife has always centered on the words
in the parable of Dives and Lazarus: "Between us and you there is a
great gulf fixed" (Luke 16:26). The conviction that eternity for all of us
is determined by what we do in this life, and that nothing after
death—with the possible exception, in Roman and Orthodox tradition,
of prayers and masses or other good works offered up for the faithful
departed—can effect our eternal destiny has defined life's drama
as seen by the church (as well as by the mosque). The traditional
theological defense of the eternity of infernal punishment drew on the
idea that after death the will is fixed; it is no longer possible to repent,
to reform, to be converted, to alter one's ingrained character.
Dante's damned sinners constantly repeat in death the sorts of action
to which their earthly vices habituated them.

As we saw, Swedenborgianism undermined this by blurring the
boundaries between life and death. Swedenborg crosses back and
forth (in spirit, at least) between the two realms on occasions almost
too numerous to count. The inhabitants of the spirit world—i.e., the
dead who have not yet definitively become angels—are for a while
not even aware that they have died. That there is no great gulf, that
the two worlds are permeable with only thin partitions dividing the
living from the dead, that the dead can be thought of a being "in the
next room," in effect defines the modern notion of heaven, as does

the idea of the possibility of permanent growth in the next life.[1] The ancient fear of permeability, which made the Mesopotamians anxious to be sure that the dead were securely locked up in the underworld, has turned into the benign idea that the dead are really quite like the living, that death is continuous with life, or even that death does not really occur at all.

We can also trace to Swedenborg the idea that an eternity spent praising God would be unutterably *boring*. What we can hope to do in heaven is to pursue our favorite pastimes—which will be the best means of improving spiritually. Although Swedenborg himself was God-intoxicated, those influenced by his doctrines tended to treat God as a sort of optional extra.

A second development that grows ultimately out of Swedenborgianism, but mingled with ideas of science, is Spiritualism—the attempt regularly, systematically, and using empirical methods, to communicate with the dead.

An unconscious Swedenborgianism entered the mainstream imagination almost without resistance in a book that was immensely popular in America, England, and other English-speaking countries in the late nineteenth century. *The Gates Ajar*, by Elizabeth Stuart Phelps, first published in 1869, sold 180,000 copies here and in America and went into fifty-five editions.It answered a spiritual need in the United States after the losses suffered by so many families during the Civil War—just as Spiritualism answered a similar need in Britain after the First World War.

The Gates Ajar takes the form of the spiritual diary of a young woman whose beloved brother, Royal, has been killed in battle. The young woman, Mary Cabot, refuses all comfort, doubts God's providence and even his goodness, and rebels against the orthodox teaching of an austerely God-centered, hymn-singing heaven as expounded by her local pastor. She is finally saved by Aunt Winifred, who comes to live with her, and who inculcates in her a belief in a different sort of heaven, one where the pleasures and activities of this world are not devalued—in other words, something like the heaven of Emanuel Swedenborg.

The Gates Ajar has some pretty easy satire at the expense of traditional Christian teaching. The pastor, the Reverend Bland, preaches that the "employments of heaven" will consist solely in studying the character of God: "[Bland] enlarged upon this.... There was something about adoration and the harpers harping with their harps, and the sea of glass, and crying, Worthy the Lamb! And a great deal more that bewildered and disheartened me."[2] Bland teaches that, in comparison with God, all other delights will pall. He quotes with approval a man who, on being asked whether he hopes to see in heaven the wife of his youth, replies: "I expect to be so overwhelmed by the glory of the presence of God, that it may be thousands of years before I shall think of my wife."

Aunt Winifred figures as an intellectually superior woman who can always confound the good pastor with an apt quotation from scripture, or, where that is lacking, from the latest German scholar. She does not mention Swedenborg save to deny—unconvincingly—that she is a Swedenborgian. Yet the Swedish seer is behind every idea in the book—that the dead brother is not gone but only "out of sight"; that we become angels in the next life; that a spirit body is enclosed within the material one. Death is simply the slipping off of the outer body as a husk slips from its kernel. She even quotes a Professor George Bush to the effect that it takes a material body, a spiritual body, and a soul to make a man—which is interesting in that it is just about a revival of the beliefs of the ancient Egyptians.[3]

In heaven there will be mountains, trees, flowers, eating, and drinking; and houses—not houses made of oak and pine and nailed together but a more spiritual, Platonic idea of a house.[4] Aunt Winifred causes scandal when she tells a girl in the Sunday school she teaches that she will be able to have her piano in the next world—arguing, logically enough, that if there are harps, there is no good reason to exclude other musical instruments. Indeed, she promises symphonic performances, no doubt under the best of the dead conductors.

Phelps pokes fun at the idea of a spiritual heaven by having it defended by a (more or less literally) clodhopping farmer in the middle of his potato field. He is a deacon of the Reverend Bland's church. The passage is worth quoting for its hilariously unconscious snobbery:

> "What *do* you suppose people will do in heaven?" she asked again.
>
>   "Glorify God," said the Deacon . . . glorify God, and sing Worthy the Lamb! We shall be clothed in white robes with palms in our hands . . . such employments as befit sinless creatures in a spiritooal [*sic*] state of existence."
>
>   "Now, Deacon Quirk," replied Aunt Winifred, looking him over from head to foot,—old straw hat, calico shirt, blue overalls, and cowhide boots, coarse, work-worn hands . . . "just imagine yourself, will you? Taken out of this life this minute as you stand here in your potato field . . . with a green branch in one hand and a singing book in another."

Instead, there is going to be a decidedly *haut bourgeois* heaven, in which the Heine-quoting Aunt Winifred will be thoroughly at home. Instead of simple farmers singing Worthy the Lamb! there will be symphony concerts and educational trips to Jupiter. To be fair, Aunt Winifred does allow that the transition to the next life will purify Quirk of his grossness and wonderfully refine him. There may even be some kinds of agricultural employment, or even some sorts of machinery for a mechanically minded American peasantry to improve upon.[5]

The chief appeal of this thin little book must indeed have been that it offered its readers a painless transition to a better world, with no fear of hellfire, a world where they would meet their loved ones and carry on with an improved version of the lives of the better sort.

The other main legacy of Swedenborg, Spiritualism, also imagines a next life that is a continuation of the present one. It, too, offers hope that the transition between the two worlds will be easy, and that there is no fear of postmortem punishments. Its chief innovation is that it offers an empirical method for getting in touch, systematically, with the dead. In its palmiest years, Spiritualism penetrated high society and attracted the serious attention of distinguished minds. The beginnings of Spiritualism can be dated with remarkable accuracy. On March 31, 1848, two children, Katie and Maggie Fox, aged twelve and fourteen respectively, decided to play a trick on their devout Methodist parents in their house in Hydesville, New York. The family had only recently moved into the house, which had the reputation of being haunted. The children decided to frighten the rest of the family into believing that this was so. They found that they were able, by snapping and cracking their fingers and toes, to set off strange knocking noises in various parts of the house. The parents would ask the "spirits" their children's ages—and raps would duly be heard giving the correct ages, including the age of a child who had died in infancy. The Fox parents were completely deceived; news of the supernatural happenings spread, and modern Spiritualism was born. Their much older sister, a Mrs. Underhill, turned up and took them on a tour of the United States, attracting the "most prominent theologians, physicians and professional men of all kinds, as well as great crowds everywhere." Forty years later the girls publicly admitted to the hoax—but few took any notice. Mrs. Underhill, indeed, flew into a passion and told Katie that she wished to establish a new religion, and that she had always received spirit messages herself. The Fox manifestations went on being quoted by leading apologists for Spiritualism well into the twentieth century.[6]

The importance of raps and knocks is one of the curious things about Spiritualism. Then there are tables that turn, stand on end, move about the room, and levitate. This was not how the dead were anciently seen to have communicated, but something entirely new. It gave Spiritualism a character that it has retained ever since—an indoor performance, mysterious noises resembling telegraphic messages in Morse code, the sense that the other world is separated from us by a wall. It is singular that the whole fashion of the cult should have been set by a couple of girls cracking their joints.

Only a few years later, in 1854, still more marvelous events took place in Massachusetts, at the house of Josiah Gridley.[7] Gridley, while adopting these newly discovered essential tools of modern spiritualism—rappings, knockings, table-turning, and the medium—mixed it with good old-fashioned, malicious spirits. Gridley's medium is an "illiterate" young man, chosen because out of the many thousands of rappings and knockings heard in the house during the séances, a vast number occur around the chair in which the young man sits.

The Gridley manifestations did not represent the future of Spiritualism precisely in that they are suffused with an old-fashioned sense of the presence of evil. Much of the opening part of the book describes the devil's persistent attempts to get hold of people, and his being rendered impotent by a pure Presbyterian female. The young "illiterate" who is chosen to be the medium represents the forces of good. The table-turnings represent the "commence-ment of the battle of the Great Day of God" with the forces of evil. The heavenly host is "commissioned to train and perfect mediums and circle in goodness and purity all over the earth" while on the other hand all the wicked upon the earth—including "the bigots of the churches"—will combine with "Apostate Spirits . . . [to] encompass the Camp of the Saints" (ibid., 21).

Two of the Apostate Spirits, Joshua and Jane, set themselves to make life difficult for the medium. Evil spirits enter into people by a jet of electromagne-tism (ibid., 65). With his feet Joshua strikes the young man in the pit of the stomach, and by utilizing the power of electricity "palsies" his heart and lungs, and completely immobilizes him. Jane has less electromagnetic power, and contents herself merely with pinching the foot of Gridley's daughter (ibid., 25).

In life, Joshua had been a bestial fellow and an alcoholic. And as, in Pope's words, the "love of Ombre" survives into the next world in the spirits of fashionable ladies,[8] so Joshua takes his addiction to the bottle into the next world ("his love of rum in the former [life] was by no means diminished by his transfer to the world of spirits"). Fortunately for him, he can satisfy his cravings by entering the body of "any drunken brute."

Gridley is not only a spiritual descendant of good Massachusetts Puritans (whose devout belief in evil spirits gave rise to the Salem witch hunts) but also a medical man. His interest in the Beyond is, therefore, a curious mixture of his religious and medical preoccupations:

"Neighbor Strong,—you died of pulmonary disease? "Yes." Did you suffer in your lungs after you left the body? "Certainly I did, and though it is now about twenty years since, I am still shorter in breath than if my lungs had always been sound. I enjoy what I call good health and sound lungs, but it would put me out of breath to travel with friend Bryant, as fast as he could go with ease."[9] (It should be noted that friend Bryant, according to his own postmortem testimony, normally achieves a rate of sixty feet per second.)

Gridley interrogates a female spirit, Lavinia, who had died of consumption, and is now in the Fifth Circle (where the "stings of death are plucked away"): "are your lungs sound? "In the fifth degree we outgrow our diseases much faster than they do who are in the lower degrees. I think my lungs are nearly, if not quite sound. . . . I used to sing on earth, and do so here; but I cannot use the organs of your Medium for that purpose. I am not strong enough in the vital parts" (ibid., 50).

Gridley also performs a medical examination on a laborer who had died after being dragged by a locomotive, his head striking sleeper after sleeper. His spiritual body took ten hours to separate from his material one because the material and spiritual heads were smashed into one another. Though it is now five years since the injury, his head has ever been and is still tender (ibid., 51).

Hundreds of spirits visit the Gridley household—including Lafayette and George Washington. Washington mentions that he thinks that the disputes leading to the War of Independence could not have been settled peacefully. The evil spirits employ all their powers of electromagnetism to attack the unfortunate medium: "The current was so strong that full twenty times it has punctured the skin, as the buttons of the battery are known to do when it is run with great power, the whole size of the Medium's hand . . . so that the bloody serum would ooze out and form a scab in three minutes" (ibid., 71).

It is a curious medley. The spirits are frequently, if oddly, malign. There certainly is a throwback to Salem and the powers of evil. At the same time there are those features typical of modern Spiritualism—the "scientific" interest in electromagnetism and mesmerism; the tables moving; the interrogations about the exact current state of health of the departed. There is a definite anticipation of one of the most characteristic phenomena of Spiritualism— the unsurprisingness of the messages from the Beyond. Did it need a spirit, come from the grave in the shape of George Washington, to uphold the orthodox American belief—that the War of Independence was inevitable?

A New Revelation?

Indeed, it is the attempted union of the paranormal (to use a phrase popularized in the early twentieth century to avoid the connotations of "supernatural") with everyday experience that most clearly marks the Spiritualist movement of the period as something new. Beginning as an American craze, once imported into England not only did it appeal to ordinary people, but it soon captured many of the upper middle classes and the nobility who wanted empirical confirmation of faith, comfort in bereavement, and also the assurance that they were giving their allegiance to something intellectually, morally, and even theologically respectable. The combination of these needs with this insistence on intellectual respectability turned Spiritualism into a serious movement, even an alternative religion.

The sense that a whole new world of energy—psychic energy, which was often assumed to have some connection with electricity—was about to be untapped, or was even now being untapped, was a strong theme. The medium would be a sort of wireless receiver picking up impulses from the spiritual ether. This sudden new discovery of a benevolent power that had lain there all around us for millennia scarcely noticed, was exhilarating. (Spiritualism of course antedates the invention of radio). Astonishing claims were made for the new faith. Sir Arthur Conan Doyle, creator of Sherlock Holmes (whom one could imagine investigating Spiritualistic phenomena with well-directed skepticism), was an enthusiastic propagandist for Spiritualism. Critics might claim that the phenomena produced by the mediums and their spirit guides were trivial, centering as they did on rappings, table-turning, and automatic writing. Sir Arthur's response is that this was true of many scientific advances. Did not the fall of a humble apple herald the discovery of gravity? Did not the twitching of frogs' legs in a laboratory open up "the train of thought and experiment which gave us electricity"? Did not the boiling of a kettle lead to the steam-engine? (ibid.).

The manifestations that Sir Arthur appealed to as the equivalent of the twitching of frogs' legs happened to be the rappings, snappings, and crackings of Katie and Maggie Fox (which were indeed produced by tendons and muscles in the legs), or, as Sir Arthur put it, "the lowly manifestations of Hydesville [which] have ripened into results which have engaged the finest group of intellects in this country during the last twenty years, and which are destined, in my opinion, to bring about far the greatest development of human experience which the world has ever seen" (ibid.).

Table-tilting, through which spirit-communication was supposed to be achieved, became one of the special characteristics of the new movement. The tables certainly seemed to take on a life of their own: "The table rocked to and fro with a pleased motion. . . . The table now seemed to wish to get into Lady Lodge's lap, and made most caressing movements to and fro, as if it could not get close enough to her. . . . It found a corner of the skirting board, where it could lodge one foot about six inches from the ground. It then raised the other three level with it in the air; and this it did many times, seeming delighted with its new trick. . . . They enjoyed the joke together, and the table shook as if laughing."[10] Tables certainly had a central place in the affections of the Spiritualist movement. Perhaps one ought to say that they had a particular affection *for* the Spiritualist movement: "A table can exhibit hesitation, it can seek for information, it can welcome a newcomer, it can indicate joy or sorrow, fun or gravity, it can keep time with a song as if joining in the chorus and most noticeably of all it can exhibit affection in an unmistakable manner."[11] (The table indeed seems moved by a desire for what the magazine, *Private Eye*, describes as a "leg-over.")

It is certainly true that the immense claims made by Spiritualism, both as a science and a new religion, attracted the loyalty or at least the sustained interest of an astonishing array of distinguished people from the arts and sciences, from philosophy, from public life in the nineteenth and early twentieth centuries. If we put together members of the Society for Psychical Research and known sympathizers of Spiritualism (who often, of course, overlapped), we find that they include Ruskin; Elizabeth Barrett Browning (but certainly not her husband, Robert Browning); the King's College, Cambridge don and socialite, Oscar Browning; the Reverend Charles Lutwidge Dodgson—alias Lewis Carroll; John Addington Symons; W. E. Gladstone; Arthur Balfour; Oscar Wilde and Mrs. Oscar Wilde; Sir Frederick Leighton; the Ranee of Sarawak; William James; the Cambridge philosophers C. D. Broad and Henry Sidgwick; F. W. H. Myers; Gilbert Murray; Janet; Lombroso; Bergson; Goldsworthy Lowes Dickinson; Sir Arthur Conan Doyle; and W. B. Yeats. The Society for Psychical research, largely Cambridge-based, brought out a yearly journal of *Proceedings*, which detailed the activities of earnest and distinguished men and women who conscientiously spent the night in haunted houses, attended séances and table-turnings, scrutinized the gnomic messages given in automatic writing, and attempted to outwit mediums possessed of a cunning undreamed of by unworldly dons and their wives.

Indeed, the *Proceedings* were compromised from the beginning by the scarcely concealed faith of these would-be objective investigators. The immensely distinguished Henry Sidgwick, president of the Society for Psychical Research for some years, set the tone in an inaugural address: "That the dispute as to the reality of these marvelous phenomena [i.e., thought-reading, clairvoyance, mesmerism "and the mass of obscure phenomena commonly known as Spiritualistic"],—of which it is quite impossible to exaggerate the scientific importance, if only a tenth part of what has been alleged by generally credible witnesses could be shown to be true,—I say it is a scandal that the dispute as to the reality of these phenomena should still be going on."[12]

Spiritualism was to change the world; it was a new revelation, which would turn life upside down. Christianity itself must change by accommodating to it,

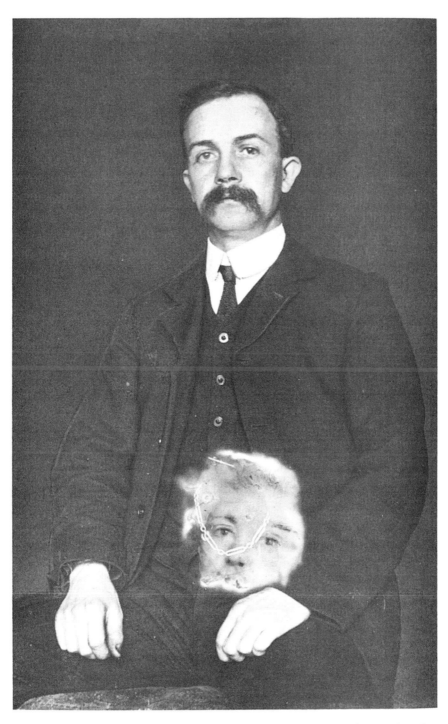

An ectoplasmic emanation from the spirit world. From Cyril Permutt, *Photographing the Spirit World* (Aquarian Press, 1988).

or perish.[13] Spiritualism would transform utterly our understanding of death, turning the experience of it into something really rather pleasant ("The departed all agree that passing is usually both easy and painless, and followed by an enormous reaction of peace and ease).[14] It would confirm the existence of angels and the Roman Catholic doctrine of purgatory, but not hell, which would drop out of consideration (ibid., 69–70). Above all—and this is the enduring source of Spiritualism's appeal in a consciously scientific age—it makes religion "no longer a matter of faith, but of actual experience" (ibid., 51). Doubting Thomas wanted to put his finger into Christ's side; Spiritualist believers will hear the tappings and rappings of the dead, their voices transmitted through the Spiritualist medium; they will feel the astonishing force of the levitating table and, if especially privileged, will see the spirits of the deceased issuing in the form of "ectoplasm" from the medium's mouth or other orifices.

Some of the most eminent Spiritualists in the early twentieth century had lost sons in the Great War. Among these were Sir Arthur Conan Doyle himself and Sir Oliver Lodge, author of a book called *Raymond, or Life and Death* (1916), which took the form largely of spirit letters from his dead son. He believed the book to contain unanswerable evidence that the dead survive and communicate. Spiritualist propagandists and believers of the period return repeatedly to the hideous tragedy of the First World War. Very many of those seeking consolation from the mediums are parents bereaved in the conflict.

Sir Arthur Conan Doyle believed that the war, with its unparalleled casualties, had itself caused a "breaking down of walls between two worlds, a direct, undeniable message from beyond, a call of hope and guidance to the human race at the time of its deepest affliction." It is a new revelation in course of delivery to the human race, the greatest since the Protestant Reformation (ibid., 49–50, 131).

The new revelation was cavalier with centuries of Christian doctrine—although virtually all the Spiritualists professed themselves to be Christians. Conan Doyle's explorations of the spirit world persuaded him that certain doctrines needed to be, at the very least, modified. Indeed, virtually all of the characteristic Christian teachings are to be swept away in the face of the New Revelation. Sir Arthur finds no evidence of a Fall and concludes that there can therefore be no such thing as the atonement, redemption, original sin. Too much has been made of Christ's death—after all, plenty of people die for their convictions: "Thousands of our lads are doing it at this instant in France." No, it is Christ's life that we should concentrate on—"a life full of easy tolerance for others, of kindly charity, of broad-minded moderation, of gentle courage, always progressive and open to new ideas . . . although he did occasionally lose his temper" (ibid., 72–73). Hell "drops out altogether, as it has long dropped out of the thoughts of every reasonable man" (ibid., 89–90).

What, then, is the content of this new and momentous revelation? What do we learn about the Beyond? How is this great new power—"the greatest new development in the history of mankind" (ibid., 131–32)—to manifest itself? What is the new wisdom?

It undeniably disappoints. The teachings of the spirits mix the truistic with the eccentric. The Reverend William Stainton Moses, member of the Society for Psychical Research, wrote a book containing nearly three hundred pages of messages from different spirits. They agree in deprecating war—"the product of your lust for gain, your ambition, your angry, proud, vengeful passions . . . Bad! All bad!"[15] They abhor addiction to the bottle, which leads to "the unpardonable sin"— "Round the gin-shops of your cities, dens of vice, haunted by miserable besotted wretches . . . hover the spirits who in the flesh were lovers of drunkenness and debauchery" (ibid., 27). They suggest that Spiritualism will reform Christianity just as Christ reformed ancient Judaism (ibid., 143). And they deprecate the vicious tendency of Bank Holidays and other national festivals. The celebrated (and by then deceased) medium, Daniel Dunglas Home, gets in touch but makes the mistake of choosing Epsom Downs on Derby Day on which to do so. He explains that he has difficulty in coming through, because on that day of low festivities, spirit communications are interfered with by antagonistic spirits who hover over the "vast masses whose passion of cupidity is excited to an enormous degree" and who are stimulated by the presence of thousands of bodies "wildly excited by intoxicating drinks." Not that the spirits are against all bodily pleasures. They advocate a Third Way: "A body wasted by fasting is not in any way profitable: but neither is a body which is clogged by over-indulgence" (ibid., 44). The spirits tend to mix the trite with the dogmatic: "All truth is mixed with error"; "The mutilation of the body does not harm the spirit, except by the rude shock" (ibid., 214–15).

Conan Doyle reveals through his spirits that death is usually both easy and painless. The deceased often do not know that they are dead (an idea, of course, of Swedenborg's). Although their new and amazing experience tends to preoccupy them, they nevertheless try immediately after death to appear to and kiss the lips of those they love.[16] The terrors of death, then, are removed, while family pieties remain.

Although the dead can and do communicate with the living by means of automatic writing, one should not expect them to do this assiduously, for they have better things to do and enjoy.[17] A certain Miss Julia Ames passed over and in her enthusiasm for keeping in touch with the world she had left behind, proposed setting up a Bureau of Communication. But after fifteen years she admitted that the other spirits were simply not interested, since by then their own loved ones had all passed over as well (ibid., 96). A wife learns from her deceased husband that a pet dog that had unaccountably vanished had passed over to join him, because "All things which love us and are necessary to our happiness in the world are with us here" (ibid., 157). (This would, of course, give heart to lovers of money in this life who may have been disturbed by Christ's remarks about the camel and the eye of a needle.)

Religious skeptics of a positivistic cast of mind have always suggested that a belief in immortality is simply wish fulfillment. Yet when one looks at the history of such beliefs, we see that they are much more complex. There is fear at least as much as hope. Indeed, the imagination of suffering and punishment in a future state has probably terrified more people throughout the ages than the hope of heavenly bliss has consoled. Hell has been more imaginable than heaven. But Spiritualism has been different. The future life is not urgently related to our moral performance in this one. Life is no drama in which we make the momentous choices that determine our eternal destiny. The agony of death is not a prelude to rebirth for the virtuous. There *is* no agony of death. Death is pleasant, not a thing of terror. Our passage into the next world is gradual, almost imperceptible, not a shocking dissolution of our bonds with all we know. Nobody is damned—hell indeed "drops out altogether."

There is no energy in the apprehension of the Beyond, or in this gentle stream of wishful thinking. Although much of the doctrine derives from Swedenborg, there is none of his vividness, no surprising and odd revelations etched with the clear eye of the seer. Instead, the deceased try to get in touch with the living either through code messages or what most resembles a poor telephone line. (Indeed, the dead seem to be reduced to the faintly gibbering spirits, or *eidola*, of Homer.) The laboriously tapped-out messages in automatic writing are obscure, fragmentary, and commonplace. Daniel Dunglas Home— probably the most famous medium in the history of Spiritualism—would receive messages ranging from "God is love" to "Remember, Dan must not sit on a silk cushion while this hot weather lasts."[18]

Dons among the Spirits

From the beginning, the whole Spiritualist setup was singular. So used have we become to the medium, tables that hover, weave, and dive, messages through rappings, knockings, and automatic writing, ectoplasmic materializations, that we may forget that these are, essentially, new phenomena. Ghosts appeared in the past in all sorts of ways and in all sorts of places—in open fields, on housetops, in the sky, groaning, rattling their chains or whatever. They often spoke *in propria persona* rather than through the voice of someone else. They appeared in dreams—as they rarely do in Spiritualist manifestations. A medium was not usually necessary, except when this took the obvious form of witchcraft, as with the three weird sisters and Macbeth, or the witch of En-dor raising the spirit of Samuel.

Ghosts and spirits are culture-specific. Spiritualism sets up its own, singular, ghost culture. The medium is in control, and would not be in control if the spirits communicated in the open or in dreams. The medium is conjuror, magician, priest, shaman. What is astonishingly obvious is that virtually all of the manifestations—the table-turning, the automatic writing, the rapping, the ectoplasm—have the *form* (whether or not this represents the reality) of conjuror's tricks. Quite obviously, the medium is on stage; but in this case, the audience is expected genuinely to believe in the illusions rather than simply to enjoy the entertainment. That the mediums so obviously play the part of members of the Magic Circle, yet demand not to be seen through, could strike one as a piece of glorious impertinence. If you want to be believed, why surround yourself with all the paraphernalia of stage conjuring-tricks?

And the members of the Society for Psychical Research—Cambridge dons and their wives, well educated but innocent, devoted to painfully laborious empirical procedures—had no idea that what might be needed for this sort of investigation are skills of a quite different order: those possessed by magicians, conjurors, and fraudulent practitioners who know all the tricks of the trade.

This shows itself from the beginning. In volume 1 of the *Proceedings*, a committee, which includes Mrs. Henry Sidgwick, reports on a haunted house. A young artist had been painting the portrait of a spirit that had appeared to him more than a hundred times (more sittings than even Lucien Freud would require.) The committee reported that it was impossible to doubt the good faith of the artist, since "he was perfectly clear in his account." That he actually saw what he described "is a matter which, in our judgment, did not admit of doubt."[19]

Since it is impossible to doubt the veracity of the artist, who had depicted "a young man...with the right arm torn away from the shoulder, and a strangely mournful, pleading expression in the eyes" (a very natural consequence of his condition, one might have thought), and since the committee members are cautious empiricists, they conclude that the vision must have been "an hallucination arising from some morbid condition of the subject." They simply do not take seriously the possibility that it is a hoax.

This readiness to be certain that "the circumstances were such as to preclude all possibilities of deception" is found again and again. True, they sometimes detect, or at least report the detection of fraud. They accept a report that shows that the famous Theosophist seer, Madame Blavatsky, arranged a secret panel in a shrine in Madras through which fake letters from a spirit "Mahatma" could be introduced. They accept, also, the report by a defector that one of Blavatsky's astral journeys did not take place. They laboriously assemble, over two hundred pages, evidence that flowers miraculously showered on devotees from a spirit Mahatma on a balcony were faked.[20]

Yet the overwhelming probability that the mass of startling phenomena they investigate is most economically to be explained by fraud seems rarely to occur to them. Instead, they look, first, to natural causes, but are often impatient to find paranormal ones. F. W. H. Myers, a pillar of the Society for Psychical Research, was adept at cloaking with scientific-sounding terminology his undoubted faith in ghosts: "Let us attempt...a truer definition [of ghosts.] Instead of describing a 'ghost' as a dead person permitted to communicate with the living, let us define it as *a manifestation of persistent personal energy,*—or, as an indication that some kind of force is being exercised after death which is in some way connected with a person previously known on earth."[21]

The personal energy so persistently manifested seems rather often to have been that of a skillful medium, for the spirits are addicted to parlor tricks: "a pair of salad tongs of Sèvres manufacture [was] brought from the drawing room through two closed doors."[22] "Dickie [a spirit] brought a small croquet ball from the next room and a handful of lozenges from the bedroom.... Imperator [an important spirit] had sent the manifesting spirit to fetch the articles in order to show Dr. Thomson the power."[23] A second display follows of "some Guimaave lozenges from my bedroom, four dominoes from a box in the dining room, and a heavy clip with receipted bills from Dr. Thomson's room." Presumably Dr. Thomson was convinced.

Three investigators from the society confined a famous (and now famously fraudulent) medium—Eusapia Paladino–on a small Italian island. There she produced all sorts of astonishing phenomena, including movement at a distance. The researchers concluded that she could not possibly have used any underhand methods. Yet they themselves had no skill in detecting such methods when faced with impossible marvels. It was not the members of the Society for Psychical Research who did the most convincing work uncovering frauds, but more worldly skeptics, especially magicians, conjurors, and members of the Magic Circle.

In his book *Behind the Scenes with the Mediums*, the American David P. Abbott, detailed many of the tricks of the trade—the envelopes with false backs in which "automatic writing" was concealed; how mediums would pump people of a town for details about their clients' dead loved ones, which would then be miraculously served up to the bereaved; how "ectoplasm" was really muslin painted in Balmain's Luminous Paint; how action at a distance was faked; how materialized spirits might be children let down from ladders in the ceiling or up from trap doors; and how confederates behind the scenes and in the audience were often essential to the success of the deception. He also pointed to the dominance of instant fashions—as soon as one medium developed the novel idea of having a Spirit Guide (usually a "Red Indian"), the fashion instantly spread throughout the country, as did the useful fad for séances held in darkness.[24]

Mr. Sludge the Medium

The case that most called out for the skepticism of experts in conjuring was that of David Dunglas Home [1833–86], a medium whose powers outstripped those of all the others. Home was of humble Scottish birth, was taken to the United States in childhood, and returned to England as a young man to take up his career in Spiritualism. He claimed to be related to the Earl of Home (a claim that the creator of Sherlock Holmes accepted credulously, even though Home was manifestly proletarian) and even to be descended from nobility who fought in 1513 at Flodden Field. Home walked with emperors and tsars, lost the common touch, lived a life of luxury, was enthusiastically received in the grandest houses, and achieved the notoriety of being exposed and lampooned in a poem by Robert Browning. In the *Proceedings of the Society for Psychical Research*, there are two lengthy accounts of the wonders achieved by D. D. Home.[25] The latter occupies nearly one hundred and fifty pages of the journal. Both are entirely uncritical.

Some of the revelations that the Spirit communicates to Home are on scientific and ideological matters.

> Question: "Are not the sun's rays composed of something more than light?" [The Spirit answers] "Of light only, and an elastic wave of electricity that precedes the light." Question: "Is not the sun hot?" "No, the sun is cold; the heat is produced and transmitted to the earth by the rays of light passing through various atmospheres. (*Proceedings*, 86, 158)

The Spirit shares beliefs about eugenics that were common in progressive circles at the time: "It is wrong to allow persons to marry who are not properly fitted to perpetuate their race. By allowing perfect freedom of marriage, crime and disease become perpetuated, and the lower and imperfect form becomes too permanent. Such as are imperfect should be put aside, cared for, pitied, but not allowed to perpetuate by marriage" (ibid., 89).

But in the midst of these high speculations, the Spirit does not lose sight of the welfare of the medium: "You have caught cold in that gambling room, sitting at the table in the large room near the door, there is a strong current of cold air there" (ibid., 99).

However, the main interest is in the incredible phenomena that surround Home. One thing he could do was alter his bodily dimensions, rather in the manner of Alice in Wonderland. Normally five feet ten inches tall, he grows, on one occasion, to six feet six inches so that "there was a space of four inches between his waistcoat and the waistband of his trousers. He appeared to grow also in breadth and size all over" (ibid., 63).

On another occasion, Home takes up a piece of red-hot charcoal in a "fine cambric handkerchief," with no ill effects to himself and not many for the handkerchief. A white luminous cloud comes out of some heliotrope and advances to the hand of one of the female members of the séance.[26] He picks up, with one hand, an accordion, which has already shown signs of liveliness: "Mr. Home got up and stood behind in full view of all, holding the accordion out at arm's length. We all saw it expanding and contracting, and heard it playing a melody. Mr. Home then let go of the accordion, which went behind his back and there continued to play; his feet being visible and also his two hands, which were in front of him."[27] Home's (or his possessing spirit's) ability to produce ravishing music on the accordion is often attested to: one witness says it was like a beautiful voluntary played on an organ. However, the range of pieces performed (if we go by the record) was limited, consisting of "Home, Sweet Home," "Ye Banks and Braes," "The Last Rose of Summer," and, on one occasion only, "Oft in the Stilly Night."

Home's greatest performance was a piece of levitation. In 1871 in the presence of three witnesses, he "went into a trance, and in that state was carried out of the window in the room next to where we were, and was brought in at our window. The distance between the windows was about seven foot six inches. . . . We heard the window in the next room lifted up, and almost immediately after we saw Home floating in the air outside our window. The moon was shining full into the room . . . he remained in this position for a few seconds, then raised the window and glided into the room feet-foremost and sat down. . . . The window is about seventy feet from the ground."[28]

A Magician among the Spirits

Harry Houdini was the most celebrated magician and escape artist of all time. His best known performances included his being chained up and locked in a box that was then submerged in water. His astounding ability to escape within minutes, or even seconds, led some people to believe that he actually possessed supernatural ("paranormal") powers himself. Spiritualists often tried to insinuate that, and claim him as one of their own, hoping that his exploits would cast credit on their own performances.

However, Houdini was consumed with a passionate determination to show up the mediums and explode the whole Spiritualist imposture. His premise was simple: if he could reproduce all the occult phenomena of Spiritualism and demonstrate publicly how it was done, it followed by the application of Occam's razor that there was no need to go to supernatural explanations. And Occam's razor would certainly allow—probably point to—widespread trickery. Houdini paid particular attention to D. D. Home.

A piece of trickery by Home inspired one of Browning's dramatic monologues, "Mr. Sludge the Medium," a savage attack on the fraudulent practices of the mediums, represented by a cowardly, low-born trickster who was certainly based on Home. Browning's wife, Elizabeth Barrett Browning, had fallen under the influence of Spiritualism and of Home, which alarmed Browning. The poet attended one of Home's séances where a face was materialized, which, Home's spirit guide announced, was that of Browning's dead son. Browning seized the supposed materialized head, and it turned out to be the bare foot of Home. The deception was not helped by the fact that Browning never had lost a son in infancy. Browning's living son wrote a letter to the *Times* in which he said that "Home was detected of a vulgar fraud." Elizabeth Barrett Browning's faith in Spiritualism was dented because she had been deceived by a "trusted friend." As the son put it, "The pain of the disillusion was great, but her eyes were opened and she saw clearly."

Eyes were opened on other occasions. The *Proceedings of the Society for Psychical Research*, usually uncritical of Mr. Sludge, do contain some "Thoughts on D. D. Home"—that "alpha and omega of physical Spiritualism with whom modern Spiritualism must stand or fall."[29] Home's bare feet served him well, it seems. Count Perovsky-Petrovo-Solovo described how Home was caught in the act of tricking Eugenie, empress of the French. In his séances Home wore thin shoes, easy to take off and draw on, and also cut socks that left the toes free: "At the appropriate moment he takes off one of his shoes and with his foot pulls a dress here, a dress there, rings a bell, knocks one way and another, and, the thing done, quickly puts his shoe on again."[30]

Home had been living on intimate terms with the emperor and empress for over a year before he ruined his reputation by getting caught out. At the beginning, he gave value for money. His very first séance was visited by Napoleon, Marie Antoinette, Queen Hortense, Rousseau, Pascal, and St. Louis, who all chatted intimately, through Home, to the assembled company.[31] He held a séance at Court, sitting between Eugenie and Napoleon III. A General Fleury, suspecting some conjuring trick, asked leave to withdraw but returned unobserved by another door behind Home: "He then saw the latter open the sole of his right shoe, leave his naked foot some time on the marble floor, then suddenly with a rapid and extraordinarily agile movement, touch with his toes the hand of the Empress, who started, crying 'The hand of a dead child has touched me!' General Fleury came forward and described what he had seen. The following day Home was embarked at Calais, conducted by two *agents*; the order was to keep the incident secret."[32]

Home's had been a dazzling success (comparable with Rasputin's) at the Russian Court, where he lived for weeks in the tsar's palace. During his stay in Russia, he met a beautiful young noblewoman and married her, with the tsar's approval. He developed a passion for precious stones. "On the third finger of the left hand he wore an immense solitaire, which flashed imperial splendors with every movement; above that a sapphire of enormous size; on the other hand was a large yellow diamond and a superb ruby set in brilliants."[33] All these jewels seem to have been given to Home by his admirers for, although he took no money for his performances, he was supported in continuous luxury and showered with gifts.

As Home was a brilliant expositor of the Spiritualist art of materialization, so he was an adept at the rarer practice of *dematerialization*. Physical objects were made to disappear into the spirit world. On one occasion he "dematerialized" a splendid row of emeralds of great value. However, the spirits seemed to have taken a liking for them, because they were not returned to this world at the end of the séance. The chief of police organized a search, and "the dematerialized emeralds were found materializing in [Home's] coat-tail pocket." Home intimated that the jewels had been placed there by an evil spirit—but he had to leave Russia (ibid., *Magician Among the Spirits*, 43–44).

At the age of thirty-three Home succeeded in captivating a seventy-five-year-old widow, from whom he extracted sixty thousand pounds as a result of his summoning up the spirit of her late husband who urged her to sign over the money to Home. A law case followed, in which Home was found to have acted fraudulently and compelled to return all the money, which did not prevent the eminent scientist and devotee of Spiritualism, Sir William Crookes, describing Home as "one of the most lovable of men—whose perfect genuineness is above suspicion" (ibid., 45–46). Crookes almost invariably found the Spiritualistic practitioners to be above suspicion. Houdini offered to reproduce Home's window trick in the presence of Spiritualist believers, but his offer was not taken up. The truth was that however overwhelming the evidence of Home's trickery was, the believers seem to have been emotionally unable to confront the evidence.

Home died from "a terrible spinal disease." Houdini, who denounced Home as a humbug, a pervert, and a moral degenerate, insinuates that this was syphilis. Madame Blavatsky, however, thought that it was "brought on through his intercourse with the Spirits" (ibid., 49).

Spiritualism and the Great War

We have already suggested that the horrors of the First World War (1914–18) gave an immensely powerful impetus to the Spiritualist movement. Countless bereaved parents, in many cases crazed with grief, desperately grasped the chance offered to them by mediums for contact with their dead sons.

A famous book setting out the Spiritualist message in a way that had enormous appeal at the time (it was published in 1916 and went through thirteen editions by 1922) was *Raymond, or Life and Death* by Sir Oliver Lodge. Second Lieutenant Raymond Lodge was the youngest son of Sir Oliver Lodge—a prominent Spiritualist, Fellow of the Royal Society, and member of the Society for Psychical Research. Raymond volunteered for service in September 1914; he was in the trenches at Ypres in 1915. He was struck by a shell fragment in the attack on Hooge Hill, September 14, 1915, and killed.

Sir Oliver's book starts like many a memorial of a dead son or brother that appeared after the Great War. There are letters home from Raymond—cheerful, plucky letters giving no hint of fear or danger. Then there is the telegram from the War Office to his parents with the news of his death, with condolences from Lord Kitchener; another from the king and queen regretting his loss to his parents and to the army. Letters follow from his fellow officers with memories of comradeship and describing the circumstances of his death. There is also a group photograph of Raymond with about fifteen of his brother officers.

Which is where the story proper begins. A medium abroad had said something to a friend of Lady Lodge about a group photograph, before Lady Lodge had heard anything about it. And, a week or two before Raymond's death, messages from the (deceased) Spiritualist, F. W. H. Myers, were reported to Lady Lodge. They referred to Horace's Ode 17 in book 2 of the Odes, one of two poems where Horace records how near he came to being brained by a tree, which suddenly fell on him, but was protected by Faunus, defender of poets, who with his right hand "lightened" the stroke. The message mentions "Faunus," and the "spirit Guide," who reveals himself as Verrall, late professor of Greek at Cambridge, and helpfully recommends that Lady Lodge ask his (Verral's) widow, also a classicist, what it means. Mrs. Verrall duly explains the poem, and Lady Lodge assumes that the interpretation is that a dangerous threat will be averted from Raymond—that F. W. H. Myers would intervene to protect the boy from the blow. But the boy is killed.

As for the group photograph, one does turn up after Raymond's death. The message had referred to someone leaning on Raymond and, sure enough, an officer sitting behind Raymond, who is himself sitting cross-legged on the ground, seems to be leaning on him with his arm. (Another photograph turned up with the officer's *leg* apparently over Raymond's shoulder. Both photographs seem suspiciously doctored, with both leg and arm looking awkward and elongated.)

There is an obvious reaction to all this. The first séance, in which it seemed that a spirit was to ward off a blow, was obviously designed to comfort and reassure Lady Lodge—with a prophecy that turned out to be false. It should have damaged her faith in the medium, rather than strengthening it. The group photograph is neither here nor there—officers were always having their group photographs taken, and Raymond, as a twenty-six-year-old 2nd Lt. and therefore quite junior, would be likely to be in the front row sitting cross-legged on the ground. But such were the Rorschach blots that Spiritualism joined up to produce its revelations; and on such a foundation was the structure of Raymond's posthumous existence reared.

Sir Oliver Lodge was already a convinced Spiritualist, and these bits of "evidence" from the mediums set him on the track of what he believed would be a momentous message for humanity. He and Lady Lodge attended séances anonymously and found that the mediums seemed to know something about Raymond. Then messages from Raymond himself begin, usually through table-turning and automatic writing. Most of the rest of the book consists of these. The messages are quite numerous, for Raymond is extremely communicative. These are the sorts of communication that make up his message for humanity:

He didn't think when he waked up first that he was going to be happy, but now he is and says he is going to be happier. He says that as soon as he is more ready, he has got a great deal of work to do...

He seems to know what the work is. The first work he will have to do will be helping those who are passing over in the War. He knows that when they pass on, they still feel a certain fear... some even go on fighting; at least they want to; they don't believe they have passed on. So that many are wanted where he is now, to explain to them and help them and soothe them.[34]

Clearly this is designed to comfort the parents with the news that Raymond is not only alive but still doing a useful, and patriotic, job. Raymond died unmarried, a sadness for any parent. So there comes this report in a séance: "He is bringing a girl with him now—a young girl, growing up in the spirit world. She belongs to Raymond; long golden hair, pretty tall, slight, brings a lily in her hand" (ibid., 159).

In subsequent séances Raymond begins to describe heaven or the spirit world. He says it will be fifty times more interesting than the earth plane: "There is such a big field to work in" (ibid., 160). He is in "a house built of brick, and there are trees and flowers and real mud that gets you muddy. But the night doesn't follow day in quite the way it does here" (ibid., 184).

"Raymond" goes on to prophesy the progress of the war. After some gnomic remarks about Romania, he says that he sees better prospects for the war. "On all sides now more satisfactory than it has been before. All agree that Russia will do well.... They are going to show what they can do" (ibid., 185).[35]

He gives his views on cremation. He is against it, because it makes the parting of the spirit body from the material one harder (ibid., 196). He reveals that "over there" they manufacture cigars not, as we do here, out of solid matter "but out of essences, and ether, and gases."[36] He assures his mother that he will be in the house all day on Christmas day, and so will thousands of others of the dead soldiers (ibid., 197).[37] He expresses a masculine embarrassment at having to wear the normal heavenly clothes: "Can you fancy me in white robes?... I didn't care for them at first, and I wouldn't wear them... I don't think I will ever be able to make the boys see me in white robes" (ibid., 189).

Raymond keeps insisting how interesting his new world is, far more exciting than the one he has left behind. But the descriptions of this world are sadly thin, there is nothing that seizes the attention or surprises (unlike the visions of Swedenborg). There are simple family pieties, conventional wisdom about the progress of the war, gently eager patriotism, a milk-and-water Christianity—and little else. The disproportion between what is being offered as the testimony of one who ranges over many worlds and spheres of being and what is actually achieved could scarcely be greater.

The success of *Raymond* spawned many imitators. In *The Children of Heaven*, and *The Outlands of Heaven*[38] the Reverend G. Eustace Owen claimed to describe a whole world "beyond the Veil."[39] The whole account purports to be dictated by spirit guides. These spirits normally visited Mr. Owen in his vestry, until the pressure of curious visitors, drawn by the fame of his Spiritualist books, forced him to receive them in the vicarage, where the reception was nothing like as good. *The Children of Heaven* describes how dead children are trained in heaven and how they learn to play the heavenly games. They gather in a *Pleasaunce*, where some learn to levitate, while others "descend to the sward" and call them back, so that "they have to descend in like manner, eyes closed, on to the exact spot whereupon they stood at the beginning of the game."[40] Another child balances "a large opal ball" on a wand and pushes it to other children. If anyone drops the ball he has to descend to the sward. (This sedate game seems much less lively than quidditch in *Harry Potter*.) The older children "gather in some spot appointed. There they converse, interchanging their mental beauties in love. So do they become the more in unison of purpose and in the focus of their energizing."[41]

The Outlands of Heaven describes the system of spheres through which people rise or fall (even into a sort of hell). There are prominent spirits called by names such as Wulfhere and Shonar. Wulfhere is a female mother-leader who puts down uppity men who yearn for a male-dominated heaven, for she has "strength to rule you and guide you as a mother shall order her family of babes." As well as the insipid narrative, there are some Spiritualist scientific doctrines. We learn that mind waves produce the atom, and that the average African lives in squalor because his mind waves have less spiritual dynamism than those of Europeans. Samuel Johnson said that criticism wastes its efforts when directed at "unresisting imbecility." These books mix something approximating to imbecility with an appeal to easy credulity. The colorless worlds described are presented not as science fiction, nor as children's yarns, but as revelations from the spirit world. The belief that all Spiritualists held in common—that the dead and their world are near at hand, even all around us, and that theirs is a world, which in many ways replicates our own—is what gives warrant to, even demands, the attempt to describe that world, betrayed by a notable lack of imagination.

A Writer among the Spirits

There is at least one attempt to describe the world implied by Josiah Gridley, Elizabeth Phelps, Oliver Lodge, Eustace Owen, and the whole throng of Spiritualist seers that does not suffer from imaginative poverty. It was written as a romp and a satire. Mark Twain's excellent jeu d'esprit, *Captain Stormfield's Visit to Heaven,*[42] brings a refreshing sense of detail entirely lacking in the works of the believers. We first meet the late Captain Stormfield, a tough old salt, while he is racing a comet "at about a million miles a minute." Stormfield discovers that heaven is inconceivably vast, for it includes plenty of galaxies beyond our own. Asked at the gates where he is from, he first names his city, then his state, then America, then the world—to be met with blank looks, The world is one insignificant dot in the universe. Eventually he gets to the right place, but finds that very few people there speak English, because the American continent includes all those who had lived there for hundreds of thousands of years before the white man arrived on the scene.

It is explained to Stormfield by a friendly American spirit that heaven is not a democracy. Heaven "is Russia—only more so. There's not a shadow of a republic about it anywhere. There are ranks here. There are viceroys, princes, governors, sub-governors, sub-sub-governors, and a hundred orders of nobility, grading along down from gran-ducal archangels, stage by stage, till the general level is struck, where there ain't any titles." As for the prophets and patriarchs, "just to get a two-minute glimpse of one of them is a thing for a body to remember and tell about for a thousand years. Why, Captain, just think of this: if Abraham was to set his foot down here by this door, there would be a railing set up around this foot-track right away, and a shelter put over it, and people would flock here from all over heaven, for hundreds and hundreds of years, to look at it."[43]

Twain's satire finds its target. If there is another world, parallel to this one, to which we go after death, it might well not replicate what a particular generation or nation most values in our present world. In Swedenborg, at least, there is *some* element of surprise, some sense that the higher reality and its values might in sharp ways differ from our present ones. In Phelps, and then the Spiritualists, there is no such sense, only a pallid copy of our present existence—reversing, in effect, Plato's idea that the present world is an imitation of something more real. The Spiritualists, indeed, are astonishingly attached to material possessions. How interested the spirits are in lozenges, dominoes, Sèvres salad tongs, silk cushions, croquet balls, cigars, claw-legged occasional tables, pianofortes—the whole world of object-packed, comfortable, upper-middle-class living!

The ideas about heaven and hell that we find in Christianity (and in Islam) are filled with the conviction that there is some vast conflict between the kingdom of heaven and the kingdom of this world. Persons in this world are sinners, are enslaved by evil passions, false beliefs, the powers and glamour of the world and the flesh. The kingdom of heaven is within you if you can re-order your soul to a condition of calmness, peace, benignity, long suffering, charity—the "gifts of the spirit." In doing this one sets oneself against the world and its practices. The afterlife imagined by the Spiritualists, having given up the philosophical Idealism that gave, at least, some spiritual and intellectual stiffening to Swedenborgianism, is pallid, preoccupied with petty materialism and small anxieties; the pain of loss and the hope that this can be repaired by inconsequential chat with the deceased through the spirit medium.

The final words about Spiritualism might as well be those of T. H. Huxley. Invited to show an experimental interest in Spiritualistic phenomena, he declined, in a letter to the Council of the Dialectical Society: "The only good that I can see in a demonstration of the truth of "spiritualism" is to furnish an additional argument against suicide. Better live a crossing sweeper than die and be made to talk twaddle by a 'medium' hired at a guinea a séance."[44]

17

Scoring in Heaven

An Etiolated Vision

There the story ends. With one or two exceptions, the twentieth century evolved no new ideas about the next life. The last century may have been most fruitful in producing earthly hells, but it added nothing theoretically to the concept of evil. Indeed, paradoxically and contrary to mass experience, this was the century when belief in the reality of evil tended to drop out of public discourse—and especially from the language of religion. From the nineteenth century on, theologians have been more and more engaged in demythologizing religion. In the twentieth century, to deconstruct the myths of traditional religion came to be seen as the chief task of critical theology. Christ's miracles, his bodily resurrection and ascension were symbols, myths, or allegories behind which a deeper—and more acceptable—Christian message lurked. The Resurrection could not be understood as being based on evidence such as the empty tomb. It could not be understood historically at all.

True, "King Bomba's lazzaroni foster yet the sacred flame."[1] Fundamentalists retain full-blooded faith in heaven and hell. But the gap between Christian fundamentalism and Christian theology has become unbridgeable.[2] Two-thirds of adult Americans apparently believe in a life after death.[3] Seventy-one percent believe that there is a heaven, and 93 percent think they have an excellent, good, or fair chance of getting there. (Fifty-three percent believe in hell, "to which people who have led bad lives without being sorry are eternally damned." Gallup seems, explicably, not to have asked them about their excellent, good, or fair chances of getting to hell.)[4] In heaven there will be love between people, and we will be happy. A substantial minority believe that we will see friends, relatives, and spouses, that we will live for ever, that crippled people will be whole, and that we will grow spiritually. Strangely enough, 5 percent think that in heaven there will be total darkness.[5] A surprisingly small number (5 percent again) think that heaven will be "boring." However, among "leading scientists" only 8 percent believe in heaven, and 4 percent in hell.[6] (It might be worth noting that nearly a quarter of Americans also believe in reincarnation, and half of all males think there is human life on other planets.)

This contrasts as sharply as could be with attempts by professional theologians to make sense of the ancient doctrines. St. Paul said that without the resurrection of Christ, the Christian hope was vain (1 Cor. 15:13–22). But all the ingenuity and verbal dexterity of the great Karl Barth can hardly convince the reader that he has formulated a coherent, let alone a clear doctrine about that. Barth takes Paul's insistence that resurrection is essentially connected with the overcoming of sin as part of an argument that Christ's rising from the dead cannot possibly be understood by Paul as an historical event.[7] He takes Paul's words—"If there be no resurrection of the dead, then is Christ not risen" (1 Cor. 15:13)—and argues that the "historical fact," the resurrection of Jesus, stands and falls by the resurrection of the dead generally—and the general resurrection cannot be an historical fact, because it can emerge only "on the confines of history, on the confines of death."[8] For Barth, resurrection, whatever it might be, cannot be the prolongation or restoration of life that has any intelligible continuity with life as we know it here and now. It cannot take place within time, within history, and therefore it cannot be an historical fact, supported by historical evidence. It can be understood only as part of the whole Christian hope in God. Indeed, it comes close to being nothing more than hope in God. Human resurrection, therefore, cannot be thought of as a future event. It is "the termination of history, history at the termination of the story, of the life story of the individual as well as the story of the world and of the church, in fact, even of natural history, in a possibility beyond those known to us, but always as new, unknown further possibilities linking up with the latter in continuous succession, perhaps amid unparalleled catastrophes, surpassing and perpetuating them upon a higher plane."[9] If that is so, it is hard to see how it can be any sort of event at all. In which case, what is it? It seems to be a pure absence.

It seems that what Barth is saying is that Paul is speaking of the end of this earthly man and his world: "In other words, Barth defines the life of the believer as life characterized by faith in Christ's resurrection and hope for his own resurrection." The words are those of one of the great New Testament scholars of the early twentieth century, Rudolf Bultmann.[10] Barth (in Bultmann's understanding of him) interprets the witnesses to Christ's resurrection whom Paul cites (the twelve apostles, five hundred of the brethren at once, etc.) as simply witnesses to the hope and faith of the primitive church.[11] Bultmann finds this artificial and tortuous. He agrees, however, with Barth that Paul thinks that the being of man as such is a being of the "body" and of "death," and that the being of the Christian man is characterized by the "body" and by the future of "life."[12]

I am not sure which of the two, Barth or Bultmann, is the more tortuous. What emerges from both of them is that the faith they subscribe to does not envisage resurrection—that of Christ or of human beings in general—as an event in time, or even out of time, or after time. It seems to be something that cannot be captured in temporal terms at all. Therefore, from the commonsense point of view, it cannot be something that happens, something with a before and after. The only thing it can be is a life as we live it now—one characterized by an overwhelming trust in God—as distinct from believing that he will bring something about; and a sense that the life of man, untransfigured by Christ, is no better than death.

This may or may not be a correct representation of two writers, one of whom is undeniably obscure and the other hardly a model of lucidity, but we are plainly faced with an example of what Bultmann calls "demythologizing."[13] The idea is that if we strip away from the New Testament certain elements that as moderns we are bound to regard as impossible—Christ's coming back to life, his ascending to heaven, his virgin birth, his miracles—then we will be left with a message that, correctly understood, illuminates our predicament as human beings in the most general way.

The trouble is that it is only because these stories as literally understood have had emotional and spiritual power that anyone troubles to demythologize them. It seems unlikely, were we to start from the demythologized versions of the resurrection story, that we could be persuaded to take much interest in it—any more than most of us do in the elaborate allegorical word-spinnings of the ancient Gnostics. The considerable disparity between verbal elaboration and lucidity of content that we find in Barth, Bultmann, and other demythologizing theologians does suggest an attempt to cling on to the Christian emotions while withholding full assent to what the great majority of Christians throughout the ages were actually moved to believe. Whether this be the only way for intelligent moderns to proceed, it has nevertheless led to that cleavage between theology and popular religion that characterizes modern Christianity.[14]

Mormon Certainties

The United States has been fertile in the development of ideas about death in the modern imagination. It has seen both the sunniest denial that death exists, and a reaffirmation of fundamentalist beliefs in the most literal versions of resurrection. These have grown as though the modern professional theologians never wrote. The Mormons, for instance, teach that children who die before they reach mature years are resurrected in the form in which they would have appeared had they lived to grow to maturity in the flesh "or to develop their physical bodies to the full stature of their spirits."[15] They will have a beauty of the type most admired by Americans. A son who died in babyhood appears to his mother to comfort her: "His height was about that of my husband, but his frame was larger. His hair was sandy-colored with a soft wave in it, and his jaw square and muscular."[16] "Brother Kimble" gives his own corroborative testimony: "He saw the righteous gathered together in the spirit world, and there were no wicked spirits among them. He saw his wife . . . She came to him, and he said that she looked beautiful and had their little child, that died on the Plains, in her arms, and said, 'Mr. Grant, here is little Margaret; you know that the wolves ate her up, but it did not hurt her; here she is all right.'"[17]

Mormonism seems to mix ideas akin both to Spiritualism and to Swedenborgianism. There is only a thin veil separating this world from the next so that the dead are not far from us; paradise is a place where the spirit grows and learns, and acts with renewed capacity, vigor, and enthusiasm;[18] angels are former human beings; the celestial kingdom is divided into a number of heavens or degrees, from the "Paradise of the Righteous" to the Celestial City, in which there are degrees of glory.[19] Like the Spiritualists, Mormon writers commonly insist that the moment of death is an easy and painless experience.[20] (Nonbelievers often suggest that religion contradicts the facts of experience. This confidence of Mormons and Spiritualists about the essentially pleasant nature of death conflicts with experience possibly more than any other religious dogma.) Mormonism imagines an afterlife that is even more solidly material than that of Swedenborg. The fields and woods, delicious streams and verdure, palatial buildings are all described in detail. God's own residence, as one might expect, is a particularly notable structure within the Celestial City—a mansion of white stone, clothed with fire and intense light, and having engraved upon it an enormous letter B.[21] Animals will be resurrected, with the disturbing prospect of millions of domestic pets fouling the whiteness of the Celestial City.

Many Mormons seem to have had near-death experiences, or even to have died and been allowed to come back and describe what they saw. In particular, there have been many sightings of Jesus Christ himself. Nearly all these have in common that he is tall, well built, and handsome, with wavy light to blond hair, and piercingly blue eyes.[22] In other words, he is close to the Charleton Heston ideal. None seems to have seen him as looking Semitic—shortish, say, with prominent nose and piercing dark eyes. That notable anti-Semite, Stuart Houston Chamberlain, argued that it is impossible that a figure as noble as Jesus Christ could possibly have been a Jew—he must have been Aryan.[23] The image, if not the idea, lives on in Utah.

The Mormons are equally happy to describe hell, in which they solidly believe, but which is not quite as horrific as the most traditional Christian hells. In heaven, though, families will be resurrected and reunited, for "Marriage and the family unit were intended by God to be eternal."[24] Here we come to a Mormon doctrine, which can indeed be regarded as a new idea about the future life—"sealing." Couples can be sealed in a special Mormon ritual that consecrates certain marriages to last even beyond death, and will live reunited and engendering offspring for all eternity. This is a belief that seems unique to Mormonism and which, incidentally, emphasizes how remote the religion is from orthodox Christianity.

For a start, Mormons believe that God the Father was once a man who through living an exemplary life attained godhead. God has a body like ours, although a very much superior one.[25] He married a woman—"The Heavenly Mother"—who gave birth to his spirit children who were then sent to earth to inhabit bodies of flesh and blood. These children in turn, if they are good Mormons, will become gods themselves and will give birth to spirit children who will rule their own planets.[26] Some Mormons seem to have believed that God the Father is the (possibly final) product of an infinite series of celestial couplings.[27] Without going into the details of these particular beliefs, we plainly gather that for Mormons families (at least of the true believers) are of their nature eternal, and that the whole Mormon family of believers can itself exist throughout eternity. Some fundamentalist Mormons, still attached to polygamy, look forward to a polygamous futurity with every husband living with all the wives to whom he has been sealed. In this they may well be joined by Jesus Christ whom they believe to have been married (since a celibate Jesus wholly contradicts the Mormon ethos) to Mary Magdalene, Martha, and possibly other women followers.

The sealing ceremony involves the bride and groom meeting in a special sealing room in the temple, hearing words of encouragement and instruction from a temple official, and kneeling facing each other, each before a mirror, which thus reflects their image endlessly, symbolizing the eternity of their union and their membership of a family that stretches to ages eternal.

These ideas face an apparently great scriptural obstacle in those words of Jesus Christ that those who rise from the dead "neither marry, nor are given in marriage; but are as the angels which are in heaven."[28] The whole spirit of Mormonism is splendidly against such an unfleshly picture of the future life, just as it opposes a God who is pure spirit. Yet it gets around Christ's words without too much difficulty, for those who rise from the dead indeed do not marry. They have already been married on earth for all eternity at a special service in a Mormon temple. The formula "till death us do part" refers only to the tragic condition of those who have not been sealed. Any woman to whom a man has been sealed—any number of women, indeed—remain his wives eternally. If a woman has been sealed to a man in a temple and he dies, she may marry another man. But her first husband is her celestial, eternal spouse, while the second is her husband only until the parting by death. It seems that the Church of Jesus Christ of Latter-day Saints has not clarified the question whether there can be polyandrous as well as polygamous celestial marriages. Brigham Young said that eternal marriage "is the thread which runs from the beginning to the end of the holy Gospel of salvation—of the Gospel of the Son of God: it is from eternity to eternity."[29]

Just as the Mormon Church has power to seal spouses, so it can seal children to their parents, so that the whole family will be together forever in eternity. Not only that, it can also baptize into the Mormon Church any or all the ancestors of current Mormons, and then seal them all in the same way. As an official Mormon publication freely admits, this is not an easy task: "It requires faith and commitment, and a lot of hard work." But it is a task worth doing and consecrates what is at the heart of Mormonism—the family, which is based on "faith, prayer, repentance, forgiveness, respect, love, compassion, work and wholesome recreational activities."

Before being admitted as a state of the Union, the Mormon state of Utah had officially to abjure polygamy. Yet in its overwhelming emphasis on the family, its optimism, wholesome materialism and work ethic, and, of course, in its core belief that Jesus Christ paid a special visit to North America after his resurrection, it is and always was emphatically American. To cynical Europeans, though, this prospect of a union that nothing—not even the separation of soul and body—can dissolve, may add a new terror to death.

Be Happy

There is a secular (but not consciously antireligious) tradition that also knows none of the doubts of the theologians. In a chapter 4 we looked at ancient

Greek and Latin epitaphs as a source of popular attitudes to life, death, and the afterlife. Modern cemeteries—especially in the United States, where greater freedom reigns in remembering the dead than in England or Europe generally—are also informative. In America there is very often the purest secularism, in the celebration of life rather than mourning or recognition of death. There is pride (sometimes boastfulness) in a profession followed: "William S. Schafner... Dalton's No. 1 Disc Jockey"; "John Denny was a descendant of a long line of millers. His four sons followed in this profession." An enthusiastic bowler has a representation of falling tenpins on his grave. The tombstone of another lover of bowling, who died at the age of thirty-one, has the figure of a young man knocking the pins down, with the simple legend: "Scoring in heaven."[30]

> O dark dark dark. They all go into the dark,
> The vacant interstellar spaces, the vacant into the vacant,
> The captains, merchant bankers, eminent men of letters....
> ... Distinguished civil servants, chairmen of many committees,
> Industrial lords and petty contractors, all go into the dark ...[31]

Many American epitaphs proudly recall the details of a career. One epitaph informs the passerby that the dead man was "awarded DAR Americanism Medal, November 1960," and that he was "Breeder of Champion Dobermans." One Maurice A. Strickland carries pride in profession and lifetime's achievement very far. Instead of the list of virtues that we find on tombs of the eighteenth century, he has a *curriculum vitae*. We learn that he was Beta Gamma Sigma, and Delta Mu Delta, earned a bachelor of science degree from the University of Georgia, an MBA and PhD from New York University, Fellow of the College of Surgeons; had honorary or practical connections with American Dermatology, Rider Wisdom Hall of Fame, the American Cancer Society, the International Society of Cosmetic Surgeons, the English Royal College of Medicine; that he was in *Who's Who in America*, and *Who's Who in World Business*; that he was a member of the Chamber of Commerce, Delta Sigma Phi, and a Rotarian.[32]

Far from thinking of earthly human life as a form of death (as Barth and St. Paul do), many modern Americans have gone so far in celebrating being alive as to deny that death exists. At any rate, they have wanted to take away from it all its terrors. This famously comes out in the American replacement of the traditional cemetery with the memorial park. David Charles Sloane quotes the words of one of the pioneers of the memorial park: "In 1915 J. J. Gordon wrote in the *Cemetery Beautiful* of "The Ideal Cemetery—Memorial Park." His ideal design included a five-acre central park and an ornamental entrance, neither of which had visible monuments or markers. Gordon reminded his readers of the response of Americans to most memorials: "Few but have felt the chill that strikes the heart when standing in the office of some cemetery, even the most beautiful, and seeing the gleaming monuments, silent reminders of the shortness of life. [In the Central Memorial Park] there is no note of sadness. The flowers fling their fragrance far and wide, the fountains tinkle merrily and it is a beautiful park and the onlooker enjoys it."[33]

For the first time in human history, cemeteries were to be places of joy rather than sorrow. Sadness was to have no place: "Superintendents wanted cemeteries to be places of celebration and joy, but the monuments evoked death. They found it difficult to believe in the older vision of the cemetery. Superintendents, along with their customers, wanted a new cemetery that would truly be without gloom."[34] Hence—no monuments.

Famously, this reached its apogee in the philosophy of the man who inspired the most celebrated of all modern American cemeteries, Hubert Eaton, founder and ideologist of Forest Lawn Memorial Park, California. His credo was issued in 1917:

> I shall Endeavour to build Forest Lawn as different, as unlike other
> cemeteries as sunshine is unlike darkness, as Eternal Life is unlike
> Death . . . a great park. Devoid of misshapen monuments and other
> customary signs of earthly Death, but filled with towering trees,
> sweeping lawns, splashing fountains, singing birds, beautiful
> statuary, cheerful flowers; noble memorial architecture, with interiors
> of light and color, and redolent of the world's best history and
> romances . . . a place where lovers new and old shall love to stroll and
> watch the sunset's glow . . . where schoolteachers bring happy
> children.[35]

There were to be works of art—frequently "exact" reproductions of European masterpieces, such as Michelangelo's *David*, Thorvaldsen's *The Christus*, and a gigantic stained-glass magnification of Leonardo's *Last Supper*. The first *David*, to which a fig leaf had been added, was unfortunately knocked down in an earthquake. Its replacement had no fig leaf, which led to vehement objections by visiting groups of ladies.[36] There was also a replica of the church at Stoke Poges, in Buckinghamshire, where Gray had been inspired to write his "Elegy in a Country Churchyard." This would be used for weddings. (In a graveyard devoted to happiness, and where the notion of death was suppressed, what could be more natural than young couples wanting to celebrate their nuptials? As Hubert Eaton put it: "in so far as possible all evidences of death should be eliminated and . . . this building should be a creation of art.") The works of art were to be surrounded by sections of lawn, with no graves visible, bearing names such as Kindly Light, Whispering Pines, Graceland, Eventide, and Sunrise Slope.[37]

Eaton summarized the Forest Lawn *credo* thus: "[Let] no bleak tombstone mar its beauty.... Today religion is gladsome, radiant, it speaks in terms of the Beatitudes, of joyousness, and the smiling Jesus."[38]

Such fatuity could only await the simoom of satire coming from afar. The most celebrated celebration of Forest Lawn is Evelyn Waugh's novella, *The Loved One* ("loved one" being the Forest Lawn euphemism for a corpse). The work is set in a California memorial park called Whispering Glades. Inside the Golden Gates of the cemetery ("the largest gates in the world") the novel's hero finds a semicircle of golden yew, a wide gravel roadway, and an island of mown turf "on which stood a singular and massive wall of marble sculptured in the form of an open book." In letters a foot high was incised:

THE DREAM

Behold I dreamed a dream and I saw a New Earth sacred to HAPPINESS. *There amid all that Nature and Art could offer to elevate the Soul of Man, I saw the Happy Resting Place of Countless Loved Ones. And I saw the Waiting Ones who still stood at the brink of that narrow stream that now separated them from those who had gone before. Young and old, they were happy too. Happy in Beauty, Happy in the certain knowledge that their Loved Ones were very near, in Beauty and Happiness such as the earth cannot give.*

I heard a voice say: "Do this."

And behold I awoke and in the Light and Promise of my DREAM *I made* WHISPERING GLADES.

ENTER STRANGER *AND* BE HAPPY.

And below, in vast cursive facsimile, the signature:

WILBUR KENWORTHY, THE DREAMER.[39]

Whispering Glades also has reproductions of famous works of art and of European buildings (for instance, a "perfect replica of an old English Manor" constructed of Grade A steel and concrete, certified proof against fire, earthquake, and nuclear fission). And it has a Wee Kirk o' the Heather where young people court and are married.

Waugh's exuberant comedy is, of course, wholly accurate in its portrayal of the philosophy that stands behind Forest Lawn and the mixture of paganism, spiritualism, Swedenborgianism, and infantile optimism that inspired what came to be called "The American Way of Death."[40] Perhaps, though, the most potent immediate influence was that combination of Romanticism and liberal theology that became so powerful in America in the later nineteenth century. Since man is part of nature, should we not see death as a beneficent reunion of the human being with mother earth? A funeral should not be like a funeral, but "more like some wonderful canvas representing a spring festival, with lovely groups and garlands against the tender greenery of the dainty season."[41] Death is natural—so why feel sad about it? Nature should teach us not to think about death at all—so there must be no funerary mounds in cemeteries to remind us of our dread last end. Indeed, we must not think of our last end (assuming we fall into the mistake of thinking about it at all) as dread. The *Ladies Home Journal* noted approvingly that in a "lawn cemetery" there was "none of the grewsomeness [*sic*] which is invariably associated with cemetery lots. ... No grave mounds are used, so save the headstones, there is nothing to suggest the presence of death."[42] The romantic naturalism of the lawn cemetery banishes any cheerless thought: "Using those trees that inspire joy and gladness and help us forget trouble ... make the surroundings cheerful and bright. ... Kill off every plant and remove everything you see that suggests sadness."[43]

The custom of having the sexton drop clods of earth onto the coffin as the minister repeats "ashes to ashes and dust to dust" is antiquated and revolting. How can it be agreeable to the mourners and their friends to hear a shovelful of dirt rattling down as a last memory of the departed?[44]

Liberal theology comes into this when it teaches Christians to play down any doctrine of original sin, then of sin and therefore of any fear of the future state. It becomes assumed that the departed will have gone to heaven—and so there is no rational grounds for mourning and grief. The two motives, coming together, merge into the strangely unfeeling sentimentalism that reaches a climax in Forest Lawn. Indeed, a direct endorsement of that movement of sensibility that led to Forest Lawn—astonishingly prophetic of the forms it would take, even unto Waugh's *The Loved One*—was given as early as 1907, when the Reverend Calvin T. Blackwell addressed the National Funeral Directors Association and described their work as:

> the highest development of our American life; for in no occupation
> has there been such a wonderful advance from crudity to the articulate
> and aesthetic as in yours. ... You have changed that somber black into
> buff and gray; you have changed that monotonous white of the flowers
> by a dash of color; you have removed the artificial, repulsive attitude of
> the dead and given us in its stead inviting quiet and repose. You have
> taken the stiffness of the old shroud, and converted in into the soft
> robe of the death slumber. You have made the casket so attractive[45]
> that it almost woos us of the living to lie down to the dreamless sleep;

you have even cushioned the lid of the coffin so that the falling of the clod may not send from the tomb a doleful sound. By your touch you have even changed the dark valley of death into the "sunny side."[46]

Armageddon

De facto secularism, liberal religion, and a sunny optimism about futurity (which the Mormons largely share) has not had all its own way in modern American religion, for the fundamentalist Christian movement has set itself to revive an uncritical scriptural literalism. The best-selling preacher, Hal Lindsey, wants to go back even beyond St. Augustine, whom he accuses of starting the rot by allowing that prophecy (for instance, of the thousand-year reign of Christ upon earth) should be interpreted not literally but allegorically. For Lindsey, scripture, and especially the *Revelation of St. John*, foretells the future with absolute accuracy. In particular, it foretells a coming Armageddon that should have happened by now, since Lindsey seemed to have expected it some time around 2000. There would be certain catastrophic events that presage the coming of Antichrist. Arab armies would attack Israel. This would encourage the Soviet Union (as it then was) to attack the Middle East as a whole, pursuant to their long-term aim of world domination. Two hundred million Chinese would then assault both the Soviet Union and the Middle East. All this would precipitate nuclear war, including nuclear missiles, as a result of which one third of the earth's surface, with its grain, grasses, and trees would burn up. One third of the world's population would perish.[47] This would be the Tribulation, prophesied by scripture, to last seven years.

Antichrist will turn up in Jerusalem, make a pact with the Jews to restore the Temple and its ancient ceremonies, including animal sacrifice. After a few years he will break his word, and reveal himself as a new Roman emperor, his power deriving from the countries of the European Union (or the Common Market, as it was when Lindsey wrote in 1983). He will rule for a time and persecute the Christians, just as certain Roman emperors did.

But then Christ will be made manifest in his Second Coming and will end the Tribulation. Then will be the Rapture—"the coming of Christ for the Church in which he instantly catches all living believers to meet him in the air and translates them into immortal bodies without experiencing physical death." The thousand-year reign on earth of Christ ensues, to be followed by Eternity and the end of time.[48] The Rapture will indeed happen, as St. Paul suggests, "in the twinkling of an eye." It will be much more impressive than a takeoff of the space shuttle.[49] And, one assumes, less risky.

The Reign of Antichrist. Luca Signorelli, San Brisio Chapel, Orvieto, Plate 4.

Rapture theory has become a major theme among evangelical Protestants, above all in the United States. Their beliefs include conservative social and political positions, combined with passionate support for Israel, and a systematic correlation of biblical texts with current politics and international affairs. The signs of the coming end of the world are mostly traditional, but they include some up-to-date ones as well. The behavior of OPEC, the downward spiral of the dollar, crisis in world banking, rises in the price of oil and gold, pressures on Israel to acquiesce in the creation of a Palestinian state (all in 2008) are signs of the coming end.[50] The evolution of the European Union is also a source of prophetic insight. The original Common Market started with six states, but was then joined by the United Kingdom, Denmark, Ireland, and Greece—making ten countries. This clearly corresponds to the Beast in Revelation, who has ten horns.[51] (The Beast also has seven heads, is also a leopard, has the feet of a bear, the mouth of a lion, and the power of a dragon (Rev. 13:1–2). This possibly indicates the well-known bureaucratic inertia of the EU; while the power of a dragon—the dragon alone of the beasts mentioned being mythical—might allude to its equally well-known military impotence.) Indeed, Rapture theory aims at being an exact science. The *Prophetic Top Ten* gives an exhaustive list of the current indications that the last days are approaching: (1) Iran's nuclear program, (2) "Putin's grab for power in Russia," (3) the supply of oil, (4) the subprime loan crisis, (5) the declining dollar, (6) the rise of China, (7) global terrorism, (8) "nation ID initiatives," (9) global weather changes, and (10) tension between Israel and Syria. The tenth sign, incidentally, is especially felicitous, because it is on a minaret of the Ummayid Mosque in Damascus that Christ and Mohammed will stand together—according to Muslim tradition—to judge mankind at the Last Day.

The role of Israel in Rapture theory is of particular interest. In general the rapturists are passionately pro-Israel and hostile to Islam, and indeed to Arabs. The establishment of the modern State of Israel reflects a divine providence and will manifest the power of God, who will save Israel when all her friends desert her. This support of Israel is, however, ambiguous, for it is based on the belief that the existence of Israel is itself a sign of the coming end, and that just before the end the Jews will convert to Christianity.

Enter Antichrist: He will be the crucial agent in the coming of the final days, Jesus having come in the air to "Rapture his Church to be with him in heaven," Antichrist will appear as a political leader. A popular series of Christian works of prophetic fiction dramatizes this.[52] Antichrist in these books is one Nicolae Carpathia, former president of Rumania and (more sinisterly) former secretary-general of the United Nations. His body is inhabited by Lucifer, who gives him his power and occasionally provides dramatic visual effects. Carpathia does indeed help the Jews rebuild a spanking new Temple (Solomon's rather than the apparently grander one later built by Herod.) To this end he makes a pact with the Jews for seven years, but then breaks it and enters into alliance with the European Union.

Carpathia is by now not well disposed to the Jews, most of whom have become Christians anyway. ("Millions around the world, most of them Jews, were acknowledging Jesus as the Messiah.")[53] He occupies the holy places with an enormous army. He is opposed by some tough and well-armed Americans, and also by the Rabbi Rosenzweig, a Jew converted to Christianity who has the useful power of turning water into blood.[54] After many violent conflicts in which tens of thousands are incinerated, blown up, or at the least afflicted with boils, the stars fall from the sky, Christ returns in glory, destroying Antichrist (which presumably persuades the remaining Orthodox Jews to convert), and the world ends.

As Jesus had foretold, the Second Coming is an immense contrast to his obscure birth in the stable at Bethlehem. One of the characters in *Glorious Appearing* finds the words for it: "'This is sure different from the last time Jesus came,' Naomi said. 'Beside that time we weren't ready, it happened in the twinkling of an eye. Apparently God's going to play this one for all its worth.'"[55]

The *Dajjal:* Muslim Apocalyptics

From the above account it might seem that in the modern world Muslims are more prophesied against than prophesying. But that would not be correct—Muslims themselves have a long tradition of apocalyptic writing. It begins in ancient times when many *hadith* prophesying the Last Day and the tribulations that will accompany it were attributed to Mohammed. It has also enjoyed a revival in recent times, when some Muslim attempts to read the signs of the end of the world, and decipher scripture in order to predict how events will unfold, provide a remarkable mirror image of the efforts by the Rapture theorists.

Islam has from earliest times believed that the last days will include the coming of the Antichrist. In Arabic he is called the *Dajjal.* His essential mission will be to destroy the conquests of Islam and slaughter Muslims. It seems that he will not be as glamorous as Nicolae Carpathia. Indeed, if we are to go by the *hadith* he will be quite unprepossessing. He will have twisted, contracted hair, and will be blind of the right eye, which will be like a floating grape.[56] He will be a Jew[57]—a fact that he will hardly be able to keep secret, given that he will be followed about by "seventy thousand Jews of Isfahan wearing Persian shawls."[58] Any remaining uncertainty about his identity will be removed by the fact that on his forehead will be the letters *k.f.r* (*kafir*—pagan, infidel).[59] Nevertheless he is destined to deceive millions.

Islam has classically distinguished between the "Greater Signs" of the Last Day, and the "Lesser Signs." The Greater Signs have included: the Euphrates uncovering a mountain of gold, over which people will fight, 99 percent of them dying in the process; the conquest by the Muslims of Constantinople; the rising of the sun in the west; the appearance on earth of Gog and Magog; a great fire in the Hijaz, which will illuminate the necks of camels of the Busra; and the appearance of the horns of Satan.[60] A more obscure sign will be that Muslims will fight with people wearing shoes of hair, having faces like hammered shields, with red complexions and small eyes.[61]

When he appears on earth the *Dajjal* will perform miracles—such as causing rain to fall and filling the udders of goats and cows with a great deal of milk. He will also demand that people surrender to him their treasures—and their treasures will then collect themselves before him like a swarm of bees. He will also start killing young men purely for the pleasure of it. But then, just as he is rejoicing in his power, Jesus, son of Mary, will descend at the white minaret of the Ummayad mosque in Damascus, and kill him.[62]

The early Muslim prophecies of the last days were preoccupied with the struggles during and after the lifetime of Mohammed—especially with the Byzantine Empire. However, a new school of Muslim apocalyptic writing has sprung up—mostly inspired by the catastrophic defeats of Arabs at the hands of Israelis in the wars of 1948 and 1967.[63] What is novel about this school is that, like some Evangelical Christian apocalypticists, it tries to decipher the present time and predict the future; and—quite contrary to Islamic tradition (indeed, explicitly forbidden)—it presses into service texts from the Hebrew Bible and the New Testament.[64]

The current Muslim popular apocalypticists—denounced as unscholarly or heretical by most established scholars in Islamic countries—sprang into prominence with Muslim defeat and impotence, especially in the Middle East; with trying to predict from scripture the ultimate defeat and destruction of the enemies of Islam; and with an all-encompassing conviction that they are victims of a Jewish world conspiracy. In effect, the Jews occupy the place that the Rapture theorists implicitly reserve for the Muslims—although it must be said that the role of the Jews in the worldview of the Muslim apocalypticists is vastly more sinister than that of the Muslims in the Evangelical Christian prophetic scheme.

Conspiracy theory is certainly a powerful form of political thinking in the Middle East—not altogether without reason. Contemporary Muslim apocalypticists take conspiracy into some very dark realms of thought indeed. The world is under the sway of a secret government of Jews, who use Christians—particularly Americans—to carry out their designs. Modern Israel and the Jews are Gog and Magog, engaged in a conspiracy against the good of the whole human race, but especially against Muslims. This Jewish world conspiracy (so the theory goes) lies behind the earlier rise of Communism, behind pornography, secularism, the destruction of family values, and all irreligion.[65] Jesus was a great and good prophet, but the Jew, St. Paul, perverted his teaching, invented the religion of Christianity, and foisted it on the Gentile world.[66] The end of the world will see the return to earth of Jesus, who will kill the *Dajjal*, and large numbers of Jews (and some Christians), recover Jerusalem and Palestine, and eventually extend Muslim dominion over the whole earth. The Jews have been gathered together in Israel just so that Allah can destroy them. Those Jews who are not killed at the final battle in the Holy Land will convert to Islam.

Like earlier Muslim commentators, the modern apocalypticists distinguish between the Lesser and Greater Signs of the end. Among the Lesser Signs are the construction of tall buildings, the use of cosmetics and musical instruments, and the invention of the motor car.[67] A writer by the name of

Mustafa Murad adds some even more vivid Lesser Signs: each man will have fifty women; animals will talk; a shoe will tell its master about the infidelities of his wife.[68] Mixing Muslim with Hebrew and Christian scriptures, the apocalypticists find many modern equivalents for the Four Beasts of the book of Daniel, and from the *Apocalypse* the Scarlet Woman, and Antichrist (*Dajjal*). Of the Four Beasts of Daniel, the lion is the British Empire, the bear is the Soviet Union, the leopard is the United States, and the terrifying fourth beast with ten horns is the European Community.[69] (Here Muslim apocalyptics tends to coalesce with the Rapture theorists. Another shared outlook is extreme distrust of the United Nations, especially the Security Council.) As for the Scarlet Woman of Revelation—that is obviously Babylon, which in turn is obviously the United States. Further evidence is provided by the Stars and Stripes itself—for the robe of the harlot is scarlet, and there are indeed red stripes on the American flag. Most of the candidates for Antichrist are also American, including Henry Kissinger, Burt Lancaster, and Clint Eastwood.[70]

The End of the World cannot take place until Israel has been replaced with a Muslim state, with Jerusalem as its capital. So the return of Jesus and the vanquishing of the Antichrist will lead not to the consequences looked to by the Rapture theorists (except perhaps for the final conversion of the Jews—but to Islam rather than Christianity) but to a worldwide Muslim caliphate, ruling from the Holy City and eternally dispensing justice to a grateful mankind.

Bishop Grigorius and the Final Days

But let us end by returning to the beginning, to the early Christian centuries, to a more quietly traditional, but no less literal, recounting of the same thing from a different perspective; and to a personal reminiscence.

I was in Cairo early in the 1990s and had had many conversations with Muslims, both liberal and fundamentalist. I had also talked to Copts, and found that they were intensely anxious about the future, fearing the apparently ever-increasing militancy of radical Islam. Along with a Catholic priest working in Egypt, I was taken to meet a famous Coptic bishop.

We met Bishop Grigorius, a man in his eighties, with the usual magnificent beard of the Coptic clergy, in the "Vatican" (as Copts refer to it) of the Coptic Church in Cairo—the compound that was also the residence of Pope Shenouda, leader of the church. The compound was heavily guarded by soldiers. It contains the new cathedral, which houses those few remains of St. Mark left by the Venetians when they stole the body, and a few more returned as a gesture of good will by Pope Paul VI.

In fact it is not anything like the Vatican but resembles more a large social club where Copts meet to be together, to stroll in the central square, or to visit a bookshop that sells holy pictures, photographs of past popes, cassettes of Coptic music, and similar souvenirs.

Bishop Grigorius was reputed to be the greatest of all Coptic scholars and theologians then alive, and one of the greatest of all time. When one remembers that Origen was a Copt, this was a striking claim. The bishop took a higher degree at Birmingham University and was the first "Bishop of Higher Theological Studies, Coptic Culture and Academic Research." He was the author of many books and booklets on all aspects of Coptic theology, history, and liturgy.

His large drawing room/study was full of books, filing cabinets, and religious art, including a "God is Love" clock and a Sacred Heart clock.

At first our interview was unpromising. Whenever I asked a question, Bishop Grigorius took the trouble to move with some effort to his filing cabinets, rifle through them, and present me with a booklet—usually in Arabic—which he had written on the subject. The booklets included his account of the Monophysite question, the Trinity, and the activities of Coptic missionaries in sixth-century Ireland.

I learned that—contrary to a *canard* put about by Evelyn Waugh—the Copts do not regard Pontius Pilate as a saint, not even in Ethiopia: "Pilate a saint? No—I don't think so. The centurion at the foot of the cross—Longinus—now he *is* a saint." We touched briefly on the question—fundamental to the separation of the Copts from the larger church in the fifth century—whether Christ is "in two natures" (*en dusi phusiois*) or "out of two natures" (*ek duon phusion*). I learned about the procedure of electing the Coptic pope. Three names are put into a chalice, and a child draws out one of the names. He is then pope.

The bishop then talked of Muslims who do not believe the Qur'an to be the word of God—among whom he included the Shiites. "You may have other questions..."—then back to the files for another pamphlet, the one on Monophysitism: "There is another point I wish to clarify."

Then he turned to the fundamentalists: "Most Muslims are against the fanatics—they think they are evil. The fanatics think the Copts are *kafirs* [i.e., infidels, pagans] and that they must go to hell, just like atheists. The fanatics are eager to condemn. A Muslim has just been condemned for asking a question, in a newspaper article, about Mohammed's ascent to see God in the seventh heaven. He asked: 'Did the Prophet go to see God in body or in spirit?' For his best loved wife, Aisha, said of the night on which Mohammed saw God: 'He did not leave my neck or breasts that night.'"

Time was passing, and our conversation had no clear direction. I asked a final question: "Do the Copts fear for the future?" It was then that the interview moved in a new and unexpected direction. The bishop gave me a glance, lifted his gaze to the ceiling, closed his eyes, and began to speak. Without reserve or the discreet silences I had become used to in Copts speaking on sensitive subjects, there came forth a comprehensive view of the religious situation in Egypt, indeed the world. It was the voice of Coptic, of fifth-century Christianity, besieged, but with hope drawn from prophecy:

> We believe that the Second Coming of Christ is at hand. Therefore the fanatics will not triumph in the end. These will be the signs that the last days are near. War must break out between Jews and Arabs. There will be earthquakes and other portents, as foretold in the scriptures. Also we shall see Antichrist. Now these signs are actually at hand.
>
> There was a great earthquake [in Cairo in 1992]. And now millions of Jews are coming back into Palestine from Russia and America. They are coming in order to rebuild the Temple. But the Temple was on the site where the El Aqsa mosque now stands—whence Mohammed ascended to heaven. So there must be war between Arabs and Jews.
>
> Our Lady appeared in Egypt in 1968. In all her apparitions she looked terribly sad. Something terrible and tragic was going to happen. Some people believe that this was the birth of Antichrist. Antichrist will have to be at least thirty years old when he appears. Therefore he will be made manifest in 1998 or thereabouts [i.e., thirty years after the apparitions of Our Lady]. The Epistle of St. Paul to the Thessalonians speaks of Antichrist. The devil will give him all power.
>
> Antichrist will not respect the United Nations—he will think of himself as the real Christ-king. He will be a wicked man in whom the devil himself dwells. His time will be as stated in the Apocalypse—three and a half years. He will abolish all religions other than the worship of himself, for he will hate religion. He will claim to be God himself.
>
> Now Christ has said that the Second Temple had to be destroyed. The Jews are awaiting the Third Temple. Antichrist will build this temple, and will take it to be his throne. After three and a half years, the real Christ will return, and will destroy Antichrist with something celestial. Then the Jews will ask to become Christians—according to the words of St. Paul in Romans 11. The Jews will believe in Christ, and Christianity will become the religion of the whole world—as the

prophet Daniel says in his second chapter. All this will happen around the year two thousand—I am not quite sure. No one can tell exactly when.

So the Muslims will not succeed in making Islam the sole world religion. Muslim plans for world domination—especially for domination here in Egypt—will never finally succeed.

The bishop opened his eyes, gave me a perceant glance, and lifted his eyes and arms toward heaven: "Christ is the real ruler of the whole world. Not a bird falls from heaven without his permission. So I do not think the Muslim triumph is—inevitable."

A schoolboy—one of a poor Muslim family I had become friendly with in a village in Upper Egypt:

"What do you think of the story that all the newspapers are full of?"
"What story?"
"It is famous all over the world. A grove of trees in Germany was found miraculously to have formed the Arabic script for 'God is one God and Mohammed is his prophet.' And exactly the same thing happened in Japan."

Epilogue

In *A Portrait of the Artist as a Young Man* James Joyce had presented orthodox Catholicism in effect as one of several stages through which his hero, Stephen Dedalus, passes on his way to maturity. As a boy he had listened, terror struck, as adults had argued violently about Charles Parnell and Irish nationalism over Christmas dinner. The argument is strident, often coarse, and presents people going over well-worn topics, working themselves up into a rage almost as an act of will. Yet the young Stephen is powerfully affected. In guilty anticipation of Father Arnall's sermons on hell "Stephen's heart had withered up like a flower of the desert that feels the simoom coming from afar." Under the impact of the sermons, he finally forces himself to go to confession, and then receives Communion. He proceeds to practice mortifications of flesh and spirit, and to live a life of carefully aesthetic piety, praying before the Blessed Sacrament using "an old neglected book written by Saint Alphonsus Liguori, with fading characters and sere foxpapered leaves," and identifying with "the attitude of rapture in sacred art, the raised and parted hands, the parted lips and eyes as of one about to swoon."[1]

Joyce is not satirizing the young Stephen, nor his religious beliefs. At every stage of Stephen's life he is given the words and attitudes right for his age, and they are never judged from the standpoint of one looking back with superior wisdom. Yet Joyce, if not a satirist, is an ironist. Stephen's fear of hell and his piety have to be lived through and outgrown. Joyce's insinuation is that it is only as an artist that his hero will have come fully to himself, will outgrow the opinions, feelings, and doctrines imposed upon him in childhood and youth, and go "to encounter for the millionth time the reality of experience and to forge in the smithy of my soul the uncreated conscience of my race."[2]

Joyce's—and Stephen's—fidelity to experience means that all dogmatic certainties—his father's and his friends' Irish nationalism, his mother's love, Catholicism—dissolve. Irish Catholicism with its rigidities of idealism is peculiarly suited to be the object of his irony, because fidelity to experience means that we come to feel that the only possible stance to take up is "a recognition, implicit in the expression of every kind of experience, of other kinds of experience which are possible."[3] Those are the terms (we remember) in which T. S. Eliot defined metaphysical wit. They help to describe the powerful apparent ease with which Joyce stands both within and outside a religious and moral tradition, and perhaps insinuate that this is the only way in which a modern person can be intelligently true to his experience. Indeed, Eliot also insinuates that where belief finds literary expression, we can best situate it in a sort of third realm, between actual assent and mere imagining. In denying that we know anything of what Shakespeare actually thought, he writes that "all great poetry gives the illusion of a view of life,"[4] that what might seem like beliefs in Shakespeare and Dante "are merely gigantic attempts to metamorphose private failures and disappointments."[5] The business of Shakespeare (and presumably Dante as well) was "to express the greatest emotional intensity of his time based on whatever his time happened to think."[6]

Both Joyce and Eliot seem to be offering a way of entering into systems of thought, feeling, and belief free from any need to affirm or deny. Eliot seems, indeed, to see the possibility of this freedom as helping us to understand the point of view of the religious believer. Writing of Pascal, he says that the Christian thinker—"the man who is trying consciously and conscientiously to explain to himself the sequence that culminates in faith"—finds the world to be inexplicable by any nonreligious theory.[7] But to find the world explicable is to correlate our understanding of it with "the moral world within." For Eliot the type of the unbeliever is Voltaire—"the greatest skeptic of all"—because he is willing to subordinate the moral world within by referring all beliefs to universal criteria of rationality as those are defined by the Enlightenment.

We do not have to takes sides with either Pascal or Voltaire, but we might be able to agree that Eliot does seem to have caught a necessary condition of religious belief. We are rightly skeptical about the moral world within since we know how many crimes have been committed in its name. But those individuals, those cultures that have been most serious in their beliefs about postmortem punishments and rewards are also those for whom the choice between good and evil has a momentous, even cosmic significance. For good or ill they have regarded the moral world within with the utmost seriousness. The Abrahamic faiths, and the religion of the ancient Egyptians, assuming as they do an overarching moral law, carry with them a heightened sense of good and evil choices that makes their ideas about the afterlife seem virtually inevitable. An ethic of the virtues—as systematized by Aristotle, for instance—does not naturally support moral idealism. On the whole the Greek and Roman world (with exceptions such as the Stoics and Platonists) was not hospitable to moral idealism, and did not evolve urgent fears and hopes about life after death.

It could be that the decline of belief in heaven and hell in our own time flows less from a change in convictions about how the world is, and more from changes in the moral world within. Many reject, for instance, any idea that punishment is justified simply as the exercise of justice, rather than as aiming at reform and rehabilitation (as Origen himself argued). This is often taken as a sign of an advance in rationality. Against that, Nietzsche argued that far from signaling progress this merely argues a loss of nerve: "There comes a point of morbid mellowing and over-tenderness in the history of society at which it takes the side even of him who harms it, the *criminal*, and does so honestly and wholeheartedly. Punishment: that seems to it somehow unfair—certainly the idea of 'being punished'—and 'having to punish' is unpleasant to it, makes it afraid. 'Is it not enough to render him *harmless*? Why punish him as well? To administer punishment is itself dreadful!'"[8]

Nietzsche deals only in possible points of view, what he calls "perspectives." His great achievement is to suggest how complex the relations are between how we see and interpret the world around us and what Eliot called "the moral world within." It is certainly true that those in the modern world who hold most convincedly to the old religious beliefs about the afterlife—Muslims, for instance, as well as Christian Evangelicals and resurgently orthodox Catholics—are also those who cleave to the old moral codes.

Modernists are typically skeptical about heaven and hell, as well as almost any absolute code of morality, and we are in effect their heirs. A characteristic feeling of educated moderns is that the conviction among, say, Muslims and Evangelical Christians that moral judgments are about our eternal fate is not quite grown-up and certainly unenlightened. And as chapter 17 suggests, this may often in fact be the case. Yet such a dismissive attitude may be superficial and misguided. In forming ideas about heaven and hell we may well be doing something serious, something that most of our ancestors have done. We may be contemplating seriously what we believe about our own conduct—sitting in judgment, as it were, upon ourselves in order to decide what things we finally value. The temptation to engage in irony is there—and in parts of this book I have consciously encouraged it, for it is very often justified and sometimes irresistible—but in the end it must indeed be resisted. Necessary as it may be, it cannot show us the whole truth.

It could be that in following the history of the extraordinarily varied ideas people have had about the future life, future punishments for the wicked and bliss for the good, we will find that the best compass we can have will not be some idea about how reasonable or risible such beliefs are, judged by a yardstick of the rational that we bring to bear from the outside but rather a sense of how deeply they mirror our own most sincere self-consciousness, most courageous self-judgment. Our image of heaven and hell is finally an image of how we judge ourselves.

Notes

Note: All biblical references are from the Authorized (King James) Version unless otherwise noted.

PROLOGUE

1. Browning, "Bishop Blougram's Apology."
2. Of which the Oath against Modernism, imposed on all priests by Pius X, is a notable example.
3. Joyce, *Portrait*, chap. 3.
4. Newman, *Grammar of Assent*, chap. 2, 18. For Newman, real as distinct from notional assent is accompanied with emotion, vitality. It is characteristic of real assent that it is "warm" or "vital" and engages our emotions and not merely our intellect. Real assent is not to a notion, but to an object. A child's belief in his mother's veracity "is to him no abstract truth or item of general knowledge, but is bound up with that image and love of her person which is part of himself."
5. Joyce, *Portrait*, chap. 3.
6. *Odyssey* 11, 576–600.
7. *Aeneid* 2, 580–627.
8. Chap. 5, 120–21.
9. See Newman, *Apologia Pro Vita Sua*, chap. 5.
10. Camporesi, *Fear of Hell*.
11. Ibid., 108–9, quoting A. Valeschi, *Quaresimale* [Leghorn 1847].
12. Augustine, *De Vera Religione*, 69ff; *Enarrratio in Psalmos*, bk. 8, chap. 13; *De Trinitate*, bk 12, chap. 14. See John Burnaby, *Amor Dei*, 185, and John Casey, *Pagan Virtue*, 199.

13. Joyce, *Portrait*.

14. Matt. 10:28: "And fear not them which kill the body, but are not able to kill the soul: but rather fear him which is able to destroy both soul and body in hell." See also Matt. 16:26; Mark 8:36; Luke 9:25.

CHAPTER 1

1. See the old Roman Catholic "penny catechism," questions 3 and 4: "Is this likeness to God chiefly in my body or in my soul?" "It is chiefly in my soul." "Of which should you take most care, your body or your soul?" "I should take most care of my soul, for Christ has said 'What doth it profit a man to gain the whole world and suffer the loss of his own soul?'"

2. Aquinas, *Summa Contra Gentiles* 2, 79.

3. Spinoza, *Ethics* 3, props. 6–10. See also Unamuno, *Tragic Sense of Life*, 54.

4. Plato, *Apology* 40, C–E.

5. Lucretius, *De Rerum Natura* 3, 830–931.

6. *Iliad* 6, 464–65. A literal translation of Hector's words: "But let me be dead, and let the heaped-up earth cover me ere I hear thy cries as they hale thee into captivity." Pope's freer translation (*The Iliad of Homer* 6, 590–93) supports my possibly more tendentious interpretation:

> May I lie cold before that dreadful day,
> Press'd with a load of monumental clay!
> Thy *Hector*, wrapt in everlasting sleep,
> Shall neither hear thee sigh, nor see thee weep.

7. For Nietzsche's development of the concept of the slave morality, see, e.g., *Beyond Good and Evil*, pts. 5–7, 9.

8. A formula of the ancient Egyptians—see chap. 2, *After Lives*, "Egypt."

9. Vulliamy, *Immortal Man*, 139.

10. Pascal Khoo Thwe, *From the Land of Green Ghosts*, 93–94.

11. Vulliamy, *Immortal Man*, 139.

12. Explicitly forbidden to the ancient Jews: "Ye are the children of the Lord your God: ye shall not cut yourselves, nor make any baldness between your eyes for the dead" (Deut. 14:1).

13. J. G. Frazer, *Belief in Immortality*, vol. 1, 135. Frazer here is describing the mourning customs of the Narrinyeri of southeastern Australia. Possibly this suffers from the overrationalizing explanation of the outsider addicted to finding causes for alien behavior. That belief in immortality often seems to originate in attitudes to the dead, rather than hopes for oneself, still seems well based.

14. See Colin Thubron, *In Siberia*, 97–107.

CHAPTER 2

1. Taylor, *Death and the Afterlife in Ancient Egypt*, 12; Quirke, *Ancient Egyptian Religion*, 14.

2. Mercer, *Religion of Ancient Egypt*, 316.

3. Lichtheim, *Moral Values in Ancient Egypt*, 67; Mercer, *Religion of Ancient Egypt*. "O you that love life and hate death" was normally followed by a prayer for the dead." (See Morenz, *Egyptian Religion*, 187.) A notice in the Egyptian Museum in Cairo informs the visitor that it possesses five hundred stelae from the Middle Kingdom of the following form: "you priests of every rank, you do your duty to your children if you say: 'here is an offering to Osiris Khentamentit . . . thousands of offerings appeasing thy voice, bread, beer, meats, fowl, incense, perfume and sweet breezes from the North, all things good and pure that heaven creates and gives the earth, and that the Nile brings. O you who are still on earth and pass this stone, you who love life and hate death, make offerings of fruit, fowl and meats to Osiris on behalf of the child buried here'" [translated from the French].

4. Mercer, *Religion of Ancient Egypt*, 47.

5. Morenz, *Egyptian Religion*, 186.

6. A. J. Spencer, *Death in Ancient Egypt*, 149.

7. See Morenz, *Egyptian Religion*, 153, 202.

8. Brandon, *Judgment of the Dead*, 10–11.

9. Mercer *Religion of Ancient Egypt*, 207.

10. Lichtheim, *Moral Values*, 41.

11. Stephen Quirke suggests that the concept of a general judgment of the dead becomes current after 1800 BC when the *Coffin Texts* were still in use with the old view of an afterlife without a judgment of the dead: "In the new tradition the judgment of the dead was not the trial for one incident as in a modern law court [and in the Coffin Texts] but an assessment of the entire being, the entire earthly life, of an individual. Each person was taken before Osiris, god of the dead, and his or her heart weighed on scales against the measure of the Right." Quirke, *Ancient Egyptian Religion*, 162.

12. Brandon, *Judgment of the Dead*, 15.

13. Ibid.

14. Ibid.

15. Ibid.

16. Lichtheim, *Ma'at in Egyptian Autobiographies*, 85, 94.

17. Brandon, *Judgment of the Dead*, 42–44, quoting G. Lefebvre, *Le Tombeau de Petosiris*, vol. 1, 136, 54 (inscription 81, vol. 2, 16–22). It has been suggested that there might even be a Jewish influence on the Egyptian story. Lefebvre juxtaposes texts from the tomb of Petosiris with similar texts from the Wisdom literature of the Old Testament: "Whoever walks in your path, he will not stumble; since I have been upon the earth up to this day whence I arrived in the perfect regions [i.e., in Amentit], no fault has been found in me."

Cum adhuc junior essem . . . quaesivi sapientiam . . . ambulavit pes meus iter rectum, a juventate mea investigabam eam . . . Zelatus sum bonum et non confundar" (Ecclus./Sirac 51, 18–24).

["Good is the way of him who is faithful to God; he is blessed who turns his heart towards the godhead (*elle*)."]

"Beati omnes qui timent Dominum, qui ambulant in viis ejus" [Ps.128:1]—Gustave Lefebvre, *Le Tombeau de Petosiris*, 3 vols., 37–38.

18. Matt. 19:24; Mark 10:25; Luke 18:25.

19. Lichtheim, *Autobiographies*, 50–51.

20. This is a modern title of a work known to the Egyptians as *The Book of Going Forth by Day*.

21. Allen, *Book of the Dead: Studies in Oriental Civilization*, no. 37, spell 125. Egyptologists include these denials under the general category of "negative confessions": "Forty-two deities heard the deceased protest innocence of crimes against the divine and human social order, from sexual misconduct to lying and cheating to blasphemy." Quirke, *Ancient Egyptian Religion*.

22. The heart, rather than the brain, was the seat of intellect, memory, and the moral sense (see John H. Taylor, *Death and Afterlife*, 17). The heart had to be preserved and kept within the body at mummification. The brain was usually drawn out through the nose.

23. Allen, *Book of the Dead*, spell 30. See also Brandon, *Judgment of the Dead*, 37–38. (I have blended Allen's version of spells 30 A and B with Brandon's version.)

24. Spencer, *Death in Ancient Egypt*, 146.

25. Allen, *Book of the Dead*, spell no 125; Spencer, *Death in Ancient Egypt*, 147.

26. See Spencer, *Death in Ancient Egypt*, 144.

27. Ibid., 145.

28. Quirke (*Ancient Egyptian Religion*, 158) denies that there is democratization. Rather it is Pharaoh who allows certain of his followers the privilege of immortality: "The label 'democratization' thus reverses the historical direction of the trend; the 'people' do not intrude into royal power, on the contrary the role of king intrudes into the burial customs not of the 'people,' but of those subjects who were sufficiently well placed to commission for their tombs and chapels texts and images for the afterlife." Morenz speaks of "democratization" on the grounds that the Egyptian heaven was "opened up to commoners." Morenz, *Egyptian Religion* 204–5.

29. Mercer, *Religion of Ancient Egypt*, 322.

30. They are found in the Old Kingdom Pyramid of King Unas, ca. 2400 BC, in the Fifth Dynasty, i.e., preceding the Sixth Dynasty Pyramids of Cheops, Chephren, and Mycerinus at Giza. Some have found aspects of these early texts primitive—or "barbarous gibberish": "The impression of savagery is increased when we find that the dead king [Unas] is to kill the gods and to fatten upon them; "the old gods shall be thy food in the evening," and we have the weird picture of the dead king boiling the bones of the gods in a cauldron to make his bread. The arrival of the dead ruler is to be the signal for general commotion and fear on the part of the denizens of the other world: "heaven opens and the stars tremble when this Unas cometh forth as a god."

31. Faulkner, *Ancient Egyptian Pyramid Texts*, utterance 215.

32. Or "I have put truth in the place of error" (Brandon, *Judgment of the Dead*, 11).

33. Quirke, *Ancient Egyptian Religion*, 175.

34. Mercer, *Religion of Ancient Egypt*, 45–46.

35. Taylor, *Death and Resurrection in Ancient Egypt*.

36. Ibid.

37. See Quirke, *Ancient Egyptian Religion*, 144.

38. Mercer, *Religion of Ancient Egypt*, 44.

39. Quirke, *Ancient Egyptian Religion*, 106.

40. Mercer, *Religion of Ancient Egypt*, 45.

41. Taylor, *Death and Resurrection in Ancient Egypt*, 19.

42. Quirke, *Ancient Egyptian Religion*, 106.

43. Taylor, *Death and Resurrection in Ancient Egypt*.

44. Mercer, *Religion of Ancient Egypt*, 41.

45. Ibid., 42.

46. Ibid., 316.

47. Herodotus 2, 85–90.

48. Mercer, *Religion of Ancient Egypt*, 46.

49. Zandee, *Death as an Enemy*, 55.

50. Faulkner, *Pyramid Texts*, utterance 210 (127–28).

51. Faulkner, *Ancient Egyptian Coffin Texts*, vol. 3, spell 1012.

52. Ibid., spells 1012–13.

53. Allen, *Book of the Dead*, e.g., spells 32, 51, 52, 53 ("spell for not eating shit in the god's domain"), 82, 116, 124, 189.

54. Faulkner, *Coffin Texts*, spell 1021.

55. Ibid., spells 1054, 1055, 1084.

56. Wallis-Budge, "Book of Am Tuat," vol. 1, 59.

57. Wallis-Budge, "Book of Gates" (The Sarcophagus of Seti 1, Sir John Soane Museum), vol. 2, 98–99.

58. Ibid., 235.

59. Wallis-Budge, "Book of Am Tuat," 246.

60. Wallis-Budge, "Book of Gates," 200.

61. Wallis-Budge, "Book of the Dead," spell 175.

62. Ibid., spells 149, 178.

63. Ibid., spell 149. (Possibly this has something to do with the amount of feasting that will go on in the afterlife.)

64. Faulkner, *Pyramid Texts*, utterance 223.

65. Wallis-Budge, "Book of Gates," 186–87.

66. Morenz, *Egyptian Religion*, 195. See Herodotus 2, 78: "At rich men's banquets, after dinner a man carries around an image of a corpse in a coffin, painted and carved in exact imitation, a cubit or two cubits long. This he shows to each of the company, saying: 'Drink and make merry, but look on this; for such thou shalt be when thou art dead.'"

67. Tomb of Nefer-Hotep, end of the Amarna [i.e., Akhnaton] period. Morenz, *Egyptian Religion*, 187.

68. Zandee, *Death as an Enemy*, 2.

69. Morenz, *Egyptian Religion*, 188.

70. Homer *Odyssey* 11, 488–91; Morenz, *Egyptian Religion*, 189.

71. Morenz, *Egyptian Religion*, 192.

72. As Morenz does. Ibid., 189.

73. Ibid., introduction.

74. Eliot, "Andrew Marvell," in *Selected Essays*, 303.

75. Mercer, *Religion of Ancient Egypt*, 102–3.

76. Wallis-Budge, *Osiris*.

77. Accounts of Osiris are to be found in classical writers, including Plutarch (*Moralia*) and Diodorus Siculus [bk. 1, chap. 2] as well as in the Egyptian texts.

78. Mercer, *Religion of Ancient Egypt*. See A. H. Gardner, "The Contending of Horus and Seth," *Chester Beatty Papyri No. 1* [London 1931]. At Philae there is a relief of Osiris in which corn is seen growing out of his mummified body. See Wallis-Budge, *Osiris*, 58.

79. Wallis-Budge, *Osiris*, 78–80. However, Quirke suggests that Osiris cannot be the god for all mortal men, for he was strictly speaking the god not of the dead in general but of the *blessed* dead, the dead who had led good lives. Indeed, in the surviving records of texts and images formulated for the wealthier sections of society, the blessed dead are defined still more narrowly as those who had received a good burial including the costly procedure of being mummified. "Since mummification involved immersion in a tub of dry natron, wrapping in fine (if never new) linen strips, and dousing with unguents and resins, it was, even at the cheapest end of the market, an expensive business, and can never have been available to the very poor." Quirke, *Ancient Egyptian Religion*, 52.

80. Herodotus 2, 5.

81. Most famously presented in Mozart's *Magic Flute*.

82. See Quirke, *Ancient Egyptian Religion*, 25.

83. Ibid., 26.

84. Ibid.

85. Ibid., 36.

86. Morenz, *Egyptian Religion*, 168.

87. Quoted by Quirke, *Ancient Egyptian Religion*, 51.

88. Lichtheim, *Autobiographies*, 55.

89. Pritchard, "A Song of the Harper," 467.

90. Quirke, *Ancient Egyptian Religion*, 67.

91. Eliot, *After Strange Gods*, 43.

CHAPTER 3

1. Kramer, *Sumerian Mythology*, 12. I use translations of the "standard" version of the Babylonian Gilgamesh epic, written in Akkadian, other Babylonian texts, and Sumerian poems about "Bilgames," (i.e., Gilgamesh). I almost always quote from the Penguin version, translation and notes by Andrew George, which is the best version for the general reader. (Those interested in the definitive scholarly edition with translation, along with original Sumerian and Akkadian texts, see the two-volume Oxford edition by George, *Babylonian Gilgamesh Epic*.)

2. George, *Epic of Gilgamesh*, chap. 1, tablet 1; and Dalley, *Myths from Mesopotamia*, tablet 1. "Resigned" is Dalley's translation, and "found peace" is George's.

3. See Heidel, *Gilgamesh Epic*, 170.

4. Brandon, *Man and His Destiny*, 75. The goddess, Ishtar, went down to the netherworld, and vowed that unless the doorkeeper opened the gates she would "smash the doorpost, and unhinge the gates" and "lead up the dead, so that they may eat the living." The Mesopotamians seem to have been very anxious to keep the dead safely under lock and key, lest they pour fearfully into the world of the living.

5. Heidel, *Gilgamesh Epic*, 60.

6. Dalley, *Myths*, tablet 1.

7. George, *Epic of Gilgamesh*, chap. 1, tablet 1.

8. For the incessant contests, see George, *Epic of Gilgamesh*, chap. 1, tablet 1; for the piggyback rides, see ibid., chap. 5 ("Bilgames and the Netherworld," or "In those days, those far-off days") for Sumerian versions of the story. The game sounds rather like polo but played on the backs of young men rather than horses! This notion might be born out by the fact that in a later story Gilgamesh drops into the netherworld a ball and a mallet.

9. Dalley, *Myths*, 1.

10. George, *Epic of Gilgamesh*, chap. 1.

11. Probably a rather grand temple prostitute.

12. George, *Epic of Gilgamesh*, chap. 1, tablet 2.

13. Ibid.

14. "The concept of defilement through sexual experience is one that tallies with a widespread human belief that sexual knowledge brings the end of innocence. The idea that ejaculation engenders weakness is also common. On his deathbed Enkidu uses telling language in lamenting this first step in his transformation from animal to human state. He was "pure and undefiled" . . . but [Shamhat] made him feel "diminished and degraded" George, *Babylonian Gilgamesh*, vol. 1, 451.

15. George, *Epic of Gilgamesh*, chap. 1, tablet 1. That a homosexual interpretation of the relation between Gilgamesh and Enkidu is probable in the Akkadian version of the epic is argued by George, following A. D. Kilmer, *Babylonian Gilgamesh*, vol. 1. 452, 529.

16. George, *Epic of Gilgamesh*, bk. 1, tablet 6.

17. And Gilgamesh has a divine mother.

18. George, *Epic of Gilgamesh*, bk. 1, tablet 7.

19. Ibid.

20. Ibid.

21. Ibid.

22. Ibid., tablet 10.

23. The account of this meeting is not contained in the "standard" version of the Gilgamesh epic, but in George, *Epic of Gilgamesh*, chap. 2 ("Babylonian Texts of the Early Second Millennium BC, Tablet reportedly from Sippar"), 122–26.

24. George, *Epic of Gilgamesh*, chap. 11.

25. In the story of the flood in Genesis, the water seems to be thought of as not simply falling from the heavens but as being produced also from the breaking open of the fountains of the deep, i.e., the waters that were believed to lie under the earth.

26. Brandon, *Man and his Destiny*, 70, 94.

27. Matt. 7:27: "Which of you by taking thought can add one cubit to his stature?"

28. Moran, "The Epic of Gilgamesh," *Canadian Society for Mesopotamian Studies* 22, 15–22. See George, *Epic of Gilgamesh*, 52.

29. George, *Epic of Gilgamesh*, chap. 5, "The Sumerian Poems of Gilgamesh," *Bilgames and the Netherworld*.

30. There are one or two places where misdeeds in this world seem to lead to punishment in the next. A man who made his parents sigh with sorrow is beset with "one thousand Amorites, his shade cannot push them off with his hands, he cannot charge them down with his chest." George, "Bilgames and the Netherworld," *Babylonian Gilgamesh*, vol. 2, 777.

31. The great archaeological excavator, Sir Leonard Woolley, actually discovered, or thought he had discovered, the Flood at Ur. He sunk a deep shaft and found many strata of shards, pots, and other evidence of human habitation, and then, farther down, several feet of pure alluvial mud. Below that were more strata of pots, etc. Woolley's wife, invited to give an opinion, immediately said "It's the Flood, of course." Current opinion, alas, holds that this was an inundation more localized than that described either in Genesis or in Sumerian and Babylonian mythology. See Woolley, *Ur Excavations*.

32. Lambert, "Dialogue of Pessimism," 145, 147, lines 10–16, 46–52.

33. Pritchard, "Dialogue about Human Misery," 439–40, lines 71–74, 256–57.

34. Lambert, "The Poem of the Righteous Sufferer," tablet 1.

35. Langdon, *Babylonian Penitential Psalms*.

36. Lambert, "The Poem of the Righteous Sufferer," tablet 2.

37. Ibid., tablet 3.

38. Langdon, *Babylonian Penitential Psalms*, 61.

39. Of course, Job may seem incomparably grander to us because we have a continuous history of commentary and superb translation, both of which are lacking in the case of Babylonian literature.

40. The Hebrew text has "Bless God." This is a euphemism, aiming to avoid writing the evil word "curse" next to the sacred name. I owe this information to Dr. Cally Hammond.

41. "Marvellous" seems to means that God's power is a thing to be marveled at. For Job's ambivalence toward God's absence and his oppressive presence, see Crenshaw, *Whirlwind of Torment*, 60–61.

42. Job's insistence on his own sinlessness could even be seen as a challenge to God to make himself manifest and justify himself. If Job is lying, this is an impossible defiance, and God *must* act to challenge the deceit.

43. He will return to the stuff of which man is made: "For dust thou art, and unto dust thou shalt return" (Gen. 3:19); "Then shall the dust return to the earth as it was: and the spirit shall return unto God who gave it" (Eccles. 12:7).

44. Here I follow Brandon, *Man and His Destiny*, chap. 4, 106–52. For an account of these topics systematically opposed to that of Brandon, see Heidel, *Gilgamesh Epic*, esp. 142, 147–48, 173–76, 185–86, 193–94, 203–4, 211–14, 217–18, 222–23. Who can decide, where doctors disagree?

45. Brandon, *Man and His Destiny*, 119, referring to M. Noth, *Das System der Zwolf Stamme Israels*, 58; W. F. Albright, *From Stone Age to Christianity: Monotheism and the*

Historical Process (Baltimore: Johns Hopkins University Press, 1948), 215;
H. H. Rowley, *From Joseph to Joshua: Biblical Traditions in the Light of Archaeology*
(Oxford: Clarendon, 1948), 45, 102–3, 126–29; Charles, *Critical History of the Doctrine
of a Future Life*, 9–10.

46. In later times, *Sheol* got divided into compartments, one of which contained infernal punishments for the wicked.

47. See Brandon, *Man and His Destiny*, 122, but see Heidel, *Gilgamesh Epic*, 182.

48. Brandon, *Man and His Destiny*.

49. See Lev. 21:5; 19:28; Deut. 14:1–2.

50. Brandon, *Man and His Destiny*, 121.

51. This is the opinion of Heidel, *Gilgamesh Epic*, 179–84.

52. Heidel, *Gilgamesh Epic*, 211.

53. Heidel vehemently defends the traditional Christian interpretation: "Job unwaveringly maintains his innocence and solemnly affirms that, although all other hope is vain, God himself, his Redeemer, will vindicate him and free his name from reproach.... He will do this ... by resurrecting Job's body, and by elevating him to blessed communion with God" (214–14).

54. The passage—so crucial in the development of thought about a resurrection of the body—has been described as "textually, one of the most corrupt pericopes in the Old Testament." Cox, *Triumph of Impotence*, 87. The "redeemer" seems widely interpreteted to be a Vindicator—someone, possibly God, who will vindicate Job's life (i.e., his innocence of hidden sins) after his death. It has been suggested that we have here a momentary conviction by Job that after his death he will enjoy a vision of God, and that this shows that the idea of a future life "was in the air" at that time. Charles, *Critical History*, 71–73. Crenshaw (*Whirlwind of Torment*, 74) writes that Job is using ambiguous language here: "He is standing on the horizon and peering into the unknown; therefore he cannot speak with utter precision about what is to be. Vaguely he sees his vindicator standing on the dust, and when Job tries to describe his own condition words fail him. It seems that death has occurred, but somehow he beholds God, no longer an enemy.... The thought that God is at Job's side overwhelms him, and he perceives strange movements within his heart." It would seem that it is not only Job's language that is ambiguous.

55. See Dell, *Book of Job*; Cox, *Triumph of Impotence*.

56. See Gen. 22:1–13.

57. In the opinion, at any rate, of many scholars.

58. Except for a passage in 2 Maccabees, where dead Jewish soldiers are prayed for. Maccabees is regarded in the Protestant tradition as apocryphal. The Roman Catholic Church has used this passage as an argument for purgatory and prayers for the dead.

59. Josephus, *Antiquities of the Jews*, chap. 1.

60. Levenson, *Resurrection and the Restoration of Israel*, 72–77.

61. Ibid., 30, quoting Rabbi Simai.

62. Ibid., 22.

63. Ibid., 75–78, 107.

CHAPTER 4

1. George, *Epic of Gilgamesh*, Tablet 2, 187; see also Griffin, *Homer on Life and Death*, 92.

2. Horace, *Odes* 3, 30, "*dum Capitolium / scandet cum tacita virgine pontifex*"—"so long as the Pontiff climbs the Capitol with the silent Vestal."

3. Milton, "Lycidas."

4. *Psucho* is to "blow"; the Latin words for soul or shade—*animus* and *anima* are cognate with the Greek word *anemos*—"wind."

5. Burkert, *Greek Religion*, 195.

6. Burkert, 195. He calls the two scenes—the appearance of Patroclus and the journey to Hades—"decisive."

7. See Albinus, *House of Hades*, 73.

8. Burkert, *Greek Religion*, 197.

9. Ibid., 196. This refers to *Iliad* 20, 61–65. The overturned stone with its putrefaction and teeming larvae is Burkert's excellently creative addition to the words of Homer.

10. Jaeger, *Paideia*.

11. *Iliad* 22, 105–25.

12. Jaeger, *Paideia*, 7–10.

13. Cumont, *After Life in Roman Paganism*, 167.

14. Hesiod, *Works and Days*, 167–73; Burkert, 198.

15. MacIntyre, *After Virtue*, 124.

16. Thucydides, *Peloponnesian War* 2, 43.

17. Aristotle, *Nicomachean Ethics*, 1116a.

18. Pound, *Cantos*, Canto 1.

19. Griffin, *Homer on Life and Death*, 93.

20. Ibid., 91.

21. Shakespeare, *Henry IV*, 1.5.2, 131–35.

22. Griffin, *Homer on Life and Death*, 98, 102.

23. Wittgenstein, *Lectures and Conversations*, 51.

24. Farnell, *Greek Hero Cults*, 397–98.

25. Cumont, *After Life in Roman Paganism*, 15, a free translation of:

> *O Charida ti ta nerthe?—Polu skotos—Hai d' anodoi ti?*
> *Pseudos—Ho Pluton?—Muthos—Apolometha.*

26. Rice and Stambaugh, *Sources*, 240.

27. Simonides, *Palatine Anthology* 7.253 [frag. 118 Palatine Anthology] quoting Diehl, in Rice and Stambaugh, 241.

28. Ibid. (Simonides *Palatine Anthology* 7 7.251 [frag. 121]).

29. Ibid. (frag 22 in Diehl).

30. Griffin, *Homer on Life and Death*, 140–43.

31. G. Kaibel, *Epigrammata Graeca*, in Rice and Stambaugh, 243.

32. Lattimore, *Themes in Greek and Latin Epitaphs*, 77.

33. Kaibel, *Epigrammata Graeca*; Rice and Stambaugh, 244–45.

34. Cumont, *After Life in Roman Paganism*, 10.
35. Ibid.
36. Lattimore, *Themes in Greek and Latin Epitaphs*, 162–63.
37. Ibid., 194, 197.
38. NCE 193 Villa Aldobrandini, 2nd half first century AD.
39. Delfini collection, second century AD.
40. Coll. of Instituto Archaeologico Germanico, second century AD. Epitaph of Geminia Agathe Mater [the preceding four notes were taken by the author in the Capitoline Museum in Rome where replicas of these inscriptions were on display. The information I have given is what the notes provided].
41. Cumont, *After Life in Roman Paganism*, 28: "dum vixi, bibi libenter; bibite vos qui vivitis."
42. Ibid., 11–12.
43. Theognis, *Elegies*, 425.
44. Sophocles, *Oedipus at Colonus*, 1224–26.
45. Mimnermus of Colophon, in Stobaeus, *Eclogae* 4. 34.12; frag. 2 in M. L. West, "Iambi et Elegi Graeci II," in Rice and Stambaugh, 221–22.
46. Farnell, *Greek Hero Cults*, 399. He is writing of "the pious Greek."
47. Pausanias, *Description of Greece* 4, bk. 10, 25–31.
48. Ibid., 28, 4.
49. Ibid., 31.
50. Plato, *Republic* 1, 5.
51. Guthrie, *Orpheus and Greek Religion*, 152–53.
52. Lucretius, "Prologomena," *De Rerum Natura* 3, 69.
53. Spinoza, *Ethics*, pt. 3, On the Origin and Nature of the Emotions, prop. 2.
54. Samuel Johnson, *Vanity of Human Wishes*.
55. Catullus 5, 1–6. Compare Herrick:

> So when or you or I are made
> A fable, song or fleeting shade,
> All love, all liking, all delight
> Lies drowned with us in endless night.
> Then while time serves, and we are but decaying,
> Come, my Corinna, come, let's go a-Maying.

56. Housman, *Collected Poems and Selected Prose*, 494.
57. Ibid.
58. Cornford, "Mystery Religion," *Cambridge Ancient History*, vol. 4, 524.
59. Ibid., 531.
60. Guthrie, *Orpheus and Greek Religion*, 148.
61. Ibid.
62. Plutarch *Moralia* 5, 364, 34.
63. *Diodorus Siculus* 1, 96, 4–6.
64. Guthrie, *Orpheus and Greek Religion*, 31.
65. Milton, "Lycidas," in *Poems*.

66. Cornford, "Mystery Religion," 533.

67. Plato *Laws*, 782C.

68. Guthrie, *Orpheus and Greek Religion*, 201.

69. Ibid. Farnell, *Greek Hero Cults*, 385: "the eschatological promise of Orphism was anti-social in its tendency . . . this gospel laid stress solely on the salvation of the individual through purity and asceticism." He cites the *Hippolytus* of Euripides in which Thesus "taunts his son [Hippolytus] with "the pharisaic hypocrisy of his Orphic holiness, his ritualistic sanctimoniousness and the inward uncleanness of his soul" (384).

70. Guthrie, *Orpheus and Greek Religion*, 269–70.

71. Ibid., 242.

72. They had a theogony that explained this. In brief, Zeus declared the infant god, Dionysus, to be king of a new generation of gods. The jealous Titans, things of earth, attacked the infant god, slew him, and tore his body to pieces. Zeus saved the heart, ate it, and thus resurrected Dionysus. But the Titans had actually eaten of the flesh of Dionysus, so Zeus hurled a thunderbolt at them and burned them all up. The human race sprang from the barbecued Titans—so human beings are evil and sprung from earth, like the Titans, but also have something divine in them—the flesh of Dionysus. Therefore human beings are the children both of earth and of the starry heavens.

73. Cornford, "Mystery Religion," 537.

74. Guthrie, *Orpheus and Greek Religion*, 175.

75. Ibid., 171–75; Ferguson, *Greek and Roman Religion*, 162–63; Burkert, *Greek Religion*, 293–95.

76. Ferguson, *Greek and Roman Religion*, 162–63.

77. Ibid., 164.

78. Ibid. The kid falling into milk could recall the story that Dionysus, trying to escape the Titans, transformed himself into several animals, including a kid. But it may just mean immense good fortune.

79. Here I have blended together ideas from the Orphics, the Pythagoreans, Plotinus, etc. The syncretism of the ancients gives some justification for this. The idea of future felicity was made up of a congeries of such ideas. See Cumont, *After Life in Roman Paganism*, 182–213.

80. Ibid.

81. Pindar, *Olympian Odes* 2, 57–72; Ferguson, *Greek and Roman Religion*, 161–62.

82. Eliot, "The Dry Salvages V," *Four Quartets*.

83. Plato, *Phaedo*, 65D.

84. Plato, *Gorgias*, 493A; Guthrie, *Orpheus and Greek Religion*, 161.

85. MacIntyre, *Short History of Ethics*, 32.

86. Plato, *Symposium*, 216–23; *Phaedo*.

87. *Symposium*, 220B–223D; *Phaedo*, 117–18; See also Martha Nussbaum, *Fragility of Goodness*, 183, 199.

88. Plato, *Symposium*, 218A.

89. Ibid., 216B.

90. Plato, *Gorgias*, 486A–C.

91. Guthrie, *Orpheus and Greek Religion*, 239.

92. Plato, *Symposium* 210 E–211 B, C–D.

93. See chap. 1, 14, and this chapter, 101.

94. Aquinas *Summa Theologiae* 1a, 77, 8, and 1a, 89, 2.

95. Ibid.

96. The idea of a postmortem existence as a sort of impersonal intellectual activity seems to have been a doctrine of the most famous predecessor of Aquinas, the Arab philosopher Averroes. This may be why the doctrines of Averroes were looked on with extreme suspicion by the Roman Catholic Church, a suspicion that extended for a time to Aquinas himself.

97. Kenny, *Aquinas*, 47–49.

CHAPTER 5

1. Joseph Klausner (*Jesus of Nazareth*, 370–76) sees this, from a Jewish perspective, as a severe limitation in the teachings of Jesus.

2. This saying of Jesus is paralleled by a saying in a Dead Sea Scroll, which describes two people, one fairly good with six parts of light against three parts of darkness; and another very wicked, having eight parts of darkness and only one part of light, Dead Sea Scroll (4Q186); see Vermes, *Authentic Gospel of Jesus*, 94–95. The words of Jesus involve an absolute opposition that goes beyond anything in this scroll.

3. The other forms are prophet and priest.

4. Arnold, *Culture and Anarchy*, chap. 4, 165, 168.

5. The earliest revelations of the Qur'an have a comparable urgency about hell and repentance, e.g., suras 85, 87, 89, 90, 92, 96, 99, 101, 102, 104, 111.

6. Brandon, *Judgment of the Dead*, 99–120.

7. Bernstein, *Formation of Hell*, 207–24.

8. This is plainly a reference to Isaiah's "for their worm shall not die, neither shall their fire be quenched" (Isa. 66:24).

9. Bernstein, *Formation of Hell*, 231–33.

10. Ibid., 232.

11. Ibid., 239.

12. Ibid., 236–37.

13. Hume, e.g., *Enquiry Concerning the Principles of Morals*, sec. 8, 207–8.

14. As distinct from the traditions that later went into the Synoptic Gospels, and which may contain much of the actual teaching of Jesus.

15. My account of St. Paul's doctrine of postmortem punishment is substantially indebted to Bernstein, *Formation of Hell*, 207–24.

16. Bernstein finds this to be Paul's one reference to Hades—i.e., hell, reading the text as "O death [*thanate*], where is thy victory? O death [*hade*] where is thy sting?" and comments "it is sufficient to note that the point of Paul's only reference to Hades is to celebrate its impotence!" "*Hade*" seems to be a variant reading in the Greek text, which otherwise repeats *thanate*.

17. Bernstein, *Formation of Hell*, 221.

18. A mystic with such a hope was Julian of Norwich—"All shall be well, and all manner of things shall be well."

19. Bernstein, *Formation of Hell*, 214.

20. The apostles ask the risen Christ: "Lord, wilt thou at this time restore the kingdom to Israel?" (Acts 1:6).

21. See Brandon, *Judgment of the Dead*, 221–22.

22. Ibid., 101.

23. Vermes, *Authentic Gospel of Jesus*, 193–94, 388.

24. Brandon, *Judgment of the Dead*, 105–6.

25. Ibid., 105.

26. Klausner, *Jesus of Nazareth*, 477.

27. The man who actually did so—Cyrus the great—was regarded by the Jews as having been sent by God (Isa. 45:1).

28. From which Pope Benedict XVI, however, dissents in his book *Jesus of Nazareth*, where he aims to reconnect the Jesus of the Synoptic Gospels with the Christ of the church.

29. Elliott, *Apocryphal New Testament*, 594–95.

30. Assuming the current dating of John's Gospel to the end of the first century is correct.

31. Elliott, *Apocalypse of Peter*. The *Apocalypse* consists of two varying texts, the "Ethiopic" and the "Akhmim."

32. Ibid., 603–4 I have freely mingled the "Ethiopic" and "Akhmim" texts here and elsewhere.

33. Ibid., 603.

34. Ibid., 604. (The punishment also of enemies of the church by their being eaten by worms will become a popular Christian theme.)

35. Aquinas, *Summa Theologiae*, 3a, suppl., qu. 94, art 3. The passage quotes Ps. 57:11 (Vulg.): "The just shall rejoice when he shall see the revenge: he shall wash his hands in the blood of the sinner" (Douay trans.).

36. *Apocalypse of Peter*, 605.

37. Pound, *Cantos* XIV–XVI.

38. *Acts of Thomas*, chap. 57.

39. Joyce, *Portrait of the Artist*, chap. 3.

40. *Apocalypse of Peter*, 605. (I have again conflated the two texts.)

41. "twas this flesh begot / These pelican daughters." *King Lear* 3.4.74–75.

42. *Apocalypse of Peter*, 610.

43. Ibid., 601.

44. There is also a remarkable verse in 1 Tim. 4:10: "For therefore we both labour and suffer reproach, because we trust in the living God, who is the Saviour of all men, specially of those that believe." This even seems to undermine the strictest doctrine of justification by faith alone. However, most biblical scholars do not include this book among the genuinely Pauline writings. (I am indebted to Cally Hammond for drawing my attention to this text.)

45. *Apocalypse of Peter*, 601.

46. *Apocalypse of Paul*, 616.

47. Ibid., 623.

48. Ibid., 626.

49. Ibid.

50. Ibid., 626–27.

51. Derived from the four rivers of paradise of Genesis, here the "Pison" (honey), the "Gion" (oil), the Euphrates (milk), and the Tigris (wine).

52. *Apocalypse of Paul*, 633.

53. Ibid. (i.e., 633).

54. See Isa. 6:6–7: "Then flew one of the seraphims unto me, having a live coal in his hand . . . and he laid it upon my mouth."

55. Dante *Inferno*, Canto 3, 34–51

56. Elliott, *Apocalypse* 3, 15–16.

57. Dante, *Inferno*, Canto 3, 34–51.

58. Dante, *Divine Comedy* (Singleton, "Commentary"), 52.

59. *Apocalypse of Paul*, 634.

60. Ibid., 637.

61. Ibid., 638.

62. Ibid.

63. Ibid., 639. The actual words are "on the day on which I arose from the dead." If this means *only* Easter Sunday, rather than every Sunday (the latter being the usual interpretation) the concession would have the purely dramatic quality of the sternest possible mercy.

64. W. H. Auden, "Hymn to St. Cecilia," Music, Benjamin Britten, 1940–42.

65. The *De Spectaculis* is therefore much earlier than the *Apocalypse of Paul*, which dates from the late fourth century.

66. Swete, *Patristic Study*, 59.

67. Gibbon, *Decline and Fall of the Roman Empire*, chap. 15.

68. The Flavian Amphitheater (the Colosseum).

69. Or "assemblage of the Gentiles"—for the church is the New Israel.

70. The Jove who in the shape of a swan raped Leda.

71. All the actors were male.

72. The soul swayed by the love that belongs to the Popular Aphrodite (Pandemou Aphrodites), Plato, *Symposium* 181A–B.

73. Gibbon, *Decline and Fall of the Roman Empire*, chap. 15.

74. Lactantius, *Divine Institutes*, vol. 49.

75. Probably written around 314–15.

76. Probably written around 314.

77. Cross and Livingstone, eds. *Oxford Dictionary of the Christian Church*, s.v. "Lactantius," 942.

78. Virgil, *Aeneid*, bk. 6.

79. *Sibylline Oracles* 8.239; Lactantius 7, 16.

80. *Sibylline Oracles* 5.107–10.

81. Ibid., frag. 3.

82. Lactantius 7, 24, drawing on Isa. 30:26.

83. Ibid., All these images are taken from the *Sibylline Oracles*.

84. Virgil, *Fourth Eclogue*, 38–41.

85. An alternative tradition holds that his amazing chastity came from his use of drugs.

86. Origen, *First Principles*, introduction, v.

87. Ibid., 53 n3. *First Principles* was translated from the original Greek into Latin by Rufinus who, however, bowdlerized it by suppressing or toning down the more "heretical" passages.

88. Origen, *First Principles*, 326, n1: "that all rational natures, that is, the Father, the Son and the Holy Spirit, all angels, authorities, dominions and other powers, and even man himself in virtue of his soul's dignity, are of one substance" (Jerome, *Ep. Ad Avitum* 14). And Jerome considers this to be a "gross impiety."

89. Ibid., 65, 146 (Greek text only), 251, and especially 243 where Origen talks of the "prefect restoration of the whole creation." The word "apocatastasis" was used earlier by St. Clement of Alexandria and, meaning simply "salvation," by Philo of Alexandria. See Chadwick, *Early Christian Thought*, 146, n126.

90. Some of these opinions are not to be found in the extant text of Origen, but are taken from the Anathemas issued against him at the Council of Constantinople.

91. Aristotle, *Nicomachean Ethics*, 1103a–1103b.

92. Origen, *Contra Celsum* 5, 23, 281.

93. Origen *Contra Celsum*, 86.

94. See ibid., 218.

95. Origen, *First Principles*, 141.

96. Isa. 66:24: "for their worm shall not die, neither shall their fire be quenched."

97. Origen, *Contra Celsum*, 141, Isa. 50:11 The verse reads in full: "Behold, all ye that kindle a fire, that compass yourselves about with sparks: walk in the light of your fire, and in the sparks that ye have kindled. This shall ye have of mine hand; ye shall lie down in sorrow."

98. Ibid., 142.

99. Matt. 25:41; Origen, *First Principles*.

100. See Origen, *First Principles*, 142, n3 (Jerome, *Ep. Ad Avitum* 7).

101. These thoughts are found only in the Greek text, as preserved by one of Origen's critics. Rufinus, in the Latin text, has simply: "Let these remarks which we have made at this point, to preserve the order of our discourse, in the fewest possible words, suffice for the present."

102. See Origen, *First Principles*, introduction, xx (Jerome, *Ep. Lxxxxiv ad Pammachium et Oceanum*).

103. The notion of "conversion" does seem far from the spirit of Aristotle's account of choice.

104. A principle he derives from the Jewish scholar and philosopher Philo of Alexandria.

105. For the distinction between "notional" and "real" assent, see Newman, *Grammar of Assent*, pt. 1 chap. 4, and prologue, n4, 405.

106. Satisfaction is the temporal punishment due to sin when the guilt has been forgiven. Penance is a typical requirement.

107. Qur'an (trans. Arberry), sura 17.

108. Sahi Muslim, *Hadith* 6813, 6811.

109. Imam 'Abd ar-Rahim ibn Ahnad al-Qadi, *Islamic Book of the Dead*, 104.

110. Ibid., 78–79.

111. Imam 'Abdallah Ibn 'Alawi Al-Haddad, *Lives of Man*, 56.

112. Idleman- Smith and Haddad, *Islamic Understanding*, 37.

113. 'Abdallah Ibn 'Alawi Al-Haddad, *Lives of Man*, 44.

114. Ibid., 36.

115. Ibid., 75 (and see translation of Sahih Muslim, Book 40, Numbers 6815, 6816).

116. Ibid., 42 (and see Sahi Muslim Book 40, number 6862).

117. 'Abd ar-Rahim ibn Ahmad al-Qadi, *Islamic Book of the Dead*, 27.

118. Ibid., 34, quoting the sixteenth century writer 'Abd al-Wahhab Sha 'rani.

CHAPTER 6

1. See Wicksteed, *Dante and Aquinas*, 114–18.

2. Aristotle, *Poetics*, 1460a, 25–30.

3. Jonathan Swift, *Gulliver's Travels*, pt. 3, chap. 1.

4. T. S. Eliot takes this image as quintessential in distinguishing the Dantean from the Shakespearian imagination, "Dante," *Selected Essays*, 243–44.

5. See *After Lives*, chap. 5, 204–15.

6. Eliot, "Shakespeare and the Stoicism of Seneca," *Selected Essays*, 136.

7. Benvenuto's Commentary on Dante, quoted in Dante, *Divine Comedy* (hereafter as Singleton, "Commentary"), 5.

8. Ibid.

9. Singleton, "Commentary," 10–11; see also *Inferno* (Carlyle/Oelsner), 11.

10. See Elliott, *Apocryphal New Testament*, chap. 5, 214–15.

11. "Who is more impious than he who sorrows at God's judgment?" *Inferno* 20, 27.

12. *Inferno* 28, 142 This is in fact the only occasion on which Dante actually uses the term.

13. Aquinas, *Summa Theologiae* 2a2ae, 61, 4. This is a version of the *lex talionis* (an eye for an eye) mediated through Aristotle, *Ethics* 1132b. Aristotle uses the term *antipeponthos*, which can be rendered as "reciprocity." Aquinas's word is *contrapassum*. See Singleton, "Commentary," 523. Since, here, justice is being rendered by God, this does not contravene the Christian precept "turn the other cheek."

14. In an earlier tradition, Cerberus was actually a devourer of the dead—hence, *kreoboros*, eater of flesh (Singleton, "Commentary," 97). This even resembles the activities of the dog-headed Anubis in the Egyptian underworld.

15. Aquinas, *Summa Theologiae* 2a2ae, 148, 6 (Singleton, "Commentary," 105).

16. Ibid.

17. Ibid., 2a2ae, 148, 2.

18. Ibid., 2a2ae, 148, 5 (the reference is to Aristotle, *Ethics* 1099a7 and 1177a22).

19. Ibid., 148, 2.

20. Singleton, "Commentary," 98.

21. Singleton, "Commentary," 126: Violent rage is natural in a dog, but not natural in a man.

22. Aquinas, *Summa Theologiae* 2a2ae, 158, 5.

23. Ibid., 1a2ae, 46, 7.

24. Ibid., 1a2ae, 46, 6. Aquinas here refers to Aristotle, *Rhetoric* 1382a14.

25. Aquinas, *Summa Theologiae* 2a2ae, 35, 1.

26. Ibid.

27. Ibid., 2a2ae, 35, 2.

28. Ibid., 2a2ae, 35, 4.

29. Baudelaire, *Pleiade*, vol. 1, 656. For the *Fuses* reference I am indebted to Nicholas Hammond.

30. "Baudelaire," *Selected Essays*, 423. In the same paragraph Eliot writes of Baudelaire's *ennui* as "a true form of *acedia*, arising from the unsuccessful struggle towards the spiritual life."

31. Dante is here quoting the words of Orosius, author of the *Historiarum adversum paganos libri VII*, one of Dante's chief sources on ancient history, and who takes this rather surprising view of Alexander the Great. See Singleton, "Commentary," 196–97.

32. The passage may in part imitate one in Seneca's *Hercules Furens*. See Singleton, "Commentary," 204–5.

33. The passage imitates one in Virgil, *Aeneid* 3, 22–48.

34. Singleton, "Commentary," 227.

35. Proust, [*A la recherché*], *Remembrance of Things Past*, vol. 4: *Cities of the Plain*. pt. 1. Turning their heads like Lot's wife "they engendered a numerous progeny with whom the gesture has remained habitual."

36. *Politics* 1258b5, quoted by Aquinas, *Summa Theologiae* 2a2ae, 78, 1.

37. Ibid.

38. Assuming that we think of the mind of Ezra Pound as not representatively "modern."

39. This was improved in a midwestern newspaper of the time to "Myrtle Dante assures us . . ."

40. Spinoza would put it that way as well. The final sentence of the *Ethics* runs: "all noble things are as difficult as they are rare."

41. Aquinas, *Summa Theologiae* 2a2ae, 35, 4.

42. Aristotle, *Nicomachean Ethics*, 1116a–1116b.

CHAPTER 7

1. The Manicheans seem to have been influenced by the Zoroastrian idea of a cosmic struggle between two eternal beings.

2. Augustine, *Against Julian*, 1, 9, 51: "the root of evil cannot arise from anywhere else or be anywhere else except from and in a rational nature, for a rational nature cannot be anything but a gift of God. But, since it was created from nothing by the supreme and unchanging Good, so that it might be a good, even though changeable, its falling away from the Good by which it was created is the root of evil from it or in it, because evil is nothing else but privation of good."

3. *Hic est enim calix sanguinis mei novi et aeterni testamenti qui pro vobis at pro multis effundetur in remissionem peccatorum*, Matt. 26:27–28, Mark 14:23–25, Luke 22:20.

4. Book of Common Prayer (1662), "A General Confession" (Morning and Evening Prayer).

5. Julian of Eclanum, quoted by Augustine, *Against Julian*, bk. 3, chap. 21, 42.

6. The Douay version reads "the heart is perverse above all things."

7. Augustine, *Against Julian* 2, 7, 20. Here Augustine is quoting St. Ambrose of Milan.

8. Augustine, *Against Two Letters of the Pelagians*, bk. 1, chap. 32, 387 (vol. 5).

9. Milton, *Paradise Lost*, bk. 9, 1027–34. This imitates a passage in the *Iliad* where Hera successfully inflames the desire of Zeus.

10. Chrysostom, *Homilia 9, in Genesim*, in *Against Julian*, bk. 1, 6, 30.

11. Milton, *Paradise Lost* 3, 98–99.

12. T. S. Eliot, "Little Gidding," 3.

13. Julian of Eclanum, quoted by Augustine [*Op. Imp.*3, 67 sq], in Brown, *Augustine of Hippo*, 387–88.

14. Luther, *Bondage of the Will*, 247.

15. Erasmus, *De Libero Arbitrio*, 24.

16. Erasmus, *Hyperaspistes*, bk. 1, 184.

17. Erasmus, *De Libero Arbitrio*, 24.

18. See pp. 188–89.

19. The *Institutes* was first published in Latin in 1539; Calvin's own French translation appeared in 1541.

20. T. S. Eliot, "Cousin Nancy" (after Ralph Waldo Emerson).

21. Augustine, *Confessions*, bk. 7, chap. 13.

22. Augustine, *Enchiridion*, chaps. 11–15.

23. Calvin, *Institutes*, vol. 1, chap. 1, 36.

24. Aquinas, *Summa Theologiae* Ia 23, 3.

25. Calvin, *Institutes* 2, chap. 6, 263. Calvin singles out for particular censure Peter Lombard and Bernard of Clairvaux.

26. Augustine, *Letters*, 165; Calvin, *Institutes* vol. 2, chap. 8, 265.

27. Calvin, *Institutes*, vol. 2, chap. 2, sec. 12, 306.

28. One might have thought that this puts human nature in a good light. However, these accomplishments do not count against man's spiritual and moral depravity. Compare Kant: "Intelligence, wit, judgment, and the other *talents* of the mind . . . or courage, resolution, perseverance, as qualities of temperament, are undoubtedly good and desirable in many respects; but these gifts of nature may also become extremely bad

and mischievous if the will which is to make use of them . . . is not good." Kant, *Fundamental Principles of the Metaphysic of Morals*, sec. 1.

29. That is the characterization of Calvin adopted by the Roman Catholic Church. An alternative account of his argument is this: God foresaw the fall of Adam, inasmuch as he willed it. In sinning, Adam involved all mankind in his corruption, bequeathing to them a perverse will to rebel against God. Hence, every individual wilfully chooses to sin, and this cannot be excused as the result of an inherited taint. For Calvin's discussion, see the *Institutes* 3, 23 and 24.

30. We might notice here an Augustinian remark by a great twentieth-century thinker: "Anyone who listens to a child's crying and understands what he hears will know that it harbors dormant psychic forces, terrible forces different from anything commonly assumed. Profound rage, pain, and lust for destruction." Wittgenstein, *Culture and Value*, 2.

31. Aristotle, *Nicomachean Ethics*, 1110b1–1111a5.

32. For "desirability characterizations" see Anscombe, *Intention*, 70–78.

33. Davidson, "How is weakness of the will possible?" 33–36.

34. Plato, *Protagoras*, 357C–E.

35. Sartre, *Being and Nothingness*, pt. 3, chap. 3.

36. Newman, *Apologia Pro Vita Sua*, chap. 5.

37. Tanner, *Council of Trent*.

38. Ibid., "Canons Concerning Justification, Canon 4," 679.

39. Palmer, *Catholics and Unbelievers*, 24–25.

40. Ibid., 27.

41. Ibid., 35.

42. Ibid., 37.

43. *Catechism of the Catholic Church*, 237.

44. Ibid., 432–39.

CHAPTER 8

1. As pointed out by Camporesi in *Fear of Hell*.

2. Drexel, *Considerations*. The first English translation of Drexel's *De aeternitate considerationes* seems to have been as early as 1632.

3. Like the vision of St. Catherine of Siena; see n. 13, this chapter.

4. Drexel, *Hive of Devotion*, 284.

5. Drexel, *Infernus Damnatorum carcer et rogus, aeternitatis* (author's trans.).

6. Ibid. [Colon. Agrippinae: apud Bernard Gualteri, 1632] "si aeternae mortis damnentur trigefies aut etiam centies mille milliones hominum, sive, 100,000,000,000. Flammeus autem hic carcer, secundum omnem altidudinis, latidudinis, ac longitudinis dimensionem, unum milliare Germanicum complectatur, satis omnino spatii habebit, ad obstupescendum illum numerum hominum complectendum. . . . Atque grex damnatorum canes illi ac porci in arcto habitabunt, eruntque sicut uvae in torculari, aut salsae haleces in orca, aut sicut lateres in furnace calcaria, aut sicut

agna in rogo, aut sicut prunae in ignitabulo, aut sicut oves jugulatae in macello; arcte scilicet et compresse vincientur."

7. I am grateful to Nicholas Hammond for that detail.

8. Bourdaloue, "*Sur L'Enfer*," 552.

9. Pope, "Epistle to Burlington," in *Complete Works*.

10. Calvin, *Institutes*, 2, viii, 42.

11. Dawes, *Greatness of Hell Torments*, 4.

12. The original title reads "Christopher Love, *Heaven's glory, Hell's terror, or, Two Treatises: the one concerning the glory of the saints with Jesus Christ as a spur to duty: the other of the torments of the damned as a preservative against security/* by that late faithful servant of Jesus Christ, Mr. Christopher Love."

13. Which existed, however, in earlier times. St. Catherine of Siena had a vision in which she saw souls falling into purgatory like autumn leaves into a river; souls falling into hell like snowflakes onto the ground. Of souls ascending into heaven she saw but three.

14. Love, *Hell's Terror*, 213.

15. Psalm 58:10: The righteous shall rejoice when he seeth the vengeance: he shall wash his feet in the blood of the wicked" (KJV).

16. Lucretius, *De Rerum Natura*, bk. 2, 1–4.

17. Baxter, *Saints Everlasting Rest*, 63; see Almond, *Heaven and Hell in Enlightenment England*. 97.

18. Jonathan Edwards, *Works of President Edwards*, vol 4, 291; quoted in Baxter, *Saints Everlasting Rest*, 98,

19. Burnet's rebuke occurs in *Hell's Torments Not Eternal*.

20. See Camporesi, *Fear of Hell*, chap. 6.

21. "*sudden glory*, is the passion which maketh these grimaces called LAUGHTER; and is caused either by some sudden act of their own, that pleaseth them; or by the apprehension of some deformed thing in another, by comparison whereof they suddenly applaud themselves." Hobbes, *Leviathan*, pt. 2, chap. 6.

22. Love, *Hell's Terror*, 258.

23. Joyce, *Portrait of the Artist*, 126–27.

24. Love, *Hell's Terror*, 270.

25. Bunyan, *Resurrection of the Dead*, vol. 3.

26. Ibid., 216–17.

27. Ibid., 248–49.

28. Bunyan, *A Few Sighs*, 271.

29. Newman, *Apologia Pro Vita Sua*, chap. 5, 247.

30. Vincent, *Fire and Brimstone*.

31. Ibid.

32. Milton, *Paradise Lost*, 1, 63.

33. Vincent, *Fire and Brimstone*, 102–3.

34. Ibid., 109–10.

35. *Works of Lucian*, vol. 1, *Menippus*, trans. A. M. Harmon (London: Loeb, 1913).

36. Swinden, *Enquiry into the Nature and Place of Hell*.

37. Dawes, *Eternity of Hell Torments*, 7.

38. "Hell is not mentioned as being created in the six days of creation; Solomon was wiser than all men, yet he never mentions hell." Richardson, *Discourse of the Torments of Hell*, 33.

39. "fire is light—hell is darkness." Hence any fire in hell is not corporeal. And "they say the absence of God is the greatest torment in hell; corporal fire is a greater torment to the body than the absence of God," Corporal fire consumes, but that of hell is said to last for ever. Corporal fire can be quenched—it "goeth out without wood." Ibid.

40. Burnet, *Hell's torments not eternal*.

41. Whiston is correct. The Greek text does indeed have *en to hade*, Luke 16:23.

42. Whiston, *Eternity of Hell Torments Considered*, 121.

CHAPTER 9

1. The Church claimed scriptural warrant for this in Christ's words to his disciples: "Whose soever sins ye remit, they are remitted unto them; and whose soever sins ye retain, they are retained" (John 20:23).

2. "The whole structure of mortuary provision of masses, alms, pilgrimage, and the adornment of churches and images, which to a greater or lesser degree characterized almost all the wills of fifteenth- and early sixteenth-century English men and women, was raised on the belief that such largesse would hasten the soul's passage through the pains of Purgatory." Duffy, *Stripping of the Altars*, 338.

3. Tanner, "Council of Trent." Trident. Sess. xxv.init.. 238.

4. Le Goff, *Birth of Purgatory*, 12.

5. Hall, *Doctrine of Purgatory*, 332.

6. Milton, *Paradise Lost* 2, 1027 "boiling gulf" and the parable of Dives and Lazarus—"great gulf."

7. Hartcliffe, *Discourse Against Purgatory*, 11, and Milton, *Paradise Lost*, 2.

8. Hall, *Doctrine of Purgatory*, 284.

9. Leslie, *Saint Patrick's Purgatory*, xv.

10. *Hamlet* 1, 5, 135. Old Hamlet makes it plain that his soul is detained in purgatory.

11. O'Sullivan's *Compendium of the Catholic History of Ireland*, vol. 1, lib ii, chap. 3, 24, quoted in Hall, *Doctrine of Purgatory*, 221.

12. Until modern times the faithful were allowed, on All Souls' Day, a plenary indulgence, applicable to the dead, on every visit to a church. The present writer recalls taking part in the practice—not uncommon—of going in and out of church every few minutes, gaining the indulgence on each visit. Having gone through all his deceased relatives, his application of indulgences began to range through recorded history, eventually taking in Julius Caesar and Herod the Great.

13. Duffy, *Stripping of the Altars*, 339.

14. 2 Macc. 12:41–46 (Apoc.). See also White, *Middle State of Souls*, 7.

15. White, ibid.; 1 Cor. 15:29. St. John Chrysostom attributed this practice to the Marcionites and the Montanists.

16. Thomas White, *Middle State of Souls*, 18–19.

17. Hartcliffe, *Discourse Against Purgatory*, 15.

18. Ibid., 16.

19. Kant, *Critique of Practical Reason*, Analytic of Pure Practical Reason, theorem 5, problem 2.

20. John Gother, *Papist Misrepresented and Represented*, 58.

21. Origen, *First Principles*, 143.

22. Ibid., 142.

23. White *Middle State of Souls*, 86.

24. Ibid., 102.

25. Catherine of Genoa, *Treatise on Purgatory* 1, 17–18.

26. Ibid.

27. Certain English Protestant theologians thought that an additional pleasure was that the saved, in observing the damned, blessed (as it were) their lucky stars. But that would certainly involve a strong sense of self.

28. Catherine of Genoa, *Treatise on Purgatory* 2, 18–19.

29. White, *Middle State of Souls*, 102.

30. Crashaw, "A Hymn to the Name and Honour of the Admirable Saint Theresa," in *Works*.

31. See Casey, *Pagan Virtue*, 12.

32. Catherine of Genoa, *Treatise on Purgatory* 10, 27.

33. Ibid., 11, 28.

34. Hall, *Doctrine of Purgatory*, 220–21.

35. Le Goff, *Birth of Purgatory*, 334.

36. Ibid., 292–93.

37. Dante, *Purgatorio*, Canto 5, 103–8.

38. Dante, *Divine Comedy* (Singleton), Commentary on *Purgatorio*, 104; and Aquinas on contrition as tearful, *Summa Theologiae* 3, Suppl., q 1, a.1,resp.; see also Dante, *Divine Comedy* (Singleton), 758–59.

39. Note the words of Belacqua, punished for sloth, in Canto 4, 132–35; and of Forese, punished for gluttony, whose wife, by her floods of tears, devout prayers and sighs "has brought me from the slope where they wait, and set me free from the other circles." Dante, *Purgatorio*, Canto 23, 88–90.

40. Le Goff, *Birth of Purgatory*, 339.

41. Aquinas, *Summa Theologiae* 2a2ae, 36, 2.

42. Ibid., 3.

43. Ibid.

44. A virtue that also characterizes Marge Simpson.

45. Aquinas, *Summa* 1a2ae 48, 2.

46. Eliot, *Complete Poems and Plays*, 207.

CHAPTER 10

1. Those of the pyramids of King Wenis at the end of the Fifth Dynasty and of the rulers of the Sixth Dynasty. See Faulkner, *Ancient Egyptian Pyramid Texts*, preface, v.

2. Wright, *Early History of Heaven*, 6.

3. Ibid., 8–10.

4. Ibid., 10–16.

5. Faulkner, *Pyramid Texts*, utterance 214.

6. See Faulkner, *Ancient Egyptian Book of the Dead*, introduction, 11.

7. Wright, *Early History of Heaven*, 6.

8. Allen, introduction to *Book of the Dead*, 12.

9. Faulkner, *Ancient Egyptian Coffin Texts*, vol. 1, spell 306.

10. Pope, "The Dunciad" in *Works*, vol. 1, 51.

11. Faulkner, *Pyramid Texts*, utterance 210, *Coffin Texts*, vol. 3, spell 1012, 49–50. See also chap. 2, *After Lives*.

12. Allen, *Book of the Dead*, spells 32, 51, 52, 53, 82, 116, 124, 189.

13. Faukner, *Coffin Texts*, spell 197. See also chap. 2, n62, *After Lives*; Zandee, *Death as an Enemy*, 55.

14. Ibid., *Coffin Texts*, spell 210.

15. Allen, *Book of the Dead*, spell 6. See also chap. 2, *After Lives*.

16. Faulkner, *Coffin Texts*, spell 278.

17. Allen, *Book of the Dead*, spell 75.

18. Ibid., spell 80.

19. Wallis-Budge, *Egyptian Heaven and Hell*, vol. 3, 65, 67.

20. Wright, *Early History of Heaven*, 29–31, quoting Kramer "Death and Netherworld According to the Sumerian Texts," in *Sumerian Mythology*.

21. Pritchard, "Descent of Ishtar to the Underworld," 107.

22.   *Thammuz* came next behind,

     Whose annual wound in *Lebanon* allur'd

     The *Syrian* Damsels to lament his fate

     In amorous ditties all a Summers day,

     While smooth *Adonis* from his native Rock

     Ran purple to the Sea, suppos'd with blood

     Of *Thammuz* yearly wounded." (Milton, *Paradise Lost* 1, 446–52)

23. I have mixed elements of the Babylonian (Pritchard) with the Sumerian versions. For a translation of the Sumerian version, see Kramer, *Sumerian Mythology*, 88–96.

24. Kramer, "Dilmun, the Land of the Living," 18–19.

25. Langdon, *Sumerian Epic of Paradise*, Obverse 1.

26. Ibid., Obverse 2.

27. Ibid., 8–9.

28. Kramer, "Dilmun, Land of the Living," 26.

29. Langdon, *Sumerian Epic of Paradise*, 54.

30. Milton, *Paradise Lost* 11, 824–35.

31. Kramer, *Sumerian Mythology*, 63–64.

32. Wright, *Early History of Heaven*. 43.

33. Ibid., 63ff.

34. Ibid., 63.

35. Ibid.; Mic. 4:5. The Authorized (KJV) Version reads: "For all people will walk every one in the name of his god, and we will walk in the name of the LORD our God for ever and ever."

36. 1 Sam. 28. It seems likely that the scene in Macbeth where the witches call up images of the future kings of Scotland and England is influenced by the account of the witch of En-dor calling up Samuel. Macbeth's fate will be Saul's—but the witches deceive him.

37. McDannell, *Heaven*, 6.

38. Ibid., 1–2.

39. Ibid., 8–9.

40. See chap. 3, *After Lives*, "Mesopotamia and Israel."

41. The tombs of the Persian kings, including Darius the Great and Xerxes, at Nakht-i-Rustum, and of Cyrus himself at Passagardae, do not fit this account.

42. McDannell, *Heaven*, 12.

43. 1 Enoch 14 (*The Book of Watchers*), *Apocryphal Old Testament* (Sparks/Knibb).

44. See Himmelfarb, *Ascent to Heaven*, 15.

45. 1 Enoch 18, *Apocryphal Old Testament* (Sparks/Knibb).

46. Ibid.

47. Ibid.

48. Gibbon, *Decline and Fall*, chap. 16.

49. 2 Enoch 9, *Apocryphal Old Testament* (Pennington).

50. See Himmelfarb, *Ascent to Heaven*, 4.

51. 2 Enoch 17, *Apocryphal Old Testament* (Pennington).

52. Himmelfarb, *Ascent to Heaven*, chap. 1.

53. Wright, *Early History of Heaven*, 209.

54. 2 Enoch 17, *Apocryphal Old Testament* (Pennington).

55. Philo, *On the Creation*, 3, 13–14; *Philo, in Ten Volumes*, vol. 1.

56. Philo, *On the Creation*, 23, 69–71.

57. Philo, *On the Giants*, 23, 12–16; *Philo, in Ten Volumes*, vol. 2.

58. Philo, *On Dreams*, 1, 22, 133–41; *Philo, in Ten Volumes*, vol. 5.

59. Philo, *On Dreams*, 1, 32, 184–86.

60. McDannell, *Heaven*, 18.

61. Philo, *Embassy to Gaius*, 44 349–45 367; *Philo, in Ten Volumes*. vol. 10,

62. Augustine, *City of God*.

63. *Othello* 5, ii, 347–49.

64. *Justus quidem tu es, Domine, si disputem tecum . . .*; see Jer. 12:1.

65. Augustine, *Confessions*, bk. 9, x, xi.

66. McDannell, *Heaven*, 37–44.

CHAPTER II

1. See chap. 5, *After Lives*, "Christian Beginnings," 129–30.

2. Irenaeus of Lugdunum, *Against Heresies*.

3. McDannell, *Heaven*, 50.

4. Irenaeus, *Against Heresies* 5, 5.

5. Bynum, *Resurrection of the Body*, 61.

6. This is often attributed to St. Augustine but seems more probably to have a Gnostic provenance.

7. Irenaeus, *Against Heresies* 5, 26.

8. McDannell, *Heaven*, 48.

9. Ibid., 53.

10. Augustine, *Confessions*, 1, vii.

11. Aristotle, *De Generatione Animalium*, bk. 4.

12. Augustine, *City of God* 22, 17.

13. Bynum, *Resurrection of the Body*, 100, quoting Augustine, sermon 243.

14. Tertullian, *De Resurrectione*, chap. 58.

15. Augustine, *City of God* 22, 18.

16. Wittgenstein says: "my attitude toward him is an attitude toward a soul. I am not of the *opinion* that he has a soul." *Philosophical Investigations* 2, iv.

17. Qur'an, sura 19. See also sura 78.

18. Kitab Al-Jannat wa Sifat Na'imiha wa Ahliha. no. 6784, *Book Pertaining to Paradise*, bk. 40.

19. Ibid., no. 6790.

20. Ibid., no. 6804.

21. Ibid., 6792.

22. 'Abd Ar-Rahim Ibn Ahnad, *Islamic Book of the Dead*, 127–28.

23. *Book Pertaining to Paradise*, nos. 6796, 6797, 6798; also *Islamic Book of the Dead*, 124.

24. *Book Pertaining to Paradise*, no. 6808.

25. Idleman-Smith and Haddad, *Islamic Understanding*, chap. 4, 113–35.

26. 'Abd Ar-Rahim Ibn Ahnad, *Muslim Book of the Dead*, 130.

27. Ibid., 134.

28. This is strongly argued by Asin, in *Islam and the Divine Comedy*, where he traces an Islamic influence upon Dante. But he is forced to conclude that these later traditions represent a departure from what he considers to be the "coarse and sensual materialism of the paradise" depicted in the Qur'an. Ibid., 136.

29. 'Abdallah Ibn 'Alawi, *Lives of Man*, 80–81.

30. Ibid., 82.

CHAPTER 12

1. T. S. Eliot, "Dante," *Selected Essays*.

2. Singleton, "Commentary," 212, quoting C. H. Grandgent.

3. Ibid., 222.

4. It is widely assumed that in the Ptolemaic system the earth is the center of the universe because the sun and stars circle around it. This is not really true. The earth is at the farthest point from God; and hell, which is at the center of the earth, is the absolute farthest point. The true center is God, the Unmoved Mover, out of love for whom "the sun and the other stars" circle eternally.

5. Singleton, "Commentary," 238–39.

6. St. Bonaventure, *Soliloquium* 4, v, 27; Singleton, "Commentary," 243.

7. Singleton, "Commentary," quoting Grandgent.

8. Anthony Kenny, *Aquinas*, 48.

9. Coplestone, *Aquinas*, 160.

10. Aquinas, *Summa Contra Gentiles* 4, 79.

11. Singleton, "Commentary," 244.

12. Eliot, "Dante," *Selected Essays*, 269.

13. Ibid., 258.

14. Aristotle, *Metaphysics* 1072b, 20–30.

15. Bernard of Clairvaux, *On Consideration*, bk. 5, 12, 25.

16. Ibid.

17. Dante, *Convivio* 2 iv, 9–13; see Singleton, "Commentary," 473–74.

CHAPTER 13

1. Dante, *Paradiso* 33, 85–87.

2. McDannell, *Heaven*, 119.

3. Jean Delumeau, *History of Paradise*, 9.

4. Ibid., 12–13.

5. Ibid., 55.

6. Harry Levin, *Myth of the Golden Age*, 183.

7. Christopher Ricks writes well of this nostalgia in *Milton's Grand Style* (149): "Nowhere else in the poem, not even at the magnificent moments when Milton lavishes his full luxuriance on the Garden, do we so yearn for Paradise. And of Milton's touching oxymorons, perhaps the greatest is the title of his epic."

8. Lorenzo Valla, *De Vero Falsoque Bono*, 201–2. The first version of the dialogue was published in 1431.

9. Ibid., 287.

10. Virgil, *Aeneid* 7, 809.

11. See also Virgil, *Aeneid* 6, 820–23.

12. Savonarola, *Compendium of Revelations*, 246–47. See also McDannell, *Heaven*, 118–19.

13. McDannell, *Heaven*, 126–27; Harrison, *Pastoral Elegy*. This is, of course, a pastoral poem, so the images of the Elysian Fields need not in themselves testify to changing ideas of the Christian heaven.

14. Erasmus, "The Apotheosis of Caprio," in *Familiar Colloquies*, vol. 1, 216–17.

15. Dante, *Inferno*, Canto 4, 90–99.

16. Cicero, *Republic*, vol. 1, 1, 2.

17. Cicero, *Somnium Scipionis*, in *Republic*, vol. 6, 12.

18. Cicero, *De Senectute* 23, 83–84.

19. Nietzsche, *Antichrist*, 61; *Genealogy of Morals* 1, 16; *Ecce Homo*, "The Case of Wagner," 2.

20. Luther, *Table Talk*, 347.

21. Ibid., 19, 50, 81, 189.

22. This comes from a brief note Pascal wrote describing a religious experience he had on November 23, 1654: "Fire. God of Abraham, God of Isaac, God of Jacob, not of the philosophers and schoolmen . . ."

23. Luther, *Table Talk* (June 4, 1539), 358–59.

24. McDannell, *Heaven*, 148.

25. Ibid., 153.

26. Calvin, *Institutes* 1, 1, 1.

27. McDannell, *Heaven*, 148.

28. Ibid., 155.

29. Aquinas, *Summa Theologiae* 1, 2, suppl. xciii, 3.

30. Calvin, *Institutes* 3, 11.

31. Luther, *Commentary on 1 Corinthians*, 170.

32. Luther also says, ambiguously, that "persons such as husband and wife will remain, and also the entire human race as it was created."

33. Luther, *Table Talk*, no. 305, 41.

34. Ibid., no. 3901, 291.

35. Ibid., no. 5386, 416.

36. Luther, *Commentary*, 172.

37. *Table Talk*, no. 5468, last entry (February 16, 1546), 476.

38. Ibid., no. 5537, 448.

39. Luther, *Bondage of the Will*, trans. Philip S. Watson in collaboration with Benjamin Drewery, in Luther's *Works*, vol. 33, 247 (Philadelphia, 1972.)

40. *Oxford Dictionary of the Christian Church*, s.v. "Francis de Sales."

41. His other is the *Introduction to a Devout Life*.

42. Francis de Sales, *Love of God*, 6.

43. Plato, *Symposium*, 210–12.

44. Baxter, *Saints' Everlasting Rest*, 166–77.

45. John Hampden and John Pym were English Parliamentarians who were fiercely opposed to Charles I and Episcopacy and fought on Parliament's side against the king in the English Civil War.

46. Ibid.

47. Beveridge, *Happiness of the Saints*.

48. Blake's illustrations to Blair's *The Grave*, plate 10.

49. Ibid., plate 11.

50. Ibid., plate 12.

CHAPTER 14

1. Overton, *Man Wholly Mortal*. See the bibliography for the complete (and sprightly) title.

2. The Royal Society of London for Improving Natural Knowledge, founded 1660.

3. Isaac Watts, *World to Come*.

4. Watts has read his Milton (*Samson Agonistes*, 92–96):

> . . . if it be true
> That light is in the Soul,
> She all in every part; why was the sight
> To such a tender ball as th'eye confin'd?
> So obvious and so easie to be quencht,
> And not as feeling through all parts diffus'd,
> That she might look at will through every pore?

And:

> So much the rather thou Celestial Light
> Shine inward, and the mind through all her powers
> Irradiate, there plant eyes, all mist from thence
> Purge and disperse. (*Paradise Lost* 3, 51–54)

Watts indeed quotes *Paradise Lost* on the darkness of Hell as one of its chiefest terrors. It is the devils and the damned who are in darkness.

5. Watts, *Death and heaven*.

6. Aquinas, *Summa Contra Gentiles*, bk. 4.

7. See, for example, sura 36.

8. Burnet, *State of the Dead* . . . "with remarks . . . and an answer to all the heresies within" (Matthias Earbery, trans.).

9. Burnet, *Sacred Theory of the Earth*.

10. Burnet, *State of the Dead*, 120.

11. Earbery, in one of his "answers to all the heresies within": "the Doctor was a great enemy to old women."

12. See Gearing, *Prospect of Heaven*, 121.

13.

> for ev'n in Heav'n his looks and thoughts
> Were always downward bent, admiring more
> The riches of Heav'ns pavement, trodd'n Gold,
> Than aught divine or holy else enjoyd
> In vision beatific (*Paradise Lost* 1, 680–84)

14. Basil Willey, introduction to Burnet's *Sacred Theory*.

15. Burnet, *Sacred Theory*, 75, quoting Psalms 24:2 and 136:6.

16. Rowe, *Friendship in Death*, 4.

17. Ibid.

18. Milton, *Paradise Lost*, bk. 6, 749–66.

19. Ibid., 4, 236–63.

20. Rowe, *Friendship in Death*.

21. Ibid., 11.

22. Ibid.

23. Waugh, *The Loved One*.

24. Rowe, *Friendship in Death*, 14–15.

25. Ibid., 32.

26. Asgill, *An Argument Proving*.

27. Almond, *Heaven and Hell*, 54.

28. Defoe, *Enquiry into the Case of Mr. Asgill's General Translation*.

29. Anonymous, *Account of Mr. Asgill's Strange and Wonderful Translation*.

30. Ibid., 9.

31. To the Great Fire of London.

32. Ibid., 10.

CHAPTER 15

1. Bernhard Lang, introduction to *Heaven and Its Wonders and Hell, Drawn from Things Heard and Seen*, by Emanuel Swedenborg. The book reviewed by Goethe is *Ausichten in die Ewigheit* by Johann Kaspar Lavater.

2. Lang, intro., 10.

3. Kant, *Dreams of a Spirit Seer*, 101.

4. Ibid., 95. Kant wrote a letter to Charlotte Von Knobloch with a fuller version of this story, and also two others that related to Swedenborg's supposed ability to communicate with the dead.

5. Carlyle, "The Hero as Prophet," in *On Heroes and Hero-Worship*, 42.

6. See T. S. Eliot, "Blake," in *Selected Essays*, 320.

7. McDannell, *Heaven*.

8. Swedenborg, *Heaven and Hell*, sec. 33.

9. McDannell, *Heaven*.

10. Aristotle, *Poetics*, 1459a.

11. Blake, "Auguries of Innocence," 1–4.

12. Ibid., "Marriage of Heaven and Hell."

13. Ibid., "Proverbs of Hell," "Marriage of Heaven and Hell."

14. Both are discussed by McDannell in, *Heaven*, 195–216.

15. Ibid., 195.

16. Ibid., 196.

17. Swedenborg, *Heaven and Hell*, 547.

18. Kant's summary, *Dreams of a Spirit Seer*, 110; Swedenborg, *Heaven and Hell*, 59, and *Arcana Coelestia*, 4219, 4224.

19. Swedenborg, *Heaven and Hell*, 65.

20. Swedenborg, *Worlds in Space*, 13.

21. Ibid., 79.

22. Ibid., 163–65.

23. As Kant pointed out in *Dreams of a Spirit Seer*, 108. I have drawn upon Kant's excellently succinct account of Swedenborg's metaphysics.

24. Kant, *Dreams of a Spirit Seer*, 107.

25. Swedenborg, *Heaven and Hell*, 89.

26. Swedenborg, *Spiritual Diary*, vol. 1, sec. 154.

27. Swedenborg, *Heaven and Hell*, 416.

28. See Swedenborg, *Worlds in Space*. First published in Latin 1758, largely taken from *Arcana Coelestia* (1749–56).

29. Swedenborg, *Heaven and Hell*, 17.

30. Hegel, *Philosophy of Mind*, sec. 396, 401. See Sartre: "Every human fact is significant, and to rob it of its significance is to rob it of its status as a human fact." *Sketch for a Theory of the Emotions*, 27.

31. Milton, *Paradise Lost*, 4, 303.

32. Swedenborg, *Heaven and Hell*, 51.

33. See T. S. Eliot, "Hamlet," in *Selected Essays*, 145.

34. Kant, *Dreams of a Spirit Seer*, 108.

35. Swedenborg, *Heaven and Hell*, 54.

36. This is more or less what Socrates thinks idealized homosexual love procreates; see *Symposium* 208D–212B.

37. Swedenborg, *Heaven and Hell*, 337.

38. Swedenborg, *Spiritual Diary*.

39. Swedenborg, *Heaven and Hell*, 414.

40. The full title of which is *The Delights of Wisdom on the subject of Conjugial Love followed by The Gross Pleasures of Folly on the Subject of Scortatory Love*. "Conjugial" is a word of Swedenborg's coinage, denoting the highly erotic but chaste love that is his ideal. "Scortatory" is another coinage and means, in effect, promiscuous sexual attraction.

41. John Wesley, *Works*, vol. 4, 149–50.

42. Ibid.

43. McDannell, *Heaven*, 225.

44. Swedenborg, *Conjugial Love*, chap. 1, 15–16.

45. Milton, *Paradise Lost* 8, 618–29.

46. Swedenborg, *Conjugial Love*, chap. 3, 55.

47. Homer, *Odyssey* 11, 198–203.

48. Song of Songs, 2:9, 5:15, 4:12 (Douay).

49. Swedenborg, *Conjugial Love*, chap. 5, 97.

50. Wesley, "Letter to Miss Ritchie," Feb. 12, 1779, *Works*, vol. 13, 62.

51. Aristotle, *Poetics*, 1460a, 25–30.

CHAPTER 16

1. A point made by McDannell in *Heaven*, 276.

2. Phelps, *Gates Ajar*, 49.

3. Ibid., 79. Professor Bush, in *Anastasis*, does indeed argue along these lines.

4. Ibid., 97.

5. Ibid., 107, 120.

6. For the account of the Fox children, the career of Katie Fox, and her subsequent recantation, see Harry Houdini's *Magician Among the Spirits*, 1–11. On the day on which Katie Fox was expected to make her public recantation, along with detailed accounts of "how the trick was done," she was kept closely guarded in her hotel lest there should be attempts by certain mediums to kidnap her. Sir Arthur Conan Doyle approvingly called the Hydesville manifestations "the starting point of modern spiritualism." Doyle, *New Revelation*, 43.

7. Gridley, *Astounding Facts*.

8.
> Her Joy in gilded Chariots when alive,
> And love of *Ombre*, after Death survive.
> (Pope, "The Rape of the Lock," Canto 1, 55–56)

9. Gridley, *Astounding Facts*, 50.

10. Lodge, *Raymond*, 220–24; Mercier, *Spiritualism and Sir Oliver Lodge*, 121.

11. Mercier, *Spiritualism and Sir Oliver Lodge*, quote by Houdini, 206.

12. Sidgwick, Presidential Address, *Proceedings of the Society of Psychical Research*, 1852, 8. See also Barrett, *On the Threshold*.

13. Doyle, *New Revelation*, 70.

14. Ibid., 85. This claim that the moment of death is usually pleasant became a recurrent theme in Spiritualist writings. Sir Oliver Lodge records a piece of "automatic writing": "The look of ecstasy on Mrs. Piper's face at a certain stage in the waking process is manifestly similar to that seen on the faces of some dying people; and both describe the subjective visions as of something more beautiful and attractive than those of earth." Lodge, *Survival of Man*, 114. A critic of Lodge wrote, in rebuttal: "As a medical man of many years' residence in medical institutions, I am sure I have seen very many more dying people than Sir Oliver Lodge has; and I have never yet witnessed a look of ecstasy on the face of a dying person." Mercer, *Spiritualism and Sir Oliver Lodge*, 60.

15. Moses, *Spirit Teachings*, 22.

16. Doyle, *New Revelation*, 86–87.

17. Ibid., 132–33. "If your boy were in Australia, you would not expect him to continually stop his work and write long letters at all seasons. Having got in touch, be moderate in your demands."

18. Crookes, "Record of Seances with D. D. Home," in *Proceedings of the Society for Psychical Research*, 1924–25, vol. 35, 70.

19. Sidgwick, *Proceedings of the Society for Psychical Research*, 1884, vol. 1, 162.

20. Ibid., "On Phenomena Connected with Theosophy," in *Proceedings*, 1885, vol. 3, 204, 209.

21. Ibid. *Proceedings*, 1889, vol. 6, 15.

22. Ibid., "The Experiences at Seances of W. Stainton Moses," in *Proceedings*, 1893–94, vol. 9, 297.

23. Ibid., *Proceedings*, 1893–94, vol. 9, 298.

24. Abbott, *Behind the Scenes*. 54, 236–52.

25. Crookes, "Notes of Seances with D. D. Home," in *Proceedings*, 1889–90; and "Record of séances with D. D. Home (detailing séances from 1867–69)," in *Proceedings*, 1924–25, vol. 35.

26. Crookes, *Notes of Seances*, 108.

27. Ibid., 102–3, 113.

28. Barrett, *On the Threshold*, 70–71; see also *Proceedings*, 1924–25, vol. 35, 156–57, for another account.

29. Frank Podmore, the historian of Spiritualism, quoted by Count Petrovsky-Petrovo-Solovo in "Some Thoughts on D. D. Home," in *Proceedings*, 1930, vol. 114.

30. Ibid., 248.

31. Massey, "The Great Spiritual Case," Lyon v. Home," *Illustrated Police News* (1868).

32. *Proceedings*, 1930, vol. 114, 251.

33. Houdini, *Magician Among the Spirits*, 43.

34. Lodge, *Raymond*, 126.

35. It says something for Sir Oliver Lodge's frankness that this prophecy was not omitted in the revised edition of *Raymond* published in 1922.

36. The medium was female and possibly not a cigar smoker. We learn, however, that "the chaps who try these cigars give them up after a few attempts."

37. It may be worth remembering that this is only one year after the famous "Christmas truce" of 1914.

38. These were two of a series titled The Life Beyond the Veil.

39. Tennyson's use of "behind the veil, behind the veil" in *In Memoriam* 56—a poem of almost unassuageable grief for the dead Arthur Hallam—suggests an influence either on or by Spiritualism.

40. Owen, *Children in Heaven*, 71.

41. Ibid., 74.

42. Twain (Clemens) died in 1910, but the short story in booklet form was published in 1909, the last ever published by that author.

43. Twain, *Captain Stormfield's Visit*, 82–83.

44. "That the glory of this world in the end is appearance leaves the world more glorious, if we feel it is a show of some fuller splendour; but the sensuous curtain is a deception and a cheat, if it hides some colorless movement of atoms, some spectral woof of impalpable abstractions, or unearthly ballet of bloodless

categories." F. H. Bradley, *Principles of Logic*. (See T. S. Eliot, "Francis Herbert Bradley," in *Selected Essays*, 447.)

CHAPTER 17

1. Browning, "Bishop Blougram's Apology."

2. The same clearly does not apply to Islam.

3. Gallup, *Adventures in Immortality*, 3. But only 54 percent of nonwhites share this faith (183).

4. Ibid., 185–91.

5. Ibid.

6. Ibid., 207.

7. Barth, *Resurrection of the Dead*, 122–23.

8. Ibid., 140–41.

9. Ibid.

10. Bultmann, "*Karl Barth: The Resurrection of the Dead*," in *Faith and Understanding*, 67.

11. Ibid., 84–85.

12. Ibid., 87.

13. See Bultmann, *New Testament and Mythology and Other Writings*.

14. See McDannell, *Heaven*, chap. 10.

15. Hill, *Angel Children*, 41, quoting the Mormon bishop Edward Hunter.

16. Ibid., 54.

17. Ibid., 43.

18. Hill, 15, 18.

19. Ibid., 73, 126.

20. Crowther, *Life Everlasting*, 53.

21. Ibid., 465–67.

22. Ibid. One witness says that his hair was brown, and another that it was "brownish-golden"—but all agree on the piercing blue eyes.

23. Chamberlain, *Foundations of the Nineteenth Century*, 200–213.

24. Millett, *Life Beyond Death*, 98.

25. "God has a body that looks like yours, though His body is immortal, perfected, and has a glory beyond description." *God is your loving heavenly father*, Truth Restored, www.Mormon.org/eng/basic-beliefs/the-restoration-of-truth (defunct).

26. McGann, *Implications of Mormon Eternal Progression*.

27. Pratt, *Seer*, 132.

28. Mark 12:25. See also Matt. 22:30, Luke 20:35.

29. Young, *Discourses*, 195.

30. Lucinda Bunnen and Virginia Warren Smith, *Scoring in Heaven* (New York: Aperture Books, 1991). [unpaginated].

31. Eliot, "East Coker," no. 3, *Four Quartets*, in *Complete Poems and Plays*.

32. Laugs and Kletke, *American After Life*, 74.

33. Quoted by Sloane, in *Last Great Necessity*, 160–61.

34. Ibid., 161.

35. Ibid., 167.

36. Mitford, *American Way of Death Revisited*, 102.

37. Sloane, *Last Great Necessity*, 170–71.

38. Ibid., 174.

39. Waugh, *Loved One*, 35.

40. And which became the title of a study of American funerary customs by Jessica Mitford.

41. See Farrell, *Inventing the American Way of Death*, 183.

42. Ibid., 121.

43. Ibid., 132.

44. Ibid., 135.

45. The point of the "casket" was to avoid that suggestion of death that the coffin, following as it does the form of a human body, makes inescapable.

46. Farrell, *Inventing the American Way of Death*, 181. Is it even possible that Blackwell was being wickedly satirical? It would be the only creditable explanation. "Sunny Side" was part of the title of a well-known morticians' journal with the title of *Casket and Sunny Side*.

47. See Lindsey, *Rapture: Truth or Consequences*.

48. Ibid., 24.

49. Ibid., 40.

50. See *Rapture Ready*, March 24, 2008, 3, www.radosh.net.

51. Ibid., March 25, 2008, 1–2.

52. See Lehay and Jenkins, Left Behind series, esp. *Desecration, The Remnant,* and *Glorious Appearing*. The series claims to have sold in excess of fifty million copies.

53. Lehay, *Glorious Appearing*, 71.

54. One of the more up-to-date signs of the coming end is the millions of hits from converts on Dr. Rosenzweig's website.

55. Lehay, *Glorious Appearing*, 132.

56. Sahih Muslim, trans. Abdul Hamid Siddiqui, bk. 41, *Book Pertaining to the Turmoil and Portents of the Last Hour* (Kitab Al-Fitan wa Ashrat As-Sa'ah), nos. 7005, 7015.

57. Ibid., no. 6995.

58. Ibid., no. 7034.

59. Ibid., no. 7007.

60. Ibid., nos. 6918, 6922, 6924, 6931, 6932, 6935, 6937.

61. Ibid., nos. 6597–6960. This appears to refer to the Turks—who nevertheless turned out to be the conquerors of Constantinople.

62. Ibid., no. 7015.

63. See Cook, *Contemporary Muslim Apocalyptic Literature*.

64. Ibid., 15.

65. Fahd Salim, *Kashf al-sirr al-ta'rikhi Yahud al-yawm hum Yahuj wa-Majuj wa-iqtaraba al-wa'd al-haqq*, quoted in Cook, *Contemporary Muslim Apocalyptic Literature*, 19.

66. Said Ayyub, *Al-Masih al-Dajjal*, quoted in Cook, 20–21.

67. See Cook, *Contemporary Muslim Apocalyptic Literature*, 50–51.

68. Mustafa Murad, *Mata taqum al-sa'a*, quoted in Cook, 54.

69. B. Bashir Muhammad 'Abdallah, *Zilzal al-ard al-'azim*, quoted in Cook, 42.

70. Safar Ibn 'Abd al-Rahman al-Hawali, *Wa'd Kissinjir wa-l-ahdaf al-Amrikiyya fi al-khalij* quoted in Cook, 163.

EPILOGUE

1. Joyce, *Portrait of the Artist*, 155.

2. Ibid., 257.

3. Eliot, *Selected Essays*, 303.

4. Eliot, "Shakespeare and the Stoicism of Seneca," in *Selected Essays*, 135.

5. Ibid., 137.

6. Ibid.

7. Eliot, "The *Pensees* of Pascal," in *Selected Essays*, 408.

8. Nietzsche, *Beyond Good and Evil*, sec. 201.

Bibliography

All biblical quotations are from the Authorized (King James) Version of the Bible, unless otherwise noted.

Abbott, David P. *Behind the Scenes with the Mediums*. London, 1907.

'Abd Allah ibn 'Alawi Al-Haddad, Imam. *The Lives of Man*. Quilliam Press, 1991.

'Abd 'ar-Rahim ibn 'Ahmad Al-Qadi, Imam. *The Islamic Book of the Dead: A Collection of Hadith on the Fire and the Garden*. Translated by A'isha 'Abd 'al-Rahman al Tarjumana. Norwich, Norfolk: Diwan Press, 1977.

Albinus, Lars. *The House of Hades: Studies in Ancient Greek Eschatology*. Aarhus, 2000.

Albright, W. F. *From Stone Age to Christianity: Monotheism and the Historical Process*. Baltimore: Johns Hopkins University Press, 1948.

Allen, Thomas George, trans. *The Egyptian Book of the Dead; or The Book of Going Forth by Day*. Chicago, 1974.

Allen, William. *A Defense and Declaration of the Catholike Churches Doctrine touching purgatory*. Antwerp, 1565.

Almond, Philip C. *Heaven and Hell in Enlightenment England*. Cambridge, 1994.

Anonymous. *An Account of Mr. Asgill's Strange and Wonderful Translation, Which will happen upon the Twelfth of July Next*. London, 1704.

Anscombe, Elizabeth. *Intention*. Oxford: Blackwell, 1957.

Apocryphal Old Testament. Edited by F. J. Sparks. 1 Enoch, translated by M. A. Knibb. 2 Enoch, translated by A. Pennington. Oxford, 1984.

Aquinas. *See* Thomas Aquinas, Saint.

Aristotle. *De Generatione Animalium*. Translated by D. M. Balme. Oxford, 1972.

———. *Metaphysics*. Edited and translated by W. D. Ross. Oxford, 1928.

Aristotle. *Nicomachean Ethics*. Translated by W. D. Ross. Oxford, 1915.

———. *Poetics*. Translated by I. Bywater. Oxford, 1909.

———. *Rhetoric*. Translated by W. D. Ross. Oxford, 1924.

Arnold, Matthew. *Culture and Anarchy*. Edited by R. H. Super. In *Complete Prose Works of Matthew Arnold*. Michigan, 1965.

Asgill, John. *An Argument proving, that according to the Covenant of eternal life revealed in the scriptures, man may be translated from hence into that eternal life, without passing through death, although the human nature of Christ himself could not be thus translated till he had passed through death*. London, 1700.

Asin, Miguel. *Islam and the Divine Comedy*. Translated by Harold Sutherland. London, 1926.

Augustine, Saint. *Against Julian*. Translated by Matthew A. Schumacher. New York, 1957.

———. *The City of God*. Translated by Henry Bettenson. Penguin, 1972.

———. *Confessions*. Translated by F. J. Sheed. London, 1944.

———. *De Libero Arbitrio*. Translated by Anna S Benjamin and L. H. Hackerstaff. Indianapolis, 1964.

———. *De Trinitate*. Translated by Stephen J McKenna. Washington, 1970.

———. *Enchiridion*. Translated by J. F. Shaw. Edinburgh, 1883.

———. *On Marriage and Concupiscence. The Good of Marriage. On the Predestination of Saints. On the Good of Perseverance. Against Two Letters of the Pelagians*. Edited by Philip Schaff. In *A Select Library of Nicene and Post-Nicene Fathers of the Church*. Michigan, 1971.

Baudelaire, Charles. *Complete Works*. Paris: Gallimard, 1975.

Barth, Karl. *The Resurrection of the Dead*. Translated by H. J. Stenning. London, 1933.

Barrett, Sir William. *On the Threshold of the Unseen*. London, 1917.

Bashir, Muhammad Abdallah. *Zilzal al-ard al-'azim*. Cairo, 1994.

Baxter, Richard. *The Saints' Everlasting Rest*. Edited by.William Young. London, 1907.

Bernstein, Alan E. *The Formation of Hell—Death and Retribution in Ancient and Early Christian Worlds*. London, 1993.

Bernard of Clairvaux, Saint. *On Consideration*.

Beveridge, William. *Of the Happiness of the Saints in Heaven*. London, 1690.

Blair, Hugh. *The Grave*. London, 1783.

Blake, William. "Auguries of Innocence"; "The Marriage of Heaven and Hell." *Poetical Works of William Blake*. London, 1906.

Bonaventure, Saint. *Soliloquium*. London, 1655.

Bourdaloue, Louis. "Sur L'Enfer." Translated by John Casey. In *Oeuvres de Bourdaloue*. Paris, 1707–21.

Brandon, S. G. F. *The Judgment of the Dead*. London, 1967.

———. *Man and His Destiny in the Great Religions*. Manchester, 1962.

Brown, Peter. *Augustine of Hippo*. London, 1967.

Browne, Sir Thomas. *Religio Medici*. London, 1909.

Browning, Robert. "Bishop Blougram's Apology." In *Poetical Works of Robert Browning*. London, 1889.

Bultmann, Rudolph. *New Testament Mythology and Other Writings*. London, 1985.

————. "Karl Barth: The Resurrection of the Dead." In *Faith and Understanding*, translated by Louise Pettibone Smith. London, 1969.

Bunyan, John. *The Resurrection of the Dead*. Edited by J. Sears McGee. In *Miscellaneous Works of John Bunyan*. London, 1976.

————. *A Few Sighs from Hell*. Edited by J. Sears McGee. In *Miscellaneous Works of John Bunyan*. London, 1976.

Burkert, Walter. *Greek Religion Archaic and Classical*. Translated by John Raffan. Oxford, 1986.

Burnaby, John. *Amor Dei*. London, 1938.

Burnet, Thomas. *Hell's torments not eternal*. London, 1739 (being a translation of part of *De statu mortuorum et resurgentium tractatus*). London, 1729.

————. *Of the State of the Dead, and of Those That Are to Rise* (*De Statu Mortuorum at Resurgentium Tractatus*). Translation by Matthias Earbery. London, 1728.

————. *The Sacred Theory of the Earth* (*"Containing an Account of the Original of the Earth, and of all the General Changes which it hath already undergone or is to undergo, Till the Consummation of all Things"*). London, 1691.

————. *The Sacred Theory of the Earth*. Introduction by Basil Willey. London, 1965.

Bury, J. B. "Mystery Religion and Pre-Socratic Philosophy." In *The Cambridge Ancient History*. Cambridge, 1924–.

Bush, George. *Anastasis, or, the Doctrine of the Resurrection of the Body rationally and scripturally considered*. London, 1845.

Bynum, Caroline Walker. *The Resurrection of the Body in Western Christianity, 200–1336*. New York: Columbia University Press, 1995.

Callimachus, *Epigrams*. Oxford 1934.

Calvin, John. *Institutes of the Christian Religion*. Edited by John T. McNeill. Translated by Ford Lewis Battles. Library of Christian Classics. Philadelphia: Westminster, 1960.

Camporesi, Piero. *The Fear of Hell*. Cambridge, 1991.

Carlyle, Thomas. *On Heroes and Hero-Worship and The Heroic in History*. London, 1840.

Casey, John. *Pagan Virtue: An Essay on Ethics*. Oxford, 1990.

Catechism of the Catholic Church. London, 1994.

Catherine of Genoa, Saint. *Treatise on Purgatory*. Translated by Charlotte Balfour and Helen Douglas Irvine. London, 1946.

Catullus. *Poems of Caius Valerius Catullus*. Translated by F. W. Cornish. London: Loeb, 1962.

Chadwick, Henry. *Early Christian Thought and the Classical Tradition*. Oxford, 1966.

Chamberlain, Stuart Houston. *The Foundations of the Nineteenth Century*. London, 1911.

Charles, R. *A Critical History of the Doctrine of a Future Life*. London, 1913.

Cicero. *De Senectute*. Translated by William Armstead Falconer. London: Loeb, 1971.

————. *Republic*. Translated by Clinton Walker Keys. Oxford, 1998.

Cook, David. *Contemporary Muslim Apocalyptic Literature*. Syracuse, NY: Syracuse University Press, 2005.

Coplestone, Frederick. *Aquinas*. Penguin, 1975.

Cornford, F. M. "Mystery Religion and Pre-Socratic Philosophy." In *The Cambridge Ancient History*, edited by J. B. Bury. Cambridge, 1924.

Cox, Dermot. *The Triumph of Impotence: Job and the Tradition of the Absurd*. Rome: Universita Gregoriana, 1978.

Crashaw, Richard. *The Poems, English, Latin, and Greek, of Richard Crashaw*. Oxford, 1957.

Crenshaw James, L. *A Whirlwind of Torment*. Philadelphia, 1984.

Crookes, William. "Record of Seances with D. D. Home." In *Proceedings of the Society for Psychical Research*. Vol. 35, 1924–25.

Cross, F. L., and E. A. Livingstone. *A Dictionary of the Christian Church*. Oxford, 1997.

Crowther, Duane S. *Life Everlasting*. Utah, 1997.

Cumont, Fransz. *After Life in Roman Paganism*. New Haven, CT: Yale University Press, 1922.

Dalley, Stephanie, trans. *Myths from Mesopotamia*. Oxford, 1998.

Damon, S. Foster, ed. *Being William Blake's Illustrations for Blair's "The Grave," Arranged as Blake Directed*, with commentary by Damon. Providence, RI: Brown University Press, 1963.

Dante Alighieri. *La Divina Commedia*. Translation with commentary by Charles A. Singleton. Princeton: Princeton University Press, 1977.

———. *La Divina Commedia*. Translation and argument by J. A. Carlyle. Notes by Rev. H.Oelsner. Temple Classics, London, 1867.

Davidson, Donald. "How is weakness of the will possible?" In *Essays on Action and Events*. Oxford, 1980.

Dawes, Sir William. *The Greatness of Hell Torments*. London, 1707.

Dead Sea Scrolls. Translated by Geza Vermes. London, 1997.

Defoe, Daniel. *An Enquiry into the Case of Mr. Asgill's General Translation*. London, 1717.

Dell, Katherine, J. *The Book of Job as Sceptical Literature*. Berlin, 1991.

Delumeau, Jean. *History of Paradise*. Translated by Matthew O'Connell. New York: Continuum, 1995.

de Sales, Francis. See Francis de Sales, Saint.

Diehl, E. *Anthologia Lyrica Graeca*. Leipzig, 1925.

Diodurus Siculus [Historical Library]. 6 vols. Translated by C. H. Oldfather. London: Loeb, 1933–1954.

Doyle, Sir Arthur Conan. *The New Revelation*. London, 1918.

Drexel, Jeremias. *The Considerations of Drexelius upon Eternity*. Translated by S. Dunster. London, 1710.

———. *The Hive of Devotion*. Translated by one of the Fellows of Trinity College. London, 1647.

———. *Infernus Damnatorum Carcer et Rogus, Aeternitatis*. Bernhard Walther, 1632 (Colon. Agrippinae: apud Bernard Gualteri 1632).

Dryden, John. *Virgil's Aeneid*. Oxford, 1958.

Duffy, Eamon. *The Stripping of the Altars*. New Haven, CT: Yale University Press, 1992.

Eliot, T. S. *After Strange Gods*, 1934.

———. *Complete Poems and Plays*. London, 1969.

———. *Selected Essays*. London, 1932.

Elliott, J. K., trans. *The Apocryphal New Testament*. Oxford, 1993.

Erasmus, Desiderius. *De Libero Arbitrio*. Edited by Charles Trinkhaus. Translated by Peter Macardle and Clarance H. Miller. Toronto, 1999.

———. *Familiar Colloquies*. Translated by N. Bailey. London. 1900.

———. *Hyperaspistes*. Toronto, 1999.

Euripides. *Iphigenia at Aulis*. translated by David Kovacs. London, 2002.

Fahd, Salim. *Kashf al-sirr al-ta'rikhi Yahud al-yawm hum Yahuj wa-Majuj wa-iq-taraba al-wa-'d al-haqq*. Cairo, 1998.

Farnell, L. R. *Greek Hero Cults and Ideas of Immortality*. Oxford, 1921.

Farrell, James J. *Inventing the American Way of Death*. Philadelphia, 1980.

Ferguson, John. *Greek and Roman Religion, a Source Book*. Park Ridge, NJ: Noyes Press, 1980.

Faulkner, R. O. *The Ancient Egyptian Book of the Dead*. New York, 1972.

———. *The Ancient Egyptian Coffin Texts*. Warminster, 1978.

———. *The Ancient Egyptian Pyramid Texts*. Oxford, 1969.

Francis de Sales, Saint. *The Love of God*. Translated by Vincent Kearns. London, 1962.

Frazer, J. G. *The Belief in Immortality*. London, 1913.

Gallup, George Jr. With the assistance of William Proctor. *Adventures in Immortality*. London: Souvenir Press, 1983.

Gardner, A. H. "The Contending of Horus and Seth." *The Chester Beatty Papyri No 1* London, 1931.

Gearing, William. *A Prospect of Heaven*. London, 1673.

George, A. R., ed. and trans. *The Babylonian Gilgamesh Epic*. Oxford, 2003.

———. *The Epic of Gilgamesh*. Penguin, 1999.

Gibbon, Edward. *The Decline and Fall of the Roman Empire*. Edited by J. B. Bury. London, 1909.

Gother, John. *A Papist Misrepresented and Represented or a Twofold Character of Popery*. London, 1685.

Gray, Thomas. "Elegy Written in a Country Churchyard."

Gridley, Josiah. *Astounding Facts from the Spirit World*. Massachusetts, 1854.

Griffin, Jasper. *Homer on Life and Death*. Oxford, 1983.

Guthrie, W. K. *Orpheus and Greek Religion*. London, 1935.

Hall, H. R. *The Ancient History of the Near East*. London, 1913.

Hall, William John. *The Doctrine of Purgatory and the Practice of Praying for the Dead: as maintained in the Romish Church*. London, 1843.

Harrison, Thomas Perrin, ed. *The Pastoral Elegy: An Anthology*. Translations by Harry Joshua Leon. Austin: University of Texas Press, 1939.

Hartcliffe, John. *A Discourse Against Purgatory*. London, 1685.

Hegel, G. W. F. *Philosophy of Mind*. Translated by William Wallace. Oxford, 1971.

Heidel, Alexander. *The Gilgamesh Epic and Old Testament Parallels*. Chicago, 1946.

Herodotus. *History*. London: Loeb, 1925.

Hesiod. *Works and Days*. Translated by Glenn W. West. London: Loeb, 2006.

Hill, Mary V. *Angel Children*. Salt Lake City: Brigham Young University Press, 1973.

———. *The Life Beyond*. Salt Lake City: Brigham Young University Press, 1973.

Himmelfarb, Martha. *Ascent to Heaven in Jewish and Christian Apocalypses*. Oxford, 1993.

Hobbes, Thomas. *Leviathan*. Edited by Michael Oakeshott. Oxford: Blackwell, 1957.

Homer, *Iliad*. Translated by A. T. Murray. London: Loeb, 1924.

Homer. *Iliad. Odyssey.* Translated by A. T. Murray. London: Loeb, 1919.

Hopkins, Gerard Manley. "Thou art indeed just Lord." In *The Complete Poems: With Selected Prose.* Intro. by Robert Van de Weyer. London, 1996.

Horace. *Odes* 3, 4. London: Loeb, 1927.

Houdini, Harry. *A Magician Among the Spirits.* New York, 1924.

Housman, A. E. *Collected Poems and Selected Prose.* Edited by Christopher Ricks. Penguin, 1988.

Hume, David. *An Enquiry Concerning the Principles of Morals.* Edited by L. A. Selby-Bigge. Oxford, 1902.

Idleman-Smith, Jane, and Yvonne Yazbeck Haddad, *The Islamic Understanding of Death and Resurrection.* Albany, NY: SUNY Press, 1981.

Irenaeus of Lugdunum. *Against Heresies.* Translated by John Keble. Oxford, 1872.

Jaeger, Werner. *Paideia.* Translated by Gilbert Highet. Oxford: Blackwell 1965.

Joyce, James. *A Portrait of the Artist as a Young Man.* London, 1956.

Johnson, Samuel. *The Vanity of Human Wishes.* Works of Samuel Johnson. Vol. 6. *Poems.* Edited by G. Milne. New Haven, CT: Yale University Press, 1964.

Josephus. *Antiquities of the Jews.* Translated by William Whiston. Edinburgh, 1826.

Kant, Immanuel. *Critique of Practical Reason* Translated by Lewis White Beck. New York, 1956.

———. *Dreams of a Spirit Seer Illustrated by Dreams of Metaphysics.* Translated by Emanuel F. Goerwitz. Edited by Frank Sewall. London, 1900.

———. *Fundamental Principles of the Metaphysic of Ethics.* Translated by T. K. Abbott. 10th ed. London, 1965.

Kenny, Anthony. *Aquinas.* Oxford, 1980.

Khoo Thwe, Pascal. *From the Land of Green Ghosts: A Burmese Odyssey.* London, 2002.

Kitab Al-Fitan wa Ashrat As-Sa'ah. The Book Pertaining to the Turmoil and Portents of the Last Hour. Translated by Sahih Muslim. Center for Muslim-Jewish Engagement, University of Southern California, 2007–2009. (See Sahih Muslim.)

Kitab Al-Jannat wa Sifat Na'imiha wa Ahiha. The Book Pertaining to Paradise, Its Description, Its Bounties, and its Inmates. Translated by Sahih Muslim. Center for Muslim-Jewish Engagement, University of Southern California, 2007–2009. (See Sahih Muslim.)

Klausner, Joseph. *Jesus of Nazareth.* Translated by Herbert Danby. London, 1929.

Kramer, Samuel Noel. *Sumerian Mythology.* Philadelphia, 1962.

———. "Dilmun, the Land of the Living." *Bulletin of the American Schools of Oriental Research.* December 1944.

Lactantius. *De Mortibus Persecutorum.* Translated by Sister Mary Francis McDonald. In *Lactantius, Minor Works.* Catholic University of America, 1965.

———. *The Divine Institutes.* Translated by Sister Mary Frances McDonald. In *The Fathers of the Church.* Catholic University of America, 1964.

Lambert, W. G., ed. and trans. "A Dialogue of Pessimism"; "The Poem of the Righteous Sufferer." In *Babylonian Wisdom Literature.* Oxford, 1960.

Langdon, Stephen. *Babylonian Penitential Psalms.* In *Oxford Editions of Cuneiform Texts.* Paris, 1927.

————. *Sumerian Epic of Paradise, the Flood and the Fall of Man*. Philadelphia, 1915.

Lattimore, Richmond. *Themes in Greek and Latin Epitaphs*. Illinois, 1942.

Laugs, Martha, and Danial Kletke. *American After Life*. Munich: Kayhoff, 2000.

Lefebvre, Gustave. *Le Tombeau de Petosiris*. Cairo, 1924.

Le Goff, Jacques. *The Birth of Purgatory*. Translated by Arthur Goldhammer. Chicago, 1984.

Lehay, Tim, and Jerry B. Jenkins. *Desecration*. Coldstream, IL: Tyndale House, 2001.

————. *Glorious Appearing*. Coldstream, IL: Tyndale House, 2004.

————. *The Remnant*. Coldstream, IL: Tyndale House, 2002.

Leslie, Shane. *Saint Patrick's Purgatory*. London, 1932.

Levenson, Jon. D. *Resurrection and the Restoration of Israel: The Ultimate Victory of the God of Life*. New Haven, CT: Yale University Press, 2006.

Levin, Harry. *The Myth of the Golden Age in the Renaissance*. Oxford, 1972.

Lichtheim, Miriam. *Ancient Egyptian Autobiographies Chiefly of the Middle Kingdom*. Freiburg, 1988.

————. *Ma'at in Egyptian Autobiographies*. Freiburg, 1992.

————. *Moral Values in Ancient Egypt*. Freiburg, 1997.

Lindsey, Hal. *The Rapture: Truth or Consequences*. Prentice Hall, 1983.

Lodge, Sir Oliver. *Raymond, or Life and Death*. London, 1916.

———— *Survival of Man: A Study in Unrecognized Human Faculty*. London, 1909.

Love, Christopher. *Heaven's Glory, Hell's Terror*. London, 1653.

Lucretius. *De Rerum Natura*. Edited and translated by Cyril Bailey. Oxford, 1947.

Luther, Martin. *The Bondage of the Will*. Translated by Philip S. Watson in collaboration with Benjamin Drewery. In *Luther's Works*. Philadelphia, 1972.

————. *Commentary of 1 Corinthians*. Vol. 28. Translated by Edward Sittler. St. Louis. 1973. In *Luther's Works*.

————. *Table Talk*. Translated by Theodore G. Tappert. Vol. 54. In *Luther's Works*.

Macintyre, Alasdair. *After Virtue*. London, 1981.

————. *A Short History of Ethics*. New York, 1966.

Massey, Gerald. "The Great Spiritual Case." *Illustrated Police News*. London, 1868.

McDannell, Colleen, and Bernard Lang. *Heaven, a History*. London, 2001.

Mcgann, Vincent. *The Implications of Mormon Eternal Progression*. Utah: Spotlight Ministries, 2003.

Mercer, S. A. B. *The Religion of Ancient Egypt*. London, 1949.

Mercier, Charles A. *Spiritualism and Sir Oliver Lodge*. London, 1917.

Millett, Robert L., and Joseph Fielding Mckonkie. *The Life Beyond Death*. Utah, 1986.

Milton, John. *Poems*. Edited by H. Darbishire. Oxford, 1952.

Mitford, Jessica. *The American Way of Death Revisited*. London: Virago, 2000.

Moran, William. L. "The Epic of Gilgamesh: A Document of Ancient Humanism." *Bulletin, Canadian Society for Mesopotamian Studies* 22. Toronto. 1991.

Morenz, Siegfried. *Egyptian Religion*. London, 1960.

Moses, William Stainton. *Spirit Teachings*. London, 1894.

Mustafa Murad. *Mata taqum al-sa 'a*. Cairo, 1997.

Newman, John Henry. *Apologia Pro Vita Sua*. London, 1900.

————. *A Grammar of Assent*. Oxford, 1985.

Nietzsche, Friedrich. *The Antichrist*. Translated by Walter Kaufmann. New York, 1954.

———. *Beyond Good and Evil*. Translated by R. J. Hollingdale. Penguin, 1973.

———. *Ecce Homo*. Translated by Walter Kaufmann. New York, 1969.

———. *Genealogy of Morals*. Translated by Walter Kaufmann. New York, 1969.

Nussbaum, Martha. *The Fragility of Goodness*. Cambridge, 1986.

Origen. *Contra Celsum*. Translated by Henry Chadwick. Cambridge, 1956.

———. *First Principles (De Principiis)*. Translated by G. W. Butterworth. Oxford, 1936.

Overton, Richard. *Man Wholly Mortal, or, A treatise wherein 'tis proved, both theologically and philosophically, that as a whole man sinned, so whole man died: with doubts and objections answered and resolved, both by Scripture and reason*. London, 1675.

Owen, Eustace G. *The Children of Heaven. The Outlands of Heaven. Life Beyond the Veil*. London, 1923.

Oxford Dictionary of the Christian Church. Edited by F. L. Cross and E. A. Livingstone. Oxford, 1997.

Palmer, R. R. *Catholics and Unbelievers in Eighteenth Century France*. Princeton, 1939.

Pausanias. *Description of Greece*. Translated by W. H. S. Jones. London: Loeb, 1935.

Petrovsky-Petrovo-Solovo, Count. "Some Thoughts on D. D. Home." In *Proceedings of the Society for Psychical Research*. Vol. 114. 1930.

Phelps, Elizabeth Stuart. *The Gates Ajar*. Cambridge, MA: Harvard University Press, 1964.

Philo of Alexandria. *On the Creation*.

———. *On Dreams*.

———. *The Embassy to Gaius*.

———. *On the Giants*.

———. *Philo in Ten Volumes and Two Supplementary Volumes*. Translated by F. H. Colson and G. H. Whittaker. London: Loeb, 1929.

Pindar. *Olympian Odes*. Vol. 2. Translated by Sir John Sandys. London: Loeb, 1937.

Plato. *Apology*. Translated by H. N. Fowler. London: Loeb, 1914.

———. *Gorgias*. Translated by W. R. M. Lamb. London: Loeb, 1925.

———. *Laws*. Translated by R. B. Bury. London: Loeb, 1967.

———. *Phaedo*. Translated by H. N. Fowler. London: Loeb, 1914.

———. *Protagoras*. Translated by W. R. M. Lamb. London: Loeb, 1924.

———. *Republic*. Translated by Paul Shorey. London: Loeb, 1937.

———. *Symposium*. Translated by W. R. M. Lamb. London: Loeb, 1925.

Plutarch. *Moralia*. London: Loeb, 1927.

Pope, Alexander. *Works*. London, 1752.

Pound, Ezra. *Cantos*. London, 1954.

Pratt, Orson. *The Seer*. Washington, DC, 1854.

Pritchard, J. B., trans. and ed. "The Descent of Ishtar to the Underworld." In *Ancient Near Eastern Texts Relating to the Old Testament*. Princeton, 1969.

———. "A Dialogue About Human Misery." In *Ancient Near Eastern Texts*.

———. "A Song of the Harper." In *Ancient Near Eastern Texts*.

Proceedings of The Society for Psychical Research. Vols. 1, 3, 6, 9, 35, 114. London, 1904–30.

Proust, Marcel. *A la recherché du temps perdu*. Translated by C. K. Scott-Moncrieff and Terence Kilmartin. Penguin, 1983.

Qu'ran. Translated by Tarif Khalidi. Penguin, 2008. (*Koran*. Translated by Arthur J. Arberry. Oxford, 1964.)

Quirke, Stephen. *Ancient Egyptian Religion*. London, 1997.

Ratzinger, Joseph (Pope Benedict XVI). *Jesus of Nazareth*. Translated by Adrian J. Walker. London, 2007.

Rice, David G., and John Stambaugh. *Sources for the Study of Greek Religion*. Missoula, MT: Scholars Press, 1979.

Richardson, Samuel. *A Discourse of the Torments of Hell*. London, 1658.

Ricks, Christopher. *Milton's Grand Style*. Oxford, 1967.

Rowe, Elizabeth. *Friendship in Death*. London, 1818.

Rowley, H. H. *From Joseph to Joshua: Biblical Translation in the Light of Archaeology*. Oxford: Clarendon, 1948.

Safar Ibn 'Abd Al-Rahman Al-Hawali. *Wa'd Kissinjir wa-l-ahdaf al-Amrikiyya fi al-khalij*. Cairo, 1992.

Said Ayyub. *Al-Masih al-Dajjal*. Cairo, 1987.

Sahih Muslim. *Hadith*. Books 39–41. Los Angeles: University of Southern California Press, 2007.

Sartre, Jean Paul. *Being and Nothingness*. Translated by Hazel Barnes. London, 1957.

———. *Sketch for a Theory of the Emotions*. Translated by Philip Mairet. London, 1962.

Savonarola, Girolamo. *Compendium of Revelations*. In *Apocalyptic Spirituality*. Translated by Bernard McGinn. London, 1980.

Shakespeare, William. *Works*. Oxford, 1986.

Sidgwick, Henry. "Address to the Society for Psychical Research." In *Proceedings of the Society of Psychical Research*, July 17, 1852, vol 1.

Singleton, Charles A. Commentary and translation. *Dante's La Divina Commedia*. Princeton: Princeton University Press, 1977.

Sloane, David Charles. *The Last Great Necessity*. Baltimore: Johns Hopkins University Press, 1991.

Sophocles. *Oedipus at Colonus*, trans. Robert Fitzgerald. Chicago, 1941.

Spencer, Jeffrey A. *Death in Ancient Egypt*. New York: Penguin, 1982.

Spinoza, Benedict de. *Ethics*. Translated by James Gutman. New York, 1955.

Stanford, Peter. *Heaven: A Traveller's Guide to the Undiscovered Country*. London, 2002.

Swedenborg, Emanuel. *Arcana Coelestia* (1749–56). Edited by John Elliott. London: Swedenborg Society, 2004.

———. *The Delights of Wisdom on the Subject of Conjugial Love followed by The Gross Pleasures of Folly on the Subject of Scortatory Love*. Translated by John Chadwick. London, 1996.

———. *Heaven and Its Wonders and Hell, Drawn from Things Heard and Seen*. Translated by George F. Dole. West Chester, PA: Swedenborg Foundation, 2000.

———. *The Spiritual Diary*. Translated by George Bush and John H. Smithson. London, 1853–1902.

Swedenborg, Emanuel. *On the Worlds in our Solar System called Planets and on the Worlds in the Starry Sky and on their Inhabitants, also on the Sprits and Angels there from what has been seen and heard.* Translated by John Chadwick. London, 1997. (Cited as *Worlds in Space*, chap. 15.)

Swete, H. B. *Patristic Study.* London, 1902.

Swift, Jonathan. *Gulliver's Travels.* London, 1934.

Swinden, Tobias. *An Enquiry into the Nature and Place of Hell.* London, 1714.

Sibylline Oracles. Edited by H. N. Bate. London, 1918.

Tanner, Norman P., ed. *Council of Trent.* Vol. 2 of *Decrees of Ecumenical Councils.* London, 1996.

Taylor, John. *Death and the Afterlife in Ancient Egypt.* London, 2001.

Tertullian. *Apologeticus.* Translated by T. R. Glover. London, 1966.

———. *De Resurrectione.* Translated by Earnest Evans. London, 1960.

———. *De Spectaculis.* Translated by T. R. Glover. London, 1966.

Theognis. *Elegies.* Translated by Dorothea Wender Harmondsworth: Penguin, 1973.

Thomas Aquinas, Saint. *Summa Contra Gentiles.* Notre Dame, 1975.

———. *Summa Theologiae.* Edited by T. Gilby. London, 1972.

Thubron, Colin. *In Siberia.* London, 1999.

Thucydides. *The Peloponnesian War.* Translated by Charles Foster Smith. London: Loeb, 1919.

Twain, Mark. *Captain Stormfield's Visit to Heaven.* New York, 1909.

Unamuno, Miguel de. *The Tragic Sense of Life.* Translated by J. E. Crawford Flitch. London, 1921.

Valla, Lorenzo. *De Vero Falsoque Bono.* Translated by A. Kent Hieatt and Maristella Lorch. New York: Abaris Books, 1977.

Vermes, Geza. *The Authentic Gospel of Jesus.* New York: Penguin, 2004.

Vincent, Thomas. *Fire and Brimstone from Heaven.* London, 1670.

Virgil. *Aeneid.* London: Loeb, 1999.

———. *Eclogues.* London: Loeb, 1999.

Vulliamy, C. E. *Immortal Man.* London, 1926.

Wallis-Budge, E. A., trans. "The Book of Am Tuat"; "The Book of Gates." In *The Egyptian Heaven and Hell.* London, 1906.

———. *Osiris: The Egyptian Religion of Resurrection.* London, 2002.

Watts, Isaac. *Death and heaven, or the Last Enemy Conquer'd, and separate spirits made perfect: attempted in two funeral discourses, in memory of Sir John Gartopp Bart. And his lady, deceased.* London, 1736.

———. *World to Come, or, Discourses on the joys or sorrows of departed souls at death, and the glory or terror of the resurrection: to which is prefixed, An essay toward the proof of a separate state of souls after death.* London, 1813.

Waugh, Evelyn. *Decline and Fall.* London, 1928.

———. *The Loved One.* London, 1948.

Wesley, John. *Works.* Vols. 4, 12. Grand Rapids, MI, 1958.

Whiston, William. *The Eternity of Hell Torments Considered.* London, 1740.

White, Thomas. *The Middle State of Souls, From the Hour of Death to the Day of Judgment.* London, 1659.

Wicksteed, Philip H. *Dante and Aquinas.* London, 1913.

Wilson, A. N. *Paul: The Mind of the Apostle.* London, 1997.

Wittgenstein, Ludwig. *Culture and Value.* Translated by Peter Winch. Oxford: Blackwell, 1980.

———. *Lectures and Conversations on Aesthetics, Freud and Religious Belief.* Edited by Cyril Barrett. Oxford: Blackwell, 1966.

———. *Philosophical Investigations.* Translated by Elizabeth Anscombe. Oxford: Blackwell, 1958.

Woolley, Sir Leonard. *Ur Excavations.* London, 1963.

Wright, J. Edward. *The Early History of Heaven.* Oxford, 2000.

Young, Brigham. *Discourses.* Edited by John A.Widtsoe. Utah, 1971.

Zandee, Jan. *Death as an Enemy: According to Ancient Egyptian Conceptions.* Translated by W. F. Klasens. Leiden, 1960.

Index

Note: Page numbers in *italics* refer to illustrations.